THE WATERLOO MEDAL ROLL

Compiled from the Muster Rolls

THE NAVAL AND MILITARY PRESS
MCMXCII

This edition of

THE WATERLOO MEDAL ROLL

first published 1992 by

THE NAVAL & MILITARY PRESS LTD.,
DALLINGTON,
EAST SUSSEX

ISBN 1 897632 11 8

I N D E X

GENERAL and STAFF OFFICERS

WATERLOO

Field Marshall	HIS GRACE the DUKE OF WELLINGTON K.G. G.C.B.

Aides de Camp

Lt. Colonel	LORD FITZROY J.H. Somerset K.C.B. 1st Gds.
Lt. Colonel	JOHN FREMANTLE C. Gds.
Lieutenant	LORD GEORGE LENNOX HENRY PRINCE OF NAJSAN USINGEN 9th Drags.
Major	HON. H. PERCY 14th Drags. Extra
Captain	LORD A. HILL half pay Extra
Lieutenant	HON. G. CATHCART 6th D. Gds. Extra
General	HIS ROYAL HIGHNESS THE PRINCE OF ORANGE G.C.B.
Lt. Colonel	EARNEST BARON TRIPP 60th Foot
Captain	LORD J.T.H. SOMERSET 60th Foot
Captain	HON. FRANCIS RUSSELL 60th Foot
Major	CHARLES EARL OF MARCH 52nd Foot Extra
Lieutenant	HENRY WEBSTER 9th Lt. Drgs. Extra
Lt. General	EARL OF UXBRIDGE G.C.B.
Major	WM. THORNHILL 7th Hussars
Captain	HORACE SEYMOUR 60th Foot
Captain	THOMAS WILDMAN 7th Hussars Extra
Captain	JAMES JOHN FRASER 7th Hussars Extra
Lt. General	LORD HILL G.C.B.
Lt. Colonel	CLEMENT HILL R.H. Gds. Payne Collection 1911 Blue
Major	RICHARD EGERTON 34th Foot
Major	C.H. CHURCHILL 1st Gds.
Captain	DIGBY MACKWORTH 7th Foot
Captain	HON.ORLANDO BRIDGMAN 1st Gds. Extra
Captain	JOHN TYLER 93rd Foot
Captain	NEWTON CHAMBERS 1st Gds.
Captain	BARRINGTON PRICE half pay Extra
Lt. General	SIR HENRY CLINTON G.C.B.
Captain	FRANCIS DAWKINS 1st Gds.
Baron	CHARLES BARON ALTON K.C.B.
Lieutenant	WM. HAVELOCK 43rd Foot
Lt. General	HON.SIR CHARLES COLVILLE G.C.B.
Captain	JAMES JACKSON 37th Foot
Lieutenant	FREDK.WM. FRANKLAND Queens Foot
Captain	LORD JAMES HAY 1st Foot Gds. Extra
Major General	BARON VICTOR ALTEN
Lieutenant	H. BARON ERSTOFF 2nd Hussars K.G.L.
Major General	SIR I.O. VANDELEUR K.C.B.
Captain	WM. ARMSTRONG 19th Lt. Drags.
Major	MICHAEL CHILDERS 11th Drags. Bde. Maj.
Major General	GEORGE COOK
Captain	GEORGE DESBROWE 1st Foot Gds. H. Caskell's coll. 1908
Ensign	AUGUSTUS CAYLER C. Gds. Extra
Major General	SIR JAS. KEMPT K.C.B.
Captain Hon.	CHARLES GORE 85th Foot
Major General	WILHEM DE DORNBERG K.C.B.
Captain	AUGUSTUS KRAUCHENBERG 2nd Hussars K.G.I.
Major General	SIR E. BARNES K.C.B.
Major	ANDREW HAMILTON 4th W.I. Reg.
Sir	DENIS PACK K.C.B.
Lt. Colonel	BRAITHWAITE CHRISTIE 5th D. Gds.
Major	DE LACY EVANS 5th W.I. Reg. Extra
Major General	SIR JOHN BYNG K.C.B.
Captain	HENRY DUMARESGE 9th Foot
Major General	LORD R.E.H. SOMERSET K.C.B.

Lieutenant	HENRY SOMERSET 13th Hussars
Captain	GEO.W.W. VILLIERS R.H. Gds. Blue Bde. Maj.
Major General	SIR JOHN LAMBERT K.C.B.
Lieutenant	THOMAS BAYNES 39th Foot
Lt. Colonel	HENRY G. SMITH 95th Foot Bde. Maj.
Major General	SIR COLQUHOUN GRANT K.C.B.
Lieutenant	RAPLH MANSFIELD 15th R. Hussars
Captain	CHARLES MORAY half pay Extra
Captain	CHARLES Jones half pay Bde. Maj.
Major General	SIR JAMES LYONS K.C.B. Sold at Christies 1913
Lieutenant	JAS. MCGLASHAM 2nd Lt. Batt. K.G.L.
Major General	PERIGRINE MAITLAND
Captain	GEORGE RICHTER 1st Ceylon Bde. Maj.
Major General	GEORGE JOHNSTONE
Captain	CHARLES GEORGE GRAY 95th Foot
Captain	JAS. GUNTHROPE 1st Gds. Bde. Maj.
Captain	STEPHEN HOLMES 78th Foot Bde. Maj.
Major General	FREDERICK ADAM
Captain	CHARLES YORKE 52nd Foot
Major	THOMAS H. BLAIR 91st Foot Bde. Maj.
Major General	SIR COLIN HALKETT K.C.B.
Captain	GUSTAVUS BARON MARSCHALK K.G.L. 1st Lt. Batt.
Lieutenant	ALEX. HOME 2nd Lt. Batt.
Major General	SIR RICHARD HENRY VIVIAN K.C.B.
Captain	EDWARD KEANE 7th Hussars
Captain	THOMAS NEAL HARRIS half pay Bde. Maj.
Lieutenant	CHARLES A. FITZROY R.H.G. Blue Extra
Colonel	SIR JOHN ELLEY
Colonel	FREDK. BARON DE ARENTSSCHILD K.C.B.
Colonel	SIR GEORGE WOOD KNT.
Captain	MAURITZ DE CLOUDT staff K.G.L. Bde. Maj.
Captain	HENRY BAYNES R.A. Bde. Maj.
Captain	GEORGE BLACK 54th Foot Bde. Maj.
Captain	GOTTFRIED DE EINEM staff K.G.L. Bde. Maj.

<u>Military Secretary</u>

Lt. Colonel	LORD F.J.H. SOMERSET G.C.B. 1st Gds.

<u>Adjutant General</u>

Major General	SIR E. BARNES K.C.B.

<u>Deputy Adjutant General</u>

Colonel	SIR JOHN ELLEY K.C.B. R.H. Gds. Blue

<u>Assistant Deputy Adjutant General</u>

Lt. Colonel	JOHN WATERS unattached
Lt. Colonel	SIR GEO.H.F. BERKLEY K.C.B. 35th Foot
Lt. Colonel	SIR GUY CAMPBELL BART. 6th Foot
Lt. Colonel	SIR THOS.NOEL HILL K.C.B. 1st Gds.
Lt. Colonel	DELANCEY BARCLAY 1st Gds.
Lt. Colonel	HENRY WILLOUGHBY ROOKE 3rd Foot
Lt. Colonel	SIR JOHN MAY K.C.B. R.A.
Major	H. CAMPBELL WYLLY 7th Foot
Major	GEORGE EVATT 55th Foot
Major	WM. LINDSAY DARLING half pay
Major	F.L. BREYMANN 8th L. Batt. K.G.L.
Captain	HON. E.S. ERSKINE 60th Foot
Captain	LORD CHARLES FITZROY 1st Gds. Payne Collection 1910
Captain	CHARLES A.F. BENTINCK C. Gds.

<u>Deputy Assistant Adjutant General</u>

Captain	H.S. BLANKLEY 23rd Foot Glendings sale Jan.1910
Lieutenant	JAMES H. HAMILTON 46th Foot
Lieutenant	JOHN HARFORD 7th R.V.B.

<u>Attached to Lieut. General Baron Alten's Staff</u>

Lieutenant	EBERHARD GERSTLACHEN 3rd Hussars K.G.L.
Major	AUGUSTUS HEISE 2nd L. Batt.

<u>Deputy Judge Advocate</u>

Lt. Colonel	STEPHEN GOODMAN half pay

Assistant Quartermaster General

Colonel	HON. ALEX ABERCROMBY C. Gds.
Colonel	F.B. HARVEY 14th L/ Drag.
Lt. Colonel	ROBT. TORRENS 1st W.I. Reg.
Lt. Colonel	SIR CHARLES BROKE K.C.B. Permanent
Lt. Colonel	SIR JEREMIAH DICKSON K.C.B. Permanent
Lt. Colonel	LORD GREENOCK Permanent
Lt. Colonel	JOHN GEORGE WOODFORD 1st Ft. Gds.
Lt. Colonel	COLQUHOUN GRANT 11st Foot
Lt. Colonel	SIR WM. MAYNARD GOMM K.C.B. C. Gds.
Lt. Colonel	SIR H.H. BRADFORD K.C.B. 1st Ft. Gds.
Lt. Colonel	SIR GEO. SCOVELL K.C.B. 67 Corps.
Lt. Colonel	DAWSON KELLY 73rd Foot
Lt. Colonel	WM. CAMPBELL 23rd Foot
Lt. Colonel	CHARLES BECKWITH 95th Foot
Major	HON. G.L. DAWSON 1st D. Dgs.
Major	JAMES SHAW 43rd Foot

Deputy Assistant Quartermaster General

Captain	EDWD.T. FITZGERALD 25th Foot Payne collection 1911
Captain	HENRY GEO. MACLEOD 35th Foot
Captain	W.G. MOORE 1st Ft. Gds.
Captain	GEORGE HILLIAS 74th Foot
Captain	JAMES GRASER 9oth Foot
Captain	WM. GORDON CAMERON 1st Gds.
Captain	FRANCIS READ R. Staff Corps.
Lieutenant	PETER BARAILLER 33rd Foot

Commandant of Head Quarters

Colonel	COLIN CAMPBELL K.C.B. C. Gds.

Assistant Provost Marshall

Serjeant	WILLIAMSON 1st Ft. Gds.
Serjeant	PITCATHLY 54th Foot
Serjeant	SIMPSON 2nd L. Batt. K.G.L.
Serjeant	GARMAN C. Gds.
Serjeant	LUBSCHEWITZ K.G.L. 2nd Hussars
Serjeant	DAVIS 51st Foot
Serjeant	PHITICH 1st Ft. Gds.
Serjeant	VINTZENS 8th L/Batt. K.G.L.
Serjeant	WILLIAMS 4th Foot

* * *

RETURN OF GENERAL and STAFF OFFICERS serving in FLANDERS

Field Marshall	HIS GRACE the DUKE of WELLINGTON K.G. G.C.B.

Aides de Camp

Lt. Colonel	LORD F. SOMERSET 1st Gds. (My Secy)
Lt. Colonel	FREMANTLE C. Gds.
Lt. Colonel	CANNING 3rd Gds.
Lt. Colonel	HON. SIR A. GORDON 3rd Gds.
Lieutenant	LORD G. LENNOX 9th Lt.Drgs. H. PRINCE of MAJSAN USINGEN
Lt. Colonel	HON. H. PERCY 14th Lt. Drgs. Extra
Captain	LORD A. HILL Half pay Extra
Lieutenant	HON. G. CATHCART 6th D. Gds. Extra
General	HIS ROYAL HIGHNESS THE PRINCE OF ORANGE G.C.B.
Lt. Colonel	TRIPP 60th Foot
Major	LORD J. SOMERSET half pay
Captain	F. RUSSELL half pay
Major	EARL OF MARCH 52nd Foot Extra
Lieutenant	WEBSTER 9th Lt. Drgs. Extra
Lt. General	THE EARL OF UXBRIDGE
Lt. Colonel	THORNHILL 7th Hussars
Captain	SEYMOUR 60th Foot
Captain	WILDMAN 7th Hussars Extra
Captain	FRASER 7th Hussars Extra
Lt. General	LORD HILL G.C.B.
Lt. Colonel	C. HILL R.N.G. Blue
Lt. Colonel	EGERTON 36th Foot
Lt. Colonel	CHURCHILL 1st Guards
Captain	MACKWORTH 7th Foot
Captain	HON. O. BRIDGMAN 1st Guards Extra
Lt. General	SIR THOMAS PICTON
Major	TYLER 93rd Foot
Captain	CHAMBERS 1st Guards
Captain	PRICE half pay Extra
Lt. General	SIR H. CLINTON G.C.B.
Captain	J. DAWKINS 1st Guards

Lt. General	COUNT ALTEN K.C.B.
Lieutenant	HAVELOCK 43rd Foot
Lt. General	SIR C. COLVILLE G.C.B.
Major	JACLSON 37th Foot
Lieutenant	FRANKLAND Queens
Captain	LORD J. HAY 1st Foot Gds. Extra
Major General	V. ALTEN
Lieutenant	B. ESTORFF 2nd Hussars K.G.L.
Major General	SIR I.O. VANDELEUR K.C.B.
Captain	ARMSTRONG 19th Lt.Drgs.
Brigade Major	
Lt. Colonel	CHILDERS 11th Lt.Dgs.
Major General	COOKE
Aides de Camp	
Captain	DISBROWE 1st Ft. Gds. Payne collection 1911
Ensign	CAYLER C. Gds. Extra
Major General	SIR J. KEMPT K.C.B.
Captain	HON. C. GORE half pay
Brigade Major	
Captain	C. EELES 95th Foot
Major General	DORNBERG K.C.B.
Aides de Camp	
Captain	KRANCHENBERG 2nd Hussars K.G.L.
Brigade Major	
Captain	DE BOBENS Staff K.G.L.
Major General	SIR E. BARNES K.C.B.
Aides de Camp	
Lt. Colonel	HAMILTON 4th W.I. Reg.
Major General	SIR W. PONSONBY K.C.B.
Lieutenant	B. CHRISTIE 5th Dn. Gds.
Lt. Colonel	EVANS 5th W.I. Reg. Extra
Brigade Major	
Major	REIGNOLDS 2nd Drgs.
Major General	SIR J. BYNG
Captain	STOLHEST 3rd Gds.
Major General	SIR D. PACK
Captain	C. SMITH 95th Foot
Major General	LORD E. SOMERSET
Captain	VILLIERS R.H.G. Blue
Major General	SIR J. LAMBERT
Lt. Colonel	H.G. SMITH 95th Foot in poss. Mrs. Lambert (niece) Jan. 1909
Major General	SIR C. GRANT
Captain	JONES half pay 15th Hussars
Major General	LYON sold at Christies 1913
Captain	RICHTER 1st Ceylon
Major General	P. MAITLAND
Major	J. GUNTHORPE 1st Gds.
Major General	G. JOHNSTONE
Captain	S. HOLMES 78th Foot
Major General	F. ADAMS
Aides de Camp	
Major	H. DUMARESQ 9th Foot
Major	L. ESTRANGE 71st Foot
Lieutenant	H. SOMERSET 18th Hussars
Lieutenant	BAYNES 39th Foot Payne collection 1911
Lieutenant	MANSFIELD 15th Hussars
Captain	MORAY Extra
Lieutenant	GLASHAM 2nd L. Batt. K.G.L.
Ensign	LORD HAY 1st Gds.
Captain	GRAY C.B. 91st Foot
Captain	YORKE 52bd Foot
Captain	MARSCHALK 1st Lt. Bn. K.G.L.
Lieutenant	A. HOME 2nd Lt. Bn.
Captain	E. KEANE 7th Hussars
Lieutenant	FITZROY C.A. R.H.G. Blüe Extra
Brigade Major	
Lt. Colonel	BLAIR 91st Foot
Major General	SIR C. HALKETT K.C.B. Whitaker Collection 1908
Captain	CROFTON 54th Foot
Major General	SIR H. VIVIAN
Captain	HARRIS N. half pay
Colonel	SIR J. ELLEY K.C.B.
Colonel	SIR W.DE LANCEY
Colonel	SIR F. ASENTSCHILDT
Captain	DE CLOUDT Staff K.G.L.
Colonel	SIR GEO. WOOD

* * *

4th Brigade Division 4

Brigade Majors

Captain	DE CLOUDT Staff K.G.L.
Captain	BAYNES R.A.
Captain	BLACK 54th Foot
Captain	EINEM Staff K.G.L.
Captain	WEIGMANN Staff K.G.L.

Military Secretary

Lt. Colonel	LORD J.R. SOMERSET 1st Gds.

Adjutant General

Major General	SIR E. BARNES K.C.B.

Deputy Adjutant General

Colonel	SIR J. ELLEY R.H.G. Blue

Assistant Deputy Adjutant General

Lt. Colonel	JOHN WATERS unattached
Lt. Colonel	SIR GEO. BERKELEY 35th Foot
Lt. Colonel	SIR GUY CAMPBELL 6th Foot
Lt. Colonel	SIR N. HILL 1st Gds.
Lt. Colonel	BARCLAY 1st Gds.
Lt. Colonel	ROOKE 3rd Gds.
Lt. Colonel	SIR J. MAY R.A.
Lt. Colonel	CURRIE 90th Foot
Lt. Colonel	WYLLY 7th Foot
Major	EVATT 55th Foot
Major	DARLING half pay
Major	BREYMANN 8th L.Batt. K.G.L.
Major	HON. E.S. ERSKINE 60th Foot
Major	LORD C. FITZROY 1st Gds.
Major	BENTINCK C. Gds.

Deputy Assistant Adjutant General

Caotain	BLANKLEY 23rd Foot
Captain	HON. W. CURZON 69th Foot
Lieutenant	HAMILTON 46th Foot
Lieutenant	HURFORD 7th R.V. Bn.
Lieutenant	GERSTLACHER 3rd Hrs. K.G.L.

Attached to Lieut.General Bn. Alten Staff

Major	HEISE 2nd Lt.Bn. K.G.L.

Deputy Judge Advocate

Lt. Colonel	GOODMAN half pay

Deputy Quartermaster General

Colonel	SIR W. DE LANCEY Permanent

Assistant Deputy Quartermaster General

Colonel	HON. A. ABERCROMBY C. Gds.
Colonel	HARVEY 14th Lt.Drgs.
Lt. Colonel	TORRENS 1st W.I. Reg.
Lt. Colonel	SIR C. BROKE Permanent
Lt. Colonel	SIR J. DICKSON Permanent
Lt. Colonel	LORD GREENOCK Permanent
Lt. Colonel	I.G. WOODFORD 1st Ft.Gds.
Lt. Colonel	C. GRANT 11st Foot
Lt. Colonel	SIR W. GOMM C. Gds.
Lt. Colonel	SIR H. BRADFORD 1st Ft. Gds.
Lt. Colonel	SIR G. SCOVELL Cy. Staff Corps.
Lt. Colonel	D. KELLY 73rd Foot
Lt. Colonel	W. CAMPBELL 23rd Foot
Lt. Colonel	CHAS, BECKWITH 95th Foot
Major	DAWSON 1st Dn. Gds.
Major	I. SHAW 43rd Foot

Deputy Assistant Quartermaster General

Captain	FITZGERALD 25th Foot
Captain	H.G. MCLEOD 35th Foot
Captain	W.G. MOORE 1st Ft.Gds.
Captain	HILLIER 74th Foot
Captain	FRASER 90th Foot
Captain	W.G. CAMERON 1st Gds.
Captain	READ R. Staff Corps.
Lieutenant	P. BARRAILLER 33rd Foot

Commandant of Head Quarters

Colonel	SIR C. CAMPBELL C. Gds.

Assistant Provost Marshall

Serjeant	WILLIAMSON 1st Ft. Gds.
Serjeant	PITCATHLY 54th Foot
Serjeant	SIMPSON 2nd Lt.Bn. K.G.L.
Serjeant	GARMAN C. Gds.
Serjeant	LUBCHEWITZ 2nd Hrs. K.G.L.
Serjeant	DAVIS 51st Foot
Serjeant	PHITHEON 1st Ft. Gds.
Serjeant	VINTZENS 8th Lt.Bn. K.G.L.
Serjeant	WILLIAMS 4th Foot

* * *

1st LIFE GUARDS

Major & Lt. Colonel	SAMUEL FERREOR Killed
Captain	JOHN WHALE Wounded
Captain	MONTAGUE LIND Killed
Captain	EDWARD KELLY Wounded
Captain & Major	JOHN BERGER
Lieutenant	GEORGE RANDALL
Lieutenant	WILLIAM MAYNE Payne Collection 1911
Lieutenant	WILLIAM RICHARDSON Wounded

Sub. Lieut.	CHARLES COX Wounded
Sub. Lieut.	GEORGE STOREY
Ass.Surgeon	RICHARD GOUGH
Ass.Surgeon	J.H. JAMES
Vety.Surgeon	FRANCIS DALTON
Paymaster	WILLIAM BANKS
Qr.Master	JOHN RAMSDEN
Qr.Master	WILLIAM DOBSON Wounded
Qr.Master	JOHN SLINGSBHY Killed
Qr.Master	JOSEPH TOWERS Killed
Corporal	WILLIAM AITKIN
Corporal	WILLIAM ALLEN
Private	JOHN ATKINSON
Private	RICHARD AKRILL
Private	JOHN ASHTON
Private	WILLIAM ANDERSON
Private	JAMES ALLEN Killed
Private	JOHN AMISON
Private	WILLIAM AUSTER Wounded
Corporal	JAMES ALLEN Littledale sale Nov.1910
Private	SAMUEL ASHFORD
Private	JOHN ASPINELL
Private	EDWARD ANDERSON
Private	JOHN ALEXANDER Killed
Private	JOHN BOARDMAN
Private	ROBERT BERNES
Private	JAMES BILLEN
Private	HENRY BARRET Wounded
Private	RICHARD BAKER Killed
Private	JAMES BLACK Wounded
Private	JOHN BESWICK Wounded
Private	JAMES BROOKS Wounded
Private	JOHN BRADLEY
Private	WILLIAM BUTTERWORTH
Private	JOHN BUCKLEY
Private	WILLIAM BIRKETT
Private	JOHN BORHAM
Private	JOHN BRIGGS
Private	SAMUEL BALL
Private	ZACHY. BOCOCK
Private	JAMES BESWICK Wounded
Private	JAMES BURRELL Wounded
Private	DENNIS BARRET Wounded
Private	JOSEPH BRADLEY Killed
Cpl. Major	WILLIAM BISHOPP Wounded
Private	JOHN BRIDGE
Private	SAMUEL BATES Wounded Payne collection 1911
Private	MATTHEW BROWN
Private	EDWARD BIRTLES
Private	SAMUEL BRUCEGIRDLE
Private	WILLIAM BROOKS
Private	JOSEPH BOTTOMLEY
Private	THOMAS BRUNTON
Corporal	RICHARD COULTER Wounded
Private	MATTHEW CHARLTON
Private	BENJAMIN CALDICOTT
Private	WILLIAM CURTIS
Private	ABRAHAM CLARKE Killed
Private	ALEXANDER COUPER Wounded
Private	ROBERT CALDER
Private	DAVID CLAYLAND
Private	STEPHEN CLIFFE Wounded
Private	ANGUS CAMERON
Corporal	JOHN CARTER Wounded
Private	STEPHEN CRANBROOK
Private	JOHN CHAPMAN Killed
Private	ISSAC CARLING Wounded
Private	RICHARD DIXON
Private	JAMES DIXON
Private	GILL DIXON
Private	ROBERT DAWSON
Private	JOHN DINSDALE
Private	JOHN DENBY Wounded Cheylesmore collection
Private	OWEN DINSDALE
Private	MICHL. DRURY Wounded
Private	THOMAS EASTON Wounded
Private	JOHN EGGINS
Trumpeter	JOHN EDWARDS
Private	RICHARD EASTWOOD
Private	JAMES EDMONSON Wounded
Trumpeter	JOSEPH FRECK
Private	ROBERT FALCONER
Private	ROBERT FLETCHER Wounded Glendinings sale Jan.1913
Corporal	CHIRSTOPHER FORGE
Private	WILLIAM FRANKLIN
Private	JAMES FORSYTHE
Private	JAMES FARNEY Killed
Private	THOMAS FELE Killed
Private	JOHN FLEMMING
Private	GEORGE FORD Wounded
Corporal	JONATHAN GLOSSOP Wounded
Private	ROBERT GRAHAM Wounded
Private	THOMAS GREGSON Wounded
Private	THOMAS GOODWIN
Private	EDWARD GUEST
Private	THOMAS GARDNER Col.Gaskell's sale May 1911

Private	JOHN GILL Killed
Private	JONATHAN GLEDHILL
Private	JOHN GRAYLING
Private	JOSHUA GLEDHILL
Private	THOMAS GILES
Private	WILLIAM GILL Wounded
Private	JEREMIAH GARSIDE
Private	WILLIAM GIBSON Killed
Private	THOMAS GRATON
Private	WILLIAM GADD Day sale April 1910
Corporal	JONATHAN HOLDEN
Private	GEORGE HORROS Wounded
Corporal	GEORGE HIGSON
Private	WILLIAM HUDSON
Private	JONATHAN HESLOP
Private	WILLIAM HUMPHRIES Wounded
Private	WILLIAM HOLMES Killed
Private	CHARLES HOPWOOD
Private	JOHN HAMILTON
Private	JOHN HAMILTON (Jnr)
Private	JOHN HEYWOOD
Private	JOHN HERBERT
Private	WILLIAM HARDY Wounded
Private	ROBERT HARDCASTLE
Private	DANIEL HERDSMAN
Private	MOSES HERWOOD
Private	JOHN HAUGHTON
Private	JOHN HERDSMAN Wounded
Private	JOSEPH HIBBET
Private	JAMES HYDE
Private	JOHN HIGGINSON Killed
Private	STEPHEN HUDSON
Private	WILLIAM HEATON Killed
Private	JOHN HEYWOOD (Jnr) Killed
Private	JOHN HARPER
Private	JOHN INGHAM
Private	DAVID JOHNSON H.Gaskell's Collection 1908
Private	WILLIAM JONES
Private	JAMES JOY Payne Collection 1911
Private	ELY JOWETT
Corporal	JAMES KNOWLES Killed
Private	JAMES KNOWLES Killed
Private	DANIEL KENZIE Wounded
Private	WILLIAM KENYON Wounded on sale Baldwin's 1912
Private	WILLIAM KERSHAW
Private	WILLIAM KEATES Wounded
Private	THOMAS KENYON
Private	WILLIAM KIRBY
Private	HARTLIB KERSHAN Wounded
Private	JOSEPH LILEY Wounded
Private	JAMES LOVET
Private	RICHARD LANCASTER
Private	JOHN LEES Wounded
Private	JAMES LOW Wounded
Private	JOSHUA LILEY Wounded
Private	THOMAS LORD (Snr)
Private	JOHN LOYD
Private	THOMAS LORD
Private	JOHN LOMAS Killed
Private	JOSEPH MAYCOCK
Private	GODFREY MOLT
Private	WILLIAM MAUDE
Private	THOMAS MORLEY
Corporal	WILLIAM MILES
Private	JOHN MATTISON Col.Murray's collection
Private	DAVID MILLER
Private	THOMAS MOULSTON
Private	JOHN METCALFE
Private	THOMAS MILES Wounded
Private	THOMAS MURFIN
Private	ANTHONY MAGGS
Private	JOHN MORRISON Killed
Private	ARCHIBALD MOFFAT
Private	HUGH MCLEAN Killed
Private	JOHN NAIRNE
Private	RICHARD NUTALL
Private	CHARLES NEWLAND
Private	JOSPEH OATES Killed
Private	JAMES OCKWOOD Needes collection 1908
Private	THOMAS PARKINSON
Private	JOSEPH PICKLES Killed
Private	JOHN PARTINGTON
Private	CHRISTOPHER POTTER Killed
Private	JOSEPH POLLARD
Private	THOMAS PERRY
Private	WILLIAM PEPPERALL
Private	DANIEL PENNY
Private	GEORGE PICKET or PESKET Fleming collection 1871
Private	THOMAS PATON
Private	JOHN PEARMAN
Private	GEORGE RUDD
Private	JAMES ROSS
Private	BENJAMIN ROGERS

Private	WILLIAM RYDER
Private	EDWARD RUTHERFORD Wounded
Private	ROBERT RAINFORD Wounded
Private	WILLIAM RUTLAND Wounded
Private	THOMAS RUTHERFORD
Private	GEORGE RICHARDSON
Private	THOMAS RICHDALE Wounded
Private	WILLIAM RUDFORD Wounded
Private	JOHN ROBINSON
Private	WILLIAM ROBINSON
Private	THOMAS STEHFOX Killed
Private	JAMES SANDERSON
Private	WILLIAM SMITH Glendinings sale 25th Oct. 1907
Private	THOMAS SYKES
Private	PETER SEARGILL Killed
Private	JOHN SWIFT
Private	JOSEPH SUTTON
Private	WILLIAM SELBY
Private	JOSEPH SMITH
Private	JOHN STARR Walter's sale June 1913
Private	EDMOND SPICER
Private	GEORGE SEARGILL
Private	ELY SUTCLIFFE
Private	JOHN STEPHENSON Killed
Private	RICHARD SMITH
Private	THOMAS SHIPLEY Wounded
Private	JOSEPH STEEL
Private	ROBERT SLINGER
Private	JOHN SCOTT
Private	GEORGE THORNBOROUGH
Private	WILLIAM THORNTON
Private	THOMAS THOMAS
Private	WILLIAM THORN
Private	JOHN TURNER Wounded
Private	DAN TURNER
Private	WILLIAM TAYLOR
Private	JOHN THORP Chadwick sale Nov. 1912
Private	WILLIAM THOMAS Killed
Private	JOHN TERRAN
Corporal	WILLIAM USHER
Corporal	JAMES WILSON Wounded Galway Foley coll. 1910
Private	JOHN WALKER Wounded Whitaker coll. 1908
Private	THOMAS WILCOX Col. Gascoigne's coll.1909
Private	JOHN WINTERBOTTOM
Private	ELY WALKER Wounded
Private	JAMES WOOD Wounded
Private	JOHN WORTHINGTON
Private	JOHN WILSON
Private	JAMES WALKER Wounded
Private	NATHANIEL WRIGHT
Private	JAMES WILD Gaskell Coll.1908
Private	JOSEPH WADDINGTON
Private	WILLIAM WILSON
Private	JOHN WHITE
Private	GEORGE WHITEHEAD
Private	ROBERT WANDE
Corporal	THOMAS WHARRIE Killed
Corporal	WILLIAM H. WEAVER
Private	RICHARD WATKIN
Private	JAMES WALKER (Jnr)
Private	CHARLES WYLDE
Private	JAMES WEEDON
Private	ROBERT WHITEHEAD
Private	JOHN WHITEHEAD
Corporal	JOSEPH WILKINSON
Private	JOHN WARE
Private	JOHN WINTER
Private	LAURENCE YOUNG

* * *

2nd LIFE GUARDS

1st Major Lt. Colonel	LOYGON
Captain & Bt.Major	BOYCE
Captain	HON. H.E. IRBY
Captain & Lt. Colonel	R. FITZGERALD Killed
Captain & Lt. Colonel	J.P.M. KENYON
Lieutenant	R. MEARES
Lieutenant	WM. ELLIOTT Actg.Paymr.
Lieutenant	S. WAYMOUTH
Lieutenant	CHAMBRE BARTON
Sub.Lieut.	A.P. KENYON
Sub. Lieut.	THOMAS MARTIN
Sub. Lieut.	M. INNES H.Gaskell's collection 1908
Sub. Lieut.	JOS. CLUES
Surgeon	S. BROUGHTON
Ass.Surgeon	T.J. DRINKWATER
Vty.Surgeon	JEREMIAH FIELD
Qr.Master	JAMES FERMOR
Qr.Master	JOHN BERGAN
Qr.Master	CHAS. BARTON

Cpl. Major	ELLINGTON JOHN A.A.Paynes Coll. 1908
Corporal	CALAH JOS.
Corporal	WAINWRIGHT NATHL.
Corporal	ACOMB JOHN Galway Foley Coll. 1910
Corporal	HOLDING HENRY
Corporal	POWELL WM.
Corporal	HODGSON WM.
Corporal	MYCOCK JOS.
Corporal	
Corporal	DEAKEN CHAS.
Corporal	DEE JAMES Glenings sale 25th Oct. 1907
Corporal	DEE JAMES
Corporal	WEBSTER WM. Whitaker Collection 1908
Trumpeter	HARRIS CHARLES
Trumpeter	BARWICK THOS.
Trumpeter	MILLS ROBT.
Trumpeter	TAYLOR JAS.
Private	ARCHER JOHN
Private	ADAMS ANDREW Col. Gaskell's sale May 1911
Private	ARMSTRONG MICHAEL
Lt.Corporal	ATKINSON WM.
Private	ADDY JOHN
Private	ARKINS WILLIAM
Private	ACROYD SAMUEL
Private	BARKER JOHN
Private	BROWN WILLIAM on sale Fenton's March 1910
Private	BEAMOND JOHN Payne collection 1911
Private	BEATHAM GEORGE
Private	BEATHAM CHARLES
Private	BRADLEY DAVID
Private	BOTT JAMES
Private	BRADBURY FRANS.
Lc.Corpl.	BROWN WILLIAM
Private	BULL CALEB
Private	BEAMOND WILLIAM
Private	BEAMOND THOMAS
Private	BIRDSELL JOHN
Private	BICKERDIKE FRANS.
Private	BERRY EDWARD Gaskell collec. 1908
Private	BELL THOMAS
Private	BUTTERWORTH JOHN
Private	BALL GEORGE
Private	BAXTER JOHN
Private	BUGG ROBERT
Private	BRISKHAM THOMAS
Private	CAVE ROBERT
Private	CHAPMAN JOHN
Private	CLEGG THOMAS
Private	CLAYTON JOHN
Private	CHURCH JASPER
Private	CHILD JOHN
Farrier	CLAYTON GEORGE Cheylesmore Collection
Lc.Corpl.	COOK THOMAS
Private	CHAPMAN WILLIAM
Private	CHAPELL LSSAC
Private	CARTER PHILIP
Private	DENTON WILLIAM
Private	DAWSON SAMUEL
Private	DENTON WILLIAM
Lc.Corpl.	DARBY ISSAC
Private	DENISON JOHN Day sale April 1910
Private	DRISDALE JAMES
Private	ENSOR THOMAS
Private	FIELDING JOHN
Private	FOSTER WILLIAM
Private	FIRBY THOMAS
Private	FRANKLAND JOHN
Private	GREY THOMAS
Private	GRIVES JAMES
Private	GOBIN FRANS.
Private	GIFFORD JAMES
Private	GORE ROBERT
Private	GILL HENRY
Private	GILLETT GEORGE
Private	GODLEY SAMUEL
Private	GRIMSTER PETER
Private	GREENHALCH THOMAS
Private	GIBBINS WILLIAM
Private	GIBSON THOMAS
Private	GERRATT GEORGE
Private	GLADALL ELY
Private	HUTCHINSON MATTHEW
Private	HARDY THOMAS
Private	HOLLAND THOMAS
Private	HOGSFLESH JOHN
Private	HOWSON RICHARD
Private	HENSHALL WILLIAM
Private	HIRD JOHN
Private	HARTLEY GEORGE
Private	HAMMOND GEORGE
Private	HUNT JOHN
Private	HORSFALL WILLIAM

Private	HORNER JAMES
Private	HOOPER JOHN
Private	HAMSON WILLIAM Needes Collection 1908
Private	HOGSFLESH HENRY
Private	HINDLEY JAMES
Private	HORN WILLIAM
Private	HOWARTH JOHN
Private	HEBDEN THOMAS
Private	HOLMES THOMAS
Private	JOHNSON JOHN (Snr)
Private	JONES WILLIAM
Private	JOHNSON JOHN (Jnr)
Private	JENKINS ROBERT
Private	JOY JAMES
Private	JONES ABEL
Private	KING JAMES
Private	KERSHAW JONATHAN
Farrier	KILMORE MICHAEL
Private	KING WILLIAM
Private	LORD JOSEPH
Private	LEIGH WILLIAM
Farrier	LAMMIE JAMES
Private	LINDLEY JOHN
Private	LUCAS JOSEPH
Private	LEVITT CHARLES
Private	LETTER HUGH
Private	LOMAX JOHN
Private	LOWE JOSEPH
Private	MOTT PETER
Private	MARSLAND PETER
Private	MILNER WILLIAM
Private	MCLANE ANDREW
Private	MORLEY WILLIAM
Private	MARSDEN JOSEPH
Private	MOORE JAMES
Private	MASTIN WILLIAM
Private	MASON HENRY Glendinings sale 28th Feb.1908
Private	MATTHEWS JOSEPH
Private	PEPPER SAMUEL
Farrier	PAYNE EDWARD
Private	PICKERING GEORGE
Private	PRINCE JAMES
Private	PLAYFORD THOMAS
Private	PENDLEBURY THOMAS
Private	PEATE JOHN
Private	RICHARDSON THOMAS
Private	REED WILLIAM
Private	STOLLARD WILLIAM
Private	SIMPSON JAMES
Farrier	SANDY WILLIAM
Private	SANDERS Henry
Private	SUTCLIFFE THOMAS
Private	STANFIELD JAMES
Private	STRETON EDWARD Col. Murray's collection
Armr.	SHOULDS MICHAEL
Private	SHEPARD SAMUEL
Farrier	THOMPSON ALEX.
Private	TILFORD WILLIAM
Private	TRELFALL WILLIAM
Private	TWAITE JOHN
Private	WALKER JOSEPH
Private	WASDEN THOMAS
Private	WATSON PETER
Private	WILSON GEORGE
Private	WILLIAMSON JAMES
Private	WINTERBOTTOM THOMAS
Private	WOODS RICHARD
Private	WRIGHT EDWARD
Private	WILKINSON JOHN
Private	WRIGHT THOMAS
Private	WELCH RICHARD
Private	WILSON RICHARD
Private	WILLIAMS WATKIN
Private	WELLS JAMES
Private	WRAGG JAMES
Private	WEATHERALL JOHN In poss. W. Wetherill Willfred June Castle Eden
Private	YATES JOHN
Private	YOUESON JOHN

* * *

ROYAL REGIMENT OF HORSE GUARDS

Captain Thoyts Troop

Lt. Colonel	SIR R.C. HILL Wounded Payne collection 1911
Major	R.C. PACKE Killed
Captain	J. THOYTS
Lieutenant	G. SMITH
Lieutenant	H.E. BOATES
Cornet	T.H. PICAIRD Whitaker Collection 1908
Surgeon	D. SLOW Gray Collec.1908
Vety.Surgeon	J. SIDDALE Payne Collection 1911
Qr.Master	THOMAS FARLEY
Qr.Master	JONAS FARLEY

Corporal	WHITTAKER JOHN
Corporal	NEWTON WILLIAM Payne Collection
Corporal	LEDSUM CHARLES A. Cook Forfar Sept. 1908
Corporal	MILLER JOHN
Corporal	HEARSLEY ANDREW
Trumpeter	HIGGINS THOMAS
Private	ARMYTAGE THOMAS
Private	BASTOW JOSEPH
Private	BURNHAM ROBERT
Private	BACKHOUSE JOHN
Private	BARLOW JOHN
Private	BARRATT ROBERT
Private	BUTTERFIELD THOMAS
Private	BINGLEY JOHN
Private	COOPER RICHARD
Private	COOK WILLIAM Missing
Private	CLEMENTS WILLIAM
Private	CHEETHAM FRANCIS
Private	DARBY DANIEL Missing
Private	ELLISHAM CHARLES
Private	EDWARDS JOHN
Private	EDMONDSON DAVID
Private	GREASLY WILLIAM
Private	GRAYSON BENJAMIN
Private	GREENSMITH RICHARD Missing
Private	HANSON GEORGE
Private	HOULDSWORTH JOSEPH
Private	HOLLINGSWORTH RALPH
Private	HAINSWORTH JOHN
Private	HOYLE ISSAC
Private	HAYWARD WILLIAM
Private	HOYLAND GEORGE
Private	MORTON THOMAS
Private	MATTHEWS WILLIAM
Private	NEWTON HENRY
Private	PILGRIM JOSEPH Missing
Private	POLLARD WILLIAM Missing
Private	ROGERSON JAMES Missing
Private	RUDKIN JOSEPH
Private	SMITH JOHN
Private	SCHOFIELD RAMSDEN
Private	SMITH SAMUEL
Private	SHAW JOHN
Private	STEVENS JOSEPH
Private	SLACK JOHN
Private	TAYLOR BENJAMIN
Private	TURNER ALEXANDER
Private	TAYLOR CHARLES
Private	WILLETT ABRAM
Private	WHITTAKER JOHN
Private	WIGZEL GEORGE
Private	WHITTAKER JONATHAN
Private	WOODHEAD JOSHUA
Private	WEBB JOHN
Private	WILD WILLIAM
Private	WHITAKER THOMAS
Private	WOOD ROBERT
Private	WOOLLAM JOHN
Private	WALTON JOHN
Private	WHITEHEAD RICHARD
Private	WATMOUGH JAMES Missing
Private	WHYMAN M. JOHN

Major Drakes Troop

Captain	W.S. DRAKE
Lieutenant	W.C. SHAWE Wounded D.
Lieutenant	E.W. BOUVERIE Wounded D.
Qr.Master	WATMOUGH PETER
Corporal	CLOFT ROBERT Missing
Corporal	CART RICHARD
Corporal	DICKINSON HENRY
Corporal	MELLER JOHN
Trumpeter	RANGE WILLIAM
Private	ATKINSON RICHARD
Private	NROWN WILLIAM
Private	BOSTOCK THOMAS
Private	BISHOP WILLIAM
Private	BOARDMAN JOHN
Private	BARKER JOHN
Private	CLEMENTSON JOSEPH
Private	DYSON FREDERICK
Private	DALLMAN HENRY
Private	DRAKE THOMAS
Private	DODSON WILLIAM
Private	EDWARDS WILLIAM
Private	FREEMAN JOHN
Private	FRYER WILLIAM
Private	FOX JOHN
Private	FAIRBANKE JOHN
Priavte	FAWCETT WILLIAM
Private	FAIRBROTHER CARTER Qr.Mr. 31.5.28 Died April 1852
Private	GAWTHORP JONES
Private	GREEN WILLIAM
Private	GADD GEORGE
Private	HOULDSWORTH JOSEPH
Private	HAILEY JAMES Day sale April 1910

Private	HOLLIDAY JOHN
Private	HOYLE ROBERT
Private	KEELEY GEORGE
Private	LANCASHIRE JAMES
Private	LINTON GEORGE Glendinings sale Dec. 1908
Private	LOMAX MOSES
Private	LONGBOTTOM JAMES
Private	MIGLEY FRANCIS
Private	OSBOURNE JOHN
Private	PANLINGTON THOMAS Col. Gascoignes collection 1909
Private	PICKERING WILLIAM
Private	PARKES JAMES
Private	RAVELL JONATHAN
Private	ROWLEY WILLIAM
Private	SHEARD JOHN
Private	SMITH WILLIAM
Private	STOCKS JOSEPH
Private	SHINGLER JOHN
Private	STOTT WILLIAM
Private	SHAW ISSAC
Private	SCOTT WILLIAM
Private	WHITTAKER THOMAS
Private	BOWER JOHN Missing
Private	CHELTON WILLIAM Missing
Private	HATCH EDWARD Missing
Private	TERRY WILLIAM Missing

Lt.Col. C. Hill's Troop

Captain Lt. Colonel	HILL CLEMENT
Lieutenant	TATHWELL T.B. London 1979
Cornet	ARNOLD JAMES
Qr.Master	HARDY THOMAS
Corporal	LATCHFORD THOMAS
Corporal	FROST JOHN
Corporal	EMMOTT WILLIAM
Corporal	RAINSLEY JOHN
Trumpeter	WEBSTER ROBERT
Private	BAYNUM JOSEPH
Private	BERRY SAMUEL
Private	BASSON JOHN
Private	BERRY WILLIAM
Private	BLAMIRES GEORGE
Private	BENTLEY THOMAS Chelsea Hospital collection 1908
Private	BUTTERWORTH ROBERT
Private	BREARLY WILLIAM
Private	BOARDMAN JOHN
Private	COMER WILLIAM
Private	CORNS THOMAS
Private	DEAM WILLIAM Missing 18th June
Private	DANIELS SAMUEL
Private	DANIELS JOHN
Private	DEAN JAMES
Private	HOWCROFT PETER
Private	HALKYARD SAMUEL
Private	HARTLEY RICHARD
Private	HOWARD ELIAS Missing 18th June
Private	HALFORD WILLIAM Needes Collection 1908
Private	HALL BARTHOLOMEW
Private	HARLING CHARLES
Private	HAINES JAMES
Private	JOHNSON JOHN
Private	LAWSON JAMES
Private	LAN JOHN
Private	MADELY THOMAS
Private	MOUNTAIN GEORGE
Private	MASON SAMUEL Missing 18th June
Private	NASH JAMES
Private	NUTTER ROBERT
Private	NORTH GEORGE
Private	OGDEN SAMUEL
Private	OGDEN JOHN
Private	OAKLEY GEORGE Glendinings sale Dec. 1908
Private	PEEL ROBERT
Private	ROTHWELL JAMES
Private	REED JOSEPH
Private	RICHARDS THOMAS
Private	SIDDALL JOHN
Private	SMITH WILLIAM
Private	SHEPHERD JOSEPH
Private	SLATER GEORGE
Private	STONES SAMUEL
Private	TURNER ROBERT
Private	THOMPSON THOMAS
Private	WESTON THOMAS
Private	WILSON GEORGE
Private	WALSH JAMES
Private	WOODCOCK THOMAS Missing 18th June
Private	WATERS JOSEPH
Private	WARD BENJAMIN
Private	WALTON WILLIAM
Private	YATES PHILLIP
Private	YOUNG GEORGE Gray collection 1908

Captain Clayton's Troop

Captain	CLAYTON WILLIAM R.
Lieutenant	RIDDLESDEN JOHN B.
Lieutenant	WATSON HON. GEO. J.
Qr.Master	TROY THOMAS
Corporal	WADDELL ARCHIBALD Glendinings sale 21st July 1909
Corporal	DAWTRY JAMES
Corporal	ATHERLY GEORGE
Trumpeter	GREEN JOHN
Private	BURLEY BEMJAMIN
Private	BREARLEY JOHN
Private	BINGHAM THOMAS Gaskell's coll. 1908
Private	BULL JAMES
Private	BRIDGE SAMUEL
Private	BARKER EDWARD
Private	BATESON JOSEPH
Private	BARON HENRY
Private	BIRCH GEORGE
Private	BLACKWELL JOB
Private	BRADLEY JAMES Sotherby's Sale Dec.1910
Private	CHEETHAM THOMAS
Private	CARR JOHN
Private	CLAPHAM WILLIAM
Private	CURTIS WILLIAM
Private	DEARDEN WILLIAM
Private	EVANS THOMAS Col. Murray's collection.
Private	FORD CHARLES
Private	FIRTH THOMAS
Private	FRANKLIN JAMES
Private	FEATHERSTONE THOMAS
Private	HINCHLEY SAMUEL
Private	HAINSWORTH JOHN
Private	HANBY MICHAEL
Private	HAMPSON JAMES
Private	HASLUM JAMES
Private	HUTCHINSON JOSEPH
Private	HAY JAMES
Private	HILL JOHN
Private	JUSS ROBERT
Private	KNOWLES THOMAS
Private	LEWIN HENRY
Private	LONGWORTH THOMAS
Private	LEE THOMAS
Private	MALLARD OWEN Gray Collection 1908
Private	MORRIS HENRY
Private	MARSDEN JOHN
Private	NEWSOM JOHN
Private	OGILWAY JAMES Cheylesmore Collection
Private	OGLE WILLIAM
Private	PILGRIM JOHN
Private	PRESTON STEPHEN
Private	ROBERTS WILLIAM
Private	RAWSON JOSEPH
Private	ROTHERA SAMUEL
Private	SHAW JAMES
Private	SMITH THOMAS
Private	SKIDMORE WILLIAM
Private	TODD GEORGE Col. Gaskell's sale May 1911
Private	WILKINSON WILLIAM
Private	WILKINSON THOMAS
Private	WILTON JOHN

* * *

1st (or KING's) DRAGOON GUARDS

Captain	MICHAEL TURNER Wounded D.
Captain	JAS. F. NAYLOR
Captain	WM. ELTON
Captain	J.P. SWEENEY
Captain	ROBT. WALLACE
Captain	T.N. QUICKE
Captain	JAS. LEATHAM
Captain	WM. STIRLING
Lieutenant	R. BABINGTON
Lieutenant	R.T. HAWLEY
Lieutenant	T.C. BRANDER
Lieutenant	EDWD. HAMILL Payne Coll.
Lieutenant	W.D. IRVINE
Lieutenant	J.E. GREAVES Whitaler Collection 1908
Lieutenant	T.N. HIBBERT
Lieutenant	GEO. QUICKE
Lieutenant	T.F. MIDDLETON
Cornets	HON. H.B. BERNARD
Cornets	W.W. HUNTLEY
Qr.Master	JOHN BROWN
Surgeon	JNS. GOING
Ass.Surgeon	J.W. MACAULEY
Ass.Surgeon	R.A. PEARSON
Troop Qr.Mr.	JAMES RIGG
Regt.Sjt.Maj.	THOS. BARLOW Needes Collection 1908
P.Mr.Sjt.	HOUGHTON RICHARD

Sch.Mr.Sjt.	THOMAS JNS.
Ar.Sjt.	HALSON EDMOND
Saddler Sjt.	MISSETT ROBERT Day Sale April 1910
Troop S.Maj.	FAIRCLOUGH JAMES
Troop S.Maj.	WRIGHT EDWD.
Troop S.Maj.	LEVITT JNS.
Troop S.Maj.	LINTON THOS.
Troop S.Maj.	TRACEY JNS.
Troop S.Maj.	PAGE JAS.
Troop S.Maj.	BANKS JNS.
Serjeant	CASTLE JOS.
Serjeant	MUTTON HENRY
Serjeant	RINGLAND ROBT.
Serjeant	SHEWARD WM.
Serjeant	KENNETT RICHD. On Sale Baldwin's July 1912
Serjeant	STUBBINGS JNS.
Serjeant	BREW THOMAS
Serjeant	RICHARDSON JNS.
Serjeant	SMALLWOOD NATL.
Serjeant	STRINGER THOS.
Serjeant	ASHWORTH THOS. Sold at Glendinings 29.7.08
Serjeant	BRADBURY EMANL.
Serjeant	HOLLIS RICHD.
Serjeant.	TURNER WM.
Serjeant	ADAMS JNS.
Serjeant	BROWN WM. Glendinings sale Feb. 1911
Serjeant	HOLMES JAS.
Serjeant	POINTON THOS.
Serjeant	CHIVERS WM.
Serjeant	SMITH SAMUEL
Serjeant	SMITH WM.
Serjeant	TEBBS JNS.
Serjeant	NUTTALL ROBT.
Serjeant	VENT THOS.
Serjeant	WATTS ROBT.
Serjeant	WILSON JON.
Serjeant	COOPER JAS.
Serjeant	NUTTALL JAS.
Serjeant	SANDS THOS.
Serjeant	WARD JNS.
Serjeant	DRAKE JOS.
Serjeant	NORMAN NATHL.
Serjeant	STARKEY CHAS.
Serjeant	TUCKER JNS.L.
Corporal	DUDGEON THOS.
Corporal	OZWIN JNS.
Corporal	ROPER RALPH
Corporal	SISSON JNS.
Corporal	WHITE THOS.
Corporal	BLANCH STEPHEN
Corporal	GREEN RICHD. Glendinings sale June 1911
Corporal	HAYWOOD CHAS.
Corporal	THOMPSON GEO.
Corporal	ADAMS JNS.
Corporal	ASPINALL GEO.
Corporal	HEMMING WM.
Corporal	STEVENS GEO.
Corporal	GOODACRE WM.
Corporal	PARR JNS.
Corporal	ROLLINSON JAS.
Corporal	TAYLOR THOS.
Corporal	BRISCOE JOS.
Corporal	KIBBLE THOS.
Corporal	PERKINS THOS.
Corporal	SPELLAR JAS.
Corporal	CLARKE WM.
Corporal	HURFORD ROBT.
Corporal	JENNINGS JNS.
Corporal	WATTS RICHD.
Corporal	CLARK JNS.
Corporal	GRIPTON ROBT.
Corporal	OVENDALE GEO.
Corporal	PAGE JAS.
Corporal	BULMAN GEO.
Corporal	CLAPP JOSIAH
Corporal	SIMPSON JAS.
Corporal	TRESSLER WM. Col.Murray's Collection.
Trumpeter	DIXON WM.
Trumpeter	WATTS WM.
Trumpeter	HILLIER WM.
Trumpeter	OLIVER WM.
Trumpeter	WHEELER SAML.
Trumpeter	WILKINS ROBT. Glendinings sale Feb.1909
Trumpeter	DEATH WM.
Trumpeter	OSBOURNE WM.
Private	ABBOTTS JAS.
Private	ASHTON JNS.
Private	ASHLEY ROBT.
Private	ATHA BEJN.
Private	BATEMAN CHAS.
Private	BATTIE THOS.
Private	BEARDSLEY JAS.
Private	BINDER ROBT.

Private BRADBURY JNS.
Private BRADBURY GEO.
Private BRIDGEMAN WM.
Private BRIGHT CHAS.
Private BROWN JNS.
Private BROWN JAS.
Private BUXTON JAS.
Private CAPON HENRY
Private CLEMENTS THOS.
Private COOPER JEREMIAH
Private CROSBIE WM.
Private CUSTOBODY JAS.
Private DOWNING T.D.
Private GORDON CHAS.
Private GREENHALGH JAS.
Private GREENHALGH RICHD.
Private HASLAM WM.
Private HERBERT THOS.
Private HERDSMAN RICHD.
Private HEWITT MATTW.
Private HOLLOWAY MOSES Galway Foley Collection 1910
Private LEWIS JNS.
Private LOUGHTON JNS.
Private MAIDEN JNS.
Private MAIKEN JOSH.
Private MATHER JAS.
Private NICKSON JAS.
Private NOVIS THOS.
Private PEET WM.
Private PEMBERTON THOS. H.Gaskell's coll. 1908
Private PIPPER ISSAC
Private PIZZEY RICHD.
Private PLATT JOS.
Private POWELL J.P. Fleming Collection
Private ROE SAML.
Private SARSON WM.
Private SEAMAN STEPHEN
Private SIMPSON THOS.
Private SOPER ROBT.
Private SHAW JNS.
Private STANLEY CHAS.
Private TAYLOR GEO.
Private TEMPLE JNS.
Private TYERS THOS.
Private WAINFORD HENMAN
Private WALE WM.
Private WALKDEN ADAM
Private WEST JOB
Private WITTON JNS.
Private WOODWARD JAS.
Private WRIGHT JNS.
Private ANDREWS JNS.
Private BAPTIE ALEX.
Private BARBER JNS.
Private BARRETT THOS.
Private BERKSHIRE FRANS.
Private BEWLEY HUNTER
Private BIRCH JNS.
Private BLACKBURN HENRY
Private BLACKHURST RALPH
Private BOURNE JAS.
Private BROWN THOS.
Private CARTER JNS.
Private CARTER ISSAC
Private CHANTRY GEO.
Private COCKBURN THOS.
Private COULT THOS.
Private COOK JAS.
Private COOK JOSH.
Private CROSSWELL JNS.
Private DRY JNS.
Private ECKLEY THOS.
Private FAIRFAX JOSH.
Private FIELDHOUSE SAML.
Private FULLBROOK JNS.
Private FULLER JNS.
Private GEE PETER
Private GLOVER JOHN
Private GREEN JEREMH.
Private HALL FRANS.
Private HALE RICHD.
Private HANCOCK JNS.
Private HOLDNOW SAML.
Private JONES THOS.
Private JAMES JNS.
Private LEWIS JOSH.
Private LLOYD THOS.
Private MORLEY JOSH.
Private NEWTON WM.
Private MOSELEY JNS.
Private NUTTALL JNS. Glendinings sale Dec.1908
Private PEGG JOSH.
Private PIPER WM.
Private PREECE THOS.

Private	PRIECE THOS.
Private	PURHAM GILES
Private	ROBINSON WM.
Private	SLATER GEO.
Private	STEVENSON LEOND.
Private	STOKES JNS.
Private	SUTTON WM.
Private	VICKERS JAS.
Private	WALKER JNS.
Private	WALKER CHAS.
Private	WALKER GEO.
Private	WARD NATHL.
Private	WARREN JNS.
Private	WEST JNS.
Private	WILLIAMSON RICHD.
Private	WOODWARD WM.
Private	WOODMAN THOS.
Private	YOUNG JNS.
Private	ALETT WM.
Private	BARTTEMORE THOS.
Private	BOOTH JNS.
Private	BOTTOMS THOS.
Private	BOWER SAML.
Private	BUTCHER JNS.
Private	CHAPMAN WM.
Private	CULLAM GEO.
Private	CURTICE JAS.
Private	DEACON ROBT.
Private	DEAKIN THOS.
Private	DYSON ELY
Private	ELLIS ESAU
Private	EVANS LUKE
Private	FRANKUM JNS.
Private	FRAY WM.
Private	GASKILL THOS.
Private	GREGORY JOS.
Private	GROVES WM.
Private	HARRISON WM.
Private	HAISTE GEO.
Private	HASKER THOS.
Private	HILL JAS.
Private	HILL RAMAGE
Private	HOUGHTON JOSH.
Private	KAY JNS.
Private	KILBAND WM.
Private	LEE JNS.
Private	LOMAX WM.
Private	LYWOOD JOSHUA
Private	MARSHALL GEO.
Private	MASON THOS.
Private	MILLETT JNS.
Private	MOASS JOSH.
Private	MONGER JOSH.
Private	PARTRIDGE THOS.
Private	PERRY JNS.
Private	PICTON JNS.
Private	PINDER JNS.
Private	PINK CHAS.
Private	PREECE PHIL.
Private	ROSTHORNE EDWD.
Private	SAUNT JAS.
Private	SCHOFIELD JAS.
Private	SCHOFIELD WM.
Private	SIMPSON HENRY
Private	SMITH JNS.
Private	SYKES JOSH.
Private	TAYLOR WM.
Private	VINVENT JNS.
Private	WARD SAML.
Private	WHEATCROFT JNS.
Private	WHITEHOUSE WM. Glendinings sale 25th Oct. 1907
Private	WHITE JOSH.
Private	WHITE HENRY
Private	WILKINS THOS.
Private	WILLIAMS WM.
Private	WOODBURN WM.
Private	WRIGHT JNS.
Private	APPLETON WM.
Private	ASHTON JNS.
Private	BABB HENRY
Private	BARRELL RICHD.
Private	BATTIE JNS.
Private	BENTON WM.
Private	BLAKE THOS.
Private	BOND EDWD.
Private	BONSOR RICHD.
Private	BRADSHAW STAMFORD
Private	BRIDGE JAS.
Private	BROOKS BENJAMIN
Private	BULL JNS.
Private	BULL SAML.
Private	BUNNEY WM.
Private	CHELTON JNS.
Private	CLARK JNS.
Private	COPLEY GEO.
Private	DAKIN THOS.
Private	DALE THOS.
Private	DALRYMPLE THOS.

Private	DAVENPORT THOS.
Private	DOLTON WM.
Private	ENGLEFIELD JOSH.
Private	FAIRBROTHER WM.
Private	GIEVES HENRY
Private	GROVES EDWD.
Private	GUILFORD THOS.
Private	HALL ROBT.
Private	HARFIELD JOSH.
Private	HARRISON SAML.
Private	HUTCHISON JAS.
Private	JONES JNS.
Private	KAY JNS.
Private	LANCELY WM.
Private	LAWSON JON.
Private	LONG JOSH.
Private	LONGFIELD WM.
Private	MARTIN JAS.
Private	MATTHEWS ROBT.
Private	MEYRICK JNS.
Private	MUSSON JAS.
Private	NEWMAN EDWD.
Private	POOLE JNS.
Private	PORTER RICHD.
Private	PREECE BENJN.
Private	REED JAS.
Private	ROBINSON JNS.
Private	SHEFFIELD JNS.
Private	THOMPSON JAS.
Private	TOWERS JAS.
Private	WARD WM.
Private	WATKINS JOSH.
Private	WHITE SAML.
Private	WILLSHEE WM.
Private	WOON THOS. Col. Gaskell's sale May 1911
Private	BAGLEY CHAS.
Private	BALL BENJN.
Private	BARNETT CHAS.
Private	BIRD THOS.
Private	BODHILL EDWD.
Private	BOSSON JNS.
Private	BRIDGE BURY Gray Collection 1908
Private	CHORLEY SAML.
Private	CRANE JOHN
Private	CULLY WM.
Private	DAVIS JAS.
Private	DAVIS RICHD.
Private	DYMES JNS.
Private	FALCONBRIDGE JNS.
Private	HARRIS RICHD.
Private	HAYNES MATTW.
Private	HELPS LEOND.
Private	HEMMING EDWD.
Private	HICKMAN WM. Glendinings sale June 1912
Private	JACQUES FRANS.
Private	JAMES WM.
Private	JAMES JNS.
Private	JOHNSON WM.
Private	JOHNSON EMML.
Private	LADD GEO.
Private	LAMPORT JNS.
Private	LEADLEY JAS.
Private	LEE THOS.
Private	LORD JAS.
Private	LYNN THOMP.
Private	MOSS BENJN.
Private	NICHOLSON HENRY
Private	NICHOLSON THOS.
Private	NUTTALL JNS.
Private	PIGG WM.
Private	POPE JAS.
Private	POSTHILL JNS.
Private	RAMSDEN JAS.
Private	RAYNOR GEO.
Private	REEVES JNS. Walter's sale June 1913
Private	RIDER JNS.
Private	RIDER THOS.
Private	ROSTHORNE HENRY
Private	SACKER CHAS.
Private	SEAGRAVE WM.
Private	SIMPSON JNS.
Private	SIMMS SILAS
Private	SMITH JOSH.
Private	SMITH THOS.
Private	SMITH JOHN
Private	STACEY JAS.
Private	STANILAND REUBEN
Private	TASKER JNS.
Private	THWAITES JNS.
Private	VALANCE WM. Glendinings sale June 1911
Private	VARLEY JNS.
Private	WALDREN JNS.
Private	WARBURTON THOS.

Private	ARMSTRONG WM.
Private	BARNES JNS.
Private	BARNETT JOSH.
Private	CHINEY JNS.
Private	CRACKNELL ROBT.
Private	CUMMER CHAS.
Private	EVANS JAS.
Private	FREEMNA JOSH.
Private	GRAYSHOW JAS.
Private	HAWKYARD THOS.
Private	HAYNES CHAS.
Private	HOLMES JNS.
Private	HOWARTH CHAS.
Private	KISBIE THOS.
Private	KNIGHTS GEO.
Private	LEE WM.
Private	LEVERS TIMY.
Private	LOCK JAS. Glendingins sale July 1909
Private	LOMAX JOSH.
Private	LORD CHAS. Cheylesmore Collection
Private	MARVIN WM.
Private	MASON THOS.
Private	MARSDEN GEO.
Private	MCKEY ALEX.
Private	OLIVER WM.
Private	ORME JAS.
Private	PERKINS NATHL.
Private	PINK WM.
Private	POMFREY CHAS.
Private	POULTNEY JOSH.
Private	RAMSDEN THOS.
Private	RHODES EDMD.
Private	RIDGE JAMES
Private	SCOTT JAS.
Private	SHARPLESS JNS.
Private	SMITH SAML.
Private	STOREY JAS.
Private	SUTTON JNS.
Private	TANNER FRANS.
Private	TITLEY SAMPN.
Private	TOON JNS.
Private	WARREN RICHD. Col. Gascoignes collec. 1909
Private	WESTROOP JOSH
Private	WOOD RICHD.
Private	WOOD JOSH.
Private	WRIGHT JONN.
Private	WHITEHEAD RICHD.
Private	YOUNG WM.
Private	ARCHBOLD JNS.
Private	BELLINGER BENJN.
Private	BELL JNS.
Private	BEERSON THOS.
Private	BESTON SAML.
Private	BROWN JNS.
Private	BROWN JNS.
Private	BRAY THOS.
Private	CARTER JOSH.
Private	CALLINGHAM JAS.
Private	CARR PAT.
Private	DAVIS GEO.
Private	DEATH JAS.
Private	DENNER DAVID
Private	DIXON GEO.
Private	DOCKER JNS.
Private	ELSON THOS.
Private	EMMERSON JNS.
Private	EVATT WM.
Private	FLETCHER JAS.
Private	FOLKES WM.
Private	GADSLEY WM.
Private	GARDNER TIMY.
Private	GREENHALGH JAS.
Private	HANSLER CHAS.
Private	HEAPE WM.
Private	HILL ROBT.
Private	HOROBIN SAML.
Private	HOWITH WM.
Private	JONES RICHD.
Private	JONES WM.
Private	JEPHSON JOSH.
Private	LAWSON WM.
Private	LEVITT ISSAC
Private	LENTON WM.
Private	MAY RICHD.
Private	MCKENNA JAS.
Private	MORETON EMANL.
Private	PILGRIM JAS.
Private	POINTON WM.
Private	RICHARDSON JNS.
Private	RIDER JNS.
Private	SERJEANT JNS.
Private	SETTLE WM.
Private	SISSON SAML.
Private	STEEL JAS.
Private	STREET JNS.
Private	SUTCLIFFE JOSH.

Private	SYER STEPHEN
Private	THORNTON JAMES
Private	TUDMAN JAS.
Private	WAKEFIELD THOS.
Private	WALE JNS.
Private	WALKER EDWD.
Private	WARREN EDWD.
Private	WEBSTER RICHD.
Private	WHITE JNS.
Private	WILD EDWD.
Private	ARTINGSTALL WM.
Private	ASTON WM.
Private	BELL THOS.
Private	BARRACK WM.
Private	BARON JNS.
Private	BATEMAN WM.
Private	BEARDER JAS.
Private	BOOTH JNS.
Private	BOSWELL THOS.
Private	BRIGGS ABRAM.
Private	BROWN JAS.
Private	BROWN RICHD.
Private	BUTTERWORTH EDMD.
Private	CAPLAIN WM.
Private	CHAPPLE HENRY
Private	CRAIG ROBT.
Private	DAVENPORT ADAM
Private	DERRY JNS.
Private	DOWNHAM JNS.
Private	ELLIOTT WM.
Private	FITCH WM.
Private	GIBBONS SAML.
Private	GRIMSHAW THOS.
Private	HALL RICHD.
Private	HARRIMAN BENJN.
Private	HAWKINS JOSH.
Private	HEADINGS JNS.
Private	HEADLEY THOS. On sale Baldwin's July 1912
Private	HEWKIN ROBT.
Private	HILL GEO.
Private	HURFORD WM.
Private	JAMES GEO.
Private	KEEBLE SAML.
Private	KITCHEN ROBT.
Private	LAWDMORE HENRY
Private	LEEK JNS.
Private	LOCKY HENRY
Private	NOYES SEPT.
Private	OWEN JOSH.
Private	PATTISON WM.
Private	POET JNS.
Private	PORTER WM.
Private	PRICE EDWD.
Private	REEVES THOS.
Private	RICHARDS ABRAM.
Private	RICHARDSON WM.
Private	ROBINSON THOS.
Private	ROBINSON THOS.
Private	SHIPMAN JNS.
Private	SHARPLEY JAS.
Private	SHIRLEY WM.
Private	STARBROOK JOSH.
Private	STARKEY RICHD.
Private	STONEYSTREET JNS.
Private	TUCKER SAML.
Private	VICKERS WM.
Private	WARCOP JAS.
Private	WARD MATTW.
Private	WEBSTER SAML.
Private	WHITE WM.
Private	WYATT ATHANASA
Private	BROCKHILL WM.
Private	COUSINS WM.

* * *

1st (or ROYALS) REGIMENT of DRAGOONS

Lieut.Colonel	CLIFTON A.B.
Major	DORVILLE P. (Lt.Col)
Surgeon	STUD G.
Ass.Surgeon	ALDERTON C.R.
Ass.Surgeon	PROSSER T.
Vty.Surgeon	RYDING W.
Qr.Master	WADDELL W.
Captain	WINDSOR E.C. Killed Galway Foley Coll. 1910

Captain C.E. Radclyffe's No.1 or "E" Troop

Captain	C.E. RADCLYFFE (Lt.Col)
Lieutenant	T.R. KEILLY
Lieutenant	W. STURGESS
Troop Qr.Mr.	JAMES GILES
Py.Mr.Sjt.	SIMON GULLY
Arm.Sjt.	JOHN INGRAM
Sad.Sjt.	WILLIAM WISELEY
Serjeant	WILLIAM BROOKES
Serjeant	CHAS. H. CAMPBELL
Serjeant	THOMAS LEECH
Serjeant	WILLIAM TUCK

Corporal	THOMAS CATTON
Corporal	ADAM COLLINS
Corporal	JOHN PARTRIDGE
Trumpeter	GAINS MILLER
Private	AMBAGE WILLIAM
Private	ARROWSMITH WILLIAM
Private	AYRES JAMES
Private	BOLTON SQUIRES
Private	BOYDE THOMAS
Private	BRIERS THOMAS
Private	BREINSDON JOHN
Private	BULLOCK JAMES
Private	BURNSIDE JAMES
Private	BUTLER JAMES
Private	COOPER EDWARD
Private	CRANE THEOPHILUS
Private	CROWTHER JAMES
Private	DALSTON THOMAS
Private	DANIELS JOSEPH
Private	DEMPSTER ANDREW
Private	DICK JOHN
Private	DUEN JOHN Cheylesmore Coll. 1908
Private	EASCOTT URIAH
Private	EDNEY RICHARD
Private	ENGLAND JOHN
Private	EVANS WILLIAM
Private	FELTHAM CHARLES
Private	FERRIDGE RICHARD
Private	FIFE HUGH
Private	FLETCHER SIMON
Private	FLETCHER THOMAS
Private	FRANKLIN MOSES
Private	GLASSWICK HENRY
Private	GREY JAMES
Private	HARRIS ROBERT
Private	HARRISON JOHN
Private	HILL WILLIAM
Private	HUSSELL JOHN Glendinings sale Jan. 1910
Private	JONES WILLIAM
Private	KEELING JOSEPH Cheylesmore coll. 1908
Private	KING WILLIAM
Private	LYONS PHILIP
Private	MACK JAMES
Private	MONTFORD JOHN
Private	PATEY HENRY
Private	PERKINS FRANCIS
Private	PORTER JOHN 1st
Private	PORTER JOHN 2nd
Private	ROBERTS RICE
Private	SALTELL SAMUEL
Private	SELF SAMUEL
Private	SLATER JAMES
Private	SMITH ISSAC
Private	TAYLOR ROBERT
Private	WARD JOSHUA
Private	WHITEHEAD THOMAS

Captain Henry Rt.Carden's No.3 or "B" Troop

Captain	CARDEN HENRY R.T.
Lieutenant	BLOIS CHAS.
Cornet	MASSEY HON. JOHN
Troop Sjt.Maj.	BOYDE WILLIAM
Serjeant	DAVIS WM.
Serjeant	FORD THOS.
Serjeant	GOODALL DANL.
Serjeant	WALKER WM.
Corporal	GREEN JOHN
Corporal	MAYNARD RICHD.
Corporal	TUISLEY JOHN
Corporal	WEBB JAMES
Trumpeter	LAWSON HENRY
Private	ARROWSMITH THOS.
Private	ARTHUR SAML.
Private	BARRATT THOS.
Private	BEARD JAMES
Private	BELLOW JNS.
Private	BILSON JOSH.
Private	BROWN RICHD.
Private	BOND HENRY
Private	BUNGAY KAMES
Private	CATTON THOS.
Private	CLARKE JOHN
Private	COLE GEORGE
Private	COLEMAN JOHN
Private	COX THOMAS
Private	CRANE GEORGE
Private	DALLAN DAVID
Private	DONALD JOHN
Private	FLETCHER HENRY
Private	FOX EDWARD
Private	GIFFORD JAMES
Private	GOWERS WILLIAM
Private	HICKEY ROBT.
Private	HOLLIWELL JOHN
Private	HOLTON BENJN.
Private	JACKSON JOSEPH

Private	JEANS ROBERT
Private	JEFFRIES ROBERT
Private	JESPER JOHN
Private	KING WILLIAM
Private	MASON WILLIAM
Private	MAY PETER
Private	MAYS WILLIAM
Private	MUTTER JOHN Gray Collection 1908
Private	OLDHAM JOHN
Private	PHIPPEN ROBERT
Private	ROTHWELL JAMES
Private	RUMLEY WILLIAM
Private	SADLER WILLIAM
Private	SUTHERN JOSEPH
Private	TOMS RICHARD
Private	TREASURE LEVI
Private	WELCH JAMES
Private	WILD JOSEPH
Private	TAYLOR JOHN

* * *

Captain Ralph Heathcote's No.4 or "C" Troop

Lieutenant	OMMANEY C.
Troop Qr.Mr.	SMITH JOHN
Serjeant	ALLEN JOHN
Serjeant	RIDGE THOMAS
Serjeant	SMITH HENRY
Corporal	DALLIMERE WILLIAM
Corporal	HESLEY JOSEPH
Corporal	WEEKS JOHN
Trumpeter	LEYLAND JOHN
Private	BAKER JONATHAN
Private	BERKENSHAW GEORGE
Private	BRIERLY JAMES
Private	BROWN WILLIAM
Private	CHALL SAMUEL
Private	DAVIS WILLIAM
Private	DIXON JOHN
Private	DIXON JAMES
Private	FATHERS WILLIAM
Private	FIELDSEND THOMAS
Private	FLEMING JOHN
Private	GALLESPIE WILLIAM
Private	GARDINER JOHN
Private	GARRETT WILLIAM
Private	GLADMAN THOMAS
Private	GOMALL JOHN
Private	HALL THOMAS
Private	HALL CLIFFORD
Private	HARGRAVES JOHN
Private	HAYWOOD ROBERT
Private	HOLLIOAK JOHN
Private	HOWARTH THOMAS
Private	HUDSON CHARLES
Private	JENKINS JOHN
Private	JOHNSON WILLIAM
Private	KERSHAW JOHN
Private	MIDLER CHARLES
Private	MILNER BENJAMIN Glendinings sale April 1912
Private	PLAMER JAMES
Private	PARTON THOMAS
Private	PYWELL CHARLES
Private	RODFORD JOHN
Private	RAINS JOHN
Private	ROBINS RICHARD
Private	ROWAN JOHN
Private	SILVESTER JOHN
Private	SIMPKINS THOMAS
Private	SMITH EDWARD
Private	SMITH JOHN
Private	STERMAN STEPHEN
Private	TUCKER EDWARD
Private	WAKELIN RICHARD
Private	WARNER JOHN
Private	WEBSTER GEORGE
Private	WEST THOS. MASON
Private	WEEKS WM. THOS.
Private	WRIGHT JOHN

Captain P. Phipps No.5 or "F" Troop

Captain	PHIPPS PAUL
Lieutenant	MAGNIAC RICHARD
Troop Sjt.,aj.	BIRD WILLIAM Whitaker Coll. 1908
Serjeant	CRITCHLEY THOMAS
Serjeant	STYLES FRANCIS
Serjeant	YOUNG JAMES
Corporal	BARTLAM EDWARD
Corporal	DASORE THOMAS
Corporal	WOOD ROBERT
Trumpeter	MCLEOD HUGH
Private	ABBOTT THOMAS
Private	ASTRIDGE JAMES
Private	AYLIFFE JOHN
Private	BIGGS GEORGE
Private	BOULD JAMES
Private	BUTCHER ROBERT
Private	BUTCHER JOHN

Private	CARPENTER THOMAS
Private	CHILES JOHN
Private	COX FREDERICK
Private	CROOK THOMAS
Private	DRAPER THOMAS
Private	EDGHILL THOMAS
Private	ELSWORTH JOHN
Private	FEWINGS WILLIAM
Private	FISHER JAMES
Private	FORD JNS.
Private	GRUNDY JAMES
Private	HAND JOHN
Private	HARRISON WILLIAM
Private	HARRISON WILSON
Private	HAWKINS WILLIAM
Private	HIBBARD HENRY
Private	HISCOCKS JAMES
Private	LUKINS JAMES
Private	MURICK WILLIAM
Private	MILLER ALEX.
Private	MINTY JAMES
Private	NORRIS JOHN
Private	POPE AARON
Private	PRICE JAMES Col. Murray's collection
Private	PULLEN RICHARD
Private	ROBINS WILIAM
Private	ROWLEY JOHN
Private	SEVESTER JAMES
Private	SISTOTLE WILLIAM
Private	SILLICK WILLIAM
Private	SMITH WILLIAM
Private	SMITHERS JAMES
Private	SNELGROVE FELIX
Private	STABLES DANL.
Private	STEWART JAMES
Private	WILDING THOS.
Private	WILLIAMS JOHN 1st
Private	WILLIAMS JOHN 2nd
Private	WOODHOUSE WILLIAM

Captain C.L. Methuen's No.7 or "D" Troop

Lieutenant	WYNDOWE SAMUEL
Lieutenant	GUNNING GEORGE
Serjeant	GRANT WILLIAM
Serjeant	NOTT JOHN
Serjeant	SAXTON THOMAS
Serjeant	WEBBER WILLIAM
Corporal	COOK JAMES
Corporal	GORMAN THOMAS
Corporal	SAVAGE WILLIAM
Trumpeter	WEBB JOHN
Private	ADLAM JOSEPH
Private	ASHTON JAMES
Private	BACON JAMES H. Gaskell's Collection 1908
Private	BENTON JOHN
Private	BERRISFORD JOHN
Private	BILSBOROUGH JOHN
Private	CHEQUER WILLIAM
Private	COOPER THOMAS
Private	COUSINS JOHN
Private	DANCE WILLIAM
Private	DAVENPORT NOAH
Private	DAY JOHN
Private	DIGBY JAMES
Private	DURHAM RICHARD
Private	DURRALL JOHN
Private	DUTTON JOHN
Private	EDGE ROBERT
Private	EDMONSON WILLIAM
Private	FOSTER THOMAS
Private	FRIERS WILLIAM
Private	GALE GEORGE
Private	GALLISFORD WILLIAM
Private	HALL WILLIAM
Private	HEMERS THOMAS
Private	HILHOUSE JAMES
Private	HUTCHINGS THOMAS Glendinings sale 25th Oct. 1907
Private	ISON JOSEPH
Private	JONES WILLIAM
Private	KERSHAW JOHN
Private	KING ROBERT
Private	KINGHT THOMAS
Private	LENNARD CRISP
Private	MARTIN JOSEPH
Private	MAYHEW ROBERT With MGS offered FB NX for pair 22.9.64
Private	MILLER ALEXR.
Private	MCLEOD JOHN
Private	MORRIS JAMES
Private	PARKER JOHN
Private	PARKER JAMES
Private	SHELL JAMES
Private	SLATER HENRY
Private	WADHAM JOSEPH
Private	WALKER WILLIAM
Private	WARFOOT THOMAS

Private	WATTS RICHARD
Private	WHITE ALEXR.
Private	WHITTLE WILLIAM
Private	WILES WILLIAM
Private	WILLIAMS WILLIAM
Private	WILMOTT RICHARD
Private	WILSON JAMES

Captain A.K. Clark's No.8 or "G" Troop

Captain	CLARKE ALEXR. K.
Lieutenant	TRAFFORD S.
Lieutenant	GOODENOUGH S.
Cornet	STEVENSON S.
Troop Sjt.Maj.	SANDERSON ROBERT
Serjeant	CHURCHILL JOSEPH
Serjeant	SMITH ROBERT
Serjeant	SMITH JOHN
Corporal	BENNETT GEORGE
Corporal	DICKMAN ROBERT
Corporal	WILSON CHARLES
Corporal	WHEELER JOHN
Trumpeter	DYSON JAMES
Private	ANDERSON STEPHEN
Private	BAXTER ARTHUR
Private	BENTLEY MICHAEL
Private	BRAGE JOHN
Private	BURTON JOHN
Private	CLAPPEN WILLIAM
Private	COUSINS JOHN
Private	CROCKER JAMES
Private	CRUMSTY BRYAN Littledale sale Nov. 1910
Private	GIBBS JOHN
Private	HARBOUR WILLIAM
Private	HAWKINS THOMAS
Private	HUBBARD THOMAS
Private	JONES GEORGE
Private	LEGGATT WILLIAM Col. Gascoigne's coll. 1909
Private	LOMAX RALPH
Private	MANN WILLIAM
Private	MARTIN STEPHEN Payne Collection 1911
Private	MEYER JOHN
Private	NIGHTINGALE JOHN
Private	NOYLE JACOB
Private	PORCH JAMES
Private	PORTER WILLIAM
Private	POWELL SAMUEL
Private	PUMMELL WILLIAM
Private	RICHARDSON JOHN
Private	RIGLEY RICHARD
Private	ROTHWELL HENRY Needes Collection 1908
Private	RYLAND JOHN
Private	SAUNDERS WILLIAM
Private	SANDERSON JOHN
Private	SHAW JOHN Day Sale April 1910
Private	SIMMONDS JOHN
Private	SIMPSON WILLIAM
Private	SMITH CHARLES
Private	SMITH GEORGE
Private	SPARROW JAMES
Private	SPINDLOW EDWARD
Private	STEVENSON THOMAS
Private	THOMAS JAMES
Private	THOMPSON ROBERT
Private	TULLISON WILLIAM
Private	WADDELL ALEXR.
Private	WARD THOMAS
Private	WARING HENRY
Private	WEEKS JAMES
Private	WHEELER WILLIAM
Private	WILLIAMS JOHN
Private	WILSON JAMES

* * *

2nd (or R.N.B.) REGIMENT of DRAGOONS

Major	CLARKE J.B. Wounded
Major	HENKIN J.P. Wounded
Adjutant	MACMILLAN HENRY
Surgeon	DAUN ROBERT
Ass.Surgeon	ALEXANDER JAMES
Ass.Surgeon	YOUNG
Vty.Surgeon	TRIGG JOHN
Qr.Master	LENNOX JOHN
Py.Mr.	DAWSON WILLIAM

Captain (late Barnard's) Troop

Lieutenant	FALCONAR G.H.
Troop Sjt.Maj.	PERRIE WM.
Reg.Sjt.Maj.	CRAWFORD WM.
Py.Mr.Sjt.	BAYNE WM.
Arm.Sjt.	BRAY JAMES
Sad.Sjt.	WALLACE ALEXR.
Serjeant	GILLIES JNS.
Serjeant	PORTIOUS WM.
Serjeant	WHITE JNS.
Corporal	HALL ALEXR.

Corporal	LITCH ALEXR.
Corporal	SCOTT JNS.
Corporal	WYLIE HUGH
Trumpeter	STEVENSON HUMPHREY
Private	ATKINS JNS.
Private	ANDREWS JNS.
Private	BALLANTYNE JAS.
Private	BELL EDWARD
Private	BELL ISSAC
Private	BLAIN JNS.
Private	BROMLEY WM.
Private	BULLOCK JAS.
Private	CALLANDAR JNS.
Private	CHAMBLING JNS.
Private	CLACHAN JAS.
Private	DRUMMOND JAS.
Private	FIDDES GEO.
Private	FRAME JAS. Needes Collection 1908
Private	GIBSON JAS.
Private	HEAD HENRY
Private	JARVIE JNS.
Private	JARVIE JOSEPH
Private	KAILY DAVID Galway Foley Coll. 1910
Private	KIDD WM.
Private	KNOX JAS.
Private	LEVINGTON JNS.
Private	LUKE WM.
Private	McCREE ADAM
Private	MCMILLAM JAS.
Private	MARSHALL JNS.
Private	MATHIE DAVID
Private	MATTHEWS ROBERT
Private	NAIRNE JAS.
Private	NICHOLS THOMAS Wounded
Private	PATRICK WM.
Private	PENTLAND DAVID
Private	PRONAN WM.
Private	ROBERTSON WM.
Private	ROOD JOB
Private	ROWAN JAMES
Private	TAYLOR WM. Wounded
Private	WATSON JNS.
Private	WATT ROBERT Wounded
Private	WELLS WILLIAM Wounded
Private	WILLIAMSON WM.
Private	WILLIAMSON WM.
Private	WILSON DAVID
Private	WHITE JNS.
Private	YOUNG THOS.

Captain Payne's Troop

Captain	PAYNE EDWD,
Lieutenant	HAMILTON ARCHD.
Lieutenant	WYNDHAM CHAS.
Troop Sjt.Maj.	ROBERTSON WM.
Serjeant	BULLOCK JAS.
Serjeant	DUNN DAVID
Serjeant	MCNEIL JNS.
Serjeant	SOMERVILLE WM.
Corporal	EDWARDS GEO.
Corporal	MILWARD GEO.
Corporal	NELSON MICHAEL
Private	ANDERSON DAVID on sale Baldwin's July 1912
Private	ARMOUR ALEXR.
Private	BISHOP JNS.
Private	BORLAND ALEXR.
Private	BRAZIER JOSH.
Private	BROWN JNS.
Private	BULLOCK THOS.
Private	CAMPBELL ALEXR.
Private	CAMPBELL COLLIN
Private	CARMALY ROBT.
Private	CLARKE WM.
Private	CUNINGHAM WM.
Private	EAVES HENRY
Private	EVANS PETER
Private	FERGUS THOS.
Private	FLEMING WM.
Private	GIBSON PETER
Private	GOURLEY ALEXR.
Private	HAMILTON JNS.
Private	HART JAS.
Private	HICKLEY WM H. Gaskell's Collection 1908
Private	HILL WM.
Private	HUNTER ALEXR.
Private	INGRAM ALEXR. Littledale sale Nov. 1910
Private	LAPSLEY JAS.
Private	LEE RICHD.
Private	LEVITT WILLIAM
Private	LONGWORTH GEORGE
Private	MCKECHAY JNS. Watters sale June 1913
Private	MCLELLAND DAVID
Private	MCLEOD ALEXR.

Private	MCLINTOCK JAS.
Private	MACKIE WM.
Private	MARTIN JNS.
Private	MASTERTON JAS.
Private	MANCHLIN GEO.
Private	MERRIE WM.
Private	MILLER ROBT.
Private	PATERSON JAS.
Private	PATERSON ROBERT
Private	PATTISON HUGH
Private	PEDEN ANDW.
Private	SIFTON SAMUEL
Private	SMITH JAMES
Private	SMITH WM.
Private	SMITHERS JAS.
Private	TUCKY JOSH.
Private	WAITE JAS.
Private	WALKER JAS.
Private	WELLS FRANCIS
Private	WILLETT GEO.
Private	WILKERSON WM.
Private	WILSON WM.
Private	WILSON ROBT.
Private	WRIGHT ARCHD.

Captain E. Cheney's Troop

Captain	CHENEY EDWD.
Lieutenant	STUPART FRANCIS
Lieutenant	GAPE JAS.
Troop Sjt.Maj.	DINGWALL ALEXR.
Serjeant	CAMPBELL DONALD
Serjeant	DICKIE WM.
Serjeant	HARVEY WM.
Serjeant	RENNIE ALEXR.
Corporal	HAIR ROBERT
Corporal	LAIRD WM.
Corporal	LONG JNS.
Corporal	ROSS JAS.
Trumpeter	SIBOLD JOHN H. Grey Collection 1908
Private	ALLISON GEO.
Private	ANDERSON MATTHEW
Private	BELL ARCHD.
Private	BICKETT HUGH
Private	BRASH JNS.
Private	BURGESS CHAS.
Private	BUTTON JAS.
Private	CALDER JNS.
Private	CLARKE SAML.
Private	CRAIG ARCHD.
Private	CRIGHTON DAVID
Private	CROWE THOS.
Private	CROMBIE JNS.
Private	DICKINSON MAJOR
Private	DRYSDALE PETER
Private	FRASER JNS.
Private	GRAY GEO.
Private	GUNN WM. Day sale April 1910
Private	HAMILTON (Snr) JAS.
Private	HAMILTON (Jnr) JAS.
Private	HENDERSON DAVID
Private	HEPBURN ADAM
Private	HUBBARD WM.
Private	JOHNSON THOS.
Private	JUDD JNS.
Private	LOCHEAD WM.
Private	McCLURE ANDREW
Private	MCFARLANE ARCHD.
Private	MCINTYRE JNS.
Private	MCKENDRICK ANDW.
Private	MCKINLEY WM.
Private	MCPHERSON ALEXR.
Private	MAKIN ROBT.
Private	MANN JAS.
Private	MATHIE WM.
Private	OMAN THOS.
Private	RAMPTON DAVID
Private	RONALDS JAS.
Private	SCOTT ANDW.
Private	SCOTT JAS.
Private	SPRAIKE JNS.
Private	STIRLING JNS.
Private	STIRLING ROBT.
Private	STIRLING WM.
Private	STOBO THOS.
Private	TIMPERLY THOS.
Private	TEMPLE ROBT.
Private	THOMPSON JAS.
Private	TOMAN JNS.
Private	WALLACE JNS.
Private	WATT WM.

Captain J. Poole's Troop

Captain	POOLE JAS.
Lieutenant	WEMYSS JNS.
Troop Sjt.Maj.	RUSSELL JAS.
Serjeant	BISHOP JNS.

Serjeant	JOHNSTON RICHD.
Serjeant	STODDART THOS.
Corporal	GARDNER ALEXR.
Corporal	NELSON JAS.
Corporal	ROBERTS JNS.
Trumpeter	BUNCLE PETER
Private	ALEXANDER JNS. Payne Collection 1911
Private	BRUCE JAS. Col.Gaskell's sale May 1911, Christie 16.3.65
Private	CRAWFORD JAS.
Private	CRIAG DAVID
Private	CROWE JOSEPH
Private	DONALDSON ALEXR.
Private	ERSKINE WM.
Private	GIBSON GAVIN
Private	GIBSON JNS
Private	GILCHRIST ROBT.
Private	GOODS THOS Col Murray's Collection
Private	KENNEDY JAS.
Private	LANDER ALEXR.
Private	LEES ANDRW.
Private	LOCKS WM.
Private	LOWRIE ROBT.
Private	MCGONN DAVID
Private	MCVICAR FREDK.
Private	MILLER JNS.
Private	MUIR ANDW.
Private	NELSON JNS.
Private	NOAKES EDWD.
Private	PLAMER HENRY
Private	PHILLIPS THOS.
Private	RATCLIFFE JAS.
Private	RICHARDSON JAS.
Private	ROBERTSON THOS.
Private	ROBERTSON WM.
Private	ROWAT JNS.
Private	SALMON JNS.
Private	SCOTT MATTHEW
Private	SMELLIE ROBT.
Private	STEVENSON ROBERT
Private	TAIT ADAM
Private	THOMPSON JNS.
Private	TOVIE JAS.
Private	WARK JNS.
Private	WHITE ANDREW
Private	WILSON ROBT.
Private	WILLES WM.
Private	WRIGHT WM.
Private	YOUNG ALEXR.
Private	YOUNG NATHL.

Captain R. Verner's Troop

Captain	VERNER ROBT.
Lieutenant	MILLS JNS.
Troop Sjt.Maj.	MCMILLAN WM.
Serjeant	CLARKE WM.
Serjeant	EWART CHAS
Serjeant	TAMOCK JNS Cheylesmore Collection 1908 Christie 16.3.65
Corporal	DICKSON JNS.
Corporal	TAR SAML. Col.Gascoigne's Collection 1909
Corporal	WILSON ALEXR.
Trumpeter	REEVES JOSH.
Private	ATHERLY JNS.
Private	BROWN FRANCIS Glendinings sale Feb. 1913
Private	BROWN JAS.
Private	BROBIN JNS.
Private	BUTLER GEO.
Private	COLQUHOUN ADAM
Private	COLLIER JNS Needes June 1908
Private	CRAIG ROBT.
Private	DALZIEL JNS.
Private	DUMLOP WM.
Private	DUNN JNS.
Private	GILLIES JNS.
Private	GORDON WM.
Private	GOURLEY ROBT.
Private	GRIEG ROBT.
Private	HARKNESS JNS.
Private	HENDERSON JNS.
Private	HODKINSON HENRY
Private	JONES WM.
Private	KENMUIR SAML.
Private	KING JAS.
Private	LAND JNS. Glendinings sale Dec. 1913 Christie 16.3.65
Private	MCALL DAVID
Private	MCGEE JNS.
Private	MACKIE WM.
Private	MCNAIR WM.
Private	MATTHEWS JNS.
Private	MONTGOMERY JAS.
Private	MOORE JNS.
Private	PATTON (Snr) WM.
Private	PATTON (Jnr) WM.

Private	PARK WM.
Private	REID ROBT.
Private	REID THOS.
Private	ROSS WM.
Private	SMITH JAS.
Private	SMITH WM.
Private	SYKES WM.
Private	THOMPSON EDEN.
Private	VEAZY JNS.
Private	WALLACE ROBT
Private	WATSON THOS.
Private	WHARAN RICHD.
Private	WISE JNS.

Captain T.C. Fenton's Troop

Captain	FENTON THOS.C.
Lieutenant	GRAHAM J.R.S.
Serjeant	ANDREW JAS.
Serjeant	HAYWARD RICHD.
Serjeant	SOARS THOS.
Serjeant	SWAM WM.
Corporal	CRAIG JNS.
Corporal	DAVIS THOS.
Corporal	THOMPSON ROBT.
Corporal	MAIR JNS.
Trumpeter	BOWING HENRY
Private	ANDERSON THOS.
Private	ARKLIE JNS.
Private	ARMOUR JAS.
Private	BALLANTYNE WM.
Private	BIDDOLPH GEO.
Private	BLACKADDER ALEXR.
Private	BOULTER SAML.
Private	BOWES CUNNINGHAM
Private	BROOKES STEPHEN Littledale sale Nov.1910 Christie 16.3.65
Private	BROWN ADAM
Private	CAMPBELL JNS.
Private	CLARKE JNS. Whitaker Collection 1908
Private	CURRIE ROBT.
Private	DICK WM.
Private	DOBBIE JNS.
Private	FERGUSON JNS.
Private	GOULD JNS.
Private	GREEM JAS.
Private	HOWIE WM.
Private	HUNTER ALEXR.
Private	HUNTER HUGH
Private	HUNTER ROBT.
Private	HUTTON ARCHD.
Private	JONES JAS.
Private	KEAN ARCHD.
Private	KEAN JAS.
Private	KEEBLE SAML.
Private	KINDER SAML.
Private	LIDDLE JNS.
Private	LITTLEJOHN ROBT.
Private	MACRO JOSEPH
Private	MILLER PETER
Private	MITCHELL JNS.
Private	PEARSON WM.
Private	REID WM.
Private	ROSS JNS.
Private	SMITH WM.
Private	SWAN PETER
Private	TAYLOR JONATHAN
Private	THOMPSON ANDREW
Private	WATSON JNS.
Private	WILMOT THOS.

* * *

6th (or INNISKILLING) DRAGOONS

Lt. Colonel	MUTER JOSEPH
Major	MILLER FIENNES
Surgeon	BOLTON JOHN
Ass.Surgeon	RICKETTS WM.H.
Vty.Surgeon	VINCENT RICHD.
Qr.Master	KERR JAMES
Pay.Master	ARMSTRONG WM.
Lieutenant	BUFFS P. severely wounded 4th D.Gs.

Captain Edward Hollech's Troop

Captain	HOLLECH EDWD.
Troop Sjt.Maj.	MARSHALL MATTHEW Needes Collection 1908
Reg.Sjt.Maj.	BOYDE THOS.
Pay.Mr.Sjt.	HUNTER MAURICE
Sad.Sjt.	MITCHELL WM.
Trumpeter Maj.	GILBERT BENJN.
Serjeant	BROWN ROBT.
Serjeant	COPP CHAS.
Serjeant	CARROLL BERNARD
Serjeant	MAGAVERN FRANCIS
Corporal	HUDDLESTON JOHN
Corporal	PATTERSON JOHN
Corporal	WALTON RICHD.
Private	ALLEN WILLIAM

Private	ARMSTRONG JAMES
Private	ASPILL MICHL.
Private	BIANDON JAMES
Private	BROTHRICK MATTW.
Private	CANN RICHD.
Private	CARDIFF WM.
Private	CARRIGAN HUGH on sale Baldwin's July 1912
Private	CAVE PHILIP
Private	CRAWFORD JOSEPH
Private	CLARK JAMES
Private	CORBETT HUGH
Private	CORR FRANCIS
Private	CURLESS GEORGE
Private	DEERY WM.
Private	DUFFEY PATRICK
Private	ELLIOTT ARTHUR
Private	EWENS THOMAS
Private	GORMLEY HUGH
Private	HACKETT EDMUND
Private	HARRY GEORGE
Private	HIDGE ISSAC
Private	LEE STEWART
Private	MCLANAPHY THOMAS Galway Foley Collection 1910
Private	MELVILL JOHN
Private	MCBRIDGE PETER
Private	MCGINNES THOMAS
Private	MCMANUS JAMES
Private	MCKEWN JOHN
Private	PENN WILLIAM London 1975
Private	POTTERS ROBERT
Private	PRICE CYRUS
Private	PRICE BENJN.
Private	QUINN WILLIAM
Private	SMITH JONATHAN
Private	TRAINER CHARLES
Private	TURNER HENRY
Private	REACH MICHAEL
Private	ROBINSON RICHARD
Private	ROONEY THOMAS
Private	WRAY EDWARD

Captain William F. Hadden's Troop

Captain	HADDEN WM.F.
Lieutenant	DAWN RICHARD
Troop Sjt.Maj.	EMERSON ISSAC
Serjeant	EARLS JNS. Col. Gascoigne's Coll. 1909
Serjeant	MCMAHON HUGH
Serjeant	WILLIAMSON JAMES
Trumpeter	DEAKIN JOHN
Private	ADAMS THOMAS
Private	ARMSTRONG CHRISTOPHER Watter's sale June 1913
Private	ARTHURS JAMES
Private	ANDERSON JAMES
Private	AITCHISON JAMES
Private	BRANNON PATRICK
Private	BRISON JOHN
Private	CAMPBELL JAMES
Private	CAVANAGH THOMAS
Private	CARRON JOHN
Private	COMBS LAURENCE
Private	COX ALEXANDER
Private	CRAWLEY JOHN
Private	DAVIDSON ALEXANDER
Private	DAVIS JOSEPH
Private	DENNISON SAMUEL Col. Murray's Collection
Private	DENNISON WILLIAM
Private	FEE JAMES Sotherby's sale Feb. 1914
Private	FEE DANIEL
Private	FERRAND STEPHEN
Private	GALLEY JOHN
Private	GIBSON JOSEPH
Private	GLRN JOHN
Private	HENSON JOHN
Private	HILL WILLIAM
Private	KERRY HENRY
Private	KIDNEY JAMES
Private	KILPATRICK FRANCIS
Private	LEECH JAMES
Private	LEE THOMAS
Private	LYLE JOSEPH
Private	MILLS JAMES
Private	MOORE SAMUEL
Private	MOORE WILLIAM
Private	MANAGHAM JOHN
Private	MOSS JOHN
Private	MURPHY JAMES
Private	MCTAGGART JAMES
Private	NIDSDALE JOHN
Private	OBRIEN LAWRENACE
Private	PALMER GEORGE Glendining's Sale Feb.1914
Private	SCARLETT THOS.
Private	SMITH SAMUEL
Private	WALKER ROBERT
Private	YORK JOHN

Captain William F. Brown's Troop

Captain	BROWN WM.F.
Lieutenant	WILLETT AUG.S.
Lieutenant	PETRE HENRY
Troop Sjt.Maj.	MUSSON ALEXR.
Serjeant	CIOTHUS ROBERT
Serjeant	HANKINS WILLIAM
Serjeant	MCMAHON ARTHUR
Corporal	GRAHAM ROBERT
Corporal	MCGAVERN JOHN
Corporal	QUIN CHARLES
Trumpeter	MCGRAW JOHN
Private	BARRON JOHN
Private	BRENDON SAML.
Private	BARRY WM.
Private	CAFFREY BARTHW.
Private	CAMPBELL WILLIAM
Private	COFFEY JOHN Glendining's Sale 25th Oct. 1907
Private	COLLINS HUGH
Private	CONNALLY HENRY
Private	CONNALLY ANTHONY
Private	COSGROVE WILLIAM
Private	CORRY MICHAEL
Private	CROOKS THOMAS
Private	CURREN JAMES
Private	CARSON WILLIAM
Private	CROZIER JAMES
Private	EAGIN MARTIN
Private	FERGUSON COLIN
Private	FRAIL JOHN
Private	GARDNER THOMAS
Private	KENNEDY ROBERT
Private	KEAMS WILLIAM
Private	KEAMS JOHN
Private	KIRK WILLIAM
Private	KING RICHARD
Private	LEYONAW HUGH
Private	MONAGHAN PATRICK
Private	MCBRIDE FRANCIS
Private	MCGRENERY PHILLIP
Private	McCARTNEY HUGH
Private	MCMANUS HUGH
Private	NUGENT PETER
Private	PARKER WILLIAM
Private	ROBINSON JOHN
Private	ROE THOMAS
Private	ROE WILLIAM
Private	ROGERS WILLIAM
Private	RYANS JAMES
Private	SCALLON THOMAS
Private	SCOTT GEORGE
Private	SCOTT MATTHEW
Private	TONER JOHN
Private	TODD THOMAS
Private	TRIMBLE WILLIAM
Private	WARMSLEY WILLIAM
Private	WATSON WILLIAM
Private	WILSON HUGH
Private	YOUNG JAMES

Captain Henry Madox's Troop

Captain	MADOX HENRY
Lieutenant	LINTON JOHN
Troop Sjt.Maj.	MACUE JAMES
Serjeant	DICKERSON GEORGE Littledale sale Nov.1910
Serjeant	SLAITER THOMAS
Serjeant	SINNOTT THOMAS
Serjeant	HERRON WILLIAM
Corporal	MCDOWELL FREDK.
Corporal	WINLOW ALEXR.
Private	ALLEN ALEXANDER
Private	ARMSTRONG JOHN
Private	ANDERSON JOHN
Private	BAMFORD JOHN
Private	BENSON STEPHEN
Private	BEATS JOSEPH
Private	BLEAKLEY WILLIAM
Private	BRANCH THOMAS
Private	CONNALLY JAMES
Private	CLAYTON MATTHEW
Private	CROTHERS EDWARD
Private	DEVELAND HUGH
Private	DOWLAND HENRY
Private	FLESH JAMES Scott Earnshaw June 1912
Private	GORDON MIDLEY Payne Collection 1911
Private	HAMILTON ROBERT
Private	HAZLE JOHN
Private	HOOKS MOSES
Private	JOHNSTON ROBERT
Private	IRWIN MICHAEL
Private	IRWIN CHARLES
Private	KENT JOHN
Private	KELLY WILLIAM
Private	LIDDY THOMAS

Private	MARSHALL JOHN
Private	MATHERS THOMPSON
Private	MEXWELL JAMES
Private	MONTGOMERY JAMES
Private	MONTGOMERY WILLIAM
Private	MORTIMOW EDWARD
Private	MORTIMOW WILLIAM
Private	MURPHY ROBERT
Private	McCLAIN THOMAS
Private	McGARR JAMES
Private	McGARGIN GREGORY
Private	PORTER WILLIAM
Private	PRICE NOBLE
Private	QUIGLEY PHILLIP
Private	ROBINSON ALEXR.
Private	ROEBUCK JERRY
Private	RUTLEDGE JAMES
Private	ROGERS CHARLES
Private	ROGERS NEIL
Private	RYAN PETER
Private	SENIOR ESAU
Private	SMITH WILLIAM
Private	STENSON JAMES
Private	TONER JAMES
Private	THOMBURY JAMES
Private	WARD JOHN
Private	WORLING GEORGE

Captain Hon. S. Douglas's Troop

Captain	DOUGLAS HON.S.
Lieutenant	HASSARD ALEXR.
Cornet	ALLINGHAM JOHN D.
Troop Sjt.Maj.	LENEY WILLIAM
Serjeant	NUGENT THOMAS
Serjeant	TILDSLEY ABRAM.
Serjeant	POALER HOLLIDY
Serjeant	CORBETT MICHAEL
Corporal	DOUGHERTY FRANCIS
Corporal	MARSLOW JOHNSTON Whitaker Collection 1908
Trumpeter	GOOD ROBERT
Private	ALLISON JAMES
Private	BARRON THOMAS
Private	BARNETT FRANCES
Private	BIDDLETON WILLIAM
Private	BRUCE WILLIAM
Private	BUNCH THOMAS
Private	CARRON THOMAS
Private	CLARK THOMAS
Private	CUMMINS JOHN
Private	DAVIS WILLIAM
Private	DONALDSON WILLIAM
Private	DRUM JOHN
Private	DUNKIN HENRY
Private	EVANS THOMAS
Private	FAULKNER JAMES
Private	FOSTER WILLIAM
Private	FOX PATRICK
Private	FREEBURN ROBERT
Private	FULTON JOHN
Private	GALLAGHER JOHN
Private	GILBREATH JOHN
Private	HEAVY CHARLES
Private	HOWDEN WILLIAM
Private	HUGHES JAMES
Private	HUMPHRESS ROBERT
Private	JOHNSTON WILLIAM
Private	JOHNSTON (Jnr) JAMES
Private	JOHNSTON JNS.
Private	KING JNS. Fleming Collection 1871
Private	KEAMS WILLIAM
Private	LEECH EDWARD
Private	LEWES JOHN On sale 1975
Private	LYNCH HENRY
Private	MIDDLETON JOHN
Private	MURPHY OWEN
Private	MOODY THOMAS
Private	MORROW DAVID
Private	McCANN JOHN
Private	McCLUSKY PHILLIP
Pricate	McCREECE JOHN
Pricate	McGURK JOHN
Private	OBRIEN LAURENCE
Private	NOUGHER GILBERT
Private	PAGE HIRAM
Private	PEARSE LUKE
Private	PENFORD WILLIAM On sale at Baldwin's July 1912
Private	ROGERS PATRICK
Private	ROYAL LAURENCE
Private	TOWNSEND EDWARD mentioned by Marsland in letter 1.4.64
Private	TREACY JAMES
Private	TODD ADAM

Captain Thomas Macky's Troop

Captain	MACKY THOMAS
Lieutenant	BIDDULPH T.

Lieutenant	BLACK SAML.
Troop Sjt.Maj.	HOOPER JOHN
Serjeant	CAMPBELL ARTHUR H.Gaskell's Coll.1908
Serjeant	FOX JOHN Cheylesmore Collection 1908
Serjeant	SMITH SAMUEL Needes Collection 1908
Corporal	CARRIGAN B.
Corporal	KELLY JOHN
Corporal	McGUIRE CHRISTN
Trumpeter	EASTERBEE GEORGE
Private	ANNON WILLIAM
Private	ARMSTRONG JAS.
Private	CHURCH SAMUEL Glendinings sale 17 June 1908
Private	CLARK JOHN
Private	CLUFF JAMES
Private	COONEY JAMES
Private	CAMPBELL ROBERT Payne Collection
Private	CONNOR CHARLES
Private	CROZIER MICHAEL
Private	CULLEN LUKE
Private	DRUM WILLIAM
Private	EDWARDS WILLIAM
Private	FALLS WILLIAM
Private	FOSTER JAMES
Private	FLESH PATRICK
Private	GALWAY ROBERT
Private	GALWAY JOHN
Private	GARDNER JOHN
Private	HACKETT JAMES
Private	HUSTON JAMES
Private	HUGHES OLIVER
Private	HUGHES JAMES
Private	HURST JAMES
Private	JOHNSTON JOHN
Private	KEENEN HENRY
Private	LEE HENRY
Private	LOVE ROBERT
Private	LITTLE JAMES
Private	LINDSAY JOHN
Private	LINN PATRICK
Private	MOORHEAD JOHN
Private	MURPHY JOHN
Private	MURPHY WILLIAM
Private	McALESTER JAMES
Private	McCAFFREY NEIL
Private	McCAFFERY THOMAS
Private	McCOURT THOMAS
Private	McCARDWELL BERND.
Private	McGOWAN JOHN
Private	McGRICE JAMES
Private	McQUIRE JOHN
Private	McNAMCE JAMES
Private	NOBLE JAMES
Private	OBRIAN JOHN
Private	OBRIAN PATRICK
Private	PARKER WILLIAM
Private	PORTER CHARLES
Private	ROGERS WILLIAM
Private	SHELDON JAMES
Private	SHELDON JOHN
Private	SMITH DAVID
Private	THISTLE SAMPSON
Private	THOMPSON WILLIAM
Private	WATKINS RICHARD

* * *

7th (or QUEENS OWN) HUSSARS

Colonel	KERRISON W.E.
Major	HODGE E. Killed in Action
Major	THORNHILL WM. Staff
Captain	VEMER WM.
Captain	ROBBINS T.W.
Captain	KEANE EDWD.
Captain	HEYLIGER P.A.
Captain	WILDMAN T. Staff
Captain	FRASER J.J. Staff
Captain	ELPHINSTONE J.D.
Captain	WILDMAN WM.
Lieutenant	OGRADY S.
Lieutenant	SHIRLEY WM.
Lieutenant	GRENFELL WM. Glendinings sale 17th June 1908
Lieutenant	DOUGLAS ROBERT
Lieutenant	UNIACKE ROBERT
Lieutenant	GORDON J.R.
Lieutenant	DANIELL J.
Lieutenant	PETERS C.J.
Lieutenant	WILDMAN JNS.
Lieutenant	BEATTY FREDK.
Lieutenant	RICE J.S.
Lieutenant	TOWERS FREDK.
Pay Master	FELTON THOS.
Lt. & Adjt.	MYERS A. Wounded in action and missing
Qr.Master	GREENWOOD JNS. Whitaker Collection 1908

Surgeon	IRWIN D. Payne Collection 1911
Ass.Surgeon	CHERMSIDE R.A.
Ass.Surgeon	MOFFATT JAS.
Vty.Surgeon	DARVILLE R.
Ass.Vty.Sergeon	MAURICE A.S.
Surgeon	CALLENDAR J. Payne Collection 1911
R.Sjt.Maj.	HOULT JAMES
Trp.Sjt.Maj.	BLACKIES THOS.
Trp.Sjt.Maj.	JARVIS THOS.
Trp.Sjt.Maj.	INSTER JAMES
Trp.Sjt.Maj.	MULLER HENRY
Trp.Sjt.Maj.	RAWNSLEY ROBT.
Trp.Sjt.Maj.	SHORE JOHN
Trp.Sjt.Maj.	TONGUE GEORGE
Serjeant	BRISSETT WM.
Serjeant	VRITLER BENJN.
Serjeant	EAST DAVID
Serjeant	EDWARDS WM.
Serjeant	FULDER THOS.
Serjeant	FISHER THOS.
Serjeant	HATLIP WM. Killed in Action
Serjeant	HAYMAN JOHN Watter's sale June 1913
Serjeant	HINWOOD ROBT.
Serjeant	HOLLAND JOHN
Serjeant	HOOPER WILLIAM
Serjeant	KING CHAS.
Serjeant	MILES VINCENT
Serjeant	MANTAGUE HENRY
Serjeant	NEWMAN WM.
Serjeant	NICHOLSON WM.
Serjeant	POKE JOHN H.Gaskell's Collection 1908
Serjeant	RICHARDS JAMES
Serjeant	RIVERS ROBT.
Serjeant	ROBINSON STEPHEN
Serjeant	STARKEY JOS.
Serjeant	STRANGE WM.
Serjeant	STUMP WM.
Serjeant	WALL WM.
Serjeant	WHITE ROBT.
Serjeant	YORK JNS.
Corporal	AGENT WM.
Corporal	BADCOCK WM.
Corporal	BOWMAN GEO.
Corporal	BROADRIBB SAML.

Corporal	CURRIE JAMES Needes Collection 1908
Corporal	EASTWOOD WM.
Corporal	FRASER DAVID Died of his wounds
Corporal	GARROD THOS.
Corporal	HALL JOHN
Corporal	HARRIS GEO.
Corporal	HITCHEN JNS.
Corporal	HORSLEY JNS.
Corporal	ILTON JNS. Killed in Action
Corporal	JOHNSON HENRY Killed in Action
Corporal	LOWES JOHN
Corporal	MORTIMER JOHN
Corporal	MOSS JOSEPH
Corporal	NIGHTINGALE THOS.
Corporal	POSTINGS THOS.
Corporal	ROACH ROBT.
Corporal	ROSENTAL ANTHONY
Corporal	SKIPPE JAMES
Corporal	STONE HENRY
Corporal	WEBB JOSEPH Killed in Action
Corporal	WOODCOCK JOSEPH
Trumpeter	CRUTCHFIELD JAMES
Trumpeter	GILSON WM.
Trumpeter	LAWTON THOS.
Trumpeter	MATTHEWS BENJN.
Trumpeter	ONIRN ABRAHAM
Trumpeter	TOWNSEND JOHN
Private	ABRAMD WM.
Private	ACKROIDE WM.
Private	AISS THOS.
Private	ALFREY RICHD.
Private	ANDREWS JOHN
Private	APPLEYARD RICHD.
Private	ASHLEY JNS.
Private	ASHTON JNS.
Private	ASHLIN JNS.
Private	ATKINS JAMES
Private	ATKINS JAMES
Private	AVISS JOHN on sale at Baldwin's July 1912
Private	BAIRD JOHN
Private	BAKER PETER
Private	BAKER NOAH Killed in Action
Private	BALL JOHN
Private	BALL JOSEPH
Private	BAMFORD RICHARD
Private	BARBER JOSEPH

Private	BARLOW JOHN
Private	BARTLETT JAMES
Private	BASSETT WM.
Private	BATES THOS.
Private	BATEMAN THOS.
Private	BEADLE THOS.
Private	BECKITT THOS.
Private	BEECH JAMES
Private	BENNETT HENRY
Private	BENSTEAD JOSEPH
Private	BENSON WM.
Private	BEST WM.
Private	BESWICK JOHN
Private	BETTS WM.
Private	BOLOFIELD GEO.
Private	BOOTH JAMES
Private	BORRETT JAMES
Private	BOUTLER JAMES Killed in Action
Private	BOULTER JOSEPH
Private	BRADSHAW THOS.
Private	BREWSTER THOS.
Private	BRIDGES WM.
Private	BRILLARD WM.
Private	BROWN JONATHAN
Private	BROWN STEPHEN
Private	BROWN THOS.
Private	BROWN WM.
Private	BRUMFIELD JOSEPH
Private	BRYANT WM.
Private	BURMAN ABRAM. Died of his wounds
Private	BURTELL WM.
Private	BURTON WM.
Private	BYFORD WM.
Private	BAMBER THOS.
Private	CAMM GEO.
Private	CARNAL DAVID
Private	CARTER JAMES
Private	CASTLE JAMES
Private	CASTLE WM.
Private	CAVE JAMES
Private	CHANDLER ROBERT
Private	CHANDLER JOHN
Private	CHAPMAN JAMES
Private	CHARLWOOD GEO. Glendinings sale Feb. 1909
Private	CHATTERTON JAMES
Private	CHEADLE JAMES
Private	CHILTON JOHN Glendinings sale Oct. 1913 2.10.0
Private	CHURCH SAML.
Private	CHURCH WM.
Private	CLARE JAMES
Private	CLARKE JAMES
Private	CLARKE JAMES
Private	CLARK BENJ.
Private	CLAYTON CHAS.
Private	CLAYPOLE HENRY
Private	COCKERELL CHAS.
Private	COCKS JOHN
Private	COLLINGSWORTH SAML.
Private	COLLINS THOS.
Private	COLLINS CHAS.
Private	COOK JOHN
Private	COOPER JOHN
Private	COTTON EDWD.
Private	COURTNEY JOHN
Private	COX JOHN
Private	COXHEAD JOHN
Private	CROSSMAN ROBERT
Private	CRUTCHFIELD
Private	DALE ISSAC
Private	DALE RICHD.
Private	DALTON JOHN
Private	DAVENPORT THOS.
Private	DAVIES JOHN Glendinings sale Oct. 1913
Private	DAVIES JOHN
Private	DAVIES JOHN
Private	DAVIES GEO.
Private	DAVIES THOS.
Private	DEANE JAMES
Private	DEATH THOS.
Private	DELL JAMES
Private	DICKMAN THOS.
Private	DIMOND WM.
Private	DOREY WM.
Private	DOWLING THOS.
Private	DOWSELL ROBT.
Private	DRAKE HENRY
Private	DUNNETT JAMES Col.R.T. Gascoigne's Collection 1909
Private	DURBIN JAMES
Private	EASH JAMES
Private	EDLEY WM. Died of his wounds
Private	EGGLETON WM.

Private	ELLIOTT WM.
Private	ELSON JOHN
Private	FAIRCLOTH WM.
Private	FAVELL WM.
Private	FINCH WM. Glendinings sale Jan. 1911
Private	FISHER JOHN
Private	FISHER JOEL
Private	FISHER ROBT. Killed in Action
Private	FISH WM.
Private	FOWLER JOHN Glendinings Sale Dec.1913
Private	FOX WM.
Private	FRANKS JAMES
Private	FRASER GEORGE
Private	FRY WM.
Private	FULLBROOK WM.
Private	GAIT JOHN
Private	GARMENT WM.
Private	GARRETT THOS.
Private	GICKS JOHN on sale at Baldwin's Feb. 1910
Private	GILBERT CORNELIUS
Private	GILMORE EDWARD
Private	GEOVER THOS. Gray Collection 1908
Private	GOBLE JOHN
Private	GOOLD ROBT.
Private	GREEBE FREDK.
Private	GROVES JAMES
Private	GILBERT JOHN
Private	HAINE WM.
Private	HALLETT WM. Killed in Action
Private	HAMBLETON GEO. Glendinings sale Dec. 1913
Private	HAMLET WM.
Private	HAMMERTON WM.
Private	HANDCOCK JACOB
Private	HARMAN JOHN
Private	HARRIS SAML.
Private	HARRALL WM. Died of Wounds
Private	HASELL JAMES
Private	HASLUM WM.
Private	HATHERBY JOHN
Private	HAWKINS CHAS.
Private	HAWKINS WM.
Private	HAYES JOHN Killed in Action
Private	HEAD JOSEPH
Private	HEAL JOHN
Private	HEARN WM.
Private	HERBERT GEORGE
Private	HERRING JAMES
Private	HESSEY JAMES Gray Collection 1908
Private	HEWITT JOHN Col.Murray's Collection
Private	HILSDEN JOHN
Private	HITCHCOCK RICHD. Glendinings sale April 1912
Private	HUTCHINSON WM.
Private	HOGG ROBT.
Private	HOLLOWAY SAML.
Private	HOLLOWAY HENRY
Private	HOMAN HOWELL
Private	HONEYBOAME ROBT.
Private	HOOPER THOS.
Private	HOTT WM.
Private	HOWARD HENRY
Private	HOWARD JAMES
Private	HOWELL PETER
Private	HOWES JAMES
Private	HOYTES THOS.
Private	HUFTON JOHN
Private	HUGHES WM.
Private	HUMPHREY JAMES
Private	HUNT WM.
Private	HUNT HAMOND
Private	JACKSON HAMOND
Private	JACKSON JAMES
Private	JACKSON THOS.
Private	JACOBS HENRY
Private	JACOBS JAMES
Private	JEFFREYS THOS. Killed in Action
Private	JOHNSON JOHN
Private	JOHNSON WM.
Private	JONES ROBT.
Private	JULYAN BENJN.
Private	JULYAN JOHN
Private	KEELING JEPTHA Killed in Action
Private	KEMP MOSES
Private	KETTERICK JOHN
Private	KNAPP JOHN
Private	LAMB MATTW.
Private	LAMB ROBT.
Private	LANE JOSEPH
Private	LAPER GEO.
Private	LATTIMORE THOS.

Private	LAWSON JAMES
Private	LEEDLE MATTW.
Private	LEWIS THOS.
Private	LINTON JAS.
Private	LINNICAR RICHD.
Private	LLWELLYN THOS.
Private	LLOYD DAVID Killed in Action
Private	LLOYD JAMES Littledale sale Nov.1910
Private	LOCK HENRY
Private	LOCKYER JEWITT
Private	LOMAX JOHN
Private	LOVELL OWEN
Private	LOWDEN DAVID Died of his wounds
Private	LOWE WM.
Private	MANN JAMES Cheylesmore Coll.1908
Private	MANSFIELD THOS.
Private	MARSH JOSEPH
Private	MARSHALL GEO.
Private	MARTIN JOHN
Private	MASKELL WM.
Private	MASON JOHN
Private	MASON WM.
Private	MAY GEO.
Private	MAYS JOHN
Private	MILKINS THOS.
Private	MILLER ROBT.
Private	MILSOME GEO.
Private	MONEYPENNY JOSEPH
Private	MONK JOHN
Private	MORPHEW JOHN
Private	MORRIS WM.
Private	MORSLEN NATHW.
Private	MORTON WM.
Private	MOSS INSTINIAN
Private	MOWKES EDWD.
Private	MUNDAY JOSEPH
Private	NATH JOHN
Private	NATH GEO.
Private	NAYLOR THOS.
Private	NEAL JAMES
Private	BEILD LUKE
Private	NOBLE JOHN
Private	NORTH EDWD.
Private	OLD JAMES
Private	OLIVER RICHARD Glendining's Sale 25th Oct. 1907
Private	PARKER JAMES
Private	PARRY JOHN Galway Foley Collection 1910
Private	PARSONS HENRY
Private	PASSMORE THOS.
Private	PAYNE JAMES
Private	PEARCE JOSEPH
Private	PEARCE ROBT
Private	PEARSON WM.
Private	PEATFIELD JOHN
Private	PETERS JOSEPH
Private	PETERS WM.
Private	PHILPOT JOHN
Private	PUK THOS.
Private	PIERS PETER
Private	PIMBLE CHAS.
Private	PHIPPON JAMES
Private	PILMAN PHILIP
Private	PLANE HENRY
Private	PLATT WM.
Private	PORTER JOHN
Private	POUCHER ROBT.
Private	PRATT RICHD.
Private	PREECE BENJN.
Private	PRICE SAML.
Private	RAGG JOSEPH
Private	RASON GEORGE
Private	REED JAMES
Private	REEVES JOHN
Private	RUE THOS.
Private	RIDGER JOHN
Private	ROADLEY JAMES
Private	ROBERTS THOS.
Private	READE JAMES
Private	REDFERN JOSEPH
Private	ROBERTSON WM. Killed in Action
Private	ROBINSON WM.
Private	ROBINSON JAMES
Private	RODIMORE SAML.
Private	RODDLE ROBT.
Private	ROLFE SAML.
Private	ROWELL WM.
Private	RUDLAND JAMES
Private	RUSSELL JOHN
Private	SAINTILL JAMES
Private	SCOTT SIMON
Private	SEAGAR ROBT.
Private	SEAGS EDWD.

Private	SEGGER JOSEPH
Private	SHERMAN LESBIAS
Private	SIMMONDS JAMES
Private	SIMPSON ROBT.
Private	SINGLETON WM.
Private	SINGFORD JOHN
Private	SIVITER JOHN
Private	SKEENE DAVID
Private	SMALL WM.
Private	SMITH ROBT.
Private	SMITH WM. Killed in Action
Private	SMITH BENJ.
Private	SMITHERGALL JAMES
Private	SMITHERWAITE ALEXR. Died of his wounds
Private	SOMERSET JOHN
Private	SOUTHGATE WM.
Private	SOUTHAM WM.
Private	STACEY JOHN
Private	STANGER SAML.
Private	STAPLES JAMES
Private	STEWART JOHN
Private	STOCKFORD JOHN
Private	STORR JOSEPH
Private	STRACHAN JOSEPH
Private	STURT JAMES
Private	SUMMERS DANIEL
Private	SWANSBURY ROBT.
Private	TAIT ADAM
Private	TAYLOR JAMES
Private	TAYLOR WILLIAM
Private	THOMAS ROBT.
Private	THOMPSON JAMES
Private	THOMPSON WM.
Private	THULBY EDWD.
Private	TITTERSON WM.
Private	TORR WM.
Private	TUCKWELL JAMES
Private	TURNER JOHN
Private	WALKER JOHN
Private	WASE WM.
Private	WASF ROBT.
Private	WATTS JOHN
Private	WEAVER SAMUEL
Private	WELCH THOS.
Private	WELMORE CHAS.
Private	WESTON GEO.
Private	WEST EPHRAIM
Private	WHITEHEAD WM.
Private	WHITESMITH GEO.
Private	WHITMORE JOHN
Private	WITTINGTON CHAS.
Private	WILLIAMS RICHD.
Private	WILLIAMS JAMES
Private	WILKINS GEO.
Private	WILKINS JNS.
Private	WILSON ANDREW
Private	WILSON RICHD.CHARLES
Private	WINKS CHARLES
Private	WINTERTON WM.
Private	WITHAM ISSAC
Private	WODDOPS JAMES
Private	WOOLEY JOSEPH
Private	WILSON RICHD.
Private	WOODWARD WM.GEO.
Private	WOODLEY WM.
Private	WORKMAN SAML.
Private	WORRALL WM.
Private	WRIGHT JOHN

* * *

10th ROYAL REGIMENT of HUSSARS

Lt. Colonel	QUENTIN GEO. COL.
Lt. Colonel	MANNERS LORD R.
Major	HOWARD THE HON. F. Killed
Adjutant	HARDMAN SAML.(Lt)
Surgeon	GRANT ROBERT Attached
Ass.Surgeon	JENKS G.S. Payne Collection
Vty.Surgeon	SANNEMAN H.
Pay Master	TALLON JAS. Whitaker Collection
Captain	SHAKEPEARE Supernumerary

Captain John Garwood's Troop No.1.

Captain	GARWOOD JOHN
Lieutenant	HODGSON S.
Lieutenant	LINDSAY WM.
Troop Sjt.Maj.	THOMPSON ROBT. Col. R.T. Gascoigne's Collection 1909
Pay Mr.Sjt.	RIVETTS J.C.
Sad.Sjt.	CLARKE JAS.
Serjeant	BUSBY WM.
Serjeant	GRISDALE LEVI.
Serjeant	CLARK CHAS.
Serjeant	SACKLEY JOHN
Corporal	CRAMPHORN JNS.
Corporal	LAMBERT JNS.
Corporal	INCHES WM.
Corporal	LITTLEWOOD JOHN
Trumpeter	SMITH JOHN

Private	AILSBY JOHN
Private	ANGLES GEO.
Private	BURDEN JOHN
Private	BEAUMHERVIER RENIER
Private	BROWN JOHN
Private	BUDD JOSEPH
Private	BICKLEY WM.
Private	CASTLES JOHN
Private	CASTLES JOHN
Private	CONSTABLE GEO.
Private	CORK JAMES
Private	COREY WM.
Private	CUNNINGHAM ROBT.
Private	DOYLE JAMES
Private	DURHAM SAML.
Private	FARLEM GEO.
Private	FARROW SAMUEL
Private	FLANNAGAN THOS.
Private	FILMER EDWD.
Private	FREWER CHAS.
Private	FRYGATE WM.
Private	GREGSON JNS.
Private	GOODYEAR THOS.
Private	GLOVER SAML.
Private	GOODRIDGE THOMAS
Private	HARDING JOHN
Private	HEMMERSLY
Private	HOLLOWAY JOSH.
Private	HOWELL EDWD.CHAS.
Private	HODGES HENRY
Private	HARTES JOHN
Private	HINES JOHN
Private	HALE JAMES
Private	HARPER JOHN
Private	HOOLE WM.
Private	JENKINS JOHN
Private	JACKSON GEORGE
Private	JONES JOSH.
Private	LAMBERT GEO.
Private	LAWRENCE THOS.
Private	LONGHURST DANIEL
Private	MAGGS JOHN
Private	MORETON JNS.
Private	McKINSEY HENRY
Private	MAY JOSH.
Private	NAILOR ISSAC
Private	NEEDHAM GEO.
Private	NORRIS THOS.
Private	PALMER WM.
Private	REED JOHN
Private	ROBINSON WM.
Private	ROBINSON ROBT.
Private	RUSSELL JOSH.
Private	SMITH THOS. Watter's sale June 1913
Private	SEWELL JOHN
Private	TAYLOR JOHN
Private	THOMPSON THOS.
Private	WALTERS RICHD.
Private	WOOLDRIDGE WILLIAM

Bt. Major Taylor's Troop No.2.

Captain & Bt.Major	TAYLOR
Lieutenant	PARSONS J.W.
Lieutenant	GUNNING GEO. Killed
Trp.Sjt.Maj.	SHADWELL JOHN
Corporal	SCHULTZE JNS.
Corporal	DRUMMOND EDWD.
Corporal	SPICER WILLIAM
Corporal	COLLIER ROBT.
Serjeant	STONE THOMAS
Serjeant	SMALL J.W.
Serjeant	TOOTLE JAMES
Serjeant	VINCE WM. Sold London 1979
Trumpeter	AFFLECK WILLIAM
Private	ARUNDLE JAMES Glendinings sale Oct. 1912
Private	AVERY RICHD.
Private	BAKER JOHN
Private	CURBY JAMES Gray Collection 1908
Private	CHANDLER RD.
Private	CLARKE GEO.
Private	CONNOLLY DANL.
Private	CROUCHER HENRY
Private	DENTON THOS.
Private	DYKE RICHD.
Private	DYMOCK WM.
Private	ETHERINGTON JNS.
Private	FENNING ROBT.
Private	FITZHUGH CHAS.
Private	GAINS ABM.
Private	GOODWOOD JNS.
Private	GORE ROBT.
Private	HALT WM.
Private	GARDIMENT JNS.
Private	HADDOCK JNS.
Private	HAID GEO.
Private	HASLAM THOS.

Private	HALES JAMES
Private	HEYLING JOSEPH
Private	HINSLEY FREDK.
Private	HAILLES WM.
Private	HUICKLEY JOHN
Private	HUMPHREYS WM.
Private	HUNT GEORGE
Private	JACKSON WM.
Private	JORDAN HENRY
Private	JUDD CHAS.
Private	INGLES WALTER
Private	KEMBLE ROBT.
Private	KEON ANDW.
Private	LEVITT THOS.
Private	MARTIN 1st THOS.
Private	MARTIN 2nd THOS.
Private	MERRIOTT JNS.
Private	MATTHEWS HAM.
Private	MILLERS EDWD.
Private	MITCHELL DAVID
Private	NORRIS THOS.
Private	OSBORN WM.
Private	PAINE ISSAC
Private	PALMER THOS.
Private	PALMER WM.
Private	PETHERS THOS.
Private	PORTER CHAS.
Private	RANDALL WM.
Private	RICKARDS JNS.
Private	REDMAN RD.
Private	SEYMOUR EDWD.
Private	SHAWCROSS JOSH.
Private	SMITH JOHN
Private	SPELLES HENRY
Private	THOMAS GEO.
Private	WARREN WM.
Private	WILSON NATHL.
Private	WING WM.
Private	WIRE JACOB

Captain H.C. Stapylton's Troop No.3.

Captain	STAPYLTON H.C.
Lieutenant	CARTWRIGHT WM.
Lieutenant	HAMILTON W.C.
Trp.Sjt.Maj.	CLARKE THOS.
Serjeant	ALLEN HENRY
Serjeant	HODGES WM.
Serjeant	BARKER GEO.
Serjeant	PLOWMAN WM. Sotheby's Sale Dec. 1910
Corporal	CLEWS WM.
Corporal	OTHEN THOS.
Corporal	MARSHALL JAMES
Corporal	SMITH EDWD.
Trumpeter	MILES THOS.
Private	ACOURT FRANCES
Private	ARMITAGE GEO.
Private	ATKINS EDWD.
Private	ATTRIDGE WM.
Private	BENCE ROBT.
Private	BEWLER WM.
Private	BLACKBURN THOS.
Private	BOWLING WM.
Private	BOND THOS. Littledale sale Noc. 1910
Private	BOWLER ROBT.
Private	BRAIN WM.
Private	BIRCH WM.
Private	CHAMPOIN MARTIN
Private	CHARLTON HENRY
Private	CLARK JOSEPH
Private	COCK HENRY
Private	COSTELO EVAN
Private	DALTON SAMUEL
Private	DAVIS GEO.
Private	DAY JOHN
Private	ETHERS WM.
Private	FAIRMAINES ANTH.
Private	FRAZIER JOHN
Private	FRENCH HENRY
Private	FROST THOS.
Private	GARDINER SAML.
Private	GILLETT JNS.
Private	GILKS WM.
Private	GODDARD THOS.
Private	GRAVILLE JOSH.
Private	GREEN WM.
Private	GREEN THOS.
Private	GREEN JAMES
Private	HALL THOS.
Private	HAM JAMES
Private	HARVEY STEPHEN
Private	HEWARD WM.
Private	HILL GEO.
Private	HITCHCOCK WM.
Private	HOUSE JAMES
Private	HOLMES WM.
Private	HOPKINS JOTH.
Private	JOHNSON JAMES

Private	KEMP WM.
Private	LAURENCE JNS.
Private	LLOYD MAURICE
Private	OLDACRE THOS.
Private	PEDLEY WM.
Private	PHILLIPS ISSAC
Private	REED ABEL
Private	ROSS ROBT.
Private	RYDER WILLIAM
Private	STUART I. MAC.
Private	STILLMAN EBENEZER
Private	STONAR WILLIAM
Private	TREVOR HENRY
Private	WHEATLEY SAML.
Private	WILLSON WM.
Private	WOODWARD WM.

Captain Grey's Troop No.4.

Captain	GREY JOHN
Lieutenant	ARNOLD ROBT.
Lieutenant	BACON ANTHY.
Trp.Sjt.Maj.	SURMAN JOHN
Serjeant	FOWLER JOHN
Serjeant	UCKROWITCH JOHN
Serjeant	HUTCHINGS JOHN
Serjeant	HUGHES JOSEPH
Corporal	EDWARDS JOHN Galway Foley Collection 1910
Corporal	WILKINS JNS.
Corporal	LEE JAMES
Corporal	PRICE JAMES
Trumpeter	HUNTER JNS.
Private	ALLYFFE GEO.
Private	BARHAM STEPHEN
Private	BARKE GEO.
Private	BROWN WILLIAM Col. Murray's Collection
Private	BUCKLER SAMUEL
Private	CHADSEY JOHN
Private	CREASE ALEXR
Private	CRANFIELD 1st WM.
Private	CRANFIELD 2nd WM.
Private	COLLIER WM.
Private	COZENS BENJN.
Private	DAKIN THOS.
Private	DYPLOCK WM.
Private	DYOS RICHD.
Private	EARL RICHD.
Private	FARMER JNS.
Private	FORTH ABM.
Private	FRENCH THOS.
Private	GILBERT JNS
Private	GREAVES JAMES
Private	GOODWIN JNS.
Private	HILL GEO.
Private	HOARE CHAS.
Private	HOGSFLESH EDWD.
Private	JACKSON WM.
Private	JOHNSON PETER
Private	LAWRENCE SAML.
Private	NORTH JOHN
Private	NORTHCOTT JOHN
Private	PARROTT WM.
Private	PETTITT GEO.
Private	PETTITT WM.
Private	PRICE EVAN
Private	PILE WM.
Private	REED JAMES
Private	RUFF CHAS
Private	ROBINSON JNS.
Private	SHAOSKIE PETER
Private	SHACKLEFORD JAMES Fleming Collection 1871
Private	SHILCOCK JNS.
Private	SMITH GEO.
Private	SMITH JAMES
Private	STEVENS JAMES
Private	THORP JOHN
Private	THORLEY WM.
Private	THRING JOHN
Private	TRUTCH EDWD.
Private	TRIVETT WM.
Private	TUMBER EDWD.
Private	TINHAM JAMES
Private	VERNON JNS.
Private	UNDERWOOD SAML. Glendining's sale 25th Oct. 1907
Private	WANSTILL WM.
Private	WHITE JOHN
Private	WILKINS WM.
Private	WORTHINGTON THOS.
Private	WRIGHT CHAS. Glendining's sale Jan 1909
Private	YORK GEO.

Captain Charles Wood's Troop No.5.

Captain	WOOD CHAS.
Lieutenant	BURN H.I.
Trp.Sjt.Maj.	KINKEE FREDK. H.Gaskell's Collection 1908
Serjeant	HAITT JAMES

Serjeant	ROPER JOSEPH
Serjeant	WHITE THOS.
Serjeant	JONES JOSEPH Payne Collection 1911
Corporal	HOLMES RICHD.
Corporal	MYER HENRY
Corporal	ROBERTS JAMES
Corporal	SAWKINS WM.
Trumpeter	LATHAM CHAS.
Private	BALTROP REUBEN
Private	BALES CHARLES
Private	BURFITT EDWD.
Private	BROADBENT JOHN
Private	BROUGHTON JOHN
Private	BURTON ALEXR.
Private	BURROWS HENRY
Private	BOX THOMAS
Private	BUNCE JOSEPH
Private	BRYANT GEO.
Private	COLLINS WM.
Private	CHATFIELD JAMES
Private	CHEESLEY JAMES
Private	CLARK GEO.
Private	CLARK WM.
Private	CHANCE RICHD.
Private	CHANDLER JESSE
Private	COLEBROOK JNS.
Private	COMPTON JNS.
Private	DANIELS JAMES
Private	DAWBORN CHAS.
Private	DOWLING JNS. Missing
Private	DERRY JOSEPH
Private	FOWLER WM.
Private	FREEMAN JNS. Cheylesmore Collection 1908
Private	GRASS JOSEPH
Private	HISCOCK DANIEL Glendining's Sale Oct. 1913 4-5-0
Private	HILL JAMES
Private	HARRIS THOS.
Private	HEWSON ALLEN
Private	KENSEY JNS.
Private	KING 1st JAMES
Private	KNIGHT THOS.
Private	LEHE ERNEST
Private	MARSHALL JNS.
Private	MOULTON CHAS.
Private	NORTH JACOB
Private	OSBORN JNS.
Private	POOLE CHRISTIAN
Private	REED MATTW.
Private	RING JOHN
Private	SMITH THOS.
Private	SMITH WM.
Private	STOPFORD THOS.
Private	TAYLOR SAML.
Private	TIBBALDS JON.
Private	THOMPSON WM.
Private	VAUGHAN JAMES
Private	VINCER JOHN on sale at Baldwin's July 1912
Private	WILLIAMS THOS.
Private	WEBB WM.
Private	WEEDY JOHN
Private	WORKMAN EDWD.
Private	WOODRIDGE THOS.
Private	WHITEBREAD CHAS.
Private	WYATE JAMES

Captain H. Floyds Troop No.6.

Captain	FLOYD HENRY
Lieutenant	WALLINGTON J.C.
Lieutenant	SMITH W.S.
Trp.Sjt.Maj.	WARREN JOSEPH
Serjeant	BUCK CHAS.
Serjeant	ELLARD WM.
Serjeant	HOULDSWORTH THOS.H.
Serjeant	TRIGG JOHN
Corporal	LUCAS JESSE
Corporal	SMITH HARRY
Corporal	SWINDON EDWD.
Trumpeter	JAMES OLIVER
Private	ANDREWS RICHD.
Private	BENNETT SAML.
Private	BUSS JOHN
Private	COLE WM. Glendining's Sale 1912
Private	ELLING WM.
Private	EXALL EDWD.
Private	FARMAN JNS.
Private	GAUNT JOSH.
Private	HARRISON JOHN
Private	HEFFIELD WM.
Private	HOOLE JOHN
Private	HORTON JOHN
Private	LANE GEO.
Private	LASSITER JAMES
Private	LITTLER GEO.
Private	LEE HENRY

Private MABY AMBROSE
Private MANLY JOHN
Private MILL HENRY
Private MILNER EDWD.
Private MOREFORT MATTW.
Private MORLEY JOHN
Private MUMFORD THOS.
Private MUERHEAD ROBT.
Private PALMER JOHN
Private PORTER CHAS.
Private PROCTOR THOS.
Private REED JOHN
Private ROBERTS JNS.
Private ROBINSON WM.
Private ROLPH JNS.
Private ROSE THOS.
Private ROWLAND RICHD.
Private RYEGATE JAMES
Private SHAWE WM.
Private SIBLEY JAMES
Private SIMMS PHINEAS
Private SILVESTER JOHN
Private SMITH ROBT.
Private SNELL JAMES
Private SOPER ROBT.
Private STANLEY SAML.
Private STEVENS GEO.
Private STEVENS THOS.
Private SUTTON CHAS.
Private TAMER THOS.
Private THOMAS RICHD.
Private TRITTON JOHN
Private TRUEMAN WM.
Private TURNER WM. Watter's Sale June 1913
Private VENN ISSAC
Private WADE JOSHUA
Private WEBB HENRY
Private WEBB JNS.
Private WELLS STEPHEN
Private WATMORE JOHN
Private WHEELER CHAS.

* * *

11th REGIMENT of LIGHT DRAGOONS

Lt. Colonel SLEIGH J.W.
Major MONEY ARCHIBALD
Adjutant SICKER GEORGE
Suregon OMALLEY JAMES
Ass.Surgeon STEEL HENRY
Rgt.Qr.Mr. HALL JOHN
Pay Mr. LUTYENS DANIEL
Captain CHILDERS MICHL. Bde.Major

Captain James Bourchier's Troop

Captain BOURCHIER JAMES
Lieutenant LYE BENJAMIN
Lieutenant MILLIGAN ROBERT
Cornet JAMES O.H.
Trp.Sjt.Maj. BUTCHER GEORGE A.A. Payne's Collection 1908
P.Mr.Sjt. WILKES JOHN
Tr.Major SINGER WILLIAM
Serjeant ELLIS JOHN
Serjeant ENTWISTLE THOS.
Serjeant PARSTER JAMES
Serjeant WILSON ALEXR.
Corporal BIGGS THOMAS Gray Collection 1908
Corporal HALL JOSEPH
Corporal SMITH JOSEPH
Corporal TURNER JONATHAN
Private ABBOTTS JOHN
Private ANDERSON WILLIAM
Private BANCROFT WILLIAM
Private BECT JOHN
Private BISHOP JOHN
Private BIGGS JONATHAN
Private BRANT DANIEL
Private CARVER JOSEPH
Private COX HENRY
Private CROWDER MARK
Private DASH ROBERT
Private DAWSON WM.
Private DEAM THOMAS
Private EASTINGS ROBERT
Private FARMER JOHN
Private GIBLING JOHN Col. Gaskell's sale May 1911
Private GOODALL JOSEPH
Private GOULDING WILLIAM
Private GOOSE ROBERT
Private GREENWOOD THOMAS
Private GROVER RICHARD
Private HADWICK RICHD.
Private HALL BENJN.
Private HART JOHN
Private HARWOOD GEORGE
Private HARKER JOHN

Private	HOPKINS WILLIAM Holloway sale at Sotheby's May 1910
Private	HOWSE JOHN
Private	IRDLE JOHN
Private	JONES HENRY
Private	KAY JOSEPH
Private	KANES THOMAS
Private	KEYWORTH JOSEPH
Private	LEAVETT WILLIAM
Private	LOW EDWIN
Private	LOCKWOOD THOMAS
Private	MARTIN WILLIAM
Private	MASTERS GEORGE
Private	MOSS THOMAS
Private	NASH WILLIAM
Private	ONIBBLER THOMAS
Private	PERREY THOMAS
Private	POWELL JAMES
Private	PINK JOHN
Private	SPENCE JOSEPH
Private	STRANGE ROBERT
Private	TAYLOR EDWD.
Private	TOMPKINS THOMAS
Private	TOMKINSON WM.
Private	TURNER JAMES
Private	WADMORE ROGER
Private	WHARAM JEREMIAH
Private	WETTON JOHN
Private	WILDE CHARLES
Private	WOOD WILLIAM
Private	WOOLCOTT SAMUEL
Private	WOOLDRIDGE JOHN
Private	WOOLHOUSE GEORGE
Private	YEATES THOS.
Private	MALLABAR WILLIAM Killed in Action 18th June

Captain Benjamin Lutyen's Troop

Captain	LUTYEN BENJN.
Lieutenant	COLES RICHD. Wounded
Lieutenant	SCHREIBER GEORGE
Trp.Sjt.Maj.	GAMBLE RICHD. Gray Collection 1908
Serjeant	DIXON CHARLES
Serjeant	STUMP THOMAS
Serjeant	WALDON JOBB Wounded
Serjeant	WINKWORTH JOHN
Corporal	BETTRIDGE HENRY
Corporal	CHAPMAN GEORGE
Corporal	MILLER THOMAS
Corporal	OLIVER JOHN
Trumpeter	ELLIS JOHN
Private	ARMITAGE ISSAC
Private	BARTLETT JAMES
Private	BARBER EDWD.
Private	BENWELL WILLIAM
Private	BEECHAM BENJN.
Private	BENTLEY WM.
Private	BIGGINS WM.
Private	BRADBY JOHN
Private	BRUMLEY JOHN
Private	BRETT BENJN.
Private	BRETT JOHN
Private	BUCKLEY JOSEPH
Private	BROOK PHILIP
Private	BURNETT ROBT.
Private	BUDD RICHD. Col.Murray's Collection
Private	BURMAN MATTW. Cheylesmore Collection 1908
Private	BURVILLE CHAS.
Private	CATO JESSE
Private	COLEMAN JOSEPH
Private	CURTIS JOHN
Private	DICKMAN FRANCIS
Private	EASTWOOD JOHN
Private	ELPHEE WILLIAM
Private	FIELD RICHD.
Private	FLAXMAN JOHN
Private	FLEMMING MICHAEL Chelsea Hospital Collection 1908
Private	FORD THOS.
Private	FORD WM.
Private	FREMANTLE EZEKEL
Private	GOLLOWAY CHRISTOPHER Wounded
Private	GIBBS JOHN
Private	GRIFFIN THOMAS
Private	HIX JAMES
Private	HAGLE JOHN
Private	HOOK JOHN
Private	JAMES JOHN
Private	JENT JAMES
Private	KILNER JOHN
Private	KNIGHTON WM.
Private	LEIGHTON GEORGE
Private	MAWSON JOHN
Private	MAJOR JOHN
Private	MEMBRY EDWD. Wounded
Private	MITCHELL JOHN
Private	MORETON JAMES
Private	MOSS JAMES

Private	PARKER WM.
Private	PARKER SAML.
Private	PATTERSON JOSEPH
Private	PATRICK WILLIAM
Private	PEEL JOHN
Private	PIOTT JOHN
Private	PLETTS THOMAS
Private	RAND WILLIAM
Private	SHAKELLS SAML.
Private	SHAW JONATHAN
Private	SLEATER JOHN
Private	TINDLER ADAM
Private	WIMBOURNE THOS.
Private	WITHERS W.H.

Captain J.A. Schreiber's Troop

Captain	SCHREIBER J.A.
Lieutenant	PHILIPS EDWD. Killed in Action 18th June
Lieutenant	ROTTEN J.R.
Trp.Sjt.Maj.	KNIGHT JOHN
Serjeant	BRADDICK JOSH.
Serjeant	BREARLY WM.
Serjeant	WATTS JOHN
Serjeant	WIDDERS SAML.
Corporal	DAY GEORGE
Corporal	HIGGINS THOMAS
Corporal	LANGDALE WILLIAM
Corporal	MORGAN WILLIAM
Trumpeter	BRADLEY WILLIAM
Private	ARMITAGE BENJN.
Private	BANKS CHAS.
Private	BAMBRICK ROBERT
Private	BERESFORD CHAS.
Private	BOAST CHAS.
Private	BROWN JOSEPH Phillip's Sale
Private	BUTLER GEO.JOSEPH
Private	BUTTERWORTH JAMES
Private	CARTWRIGHT EDWD.
Private	CHAPMAN ROBERT
Private	CHILTENHAM GEORGE
Private	CROWTHER THOMAS
Private	DASH WILLIAM
Private	DRUMMOND THOMAS
Private	DUGDALE CORNELIUS Payne Collection
Private	FITTON ROBERT
Private	FOGG PETER
Private	FORD RICHD.
Private	GILLMAN JOHN
Private	HAMMOND JOSEPH
Private	JONES WILLIAM
Private	JOHNSON JOHN
Private	LANCETT JAMES
Private	LEWIS JOHN
Private	MAYS WILLIAM H.Gaskell's Collection 1908
Private	MARLOW JOHN
Private	McGRIGOR JOHN
Private	MEAD DAVID
Private	MERCHANT JOHN
Private	MORGAN JOHN
Private	MORBY WILLIAM
Private	MUNDAY JOHN
Private	MURRAY ROBERT
Private	MYERS THOMAS
Private	NEWBY JOHN
Private	OTTEY JOHN Wounded
Private	PARKINSON THOMAS
Private	PEHH HENRY Wounded
Private	PERREY JAMES
Private	PLANT SAML.
Private	PORCH JOSEPH Wounded
Private	ROVUEN JOHN
Private	SALT GEORGE
Private	SOUTHERN CHARLES Galway Foley Collection 1910
Private	SWINNERTON WILLIAM
Private	TAYLOR WILLIAM
Private	TWEEDLE WILLIAM
Private	VALLI SAMUEL
Private	WALTER GEORGE
Private	WATSON CHARLES
Private	WATSON WILLIAM
Private	WARD THOMAS
Private	WARD SAMUEL
Private	WATCH JOHN
Private	CLUVLEY EMANUEL Killed in Action 18th June
Private	GRANT JAMES Killed in Action 18th June

Captain John Jenkin's Troop

Captain	JENKINS JOHN
Lieutenant	SMITH WILLIAM
Cornet	BULLOCK HENRY
Trp.Sjt.Maj.	HAWKINS CALEB
Serjeant	ANTHONY JOHN
Serjeant	ELIVER RICHD.

Serjeant	MITCHELL ROBT.
Serjeant	TONG WILLIAM
Corporal	DARLING RALPH
Corporal	HOLLIDAY JAMES
Corporal	MOORS WILLIAM
Trumpeter	HOWSON JOHN
Private	BAKER DANIEL
Private	BARR JOSEPH
Private	BANCROFF GEORGE
Private	BELLAMY BENJN.
Private	BIRD DANIEL
Private	BODY STEPHEN
Private	BODY THOMAS
Private	BROWN WILLIAM
Private	BRERETON WILLIAM
Private	CLARK WILLIAM
Private	CONE HENRY
Private	COXON JOHN
Private	CONNORS JAMES
Private	CRUMP WILLIAM
Private	DAVIS WILLIAM
Private	DEADMAN JOHN
Private	DOXEY TIMOTHY
Private	DUNCAN ROBERT
Private	EVANS THOMAS
Private	FAWBERT GEORGE
Private	FAITHFULL JOHN
Private	FROGGARD JOSEPH
Private	GOULDSMITH WILLIAM
Private	GREEN JOHN
Private	HALMARAC SAMUEL
Private	HARGREAVES THOMAS
Private	HILL ISSAC
Private	HILL JOSEPH
Private	HOWARTH JOHN
Private	HOWSON EDWIN
Private	IND WILLIAM
Private	JONES WILLIAM
Private	JUDD GEORGE
Private	KENYON JOHN
Private	KNIGHT GEORGE
Private	LANCASTER THOMAS
Private	LANTON JOHN
Private	LEE WILLIAM
Private	LEE MATTHEW
Private	LEIGH AARON
Private	MAY WILLIAM
Private	MARLER WILLIAM
Private	MARLOW GEORGE
Private	MARTIN THOMAS
Private	MATTISON JOHN
Private	MEEDE THOMAS
Private	NORGATE WILLIAM
Private	PAYNE CHARLES
Private	PADMORE JAMES
Private	PEPLOW GEORGE
Private	ROSCOE ROBERT
Private	SHAW WILLIAM
Private	SHRIMPTON WILLIAM
Private	SMITH JOHN
Private	SMART CHAS.
Private	STACEY THOS.
Private	TIPPEN JOHN
Private	TURNER ROBT.
Private	VALLIS JAMES
Private	VICKERY JOSEPH
Private	WEBB WILLIAM
Private	WHITHAM THOS.
Private	WISE JOHN
Private	WOOD GEORGE
Private	WOODFORD ALEXR.
Private	WHARTON JAMES

<u>Captain Thomas Binny's Troop</u>

Captain	BINNY THOS
Lieutenant	MOORE JAMES Wounded
Cornet	ORME HUMPHREY
Trp.Sjt.Maj.	KNIGHT JACOB
Serjeant	BAMBRICK JOHN
Serjeant	BILLINGARY MATTW.
Serjeant	GRIMES ROBT.
Serjeant	HUDSON WM.
Corporal	AVERY JAMES
Corporal	BAALERN BENJN.
Corporal	MULLIGAN ANDREW Littledale sale Nov.1910
Corporal	ROYLE RICHARD
Trumpeter	WHEATLEY ROBERT
Private	ADAMS JOHN
Private	ADAMS JAMES
Private	BARNES JAMES
Private	BARROWS JOHN
Private	BREABY ABRAHAM
Private	BECKETT THOMAS
Private	BOWELL LUKE
Private	BROWNE STEPHEN
Private	BROUGHTON JOHN
Private	BUMSTEAD WILLIAM
Private	CANFIELD SAML.

Private	CHAPMAN CHRISTOPHER
Private	COATES WILLIAM
Private	CROOME JOSEPH
Private	CROWTHER JOHN
Private	DAWSON CHARLES
Private	EARNSHAW JOHN
Private	ENTWISTLE JAMES
Private	FRANKLIN JOHN
Private	GALLOWAY E.A.
Private	GARDINER THOS.
Private	GRAVETT RICHD.
Private	GRANGER JOHN
Private	HARDING SAMUEL
Private	HEARNSHAW GEORGE
Private	HOWGATE JOHN
Private	JACOBS THOS.
Private	JARVIS JAMES
Private	JACQUES PETER
Private	JONES WILLIAM
Private	LOCOCK ROBT.
Private	LLOYD RICHD.
Private	MYERS THOS.
Private	NEAL WM.
Private	OVERTON GEORGE
Private	POWELL JOHN
Private	RADWICK PHILIP
Private	RUDLAND WM.
Private	STINNALL GEORGE
Private	STANDFIELD THOS. Wounded
Private	STANLEY RICHD.
Private	STEERS WILLIAM
Private	STWEART THOS.
Private	STEPHENS ROBT. Col.R.T. Gascoigne's Collection March 1909
Private	STOCKTON PETER
Private	SMITH THOMAS
Private	SWIFT JOHN
Private	TAYLOR GEORGE
Private	TIBBLES THOMAS Neede's Collection 1908
Private	TRUTCH THOMAS
Private	THORNTON ABRAHAM
Private	VICKERS JAMES
Private	WALKER WILSON Wounded
Private	WEBSTER JOSEPH
Private	WHITWORTH THOS.
Private	WIGGINS RICHD.
Private	WILKINS EDWD.
Private	WILKINSON SAML. Wounded
Private	HARDING EDWD. Killed in Action 18th June

Captain James Duberly's Troop

Captain	DUBERLY JAMES
Lieutenant	WOOD FREDK.
Lieutenant	VOEUX NEBJ.DES.
Cornet	BROWN B.P.
Trp.Sjt.Maj.	HURST JOSEPH
Serjeant	HARRIS RICHD.
Serjeant	HEMMETT THOS.
Serjeant	HODGKINSON ELIJAH
Serjeant	HUMPHREYS RICHD.
Serjeant	STRONG ISSAC
Corporal	BOLDING FRIEND
Corporal	DRAYCOTT THOS. Watter's Sale June 1913
Corporal	FRAMER GEORGE
Corporal	NICHOLLS JOSH.
Corporal	POLLEY JAMES
Trumpeter	WINGROVE EDWD.
Private	BAKER BENJN.
Private	BENTLEY JOHN
Private	BERRELL WILLIAM
Private	BOARDMAN THOMAS
Private	BOLTON JOHN
Private	BULL CHARLES
Private	BRYAN HUGH
Private	CARD JOHN
Private	CROWTHER JONATHAN
Private	CRAMPTON JAMES
Private	CRAMPTON JOHN
Private	DOBBINGS CHARLES on sale at Spinks Oct. 1909
Private	EDWARDS DANIEL
Private	ELLISON PETER
Private	FEATHERS JAMES
Private	FEAR WILLIAM
Private	FIELDHOUSE BENJN.
Private	FISHER JOSEPH
Private	GREY WILLIAM
Private	GREEN CHARLES
Private	HAMPSON SAMUEL
Private	HAMMER RICHD.
Private	HARDING JOHN
Private	HIGGINSON THOS. Wounded
Private	HODGETTS THOS.
Private	JORDAN THOS.
Private	KILNER RICHD.

Private	LAWTY FRANCIS
Private	LEE JEREMIAH
Private	LEVER THOMAS
Private	LIGHT THOMAS Glendining's sale Oct. 1913 4-0-0
Private	MACKRELL JOHN
Private	MOORE EDWARD
Private	NASH JAMES Wounded
Private	ODDY JONIS
Private	OLDFIELD JAMES Glendining's sale 25th Oct. 1907
Private	PERRY JAMES
Private	PEARSON THOS.
Private	POOL JOHN
Private	RHODES TIMOTHY
Private	RUSHWORTH SAML. Whitaker Collection 1908
Private	SHARP RICHD.
Private	SIMPSON WILLIAM
Private	SMITH THOMAS
Private	SNOWBALL WILLIAM
Private	STANLEY SAMUEL
Private	STANDING JOHN
Private	STOCKHILL EDWD.
Private	SWETNAM HENRY
Private	TAYLOR WILLIAM
Private	UPSHAW JOHN
Private	VENNER JOHN
Private	WATSON STEPHEN
Private	WATMAN THOS.
Private	WEBB JOHN
Private	WELLS THOMAS
Private	WEST JAMES
Private	WHITTAKER WILLIAM

* * *

12th (or PRINCE OF WALES) REGIMENT OF LIGHT DRAGOONS

Lt. Colonel	PONSONBY HON. F.C. Colonel
Major	BRIDGER J.P. Lt.Colonel
Adjutant	GRIFFITH JOHN Whitaker Collection 1908
Surgeon	ROBINSON BENJN.
Ass.Surgeon	SMITH J.G.
Vty.Surgeon	CASTLEY JAMES
Pay Master	OTWAY WILLIAM
Captain	CRAWFORD CHARLES 2nd Ceylon Reg.Vol.

Captain Edwin Sandy's Troop

Lieutenant	VANDELEUR JOHN
Captain	SANDYS EDWIN Died of Wounds
Rgt.Sjt.Maj.	CARRUTHERS JOHN
Py.Mr.Sjt.	ISSAC THOMAS
Ar.Sjt.	GOULDING ROBERT
Sadd.Sjt.	McINTOSH JOHN
Serjeant	HOUSLEY JOSHUA
Serjeant	SUMMERS WILLIAM
Serjeant	SMITH JOHN
Corporal	LACKEY JAMES Promoted Sjt. since 18th June
Corporal	SMITH JAMES
Private	ALLEN JAMES
Private	AMOS EDWD. Promoted Trumpeter since 18th June
Private	ADGAR JOHN
Private	AITKENS EDWD.
Private	ASHMAN JOSEPH
Private	ASHCROFT JOHN
Private	BOYLE JOHN
Private	BELL JAMES Gray Collection 1908
Private	BRACKENBRIDGE THOMAS
Private	BARNES THOMAS Promoted Corporal since 18th June
Private	CARRY EDWD.
Private	CONNOLLY EDWD.
Private	COLLINGWOOD EDWARD
Private	CAMPBELL JAMES
Private	COX JOSH.
Private	CHADWICK WM.
Private	CARLISLE EBENEZER
Private	DRAYCOTT HENRY
Private	DRUM PETER
Private	EVERETT SAMUEL
Private	FINDLAY WILLIAM Promoted Corporal since 18th June
Private	GLOVER WILLIAM
Private	GUNNING THOS.
Private	GARDNER WILLIAM
Private	GRANT DONALD
Private	GRAINGER ROBT.
Private	GREEN JAMES
Private	GRIEVE JAMES
Private	HORTON WILLIAM
Private	HUGHES JOHN
Private	HALL EDWARD
Private	JONES WILLIAM

Private	KELLETT THOS.
Private	KAINE WM.
Private	LOWE WILLIAM
Private	LUMBER JOSEPH
Private	LOVE WILLIAM
Private	MAHER JAMES
Private	MILLER JOHN
Private	McKENNA JAMES
Private	McDONALD JAMES
Private	McCARTIN PETER
Private	MARTIN HENRY
Private	McMANIMAN PATRICK
Private	MOORE JOHN
Private	OMOROD LAWRENCE
Private	PRATT MICHAEL
Private	PERKINS JAMES
Private	RYAN JAMES
Private	SHIPLEY ROBERT
Private	TURNER PETER
Private	TURNER DUNCAN
Private	WITHERS SAMUEL
Private	WOOLLEY ROBERT
Private	WALL JAMES
Private	WHITLOW ADAM

<u>Captain Alexander Barton's Troop</u>

Captain	BARTON ALEXR.
Lieutenant	GOLDSMITH ALBERT
Lieutenant	SLADE J.H.
Trp.Sjt.Maj.	HOLMES WILLIAM
Serjant	BONNOR JOHN On sale at Fenton's Oct. 1909
Serjeant	YOUNG THOMAS
Serjeant	YARNELL JOHN
Corporal	PETTIGREW WILLIAM Reduced to the ranks since 18th June
Corporal	RENWICK ARTHUR
Corporal	THORPE WILLIAM
Corporal	WATSON JOHN Promoted to Serjeant since 18th June
Trumpeter	MARRIOTT JOHN
Private	ANDREWS JOHN
Private	ADAMS ISSAC
Private	ALLEN JOHN Payne Collection 1911
Private	PURKETT JOHN
Private	BLAKELEY JOHN
Private	BALE WILLIAM
Private	BIGGS WILLIAM
Private	BROWNE JAMES
Private	BROWNE WILLIAM
Private	BUST LUKE
Private	BURKE PETER
Private	CULLEN FRANCIS Promoted Corporal since 18th June
Private	CROCKETT WILLIAM
Private	CHAPMAN THOMAS
Private	CARROLL PETER
Private	CARSONS ROBERT
Private	COULSTON ROBERT
Private	COOPER THOMAS
Private	CHAMBERLAIN GEORGE
Private	CLARKE THOMAS
Private	CREERCH THOMAS
Private	CORKER ROBERT
Private	DARCEY HUGH
Private	DONNALLY JOHN
Private	FARMER JOSH.
Private	GIBBONS FRANCES
Private	HEALEY GEORGE
Private	HOUGH GEORGE
Private	HALL JAMES
Private	KELLY PATRICK
Private	LINDSDALE JOHN
Private	LAWS JOHN
Private	LODGE THOMAS
Private	LAMB RICHARD
Private	McKENNA JOHN
Private	McARTHUR DANIEL
Private	McARTHUR JOHN
Private	MATTHEWSON MALCOM
Private	MARTIN JAMES
Private	PYM FRANCIS
Private	PEARSON THOMAS
Private	REACHLON WILLIAM Watter's Sale June 1913
Private	RAMSAY DAVID
Private	RUTLEDGE JOHN
Private	SMITH PETER
Private	SALISBURY JOHN
Private	SUTON EDWD.
Private	SHAW JAMES
Private	SMITH THOMAS Col.R.T. Gascoigne's Collection March 1909
Private	STEWART CHARLES
Private	SHEERER THOMAS
Private	SMITH SAMUEL
Private	SCOTT ANDREW

Private	TAILBY JOHN
Private	THORPE FRANCIS
Private	TAILBY WILLIAM Promoted Corporal since 18th June
Private	TAYLOR WILLIAM
Private	TYLER WILLIAM
Private	WILCOX EDWD.
Private	WINGATE JAMES
Private	WHITE SAMUEL

Captain Samson Stanwell's Troop

Captain	STANWELL SAMSON Major
Lieutenant	CHATTERTON JAMES
Lieutenant	LANE ABRAHAM
Trp.Sjt.Maj.	HUGHES MICHAEL
Serjeant	COLLINS ROBERT
Serjeant	SPARROW JAMES
Serjeant	WHITE JOHN Promoted Trp.Sjt.Maj. since 18th June
Corporal	KIRBY JOHN
Corporal	HEALY THOMAS Promoted Sjt. since 18th June
Corporal	McCORMICK PATRICK
Corporal	SMEETON WILLIAM Promoted Sjt. since 18th June
Trumpeter	BEAVER GEORGE
Private	ARMSTRONG JAMES
Private	AMONS WILLIAM
Private	BYRNE FRANCIS
Private	BURKE PATRICK
Private	BYRNE PETER
Private	BUTLER WALTER
Private	BONSO JOHN
Private	BIGGAN SOLOMON Glendining's sale 25th October 1907
Private	BARNETT JOHN
Private	BELL GEORGE
Private	CUMMINGS CHARLES
Private	CADMAN THOMAS
Private	CLAYLAND THOMAS
Private	COOPER WILLIAM
Private	CHADWICK JOHN
Private	COSBY WILLIAM
Private	CLAYNE JOHN
Private	DIGHT HENRY
Private	DOOLAN TIMOTHY
Private	DICKENSON THOMAS
Private	FOX JAMES
Private	FARRELL PETER
Private	GREEN THOMAS
Private	GREENSHIELDS JAMES
Private	GRAHAM ROBERT
Private	HARRISON WILLIAM
Private	HOWARD JOHN
Private	HILLHOUSE JAMES
Private	HOULAGHAN MICHAEL
Private	JORDAN THOMAS
Private	JONES JOHN
Private	JEFFERY HENRY
Private	KNUCKY GEORGE
Private	KENWORTHY ELIJAH
Private	LONGHAM HENRY
Private	LYONS PETER
Private	MEADE JOHN
Private	MAHON THOMAS
Private	McJENNETT THOMAS
Private	MILLER ROBERT
Private	McNAMARA EDWARD
Private	MUSSON ERAS.
Private	McMILLEN JOHN
Private	McQUIRE JOHN
Private	ROBERTS ROBERT
Private	ROBINSON JOHN
Private	REX HENRY
Private	SMITH THOMAS
Private	SQUIRES JOSH.
Private	THOMPSON BENJ.
Private	THORNTON THOMAS Promoted Corporal since 18th June
Private	THOMPSON RICHARD
Private	WARD ROBERT
Private	WARD RICHARD
Private	WIGGANS JOHN Promoted Corporal since 18th June
Private	WHITE WILLIAM

Captain G.F. Erskine's Troop

Captain	ERSKINE G.F.
Lieutenant	HAY WILLIAM
Serjeant	BULL RICHARD
Serjeant	FEARN JOHN
Serjeant	LEE ROBERT
Corporal	BLACK CHAS. Promoted Serjeant since 18th June
Corporal	PENNISTON JOHN
Corporal	SILVEY THOMAS Promoted Serjeant since 18th June
Private	AUGHEY PHILLIP
Private	ABRAHAM THOMAS

Private	ABRAHAM WILLIAM Galway Foley Collection 1910
Private	BYRNE SYLVESTER
Private	BARTON BENJAMIN
Private	BROWNLIE WILLIAM
Private	BRINDLEY THOMAS
Private	CLIFFORD STEPHEN Littledale sale Nov.1910
Private	CURRAN JOHN
Private	CONNERS MICHAEL
Private	CHAPMAN SAMUEL Day Sale April 1910
Private	COLES PETER
Private	DELANEY DANIEL
Private	DURANCE THOMAS
Private	DOOLAN JAMES
Private	DYER MOSES
Private	DUNNEGAN RICHD.
Private	FOREST JOHN
Private	FROST JOSH.
Private	FINNECY DENIS
Private	FERGUSON ALEXR.
Private	HARMSBY EDWARD
Private	HICKLING JAMES
Private	HENDERSON GEORGE
Private	IRWIN JOHN
Private	JACKSON CHARLES
Private	KENT WILLIAM
Private	LYNAN PATRICK
Private	LOUGHMAN MATTHEW
Private	LYONS JOHN
Private	LUCKNEY ROBERT
Private	McDONALD PHELIX
Private	MADDISON JOSEPH
Private	MURPHY JAMES
Private	MURPHY EDWARD
Private	McCALLAN GEORGE
Private	MOORE THOMAS
Private	McGARRIGLE JOHN
Private	MULMER SAMUEL
Private	NORRIS WILLIAM
Private	NEILL HENRY H.Gaskell's Collection 1908
Private	OCALLAGHAN MICHAEL
Private	POWERS EDWD.
Private	PEACH JOHN Promoted Corporal since 18th June Col.Murray's Coll. 1908
Private	STURGESS JOHN
Private	SULLIVAN JOHN
Private	SNIPE JOHN
Private	SMITH JOB
Private	STOBO JOHN Promoted Corporal since 18th June
Private	TIERNEY WILLIAM
Private	THOMPSON JOHN
Private	WILDMAN GEORGE
Private	WILSON WILLIAM
Private	WOODWARD JOSEPH
Private	HALL SAMUEL Cheylesmore Collection 1908
Private	HAYES JOHN

Captain Henry Andrew's Troop

Lieutenant	HEYDON WM.
Trp.Sjt.Maj.	WILLISS GEORGE
Serjeant	CARTWRIGHT DAVENPORT
Serjeant	MADDEN MICHAEL
Serjeant	WILSON JAMES
Corporal	HONAN MICHAEL Promoted Serjeant since 18th June
Corporal	HARROLD WILLIAM Reduced to the Ranks
Corporal	RENDER WILLIAM
Trumpeter	HOLLAND JOHN
Private	ALLEN JOHN
Private	ANTHONY JAMES
Private	BEVERIDGE DAVID
Private	BROOKHOUSE WILLIAM
Private	BARRY THOMS.
Private	BENNETT HAMILTON
Private	CRAWFORD JOSEPH
Private	CARMICHAEL NEIL
Private	CAMPBELL DAVID
Private	DARCEY PATRICK
Private	DALTON WILLIAM
Private	DUNCAN ROBERT
Private	ELLINGSWORTH JOHN
Private	GULAN DAHL.
Private	HEANEY DANIEL
Private	HANLON JOHN
Private	JAMES THOMAS
Private	KERR WILLIAM
Private	LONSBY RICHARD
Private	LITTLE JOHN
Private	LIGHTON WILLIAM
Private	LOUGHAM WILLIAM
Private	LITTLE PATRICK
Private	McLOUGHLIN DANIEL
Private	McDONALD JAMES
Private	McNAMARA MICHAEL
Private	McFIGGIN ROBERT

Private	MAJOR JOHN
Private	McCONNELL SAMUEL
Private	MORROW JOHN
Private	MURRAY GEORGE
Private	MEANES SAMUEL
Private	ONEAL PATRICK
Private	PICKARD AMBROSE
Private	PENNY ABRAM.
Private	RAVEN JOSHUA
Private	ROBINSON JOHN
Private	SWEENEY JAMES
Private	STAPLELEY MATTHEW
Private	STIERKEY JAMES
Private	SIMPSON THOMAS
Private	SALMON JOHN
Private	STAPLEFORD DANIEL
Private	TIERNEY CHARLES
Private	VOWELL WILLIAM
Private	WATSON JOHN

Captain Houston Wallace's Troop

Captain	WALLACE HOUSTON
Lieutenant	DOWBIGGIN W.H.
Lieutenant	REED THOMAS
Trp.Sjt.Maj.	McCORKLE ANDREW
Serjeant	COOPER ANDREW
Serjeant	GRIFFITH GEORGE Promoted Troop Sergeant Major
Serjeant	IRWIN JAMES
Corporal	BRENNAN JOHN Promoted Sjt. since 13th June
Corporal	EITOR ROBERT
Corporal	FEWKES JOSH.
Corporal	SNEDDING WM.
Trumpeter	HINDS SAMUEL
Trumpeter	AUSTIN JOHN
Private	ARMSTRONG PETER
Private	BOWLER JOSH.
Private	BLAIR JOHN
Private	BLACK JOHN
Private	BRIGGS GEORGE
Private	BROOKHOUSE FRANCIS
Private	BROWN SAMUEL
Private	BENTON JAMES
Private	DOWNS MICHAEL
Private	EAST ABRAM.
PRivate	FISHER JAMES
Private	GILLIEA CHARLES
Private	GREGG JAMES
Private	HIGGINBOTTOM JOHN
Private	JOHNSTONE JAMES
Private	JOHNSTONE WILLIAM
Private	JONES JOSH.
Private	KILFOILE JOHN
Private	KIRKPATRICK LAW.
Private	KING JOHN
Private	LAVERTY JAMES
Private	LEONARD JAMES
Private	LAMETT JOHN
Private	LEESON JOSH.
Private	LOCKYER RICHD.
Private	MANUEL HUGH
Private	McARTHUR PETER
Private	McLEAN ROBERT
Private	McCLARKIN THOS.
Private	MILROSS THOS.
Private	NICHOLSON MARTIN
Private	PHIPPS WILLIAM
Private	RICHARDSON WILLIAM
Private	ROBINSON ALEXR.
Private	RONAN JAMES
Private	SAVAGE GEORGE
Private	SCOTT JAMES
Private	SKINNER THOMAS
Private	SIMMONDS RICHARD
Private	WEBB RICHARD
Private	WOOD WILLIAM
Private	WILSON THOMAS
Private	WALKER ROBERT
Private	WELLS JOHN
Private	WATTS LAWCE.
Private	WHITE WALTER
Private	WHITE JOHN
Private	WILLIAMS WILLIAM Promoted Corporal since 18th June Fleming Colection 1871
Private	WALLACE JAMES

* * *

13th REGIMENT OF LIGHT DRAGOONS

Lt. Colonel	DOHERTY Sick at Brussels Whitaker Collection 1908
Major	BOYSE S. Whitaker Collection 1908
Captain	LAWRENCE B.
Captain	DOHERTY J.
Captain	MACALISTER J.
Captain	BOWERS M.

Captain	GREGORIE C.
Captain	GOULBURN F.
Lieutenant	MOSS J.J. H.Gaskell's Collection 1908
Lieutenant	DOHERTY G. Whitaker Collection 1908
Lieutenant	DROUGHT J.H.
Lieutenant	BOWERS C.
Lieutenant	McLEAN A.T.
Lieutenant	NESBITT R.
Lieutenant	TURNER W.
Lieutenant	MILL JAMES
Lieutenant	PACKE G.H.
Lieutenant	ACTON H.
Lieutenant	WALLACE J.
Lieutenant	IRVING J.E.
Cornet	WAKEFIELD J.
Pay Master	STRANGE A.
Surgeon	LOGAN T.G.
Ass.Surgeon	ARMSTRONG A.
Vty. Surgeon	CONSTANT J.
Qr.Mr.	MINCHIN W.
R.S.Maj.	PRING GEORGE
Trp.S.Maj.	AYSCOUGH ROBT.
Trp.S.Maj.	BROMWICH RICHD.
Trp.S.Maj.	KINFOOT MATTW.
Trp.S.Maj.	MUIRLAND JAMES
Trp.S.Maj.	ROSSER THOS.
Trp.S.Maj.	WELLS EDWD. Needes Collection 1908
Serjeant	ARMSTRONG WM.
Serjeant	BAXTER ROBT.
Serjeant	BAXTER RICHD.
Serjeant	COX WM.
Serjeant	CAREW JAMES
Serjeant	DUDMAN THOS.
Serjeant	GREY JAMES
Serjeant	HOYE JOHN
Serjeant	HAYNE WM.
Serjeant	HIBBERT JOHN
Serjeant	INSKIP JOHN
Serjeant	KINGSLEY OWEN
Serjeant	LINTHALL WM.
Serjeant	McNAUGHTON ALEXR.
Serjeant	POWERS THOS Glendining's Sale Dec. 1909
Serjeant	ROGERS JAMES
Serjeant	SHAW WM.
Serjeant	SINGER DANIEL
Serjeant	TANNER WM.
Serjeant	WEBB WM.
Serjeant	WILSON JOHN
Serjeant	WATERS JAMES
Serjeant	WEIR GEORGE
Serjeant	WRIGHT THOMAS
Staff	NEWEY JNS. Paymaster
Serjeant	BOLISH JNS. Armourer
Serjeant	BENNETT THOS. Sadler
Corporal	ALLEN JOSEPH
Corporal	ARCHER THOS.
Corporal	BALL GEO.
Corporal	BEARD JAMES Galway Foley Collection 1910
Corporal	BUTLER MICHL.
Corporal	CORBERRY THOS.
Corporal	CORKINGS JOSH.
Corporal	EDWARDS THOS.
Corporal	GILBERT JOHN
Corporal	GADSBY MATTHEW
Corporal	HENDERSON THOS.
Corporal	HAWKINS GEO.
Corporal	HIBBERT AARON
Corporal	HAMOR ISSAC
Corporal	JONES THOS.
Corporal	KELLY JOHN
Corporal	MITCHELL STEWART
Corporal	McCOOEY JOHN
Corporal	MARSHMAN THOS.
Corporal	McELROY PETER
Corporal	McGAULTER THOS.
Corporal	NORTH THOS.
Corporal	PALMER FREDK.
Corporal	WARREN JAMES
Trumpeter	WELDON WILLIAM
Trumpeter	BRYAN RICHD. H.Gaskell's Collection 1908
Trumpeter	GRIFFITHS ELEAZER
Trumpeter	GILLIS JAMES
Trumpeter	KING KING
Private	ANKINSON FRANCES
Private	AVELING WM.
Private	ARCHIBALD EBENZER
Private	AYLIFFE GEORGE
Private	ANGELL JOHN
Private	ARMSTRONG WM.
Private	ARMSTRONG JAMES
Private	BARNET WM
Private	BARTON ISSAC

Private	BATEMAN GEO.
Private	BANKS JOSEPH
Private	BUNCE JOHN Col.Murray's Collection, Littledale Sale Nov. 1910
Private	BROWN JOHN
Private	BIRCH JOHN
Private	BOYLE DAN.
Private	BURROW THOS.
Private	BENTLEY SAML.
Private	BUSH PETER
Private	BINDON LEWIS
Private	BRIDGER JOHN
Private	BRADY NICH.
Private	BUCKLE WM.
Private	BEATTY EDWD.
Private	BRADY JAMES
Private	BROWN EDWARD Gray Collection 1908
Private	BUTT WM.
Private	BOWMAN JOHN
Private	BRIDGEMAN WM.
Private	BISHOP GEO.
Private	BROWN CHA.
Private	BROTHERTON JOHN
Private	BUNCLE PETER
Private	BANCROFT ARTH.
Private	BOWKER ROBT.
Private	BROOKS HUMPY.
Private	BRENAN MICHAEL
Private	BROKER MATTW.
Private	BUTLER BENJN.
Private	BUTLER ROBT.
Private	BAILEY JAMES
Private	BATTIS NICH.
Private	BRAND WM.
Private	BROWN JAMES
Private	BANKS RICHD.
Private	COSGROVE CORNELIUS
Private	COMERFORD JAMES
Private	CRAWLEY WILLIAM
Private	CLENDENING RICHD.
Private	COUZENS THOS.
Private	CARROL PATK.
Private	CAVEY MATTW.
Private	COOK THOS.
Private	COX JAMES
Private	CAPPER JAMES
Private	CHARLES JOHN
Private	COPELAND PETER
Private	COOKSON JOHN
Private	COOPER JAMES Cheylesmore Collection 1908
Private	COLLINGWOOD THOS.
Private	CANNON THOS.
Private	CALEY SAML.
Private	CONSLEY JOHN
Private	CREW JOSEPH
Private	CORRIGAN LEWIS
Private	CAMPBELL LAWRENCE
Private	COOK THOS.SENR.
Private	CARBERRY JOHN
Private	CREAMER MICHL.
Private	COUZINS JAMES
Private	COUGHRAN GEO.
Private	COOK THOS.
Private	CLOSURE WM.
Private	CLARKE THOS.
Private	CASEY MICHAEL
Private	COOPER JAMES
Private	CROOKS JAMES
Private	CRUTHERS WILLIAM
Private	COOK SAML.
Private	CRAWLEY EDWARD
Private	DWYER PATK.
Private	DUNN DANL.
Private	DUNN THOS.
Private	DIXON PETER
Private	DELANY JOHN
Private	DEARING WILLIAM
Private	DOYLE PAT.
Private	DAVIS THOS.
Private	DAVIS ISSAC
Private	DEACON WM.
Private	DAY THOS.
Private	DRIVER AMOS
Private	EAKINS CHAS.
Private	EAUSTACE CHRIS.
Private	EDMONDS JOHN
Private	EAST JAMES
Private	FIELD JAMES
Private	FREE RICH.
Private	FORD WM.
Private	FORD CHRIS.
Private	FERKINS THOS.
Private	FARLEY SAML.
Private	FRANKLIN JAMES
Private	FOX JOHN
Private	FABB JAMES

Private	FOWLER WM.
Private	FELLINGHAM ABRAM.
Private	GODBER WM.
Private	GININ THOS.
Private	GRAHAM GEO.
Private	GILLIGAN JAMES
Private	GETTINGS THOS.
Private	GIBBS WM.
Private	GOLDWELL WM.
Private	GREY JOHN
Private	GIBSON GEO.
Private	GILLMAN JOHN
Private	GIBBONS ARTH. Sotheby's Sale 19th June 1908
Private	GREGORY PHILIP
Private	GOLDWELL JOHN
Private	GRIERSON ALEXR.
Private	GAULEY WM.
Private	GRANT JAMES
Private	GEE JOHN
Private	GOGGINS DAVID
Private	GREY JEREMIAH
Private	HINTON JOHN
Private	HINTON WM.
Private	HEDGES THOS.
Private	HOOPER JOHN
Private	HAYWARD ROBT.
Private	HUFF EDWARD
Private	HARCOURT SAMUEL
Private	HOOK RICHARD
Private	HARLEY THOS.
Private	HANCOCK THOS.
Private	HELLAM THOS.
Private	HOPKINS OWEN
Private	HIPWELL ARTH. Gray Collection 1908
Private	HOWLAND THOS.
Private	HENLEY PATK.
Private	HEWER EDWARD
Private	HUGHES MICHL.
Private	HEATH JOHN
Private	HAYWARD THOS.
Private	HAYWARD WM.
Private	HAWKINS THOS.
Private	HANNAN JOHN
Private	HERRON MOSES
Private	HILLORY SIMON
Private	HAYGAN FRANCIS
Private	HIRSTBOROUGH ALEXR.
Private	HARDY JOSEPH
Private	HOLLIS WM.
Private	JACKSON JOHN
Private	JAMES THOS.
Private	JAMES SAML. Glendining's Sale Oct. 1912
Private	JEFFRIES JOHN Col.R.T. Gascoigne's Collection March 1909
Private	JEUSTACE CHRIS.
Private	JILLSON EDWD.
Private	JOHNSTON PETER
Private	JONES JAMES
Private	KEARNS HUGH
Private	KEEGAN JAMES
Private	KEENAN JOHN
Private	KELLY JOHN
Private	KENT JOHN
Private	KERRIGAN JAMES
Private	KETTERINGHAM GEO.
Private	KING GEO.
Private	KINTON WM.
Private	KIRVIN JAMES
Private	LACEY JOHN
Private	LANCELY RICHD.
Private	LANE JOHN
Private	LANGLEY THOS.
Private	LANGDON HENRY
Private	LAWLOR WM.
Private	LAWRENCE DAVID
Private	LEADER RICHD.
Private	LEE JOHN
Private	LEAVERS THOS.
Private	LIGHTHOLDER MARK
Private	LOOBY HENRY
Private	LOVE JOHN
Private	LYNCH LAWRENCE
Private	LYNCH EDWD.
Private	LYONS PATK.
Private	MAHAR DANL.
Private	MANLY JAS.SNR.
Private	MANLY JAS.JNR.
Private	MARKWELL SAML.
Private	MATTHEWS HENRY
Private	MAYLES WM.
Private	McCABE DENNIS
Private	McCABE GEO.
Private	McCAULEY HENRY
Private	McCLUSKEY PATK.

Private	McCLUSKEY ARTH.
Private	McLERNON JOHN
Private	McCORMICK JOHN
Private	McCRACKEN THOS.
Private	McDONALD ANDREW
Private	McENANY PATK.
Private	McGAHEY JAMES
Private	McGARRY MATTHEW
Private	McGUIRE PATK.
Private	McKENNA PATK.
Private	MEARS WM.
Private	MELLON JOHN
Private	MOFFETT WM.
Private	MOORE WM.
Private	MORAN MICHL.
Private	MORGAN JOHN
Private	MORRISON GEO.
Private	MOSS WM.
Private	MOLLEN THOS.
Private	MULLIGAN JAMES
Private	MURPHY ARTHUR
Private	MURPHY THOS.
Private	MURRY MICH.
Private	NASH SAML.
Private	NEWMAN DAVID
Private	NEWPORT EDWD.
Private	NICHOLS GEO.
Private	NUNN ROBT.
Private	OBORNE GEO.
Private	OBRIAN THOS
Private	OHARA WM.
Private	OLIVER DAVID
Private	ONEAL HUGH
Private	OSBOURNE WM.
Private	PADDIMORE WM. Glendining's Sale 17th June 1908 Dr. Gardiner 1910
Private	PAGE THOS 1st
Private	PAGE THOS 2nd
Private	PARKER PETER
Private	PARNOLD ROBERT
Private	PARSONS THOS.
Private	PATTON RICHD.
Private	PAYNE HENRY
Private	PEASGOOD JOHN
Private	PERRY JOHN
Private	PICKEN JOHN
Private	PEARSON WM.
Private	PLANK THOS.
Private	POOL THOMAS
Private	POOLTON THOS.
Private	RAHAL PETER
Private	RAINSFORD ROBERT
Private	RANDALL BENJN. Whitaker Collection 1908
Private	REID JAMES
Private	REID WILLIAM
Private	RILEY JOHN
Private	REILY WM.
Private	REILEY WM.PETER Whitaker Collection 1908
Private	REILEY DAVID
Private	REINESS CHAS.
Private	REYNOLDS WM.
Private	RICHARDSON WM.
Private	REARDON RICHD.
Private	ROBINSON WM.
Private	ROGERS WM.
Private	ROGERS MICHAEL
Private	ROOK JOHN
Private	ROONEY BERND.
Private	ROTHWELL JOHN
Private	ROURKE JAMES
Private	ROWE JAMES
Private	ROWE RICHARD
Private	RUEBOTTOM RICHD.
Private	RYDER JAMES
Private	SCOTT THOS.
Private	SCOTT HENRY
Private	SCRIVEN ROBERT
Private	SELBY MICHL.
Private	SHAW FRANCIS
Private	SHEA RICHD.
Private	SHREENAN OWEN
Private	SIMMONDS EDWIN
Private	SINCOCK WM.
Private	SMART EDWD.
Private	SMART JOHN
Private	SMITH JAMES 1st
Private	SMITH JAMES 2nd
Private	SMITH PATRICK
Private	SMITH SAML.
Private	SMITH JOHN
Private	SOMERFORD WM.
Private	SOUTHERAN RICHD.
Private	SQUIRES JOHN
Private	STEEL JAMES
Private	STINTON THOS.JNS.

Private	STOKES FRANCIS Watter's Sale June 1913
Private	STOKES WM.
Private	STONE JOSIAH
Private	STOREY JAMES
Private	STRATTON JOHN
Private	STREATON JOHN
Private	STRONGITHORN GEO.
Private	SWAN GEO.
Private	SWANSBURY ROBT.
Private	SWIFT ABRAHAM
Private	TART RICHD.
Private	TAYLOR JNS. 1st
Private	TAYLOR JNS. 2nd
Private	TAYLOR JOSEPH
Private	TURNHAM THOMAS
Private	THOMPSON FRANCIS
Private	TWELVES JOHN
Private	UNWIN ROBERT
Private	WALKER JOHN
Private	WALL JOHN
Private	WALSH JOHN 1st
Private	WALSH JOHN 2nd
Private	WARD ABRAHAM
Private	WEIBLING RICHD.
Private	WESTALL DAVID
Private	WEST JOHN
Private	WESTON SAMUEL
Private	WEYMAN HENRY
Private	WHEALAN DANIEL
Private	WHEELER JOHN
Private	WHITBREAD RENY.
Private	WHITE WM.
Private	WHITING HENRY
Private	WILDRIDGE JOHN
Private	WILSON JNS. 1st
Private	WILSON JNS. 2nd
Private	WILSON WM. 1st
Private	WILSON WM. 2nd
Private	WILSON GEO.
Private	WILLIAMS WM.
Private	WINTERS PATK.
Private	WOODS WM.
Private	WORSTENHOLME JAMES
Private	WRIGHT THOS. Glendining's Sale 25th Oct. 1907
Private	WYVELE PETER
Private	YOUNG JAMES
Private	YOUNG JOHN

* * *

15th (or KINGS) REGIMENT OF HUSSARS

Lt. Colonel	DALRYMPLE L.C.
Major	GRIFFITHS EDWIN Killed in Action
Captain	THACKWELL J.
Captain	HANCOX S. Needes Collection 1908. London 1979.
Captain	WHITEFORD J.R. Payne Collection 1911
Captain	WOODHOUSE P.
Captain	PHILLIPS F.C.
Captain	BOOTH W.
Captain	CARR J.
Lieutenant	BARRATT E.
Lieutenant	MANSFIELD R.
Lieutenant	SHERWOOD J. Killed in Action
Lieutenant	BELLAIRS W.
Lieutenant	LANE H.
Lieutenant	BYAM E.
Lieutenant	BYAM W. Payne Collection 1911
Lieutenant	DAWKINS G.A.F.
Lieutenant	DIXON H.
Lieutenant	DOUGLAS J.J.
Lieutenant	STEWART W.
Lieutenant	PENNINGTON J.
Lieutenant	BUCKLEY H. Died of wounds rec'd in action 18th June. H.Gaskell's Collection 1908
Pay.Mr.	COCKSEDGE J.C.
Lt. & Adjt.	GRIFFITH H. Lt.Col J.G. Adamson's Collection 1910
Surgeon	CARTAN F. Whitaker Collection 1908
Ass.Surgeon	JEYES S.
Ass.Surgeon	GIBNEY W.
Vty.Surgeon	DALLWIG
R.Sjt.Maj.	HICKMAN CHAS.
Trp.Sjt.Maj.	GREASLEY WM.
Trp.Sjt.Maj.	CHETTLE GEO.
Trp.Sjt.Maj.	HEARD DANL.
Trp.Sjt.Maj.	WILLIAMSON JAMES
Trp.Sjt.Maj.	DAWES WM.
Trp.Sjt.Maj.	HERVEY JAMES
Staff Sjt.	JOHNSON JOHN
Staff Sjt.	SYMES JOSH.
Staff Sjt.	HYDE WM.
Serjeant	ALBERT GEORGE
Serjeant	BISHOP JAMES
Serjeant	BRIND JOSEPH
Serjeant	CARR JOSEPH
Serjeant	CLARKE SAML.

Serjeant	CROFTS GEORGE
Serjeant	DUVALL WILLIAM
Serjeant	FARR WILLIAM
Serjeant	GIDDINGS WILLIAM
Serjeant	HARDY LAURENCE
Serjeant	HOLTON RICHD.
Serjeant	HUBBARD JACOB Killed in Action 18th June
Serjeant	LOVEGROVE JOSEPH
Serjeant	MONRO R.D. Killed in Action 18th June
Serjeant	MOULDER WILLIAM
Serjeant	NEWELL THOS.
Serjeant	PAGE RICHD.
Serjeant	PROUTING WILLIAM
Serjeant	SCOTT JOHN Cheylesmore Collection 1908
Serjeant	WINTERFIELD J.F.
Serjeant	WRIGHT SAML.
Corporal	BAILEY EDWD.
Corporal	BARTER GEO.
Corporal	BENNETT THOS.
Corporal	BURDEN H.O.
Corporal	CLARKE JOHN
Corporal	COCKHEAD JOHN
Corporal	DAY JOHN
Corporal	DAWKINS JAMES
Corporal	FISHLOCK JOHN
Corporal	FRENCH AMOS
Corporal	FISHER WILLIAM
Corporal	HALL JOHN
Corporal	HANDFORD RICHD.
Corporal	HOWARTH JOHN
Corporal	LAND THOMAS
Corporal	MORLEY RICHD.
Corporal	STILLWELL SAMUEL
Corporal	SWANN WILLIAM
Trumpeter	BOWLES WILLIAM
Trumpeter	BRITAIN WM.T.
Trumpeter	HANDLEY HUNTN.
Trumpeter	NESLER AUGUST
Trumpeter	PHISSIN HENRY
Private	ADAM JAMES
Private	ALLEN CHARLES
Private	ALLUM JONATHAN
Private	ALSOP GEORGE
Private	ANDREWS JOHN
Private	ARTHUR WILLIAM
Private	ASHTON GEORGE
Private	ASPDEN JOHN
Private	BACON THOS.
Private	BAILEY JOSEPH
Private	BAILEY GEORGE Died of wounds rec'd in Action 18th June on 19th July in Genl.Hosp. Antwerp.
Private	BAKER CHAS.
Private	BAKER JOHN
Private	BARKER GEORGE
Private	BARTLETT GEORGE
Private	BARNARD ROBT.
Private	BARNES CHAS.
Private	BASTARD JAMES
Private	BECK THOMAS
Private	BEVIS JOHN
Private	BEACH THOMAS
Private	BEDWELL RICHD.
Private	BECKINGHAM THOS.
Private	BENNETT JOHN
Private	BENBOW GEORGE
Private	BENSON THOS.
Private	BINDER JOHN
Private	BINGER HENRY
Private	BINGFIELD JAMES
Private	BLAKE JOHN
Private	BOND GEORGE
Private	BORAM JAMES
Private	BOOTH HENRY
Private	BOSSON JAMES
Private	BOSWORTH SAMUEL
Private	BOYDEN HENRY
Private	BOYNE CHRIS.
Private	BLACK GEORGE Killed in Action 18th June
Private	BRADBURY WILLIAM
Private	BRADSHAW JOHN
Private	BRAILSFORD WILLIAM
Private	BREWER ADAM Gray Collection 1908
Private	BRIDDOCK CHARLES
Private	BRITTON WILLIAM Glendining's Sale Nov. 1913
Private	BRIAN THOMAS
Private	BROWN JAMES
Private	BROWN JAMES Killed in Action 18th June
Private	BROWN GEORGE
Private	BROWN GEORGE
Private	BROWN DANL.
Private	BROWN RICHD.

Private	BROAD JAMES
Private	BURFORD JAMES
Private	BULBROOK WILLIAM
Private	BURROUGH JAMES
Private	BURROWS WILLIAM
Private	BUXTON HENRY
Private	BYE RICHARD
Private	BOURNE SAMUEL
Private	CARTER THOMAS Col. Murray's Collection
Private	CARNELL JOHN Killed in Action 18th June
Private	CASTLICK JOHN
Private	CHASEY WILLIAM
Private	CHALLINER JOHN
Private	CHESTERS JOHN
Private	CHELLIES ROBT.
Private	CLARKE JOHN
Private	CLARKE SAMUEL
Private	COATES CHARLES
Private	COOPER JOSEPH
Private	COOPER THOMAS
Private	COOMBS JOHN
Private	COGGINS HENRY Killed in Action 18th June
Private	CORR JAMES Galway Foley Collection 1910
Private	COLLINS WILLIAM Killed in Action 18th June
Private	COURTNAY FREDK.
Private	COTTAM JAMES
Private	COURT WILLIAM
Private	COWAP JOHN
Private	COX JAMES
Private	CRACKWELL THOMAS Glendining's Sale 21st June 1909
Private	CURL WILLIAM
Private	CURTIS HENRY Killed in Action 18th June
Private	DAINTRY ROBERT
Private	DARRELL WILLIAM
Private	DAVIS THOMAS
Private	DAVIS JOHN
Private	DALTON ROBERT
Private	DEAN THOMAS
Private	DIXON JOSEPH
Private	DIXON JAMES
Private	DOLLMAN JOHN Killed in Action 18th June
Private	DRAKE FREDERICK Died of Wounds rec'd in action 18th June on 27th June in Genl. Hosp. at Brussels

Private	DRAKE STEPHEN
Private	DREWITT EDMOND
Private	DROUGHT WILLIAM
Private	DUVALL WILLIAM
Private	EARL ISSAC
Private	EATON THOMAS
Private	EASTMAN GEORGE
Private	EASTON HENRY
Private	EDWARDS ROBT.
Private	EKINS WM.
Private	ELLIOTT JACOB Col.R.T. Gascoigne's Collection March 1909
Private	ELLIOTT ROBERT
Private	ELLIOTT WILLIAM
Private	ERRINGTON JAMES
Private	EVANS HUGH
Private	EVAN JEMKINS
Private	FAIRGROVE JOHN
Private	FIELDHOUSE CHARLES
Private	FINE JOHN
Private	FISHER THOMAS
Private	FLETCHER THOMAS
Private	FLUKE JOSEPH
Private	FORT J.W.
Private	FORD JOHN Glendining's Sale April 1909
Private	FOWLER DANIEL Sold at Glendining's 29/7/08
Private	FRANCIS WILLIAM
Private	FREEMAN WILLIAM
Private	FREELAND THOMAS
Private	FRENCH JOSEPH Killed in Action 18th June
Private	GASKILL THOMAS
Private	GILLETT THOMAS
Private	GIRLING GEORGE
Private	GODON JOHN Glendining's Sale Jan. 1911
Private	GORDON CHARLES
Private	GOLDINGAY WILLIAM
Private	GRACE JAMES
Private	GRAIR SAMUEL
Private	GRAY RICHARD
Private	GREEN JAMES
Private	GAY JOSH.
Private	HAINES GEORGE
Private	HANKIN JOHN
Private	HARDMAN SAMUEL
Private	HARDING JAMES
Private	HARDING GEORGE

Private	HARRIS THOMAS
Private	HAMPSON THOMAS
Private	HARLAND THOMAS
Private	HASLAM R.D.
Private	HAZLEHURST THOMAS
Private	HAWKE WILLIAM
Private	HAWARDEN JOHN
Private	HAYTER BENJN.
Private	HIGGINS JOSEPH
Private	HILLARY JOHN
Private	HILL JAMES
Private	HILLIWELL JOSEPH
Private	HICKSON JOHN
Private	HINSON DANIEL
Private	HODSON JOHN
Private	HOLTOM JOHN
Private	HOLMES WILLIAM
Private	HOBBS JOSEPH
Private	HOARE HENRY
Private	HOLYOAK WILLIAM
Private	HOLEHOUSE SAML.WM.
Private	HOWELL CHARLES
Private	HUBBARD JOHN
Private	HUGHES HENRY
Private	HUMPHRIE DAVID
Private	HULME JOHN
Private	HUTSONE WILLIAM
Private	HUTTON THOMAS
Private	JAMES JAMES
Private	JAMESON ROBERT
Private	JAQUIS JOHN
Private	JEFFERY JOHN
Private	JEFFERSON HENRY
Private	JNGER JOSEPH
Private	JENKINS THOMAS
Private	JOHNSON JOHN
Private	JOHNSON BENJN. Phillip's Sale
Private	JOHNSON THOMAS
Private	JONES EDWARD
Private	JONES JOHN
Private	JOYNSTON RICHARD
Private	IVES JOHN
Private	KEATLEY EDWD. Day Sale April 1910
Private	KELL JOHN
Private	KELLY JOHN
Private	KEELY WILLIAM
Private	KILLICK WILLIAM

Private	KNIGHTS GEORGE
Private	KNIGHTS ROBERT
Private	KNIGHTS JAMES
Private	KNIGHTS GEORGE
Private	LANE GEORGE
Private	LANGSTONE JOSEPH
Private	LATTER EDWARD
Private	LAWTON WILLIAM Payne Collection 1911
Private	LEACH JOHN
Private	LEAVY SAMUEL
Private	LEIGH GEORGE
Private	LENMAN THOMAS
Private	LEWIS THOMAS
Private	LIM SAMUEL
Private	LISTER JACOB
Private	LOCK JAMES
Private	LONGSHAW JOHN
Private	LOVETT GILES
Private	LUCY BENJN.
Private	LUKE JOHN
Private	MACHIN WILLIAM
Private	MADCALF THOMAS
Private	McKAT JAMES
Private	McCARTHY THOMAS
Private	McINNIS RICHARD
Private	MARTIN JAMES
Private	MATTHEWS WILLIAM
Private	MATHEWS SAMUEL
Private	MASON WILLIAM
Private	MARLOW ROBERT
Private	MEADON HENRY
Private	MILLWOOD ISSAC Gray Collection 1908
Private	MILLS JAMES
Private	MILLS MATTHEW
Private	MILTON WILLIAM Killed in Action 18th June
Private	MORGAN JOHN
Private	MORGAN SAMUEL Died of Wounds rec'd in action 18th June on 5th July in Genl.Hosp. at Brussels
Private	MORETON THOMAS
Private	MOSS THOMAS Watter's Sale June 1913
Private	MOSS THOMAS Killed in Action 18th June
Private	MORAY JOSEPH
Private	MONTEITH ANDREW Littledale Sale Nov. 1910
Private	MUSCHAMPT THOMAS

Private	NAPIER WILLIAM Killed in Action 18th June
Private	NETHERWOOD TITUS
Private	NEWBERRY WILLIAM
Private	NEWMAN WILLIAM
Private	NEWSHAM THOMAS
Private	NICHOLLS WILLIAM
Private	NORTH WILLIAM
Private	NOTT JOHN
Private	NUTBURNE SAMUEL
Private	NASH ROBERT
Private	OKILL THOMAS
Private	OSBOURNE PETER
Private	OSBOURNE WILLIAM
Private	PARKES STEPHEN
Private	PARSONS THOMAS Sold at Glendining's 29.7.08
Private	PATON ROBERT
Private	PEARSON EDWARD
Private	PEARCE THOMAS
Private	PERRIN EPHRAIM
Private	PHIPPS THOMAS
Private	PHIPPARD MATTHEW Killed in Action 18th June
Private	PHILLIPS WILLIAM
Private	PICKLES JOHN
Private	PICKETT HENRY
Private	PIKE WILLIAM Glendining's Sale 17th June 1909
Private	PLUMMER JOHN
Private	POPE THOMAS
Private	PORTER RICHARD
Private	POTTER THOMAS
Private	POWELL CHARLES
Private	POUND GEORGE
Private	PRETTY WILLIAM
Private	PRETTY GEORGE
Private	PRAGNELL GEORGE
Private	PROUTING ROBERT
Private	PROTHERS JOHN
Private	PRICE THOMAS
Private	PRICE THOMAS
Private	PUGH FRANCES
Private	PYE THOMAS
Private	RAMAGE ROBERT
Private	RAMSHIRE RICHARD
Private	REEVES WILLIAM
Private	REEVES WILLIAM
Private	REVELL EDWARD
Private	RITCHIE DONALD
Private	RICHARDSON JOHN
Private	ROBINSON WILLIAM
Private	ROOKE WILLIAM
Private	ROGERS THOMAS
Private	ROFF THOMAS
Private	ROWLEY EDWARD
Private	ROWLAND THOMAS
Private	ROSE JOHN
Private	RYDER RICHARD
Private	SALMON RICHARD
Private	SADLER JAMES
Private	SAUNDERS THOMAS
Private	SAWYER RICHARD
Private	SAVAGE SIMSON
Private	SCARRATT JOHN
Private	SELLERS JAMES
Private	SILVESTER PETER
Private	SEYMOUR JOHN
Private	SHARPS WILLIAM
Private	SHARRACK ROBERT
Private	SHIRLEY EDWARD
Private	SHELMERDYNE CHARLES Killed in Action 18th June
Private	SHEPPARD JAMES
Private	SHEPPARD JOHN
Private	SIBLEY JAMES
Private	SIMPSON JOHN
Private	SLACK RICHARD
Private	SMALL ABRAM.
Private	SMITH JOSPEH
Private	SMITH WILLIAM
Private	SMITH JAMES
Private	SMITH DAVID Killed in Action 18th June
Private	SOPER ROBERT
Private	STANDAGE WILLIAM
Private	STACEY GILES
Private	STEWART H.J. Died of wounds rec'd in action 18th June 25th July in Genl.Hosp. at Brussels
Private	STOCKWELL THOMAS
Private	STONE STEPHEN
Private	STEEDMAN WILLIAM
Private	STEPHENS JESSE
Private	SUTTON WILLIAM
Private	SUTTON SAMUEL
Private	SUMMERS JAMES
Private	SYER RICHARD
Private	TAYLOR SAMUEL
Private	TAYLOR RICHARD

Private	TAYLOR JOHN
Private	TARRANT JOHN
Private	TELLING WILLIAM
Private	TURNEY JAMES
Private	THOMPSON FREDK. Glendining's Sale March 1912
Private	THOMPSON S.H.
Private	THOMPSON SAMUEL
Private	TILFIT CONRAD
Private	TOULMINGI GEORGE
Private	TOWN SAMUEL
Private	TOWNSEND HENRY
Private	TULL WILLIAM
Private	TULL JOHN
Private	TUFFNELL J.A.
Private	TURNER JOSEPH
Private	WALLACE WILLIAM
Private	WALKER SAMUEL
Private	WARE EDWARD
Private	WARD HENRY
Private	WARRENER SAMUEL
Private	WATTS THOMAS
Private	WATTS JOSEPH
Private	WATSON THOMAS
Private	WEBB SAMUEL
Private	WEBB THOMAS
Private	WEBB JOSEPH
Private	WEBB ROBERT
Private	WELLS CHARLES
Private	WELLINGTON WILLIAM
Private	WHARTON W.B.
Private	WATMORE EDWARD
Private	WHEELER HENRY
Private	WHITROW RICHD.
Private	WHITEHOUSE SAMUEL Killed in Action 18th June
Private	WICKHAM EDWARD
Private	WHITING GEORGE
Private	WHITE JAMES
Private	WILLIAMS THOMAS
Private	WILLIAMS THOMAS Killed in Action 18th June
Private	WILKINSON DANIEL
Private	WILSON JOHN
Private	WINDSOR GEORGE
Private	WINSOR SAMUEL
Private	WOODS WILLIAM
Private	WOODS JAMES
Private	WOLLARD THOMAS
Private	WODEHOUSE JOHN
Private	WOODSALL HENRY
Private	WRIGHT STEPHEN
Private	WRIGHT JAMES
Private	YOUNG THOMAS
Private	BUDD THOMAS Died of wounds rec'd in Action 18th June, 18th June at Brussels

* * *

16th (QUEENS) REGIMENT OF LIGHT DRAGOONS

Lt. Col.	HAY JAMES
Major	MURRAY G.H.
Lt. & Adjt.	BARRA J.
Lieutenant	ASTEN W.
Lieutenant	WHEELER J.
Lieutenant	SEVINFIN F.
Lieutenant	BAKER G.
Lieutenant	BEAUCHAMP R.
Lieutenant	CRICHTON N.D.
Lieutenant	LLOYD E.B.
Lieutenant	NEPEAN W.
Lieutenant	LUARD J.
Lieutenant	HARRIS W.
Lieutenant	RICHARDSON J. placed on half pay 25th March 1816
Lieutenant	MONCKTON C.J. London 1975 placed on half pay 25th March 1816
Lieutenant	McDOUGALL E. placed on half pay 25th March 1816
Lieutenant	BECKWITH W. placed on half pay 25th March 1816
Lieutenant	POLHILL W. placed on half pay 25th March 1816
Lieutenant	NUGENT G. placed on half pay 25th March 1816
Lieutenant	HAY A. Killed in action 18th June
Surgeon	ROBINSON J.
Pay.Mr.	NEYLAND G.
Ass.Surgeon	McMULLOCK J.
Ass.Surgeon	MURRAY D.
Vty.Suregon	JONS J.
Qr.Mr.	HARRISON J.

Captain J.H. Belle's Troop

Trp.Sjt.Maj.	CLUES JNS.
R.Sjt.Maj.	BLOOD THOS. Fleming Collection 1871
Py.Mr.Sjt.	HODGSON JNS.
Arm.Sjt.	MEACHAM THOS.
Sad.Sjt.	WHITE JOSEPH
Serjeant	ASHWORTH GEORGE

Serjeant	MATTHEWS JOSH.
Serjeant	NORTON WM.
Serjeant	PLATT JAMES
Corporal	GREEN JAS.
Corporal	LAKEN JNS
Corporal	LLOYD THOMAS
Corporal	SHOOTER THOMAS
Trumpeter	WILKINSON WM.
Private	ARTHUR HENRY
Private	ASTON WM.
Private	BRAITHWAITE JNS.
Private	BROOKS THOS.
Private	CARTER CHAS.
Private	CHILDS PHIPP.
Private	COCKERAN MICHL.
Private	COMPTON JAS.
Private	COOMBY BENJN.
Private	DAILEY DANL.
Private	DAILEY PATK.
Private	DAVIES CHAS.
Private	FELLOWS JOSH.
Private	FENTON JNS.
Private	FERROL OWEN
Private	FIELDER JOHN
Private	FLETCROFT SETH
Private	GIBSON RICHD.
Private	GIBSON GEORGE
Private	GOODWIN GEORGE
Private	GREGORY JOSH.
Private	HENDERSON JNS.
Private	HEYWOOD JNS.
Private	HILTON THOS. Cheylesmore Collection 1908
Private	HITCHCOCK RICHD.
Private	HOBBS JOSH.
Private	HORSEFIELD ROBT.
Private	HOUGHTON JNS.
Private	JEYNES JNS.
Private	KENWORTHY JAS.
Private	LANG JAS.
Private	LAWTON GEORGE Galway Foley Collection 1910
Private	LEE SAML.
Private	LEES JNS.
Private	MASSER JNS.
Private	MAY HENRY
Private	McFARLOW ALEXR.
Private	MELVILLE WM.
Private	MORRIS WM.
Private	NANKEVILLE JAS Wounded 18th June
Private	NEWTON RICHD.
Private	PARKER JAS.
Private	PEARS THOS.
Private	PENDERGARB WALTER
Private	RIDSDALE THOS.
Private	RODGERSON JAS.
Private	STEINWELL WM.
Private	SILCOCK JNS.
Private	SMITH RICHD.
Private	SMITHHURST RICHD.
Private	SUNMER JNS.
Private	STEWART JAS.
Private	THISTLEWOOD GEORGE
Private	TILEY WM.
Private	TRAVIS PETER
Private	WALKER HENRY
Private	WALKER JAS.
Private	WESTFOLD THOS.
Private	WHITE BENJN. Col. R.T. Gascoigne's collection March 1909
Private	WIGNALL WM.
Private	WOOTEN WM.
Private	WOOTEN JOSH.

Captain Swetenham's Troop

Trp.Sjt.Maj.	JAGGER JAS.
Trp.Sjt.Maj.	BAXTER STEPHEN 18th June Killed in Action
Serjeant	BARROW JNS.
Serjeant	BLYTHE ABRAM
Serjeant	GRIPTON JAMES
Serjeant	WHITTAKER WM.
Corporal	COLLINS PETER
Corporal	FITZPATRICK DANL.
Corporal	McKEE ALEXR.
Corporal	TONGUE THOS.
Trumpeter	LORING JAS.
Private	ASHWORTH THOS.
Private	BARRETT WM.
Private	BARRY HENRY
Private	BEDDER WM.
Private	BERRY JAMES
Private	BOLTON HENRY
Private	BOWKER RICHD.
Private	BRADLEY WM.
Private	BROWN THOS.
Private	BUCKLEY EDWD.
Private	BULPOT ROBT.

Private	BYROM JNS
Private	CAFFERY THOS.
Private	COLES HENRY
Private	DEAN JAMES
Private	DERBYSHIRE RICHD.
Private	FROST SAMUEL
Private	GILBODY GEORGE
Private	GRIFFITHS WM.
Private	HACKERSLEY JOHN 18th June Killed in Action
Private	HALL JOSH.
Private	HARBERT THOS.
Private	HOLLAND ZACH.
Private	HOLT EDWD.
Private	HORRICK JNS.
Private	HOWARD JNS.
Private	HULME THOS.
Private	HUMPHRIES JNS.
Private	JACKSON ROBT.
Private	JOHNSON DANL.
Private	JONES THOS.
Private	KILLER JOHN
Private	LAWDER ALEXR.
Private	LAY WM.
Private	LODGE CALEB
Private	LOOBY JOHN
Private	LOWE THOS.
Private	MARSTON ISSAC
Pricate	McALL ANDREW
Private	McBRIDGE WM.
Private	MOORE JNS.
Private	MUSHROP PICKERY
Private	PRINCE JNS.
Private	RATCLIFFE THOS.
Private	RALPH ROBERT
Private	ROYLE THOS.
Private	RUSSELL WM.
Private	RYAN DENNIS
Private	SALISBURY JOHN
Private	SMITH JOHN
Private	STEVENS THOS.
Private	TAYLOR JONATHAN
Private	VINCENT WM.
Private	WELCH JAMES
Private	WHITEHEAD JAMES
Private	WHITEHEAD JOSEPH
Private	WILKINSON JAMES
Private	WILLIAMS JOHN
Private	WILLIAMSON ROBT.
Private	WOODERSON RICHD.

Captain Buchanan's Troop

Trp.Sjt.Maj.	WILDMAN THOS.
Serjeant	MAY ISSAC
Serjeant	KEARNEY ROBT.
Serjeant	MALONEY JOHN
Serjeant	WORTLEY JOHN
Corporal	CASTON WILLIAM
Corporal	McNAMARA HARRY
Corporal	MOUNT PATK. Killed 18th June 1815
Corporal	NEEDHAM ROBT.
Corporal	YOUNG GEORGE
Trumpeter	DEARDON JNS. Glendining's Sale Nov. 1913 3-7-6
Private	ASTLEY JOHN
Private	BAUME WM.
Private	BEARD JAMES
Private	BETHELL JOSH. Glendining's Sale 25th Oct. 1907
Private	BROOKS JOSHUA
Private	CAVANAGH WM.
Private	COURTS JOHN
Private	COWARD CORNELIUS Payne Collection 1911
Private	DAINTY GEORGE
Private	DAVENPORT SAML.
Private	DAVENPORT JOHN
Private	DENT THOS.
Private	DUGGAN JOHN
Private	EARDLEY WM. Watters Sale June 1913
Private	EDWARDS EDWD. on sale at Fenton's Nov. 1912
Private	FAIRCLOTH RICHD.
Private	FERGUSSON W,. Wounded 18th June 1815
Private	FIASIN JOHN
Private	FOXHALL WM.
Private	GOODMAN CHAS.
Private	GORDON WM. Killed 18th June 1815
Private	GREEN PHILIP
Private	GRIGG BENJN.
Private	HALL JOHN
Private	HASKETT JOHN
Private	HAYES WM.
Private	HAYES THOS. Needes June 1908
Private	HEYTHORP JOSH
Private	HEMP JAMES
Private	HOWARD JONATHAN Whitaker Collection 1908
Private	HULME ZACH.
Private	HULME GEORGE

Private HUNT EDWD.
Private JONES JOHN
Private JONES CALIB
Private LAKE ROBT.
Private LAMBERT
Private LAWRENT JAMES
Private LAWTON JOSH.
Private MADDOX THOS.
Private MAIDES JAS.
Private MADMONT JOHN
Private MANWARING HARVEY
Private MARTIN ARTHUR Glendining's Sale April 1912
Private McGUIRE MORRIS
Private MONTGOMERY WM.
Private MOON RICHD.
Private MORGAN THOS.
Private NUTTALL EDWD.
Private PERKINS JOHN
Private PLOWMAN MATTW.
Private RIFFS JAMES
Private STANFIELD GEORGE
Private STEEL THOS.ROBT.
Private STREET ROBT. Wounded 18th June 1815
Private SUMNER PETER
Private THOMAS WM.
Private WALTON JAMES
Private WILLIAMS THOS.
Private WILLIAMS CHAS.
Private WOODS JOHN
Private WOOLDRIDGE THOS.
Private WYNN RICHD.

Captain Tomkinson's Troop

Trp.Sjt.Maj. GREAVE GEORGE
Serjeant FLESH JOHN
Serjeant HILL TIMY.
Serjeant MOON JAS.
Serjeant WILLIAMS SAML.
Corporal GRINDRED SLEY.
Corporal HODGSON WM.
Corporal PECKER JOSH.
Corporal SMITH JOHN
Trumpeter VINCE JOSEPH
Private BAXTER WM.
Private BIRCH RICHD.
Private COLLINS JOSEPH
Private CROP WM.
Private CROUTY WM.
Private DELANEY GEORGE
Private DUFFIELD JOHN
Private DUNBAR JOHN
Private EMBERTON FRANCES
Private FILTON THOMAS
Private FLESH HUGH
Private GARDNER SAMUEL
Private HALL JOHN
Private HALLIWELL FRANCES
Private HAMMOND EDWD.
Private HANSON JOHN Killed in Action 18th June 1815
Private HARDIMAN JOHN
Private HOOLEY CHARLES
Private JAMISSON ROBERT Littledale Sale Nov. 1910
Private JOLLY JOHN
Private JONES WILLIAM Gray Collection 1908
Private LONG THOMAS
Private MALCOMB JAMES
Private MAINWARING JNS.
Private MASSEY JOSEPH
Private McGRATH ROBT.
Private McGUIRE RICHD.
Private MOON JAMES
Private MURRAY JOHN
Private NADAN PETER
Private OGDEN THOMAS
Private OGDEN JAMES
Private OLDHAM JAMES
Private PARSONS WM.
Private PARSONS THOS.
Private PAYNE THOS.
Private PICKETT JAMES
Private PRICE BENJN.
Private REYNOLDS HENRY
Private RICHARDS JOSH.
Private ROSTHORNE JOHN
Private SHELMERDINE JAMES
Private SIDDLE THOS.
Private SINISTER RICHD.
Private SKINNER RICHD.
Private SLOANE ROBT.
Private SMITH JOHN
Private STACEY CHAS.
Private TAYLOR JOHN
Private THORNBURY JOHN
Private TITTER JOSEPH

Private	TURNER KEY.
Private	VENABLES WM.
Private	WADDLE WM.
Private	WAIN JOHN
Private	WARBURTON PETER
Private	WEEDON JOHN
Private	WILSON J.B.
Private	WILSON SAML.
Private	WORTHINGTON JOHN

Captain King's Troop

Trp.Sjt.Maj.	SMITH BENJN. Payne Collection 1911
Serjeant	BEDFORD GEORGE
Serjeant	GREEN THOMAS
Serjeant	PAYNE JAMES
Serjeant	SAYERS JAMES Rt.
Corporal	GREENFIELD JAMES Wounded 18th June 1815
Corporal	LEWIS JOHN
Corporal	MARSHALL JOHN
Corporal	TROTTER JOHN
Corporal	TURNER GEORGE
Trumpeter	ROSTHORN HENRY
Private	AITKENHEAD ROBERT
Private	ALLIARD RICHD.
Private	ARMSTRONG THOMAS
Private	ARNOLD GEE
Private	BAYLEY WM.
Private	BARBER JOSH.
Private	BOGGAN NEIL
Private	BRADLEY THOS.
Private	BRADSHAW THOS. Wounded 18th June 1815
Private	BROWN JNS.
Private	BUTLER THOS.
Private	COOKSON THOS.
Private	COOPEY DAVID
Private	DANIELS THOS.
Private	DAVID ENOCH
Private	DOUGLASS WM.
Private	EADES WM.
Private	FAULKNER JOSH.
Private	FITZPATRICK ANTHONY
Private	FORRESTER JOHN
Private	GOLDING THOS.
Private	GOULD CHAS.
Private	GRIFFITHS WM.
Private	GRINDRED JOHN
Private	HORTON WM.
Private	HUDSON JOHN
Private	HURST JAMES
Private	HYDON SAML.
Private	JENKINSON HENRY
Private	KAY WILLIAM
Private	LEWIS WILLIAM
Private	LORD SAMPSON
Private	MATHEWS THOMAS
Private	McCORD JOHN
Private	MILLINGTON PETER
Private	MOORE WILLIAM Wounded June 18th 1815
Private	NUNERY PATK. Wounded June 18th 1815
Private	OSBOURNE JAMES
Private	PASHLEY JAMES
Private	PENNIERY JAMES
Private	PERCIVAL WM.
Private	PRIEE HENRY
Private	SAVAP RICHD.
Private	SERGEANT HENRY
Private	SLATER WILLIAM
Private	TATE JNS.
Private	TAYLOR JNS.
Private	THOMAS THOS.
Private	UPTON REDFORD Col.Murray's Collection
Private	WARBURTON JOHN
Private	WARD WM.
Private	WEBB WM.
Private	WEST RICHARD
Private	WILLIS JAMES
Private	WILSON RICHD.
Private	WILSON JNS 2nd.
Private	WRIGHT JAMES H. Gaskell's Collection 1908
Private	WATKINS THOS.
Private	YATES THOS.
Private	YATES JOHN

Captain Weyland's Troop

Trp.Sjt.Maj.	BIGGS JAMES
Serjeant	CANNOCK JOSH.
Serjeant	DALLY THOS.
Serjeant	FLOYD THOS.
Serjeant	HICKLINGTON JAMES
Serjeant	REAY JONATHAN Killed in Action 18th June 1815
Serjeant	TWEED WILLIAM
Corporal	COX LOT
Corporal	GWYLLAM JOSHUA

Corporal	LINCOLN THOS.
Corporal	MITCHELL WM.
Trumpeter	WILD JONATHAN
Private	BAKER EDWD.
Private	BALL WM.
Private	BARLOW ROBT.
Private	BAYLIS FRANCES
Private	BREARLEY STRETTLE
Private	BRIDGMAN WM.
Private	BURNS JOHN
Private	CANNONS JONATHAN
Private	CHADWICK THOS.
Private	CHAMBERS ISSAC
Private	CHAPMAN ROBT.
Private	CHITWOOD PHILIP
Private	CLEEKE THOS.
Private	CONNOLLY THOS. Sotheby's Sale April 1911
Private	COOPER ROBT.
Private	DAVID GEORGE
Private	DRUM PATK.
Private	DUGGETT JOHN
Private	DUNN WM.
Private	FIELD WM.
Private	GREENSMITH MARK
Private	HAWKINSON JOHN
Private	HARRIS JARVIS 18 June Killed in Action
Private	HARVBIN JOSEPH
Private	HOUSE RICHD.
Private	HOWE RICHD.
Private	LAURENCE THOS.
Private	LEWIS JOHN
Private	LORD JAMES
Private	LOXTON SAML.
Private	LYGO JOHN
Private	MASSEY LAWRENCE
Private	MITCHELL WM.
Private	MOORE GEORGE
Private	MORETON JAMES
Private	NORMAN THOS.
Private	OATS JAMES
Private	PEMBERTON JAMES
Private	PENDLETON RICHD.
Private	PERCIVAL JOHN
Private	PITMAN THOS. Wounded 18th June 1815
Private	PRICE WM.
Private	REED JAMES
Private	RILEY CORNELIUS
Private	ROBERTS ROBT.
Private	ROTHERWELL JNS.
Private	SCOTT THOS.
Private	SILLICK ANTHY.
Private	SMITH SAML.
Private	SMITH THOS.
Private	STAFFORD SAML.
Private	STORER JOSHUA
Private	STUBB SAMUEL
Private	TOMKINS JAS.
Private	WEBB CHARLES Killed 18th June 1815
Private	WEBB JOHN
Private	WILMAN HENRY
Private	WILSON JOHN
Private	WINGFIELD SAMUEL
Private	WOLTON JOHN
Private	WOODWARD JOHN

* * *

18th HUSSARS

Lt. Colonel	MURRAY HON.H.
Pay.Mr.	DEANE WM. Ordered to the rear
Surgeon	CHAMBERS WM.
Adjutant	DUPERIER HENRY
Ass.Surgeon	QUINCEY JOHN
Vty.Surgeon	PILCHER DAVID
Ass.Vty.Surgeon	PULSFORD LUCAS
Captain	JAMES GRANT (Lt.Col.)
Lieutenant	CHARLES HESSE
Lieutenant	COOTE ROBERT
Lieutenant	MACHELL J.T.
Trp.Sjt.Maj.	TROTTER ARTHUR
Reg.Sjt.Maj.	JEFFS THOMAS
Pay Master Sjt.	FOSTER ALEXR. F. Ordered to the rear
Sad.Sjt.	BUTTERS JOHN Ordered to the rear
Trumpeter Maj.	WILLIAMS THOS.
Serjeant	CORNELL JAMES
Serjeant	DONNOLLY MICHAEL
Serjeant	HAST JOHN Day Sale April 1910
Serjeant	LARKIN JOHN Col.R.T. Gascoigne's Collection March 1909
Corporal	FOX JAMES On sale at Baldwin's July 1912
Corporal	GILL WILLIAM
Corporal	OBRIEN PHILIP On Baggage
Corporal	WILKINSHAW ROBT.
Trumpeter	WALLACE ROBERT
Private	ADAMS JOHN Gray Colection 1908

Private	ANDREWS WM.
Private	ARIS JOHN
Private	BARTLETT JOSEPH
Private	BATES SAMUEL
Private	BAXTER CHARLES
Private	BRIEN THOMAS
Private	BRIMFIELD JOHN
Private	BRISTOL GEORGE With Officers Baggage
Private	CLINTON JAMES
Private	CLINTON WILLIAM
Private	COLLINS ROBERT
Private	COLLINS MALACHI
Private	CONNIGAN HUGH
Private	CREED EDWD. With Officers Baggage
Private	DOORLEY JAMES
Private	DOUCH HENRY
Private	DUFF WM.
Private	FAY JOHN With Officers Baggage
Private	HALLMAN MORRIS
Private	HILL JAMES
Private	HINDS JAMES
Private	HINDS EDWD.
Private	HOLTON JOHN
Private	JACKSON WM.
Private	JORDAN JAMES
Private	KELLY JAMES Blacksmith Wicklow Cheylesmore Collection
Private	LACHIN JOSEPH
Private	MARSHALL RICHD.
Private	McBRIEN EDWD.
Private	McDONNOUGH EDWD.
Private	McMAHON MICHL.
Private	McMAHON JAMES
Private	McNAMARA PATK.
Private	McPHAUL WM.
Private	MOORE JOHN
Private	MURPHY FRANCES
Private	NOONE JOHN
Private	OFLANAGAN STEPHEN
Private	OSBOURNE ROBERT Officers Baggage
Private	OSMAN THOMAS
Private	QUINN ARTHUR
Private	READY JAMES
Private	REECE JAMES
Private	ROOTS CHAS.
Private	ROURKE THOS. Officers Baggage
Private	RYAN JOHN
Private	SHINDAN JAMES
Private	SMITH CHARLES
Private	SYMS CHARLES
Private	TOONE GEORGE With the Forge Carts
Private	UNDERWOOD HENRY
Private	VINALL JAMES
Private	WALSH THOS.
Private	WALSH RICHD.
Private	WEBB JOSEPH
Private	WEBB WILLIAM
Private	WHITE WILLIAM
Private	WRIGHT WILLIAM
Private	YOUNG JOHN
Ass.Surgeon	PULSFORD LUCAS Absent with leave to Ostend with a sick Officer. General Hospital Brussels.
Private	DORAN WM.

Major Richard Crocker's Troop

Captain	CROKER RICHD. (M) Payne Collection 1911
Lieutenant	McDUFFIE DONALD
Lieutenant	SOMERSETT HENRY A.D.C. to Maj. Gen.Lord Edwd.Somerset
Trp.Sjt.Maj.	COLLINS JOHN
Serjeant	BACON JOHN
Serjeant	BEATTY RICHD.
Serjeant	HICKLING WM.
Corporal	PEARCE WILLIAM
Corporal	SMITH JAMES
Corporal	UPTON WILLIAM
Trumpeter	FITZPATRICK THOMAS
Private	BOURNE MATTHEW
Private	BOURKE ROBERT
Private	BOWMAN WILLIAM
Private	BROAD JOHN
Private	BUSH STEPHEN With Forge Carts
Private	BYRNE PATRICK
Private	CONNOR DARBY
Private	DAVIS JAMES
Private	DAWSON WILLIAM
Private	DUNCAN ARTHUR
Private	EYRES JOHN
Private	FLANAGAN JOHN
Private	FORBES RICHD.
Private	GOODIFF WILLIAM
Private	GREEN JAMES
Private	HAMMOND JAMES

Private	HATTON DANIEL
Private	HENNESSEY ARTHUR Officers Baggage
Private	HERRING LEMON
Private	JONES JOHN
Private	JORDAN JOHN
Private	KAVANAGH LAWRENCE
Private	KENNEDY TIMOTHY
Private	LAPPAN JOHN
Private	LAWE JOHN
Private	McGUIRE PATRICK
Private	MARKS DANIEL Officers Baggage
Private	MAXWELL JAMES Officers Baggage
Private	McCABE WILLIAM
Private	McDERMOTT WILLIAM
Private	McDONNELL ARCHIBALD
Private	McDOUGAL THOMAS
Private	MORRISON DANIEL
Private	MULLEN PATRICK
Private	MURPHY JOHN
Private	OWENS WILLIAM
Private	PEMBERTON JOSEPH Officers Baggage
Private	REEVES ABSALOM
Private	REILLY THOMAS
Private	ROACHE THOMAS Whitaker Collection 1908
Private	ROONEY OWEN
Private	RUST ERASMUS
Private	SANDS WILLIAM
Private	SCALES THOMAS
Private	SCOLES THOMAS
Private	SMITH PATRICK
Private	STANNY JOHN
Private	STARKEY WILLIAM
Private	STUBBS JOHN
Private	SUXENNY JOHN
Private	TAYLOR JOHN
Private	TILDESLEY JAMES
Private	VENABLES JAMES
Private	WAINWRIGHT WM. Camp Kettles
Private	WISE JAMES
Private	WOODGER THOS.
Lieutenant	MOLLOR C.C. Sick at Brussels in General Hosp.
Private	MACKIE JAMES

Captain Richard Ellis's Troop

Lieutenant	WALDIE JAMES
Trp.Sjt.Maj.	JEFFS WILLIAM
Serjeant	CRUISS JOS.ROBT.
Serjeant	DWYER JEREMIAH
Serjeant	HARCOURT JAMES
Serjeant	TAYLOR JOHN
Corporal	ASHALL JOHN
Corporal	KINE THOMAS
Corporal	STARK JOSEPH H. Gaskell's Collection 1908
Trumpeter	MILLER FREDERICK
Private	ANKERS RICHD.
Private	BAILEY EDWD.
Private	BOND ROBERT
Private	BRADFORD RICHD.
Private	BRIEN JOHN
Private	BRYNE MICHAEL
Private	BONFIELD JOHN
Private	CANAVAN THOS.
Private	CASTLEDINE RICHD.
Private	CLARKE GEORGE Payne Collection 1911
Private	CLARKE JAMES With Camp Kettles
Private	CONLAN MICJAEL
Private	COTTERALL EDWARD With Surgeons Instruments
Private	CREASY GEORGE
Private	DUNN FRANCIS
Private	DUNPHY JOHN
Private	EASTON WILLIAM
Private	FISH ROBERT
Private	FLETCHER JOSEPH
Private	GAINOR JAMES
Private	GLEN JOHN
Private	GORDON DAVID
Private	GREGORY THOMAS
Private	GRASBY THOMAS With PayMaster Books
Private	GRAYDON CHARLES
Private	HANLON JOHN
Private	HUNT FRANCES
Private	HUNT JAMES
Private	KEATING ROBT.
Private	KEENAN ANDREW
Private	KEYTE GEORGE Officers Baggage
Private	LAMINSON JOSEPH
Private	LINTON JOHN

Private	McLOGHLIN JAMES
Private	McMAHON JAMES Officers Baggage
Private	NOWLAND GARRETT
Private	ONEILL OWEN Galway Foley Collection 1910
Private	PARSONS JAMES
Private	PITCHFORTH JOHN Officers Baggage
Private	ROBERTS EDWARD
Private	ROBINS THOS. Officers Baggage
Private	ROCHTIGAN TIMOTHY
Private	ROSS EDWARD
Private	SCULLION MICHAEL
Private	SHEEHAN CORNELIUS
Private	SLATER HENRY
Private	SMITH DAVID
Private	STANDISH HENRY
Private	SUTTON JAMES
Private	TRAINER HUGH
Private	TUMETTY JOHN Officers Baggage
Private	WARREN WILLIAM
Private	WALTERS EUGENE
Private	WHEELER JAMES
Private	WHITE JOHN
Captain	ELLIS RICHD. On sick leave to England
Lieutenant	DUNKEN THOS. Absent with leave
Private	CARR GEORGE On Litter party Deynse

Captain J.R.L. Lloyd's Troop

Captain	LLOYD J.R.L.
Lieutenant	DAWSON (Hon) L.C. On Baggage Guard
Trp.Sjt.Maj.	DALY OWEN
Serjeant	FOWLES HENRY
Serjeant	MOUNTNEY CHARLES
Serjeant	NOBLE WILLIAM
Corporal	PLUCK MILES
Corporal	WRAY JOHN
Trumpeter	WHITE RICHARD
Private	ALLEN JOHN
Private	BAILLEY ROBERT Officers Baggage
Private	CASTLEDINE EDWD.
Private	CAVANAGH THOS.
Private	CHETTLE ROBERT
Private	CLAYTON BENJN.
Private	COLEMAN JAMES
Private	COLTON JOHN
Private	CONWAY JOHN
Private	CRASKE WM.
Private	CULLIFER SOLOMON
Private	EGAN PATRICK
Private	ELLARD THOS.
Private	EVANS GEORGE
Private	EUSTACE PHILIP
Private	EYRES JAMES
Private	EYRES ROBERT
Private	FIDLER JAMES
Private	FISHLOCK ARTHUR
Private	FLINN WM. With Forge Carts
Private	GOODWIN HENRY
Private	GREEN HENRY
Private	GRIFFITHS RICHD. Genl.Hospital
Private	HENNISSEY GEORGE
Private	HINDS ALEXR.
Private	JONES DAVID
Private	JAMES THOMAS Officers Baggage
Private	KELLY JAMES
Private	KELLY MATTHEW
Private	KEENAN JNS.BERD.
Private	KEEVERS WILLIAM
Private	KIRWAN MICHAEL
Private	LUMSDELL WILLIAM
Private	MAHONEY JAMES
Private	MAINWARING JOHN
Private	MAINWARING WILLIAM General Hospital
Private	McDOWELL WM.
Private	McGREGOR ROBT.
Private	McKNIGHT JAMES
Private	MUNROW MICHL.
Private	OAKLEY WILLIAM Officers Baggade
Private	PAYNE EDWD.
Private	PEGLER RICHD.
Private	POWELL BENJN. Officers Baggage
Private	REABY THOS.
Private	REECE JOHN
Private	ROBERTS CORNS. Col.Gaskell's Sale May 1911
Private	ROSSITER WM.
Private	SPENCE ROBERT
Private	TADD JAMES With Forge Carts. Col.Murray's Collection
Private	THOMAS EDWARD
Private	TROWER JAMES Officers Baggage

Private	WALDRON ALEXR
Private	WILLIAMS GRIFFITH Officers Baggage
Private	WILLIAMSON THOS.
Private	WOULFE JAMES
Serjeant	LUCKIN JOSEPH Sick Brussels
Private	BURNHAM JOHN Genl. Hospital Brussels
Private	HOWLEY CHARLES Absent Without Leave
Private	PLUCK JAMES On Litter Party Beynse

Captain George Luard's Troop

Captain	LUARD GEORGE
Lieutenant	GEORGE WOODBERRY
Lieutenant	PRIOR THOMAS
Trp.Sjt.Maj.	BLACK WILLIAM
Serjeant	CARROLL PATRICK On Baggage Guard
Serjeant	COLGAN MATTHEW
Serjeant	FELL JOHN
Serjeant	HUTTON JAMES
Corporal	JONES THOMAS
Corporal	WILSON GEORGE
Corporal	WOOLLEY JOHN
Trumpeter	HOGG JOHN
Private	ARMSTRONG J.R.
Private	BENTLEY LEVI
Private	BERNE JAMES
Private	BINNIONS CLINTON
Private	BLANCHARD THOMAS With Camp Kettles
Private	DIZELLE ROBERT
Private	DICKSON ALEXR.
Private	DRUMMOND WILLIAM
Private	DUNNE JOHN
Private	ELLIOTT FRANCIS Officers Baggage
Private	FITZGERALD ROBERT
Private	FLANAGAN ABRAHAM
Private	GAFFNEY JAMES
Private	GREEN WILLIAM Officers Baggage
Private	HALPIN PETER
Private	HARGETT JAMES
Private	HART HUGH
Private	HARTY PETER With sick horses
Private	HEATEY JOSEPH
Private	HILLIER WILLIAM
Private	HURST JOHN
Private	IPPER JOHN
Private	KELLY JOHN (1)
Private	KELLY JOHN (2)
Private	KING JAMES
Private	LENNON JOHN
Private	LEWES MICHAEL
Private	MAGUIRE JOHN
Private	McCABE ANDREW
Private	McCARDLE HENRY
Private	McCARTHY MAURICE
Private	McGAHY GEORGE
Private	McINTIRE MICHAEL
Private	MELLON THOMAS
Private	MILSON WILLIAM
Private	MORRIS THOMAS
Private	MOULANG CHARLES
Private	MINTON WILLAIM
Private	MINDOCK WILLIAM
Private	NUGENT JAMES
Private	PAINTER THOMAS
Private	PARRY THOMAS
Private	PENNINGTON JAMES
Private	PHELAN JOHN
Private	RAINSFORD JOHN
Private	REILLY JOHN
Private	SEWARD JAMES With Regimental Books
Private	SIMPSON CHARLES
Private	SWEENEY JOSEPH
Private	TALLON EDWARD
Private	TAYLOR MICHAEL
Private	TAYLOR HENRY
Private	TINTEE ANTHONY
Private	TIMPSON JOHNSON
Private	WINGROVE JAMES
Private	WOOLFRIES CHARLES
Lieutenant	MONINS WM. Sick to Brussels
Corporal	MURPHY HENRY On Litter Party Deynse
Private	FITZGERALD JOHN General Hospital

Captain Arthur Kennedy's Troop

Lieutenant	ROWLLS W.H.
Trp.Sjt.Maj.	FOSTER JOHN
Serjeant	LOGAN THOMAS
Serjeant	PENNOCK JOHN
Serjeant	TAYLOR ALEXR.
Corporal	DOWIE GEORGE

Corporal	GILMORE WILLIAM
Corporal	GODFREY THOS.
Corporal	LOGAN JOSEPH
Trumpeter	GOODWIN JAMES
Private	ANDREWS GEORGE
Private	ARCHER JOSEPH
Private	ASHMORE WILLIAM
Private	BLOOD JOHN
Private	BOYLE JOHN
Private	BRITTAM THOS.
Private	BYRNE VAL. Glendining's Sale 25th Oct. 1907
Private	CARPENTER EDWD.
Private	CANFIELD JOHN
Private	CLENDINNING HIGH
Private	CLOYNE JAMES
Private	COLEMAN SIMON
Private	CROWE BERNARD
Private	DAVIS JOHN
Private	DOYLE PATRICK
Private	ENNIS JOHN
Private	FALTON JOHN
Private	FARRELL DENIS
Private	FOWLKS THOS.
Private	FRANKS EVAN With Officers Baggage
Private	GRADY DENIS
Private	HAMILTON JOHN
Private	HAMMOND WILLIAM
Private	HARVEY CHRISTR.
Private	HEZELDINE JOHN
Private	HUEY WILLIAM
Private	HUMPHRIES THOS.
Private	JONES WILLIAM
Private	JONES EVAN With Officers Baggage
Private	KIRWAN JAMES
Private	LOVEJOY JAMES
Private	McGUIRE PAT.W.C.
Private	MALOWNEY DANIEL
Private	MATTMAN ROBERT Officers Baggage
Private	McCABE MICHAEL
Private	McDONNELL JOHN
Private	McMAHON RICHD.
Private	McMANUS PATRICK
Private	McNAMARA MICHL. Officers Baggage
Private	McNIGHT WILLIAM
Private	McWILLIAMS PATRICK
Private	MELLON PHILIP
Private	MITCHELL ROBERT
Private	MURPHY JAMES
Private	PHAYER JOSEPH
Private	PINNION WILLIAM Sotheby's Sale April 1911
Private	PRICE EDWARD Officers Baggage
Private	REILLY PATRICK
Private	RUSSELL JOSEPH
Private	TEMPLETON THOMAS
Private	TOOLE MICHAEL
Private	TOWNSEND ANDREW
Private	TUCKER WILLIAM Camp Kettles
Private	UNDERWOOD RICHARD Officers Baggage
Private	WALSH JOHN
Private	WEBB JAMES
Private	WEIR CHRISTR.
Private	WILLARD JOHN
Captain	KENNEDY ARTHUR By a hurt from his horse on 16th.
Lieutenant	FRENCH MOULIN Sick Brussels
Private	BAILLEY JAMES Horse destroyed for Glanders
Private	FARRELL EDWARD Horse destroyed for Glanders
Private	CARROLL EDWARD On Litter party Deynse
Private	WOODFORD WILLIAM General Hospital

* * *

23rd LIGHT DRAGOONS

Lt.Col.	LORD PORTARLINGTON (Col)
Major	J.A. CUTCLIFFE
Major	P.A. LANTOUR
Adjutant	HENRY HILL
Surgeon	S.L. STEELE
Vety.Surgeon	JOHN SHIPP
Qr.Mr.	JOSEPH CROUCHLEY Payne Collection
Pay.Mr.	DILLOW THOMAS

Captain Thomas Gerrard's Troop No.1.

Captain	GERRARD THOS.
Captain	WALLACE J.M.
Lieutenant	COXENE STEPHEN Killed Medal sent to friends
Lieutenant	LEWIS JOHN
Trp.Sjt.Maj.	LEE JAMES
Py.Mr.Sjt.	JANNAN JNS. GEO.
Arm.Sjt.	STUART THOS.
Sad.Sjt.	BENNETT JOHN

Trump.Maj.	KING WM.
Serjeant	SHARPE JOHN
Serjeant	SLACKE FRANCIS
Serjeant	WEBSTER WM.
Corporal	BOOTH HENRY
Corporal	HALL WM.
Corporal	WARD JNS.
Trumpeter	SKINNER JNS.
Private	AIREY HENRY
Private	BALLARD JAMES
Private	BENSON WM.
Private	BENCH JOSEPH
Private	BICK WILLIAM
Private	BLYTHE JOSEPH
Private	BOMFORD THOS.
Private	BOOTH JAMES
Private	BORER JAMES
Private	BORTON JOHN
Private	BRAUNSDEN FRANCIS
Private	BURNE JOHN
Private	BURKE WILLIAM
Private	COOPER WILLIAM
Private	CORDON JAMES
Private	CLARKE MOSES
Private	COSFORD THOS.
Private	CLAWSON THOS.
Private	DAVIES JOHN
Private	EWING JNS.
Private	GARSIDE RICHD.
Private	HALL JNS.
Private	HIGGINS EDWD.
Private	HOBY VINCENT
Private	HOWE JNS.
Private	HUNTER JAS.
Private	JEFFERY VINCENT
Private	JONES WILLIAM
Private	KENT JOHN
Private	LENNON JNS.
Private	MATTHEWSON DAVID
Private	MITCHELL JAMES
Private	MURPHY PETER
Private	PIGG SAMUEL
Private	PHILMORE MICHAEL Glendining's Sale 28th Feb. 1908
Private	POWER JAMES
Private	SANKEY WM.
Private	SAVAGE THOS.
Private	SEDDON JOSEPH
Private	SMITH RICHD.
Private	SMITH WILLIAM
Private	SMITH THOS.
Private	SPRUCE JOHN
Private	TONGUE JOSHUA
Private	TWINER JNS.
Private	WALSH THOMAS
Private	WALKER EDWARD
Private	WARE WILLIAM
Private	WEBSTER JNS.
Private	WHELAN PATRICK
Private	WHITWORTH GEO.
Private	WILCOX WM.
Private	WYNNE JNS.
Private	WESTON GEO. Whitaker Collection 1908

Captain John Martin's Troop No.2.

Captain	MARTIN JOHN
Lieutenant	BACON CESAR
Lieutenant	DISNEY BRABN.
Trp.Sjt.Maj.	WALKER J.G.
Serjeant	BLAKE EDWARD
Serjeant	HONSELY TIMOTHY
Serjeant	WEBSTER WILLIAM
Corporal	DINGLE ROBERT
Corporal	RUSHTON JOHN
Trumpeter	SAUNDERSON JAMES
Private	BARWELL THOS.
Private	BRIDGES RICHD.
Private	BROAD RICHD.
Private	BROWN JOHN
Private	BURKETT CHAS.
Private	BUXTON WM.
Private	CHANDLER WM.
Private	CHAPMAN EDWD.
Private	COOKSEY WILLIAM Col.R.T. Gascoigne's Collection March 1909
Private	CRAWFORD THOS.
Private	DAVIS ISSAC
Private	GALEFORD JOHN
Private	GREY CHARLES
Private	GREY GEORGE
Private	GREEN THOS.
Private	GREEN WM.
Private	HARLEY JOSEPH
Private	HICKS SAMUEL
Private	HOLDING JAMES
Private	HUMPHRIES HENRY

Private	HUBAND JNS.
Private	JARVIS THOS. Glendining's Sale Jan 1913
Private	LAWRENCE GEO.
Private	LEE CHARLES
Private	LONG WILLIAM
Private	LUMSDEN JNS.
Private	MARKS PAUL
Private	McCARRICK HENRY
Private	MANSBRIDGE FREDK.
Private	METCALFE THOS. Cheylesmore Collection 1908
Private	MOLAGHTON LUKE
Private	MOULTON JOSEPH
Private	NEWBOLD THOS.
Private	OLDHAM HUGH
Private	PERKS JOHN
Private	PEEBLES JOHN
Private	PHILLIPS JNS.SENR. On Sale at Baldwin's March 1909
Private	PHILLIPS JNS.JUNR.
Private	POWELL JACOB
Private	PRESSLAND THOS.
Private	PRINGLE JAMES
Private	REEVES ROBT.
Private	RIDGEWAY JNS.
Private	RILEY SAMUEL
Private	ROACH PETER
Private	SALT THOS.
Private	SARTIN JOHN
Private	STANTON THOS.
Private	STEPHENS MARK
Private	THORNTON HENRY
Private	TOMLINSON RICHD. Glendining's Sale Oct. 1913 2-17-6
Private	WHEATLEY THOS.
Private	WILD JNS.

Captain McNeill's Troop No.3.

Captain	McNEIL RODK.
Lieutenant	BLATHWAYT G.W.
Lieutenant	HEMMINGS WM.
Trp.Sjt.Maj.	GLYNN GEORGE
Serjeant	HALKS JOSEPH
Serjeant	PHILLIPS GEO.
Serjeant	PILKINGTON JNS.
Serjeant	PURCHASE THOS.
Trumpeter	OLDHAM WILLIAM
Private	AWLAS BENJN.
Private	BALES JOHN
Private	BROWN JAMES
Private	BROWN WILLIAM
Private	BRUBT THOMAS
Private	CASSWELL BENJN.
Private	CHAMBERS CHAS.
Private	COATES THOS.
Private	COSGROVE JOHN
Private	COULTER WILLIAM
Private	COULTER ROBERT
Private	COYLE EDWD.
Private	CULLEY HENRY
Private	DAVENPORT WILLIAM
Private	DAVIS JOHN
Private	DUDIMAN JAMES
Private	ENFIELD THOMAS
Private	FARQUHAR EDWD.
Private	FITZPATRICK THOS.
Private	FRIEND WM.
Private	GRAVES JNS.
Private	HALL MICHAEL
Private	HARRIS JOHN
Private	HARRISON THOS.
Private	HASLAM WILLIAM
Private	HAYNES THOS.
Private	HEATH CHARLES
Private	HIDGE JOHN
Private	HORRID JOSEPH
Private	HURD JOSEPH
Private	ISHERWOOD JNS. On sale at Spink's Oct. 1909
Private	JACKSON JNS.
Private	LENNAGHAN MICHL.
Private	LEES WILLIAM
Private	MOSSENAN W.F. On sale at Baldwin's March 1909
Private	MOURIN PHELIMN
Private	MILLS HARR.WM.
Private	OLDHAM ROBT.
Private	ORANGE JNS.
Private	OUSEY JNS.
Private	PENTLER SAMUEL
Private	PERRY EDWARD
Private	REYNOLDS WILLIAM Galway Foley Collection 1910
Private	REYNOLDS CHARLES
Private	RILEY JAMES
Private	RUSSELL CHARLES
Private	SPENCER JAMES

rivate	STILSON GEO.
Private	STUART ALEXR. Day Sale April 1910
Private	TIMKINS WM.
Private	THORPE THOS.
Private	WILTSHIRE GEO.

Captain Hamilton's Troop No.4.

Captain	GROVES HENRY
Lieutenant	DODWELL GEORGE In possession of Lord Sackville 1910
Lieutenant	JOHNSON ROBT.
Trp.Sjt.Maj.	RICE HENRY
Serjeant	CRADDOCK THOS.
Serjeant	HAMMOND JOHN
Serjeant	KING BENJN.
Serjeant	LING HENRY
Corporal	GETHINGS GEORGE
Corporal	PADGHAM THOS.
Trumpeter	WESTWOOD JNS.
Private	ATHERTON JOHN
Private	BEAKLEY ISSAC
Private	BOOTH THOS.
Private	BAILEY GEORGE
Private	BRADSHAW BANJN.
Private	BUCKLEY JNS.
Private	CANNIBGS WM.
Private	CASSIN JOHN
Private	COOK WILLIAM
Private	CRESSWELL HENRY
Private	VROYDON WILLIAM
Private	DENNER SAMUEL
Private	DYKE RICHD.
Private	EVANS THOS.
Private	GAMMAGE THOS.
Private	GEORGE JOHN
Private	GORMAN THOS.
Private	HASSALL THOS.
Private	HALL JOSEPH
Private	HARTLEY ROBT.
Private	HEWITT CHARLES
Private	HILDRETH RALPH
Private	HUBBARD GEO.
Private	HULME OLDCROFT
Private	JOINER JOSEPH
Private	JENKINSON JAMES
Private	KNUCKY THOMAS
Private	LUNDREGHAN THOS.
Private	McKANE JOHN
Private	MILLER JOHN
Private	MOORE MICHL.
Private	PAYNE WILLIAM
Private	PEARSON THOS.
Private	PRICE SAMUEL
Private	REEVES DAVID
Private	RIVETT GEORGE
Private	RILEY WILLIAM
Private	ROCKLEY JOHN
Private	SANDERS JNS.
Private	SCHOLES JAMES
Private	SLATER WILLIAM Fleming Collection 1871
Private	SIMPKINSON BENJN.
Private	SIDDONS THOS.
Private	SMITH JNS. SNR. Littledale Sale Nov. 1910
Private	SMITH JNS. JNR.
Private	SQUIRES JAMES
Private	SQUIRES JOSEPH
Private	TAYLOR JNS.
Private	TRIGG SAML.
Private	TURNER THOS.
Private	WALKDEN SAML.
Private	WALTON WM.
Private	WEBB JNS.
Private	WILSON ROBT.
Private	WILLIAMS ROBT.
Private	WILLIAMS CHAS.
Private	WINZER JOHN
Private	WINWARD SAML.
Private	WOOD THOS.

Captain C.W. Dance's Troop No.5.

Captain	DANCE C.W.
Lieutenant	BOLTON ANTHY.
Lieutenant	WALL J.B.
Trp.Sjt.Maj.	CHARMER WILLIAM
Serjeant	ASHBEE JOHN
Serjeant	BARRACLOUGH JOSH.
Serjeant	TAYLOR JAMES
Serjeant	WEST JOHN Watters Sale June 1913
Corporal	BOOLE JOHN
Private	ALLEN JOHN
Private	ASHWORTH ABM.
Private	BAKER JOHN
Private	BANNER THOS.
Private	BARKER THOS.
Private	BAJEANT WILLIAM

Private	BIRD RICHD.
Private	BLUNT WILLIAM
Private	BOWERS JNS.
Private	BROWN JNS.
Private	BURMAN WM.
Private	CHAMBERS WILLIAM
Private	CLARKE WILLIAM
Private	COLLARD SAMUEL Gray Collection 1908
Private	CREELY JOHN
Private	CRONE GEO.
Private	DALL THOS.
Private	DONACHIE WM.
Private	DOWIE PETER
Private	EVANS JOHN
Private	EVANS RICHD.
Private	EVANS HENRY
Private	EWLANK THOS.
Private	FREEMAN JAMES
Private	GLANVILLE THOS.
Private	HALL JOHN
Private	HALL CHAS.
Private	HAMPSTEAD JOHN
Private	HAYWOOD JOSH.
Private	HICKSON SAML.
Private	KNIGHT WILLIAM
Private	LEES CHAS.
Private	McCARTNEY BARND.
Private	McNAUGHTON JNS.
Private	MARSTEN EDWD.
Private	MARTELL CHAS.
Private	MAYER FRANCIS
Private	NEWSHAM THOS.
Private	NICHOLLS RICHD.
Private	NORTON GEO.
Private	PAGE WM.
Private	PEARSON JNS.
Private	PENNY WM. Col.Murray's Collection
Private	POLLETT WM.
Private	QUEENAN JAMES
Private	RAWSTON GEORGE
Private	SIBBART RICHD.
Private	SIMION J.B.
Private	SKIPP RICHD.
Private	SLATER WM.
Private	SMITH SIMON
Private	SMITH WM.
Private	STOCKTON JOHN
Private	WARD WM.
Private	WARRINER JNS.
Private	WHATKINSON WM.
Private	WHITE JOSEPH
Private	WHITE WM.
Private	WOOD STEPHEN Gray Collection 1908
Private	YATES JOHN

Captain P.L. Cox's Troop No.6.

Captain	COX P.L.
Lieutenant	TUDOR CHAS.
Lieutenant	BANNER JOHN
Trp.Sjt.Maj.	STRIDE JAMES
Serjeant	BEACHY WM.
Serjeant	MARSH ABM.
Serjeant	NASH GEO.
Serjeant	BACON MICHL.
Corporal	HOPWOOD THOS.
Corporal	HOPWOOD LUKE
Trumpeter	KING WM. JUNR.
Private	ALLISTON JOHN
Private	ALLSOP THOS.
Private	ARCHER JAMES
Private	ASHTON WILLIAM
Private	ASTON JAMES
Private	BARLOW GEORGE
Private	BOLTON CHAS. H. Gaskell's Collection 1908
Private	BURKETT DANIEL
Private	BORTON JOHN
Private	BOYLE JAMES
Private	CLIFFE THOS.
Private	CORCHERAN JOHN
Private	COOK JOHN
Private	CORWELL JOHN
Private	COUZINS EDWD.
Private	CROSSLEY WILLIAM
Private	DELVES THOS.
Private	DEAN GEO.
Private	DRAPER THOS.
Private	ELWINE WILLIAM
Private	FERREDAY EDWARD
Private	FERREDAY EDWARD
Private	GETHINGS EPHM.
Private	GITTINGS WM. Payne Collection 1911
Private	GOODWIN GEO.
Private	HANKS THOS.
Private	HAWKES WILLIAM

Private	HOPWOOD ROBT. Glendining's Sale 21st July 1909
Private	HOPWOOD JAMES
Private	HOWSDEN JAMES
Private	HOLLAND WM.
Private	JONES WM.
Private	INGRAM ROBT.
Private	JEFFS RICHD.
Private	LARDNER JOSH.
Private	LANE JOHN
Private	LACEY WM.
Private	PRIDDY THOS.
Private	PEDDER STEPHEN
Private	READER JOSH.
Private	REYNOLDS GEO.
Private	SAWYER JAMES
Private	SHEPHERD FRANCIS
Private	SHELTON GEO.
Private	SINGLETON JAMES
Private	STEAD JNS.
Private	STEAD GEO.
Private	STRINGER GEO.
Private	SYKES JAMES
Private	TAYLOR JOSH.
Private	TIMMS THOS.
Private	TRAVERS JAMES
Private	TURNER GEO.
Private	TURNER JAMES
Private	WALLIS MICHL.
Private	WARD WM.
Private	WEBSTER WM.
Private	WHITE JAMES

* * *

ROYAL WAGON TRAIN

Lieutenant	AITKEN WILLIAM With the detachment in France
Lieutenant	SMITH EDWARD With the detachment in France
Lieutenant	McDORVALL JOSEPH Gaskells Collection With the detachment in France 1908
Lieutenant	O'NEILL HENRY With the detachment in France
Lieutenant	PARKINSON ROBERT With the detachment in France
Lieutenant	BOTT CHARLES With the detachment in France
Lieutenant	KERR ROBERT At Croydon
Cornet	GLENDENNING THOS. Promoted Lieut. at Croydon
Cornet	FENN JOHN With the detachment in France
Vty.Suregon	CHERRY FREDERICK Whitaker Collection 1908
Lt.Colonel	THOMAS AIRD.
Trp.Sjt.Maj.	BLYTH WILLIAM With the detachment in France
Trp.Sjt.Maj.	DOUGLAS ALEXR. With the detachment in France
Trp.Sjt.Maj.	McDERMOT JOHN Promoted Cornet at Croydon
Trp.Sjt.Maj.	RUSSELL WILLIAM With the detachment in France
Serjeant	ALLEN ROBERT
Serjeant	CHIVERTON JACOB
Serjeant	CRAM ROBERT
Serjeant	DOVE HUMPHRY
Serjeant	DOUGLAS JOHN
Serjeant	HARRISON DAVID
Serjeant	KENNEDY JAMES
Serjeant	KENNEDY GEORGE Day Sale April 1910
Serjeant	McKAY ALEXR.
Serjeant	NORMAN RALPH
Serjeant	POLLOCK JAMES
Serjeant	SMITH JOHN
Serjeant	SMITH THOMAS
Serjeant	WILKINSON ROBERT
Serjeant	WILLIAMS JOHN Glendinning's Sale January 1909 72/6
Corporal	BARRY JOHN
Corporal	BILLINGSGATE HENRY
Corporal	HOLFORD ROBERT
Corporal	JACOBS JAMES
Corporal	KIMBER JOHN
Corporal	KING JOHN
Corporal	LEACH THOS. Littledale Sale Nov. 1910
Corporal	SHEARMAN JAMES
Corporal	SPENCER RICHD. Glendinning's Sale 17 June 1908
Corporal	SYMMONDS EMANL. Gray Collection 1908
Corporal	WARSTELL PETER
Corporal	YOUNG JOHN
Trumpeter	CRAIGHEAD JAMES
Trumpeter	SMITH JOHN
Art.Wheel.	TEWKS THOS.
Art.Wheel.	GOULDER JAMES
Art.Wheel.	GOULDER WILLIAM

Art.Wheel.	WALTON ISSAC
Collar Mak.	DAWS WILLIAM
Collar Mak.	FARRER CHAS.
Collar Mak.	PRESTON JERH.
Collar Mak.	MEARMAN JOHN
Blacksmith	SERAL WILLIAM Fleming Collection 1871
Farriers	ANDREWS WILLIAM
Farriers	BROWN THOMAS
Farriers	CHAPPLE JOHN
Farriers	CHECK THABUS
Farriers	NORRIS WILLIAM H.Gaskell's Collection 1908
Farriers	RUDD THOMAS
Private	ADAMS WM.
Private	ALLEM EDWD.
Private	ALLEN THOS.
Private	ALLUM ROBERT
Private	ANDREWS JOHN
Private	ANGLOIS GEORGE
Private	AITKIN JOHN
Private	AUSTIN JOHN
Private	AUSTON JOHN Col. Murray's Collection 1908
Private	BALDWIN JOHN
Private	BATT BENJN.
Private	BURROWS THOS.
Private	BORROSS ROBT.
Private	BREEZE ROBT.
Private	BLACKHOUSE JOSEPH
Private	BILLINGHAM THOS.
Private	BROOKS WM.
Private	BROOKS GEORGE
Private	BUCKMAN JAMES
Private	BUCKLE WILLIAM
Private	BOUNDS JOHN
Private	BROWN GEORGE
Private	BECKFORD EDWD.
Private	BAILY WILLIAM
Private	BLEEZE THOS.
Private	BONE JAMES
Private	BOURNE JOSEPH
Private	BOWERS HENRY
Private	BREWER JOSH.
Private	BROCK JOHN
Private	BUFFEY RICHD.
Private	BURTON WM.
Private	CALLAWAY JOSH.
Private	CAMHAM SAML.
Private	CARPENTER JESSE
Private	CHAPMAN RICHD.
Private	CHESHOLD ROBT. Galway Foley Collection 1910
Private	CHESSON JOHN
Private	CLARKE WILLIAM
Private	CLEMENTS JAMES
Private	COCK JAMES
Private	COE WILLIAM
Private	COLE ROBERT
Private	CORNISH JAMES
Private	CRAMP RICHD.
Private	CRIPPS WM.
Private	CREEK JAMES
Private	CAMPBELL RICHD.
Private	CAWTHRONE GEORGE
Private	CATTERMOLE ROBERT
Private	CHURCHMAN FRANCIS
Private	COOLING GEORGE
Private	COOKSEY THOMAS
Private	COLLINS DAVID
Private	COLES JAMES
Private	CUTTING CHARLES
Private	DENNIS JOSEPH
Private	DENNIS WILLIAM Glendinning's Sale Dec. 1913
Private	DEARLING JAMES
Private	DORAZAC JOHN
Private	DUTNELL HENRY
Private	DOW JAMES
Private	DIGBY DAVID
Private	DUFFEY JAMES
Private	EADE GEORGE
Private	EDWARDS HENRY
Private	ELLINGTON EDWARD
Private	ELLIOTT JOHN
Private	EDWARDS JAMES
Private	EDWARDS CHARLES
Private	ELLIOTT THOMAS
Private	FLOWERS JAMES Needes Collection 1908
Private	FARLEY FRANCIS
Private	FERGUSON CHARLES
Private	FERRYMAN THOMAS
Private	FRANCIS JEREMIAH
Private	FRANKLIN RICHARD
Private	FULCHER WM.
Private	FULLMAN RICHD.
Private	GOWER THOS.

Private	GRANTHAM WM.
Private	GURL WM.
Private	GICHEY JOHN
Private	GREEN WM.
Private	GOSLING WM.
Private	GARDNER ROBT.
Private	GEER JOSH.
Private	GLUSBY THOS.
Private	GRICE RICHD.
Private	GEORGE ARTHUR
Private	HOARE MATTW.
Private	HALL SAML.
Private	HARRIS JOHN
Private	HILL CALEB
Private	HOLDING JOHN
Private	HUTCHINSON WM 1st
Private	HUTCHINSON WM 2nd
Private	HARRISON JOHN
Private	HAYLETT WM.
Private	HOWARD JOSH.
Private	HINTON GEORGE
Private	HAWKINS JOSH.
Private	HALL ROBERT
Private	HURT WILLIAM
Private	HARRIS JAMES
Private	JENKINS THOS.
Private	JENNINGS JAMES
Private	JOBLIN THOS.
Private	IVES JAMES
Private	KNIGHT JOHN
Private	LACEY JOSH.
Private	LAWS EDWARD
Private	LESTER WM.
Private	LACH SAML.
Private	LILLEY JOHN
Private	LILLEYWHITE THOS.
Private	LUSH WILLIAM
Private	LAMBKIN WILLIAM
Private	LAWRENCE ROBERT
Private	LEWIS MORGAN
Private	LONG WILLIAM
Private	LOVETT GEORGE
Private	LUNDIE GEORGE
Private	MEDCALF WM.
Private	MILLARD AMBROSE
Private	MUGGERIDGE RICHD.
Private	MITCHELL JAMES
Private	MILES BENJN.
Private	MORRELL JOHN
Private	NICHOLS JOHN
Private	NORTON JAMES
Private	NASH THOS.
Private	NEAVES THOS.
Private	NEVILL JOSH.
Private	NEVILLE JAMES
Private	NEWBURY WM.
Private	NEWTON THOS.
Private	OSBOURNE WILLIAM
Private	OSTLEY MARTIN
Private	OSMER JOSH.
Private	OZMOND RICHD.
Private	OLIVER RALPH
Private	PAUL STEPHEN
Private	PHILLIPS WM.
Private	PHIPPS EDWD.
Private	PRATT PHILIP
Private	PEMBERTON JOHN
Private	PEARCE JAMES
Private	PRIEST JOHN
Private	PIGGIN JOHN
Private	PEARSON GEORGE
Private	READ JAMES
Private	ROLES BENJN.
Private	RANSOM SAMUEL
Private	SANDFORD BENJN.
Private	SAVAGE JOSH.
Private	SAY WILLIAM
Private	SIMPSON THOMAS
Private	SMART WM.
Private	SMITH JAMES
Private	SQUIRES JOHN
Private	STEMP GEO.JOHN
Private	STONES JOHN
Private	SUDDS PHILLIP
Private	SUMLER THOMAS Col.R.T. Gascoigne's Collection March 1909
Private	SUMMERS ADAM
Private	SEATON JAMES
Private	SHARP THOS.
Private	SHOULTZS JAMES
Private	SMITH RICHD.
Private	SELVIE JOSH
Private	SHREW GEORGE
Private	SALMON THOS.
Private	SHEPHERD WILLIAM
Private	SMALL JOHN
Private	SMITH WM.

Private	STACEY JOHN
Private	STONER JAMES
Private	SINGER GEORGE
Private	SHEPHERD GERSHAM
Private	SHEPHERD JAMES
Private	TAYLOR WM. 1st
Private	TAYLOR WM. 2nd
Private	TAYLOR JAMES Cheylesmore Collection 1908
Private	TRIESES WM.
Private	THOMAS WM.
Private	TUCK SAML.
Private	TROTT THOS.
Private	TURVEY EZEKIEL
Private	UXTER RICHD.
Private	VENHAM JOHN
Private	VICKERY WM.
Private	VERNDALL RICHD.
Private	WICKENTON JAMES
Private	WELBY THOS.
Private	WALLS THOS.
Private	WHITE HENRY Col.Gaskell's Sale May 1911
Private	WHITE WM.
Private	WHITE JOHN
Private	WELLS JAMES
Private	WEBB THOMAS
Private	WRIGHT JOHN
Private	WILSON JOSEPH
Private	WATCHES WILLIAM
Private	WEADT WILLIAM
Private	WESRON RICHD.
Private	WHITBY GEORGE
Private	WILKINSON WILLIAM
Private	WOOLSEY HENRY
Private	WESTON JOHN
Private	WOOD JOHN
Private	WILLIAMS WM.
Private	WILLIAMS JOHN 1st
Private	WILLIAMS JOHN 2nd
Private	WILLIAMS JOHN 3rd
Private	WILLIAMS JOHN 4th
Private	YOUART JOHN

* * *

ROYAL HORSE AND FOOT ARTILLERY

Lt.Col.&Bt.Col.	SIR GEO.A. WOOD Kt. Commdg.R.Artillery
Lt.Col.	SIR A. FRAZER K.C.B.
Maj.&Bt.Lt.Col.	A. McDONALD
Capt.& Bt.Lt.Col.	A. DICKSON K.C.B.
2nd Captain	W. PAKENHAW
Lt.Col.	CHAS. GOLD
Lt.Col.	S.G. ADYE
Lt.Col.	S. WILLIAMSON
Lt.Col.	J. HAWKER
Major	P. DRUMMOND
Capt.&Bt.Lt.Col.	SIR JOHN MAY K.C.B. A.A.G. Asst.Adjut.Genl.
2nd Captain	H. BAYNES B.Major Brigade Major

Lt.Colonel Ross's "A" Troop

Lt.Col.	ROSS H.D.
Captain	PARKER J.B.
Lieutenant	HARDINGS RICHD.
Lieutenant	DAY JAMES
Lieutenant	ONSLOWE P.V.
A. Surgeon	RUDGE EDWARD
S.Serjeant	MORETON GEORGE
S.Serjeant	FARQUHAR ALEXR.
Serjeant	UNTWORTH WILLIAM
Serjeant	FLEMMING JOHN
Serjeant	WHITEHEAD THOS.
Corporal	COOPER THOS. Discharged
Corporal	BIDDULPH RICHD.
Corporal	ARMSTRONG JOHN
Bomb.	NALL JAMES
Bomb.	CAMERON ROBERT
Bomb.	SEYMOUR J.
Bomb.	CARTER JOHN
Bomb.	UNSWORTH ABEL
Farrier	SEAKER WILLIAM Sotheby's Sale 19 June 1908
S.Smith	TAYLOR WILLIAM
S.Smith	HOWELLS ELISHA
S.Smith	JOHNSTON JAMES
Coll.Maker	BEAUMONT JOHN
Coll.Maker	RIGBY WM.P.
Wheeler	LEBBON JAMES
Trumpeter	HAILD THOS. Pensioned
Gunners	UNSWORTH ISRAEL
Gunners	SOLLEY THOMAS
Gunners	WILKIE WM. Pensioned
Gunners	COBB JAMES
Gunner	BURNS DAVID
Gunner	SLATER JOHN Pensioned
Gunner	DUNCAN JAMES Pensioned
Gunner	STENSOR JOHN Pensioned
Gunner	MORETON WM.
Gunner	HEYWOOD JOSH. Pensioned

Gunner	TAYLOR WM.	Gunner	THOMPSON GEORGE
Gunner	THOMPSON ANTHY. Pensioned	Gunner	PADMORE SAMUEL Discharged
Gunner	COOK JOSHUA	Gunner	HOOLEY PETER Discharged
Gunner	LEIGHTON STEPHEN	Gunner	MITCHELL JAMES
Gunner	EDWARDS JOHN	Gunner	TURNER PETER
Gunner	KNOTTS THOS.	Gunner	ABLETT WILLIAM
Gunner	TURNER JOHN	Gunner	CHISWORTH GEORGE
Gunner	WINTERBOTTOM JOHN	Gunner	PAWLEY EDWARD Discharged
Gunner	MILLS JOSHUA	Gunner	GREY WILLIAM
Gunner	CLARK JOHN Col.Murray's Collection	Gunner	WATSON JOHN
		Gunner	ROWE GEORGE Discharged
Gunner	FAIRBROTHER RICHD.	Gunner	GAMBLE SAMUEL Discharged
Gunner	NEWMAN THOS.	Gunner	BAXTER ANDREW Discharged
Gunner	BREWSTER JAMES	Gunner	BAGSHAWE ROBERT
Gunner	MASON ROBERT	Gunner	GUDSON JOHN
Gunner	ARAN JOHN	Gunner	PAUL GEORGE
Gunner	GARNER JAMES	Gunner	HANSTIN JAMES
Gunner	JENKINS HENRY	Gunner	GOSMAN WILLIAM Discharged
Gunner	INWOOD DANIEL	Gunner	WRIGHT JOHN
Gunner	LEES DAVID	Gunner	CRITCH WILLIAM
Gunner	GRAVES JOSEPH	Driver	NOTTRIDGE WILLIAM Pensioned
Gunner	ROBINSON JOHN	Driver	PETTICAN THOMAS
Gunner	BEATTIE JOHN	Driver	BOLTON JAMES
Gunner	IBBLE JAMES	Driver	MYLES THOS.
Gunner	BUTCHER JOSEPH Glendinnings Sale Nov. 1913	Driver	BANNISTER WILLIAM
		Driver	BLACKBURN THOS. Discharged
Gunner	BUTCHER JOHN	Driver	MITCHELL ROBERT Since Dead
Gunner	KIRKLEY ROBERT	Driver	BARNES SAMUEL
Gunner	PATTERSON GEORGE	Driver	RUSHTON RICHD.
Gunner	READ WILLIAM	Driver	DODD RICHD.
Gunner	DAVIDSON JAMES Payne Collection 1911	Driver	DIEMOND JAMES
Gunner	SAWYER JAMES	Driver	BOLTON BENJN.
Gunner	CHAMBERS JOSEPH Discharged	Driver	SIMPSON GEORGE
Gunner	CRESSEY SAMUEL	Driver	CORNS RICHD. Pensioned
Gunner	BRIDGE ROBERT	Driver	BERRY WILLIAM
Gunner	GIDNEY JOHN	Driver	HARDING JAMES
Gunner	DALLEY JOHN Discharged	Driver	SMITH QUENTIN
Gunner	UPTON JOSEPH	Driver	COPELAND WILLIAM Discharged
Gunner	BROWN THOMAS	Driver	REY JOHN Discharged
Gunner	JONES THOS. Discharged	Driver	ORSBOURNE JAMES Discharged
Gunner	AFFLECK DAVID Discharged	Driver	HINDS WILLIAM
Gunner	MAYHEW SCARLET	Driver	CHISELDINE JOHN
Gunner	GUTHRIE JOHN	Driver	PHILLIPS JOHN Discharged
Gunner	CURRY THOS.	Driver	PHILIPOTT GEORGE
Gunner	VOCE GEORGE	Driver	TORRANCE JOHN
Gunner	BAKER JOSH. Pensioned	Driver	SMITH JOHN Discharged
Gunner	EYRE JOHN	Driver	CHUTRY JOHN
Gunner	WARREN THOS.	Driver	THELWELL JOHN

Driver	BROOKS JAMES
Driver	MORETON JOHN Discharged
Driver	QUINTIN WM.
Driver	LEESON HENRY Discharged
Driver	HUTCHINSON JOHN Discharged
Driver	PEARSON JOHN Discharged
Driver	BRADLEY JOHN Discharged
Driver	GULLICK JOHN
Driver	FISHPOOL HENRY
Driver	HADDEN CHARLES
Driver	DAWSON MOSES
Driver	COOPER JOHN Discharged Glendinning's sale April 1911
Driver	BECKITT JOHN
Driver	ALLEN JOSH Discharged
Driver	MONTGOMERY GEORGE Transferred
Driver	LOVELY SAMUEL
Driver	RICE WILLIAM
Driver	CUNNINGHAM PATRICK Discharged
Driver	BARKIN WILLIAM Discharged
Driver	FORD JAMES Deserted
Driver	BLANKSBY WILLIAM
Driver	COWIN JOHN
Driver	FOX THOS.
Driver	PATTEN JOSEPH
Driver	CHARLESWORTH JOHN
Driver	SINGLETON JOSH.
Driver	KIRK DAVID Discharged
Driver	HUGES WILLIAM

Captain Mercer's "D" Troop

Captain	MERCER ALEXR.C.
2nd Captain	WEBBER WILLIAM
Lieutenant	MANNSELL JOHN
Lieutenant	BRUCE JAS. R.
A.Surgeon	AMBROSE JAMES
S.Serjeant	ROBSTON JAMES
S.Serjeant	OLIPHANT ROBT.
Serjeant	WEBSETER JOHN
Serjeant	EYRE JOHN
Serjeant	GREEN WM.
Corporal	BROWN JAMES Littledale Sale Nov. 1910
Corporal	BARTLETT THOS.
Corporal	WINTER WM.
Bombr.	TYCE ISSAC
Bombr.	ROSS ROBERT
Bombr.	McIVER DUNCAN
Bombr.	JOHNSTON JOSH.
Bombr.	LUCAS EDWD.
Bombr.	STUDSMAN DAVID
Farrier	WHITTLEY WILLIAM
S.Smith	WALLACE ROBERT
S.Smith	GILCHRIST JAMES
S.Smith	STEWART MICHAEL
Coll.Maker	THOMPSON JOHN
Coll.Maker	STAPLES SAML.
Wheeler	CLARK JOHN
Trumpeter	GRNNATCH JAMES
Gunner	BOOTH JOHN
Gunner	COCKER WM.
Gunner	ROBERTS JAMES
Gunner	ELLIS THOS.
Gunner	LAMBERTH SAML.
Gunner	CEYER JAMES
Gunner	MATTHEWS GEORGE
Gunner	JEFFERY JOHN
Gunner	COLE THOS.
Gunner	WATTON BENJN.
Gunner	BURKETT THOS.
Gunner	NEELON THOS.
Gunner	MILLWORD JOSH.
Gunner	SLADDON WM.
Gunner	SMITH JOHN
Gunner	MORRISON THOS.
Gunner	BROOKS EDWD.
Gunner	KAY THOS.
Gunner	FOLKS WILLIAM
Gunner	BUCKLAND WM.
Gunner	MANNING EDWD.
Gunner	GILL JOHN A.
Gunner	ALLEN THOS.
Gunner	SIMPSON HUGH
Gunner	WARDING WILLIAM
Gunner	WRIGHT ROBERT
Gunner	LILLEYSTONE THOS.
Gunner	BAILIE JOHN
Gunner	LAMBERTH JOHN
Gunner	DUFFY ANDW.
Gunner	OWENS THOS.
Gunner	WOOD JOHN
Gunner	BARRY JAMES
Gunner	BROWN THOS.
Gunner	BROADHURST JOHN
Gunner	REID JOHN
Gunner	BIRCHENOUGH WM.
Gunner	MARTIN HUGH

Gunner	WATE GEORGE
Gunner	JOHNSTONE JOHN
Gunner	HANNING WM.
Gunner	FITZGERALD GEO.
Gunner	STOPHER ROBT.
Gunner	McCORMACK JOHN
Gunner	ATTERWELL JOSH.
Gunner	BUCKLEY JOSH.
Gunner	McBREARTY BRYANT
Gunner	HERRON JAMES
Gunner	WILLIAMSON DAVID
Gunner	DENNISTON JAMES
Gunner	TAILOR JNS.
Gunner	STOREY THOS.
Gunner	ISHERWOOD MATTHEW
Gunner	ROBERTS JOHN
Gunner	FORTUNE WILLIAM
Gunner	NIXON WM.
Gunner	SMITH JAMES
Gunner	SMITH THOS.
Gunner	LARKIN PETER
Gunner	WILLOX JAMES
Gunner	GIBSON SAML.
Gunner	FORTUNE JOHN
Gunner	SCOTT JOHN
Gunner	DOIG DAVID
Gunner	JAMES ROBERT
Gunner	SMILLEY JOHN
Gunner	GALLASPIE JOHN
Gunner	DRYSDALE ROBERT
Gunner	FERGUSON WILLIAM
Gunner	HEDGES RICHARD
Gunner	STOREY CHRISTOPHER
Gunner	MYLES JAMES
Gunner	LOVE JOHN
Gunner	SANDS JAMES
Gunner	ROY BENJN.
Gunner	BEGGERS JAMES
Gunner	CUBITT HENRY
Gunner	ROBINSON DAVID
Gunner	BONCE WM.
Gunner	ROBINSON BENJN.
Gunner	MOTHER WM.
Gunner	HENDERSON JAS.
Gunner	AXON WM.
Gunner	MORGAN EDWD.
Driver	ASPDEAN RICHD.
Driver	BLAIR ANDW.
Driver	GREENALCH WM.
Driver	WEST JOSH.
Driver	MATTLEY WM.
Driver	ASHMORE JAMES
Driver	DURRANT WM.
Driver	HENDERSON ROBT.
Driver	NEILSON ROBT.
Driver	HALL HENRY
Driver	KIGGAN PETER
Driver	PEACH BENJN.
Driver	CHADWICK DAVID
Driver	LADD WM.
Driver	NOKES GEO.
Driver	McDONALD ROBT.
Driver	HAYWOOD HENRY
Driver	FRANCIS JOHN
Driver	LONG NATH.C.
Driver	WARD WM.
Driver	MALLISON JOSH.
Driver	HAMILTON JOHN
Driver	WHITE JOHN
Driver	GERMAIN HENRY
Driver	DOLLARS ROBT.
Driver	BLAIR JOHN
Driver	WEST WM.
Driver	GOULD RICHD.
Driver	ROBERTSON ROBT.
Driver	WILLIAMSON THOS.
Driver	FLETCHER RICHD.
Driver	McCULLOUGH THOS.
Driver	CAVE THOS.
Driver	McCARTNEY THOS. Glendinning's Sale Nov. 1913
Driver	HART HUGH
Driver	HOGERTY FRANCIS
Driver	LEE WM.
Driver	STEWART ROBT.
Driver	GILLESPIE DANIEL
Driver	ERNBUY WM.
Driver	HANGHEY OWEN
Driver	CORNET WM.
Driver	REID ARTHUR
Driver	THOM JAMES
Driver	SLAIN WM.
Driver	SMITH JNS.
Driver	BROWN JAS.
Driver	HERLEY DANIEL
Driver	BELDUM WM.
Driver	DRUZZANE THOS.
Driver	HURLEY THOS.

Driver	GREEN WM.
Driver	BORROWS JAS.
Driver	LEE THOS.
Driver	KENNEDY JOHN
Driver	LENNON ARTHUR
Driver	BUCKLEY WM.
Driver	HOLLOWAY JNS.

Lt.Colonel Gardiner's "E" Troop

Captain & Bt.Lt.Col.	GARDINER ROBT.
2nd Captain & Bt.Maj.	DYNELEY THOS.
Lieutenant	HARDING ROBERT
Lieutenant	SWABEY WM.
Lieutenant	INGLEBY WM.B.
A.Surgeon	MACDONALD ALEXR.
S.Serjeant	BAINS CHAS.
S.Serjeant	ANDREWS JOHN
Serjeant	BLEACHLY JAS.
Serjeant	HEDGE JNS.
Serjeant	WHITE JNS.
Corporal	PARLETT THOS. Pensioned
Corporal	BUXTER JAMES
Corporal	ROEBUCK NATHL.
Bombr.	WILKINSON JAMES
Bombr.	EDMUND WM. Trans. to "G" Troop
Bombr.	BROCKLEY SAML.
Bombr.	MALCOME JAMES
Bombr.	TATE ROBT.
Bombr.	GILES GEORGE
Farrier	DEVILLING JAMES
C&S Smith	MAXWELL JOHN
S.Smith	HILL JAMES On sale at Fenton & Son 1910
S.Smith	BIUNNER JOHN Discharged
C.Maker	WEBSTER THOS.
C.Maker	TANWOOD NOAH
Wheeler	FRANKLING ROBERT
Trumpeter	CHAMBERS ANDREW Pensioned
Gunner	MACKIE GEORGE Pensioned
Gunner	HANCOCK SAML.
Gunner	HAYES STEPHAN
Gunner	CUNNINGHAM ROBERT
Gunner	BLACKLEY JOSHUA Gray Coll.1908 Galway Foley 1910
Gunner	BRYAN WILLIAM
Gunner	WRIGHT WILLIAM
Gunner	BANLTEY THOMAS
Gunner	HEIGHTEN JAMES
Gunner	SCOTT JAS. Senr.
Gunner	MORELAND JOHN
Gunner	GILLOTT CHRISTR.
Gunner	JEFFERSON JOHN
Gunner	REED WM.
Gunner	SHAW THOS. Pensioned
Gunner	MUSGROVE PHILIP Pensioned
Gunner	HYNDMAN ROBERT
Gunner	EDWARDS JOHN
Gunner	STEWART JOHN
Gunner	RATCLIFF RICHD.
Gunner	SUTTON JOHN
Gunner	TAYLOR THOS.
Gunner	NORMAN THOS.
Gunner	KEELER JAMES
Gunner	DOWRING JOSH.
Gunner	McKENZIE JAMES
Gunner	PORTERS ISSAC Died 17 Aug.1815
Gunner	BLAYDON JOHN
Gunner	DAY JAMES
Gunner	EDDINGTON WM.
Gunner	DAVIS THOS.
Gunner	LEMMON ANDREW
Gunner	BARCLAY JAMES
Gunner	PRINCE ELIJAH
Gunner	EASTWOOD SETH
Gunner	VRICE JAMES Discharged
Gunner	SEARS GEORGE Discharged
Gunner	MORRIS JOHN Discharged
Gunner	RAMSEY JAMES
Gunner	CUTTER ROBT.
Gunner	LOVE JOSEPH Pensioned
Gunner	WRIGHT JOHN
Gunner	BAMFIELD HENRY Pensioned
Gunner	HAWLEY WM.
Gunner	MANN JOHN
Gunner	CAIRD JOHN
Gunner	DUDLOW THOS.
Gunner	RUSSELL THOS.
Gunner	ASHWORTH JOHN
Gunner	McLACHLANE JOHN Discharged
Gunner	GIBB JAMES Chelyesmore Collection 1908
Gunner	FENTON HUGH
Gunner	DEAN WILLIAM
Gunner	McMULLIN JOHN
Gunner	EASTON GEORGE Discharged
Gunner	POWRIE JAMES
Gunner	BAINES HENRY

Gunner	DUCKWORTH JOHN
Gunner	HAMMERSLEY SAML.
Gunner	SWANSTON JOHN
Gunner	BOARDMAN PETER
Gunner	FALKNER JOHN Needes June 1908
Gunner	DUCKSELL THOS. Discharged
Gunner	CLAYTON DANIEL
Gunner	LOCKYER HENRY
Gunner	STEWART ANDREW Discharged
Gunner	GOFF JOHN
Gunner	STENILY FRANCIS
Gunner	HILL JOHN
Gunner	SCOTT JAMES Jnr.
Gunner	BARWORTH ROBT.
Gunner	THEAKER THOS.
Gunner	BAINS FRANCIS
Gunner	CLARKE WILLIAM
Gunner	FREEMAN THOMAS
Gunner	DRINKWATER WILLIAM
Gunner	DEVILINE JOHN Discharged
Gunner	McCASEY WM.
Gunner	LAWRENCE JERE.
Gunner	ARDON BARN.
Gunner	DRINKWATER JAMES
Gunner	CRODDLAND LUKE
Gunner	ROWLAND EVAN
Gunner	BUCKLEY JOHN Discharged
Gunner	HIND WILLIAM Discharged
Gunner	MARLAND SAML. Discharged
Driver	HOPKING JOHN Pensioned
Driver	STAINES THOS.
Driver	MILLS JOHN
Driver	COLES JAMES Died 18th Nov. '15
Driver	PASHLEY GEORGE
Driver	ASPINALL MILES
Driver	HALL GEORGE
Driver	WHITE GEORGE
Driver	MORRISON WM.
Driver	COBB JOHN Discharged
Driver	FARRISH JOHN Pensioned
Driver	BARDY WILLIAM
Driver	STEPHENTON JOHN
Driver	TOMKINS SAML.
Driver	ELD THOMAS Discharged
Driver	DANE ROBT.
Driver	HALL JOHN
Driver	HOLMES ROBT.
Driver	BENNING WM.
Driver	McEWAN PETER
Driver	SUTHARD RICHD. Discharged
Driver	SPENCER GEORGE H.Gaskell's Collection 1908
Driver	CUTTER GEORGE
Driver	BOLTON WILLIAM
Driver	HANSLEY WILLIAM
Driver	COLLINS JAMES
Driver	CHAPPELL THOS. Discharged
Driver	NOORE THOS. Discharged
Driver	KANE JAMES
Driver	CURRAN CHAS.
Driver	DAVIS JOHN Discharged
Driver	ANDREWS EDWD.
Driver	GRIFFITHS SAML.
Driver	LANCASTER JOSIAH
Driver	DAVIS RICHD.
Driver	PRICE LEVIE Died 4th May 1816
Driver	KEMGAN ROBT. Discharged
Driver	PEARSON JAMES
Driver	MORGAN WILLIAM Pensioned
DRiver	ROBERTS AMBROSE
Driver	JARVIS THOS.
Driver	RICHARDSON JOHN
Driver	ELOOME GEORGE
Driver	CRAVEN JAMES
Driver	TOTHERINGHAM ALEXR.
Driver	ROBERTS THOS. Discharged
Driver	HACKETT WM.
Driver	LIDLOW ANDW.
Driver	BEEVOE ROBT. Discharged
Driver	MOTHEN THOS.
Driver	LUGH HARVEY
Driver	HART WILLIAM
Driver	PHILLIPS JOSEPH Discharged
Driver	RUSSELL THOS.
Driver	SELLERS BENJN.
Driver	CHILTON RICHD.
Driver	GRANGE THOS,
Driver	CAUPE JOSH.
Driver	HOLMES JAMES
Driver	BUNE THOS.

Lt.Colonel W. Smith's "F" Troop

Capt. & Bt. Lt.Col.	SMITH J.W.
2nd Captain	WALCOTT EDMD. H.Gaskell's Collection 1908
Lieutenant	CRAWFORD DOND.

Lieutenant	EDWARDS D.T.
Lieutenant	FOSTER HENRY
A.Surgeon	GATTY HENRY
Staff Sjt.	COCKLAND THOMAS
Staff Sjt.	WHITMAN JAMES
Serjeant	JEFFERSON RALPH
Serjeant	BLACKIE THOS.
Serjeant	CHAMBERS ALEXR.
Corporal	ACHINDACKY JAMES
Corporal	CRAVEN THOS.
Corporal	McKENZIE JAMES Cheylesmore Collection 1908
Bombr.	COOKE LAWRENCE
Bombr.	SMITH ROBERT
Bombr.	LAWREANCE JAMES
Bombr.	MILLS WM.
Bombr.	SMITH JOHN
Farrier	GIBSON JOHN
Smiths	GREENHILL WM.
Smiths	BARKER WM. Whitaker Collection 1908
Smiths	MARTIN BENJN.
C.Maker	NELSON MERRIOT
C.Maker	JOHNSTON WILLIAM
Wheeler	PARMER JONATHAN
Trumpeter	HODGE NATHANIAL Gray Collection 1908
Gunner	MILLORS THOS.
Gunner	WARDAN SAML.
Gunner	CRAIG DAVID
Gunner	FAIRCLOTH PETER
Gunner	ANDERSON FRANCIS
Gunner	WOOLHOUSE JOSEPH
Gunner	COOKE JOHN
Gunner	THORNLY WM.
Gunner	BROWN WM.
Gunner	WILLIAMSON THOS.
Gunner	HOLDING HENRY
Gunner	ASHWORTH WILLIAM Pinnoch June 1908
Gunner	FIELDING JOHN
Gunner	WRIGHT ROBT.
Gunner	STEEDMAN DAVID
Gunner	CRAVEN SAMUEL
Gunner	BENNETT THOMAS
Gunner	LEIGH JOHN
Gunner	McFARLANE JOHN
Gunner	PICKING THOS.
Gunner	HARRISON THEOPH. On sale at Baldwin's March 1909
Gunner	MILLIER HUGH
Gunner	COVELEY MATTW.
Gunner	STURGES WM.
Gunner	HALL HENRY
Gunner	SEXSMITH MATTW.
Gunner	HANE JOHN
Gunner	PLATTS THOS.
Gunner	FLETON JAMES
Gunner	WAINWRIGHT HENRY
Gunner	KEEPING EDWD.
Gunner	LUTTER JOHN
Gunner	LOVETT CHAS.
Gunner	JORDAN ADAM
Gunner	KEEPING JOHN
Gunner	HODGSON JOSH.
Gunner	BARNES EDWD.
Gunner	WILLIAMSON ROBT.
Gunner	TRAYTE GEORGE
Gunner	HALL WILLIAM
Gunner	EWBANK JOSEPH
Gunner	GREASLEY GEORGE
Gunner	HOGG WILLIAM Cheylesmore Collection 1908
Gunner	FLETCHER JOHN
Gunner	FOSTER THOS.
Gunner	STEVENS WM.
Gunner	EWWN ALEXR.
Gunner	NEW JAMES
Gunner	COLLAND WM.
Gunner	LINDSAY DAVID
Gunner	FAIRHURST HENRY
Gunner	MADGLEY JONATHAN
Gunner	WRIGHT JAMES
Gunner	HAGIN JOHN
Gunner	MACLEOD DANIEL
Gunner	MALONE JOHN
Gunner	GRIFFITHS JOHN
Gunner	SPEAK JOHN
Gunner	CADMAN ROBT.
Gunner	MERRIOTT JAMES
Gunner	JOYCE SAML.
Gunner	BENTLEY JOHN
Gunner	NEWTON JOHN
Gunner	FAINCHILD SAML.
Gunner	CROFFTS WILLIAM
Gunner	VAUGHN THOS.
Gunner	GOODWIN BENJN.
Gunner	CRONE SAML.

Gunner	BRAIN THOS.
Gunner	MILLS RICHD.
Gunner	LEASON ROBERT H.Gaskell's Collection 1908
Gunner	SMITH ROBERT
Gunner	WRIGHT JOHN
Gunner	WILLIAMS JOHN
Gunner	TAITE WILLIAM
Gunner	TURNER JOHN
Gunner	CURTIS ABRAHAM
Gunner	TERRALL SAMUEL
Gunner	PEARMAN THOS.
Gunner	WEBSTER ROBT.
Driver	ECCLES ABRAHAM
Driver	HOWARTH JOHN
Driver	MIDDLETON GEORGE
Driver	RIDER GEORGE
Driver	WILSON JOHN
Driver	ELLISON THOMAS
Driver	HAYS JOHN
Driver	BORMAN CHALLANDER
Driver	FRY JOHN
Driver	HAYWOOD JOSEPH
Driver	RICHARDSON ROBT.
Driver	MORRIS GEORGE
Driver	GOODWIN JAMES
Driver	MAIDLY JAMES
Driver	BUTLER JOHN
Driver	IRVIN JOHN
Driver	RILLEY WILLIAM
Driver	WILLIS GEORGE
Driver	GREENALCH THOS.
Driver	CULLAM WM.
Driver	MATTHEWS JOSH.
Driver	BOND HENRY
Driver	CALDWELL WM.
Driver	HARPER JOHN
Driver	LEE WILLIAM
Driver	WATSON JAMES
Driver	BRAITHWITH JOHN
Driver	BURTON DANIEL
Driver	CLARKE JOHN
Driver	ROGERS RUBEN
Driver	BARNCLIFF DAVID
Driver	BROWN MATTHEW
Driver	MITCHELL JOHN
Driver	FLAVEL JAMES
Driver	CLEGG JOSEPH
Driver	BRUNDLE ROBERT
Driver	NUTTLE JAMES
Driver	GRIFFITHS ISSAC
Driver	HODSON JAMES
Driver	BARNES JAMES
Driver	CROOKS JOHN
Driver	MATHER JOSEPH
Driver	THEAKER ANTHONY
Driver	WHITEHEAD JOSEPH
Driver	SEMLY GEORGE
Driver	BURTON GEORGE
Driver	BENNETT JOSEPH
Driver	WIDDOWSON WILLIAM
Driver	CATTAM JOHN
Driver	WRIGHT JAMES
Driver	RECK SAMUEL Sotheby's Sale April 1911
Driver	MATTHEWS SAMUEL
Driver	HORNS WILLIAM
Driver	MOFFATT WILLIAM
Driver	SIMMONDS BASSIL
Driver	SHEEPLY WILLIAM
Driver	FLETCHER RICHD.
Driver	SAVAGE THOS.
Driver	BARNES SALT.
Driver	TROTT CHARLES

Lt.Colonel A. Dickson's "G" Troop

2nd Capt.	NEWLAND ROBT.
Lieutenant	BELL WILLIAM
Lieutenant	LEATHES HY.M.
Lieutenant	HINCKS JOHN
Lieutenant	BRETON JOHN F.
A.Surgeon	HITCHINS RICHD.
S.Serjeant	HALL JOHN
S.Serjeant	PARSON HENRY
Serjeant	BURT DAVID
Serjeant	FULLER ROBERT
Serjeant	NISBITT JOHN
Corporal	JOHNSTON WILLIAM
Corporal	MARTIN JAMES Glendinning's Sale Sept. 1912 1-6-0
Corporal	GREEN WM.
Bombr.	OMEY SAMUEL Pensioned
Bombr.	OMEY NATHL.
Bombr.	EMMITT JOHN
Bombr.	ANDERSON THOS.
Bombr.	LOMAX JAMES
Bombr.	MASTERTON THOS.
Farrier	PRICE J.
S.Smith	BROWN EDWARD Cheylesmore Collection 1908

S.Smith	HEWDON JAMES	Gunner	FIFE THOS.
S.Smith	PETITT JOHN	Gunner	EWAN JOHN
C.Maker	RODHOUSE ROBT. Pensioned	Gunner	MATTHEWS JOSH.
C.Maker	ALEXANDER ROBT.	Gunner	HUGHES JOSH.
Wheeler	ROCKLIFF WILLIAM	Gunner	BERRY JOHN
Trumpeter	BOWEN HENRY	Gunner	CARLTON CHRISTR.
Gunner	PRESTON THOS.	Gunner	JOHNSTON WILLIAM
Gunner	MILLWARD JOSH.	Gunner	HILL JOHN
Gunner	BUTTERWORTH JOHN Dead	Gunner	HADFIELD JAS Senr.
Gunner	DEWSNIPS GEORGE	Gunner	BANNISTER GEORGE Pensioned
Gunner	DEATH JOHN	Gunner	HADFIELD JAS. Jnr.
Gunner	ENTOR JOSEPH	Gunner	LAMBERT JAMES
Gunner	PENDLETON ADAM Pensioned	Gunner	MARSDEN THOS.
Gunner	FULKS WILLIAM	Gunner	SMITH WM.
Gunner	GRIFFITHS RICHD. Pensioned	Gunner	BARLON GEORGE
Gunner	HOLTON RICHD.	Gunner	HUTCHINSON THOS.
Gunner	HELVIN THOS.	Gunner	HAY JOHN Pensioned
Gunner	RHIND JOHN	Gunner	CAMERY JAMES
Gunner	BURTON LINET	Gunner	HUNT PHILIP Pensioned
Gunner	PATTEN JAMES	Gunner	WARD JAMES Col.R.T. Gascoigne's Collection March 1909
Gunner	SPRINGLEY SAML.	Gunner	HAY ALEXR.
Gunner	SIMPSON PETER	Gunner	HUTCHINSON JAMES Pensioned
Gunner	WATTS WILLIAM	Gunner	BARHAM FRANCIS
Gunner	PARRY ROBERT	Gunner	FARRER JOHN
Gunner	CHAMBERS JAMES	Gunner	MARTIN THOS.
Gunner	PALFREY WILLIAM	Gunner	FARMER WM. Discharged
Gunner	ROLSTON GEORGE	Gunner	PRING THOS.
Gunner	KEEBLE NATHL.	Gunner	BURCH JAMES
Gunner	BIRKINSHAW JOSH.	Gunner	WOODS JOHN
Gunner	FELTON BENJN.	Gunner	BLAYS JOHN
Gunner	TAYLOR JOHN Whitaker Collection 1908	Gunner	CHASE EDWARD
Gunner	MULLETT ROBT.	Gunner	MARTIN WILLIAM
Gunner	PHILCOX JAMES	Gunner	SMITH ROBERT
Gunner	CHILDS WILLIAM	Gunner	CORBITT WILLIAM
Gunner	WEAVER SAMUEL	Gunner	NIXON THOS.
Gunner	COWLEY WILLIAM	Gunner	DYSON JOHN Discharged
Gunner	ALMEY GEORGE	Gunner	BELL RICHD.
Gunner	MARSHALL JOHN Pensioned	Gunner	WILLIAMS DAVID Dead
Gunner	RAIN GEORGE	Driver	HADLEIGH EDWARD
Gunner	ILLINGSWORTH JOHN	Driver	STAINER JOSEPH
Gunner	HUNTER ALEXR.	Driver	BALL THOMAS Discharged
Gunner	RYLEY JOHN	Driver	LORD SAMUEL
Gunner	WHITTLE JOSEPH	Driver	ALMOND GEORGE
Gunner	FRAIL JOHN	Driver	DIXON ROBERT
Gunner	MARTYN THOS. Pensioned	Driver	DISMOORE WILLIAM
Gunner	PRITCHARD HENRY	Driver	DALE WILLIAM
Gunner	ARMSTRONG JAMES	Driver	LODGE WILLIAM
Gunner	BLACKIE WM.	Driver	WILKINS FRANCIS

Driver	BYCOTT WILLIAM
Driver	LOWRING JAMES
Driver	WALLOCKS HENRY
Driver	ARLURN GEORGE
Driver	MAINWARING WM. Dead
Driver	MITCHELL JAMES
Driver	WRIGHT SAMUEL
Driver	FOX WILLIAM
Driver	McMANNERS BARNARD
Driver	FRAIL WILLIAM
Driver	LEVERSAGE GEORGE
Driver	EWAN MUNJO
Driver	MILLER THOS.
Driver	CLIFFORD RICHD.
Driver	HENDERSON ADAM
Driver	CRABTREE WILLIAM
Driver	CLAIL SYLVESTER Cheylesmore Collection 1908
Driver	TOWNLEY GEORGE
Driver	BROGDEN WILLIAM
Driver	GLASSFORD WILLIAM
Driver	PACKER JOSEPH
Driver	ANDREWS THOMAS
Driver	ALLCOCK JAMES
Driver	PITMAN AQUILY
Driver	BOARDMAN JAMES
Driver	GRANTHAM FRANCIS
Driver	SHELDER THOMAS
Driver	DARBYSHIRE JOHN
Driver	FULLER JAMES
Driver	CLARK THOMAS Discharged
Driver	ROSE WILLIAM
Driver	LIGHTFOOT WILLIAM
Driver	PICKISS JOHN
Driver	HILL WALKER Pensioned
Driver	CLIPSANT W.
Driver	HORSEFIELD JAMES
Driver	BENTLEY PHILIP
Driver	BENTLY JOHN
Driver	CLIPSON JOHN
Driver	DIBBIN THOS. Dead
Driver	HOPKINS ROBERT
Driver	MARCH JOSEPH
Driver	BEARDSLEY JOHN
Driver	GRASS OLIVER
Driver	WOOD JOHN Discharged
Driver	BAKER WILLIAM

<u>Lt.Colonel May's "H" Troop</u>

Captain & Bt.Major	MACDONALD ALEXR.
Lieutenant	BRERETON WM.
Lieutenant	SANDILANDS PHILIP
A.Surgeon	KENNY MATTIAS
S.Serjeant	COCKBURN SAML.
S.Serjeant	DISSINGTON JAMES
Serjeant	HORSPOOL JOHN Pensioned
Serjeant	MARSHALL PETER
Serjeant	ROBINSON JOHN Pensioned
Corporal	WHITE JOHN
Corporal	LAWTON THOS.
Corporal	SALT SIMON
Bombr.	FEWTRILL JEREMIAH
Bombr.	ROOKE RICHD.
Bombr.	SCOTT ROBT.
Bombr.	LEDGERWOOD JAS.
Bombr.	STANSON JOHN
Bombr.	HART SAML.
Farrier	BRUTTON JOHN
S.Smith	VIZACHLEY MICHAEL
S.Smith	GARDINER HENRY
S.Smith	VAUGHAN EDWD.
S.Smith	ANDERSON JOHN
C.Maker	CROOKESHANKS ALEXR.
C.Maker	WOOD GEORGE
Trumpeter	MACDONALD W.
Gunner	HUDSON JONA. Pensioned
Gunner	BENNETT JOHN
Gunner	McLEAN MALCOLM
Gunner	JOHN PIGG
Gunner	SELLARD SAMUEL Pensioned
Gunner	WHILLEY CHAS.
Gunner	WOOLSTONHOLME JOHN
Gunner	GRIMES LUKE
Gunner	ORMROD JOHN
Gunner	WARSLEY RICHD.
Gunner	PEALE JAMES
Gunner	TOOTHILL RICHD.
Gunner	MANNING JONATHAN
Gunner	SEWELL AARON
Gunner	LORD JOHN
Gunner	COTTON ROBT.
Gunner	AINSCONE THOS.
Gunner	BRADWELL JOHN
Gunner	LOCKTONE ROBT.

Gunner	MAMO ALEXR.
Gunner	PREACHER WILLIAM
Gunner	KINGHORN GEORGE
Gunner	TURNWALL THOS.
Gunner	BRANCH ROBT.
Gunner	ALLERT JAMES
Gunner	JORDAN DAVID
Gunner	WILKINSON THOS.
Gunner	MITCHIN SAMPSON
Gunner	TODD JAMES
Gunner	McKENZIE JOHN
Gunner	SHEARMAN JOHN
Gunner	TEMPLE JAMES
Gunner	SMITH WM.
Gunner	LUMAS ROBT.
Gunner	CARR JAMES
Gunner	BRYANT JOHN
Gunner	ROSE JAMES MGS Medal in collection J.O.Davies 5/5/66
Gunner	WEDGWOOD AARON
Gunner	McLENNON ALEXR.
Gunner	BEATIE ANDREW
Gunner	EARY WM. Pensioned
Gunner	REVITT HENRY
Gunner	JOHNSTONE JEREH.
Gunner	TEMPLE JOHN Discharged
Gunner	KING RICHARD
Gunner	SAMPSON JOSH.
Gunner	SUTTON JOHN
Gunner	CHALMERS WM.
Gunner	AUSTIN WM.
Gunner	MARSHALL JOSH. Discharged
Gunner	WALKER THOS.
Gunner	CASTLE JOHN
Gunner	KENNARD WILLIAM
Gunner	IRELAND JOHN
Gunner	SIMMONDS DAVID
Gunner	MacDOUGALL COLLIN
Gunner	SHORT JOSH. Discharged
Gunner	MUNN WM.
Gunner	CROSS JOHN
Gunner	CUTHBERT JAMES
Gunner	HOWE HENRY
Gunner	McGRIFFIN PHILIP
Gunner	DENNEY HUGH
Gunner	WEIR WALTER
Gunner	BOWERS CHAS.
Gunner	BELFOUR ALEXR.
Gunner	WOOD WILLIAM
Gunner	RUBIE CHAS.
Gunner	HETHERINGTON EDWD.
Gunner	HUMPHRIES JOHN
Gunner	WEMYSS JAMES
Gunner	MANN JOHN
Gunner	BILBY JOHN
Gunner	REID JAMES
Gunner	FARNELL GEORGE
Gunner	LUCAS JAMES
Gunner	SCOTT JOHN
Gunner	BECK THOS.
Gunner	LEE WILLIAM Day Sale April 1910
Gunner	LAMOX JAMES
Gunner	WILSON ALEXR.
Gunner	MOORE ARCH.
Gunner	WEBB JOSEPH
Gunner	RICHARDSON JAMES
Driver	THOMPSON JOSH.
Driver	VININGHAM JOSH.
Driver	REDFORD THOS.
Driver	BOGLE THOS.
Driver	OWEN JOHN
Driver	PAGE JOHN
Driver	TURNER CHAS.
Driver	ESSEX LEVI
Driver	CARTLEDGE SAMUEL
Driver	BLANTERIN JOSEPH Dead
Driver	MARSHALL JOSEPH
Driver	McDONALD DUNCAN
Driver	PATTERSON JAS.
Driver	JACOBS BENJN.
Driver	DAWES RICHD.
Driver	WILLIAM THOS.
Driver	GREENALCH JOHN
Driver	AXON THOS.
Driver	CLARK GEORGE
Driver	McLINCOLN SAML.
Driver	REYNOLDS GEORGE On Sale at Baldwin's March 1909
Driver	HARRIOTT MOSES
DriverJOHNSTON WILLIAM	
Driver	SMITH JAS. (Senr)
Driver	SMITH RICHARD
Driver	BURNS HENRY
Driver	BOWDALL HENRY
Driver	COLTON JOHN
Driver	GOSLING THOMAS
Driver	LACEY WM.

Driver	WOODWARD CHAS.
Driver	PEARSON JOHN
Driver	EVANS RICHD.
Driver	BIRKETT THOS.
Driver	GRANT JOHN
Driver	SKELTON JOHN
Driver	ROWLANDS JAMES
Driver	AUSEY ARNOLD Discharged
Driver	PICKERALL JAMES
Driver	BOOTH HENRY
Driver	PARKER THOMAS
Driver	MADDISON GEORGE
Driver	HAYWARD WM.
Driver	WILKS SAMUEL
Driver	ADAMS JAMES
Driver	JOHNSTON JOHN
Driver	PERRY JOHN
Driver	HORREN WILLIAM
Driver	MOTLEY RICHD.
Driver	THOMAS DAVID
Driver	JARVIS WM.
Driver	CARDIN WM.
Driver	SMITH SETH
Driver	HODGSON THOMAS Col. Gaskell's Sale May 1911
Driver	HUDSON SAML.
Driver	SMITH JOHN
Driver	KIRTON SAMUEL
Driver	SMITH JAS. Jnr.
Driver	HUNT RICHARD Discharged
Driver	BOOT JOHN
Driver	JACKSON ROBT.
Driver	NIX THOS.
Driver	BUSTLE ROBERT Pensioned Needes Collection 1908

<u>Lt.Colonel R. Bull's Troop</u>

Captain & Bt.Lt.Col.	BULL ROBERT
Lieutenant	LOUIS NATTHEW Trans. to 10th Batt.
Lieutenant	SMITH WILLIAM
Lieutenant	TOWNSEND JOHN Whitaker Collection 1908
A.Surgeon	BINGHAM JOHN
S.Serjeant	KENNEDY JAMES
S.Serjeant	MOORE NICHOLAS Pensioned
Serjeant	FALCONER JOHN
Serjeant	LIVSEY JAMES
Serjeant	ADAMS STEPHEN
Corporal	COLLIER JOHN
Corporal	BACON THOS.
Corporal	KNIGHT JAMES Pensioned
Bombr.	PARLETT THOS.
Bombr.	CUNDLE ANTHY.
Bombr.	YOUNG THOS.
Bombr.	HENDERSON CHAS.
Bombr.	BUCKLEY ROBT.
Bombr.	PATTERSON ROBT.
Farrier	STANDING ELIAS
S.Smith	SMITH JOHN
S.Smith	STEIN SAML. H.Gaskell's Collection 1908
S.Smith	SOLAN JOHN Discharged
C.Maker	WATT ALEXR.
C.Maker	ALEXANDER JAMES
Wheeler	DIXON JAMES
Trumpeter	POPLETT WM.
Gunner	DOUGLAS THOS. Pensioned
Gunner	ANNAN DAVID Pensioned
Gunner	SMITH EDMUND
Gunner	WHITING CHAS.
Gunner	DALLACHY CHAS.
Gunner	TAYLOR WM.
Gunner	SPENCER THOS. Pensioned
Gunner	HOLDING JOHN Senr.
Gunner	HUDSON WM.
Gunner	COURTNEY JAMES Glendinnings Sale Feb. 1911
Gunner	COWLEY THOS. Trans. to 10th Batt.
Gunner	RED ROBT.
Gunner	ROSTHORN JOHN
Gunner	DONAVAN JAMES
Gunner	PUGSON HENRY
Gunner	McKAY WM.
Gunner	ELMES WM.
Gunner	ARNOLD JAMES
Gunner	LOCK JOHN
Gunner	SMITH GEORGE
Gunner	TOOHEY WILLIAM
Gunner	CARBRIDGE WILLIAM
Gunner	WARD JOSH.
Gunner	COLLIER DAVID
Gunner	SKINLEY SAML.
Gunner	McINTOSH WM.
Gunner	JONES JOSH. Glendinnings Sale April 1911
Gunner	SERBUTT JAMES
Gunner	RANKIN PETER
Gunner	TABOR SAML. Oddy Collection Glendinnings Sale Nov. 1908

Gunner	DAVIS EDWD.	Gunner	FILES GEORGE Discharged
Gunner	HOLDING JNS. Junr.	Gunner	BROEN JAMES
Gunner	WRIGHT THOS.	Gunner	GRANGER JOHN
Gunner	COLLINS JOSH.	Gunner	HEWITT JOHN
Gunner	EDWARDS THOS.	Driver	HUCKLEY JOHN
Gunner	LLOYD JAMES Glendinnings Sale March 1912 - Discharged	Driver	HOCKS FRANCIS
Gunner	JONES EDWD.	Driver	PLATT JOHN
Gunner	SCOTT JOHN	Driver	WADE JAMES
Gunner	RICHARDS WM.	Driver	TERRY GEORGE
Gunner	PARKER JOHN	Driver	WITCH JOHN
Gunner	WITHARDT JOHN	Driver	MASSEY WM.
Gunner	WATERS WM.	Driver	BROWN JNS.
Gunner	JEPSON WM.	Driver	GOODWIN JOSH.
Gunner	COX EDWD. Discharged	Driver	AXON JOHN
Gunner	WRIGHT JOHN	Driver	ECCLESHAW WM.
Gunner	PURDIE THOS.	Driver	HICKSON PETER
Gunner	JENKINS THOS.	Driver	MANT WM. Payne Collection 1911
Gunner	TAYLOR JOHN	Driver	WRIGHT WM. Pensioned
Gunner	THOMPSON HUGH	Driver	MATCHELL JOHN
Gunner	GUNN ROBT.	Driver	EMMINS THOS.
Gunner	HOLDING WM.	Driver	TAYLOR RICHD.
Gunner	McKENZIE JOHN	Driver	BROWN ANDREW Discharged
Gunner	WILSON ROBT.	Driver	WOOD THOMAS
Gunner	BENTLEY JAMES Trans. to 8th Batt.	Driver	BAYNE GEORGE
Gunner	MYERS FRANCIS	Driver	STEVENS JOHN
Gunner	HALL ROBT.	Driver	FORD JAMES
Gunner	SIMPSON DAVID	Driver	FERGUSON JAMES
Gunner	SMITH ALEXR.	Driver	McGLASHAM ALEXR.
Gunner	BARRATT RICHD.	Driver	BATES WM.
Gunner	HEFFIELD JOSH Discharged	Driver	HEATH JAMES
Gunner	JONES JOHN	Driver	GILBERT THOS.
Gunner	BOGUE WM.	Driver	WHITEALL EDWD.
Gunner	GORSE JOSH.	Driver	GLANN JAMES
Gunner	FOX ROBT. Discharged	Driver	LENNARD JAMES
Gunner	LINN JOHN	Driver	SMITH JOHN
Gunner	OGDEN JOHN	Driver	FEULD ABRM.
Gunner	WILLIAMSON JOHN	Driver	GILES JOSEPH
Gunner	WILLIAMSON JAMES	Driver	WHITMORE THOS.
Gunner	WAINWRIGHT JAMES	Driver	ABBEY JOHN
Gunner	BENSON WM.	Driver	HASTINGS JAMES
Gunner	FORD WM.	Driver	WETTON JOHN
Gunner	LEES JOHN	Driver	POWELL JAMES
Gunner	McDONALD JAMES	Driver	WATERFIELD JOHN
Gunner	MARVIN GEORGE	Driver	MUTHER JOHN
Gunner	CHARLTON EDWD.	Driver	TAYLOR CHRISTR.
Gunner	TAYLOR MATTHEW	Driver	JONES THOS.
Gunner	ROBINSON ALEXR. Discharged	Driver	PURCH THOS.
Gunner	McCOWAN MICHL.	Driver	ELVIN JOHN
		Driver	LEES JOHN

Driver	SMITH JOHN B. Discharged
Driver	HEWITT DAVID
Driver	McKINNON ANGUS
Driver	GRIMSHAW ROBT.
Driver	CLARKE JOSH.
Driver	HOWARTH THOS.
Driver	YATES JAMES
Driver	THOMPSON WM. Discharged
Driver	HAGGER WM.
Driver	SPENCER JOHN
Driver	MANNERS THOS.
Driver	HATHAWOOD RICHD.
Driver	LOVELY RICHD. Discharged
Driver	DUNCAN DAVID

Major Whingate's (Rocket) Troop

Captain & Bt.Maj.	WHINGATE E.C.
2nd Captain	DANCEY C.C.
Lieutenant	WRIGHT A.
Lieutenant	STRANGWAYS THOS.
Lieutenant	WARDE FRANCIS
Lieutenant	WARD ADAM
A.Surgeon	BEARD THOS.
S.Serjeant	HILL THOS. On sale at Baldwin's March 1909
S.Serjeant	WRIGHT JAMES
Serjeant	DUNNETT DANIEL Glendinnings Sale Jan.1910 Payne 1911
Serjeant	TAYLOR MICHL.
Serjeant	THOMPSON RICHD.
Corporal	CHALKLEY ROBT.
Corporal	POTTS JOHN
Bombr.	MARKS EDWD.
Bombr.	BAYLEY THOS.
Bombr.	WAREHAM JOHN
Bombr.	WAREHAM WM.
Bombr.	BIRTLES THOS.
Bombr.	WATSON JOHN Dead
Bombr.	RANNIE ALEXR.
Farrier	SMITH JAMES
Smiths	BROTHERSTON WM.
Smiths	ROBERTS WM. Discharged
Smiths	SANDERS WM.
C.Maker	SILCOCK SAMUEL
Wheeler	WYATT WM. Discharged Whitaker Collection 1908
Trumpeter	CAMPBELL ARCH.
Gunner	GUY JOHN Discharged

Gunner	LLOYD THOS.
Gunner	BROOMHILL JAMES
Gunner	MUNROE GEORGE Deserted
Gunner	EAVES JOHN
Gunner	BOWERS BENJN Discharged
Gunner	PHILLIPS JOHN
Gunner	LEES SAMUEL
Gunner	WILLIAMS THOS.
Gunner	RAVEN JACQUES Discharged
Gunner	SPEARS JAMES Discharged
Gunner	BARNS MICHL.
Gunner	REID ANDREW
Gunner	YATES EDWD. Discharged
Gunner	LIDDLE JAMES Discharged
Gunner	SMITH JAMES Discharged
Gunner	BIRCHLEY THOS.
Gunner	SHINNELD WM.
Gunner	MAIDEN HENRY Discharged
Gunner	CURRELL WM.
Gunner	MELDROME WM.
Gunner	HENDERSON THOS.
Gunner	GORDON JOHN
Gunner	BIDDLE WM.
Gunner	ANDERSON WM.
Gunner	CAMPBELL DUG Discharged
Driver	PATTULLS JOHN
Driver	FOX GEORGE
Driver	KETLOW WM.
Driver	BATES JOHN Discharged
Driver	WARD JAMES Discharged
Driver	McDONALD ROBT. Discharged
Driver	HOLMES THOS.
Driver	MURPHY DANIEL
Driver	PALMER WM.
Driver	PINKERT THOS.
Driver	YOUNG WM. Senr.
Driver	WARDLE WM.
Driver	MOORE WM.
Driver	VAUGHAN ABRM.
Driver	WATERN RICHD. Discharged
Driver	HOTCHKINS THOS. Discharged
Driver	STRONG JOHN
Driver	KENT THOS.
Driver	RICKETT JOSEPH
Driver	GEEOM HENRY Discharged
Driver	FISHER ADOLPHUS
Driver	McKENZIE STEPHEN Discharged
Driver	PURDY JOHN

Driver	ANDERSON WM.
Driver	MELLISH JAMES Discharged Glendinning's Sale 21 July 1909
Driver	WISE SAML.
Driver	BEARD JOSH.
Driver	WALLER WM.
Driver	ATKINSON THOS.
Driver	SMITH JOHN Discharged
Driver	PORTER THOS.
Driver	LIVINGSTONE ARCH.
Driver	BAXTER THOS.
Driver	RICHARDSON JOHN Discharged
Driver	WOOD JOHN
Driver	CHISLETT THOS.
Driver	YOUNG WM. Junr.
Driver	MANSON WALTER
Driver	WARMSLEY WM. Discharged
Driver	TAYLOR JACOB
Driver	NEADON THOS Discharged Glendinning's Sale Feb.1913
Driver	EVES JOHN
Driver	ALFORD DANIEL
Driver	COCKING GEORGE Discharged
Driver	CHRISTIE ALEXR.
Driver	SNEADEN JOHN
Driver	WAINWRIGHT ENOCH
Driver	COOK TIM.
Driver	BOWLES WM. Discharged
Driver	PLOWRIGHT JOHN
Driver	MOSS JOHN
Driver	JONES BENJN.
Driver	SANDERSON JOHN
Driver	ASHWORTH MARK Discharged
Driver	McFARLINE ROBT.
Driver	DIXON JOHN
Driver	FOWLER WM.
Driver	GRAY ALEXR. Trans. to R.A. Drivers
Driver	VANDEN THOS. Whitaker Collection 1908
Driver	PARKET THOS.
Driver	WELLS WM.
Driver	MARSHALL THOS.
Driver	MURPHY JOHN
Driver	REAVES LUKE
Driver	SIDEBOTTOM THOS.
Driver	WOOLSTENHOLM THOS.
Driver	BECKETT THOS.
Driver	GRAVES THOS.
Driver	JENNINGS JOHN
Driver	LESLIE JOHN
Driver	COATES GEORGE
Driver	WHITE JOSEPH
Driver	KIRK JOHN
Driver	HOLRYDE MATTW.
Driver	CHANT JOHN
Driver	THOMLINSON THOS.
Driver	FOWLER PHILLIP
Gunner	McNEVINS JAMES Major Elliott's Rocket Troop
Gunner	EVANS JOHN Major Elliott's Rocket Troop
Gunner	ARSDEN W. Detachment Royal Horse Artillery
Gunner	GILLESPIE ROGER Detachment Royal Horse Artillery
Gunner	TICKNER WM. Detachment Royal Horse Artillery
Gunner	EDWARDS HENRY Detachment Royal Horse Artillery
Gunner	HELM JOHN Detachment Royal Horse Artillery
Driver	MADDISON S.
Gunner	SANDFORD WM.

Captain Sandhams Company

Captain	SNADHAMS CHAS. F.
2nd Captain	STOPFORD W.H.
Lieutenant	FOOT G.
Lieutenant	BAYNES GEO.McLEOD
2nd Lieutenant	JAGO DARVELL
Serjeant	OLIVER JOHN
Corporal	PRINT THOS.
Corporal	HALL SAML. Cheylesmore Collection 1908
Corporal	CLARK ANDREW
Bombr.	DENHAM ADAM
Bombr.	CLAYTON JOHN Pensioned
Bombr.	SMITH JAMES
Bombr.	MURRAY JOHN
Gunner	COXTON JOSH.
Gunner	WALKER THOS.
Gunner	WICKLIFFE EDWD.
Gunner	ATKINSON CHAS.
Gunner	POLLARD WM. Pensioned
Gunner	DEPLADGE SAML. Pensioned
Gunner	WALLON HENRY
Gunner	LISHER JAMES
Gunner	FERGUSON JOHN Pensioned

Gunner	SOWERBY JOHN
Gunner	RICHIE GEORGE
Gunner	HAGUE WM. Pensioned
Gunner	McINDOE ROBT. Pensioned
Gunner	ROBINSON ROBT.
Gunner	SKELLAT EDWD Pensioned
Gunner	PRENTICE ROBT.
Gunner	BISHOP HENRY
Gunner	KENYON THOS. Pensioned
Gunner	LLOYD EDWD
Gunner	HOPE ADAM
Gunner	MARSDEN WM.
Gunner	ANDERSON HENRY
Gunner	PORTER CUTHBERT Discharged
Gunner	TURNER EDWD. Discharged Phillips Sale J.O. Davies Coll. 5/5/66
Gunner	NICHOLLS JOHN
Gunner	STANDING WM.
Gunner	BARLOW JOHN
Gunner	LAIDLOR THOS.
Gunner	DIXON JAMES
Gunner	LISHER THOS.
Gunner	THORNE JAMES
Gunner	RUSSIN JOHN
Gunner	WADDLE GEORGE
Gunner	GREAVES PETER Discharged
Gunner	SAVAGE WM. Discharged
Gunner	MARTIN SAML.
Gunner	KERR WM. 1st
Gunner	HINDLE WM. Pensioned
Gunner	WEST WM.
Gunner	HALL THOMAS Discharged
Gunner	SALLER CHARLES
Gunner	TAYLOR RICHD.
Gunner	LAMON WM. Discharged
Gunner	MAKINSON NATHAN Discharged
Gunner	ADAMS JOHN Discharged
Gunner	HAMMOND EDWD. Discharged
Gunner	BOOTH JOSEPH
Gunner	HOWARTH JAMES
Gunner	KERSEY JOHN
Gunner	RIGBIE JOHN
Gunner	CROSSLEY BENJN.
Gunner	POTTER JOHN
Gunner	TOUCHITT SAML.
Gunner	LONGFELLOW WM.
Gunner	KERR WM. 2nd.
Gunner	FOWLER BENJN.
Gunner	CLEART THOS.
Gunner	KERR ANDW.
Gunner	RUSSELL ANDW.
Gunner	BARLOW JAMES
Gunner	FELL WM.
Gunner	GREY CHAS. Died 25 Sep.1815
Gunner	BOOTH MICHL. Discharged
Gunner	WRIGHT THOS.
Gunner	HAGUE GEORGE
Gunner	ASHTON ROBERT
Gunner	HANING WM.
Gunner	DAWSON WM.
Gunner	FALLOWS SAML.
Gunner	HIGHAM JOHN
Gunner	PARKINSON SAML.
Gunner	LARGE JAMES
Gunner	BEACKLEDGE WM.
Gunner	MONGHAM THOS.
Gunner	FLETCHER BENJN.
Gunner	ADDEY MICHL.
Gunner	SCOTT WM.
Gunner	DEVILING WM.
Gunner	GORDON WM.
Gunner	WATSON HENRY
Gunner	FINCH RICHD.
Gunner	JOHNSTONE ALEXR.
Gunner	LIGHTFOOT JOSH.
Gunner	PRACTTICE JOHN
Gunner	MOSS JOHN
Gunner	MACKINSON JOHN
Gunner	STEWART WM.
Gunner	BARKER ARTHUR
Gunner	JAGO HENRY
Gunner	STRONER WM.
Gunner	ROGERS WM.

Captain Napier's Company

Captain	NAPIER C.
Lieutenant	ANDERSON W.
Lieutenant	SHARPIN W. Promoted
Lieutenant	PRINGLE C. H.Gaskell's Collection 1908
Serjeant	HEMPFIELD WM.
Serjeant	BARTON JAMES Discharged
Corporal	PALMER JAMES
Corporal	RUTLEDGE WM.
Corporal	PETERS WM.
Corporal	CARNEY JOHN
Bombr.	ELMSLIE WM.

Bombr.	DARWEN JAMES Discharged
Bombr.	BRETT THOS. Discharged
Bombr.	ROBINSON DANIEL
Bombr.	ADDISON CHAS.
Gunner	ASHTON JOSEPH
Gunner	HUTTON JOHN
Gunner	HENRY WM. Discharged
Gunner	McALLISTER DENIS Discharged
Gunner	PEDDIE DAVID
Gunner	FENTON JOSEPH Dead
Gunner	BLUNT FRANS. Dead
Gunner	MORTON WM.
Gunner	BELL JAMES Discharged
Gunner	HYNES JOHN
Gunner	SHAND GEORGE
Gunner	SMITH THOMAS Discharged Galway Foley Collection 1910
Gunner	DERNISON JAMES Discharged
Gunner	TARBET ANDREW
Gunner	CLARKE WILLIAM
Gunner	DEMPRY WILLIAM Discharged
Gunner	HAIT JAMES
Gunner	NICHOLSON EDWD.
Gunner	TATE SAML. H.Gaskell's Collection 1908
Gunner	HALL JOHN Discharged
Gunner	JOHNSTONE JOHN Discharged
Gunner	MAGHILL ROBT.
Gunner	CLOUGH JAMES
Gunner	MILLIKIN JOHN
Gunner	MONAGHAN OWEN Discharged On Sale at Baldwin's March 1909
Gunner	CLOUGH LEWIS
Gunner	CAMPBELL JOHN Discharged
Gunner	VENABLES THOS. Dead
Gunner	MARGISON THOS.
Gunner	CARR THOS. Discharged
Gunner	ROSS JAMES
Gunner	PAGEN SIMEON Discharged
Gunner	AJOULL JOHN
Gunner	SMITH ANDREW
Gunner	REDMAN JOSH.
Gunner	BENNETT WM. Trans with Lt. Sharpin
Gunner	BALDY DAVID Discharged
Gunner	AITKINS JOHN
Gunner	LIZELAND GEORGE Discharged
Gunner	AMBROSE OBEDIAH Discharged
Gunner	WADE SAMUEL Discharged
Gunner	FRITH WM.
Gunner	McANENY OWEN Discharged
Gunner	QUIN HUGH
Gunner	BEARDON JOHN
Gunner	THOMPSON RICHD.
Gunner	CHARLTON JAMES
Gunner	BALL JOHN
Gunner	SOMERVILLE ROBT.
Gunner	MERTON ANDW.
Gunner	ROTHERY JOHN
Gunner	HOLROYDE JOHN
Gunner	LOCH WILLIAM Discharged
Gunner	BEAVER WILLIAM
Gunner	McLANE PETER Discharged
Gunner	GLADWEN LUKE
Gunner	McDEVITT JOHN Discharged
Gunner	DEVEN THOS.
Gunner	IRVINE LEWIS
Gunner	CAND ROBERT
Gunner	TRAINER PETER
Gunner	CANIGAN DANIEL
Gunner	McKEY ROBERT Discharged
Gunner	LAUGHLIN WM.
Gunner	BARTON RICHD. Discharged
Gunner	JACKSON JOHN
Gunner	WORFFE JOHN Discharged
Gunner	BROWN JAMES
Gunner	NEWSOME EDWD.
Gunner	TOOLE JOHN
Gunner	NOCKE JOSH.
Gunner	MENROE JOHN
Gunner	LAIRD JOHN Discharged
Gunner	CAMERON ANGUS
Gunner	ROBERTSON GEORGE
Gunner	MONAGHAN THOS.
Gunner	SMITH JAMES Discharged
Gunner	WORSTENHOLM WM.
Gunner	FISHER MICHL.
Gunner	PENNOCK GEORGE
Gunner	JAMES JONES With Col.Hawker
Gunner	PICKLING WM.
Gunner	MACLISH NEIL
Gunner	MOUNT PATRICK Trans. R.A. Drivers

<u>Late Major Lloyd's Company</u>

Captain	RUDYERD SAML.
Lieutenant	WELLS F.
Lieutenant	PHELPS SAML. Payne Collection 1911
Lieutenant	HARVEY WM.

Serjeant	McKENZIE WM.
Corporal	DOYLE JAMES
Corporal	ANDERSON JAMES
Bombr.	DAVIDSON JAMES
Bombr.	ALLEN WILLIAM
Gunner	SWANEY CHAS.
Gunner	LEUTH ALEXR.
Gunner	SMITH GEORGE Pensioner
Gunner	JOHNSTON HAMILTON
Bombr.	BOND JAMES On sale at Baldwin's July 1912
Bombr.	DUNBAR JOHN
Bombr.	GILLEY JOHN
Bombr.	McKENZIE ALEXR.
Bombr.	McPEAKE WM.
Bombr.	HUMPHRIES WM.
Gunner	JOHNSTONE ROBT.
Gunner	TENNING THOS.
Gunner	MOSS JAMES
Gunner	O'NEILL JAMES
Gunner	BELL ROBERT Dead
Gunner	GRAHAM CHRISTR.
Gunner	WATT GEORGE
Gunner	BLACK JAMES
Gunner	McCOURT JOHN
Gunner	KIRTON JOHN
Gunner	ROBINSON THOMAS
Gunner	McKENZIE ALEXR.
Gunner	ODDIE GEORGE
Gunner	TAYLOR ISSAC
Gunner	BROWN WILLIAM
Gunner	LOFTES WILLIAM
Gunner	FIELDING ADAM
Gunner	THOMASON WM.
Gunner	BARKER JEREH.
Gunner	TARBETT JOHN
Gunner	JOHNSTON JAMES
Gunner	CROZIER ROBERT
Gunner	FERGUSON ALEXR Dead
Gunner	CONNER WM.
Gunner	RYMER JOHN
Gunner	McCRACKEN JOSH.
Gunner	McCOW JOHN
Gunner	McCAFFREY PATRICK
Gunner	WHITAKER WILLIAM
Gunner	BOOT JOSEPH
Gunner	HASSWELLS JOHN
Gunner	HINDLE PETER
Gunner	MUTLEY JAMES
Gunner	DEAN JOHN
Gunner	RODGERS EDWARD
Gunner	CHADWICK GILBERT
Gunner	POOLE THOS.
Gunner	TAYLOR WILLIAM
Gunner	KACKSON JOHN
Gunner	KINDALL ATKIN
Gunner	CULLIP JAMES
Gunner	HEATH JAMES
Gunner	BROWN CHARLES
Gunner	BUMBOW SAML.
Gunner	BATES WM.
Gunner	HALL GEORGE
Gunner	LIDDONS RICHD.
Gunner	GOODWIN THOS.
Gunner	COX JOHN
Gunner	SMITH ISSAC
Gunner	MOORHOUSE HENRY
Gunner	RAY JOSEPH Dead
Gunner	MURREL RALPH
Gunner	BROOM JOSEPH Dead
Gunner	RICHARDS JOHN
Gunner	BAKER EDWD.
Gunner	GRIFFEN WM.
Gunner	KELBY JOSH.
Gunner	JONES THOS.
Gunner	PASSALL WM. Dead
Gunner	SANKEY THOS.
Gunner	WOOTTEN JAMES
Gunner	GILL JOHN
Gunner	PANY JOHN
Gunner	BRITAIN GEORGE
Gunner	ROBERTS RICHD.
Gunner	HARRISON THOS.
Gunner	MULCORK M.
Gunner	WALKINS JNS.
Gunner	TOWNSEND JAMES
Gunner	McCABBIN ROBT.
Gunner	WATTS THOS.
Gunner	NICHOLSON CHAS.
Gunner	PUGH WM.
Drummer	WILLIAMSON JOHN
Drummer	KEMP WILLIAM

Captain & Bt.Major Brome's Company

Captain & Bt.Major	BROME J. Payne Collection 1911
2nd Captain	PARKER J.E.G.
Lieutenant	SAUNDERS R.J.
Lieutenant	CATOR THOS. O.

2nd Lieutenant	MOLESWORTH A.C.
Serjeant	ROSS GEORGE
Serjeant	WATT ALEXR.
Serjeant	McPHERSON JOHN
Corporal	WALKER THOS.
Corporal	CRAIG ROBT.
Bombr.	TURNER JOHN
Bombr.	WHALLEY CHRISTR.
Bombr.	GUNN JOHN
Bombr.	GRAHAM WM.
Bombr.	NEALE WM.
Bombr.	RALSTONE DAVID
Gunner	REYALL RICHD. Pensioned
Gunner	WISHART GEO. Pensioned
Gunner	PATEFIELD JOHN
Gunner	BROOKS JOHN
Gunner	FORSYTH JAMES Pensioned
Gunner	ASPDEN ROBT.
Gunner	SMITH JNS. Senr.
Gunner	INCH HENRY
Gunner	HANSON JOHN
Gunner	WALLACE THOS.
Gunner	PATTISON THOS. Pensioned
Gunner	HUNNION JOHN
Gunner	BLACK WILLIAM
Gunner	GREADY THOS. Pensioned
Gunner	WORSACK GEORGE
Gunner	RATCLIFFE JAMES
Gunner	EVANS WM. Pensioned
Gunner	ASPINE DAVID
Gunner	BRAID DAVID
Gunner	HALVISO NICH. Glendinning's Sale Sept. 1912 1-18-0
Gunner	MITCHELL JOHN
Gunner	COCHRANR THOS.
Gunner	CAMPBELL THOS.
Gunner	BESWICK JOHN
Gunner	GREENAWAY ROGER
Gunner	DRAKE WM.
Gunner	BRADFORD JOHN
Gunner	HARRIS NICH. Trans. to 4th Batt.
Gunner	SIMMONDS JOHN
Gunner	GONDERTON SAML.
Gunner	BURROWS WM. Glendinning's Sale Oct. 1913
Gunner	JONES EDWD.
Gunner	ALLISON ARCH. Discharged
Gunner	LAKE DANIEL

Gunner	SMALL WILLIAM
Gunner	MILLS PETER
Gunner	DAVENPORT THOS. Pensioned
Gunner	ORR PETER
Gunner	TAYLOR JAMES
Gunner	SMART PETER
Gunner	WARREN JOHN
Gunner	GORDON JOHN
Gunner	BENBOW EDWD.
Gunner	McSKIMMERY JOHN
Gunner	SMITH JAMES
Gunner	CHARLES SAML.
Gunner	HOWARD THOS.
Gunner	FAIRCLOUGH JAMES Watters Sale June 1913
Gunner	ALLERTON THOS. Glendinning's Sale 17 June 1908
Gunner	COCKER FRANCIS
Gunner	EDDLESTONE JOHN
Gunner	CREUTHER SAML. Discharged
Gunner	WILLIAMSON ISSAC Discharged
Gunner	KNOX ISSAC Died 24 Aug.1815
Gunner	SUTHERLAND JAMES
Gunner	DITCHFIELD JOHN
Gunner	SMITH GEORGE
Gunner	HILLMAN JOSH.
Gunner	REID ROBT.
Gunner	WILLEY WM.
Gunner	ROXBURGH PETER
Gunner	SCHOFIELD ELY.
Gunner	WOOD THOS. Died 26 Dec.1815
Gunner	PATTERSON ANDREW
Gunner	FIELDING JOHN
Gunner	MELVILLE PETER
Gunner	CROWTHER WM.
Gunner	WALLHOUSE THOS.
Gunner	HEIGHTLY GEORGE
Gunner	ROBERTS JAMES Day Sale April 1910
Gunner	SMALL EDWD. Died 28 Oct.1815
Gunner	PRIESTLY JOHN Pensioned
Gunner	RICHIE JAMES Discharged
Gunner	GREENHOUSE WM.
Gunner	BRIERLY JAMES Discharged
Gunner	TURNER SAML.
Gunner	EVANS JAMES
Gunner	NEIL SAML.
Gunner	MILES FRANCIS
Gunner	SMITH JNS. Junr. Discharged
Gunner	WAYMAN THOS Discharged

Gunner	HUTCHISON SAML.
Gunner	COTTERALL WM.
Gunner	ROWLEY WM. Whitaker Collection 1908
Gunner	NEWTON GEO.
Drummer	McPHERSON DAVID
Drummer	PATTERSON GEORGE

Captain & Bt.Major Roger's Company

Captain & Bt.Major	ROGERS THOS.
2nd Captain	SCOTT THOS.
Lieutenant	COLES GEORGE
Lieutenant	DUNNICLIFFE HENRY Glendinning's Sale Feb. 1909
2nd Lieutenant	WILSON A.G.
Serjeant	BANNISTER WM.
Serjeant	BRANDON G.
Serjeant	STEPHENSON SAML.
Corporal	LUCAS JAMES
Bombr.	YULE WILLIAM
Bombr.	PEACOCK THOS.
Bombr.	KINNARD GEORGE
Bombr.	TOOLE CHRISTR
Bombr.	SCOTT ROBERT Payne Collection 1911
Bombr.	BROOKS DAVID
Gunner	PATTON ANDREW
Gunner	HALLAM GEORGE
Gunner	WARWICK DAVID
Gunner	WALKER JAMES Pensioned
Gunner	RUSSELL JOHN Pensioned
Gunner	McINDOE JAMES
Gunner	FAULKNER RICHD. Pensioned
Gunner	CHAMBERS ROBT.
Gunner	PICKUP LAWRENCE
Gunner	MOSLEY SAMUEL
Gunner	WALSH THOS.
Gunner	JERDINE ROBT.
Gunner	SWAINE RICHD.
Gunner	HERRICK JAMES
Gunner	COOPER MOSES
Gunner	KAY JOHN
Gunner	BOTTRILL JOHN
Gunner	CASHEW JOHN
Gunner	HEATH RICHD.
Gunner	STOTT JAMES
Gunner	WADSWORTH THOS.
Gunner	McKELVEY JAMES Discharged
Gunner	McDONALD ALEXR.
Gunner	DYKES PETER
Gunner	McCARDLE PATK.
Gunner	LAMBERT JOSH.
Gunner	LEVY JOHN
Gunner	HALL JOHN
Gunner	KIRKWOOD WM.
Gunner	GILMAN WM.
Gunner	WALLACE WM.
Gunner	GILL JAMES
Gunner	NEEDHAM GEORGE
Gunner	PEARSON ISSAC
Gunner	NESBITT ANDREW
Gunner	EWEN WM.
Gunner	COLEMAN WM.
Gunner	HAYS JOSEPH
Gunner	LIVINGSTONE NOBLE Missing supposed drowned
Gunner	COOPER JOSEPH
Gunner	CAMPBELL ROBT.
Gunner	SLACK EDWD.
Gunner	ELWELL GEORGE
Gunner	BOARDMAN JOHN Pensioned
Gunner	RUSHTON GEORGE Supposed dead
Gunner	CHADWICK RICHD. Died 21 Nov 1815
Gunner	WADDLE THOS.
Gunner	HAYS GEORGE
Gunner	BROOKS RICHD.
Gunner	WHITEHEAD WM.
Gunner	TOLMIE JAMES
Gunner	WESTON EDWD. Discharged
Gunner	DOUGLAS THOS.
Gunner	HOLDING HENRY
Gunner	MACKEY DAVID
Gunner	DUGALL WM.
Gunner	McCANVILLE JOHN
Gunner	ROLLS JAMES
Gunner	THOMLINSON ROBERT
Gunner	MILLER JAMES
Gunner	MARTIN JOHN
Gunner	BEEKY JAMES Discharged
Gunner	PENDLEBURY JAMES
Gunner	GOODFELLOW MATTW.
Gunner	DAWS MOSES
Gunner	GREGSON JAMES Pensioned
Gunner	McGILL ALEXR.
Gunner	RAINEY PETER
Gunner	BURNS WM.
Gunner	SUTTON WM.
Gunner	CLINCH SAML. Pensioned
Gunner	MILLON ARCH.

Gunner	GRUNDY GEORGE
Gunner	STEWART JAMES
Gunner	WARD JAMES
Gunner	ROOME WM.
Gunner	LOWRIE THOS.
Drummer	GALLOWAY JAMES

Captain & Bt.Major Unett's Company

Captain & Bt.Major	UNETT G.W.
2nd Captain	BROWN GORE
Lieutenant	LAWSON DOUGLAS
Lieutenant	MONTAGUE WILLOUGHBY
2nd Lieutenant	KETT CHAS. G.
Serjeant	COCHRAN CHAS.
Serjeant	POLLOCK WM.
Serjeant	WADDLE JOHN
Serjeant	PHELP GEORGE
Corporal	KENYON WILLIAM On Sale at Speaks June 1910
Corporal	SHEARER GEORGE
Corporal	BARNETT WILLIAM Littledale sale Nov. 1910
Bombr.	ARCHIBALD JOHN
Bombr.	KEY JAMES
Bombr.	EVANS OWEN
Bombr.	RUSSELL WM.
Bombr.	WATT JAMES
Bombr.	PICKMAN JAMES
Gunner	WHITE GEORGE
Gunner	PALMER ROBERT
Gunner	HOLBROOKE JOHN
Gunner	IRWIN WM.
Gunner	BAKER WM.
Gunner	HARDIMENT WM.
Gunner	LIPTHORNE WM.
Gunner	CLARKE WM.
Gunner	GREENFIELD THOS.
Gunner	PEARSON JAMES
Gunner	NEWBURN JOHN
Gunner	HOLT EDWD.
Gunner	LUISTEY CHRISTOPHER
Gunner	RAMSBOTTOM WM.
Gunner	WRIGHT JONATHAN
Gunner	GEREING GEORGE
Gunner	HARDGRAVES RICHD.
Gunner	POTTER WM.
Gunner	DEWER ALEXR.
Gunner	FAIRCHILD JOHN
Gunner	BENNETT GEORGE
Gunner	WRIGHT DAVID
Gunner	STINSON JOHN
Gunner	BOSWORTH WM.
Gunner	CUMMINGS THOS.
Gunner	DAVIES JOHN
Gunner	LEVESLEY THOS.
Gunner	MOAT ADAM
Gunner	BOND JOHN
Gunner	WRIGHT RICHD.
Gunner	KACKSON JONATHAN
Gunner	COYLE JOHN
Gunner	ASPINALL JOHN
Gunner	DAVIDSON HUGH
Gunner	RILEY JOHN
Gunner	ALLEN NICH. Glendinnings Sale Feb. 1911
Gunner	FRANCE WM.
Gunner	HINDLE SAMUEL
Gunner	GILLESPIE DAVID
Gunner	GRIMSHAW WM.
Gunner	BUTLER THOS.
Gunner	DISHLEY JAMES
Gunner	BLABER BENJN.
Gunner	STADHOLM JONATHAN
Gunner	WILLIAMS THOS.
Gunner	STEWART DAVIES
Gunner	HAYES THOS.
Gunner	COLLINSON JOHN
Gunner	RISEBOROUGH HENRY
Gunner	HEROD WM.
Gunner	BLYTHING JOHN
Gunner	FORSTER JOHN
Gunner	SYKES NATH.
Gunner	FINCH RICHD.
Gunner	ASPINALL ROBT.
Gunner	ASPDEN RICHD.
Gunner	VEARSEY THOS.
Gunner	BURCHALL THOS.
Gunner	INGHAM THOS.
Gunner	HARRISON JOHN
Gunner	TRAVERS WM.
Gunner	HORDLEY THOS.
Gunner	NEILLSON WM.
Gunner	McCAMMON JAMES
Gunner	HETHERINGTON HENRY
Gunner	ROBERTS GEORGE Chadwick sale Nov. 1912
Gunner	ALLEN WILLIAM
Gunner	ROWNTREE JOSEPH

Gunner	GOURLEY JAMES
Gunner	WILKINS EDWD.
Gunner	FRAZER JOHN
Gunner	MILLS WM.
Gunner	MACDONALD RICHD.
Gunner	ALSTON THOS.
Gunner	NOBLE JOHN
Gunner	DAVIDSON ROBT.
Gunner	TEENAN JOSEPH
Gunner	LYELLS THOMAS Glendinning's Sale 21 July 1909
Gunner	COLLINS PETER
Gunner	GAUNT RICHD.
Gunner	DOIG THOS.
Gunner	ASHTOR JAMES
Gunner	ATTATT JAMES
Gunner	BROWN WILLIAM
Gunner	MALHAS JOHN
Gunner	BROOMHEAD RICHD.
Gunner	WARWICK JOHN
Drummer	PENNOCK JAMES

Captain Gordon's Company

2nd Captain	SINCLAIR JAMES
2nd Captain	McBEAN F.
Lieutenant	WILSON J.A.
Lieutenant	POOLE W.H.
Serjeant	HURSTFIELD W. Pensioned
Serjeant	MILLER JOHN Col.Gaskell's Sale May 1911
Corporal	BOWMAN JAMES
Corporal	WARDLE JOHN Pensioned
Corporal	SCOTT JOHN
Bombr.	RIDDINGS JOHN Pensioned Needes Collection 1908
Bombr.	PATTERSON JOHN Pensioned H.Gaskell's Collection 1908
Bombr.	KITCHEN PETER
Bombr.	HUGHES THOS. Sotheby's sale 18 June 1909
Bombr.	ROBINSON EDWD.
Bombr.	CLARK WM.
Bombr.	TAYLOR JONATHAN
Gunner	TAYLOR NEIL
Gunner	CURRELL GEORGE
Gunner	SINCLAIR WM.
Gunner	McBRIDGE JOSH.
Gunner	HORTON JOHN
Gunner	AJOULE ALEXR.
Gunner	CROMPTON WM.
Gunner	GREENWOOD JAMES
Gunner	WARDLE WM. Discharged
Gunner	JONES MERICE
Gunner	WATSON BENJN.
Gunner	PRICE DANIEL
Gunner	SMITH SAML.
Gunner	McKAY JOHN
Gunner	FENYMENT RICHD. Discharged
Gunner	RUSSELL ANDREW
Gunner	MARSDEN JOSH. Galway Foley Collection 1910
Gunner	LAMBERT JOHN
Gunner	MILLER JAMES
Gunner	DALKIN GEORGE
Gunner	PARKER JAMES
Gunner	BINTON DAVID
Gunner	SMITH THOS.
Gunner	BARCLAY PETER
Gunner	WINSTANLEY JAMES
Gunner	TAYLOR BENJN.
Gunner	MORTON ROBT.
Gunner	WESTLAND JAMES Glendinning's sale Jan. 1909
Gunner	CURRAN JOHN
Gunner	WALKER JAMES
Gunner	TULLEY ANDW.
Gunner	SMITH JOHN
Gunner	WOOD JOSH. Gray Collection 1908
Gunner	EYEST MICHL.
Gunner	CLARK WM.
Gunner	ASKEW THOS
Gunner	BEESTON JAMES
Gunner	SANKEY JOHN Discharged
Gunner	GOODALL ANDW.
Gunner	THOMSON THOS.
Gunner	DAVENPORT BENJN.
Gunner	REYALS THOS.
Gunner	KELSO DAVID
Gunner	ARBURY JOHN Discharged
Gunner	HEWSON DENNIS
Gunner	LITCHFIELD ROBT. Discharged
Gunner	WATSON RICHD.
Gunner	RAMSEY THOS.
Gunner	HINDLE JOHN
Gunner	JACKSON JAMES
Gunner	STONE JAMES
Gunner	DRONS JAMES
Gunner	McLAUGHLIN JOHN
Gunner	STEWART THOS.

Gunner	SIMPSON THOS.
Gunner	TRADSOME JAMES
Gunner	TROTTER GEORGE
Gunner	DIXON ROBT.
Gunner	THAW JOHN
Gunner	REVEL CHAS.
Gunner	THORPE JAMES
Gunner	DAVENPORT WM.
Gunner	KEW WM. Col. Gascoigne's Collection 1909
Gunner	PENNINGTON JOHN Died 13 Feb. 1816
Gunner	COULBURN THOS.
Gunner	JACKSON JOSH.
Gunner	HACKING ROBT. Discharged
Gunner	MURPHY ALEXR.
Gunner	GILL JOHN
Gunner	PATTERSON EDWD.
Gunner	HENWORTH THOS. Discharged
Gunner	SNEDON JAMES
Gunner	DONALDSON ROBT.
Gunner	GRIFFITHS JOB
Gunner	LOVE JOHN
Gunner	ALLEN JOSH.
Gunner	McLAREN JOHN
Gunner	ROYAL ROBT.
Gunner	McDOUGAL ALEXR.
Gunner	LEEDALE JOHN
Gunner	CHAPMAN GEORGE
Gunner	GOLD JNS Pensioned
Gunner	PINDER ROBT.
Gunner	COLLIER BRYAN
Gunner	GOLDIE GEORGE
Drummer	WHARIN WM.

Detachment of Captain Ilbert's Company

Lieutenant	WOOD E.M.
Lieutenant	MAULE G.S.
2nd Lieutenant	HUME G.H.
Bombr.	WILLIAMS THEO.
Bombr.	SHERWOOD JOHN
Bombr.	MILLER JAMES
Gunner	McMURRAY WM.
Gunner	KELLY BERND.
Gunner	KELLY JAMES
Gunner	HOUGHTON CHAS.
Gunner	HARDY THOS.
Gunner	ELLIOTT WM.
Gunner	NICHOL ALEXR.
Gunner	STABLES GEORGE
Gunner	BLAKELEY ROBT.
Gunner	HEWARTH WM.
Gunner	EGAR JOHN
Gunner	ROBERTSON ALEXR.
Gunner	MULLEN WM.
Gunner	BLAIRS THOS.
Gunner	JONES JAMES
Gunner	ELISON JAMES
Gunner	McGEE ROBT.
Gunner	FORBES JAMES
Gunner	GRACEY WM.
Gunner	JOHNSTONE GEORGE
Gunner	BERRYMAN WM.
Gunner	MITCHELL ROBT.
Gunner	ADAMS WM.
Gunner	BROWNHILL THOS.
Gunner	GLOVER CHAS.
Gunner	CLARK JNS.
Gunner	NICHOLSON ROBT.
Gunner	TUDOR THOS.
Gunner	GOOLDING THOS.
Gunner	ALLEN ROBT.
Gunner	ALEXANDER WM.
Gunner	McGUIRE DANIEL
Gunner	BRIMNESS JOHN
Captain	HUTCHESSON THOS.
2nd Lieutenant	WATKIS THOS. Embarked for Gibraltar
Corporal	ROBINSON ROBT.
Corporal	CARMACHAL ROBT. Pensioned
Corporal	ASPDEN HENRY
Bombr.	SMITH JAMES
Bombr.	ANDREWS JOSH
Bombr.	McDIARMID JOSH.
Gunner	DAVIDSON WM. Pensioned
Gunner	BURGOYNE DAVID Pensioned
Gunner	RICE RICHD.
Gunner	LINCOLN WM.
Gunner	MARTIN JOHN Pensioned
Gunner	HARPER WM.
Gunner	BELL GEORGE Cheylesmore Collection 1908
Gunner	TAYLOR WM. Pensioned
Gunner	DRINKWATER EDWD.
Gunner	DAY SAML.
Gunner	PROCTOR HENRY
Gunner	MURPHY MATTW.
Gunner	CHETUNE THOS.
Gunner	HOLLIDAY JOHN

Gunner MOORE ROBT.
Gunner WILKIE JAMES Fleming Collection 1871
Gunner MASON JOHN
Gunner WINSTANLEY JAMES
Gunner MORTON SAML.
Gunner HUTCHENSON JOHN
Gunner GREAVES JOHN
Gunner CUBETT GEORGE Payne Collection 1911
Gunner ROSS DONALD
Gunner McMULLEN JAMES
Gunner McCUE JAMES Discharged
Gunner WALSH JAMES
Gunner BINGLEY ROBT.
Gunner TENNAL GEORGE
Gunner NEVILL JOSH.
Gunner BROWN JOHN
Gunner PRATT THOS.
Gunner CONNELLY WM.
Gunner ADAMSON WM. Pensioned
Gunner VICKARS WM. Glendinning's Sale 28 Feb. 1908
Gunner LANG JOHN
Gunner MORTON WM.
Serjeant RIDLEY MATTHEW 2172
Gunner TWIST SAML. Pensioned
Gunner DAVIES MICHL. Died 31 Jan. 1815
Gunner CROWTHER JOHN 2175
Gunner PILFEMAN SAML. 76
Gunner BRUBBS JAMES 77
Gunner DEVILLIN H. 78
Bombr. MURRAY EDWD.
Gunner McKEE DAVID
Gunner GALLAGHER SAML.
Gunner STEVENSON JOHN
Gunner DAWSON THOS.
Gunner SMITH ROBERT Maj. Cockburn's Co.1st Bat..
Gunner WRIGHT A. 1st Batt. Detachment
Gunner GILMORE JOHN 3rd Batt. Detachment
Gunner KNOTT DANIEL Lt.Col. May's Co. 1st Bn.

Medical Department

Surgeon POWELL JAMES
Surgeon TOGO THOS.M.
Ass.Surgeon LOEDEL H.P.
Ass.Surgeon DANIELS W.B.
Ass.Surgeon RALEIGH WALTER
Ass.Surgeon VERNER EDWD. D.

Field Train Department

Clerk of Stores BENTON THOS.
Clerk of Stores SMITH JAMES
Clerk of Stores MACBEAN JOHN
Clerk of Stores HIGGINS JOHN
Clerk of Stores NEALE EDED.
Condtr.of Stores COLLINS MATHIAS
Condtr.of Stores SAUNDERS CHAS.
Condtr.of Stores BRONN CHAS.
Condtr.of Stores GULLIMORE THOS.
Condtr.of Stores BANCE JOHN
Condtr.of Stores WILLSON JOSH.

* * *

3rd BATTALION R.A.

Major UNETT G.W.
2nd Captain BROWN G.
Lieutenant LAWSON DOUGLAS
Lieutenant MONTAGUE WILLOUGHBY
2nd Lieutenant KETT CHAS. G.
Serjeant COCKRAN CHAS.
Serjeant POLLOCK WM.
Serjeant PHILIP GEORGE
Corporal KENYON WM.
Corporal SHEARER GEO.
Corporal BARNET WM.
Bombr. ARCHIBALD JOHN
Bombr. ROY JAMES
Bombr. RUSSELL WM.
Gunner HARDIMENT WM.
Gunner CLARK WM.
Gunner GREENFIELD THOS.
Gunner NEWBURN JOHN
Gunner HOLT EDWD.
Gunner SENTERS CHRISTR.
Gunner RAMSBOTTOM WM.
Gunner GORING GEORGE
Gunner HARGREAVES RICHD.
Gunner POTTERS WM.
Gunner DEWER ALEXR.
Gunner FAIRCHILD JOHN
Gunner WRIGHT DAVID
Gunner STENSON JOHN
Gunner BOSWORTH WM.
Gunner DAVIES JOHN

Gunner LEVESLEY THOS.
Gunner MOAT ADAM
Gunner BOND JOHN
Gunner WRIGHT RICHD.
Gunner JACKSON JONATHAN
Gunner ASPINALL JOHN
Gunner DAVIDSON HUGH
Gunner RILEY JOHN
Gunner ALLEN NICHS.
Gunner FRANCE WM.
Gunner HINDLE SAML.
Gunner GILLESPIE DAVID
Gunner GRIMSHAW WM.
Gunner BUTLER THOS.
Gunner DISHLEY JAMES
Gunner STEDHOLM JONATHAN
Gunner WILLIAMS THOS.
Gunner STEWART DAVID
Gunner HAYS THOS.
Gunner COLLINSON JOHN
Gunner RISEBOROUGH HENRY
Gunner FORSTER JOHN
Gunner SYKES NATH.
Gunner FINCH RICHD.
Gunner ASPINAL ROBT.
Gunner ASPDEN RICHD.
Gunner VEARSEY THOS.
Gunner BURCHALL THOS.
Gunner INGHAM THOS.
Gunner HARRISON JOHN
Gunner TRAVERS WM.
Gunner HARDLEY THOS.
Gunner NEILSON WM.
Gunner ETHERINGTON HENRY
Gunner ROBERTS GEORGE Glendinning's Sale Oct. 1913 1-8-0
Gunner ALLEN WM.
Gunner ROWNTREE JOSEPH
Gunner GOURLEY JAMES
Gunner WILKINS EDWD.
Gunner FRAZER JOHN
Gunner MILLS WM.
Gunner McDANIEL DAVID
Gunner LYELL THOS.
Gunner NOBLE JAMES
Gunner DAVIDSON ROBERT
Gunner COLLINS PETER
Gunner GAUNT RICHD.

Gunner DOEG THOS.
Gunner ASHTON JAMES
Gunner ALLOTT JAMES
Gunner BROWN WM.
Gunner BROOMHEAD RICHD.
Gunner WARWICK JOHN
Bombr. EVENS OWEN No.2
Drummer PENNACK JAMES No.2
Serjeant WADDLE JOHN Pensioned No.3
Bombr. WATT JAMES Pensioned No.3
Bombr. PICKMAN JAMES Pensioned No.3
Gunner WHITE GEORGE Pensioned No.3
Gunner PALMER ROBERT Pensioned No.3
Gunner HOLBROOK JOHN Pensioned No.3
Gunner IRVIN WM. Pensioned No.3
Gunner BAKER WM. Pensioned No.3
Gunner LIPTHORPE WM. Pensioned No.3
Gunner PEARSON JAMES Pensioned No.3
Gunner WRIGHT JONATHAN Pensioned No.3
Gunner BENNETT GEORGE Pensioned No.3
Gunner CUMMINGS THOS. Pensioned No.3
Gunner COYLE JOHN Pensioned No.3
Gunner BLABER BENJN Pensioned No.3
Gunner HERDD WM. Died No.3
Gunner BLYTHING JOHN Discharged No.3
Gunner McCANNION JAMES Discharged No.3
Gunner ALSTON THOS. Discharged No.3
Gunner TEENAN JOSH Discharged No.3
Gunner MALPES JNS. Discharged No.3

* * *

ROYAL ENGINEERS

Colonel SMYTH JAMES CARMICHAEL Cembray
Major HOSTE GEORGE Norwich
Captain & Major of Bde. OLDFIELD JOHN Cambray
Captain STANWAY FRANK Cambray
Captain THOMSON ALEXR. Payne 1911 H.Gaskell's Collection 1908
Captain PRINGLE JOHN W. Cambray
Lieutenant WATERS M.A.
Lieutenant HEAD FRANCIS B. at Sir Jas. Burgess 25 Lower Brook St.
Lieutenant GILBERT F.Y. Cambray
Lieutenant SPERLING JOHN Cambray
Lieutenant WHITE ANDREW D. Cambray

* * *

ROYAL ARTILLERY DRIVERS

Major N. Turner's A. Troop

Lieutenant	CARTHEW WM.
Lieutenant	PHILPOTT EDWD.
Lieutenant	ROBERTS JOHN
St.Serjeant	MILL JAMES W.
St.Serjeant	BANKS JOHN
Serjeant	McEWEN DAVID
Serjeant	MILLER WM.
Serjeant	COOK THOS.
Serjeant	WILKINS JOHN
Serjeant	GILMORE ANDREW
Serjeant	CARR JAMES
Serjeant	GRAY DAVID
1st Corp	HENSHALL THOS.
1st Corp	ATKINSON THOS.
1st Corp	HEDGELAND THOS.
1st Corp	GRANT JOHN
1st Corp	NAPIER JOHN
1st Corp	FOWLER JOHN
1st Corp	SIMPSON WM.
2nd Corp	WITTLESEA WM.
2nd Corp	STEELL THOS.
2nd Corp	McGREGOR PETER
2nd Corp	JONES JOHN
2nd Corp	SPANTON JAMES
2nd Corp	HIGGINS CHAS.
2nd Corp	ALLEN WM.
2nd Corp	SMALL CHAS.
2nd Corp	BARNETT WM.
2nd Corp	SMITH JOHN
Farrier	CLARK THOS.
Farrier	HOOKER JOSH.
Farrier	MITCHELL HUGH
S.Smith	GREGORY JAMES
S.Smith	MUNIFORD JOHN
S.Smith	McVEY WM.
Jobbing Smith	KNIGHT WALTER
Collar Maker	SHEPHARD JOHN
Collar Maker	ROBERTS WM. Whitaker Collection 1908
Collar Maker	STEWART JOHN
Collar Maker	CAVE WM. Sotheby's Sale 19 June 1908
Wheeler	PERRY WM.
Wheeler	WRIGHT ARCH.
Wheeler	BEALES JOHN
Wheeler	OGILVIE CHAS.
Wheeler	SMITH JOHN
Driver	ASHTON JAMES
Driver	AUCHIE THOS.
Driver	ASPINAL THOS.
Driver	ABLE JAMES
Driver	ASH RICHD.
Driver	ADAMS CHAS.
Driver	ASHTON JAMES
Driver	ARCHER WM.
Driver	ALBERRY GEORGE
Driver	ALLCOCK JOSH.
Driver	ASHLEY JAMES
Driver	ASHTON WM.
Driver	ARCHER JOHN
Driver	BOLTON THOS.
DRiver	BARKER WM.
Driver	BROWN JOHN
Driver	BROWN JAMES
Driver	BUCKLEY JOHN
Driver	BOOTH JOHN
Driver	BENNETT JOSH.
Driver	BARNES JOSH.
Driver	BRITAIN PETER
Driver	BONSEL GEO.
Driver	BOYDLE JOSH.
Driver	BEAUMAN JOHN
Driver	BROADRIB JAMES
Driver	BUTTERWORTH RICHD.
Driver	BRYAN JNS. Sent.
Driver	BEAUMOND BENJN.
Driver	BOOTH JOSH.
Driver	BULL FREDK.
Driver	BRYAN JNS. Junr.
Driver	BRAZEWELL JNS.
Driver	BENNINGTON WM.
Driver	BANNISTER SER.
Driver	BUCKLEY JAMES
Driver	BRADLEY ROBT.
Driver	BROWN JOHN
Driver	BROMLEY STEPH.
Driver	BRYAN JNS. 3rd
Driver	CHAMBERLAIN SAML. on sale at Baldwin's March 1909
Driver	CARTER GEO.
Driver	CORDON THOS.
Driver	CLOUGH THOS.
Driver	COMMONS JOHN
Driver	CRAMPTON JOHN
Driver	CAMPBELL DANIEL

Driver	CROOKSHANK WM.
Driver	CREE DAVID
Driver	CHATTERTON JOSH.
Driver	CLARK GEORGE
Driver	CLARK WM.
Driver	CAMAMILE GEORGE
Driver	CROOKS HENRY
Driver	DWYER OWEN
Driver	DELVES SAML.
Driver	DAVIDSON ROBT.
Driver	DUCE THOS.
Driver	DOBBS WM.
Driver	DOWNS JOHN
Driver	DEAN JOHN
Driver	DUCKWORTH THOS.
Driver	DARBYSHIRE ROBT.
Driver	EYERS JOEL
Driver	EARL JOHN
Driver	ELLIOTT ROBT.
Driver	ELDER JOHN
Driver	EARL THOS.
Driver	ELLIOTT WM.
Driver	FARRELL JAMES
Driver	FOGG PETER
Driver	FINLEY WM.
Driver	FRITH JOHN
Driver	FORSYTHE JAMES
Driver	FOALKS WM.
Driver	FELTON THOS.
Driver	FORSTER THOS.
Driver	FRIEND WM.
Driver	GUDGEON WM.
Driver	GALLOW WM.
Driver	GREEN ROBERT
Driver	GRANT JOHN Payne Collection 1911
Driver	GREENAWAY WM.
Driver	GOSETREE DAVID
Driver	GULLEN JOHN
Driver	GLOVER WM.
Driver	GOODWIN SAML.
Driver	GRINROD WM.
Driver	GRUBB WALTER
Driver	GASKILL ROBT.
Driver	GEORGE WM.
Driver	GILL SAML.
Driver	GREATBATCH WM.
Driver	GRANT WM.
Driver	GODFREY THOS.
Driver	GIBBS EDWD.
Driver	HALL THOS.
Driver	HICKS THOS.
Driver	HOLLOWAY WM.
Driver	HOGDEN JOHN
Driver	HULLY JOHN
Driver	HOLLADAY THOS.
Driver	HOOKER JOHN Glendinning's Sale 1911
Driver	HIGHAM THOS.
Driver	HEADLAND THOS.
Driver	HEWETT CHAS.
Driver	HASSAM DANIEL
Driver	HUNTER ROBT.
Driver	HOWARD RICHD.
Driver	HUGHES JAMES
Driver	HORNSBY RICHD.
Driver	HINES JAMES
Driver	HOLLAND JOHN
Driver	HOWARTH WM.
Driver	IBBOTSON JOHN Fleming Collection 1871
Driver	JACKSON JAMES
Driver	JACOBS SAML.
Driver	JONES THOS.
Driver	JOHNSTON JAMES
Driver	JEFFERY JOHN
Driver	JONES GEORGE
Driver	JACQUES WM.
Driver	KING GEO.
Driver	KING THOS.
Driver	KEMPSHAW THOS.
Driver	KEATES GEO.
Driver	KENNEDY THOS.
DRiver	KEMPLAND THOS.
Driver	KEELER ALEXR.
Driver	KNIGHT WM.
Driver	LOVE MATTW.
Driver	LESSLIE THOS.
Driver	LINDSAY WM.
Driver	LUNN JOSH.
Driver	LAW ABSALOM
Driver	LONSDALE JEREH.
Driver	LEES JOSH.
Driver	LLOYD SAML. Col.Gaskell's Sale May 1911
Driver	LEA HENRY
Driver	LOMAS JOHN
Driver	MIDDLETON RICHARD
Driver	MIDDLETON JOSEPH

Driver	MARSHALL ROBERT
Driver	MOORE JOHN
Driver	MOXHAM JOSEPH
Driver	MILLS GEORGE
Driver	McKERNON OLIVER Gray Collection 1908
Driver	MINCHALL JOHN
Driver	MARSHALL JOHN
Driver	MORRIS WILLIAM
Driver	McGARRATY BER. WM.
Driver	MULLONS ROBT.
Driver	McROBIN SAML.
Driver	MILLS JOHN
Driver	McDONALD ALEXR.
Driver	McCUNE WM.
Driver	MILLS JAMES
Driver	McCOY JAMES
Driver	MILLETT WM.
Driver	MAYCOCK BENJN.
Driver	McLAUGHLIN JAMES
Driver	MOXHAM WM.
Driver	NEADIN JOSH.
Driver	NEWTON JOHN
Driver	NELSON JAMES
Driver	NAUGHTON MICHL.
Driver	NEW DANIEL
Driver	OLDFIELD JOHN
Driver	OWEN JOHN
Driver	ORRALL JOHN
Driver	OWENS JOSH.
Driver	PRYKE JOHN
Driver	PURSLAW THOS.
Driver	PLUMLEY STEPHEN
DRiver	POWELL WM.
Driver	PHEACEY JOSH.
Driver	PANKETT JOHN
Driver	PLANT MICHL.
Driver	PALETHORPE RICHD.
Driver	POTTER ROBT.
Driver	PICKFORD BENJN.
Driver	POOLE DANIEL
Driver	PRICE THOS.
Driver	REDDING GEORGE
Driver	ROLES ARCH.
Driver	REILLY JOHN
Driver	REID ROBT.
Driver	RABDLE THOS.
Driver	RUTHERFORD THOS.
Driver	SMITH BENJN.
Driver	SMITH WM.
Driver	STANFIELD SAML.
Driver	SKELTON JOHN
Driver	SAMBROOK THOS.
Driver	SMITH WM. Senr.
Driver	SCOTT PETER
Driver	SHUTTLEWORTH GEORGE
Driver	SHARP ROBERT
Driver	STONES JOSH.
Driver	SHEPHERD JOHN
Driver	SMITH WM. Junr.
Driver	TWELVETHRIDGE JOHN
Driver	TAYLOR ABRM.
Driver	TAYLOR GEORGE
Driver	THOMPSON WM.
Driver	THOMAS GEORGE
Driver	TANTUM PETER Glendinning's sale Oct. 1912 3-3-0
Driver	TAYLOR JOHN
Driver	TWIGG JAMES
Driver	TATTERSALL JAMES
Driver	TURNER WM.
Driver	THOMAS WM.
Driver	TYSON JOHN
Driver	TAYLOR FREDK.
Driver	TALBOT KIRBY
Driver	TWIGG JONATHAN
Driver	TOWNROW JAMES
Driver	TAYLOR JAMES
Driver	UNCLE BENJN.
Driver	VICKERS RICHD.
Driver	WILLIAMS JOHN
Driver	WILLIAMS FRANCIS
Driver	WHITE THOS.
Driver	WILDING SAML.
Driver	WEST JAMES
Driver	WOOLHOUSE BENJN.
Driver	WARD WM.
Driver	WHITESIDE GROVE
Driver	WEST THEOPH.
Driver	WARRING JAMES
Driver	WELLS GEORGE
Driver	WELSH JOHN
Driver	WARD JAMES
Driver	WARREN WM.
Driver	WEIR ALEXR.
Driver	WELLS JOHN
Driver	WOOD JOSEPH
Driver	WOOD JAMES

Driver	WOOD THOS.
Driver	YOUNG THOS.
Driver	YEPPS WM.
Driver	YATES WM.
Driver	SIGLEY JOHN
Driver	HARDY JAMES
Driver	SCOTT JAMES

Captain G.H. Grimes "D" Troop

1st Lieutenant	FISKE GEORGE
St.Serjeant	HOWARTH ROBT.
St.Serjeant	ONN HENRY
Serjeant	WRIGHT JOHN
Serjeant	HARPER ALEXR.
Serjeant	BOLTON THOS.
Serjeant	CHALMERS THOS.
1st Corp.	STEVENS GEO.
1st Corp	McALLISTER CHAS.
1st Corp	BRIERLY ROBT.
1st Corp	EDWARDS RICHD.
1st Corp	CRAWFORD WM.
2nd Corp	BEVERIDGE JOHN
2nd Corp	POTTER JAMES
2nd Corp	ELLIS WM.
2nd Corp	YOUNG JOHN
2nd Corp	WADE THOS.
2nd Corp	WILLIS FRANCIS
Trumpeter	MARTIN JOHN Glendinning's sale Nov.1909
Trumpeter	HARDY WM.
Farrier	SMITH JOHN H.Gaskell's collection 1908
S.Smith	JONES THOS. Glendinning's sale Oct. 1913 1-14-0
S.Smith	CRESSWELL ALEXR.
S.Smith	HOLLINS SAML.
Jobbing Sm	WALTON RICHD.
C.Maker	MINTON RICHD.
C.Maker	ILLINGWORTH JOHN
C.Maker	GAMMELL WM.
C.Maker	JORDAN JOHN
C.Maker	NEWTON EDWD.
Wheeler	BROWN THOS.
Wheeler	DAGGER JOHN
Wheeler	DOBSON THOS
Wheeler	ARMSTRONG JOSH.
Driver	ASHWORTH JOHN
Driver	ALEXANDER JAMES
Driver	ANDREWS JAMES
Driver	AUST URIAH
Driver	BENNETT THOS.
Driver	BARKER THOS.
Driver	BERRY WM.
Driver	BOUGH JOHN
Driver	BATES SAML.
Driver	BLACKBURN WM.
Driver	BOSWELL JOHN Glendinning's sale July 1911 - Phillips sale
Driver	BLOCKSAGE EDWD.
Driver	BUCKSTON JOSH.
Driver	BENYON JOHN
Driver	BAILEY JOHN
Driver	BARNES CHRISTR
Driver	BROWM WM.
Driver	BOTTOMLY WM.
Driver	BROWN STEWT.
Driver	BROOKSLY WM.
Driver	BELL ROBT.
Driver	BLAKELY JAMES
Driver	BAILES ANDREW
Driver	CROOKS JAMES
Driver	CAWLEY JOHN
Driver	CLARKE SAML.
Driver	CROWTHER JOHN
Driver	COTTERALL JAMES
Driver	CRANS JAMES
Driver	CRAY BENJN.
Driver	COLGRAVES JOHN
Driver	CROSSLEY HENRY
Driver	CAMB MARK
Driver	DAVIS THOS.
Driver	DICKMAN WM.
Driver	DONNELLY JAMES
Driver	DOUGLAS JAMES
Driver	DAVENPORT JAMES
Driver	DAVIS JOHN
Driver	DIGGLE RICHD.
Driver	EATON JAMES
Driver	EALEY JOHN
Driver	ECCLES CHRISTR
Driver	FELLOWS JOHN
Driver	GUYER EDWD.
Driver	GREGORY JOSEPH
Driver	GREY BERND.
Driver	GORDON FRANCIS
Driver	GUNN ROBT.
Driver	GILLETT WM.
Driver	GRAY GEORGE Galway Foley Collection 1910

Driver	HARROP HENRY
Driver	HOWARTH JOHN
Driver	HATTERLY WM.
Driver	HART WM.
Driver	HARDING PAUL
Driver	HUNE CHAS.
Driver	HARRIS WM.
Driver	HARRISON JOHN
Driver	HIGHAM PETER
Driver	HUTCHINSON JOHN
Driver	JERVIS WM.
Driver	JONES WM.
Driver	KEY WM.
Driver	KEYTON THOS.
Driver	LAYCOCK ANTHONY
Driver	LAWRENCE HENRY
Driver	LORD CHAS.
Driver	LEES THOS.
Driver	LEMMING THOS.
Driver	McKENZIE ALEXR.
Driver	McDONALD ROBT.
Driver	MUNRO ALEXR.
Driver	MITCHELL WM.
Driver	MARTIN ROBT.
Driver	MIDGELEY THOS.
Driver	MARSH SAML.
Driver	MILLER JAMES
Driver	McCOURT HUGH
Driver	McREYNOLDS ROBT.
Driver	MATTHEWS ALEXR.
Driver	MITCHELL JOSH.
Driver	McDONALD DUNCAN
Driver	MORTON JOHN
Driver	MOORE JAMES
Driver	McDONALD ALEXR.
Driver	PHILLIPS JOHN
Driver	PIDCOCK GEO.
Driver	PRINGLE ROBT.
Driver	POLLETT EDWD.
Driver	PORT WM.
Driver	PURVIS WALTER
Driver	PAYNE RICHD.
Driver	PLATTS GEORGE
Driver	PRIEST JAMES
Driver	POWELL JOHN
Driver	REX JOSEPH
Driver	ROWLAND THOS.
Driver	ROWLEY WM.
Driver	ROYALS THOS.
Driver	ROBERTS THOS.
Driver	RODGERS BARTHW.
Driver	RHIND WM.
Driver	REDFORD THOS.
Driver	ROBERTS JOHN
Driver	STRINGER JOSH.
Driver	SNELL JOHN
Driver	SIMPSON WM.
Driver	STACEY JOHN
Driver	SPRAY SAML.
Driver	SHARP THOS.
Driver	SMITH EDWD.
Driver	SHINGLER SAML.
Driver	SWAN HENRY
Driver	SALTER GEORGE
Driver	SPORTEN SAML.
Driver	SIFTON JOSH.
Driver	STEENSON JOHN
Driver	STANFIELD WM.
Driver	TWIFORD WM.
Driver	TURNER JOHN
Driver	TESDALE BENJN.
Driver	WAINWRIGHT GEORGE
Driver	WILCOX GEORGE
Driver	WILLIAMS THOS.
Driver	WOOD JAMES
Driver	WHALE JOHN
Driver	WATSON WM.
Driver	WILDSMITH JOHN
Driver	WEBB SAML.
Driver	WOOLARD JAMES
Driver	WHITE GEORGE
Driver	WRIGHT THOS.
Driver	WATSON WATTS
Driver	WALSH ALEXR.
Driver	YOUNG SAML.
Driver	FRIEND THOS.

Captain Henry Lane's "F" Troop

Serjeant	MORRISON JOHN
Serjeant	BROADBENT JAMES
Serjeant	ROBERTSON WM.
Serjeant	ADDERLY EDWD.
Serjeant	DUNBAR JOHN
1st Corp	MISSKIMMINS WM.
1st Corp	MALTHOUSE JAMES
2nd Corp	BROWN JAMES
2nd Corp	GRAHAM PETER
2nd Corp	KERR JOHN

2nd Corp	BALL WM.	Driver	CLARK JOHN
2nd Corp	LEES JAMES	Driver	CORBETT JAMES
2nd Corp	FINDLEY GEORGE	Driver	CARTER WM.
S.Smith	MASCORD WM.	Driver	CHARLES JOHN
S.Smith	McCOURT JAMES	Driver	CADDY JOSH.
S.Smith	YOUNG PHILIP	Driver	CHIPPETT JOHN
S.Smith	HOLT JAMES	Driver	CROOKS THOS.
S.Smith	EARNSHAW THOS.	Driver	CROXEN JAMES
C.Maker	BARRETT THOS.	Driver	CHAPMAN THOS.
C.Maker	WATTY JOHN	Driver	COOK BENJN.
Wheeler	BROWN WM.	Driver	COOK JOHN
Driver	ANDERSON JOHN	Driver	CHARLESWORTH WM.
Driver	ALEXANDER WM.	Driver	DEVLIN HUGH
Driver	ANDERSON DAVID	Driver	DUNLEAVY JOHN
Driver	ARNOLD JOSH	Driver	DOUGHTY EDWD.
Driver	ALMOND THOS.	Driver	DAY THOS.
Driver	ANDREWS THOS.	Driver	DOWTON WM.
Driver	ANDREWS DEBENOR	Driver	ENTWISTLE JOHN
Driver	ALEXANDER JOHN	Driver	EBBS PETER
Driver	BYGROVES JAMES	Driver	EDWARDS WM.
Driver	BELL GEO.	Driver	EDWARDS BENJN.
Driver	BOYLE HENRY	Driver	FULCHER THOS.
Driver	BRADY FRANCIS	Driver	FRAZER THOS.
Driver	BARMINSTER WM.	Driver	FLETCHER THOS.
Driver	BEST DANIEL	Driver	FAUGHY PATT.
Driver	BLOOME THOS.	Driver	FARQUHAR JAMES
Driver	BANNISTER DANIEL	Driver	GRIFFITHS JAMES
Driver	BOUCHANAN JAMES	Driver	GRAY ROBT.
Driver	BARNET THOS.	Driver	GATTINGS SAML.
Driver	BOUCHANAN GEORGE	Driver	GREENAWAY WM.
Driver	BRIDGES MATTW.	Driver	GRAHAM PATT.
Driver	BROADBENT SAML.	Driver	GREEN THOS.
Driver	BLACK GEO.	Driver	GREY RICHD.
Driver	BRACE JOSH.	Driver	GREENALGH ABM.
Driver	BAILEY THOS.	Driver	GREEN JOSH.
Driver	BRADSHAW SAML.	Driver	HAVRON PATT
Driver	BROWNSON JOHN	Driver	HOOF SAMUEL
Driver	BOLTON JAMES	Driver	HUDSON JOHN
Driver	BRADSHAW JAMES	Driver	HARROLD WM.
Driver	BOX GEORGE	Driver	HART HAMN.
Driver	BUCKLEY JOHN	Driver	HAYS JAMES
Driver	BOOTH ROBT.	Driver	HUNTER RICHD.
Driver	BESWICK JOHN	Driver	HICKS JOHN
Driver	CAMPBELL HUGH	Driver	HINCHCLIFF RICHD.
Driver	COURTNEY EDWD.	Driver	HANLAN EDWD
Driver	COOK JOSH.	Driver	HILTON JAMES
Driver	CARNES THOS.	Driver	HAMBLETT JOHN
Driver	CRITCHLEY JOHN	Driver	HURST JOHN

Driver	HUTCHINSON THOS.
Driver	HOOK WM.
Driver	HATTON JOHN
Driver	HAMES GEORGE
Driver	HENNY THOS.
Driver	HANNON PATT.
Driver	HASTINGS THOS.
Driver	HAWKSWORTH JOSH.
Driver	HAMMER JOSHUA
Driver	HOLMES JOHN
Driver	JONES ROBERT
Driver	JONES THOS.
Driver	JACKSON ISSAC
Driver	KENYON WM.
Driver	KIRBY JOSH.
Driver	KEATON WM.
Driver	KENNEDY JAMES
Driver	KELLSALL JNS.
Driver	KETTLE JAS.
Driver	KIRBY THOS.
Driver	LAWSON ALEXR.
Driver	LOVEGROVE WM.
Driver	LORD WM.
Driver	LEECH JAMES
Driver	LEWIS JOHN
Driver	MIDDLETON LUKE
Driver	MARSHALL WM.
Driver	MOORE SAML.
Driver	McKELVEY JAMES
Driver	McELROY MICHL.
Driver	McKINLEY WM.
Driver	MOCKER WM.
Driver	MARCER JOHN
Driver	MILLS THOS.
Driver	McCOY JAMES
Driver	McCURDY ALEXR.
Driver	McBRIDGE JAMES
Driver	MULLINEAUX THOS.
Driver	McQUILLAND RICHD.
Driver	McMANUS TERCE.
Driver	MORGAN CHAS.
Driver	MARSDEN SHAD.
Driver	MALLICE JAMES
Driver	McNALLY WM.
Driver	McCULLEN JAMES
Driver	MURPHY TIMOTHY
Driver	McFALL WM.
Driver	MASON BENJN.
Driver	McCALL JOHN
Driver	NIGHTINGALE JOHN
Driver	NEADIN THOS.
Driver	PEELING JOHN
Driver	PRIDE ALEXR
Driver	PEDLEY THOS.
Driver	PALMER JOHN
Driver	POWELL JAMES
Driver	POTTER WM.
Driver	REVILL JOHN
Driver	RAYNER JAMES
Driver	RENSHAW CHAS.
Driver	RAPPS JOSH.
Driver	RIDDLE JAMES
Driver	RILEY JAMES
Driver	REID WM.
Driver	RICHARDSON JNS.
Driver	RICHARDSON JAS.
Driver	RICHARDSON THOS.
Driver	SIFTON GEO.
Driver	SCOTT JAS.
Driver	SLATER JAS.
Driver	STEELING JNS.
Driver	STEVENSON JAS.
Driver	SMITH JAS.
Driver	SKELTON CHAS.
Driver	SMALLWOOD THOS.
Driver	SKELTON THOS.
Driver	SHAW THOS.
Driver	SMITH JOHN Glendinnings sale Jan. 1910
Driver	SYKES GEO.
Driver	SMALL ANDW.
Driver	SHEERDOWN SAMUEL
Driver	TEAS SAML.
Driver	TURTLE JOHN
Driver	TINSLEY JOHN
Driver	TASWELL JACOB
Driver	TOFT DAVID
Driver	TAYLOR WM.
Driver	TURNER ROBT.
Driver	TUFT JNS.
Driver	TATTERSALL THOS
Driver	URQUHART ALEXR.
Driver	UMFIELD WM.
Driver	VERVORS RICHD.
Driver	WHITEHEAD MICHL.
Driver	WILLETTS THOS.
Driver	WALKER ROBT.
Driver	WILCOX JOSH.

Driver	WILLIAMS JOHN
Driver	WARD JOSH.
Driver	WILKS TIMY.
Driver	YEATES GEO.

Captain W.H. Humphrey's "H" Troop

Captain	HUMPHREYS W.H.
Lieutenant	WILKINSON GEO.
Lieutenant	RICE THOS.
Lieutenant	REID THOS.
2nd Lieutenant	JUGGER JERH.
S.Serjeant	CLEMENTS WM.
S.Serjeant	LOVATT WM.
S.Serjeant	ROTHERY HENRY
S.Serjeant	ARMSTRONG JAS.
Serjeant	DUMONT PETER
Serjeant	BANNON HUGH
Serjeant	SCOBIE JAS.
Serjeant	MULLARD HEWITT
Serjeant	BELL JOHN
Serjeant	MURPHY EDWD.
Serjeant	ARMSTRONG JAMES
Serjeant	BULL JAMES
Serjeant	BROWN JOHN
Serjeant	CLARKE THOS.
Serjeant	WOOD JOHN
Serjeant	PETTRIE JOHN
Serjeant	CRAIG ALEXR.
1st Corp	BRANN WM.
1st Corp	BURK WM.
1st Corp	BICKLE ELISHA
1st Corp	BLAIR THOS.
1st Corp	BARROW WM.
1st Corp	BOON THOS.
1st Corp	BAXTER JOSH.
1st Corp	McARTHUR JOHN
1st Corp	CASSIDY WM.
1st Corp	ARMSTRONG WM.
1st Corp	McCARTNEY THOS. Glendinnings sale 21 July 1909
1st Corp	THOMPSON ROBT.
1st Corp	CURREN BENJN.
1st Corp	BANKS GEORGE
1st Corp	ANDERSON JAS.
2nd Corp	WILLIS THOS.
2nd Corp	WILSON THOMP.
2nd Corp	MARSH PHILIP
2nd Corp	TABB RICHD.
2nd Corp	GREY WM.
2nd Corp	ROUCH THOS.
2nd Corp	SADDLER THOS.
2nd Corp	BEDFORD JOHN
2nd Corp	PROCTOR JAMES
S.Smith	HARRISON WM.
S.Smith	REVILL FRANCIS
S.Smith	HART THOS.
S.Smith	WRIGHT RICHD.
S.Smith	KNOWLES JAMES
S.Smith	MADDEN JOHN
S.Smith	DICKSON ROGER
S.Smith	SANDERSON HUGH
S.Smith	WINTERS PHILIP
S.Smith	McBRIDE MATTY.
S.Smith	JONES SAML.
S.Smith	BLACKSHAW WM.
S.Smith	McCRUM VAL.
Job.Smith	HUNTER WM.
Job.Smith	THORNTON GEORGE
Job.Smith	WILLIAMS DAVID
Job.Smith	GREER JOSH.
C.Maker	PIGGOTT JOHN
C.Maker	MORROW JOSH.
C.Maker	DOWLING JOHN
C.Maker	IRWIN GEORGE
C.Maker	WILSON WM.
C.Maker	SKILL JOHN
C.Maker	DEAN JOHN
C.Maker	IRELAND JOHN
C.Maker	CURRY WM.
Wheeler	HAY JOHN
Wheeler	TOYSE JOHN
Wheeler	GRAY JOHN
Wheeler	McNUTTY WM.
Wheeler	THORNLEY JOSH.
Wheeler	GRAVES JAMES
Wheeler	HILTON JOHN
Wheeler	REANY NAVEN
Wheeler	DUNN WM.
Wheeler	MUNGAN PATT.
Driver	AUSTEN PATTEN
Driver	ASHWORTH JOHN
Driver	ABBOTT JOHN
Driver	ARMSTRONG WM.
Driver	ASHCROFT JOHN
Driver	ADAMSON GEO.
Driver	ADAMS ROBT.
Driver	BOWES JAMES
Driver	BLAIR OLIVER

Driver BROADHURST SAML.
Driver BLOOD THOS.
Driver BRIDGETT HENRY
Driver BURNS ALEXR.
Driver BURNS EDWD.
Driver BARLOW THOS.
Driver BRIDGE ABM.
Driver BONNER WM.
Driver BANNISTER WILSON
Driver BERRY RUBEN
Driver BARROW HUGH
Driver BAYNES JAMES
Driver BARNES WM.
Driver BONNER DANIEL
Driver BURNS HUGH
Driver BOURD JOSH
Driver BOYLE JOHN
Driver BOYCE JOHN
Driver BOYLE HENRY
Driver BURNS EDWIN
Driver BATES SAML.
Driver BRADSHAW JAMES
Driver BROWN ARCH.
Driver BROWNING ALEXR.
Driver BROADBENT JAS.
Driver BROWN FRANS.
Driver BRUNT SAML.
Driver BOGGIS NIGHTIN
Driver BALL WM.
Driver BETTY WM.
Driver BRIEN WM.
Driver BRADLEY JOHN
Driver BARCLAY JOHN
Driver BAGLEY PATT.
Driver BRADY THOS.
Driver BROWN ARTHUR
Driver BRANNON WM.
Driver BEAVER GEORGE Col. Murray's Collection
Driver BARKER JAMES
Driver BELLAMY JAMES
Driver BELL JOHN
Driver COOK THOS.
Driver COOK JNS.
Driver CALE JAMES
Driver COCKRAN ANDW.
Driver CARSON JOHN
Driver CALDER THOS.
Driver CARROLL WM.

Driver COMRIE WM.
Driver CAMPBELL PETER SENR.
Driver CAMPBELL PETER JUNR.
Driver CORRIGAN JOHN
Driver COURTNEY JOHN
Driver CHAMBY THOS.
Driver CLARKE WM.
Driver CONNOLLY OWEN
Driver CULLEN TER.
Driver CONROY JAMES
Driver CLEMENTS WM.
Driver CAVEN THOS.
Driver COWAN JOHN
Driver CONNER EDWD.
Driver CONNER ANDW.
Driver COMET JOHN
Driver CHEESEMAN GEORGE
Driver COCKAYNE SAML.
Driver COYLE SAML.
Driver CLIFFORD HUGH
Driver CASSERLY FRANS.
Driver CHRISTIE WM.
Driver CLIBBERG GEORGE
Driver COCKER FRANS.
Driver CHARLTON GEORGE
Driver COOEY THOS.
Driver CAMPBELL PATT.
Driver CAMPBELL ROBT.
Driver CARNEY JAMES
Driver DRABBLE SAML.
Driver DARBY HENRY
Driver DARGIN FRANS.
Driver DOWEL WM.
Driver DEACON GEO.
Driver DIFFEN JAMES
Driver DENNIS J.CHAS.
Driver DREW CHAS.
Driver DAVIS WM.
Driver DONNOLLY PATT.
Driver DELIGHT JAMES
Driver DAVIS FRANCIS
Driver DUGGIN WM.
Driver DOUGHERTY PETER
Driver DAFT SAML.
Driver DATTON JAMES
Driver DONYLUSS WM.
Driver DUNCAN WM.
Driver DEWICH JOHN
Driver EVINS DANIEL

Driver EATON JOHN
Driver EVINS JAMES
Driver ELLIS THOS.
Driver ERINSHAW WM.
Driver FINNEY JOHN
Driver FOSTER JOHN
Driver FIELDS CHRISTR.
Driver FLEMING JAMES
Driver FERRIS WM.
Driver FLEMING WM. Cheylesmore Collection 1908
Driver FARRELL EDWD.
Driver FACER JAMES
Driver FAULKNER JOHN
Driver FRAZER JOHN
Driver FLEETCROFT JAMES
Driver FULCHER ROBT.
Driver FLETCHER JOSH.
Driver FRY WM.
Driver FITZSIMMONS THOS.
Driver FORD JOHN
Driver FUILY JOHN
Driver GREY THOS.
Driver GILBERTSON JAS.
Driver GOODRILL EDWD.
Driver GREYSON JAMES
Driver GREY DANIEL
Driver GORE WILLIAM
Driver GILLEN ANTHY.
Driver GREER SAML.
Driver GILLIS WM.
Driver GUTHRICK WM.
Driver GOODWIN HENRY
Driver GREENWOOD JOB
Driver GREAVES JOHN
Driver GRAVES JAMES
Driver GREEN ROBT.
Driver GREENDAY JOHN
Driver GUDGEON JOHN
Driver GULLON WM.
Driver GILL WM.
Driver GRIBBIN JAMES
Driver GLASS JOHN
Driver GRIBBIN CHRISTR.
Driver GOYMOUR JOHN
Driver HIGNETT WM.
Driver HADDEN JAMES
Driver HARRISON LUKE
Driver HUBBARD WM.
Driver HALL WM.
Driver HADLEY WM.
Driver HARGREAVES JAS. Senr.
Driver HUDSON WALTER
Driver HAMMOND JAMES
Driver HAGEN JAMES
Driver HARRISON EDWD.
Driver HARDY THOMAS
Driver HARROLD JOHN
Driver HAMILTON JAMES
Driver HAGEN HUGH
Driver HUGHES JOHN
Driver HAUGHEY JAMES
Driver HENRY FELIX
Driver HAMILTON JOHN
Driver HANNAH JAMES
Driver HILL SAML. Littledale Sale Nov. 1910
Driver HETHERLY WM.
Driver HART WM.
Driver HARGREAVES JAS. Junr.
Driver HANSON JOHN
Driver HYDE ZACH.
Driver HARTLY JOHN
Driver HICKRY JOHN
Driver HODGES WM.
Driver HOLDING JNS.
Driver HACKNEY JOB
Driver HUNT GEO.
Driver HOLDERTON JAMES Glendinning's Sale 17 June 1908
Driver HOLMES SAML.
Driver HOLDING THOS.
Driver HEELHAM ROBT.
Driver HASLEM THOS.
Driver HAGUE WM.
Driver HAY BRUCE
Driver IRWIN HASLETT
Driver IRWIN ARTHUR
Driver ISHERWOOD JAS.
Driver JOHNSTON LANTY
Driver JOHNSTON JOHN
Driver JOHNSTON GEO.
Driver JACKITTS PETER
Driver JACKSON SAML.
Driver JONES WM.
Driver JOHNSTON JOHN
Driver JOHNSTON DAVID
Driver JOHNSTON FRANS.

Driver	JOHNSTON RICHD.
Driver	JACKSON WM. Adamson Collection 1911
Driver	JAMESON ROBT.
Driver	JARVIS WM.
Driver	JACKSON CHAS.
Driver	KEY JOSEPH
Driver	KEARNEY WM.
Driver	KIMMENS JAMES
Driver	KINGSBURY FRANS.
Driver	KEENAN WM.
Driver	KELLY BARND.
Driver	KENNEDY JOSH.
Driver	KELLY PATT.
Driver	LORD JAMES
Driver	LEE JNS.
Driver	LUCK ROBT.
Driver	LAWRENCE WM.
Driver	LAYLAND JOSH.
Driver	LITHRO JOHN
Driver	LITTLE WM.
Driver	LOWE EDWD.
Driver	LEAVER SAML.
Driver	LARKIN ARTHUR
Driver	LEES JOHN Glendinning's Sale Sept. 1911
Driver	MILLER GEO.
Driver	MULHOLLAND ROGER
Driver	MANWELL THOS.
Driver	MITCHELL JOHN
Driver	MILLS ROBT.
Driver	McNOUGHT WM.
Driver	MULHOLLAND PHIL.
Driver	McCOY JAMES
Driver	MONAGHAN JAMES
Driver	McGURK JOHN
Driver	McKELSEY JOHN
Driver	MORGAN JOHN
Driver	McDERMOT JOHN
Driver	McLOUGHLIN JNS.
Driver	MULLEN JAMES
Driver	McINTIRE FREDK.
Driver	McCLURG JOHN
Driver	McWILLIAMS ANDW.
Driver	McGEE JAMES
Driver	McGAHAN PATT.
Driver	MURRAY MOORE
Driver	MERRIOTT ROBT.
Driver	MATTHEWS JAS.
Driver	MILLER DANIEL
Driver	McCUE GEOREG
Driver	MASON WM. H.Gaskell's Collection 1908
Driver	MAITLAND JNS.
Driver	MILLINGTON WM.
Driver	MORRIS JOHN
Driver	McFARLAND JAMES
Driver	McREYNOLDS JOSH.
Driver	McBURNEY ROBT.
Driver	MOORE DAVID
Driver	McGRATH PATT.
Driver	McADAMS JAS.
Driver	MONTAGUE JOHN
Driver	MILLER JOSH.
Driver	McCANGHRY EDWD.
Driver	McGUINESS WM.
Driver	McGENIKEN GEO. Col.Murray's Collection
Driver	McCONEL GEO.
Driver	McCONNELL JOHN Glendinnings sale 17 June 1908 - Col.R.T. Gascoignes Collection March 1909
Driver	McMANUS PATT.
Driver	MURPHY SAML.
Driver	MEEHAN WM.
Driver	MOULT WM.
Driver	McLEAN JOHN
Driver	MARTIN EZEK.
Driver	McGEE WM.
Driver	MULLEN SAML.
Driver	McCREA HUGH Watters Sale June 1913
Driver	MAXWELL GEO.
Driver	MEDCALF JAMES
Driver	MURRELL JNS.
Driver	McLELLAND ANDW.
Driver	McGREGOR PATT.
Driver	NOTTRAM JNS.
Driver	McGOVERN HUGH
Driver	MURPHY WM.
Driver	McMULLEN CRAWD.
Driver	McCLUSKIE ROBT.
Driver	McCLURE SAML.
Driver	McCOURT JOHN
Driver	MARTIN ALLAN
Driver	MOORCROFT FRANS.
Driver	McGEE ARCH.
Driver	McLEAN HUGH
Driver	NICHOLLS WM.

Driver	NICHOLL THOS.
Driver	NESBITT JOHN
Driver	NEIL CHAS.
Driver	NOON GEO.
Driver	NEWBROOK WM.
Driver	NELSON JAMES
Driver	ONEAL FELIX
Driver	OWENS WM.
Driver	OATLEY JOHN
Driver	ORTEN WM.
Driver	PROVINCE JAS.
Driver	PHELAN WM.
Driver	PENTON BERND.
Driver	PAGETT WM.
Driver	PINKNEY JOHN
Driver	PERKINS JOSH.
Driver	PARKINS WM.
Driver	PARKER CHRSITR.
Driver	PINDER MARTIN
Driver	PRATT JOHN
Driver	PRIESTLY WM.
Driver	PORTER CHAS.
Driver	PICKFORD EDWD.
Driver	PATTERSON JOHN
Driver	QUINN MICHAEL
Driver	QUIN EDWD Junr.
Driver	QUIGLEY ISSAC
Driver	QUIN EDWD Senr.
Driver	QUINCE ISSAC
Driver	QUIGLEY DAVID
Driver	ROBINSON JAMES
Driver	RUSSELL ROBT. Senr.
Driver	RUSSELL ROBT. Junr.
Driver	REDDING JAS.
Driver	RODGERS JOHN
Driver	RICHARDSON FRANS. Sotheby's sale 19 June 1908
Driver	RICHMOND WM.
Driver	ROBI WM.
Driver	ROBINSON ALEXR.
Driver	ROSS JAMES
Driver	RAVEN ARCH.
Driver	ROBINSON THOS.
Driver	ROGLEY WM.
Driver	RENNY ROBT.
Driver	RODGERS EDWD.
Driver	RENSTRY JOHN
Driver	RITCHIE ROBT.
Driver	ROURKE FRANZ.
Driver	ROBINSON GEO.
Driver	ROBINSON THOS.
Driver	RODGERS JAMES
Driver	REILLY JOHN
Driver	RICHARDS JOHN
Driver	RAWSON HENRY
Driver	RUTHERFORD JOSH.
Driver	REID ADAM
Driver	ROPER JOHN
Driver	RHOADS THOS.
Driver	ROYALS CHAS.
Driver	SYKES JOHN
Driver	SURRELL WM.
Driver	SIMPSON JNS.
Driver	SUTTEN WM.
Driver	SUTTLE JOHN
Driver	SMITH MATTW.
Driver	SPENCE JAMES on sale at Baldwin's March 1909
Driver	SCOBIE RUBEN
Driver	SHANNON JAMES
Driver	SLATON JOHN
Driver	STANFORD JOSEPH
Driver	SANDOVER FRANCIS
Driver	STEVENS WILLIAM
Driver	SILBY JOHN
Driver	SHAW JAMES
Driver	SNAPE WM.
Driver	SEACH WM.
Driver	SHANNON PATT.
Driver	SIMPSON SIM.
Driver	SIMPSON WM.
Driver	SNAPE JAMES
Driver	SYKES SAML.
Driver	SPARROW EDWD.
Driver	SMITH JOHN
Driver	SLIXTON SAML.
Driver	SIMMONS THOS.
Driver	SHADDOCK SAML.
Driver	SMITH JOHN
Driver	SCHOOL JAMES
Driver	SMITH THOS.
Driver	SHIMMERINGS JOHN
Driver	SMITH HENRY
Driver	SMITH PHILIP
Driver	SIGLEY JAMES
Driver	SHARPE JAMES
Driver	SENNOTT JOHN
Driver	TATTERSALL JOHN

Driver	TOOLE WM.
Driver	TODD CHRISTR. Gray Collection 1908
Driver	TREASTER JOHN
Driver	TAYLOR EDWD.
Driver	THACKER JOSH.
Driver	THOMPSON JOHN
Driver	TOTTAM SAML.
Driver	THORP JOSH.
Driver	TODD ALEXR.
Driver	TIFFIN PORT.
Driver	THORPE GEORGE
Driver	THORPE JESSE
Driver	TRAINER JOHN
Driver	TAYE JOHN
Driver	THORNLEY WM.
Driver	THOMPSON JNS.
Driver	TOREY WM.
Driver	TOWER JOHN
Driver	VOCE WM.
Driver	VINCENT FRANS.
Driver	WRIGHT DANL.
Driver	WATSON JNS.
Driver	WEBSTER ROBT.
Driver	WALKER BENJN.
Driver	WALFORD WM.
Driver	WOOLER JOHN
Driver	WINCHESTER JOHN
Driver	WRIGHT RALPH
Driver	WISE JAMES
Driver	WATSON RICHD.
Driver	WELLS DANL.
Driver	WELLUM JERH.
Driver	WILLIAMS JOHN
Driver	WHITTAKER LAWCE.
Driver	WYLD SAML.
Driver	WILLEY RICHD.
Driver	WHARTON THOS.
Driver	WHEELER NATH.
Driver	WILSON ROBERT
Driver	WILKINSON THOS.
Driver	WILLIAMSON JAS.
Driver	WALSH WM.
Driver	WATERFIELD JNS
Driver	WHITEHEAD ROBT.
Driver	WHISKER SAMUEL
Driver	WHITMAN JOHN
Driver	WESTWOOD THOS.
Driver	WOODALL PETER
Driver	YOUNG PATT.

Ordnance Medical Officers

Surgeons	POWELL J.
Surgeons	TOGO T.N.
Surgeons	HICHENS R.
Surgeons	AMBROSE JAMES
Ass.Surgeon	McDONALD (M.D.) A.
Ass.Surgeon	KENNY (M.D.) M.
Ass.Surgeon	RUDGE EDWD.
Ass.Surgeon	BEARD THOS.
Ass.Surgeon	GATTY HENRY
Ass.Surgeon	VERNER E.D. H.Gaskell's Collection 1908 Payne 1911
Ass.Surgeon	LORDEL H.P.
Ass.Surgeon	DANIELL W.B.
Ass.Surgeon	BINGHAM JOHN
Ass.Surgeon	RALEIGH WALTER

Field Train

Ass.Comm.	BENTON THOS.
Clerk of Stores	SMITH JAMES
Clerk of Stores	McBEAN JOHN
Clerk of Stores	HIGGINS JOHN
Clerk of Stores	NEALE EDMUND Cheylesmore Collection 1908
Conductors of Stores	COLLINS MATTHIAS On sale at Febton's Nov. 1912
Conductors of Stores	SAUNDERS CHARLES
Condustors of Stores	BROWN CHARLES
Conductors of Stores	GALLEMORE THOMAS
Conductors of Stores	BANCE JOHN
Conductors of Stores	WILSON

* * *

2nd BATTN. GRENADIER GUARDS

Lt.Colonel Ftizroy Somerset's Company

Lt.& Captain	BUCKLEY THOS. EDWD.
Ensign	ALLEN GEORGE
Serjeant	TAYLOR THOS.
Serjeant	POLSON JOHN
Serjeant	JARVIS JOSH. Discharged
Serjeant	MITCHELL STEPHN. Discharged
Corporal	JONES CHAS.
Corporal	WOOD ABRM.
Corporal	JOHNSON THOS. Killed in Action 18th June
Corporal	WILTSHIRE WM.
Corporal	DICKENS JOHN

Corporal	OWENS GEORGE
Drummer	FORWARD JAMES
Private	ANBURY ABRM.
Private	ALCOCK WM.
Private	ASHWORTH PETER
Private	BURRIDGE SAML.
Private	BROOKS RICHD.
Private	BURCHETT RICHD.
Private	BROWN THOS.
Private	BROOK JOHN
Private	BOOTH SAML.
Private	BOWEN GRIFFITH Discharged
Private	BAKER HUMPY.
Private	CLARK WM.
Private	CARTER WM.
Private	CARMERON MALCOLM
Private	CLAYTON JOHN
Private	COYLE MICHL.
Private	CROWTHER ROBT. Dead
Private	COWPLEY SAML.
Private	CLARKSON THOS. Killed in Action 18 June
Private	DARLEY WM.
Private	DAWSON WM.
Private	DUSON JOHN
Private	ENNS JOHN
Private	EDWARDS DAVID
Private	EVANS EDWD.
Private	EVANS JAMES
Private	FISHWICK JAMES
Private	GWYNN RICHD.
Private	GOULDSON SAML.
Private	GIDDINS JAMES
Private	GARNEN JOHN
Private	HOLMES THOS.
Private	HOLDING JOHN
Private	HARVEY THOS.
Private	HOOD ADAM Killed in Action 18th June
Private	HURST GEORGE
Private	JANSON ENOCK
Private	JONES JONATHAN
Private	JENKINS DAVID Killed in Action 16th June
Private	LEWIS JAMES
Private	MORRIS JOHN
Private	MASON ROBT.
Private	MARTIN EDWD.
Private	MILLARD WM.
Private	MITCHELL WM.
Private	NEWTON DAVID
Private	NEWMAN MARTIN
Private	NEWING THOS.
Private	NUTT GILES
Private	PORTER WM. Died of Wounds 2nd July
Private	PROCTOR JOHN
Private	PREEN JOHN
Private	PRICE JOSH.
Private	PHILPOTT JAMES
Private	PARKMAN JOHN
Private	PAVIOUR GEORGE Killed in Action 18th June
Private	QUINNEY THOS.
Private	ROSS JOHN
Private	REESE THOS.
Private	RENSHAW JOHN
Private	RILEY HUGH Killed in Action 16th June
Private	ROBARTS THOS.
Private	RANSON ADAM Died of Wounds 14th July
Private	ROBARTS WM.
Private	SERJEANT RICHD.
Private	SMITH WM.
Private	SMITH JOSH.
Private	STEVENS EDWD.
Private	SYKES JOHN
Private	SHELLARD NATHL.
Private	THOMPSON HENRY
Private	TURNER EXPERIOR
Private	TROWER JESSE
Private	TOMPKINS JAMES Killed in Action 16th June
Private	THOMPSON FRANS
Private	THORP WM. Killed in Action 18th June
Private	TAYLOR WM.
Private	WILKINSON GEORGE
Private	WOOD BENJN.
Private	WATKINS DAVID
Private	WHITTAKER SAML.
Private	WALKER WM.
Private	WHITCROFT SAML.
Private	WOOD THOS.
Private	WARD WM.
Private	YOUNG ROBT. Died of Wounds 2nd July

Lt.Colonel Sir Henry Harding's Company

Lt.& Captain	JOHNSTONE W.F. H.Gaskell's Collection 1908
Ensign	HURD SAML.
Ensign	BARRINGTON Hon.S.S.P. Killed 18th June
Serjeant	WILKINS ANDREW
Serjeant	NOBES GEORGE
Serjeant	OGDEN ALEXR.
Serjeant	BULLOCK WM.
Serjeant	POWIS JOSHUA
Serjeant	GOTHARD WM. Discharged
Corporal	BERRY WM.
Corporal	FOGG JOHN
Corporal	TEMPEST JOHN
Corporal	EVANS JAMES Died of Wounds
Drummer	STEVENS WM.
Drummer	ATKINS WM.
Private	ADAMS THOS.
Private	ADAMS WM. Killed in Action 16th June
Private	ARNOLD JOHN
Private	ALLRIGHT JOHN Absent since 18th June
Private	BAILEY WM.
Private	BROWN AIMON Absent since 18th June
Private	BRIMFIELD SAML.
Private	BRAND GEORGE
Private	BLYTHE JOHN Absent since 18th June
Private	CLARKE JOHN
Private	CLOUGH JOSH.
Private	COATES JOHN
Private	CRUMPTON DAVID
Private	CATTERNOLD JEREH Spinks List Dec. 1908
Private	COLLETT RICHD.
Private	CANNEY JOHN Died of Wounds
Private	COVENTON GEORGE
Private	DRYDEN JOHN Killed in Action 18th June
Private	DALE WM.
Private	DAVIS SAML.
Private	DIMILOS SAML.
Private	DOUGLAS ADAM
Private	DUNK JOHN
Private	ENTWISTLE JAMES
Private	ELLIS JOSEPH
Private	EDMONDS JAMES
Private	ELLIOTT GEORGE
Private	FRITH JOHN Killed in Action
Private	FLOWER JAMES
Private	FLOWER WM.
Private	FRANCIS THOS. Discharged
Private	FINNEGAN HUGH
Private	FOREMAN JOHN
Private	GREEN JNS. Senr.
Private	GREEN JNS. Junr.
Private	GRIFFITHS RICHD.
Private	HAWKINS THOS. Died of Wounds
Private	HARRISON RALPH
Private	HODGIN WM.
Private	HICKLIN CHRSITR.
Private	HARDY WM.
Private	HUGHES DAVD.
Private	INGLES GEORGE Absent since 18th June
Private	JONES JOHN
Private	KERSHAW WM.
Private	LEWIS RICHD. Missing since 18th June
Private	LEWIS JOHN Killed in Action 16th June
Private	LEWIS JENKINS
Private	MUSSEN JAMES Killed in Action 16th June
Private	McDONALD JAMES
Private	MOORE THOS.
Private	MILLS WM.
Private	MORGAN WM.
Private	NASH ROBT.
Private	NEWMAN JAS.
Private	ORMRODYE JAMES
Private	PORTER THOS.
Private	PRIME SAML.
Private	PAGE THOS.
Private	PARKS PHILLIP
Private	RHINE CHAS.
Private	RIDING JOHN
Private	SOUTHORN ROBT.
Private	STREET RICHD.
Private	SMITH WM. Snr.
Private	SMITH WM. Junr.
Private	SHARP JOHN
Private	SHAW OLIVER
Private	STEVENS THOS.
Private	SADLER SAML.
Private	SHIPLEY WM.
Private	RICHARDSON WM.

Private	THORNTON WM.
Private	TURNER JOHN
Private	WILLIAMS WATKIN Killed in Action 18th June
Private	WOODCOCK THOS. Killed in Action 18th June
Private	WHITAKER GEORGE
Private	WEBB JAMES Senr.
Private	WEBB JAMES Junr.
Private	WILSON JOHN
Private	WILLIAMS JOHN
Private	WARDLE HENRY
Private	YEOMANS JOHN

Lt.Colonel Banlay's Company

Lt.& Captain	SIMPSON JAMES
Ensign	CAMERON DONALD
Serjeant	AYLESBURY GEORGE
Serjeant	BLINKHON BENJN.
Serjeant	OAKLEY ROBERT
Serjeant	TOWNSEND GEORGE
Serjeant	HERROCKS JOHN
Corporal	STANLEY JOHN
Corporal	HOWARTH JAMES
Corporal	HYATT ROBT.
Corporal	BEYNON REID
Corporal	CURRAN CHARLES Died of his Wounds
Corporal	WARD ROBT.
Drummer	DIXON THOS.
Drummer	PARFIT EDWD.
Drummer	GUPPY JOHN
Drummer	COPPIN WM.
Private	ANDERSON ANDREW Killed in Action 16th June
Private	ASHWORTH RICHD.
Private	ABRAHAMS WM. Killed 18th June
Private	BATEMAN JOHN
Private	BUDDING WM.
Private	BROWN ANDW. Killed 18th June
Private	BRYANT WM.
Private	BAMBER JOHN
Private	BETTS ZACH. Died of his Wounds
Private	BROADBENT RICHD. Killed 16th June
Private	BATE WM. Dead
Private	BONES JAMES
Private	BATE WM. Killed 16 June
Private	BLAND THOS.
Private	BROOKS JAMES
Private	BAKER JAMES
Private	BIRD MILES
Private	BUXTON WM.
Private	CRESSWELL WM.
Private	CAFFELL WM.
Private	CLARKE JOHN Died of his wounds
Private	CLARK NOAH
Private	COLE JOHN
Private	CANSTON JAMES
Private	CRANE ABM. Killed 18 June
Private	CORNWELL SAML.
Private	CLAYSON JOHN
Private	COATS THOS.
Private	DOWN JAMES
Private	DOBBINS WM.
Private	DICKINSON SAML.
Private	DIXON JOHN Glendinnings sale April 1912
Private	DAVIS DAVID Died of his Wounds
Private	DAVIS WM.
Private	EGGLESHAW GEORGE
Private	EAMS THOS.
Private	ELLISTON SAML.
Private	FLOAT HENRY
Private	FOWDEN WM.
Private	GOODMAN WM.
Private	GARSIDE JOHN
Private	GODWARD BENJN.
Private	GALLOWAY WM.
Private	GRIFFIN THOS.
Private	HERBERT WM.
Private	HUTCHINSON HENRY
Private	HOWER WM.
Private	HOLT THOS. Killed 18th June
Private	HAMMOND JOHN
Private	HUGHES JOHN
Private	HITCHCOCK WM.
Private	HOLDING ROBT.
Private	HOPKINS WM. Killed 16 June
Private	JONES JOSHUA
Private	KENT JOHN
Private	KNIGHT JOHN
Private	KEHOE JAMES
Private	LAWRENCE JOHN Deserted
Private	LIDBETTER JOHN
Private	MEDLICOT PETER
Private	McALPIN ROBT.
Private	MARKS GEORGE
Private	MOORE CHARLES

Private	MORRIS MAXWELL
Private	NORTH HUMPY.
Private	ORD GEORGE
Private	OSBURN ABRM.
Private	PROCTOR SAML.
Private	PATTERSON WM.
Private	PAYNE WM.
Private	ROCK DAVID
Private	RALPH DANIEL
Private	SHARP ABRM.
Private	STANDAGE JAMES
Private	SIMMAWS WM.
Private	SMITH WM.
Private	SHEPPERD CHAS. Killed 16 June
Private	SEVILL JAMES
Private	SLAYNEY DANIEL
Private	SMITH JOHN
Private	THOMPSON CHAS.
Private	WARD JOHN
Private	WARREN JOSH.
Private	WESTON DAVID
Private	WALIOT GEORGE
Private	WINTERBOTTOM JAMES
Private	WEBB GEORGE
Private	WISLEY THOS. Killed 18 June

Lt.Colonel West's Company

Captain & Lt.Colonel	OYLY Sir FRANS.D. Killed 18th June
Lt.& Captain	CLIVE EDWD.
Ensign	ST.JOHN JOSH.
Ensign	TALBOT JAMES
Serjeant	FORD JOHN Killed in Action 16 June
Serjeant	LUND JOHN
Serjeant	COMMINS ROBT.
Serjeant	WENTWORTH EDWD.
Serjeant	MILLS JOSH.
Corporal	OCKENDON JOHN
Corporal	SMITH EDWD.
Corporal	SELLOWS WM.
Corporal	EASOM JOHN
Corporal	RUSH ROBERT
Corporal	TAYLOR JOHN Killed in Action 16 June
Drummer	EAKER JAMES
Drummer	BUCK EDWD.
Private	ALLCOCK JOHN
Private	BROADBENT THOS. Whitaker Collection 1908
Private	BEE GEO.
Private	BONATTA WM.
Private	BARTON GEO.
Private	BAGG JOHN
Private	BOOTY JAMES
Private	CUSSONS WM.
Private	CHATWORTHY JOHN
Private	COLQUHONE JOHN
Private	COX JOHN
Private	CUTTS GEORGE
Private	CURLE CORNS.
Private	CORDWELL BENJN.
Private	COLE THOS.
Private	DOWSETT THOS. Col.Murray's Collection
Private	DUCK THOS.
Private	DEAL SAML. Sotheby's Sale March 1911
Private	DAVID THOS.
Private	EMBLING WM.
Private	EASTGROVE THOS.
Private	ELLIS WM.
Private	FLETCHER THOS.
Private	GRIFFEN FRANS.
Private	GROUNDWELL GEORGE
Private	GREEN THOS.
Private	GRIFFITHS BENJN.
Private	GREENWOOD THOS.
Private	HARRIS JOHN
Private	JARVIS ROBT. Killed in Action 16th June
Private	JEWELL CHAS.
Private	JONES WALTER
Private	JACOBS JOHN
Private	JACKSON ABRM.
Private	JORDAN WM.
Private	KEMPTON JOHN
Private	LANKISHIRE JAMES
Private	LLOYD RICHD.
Private	MILLS JOHN
Private	MOODY THOS.
Private	MANFIELD SAML.
Private	MARSHALL JAMES
Private	MOUNTERY JOHN
Private	NICHOLLS CHAS.
Private	OVERHALL THOS.
Private	OLD JOHN
Private	OAKES JOHN

Private	OGDEN ABRM.
Private	PRICE JAMES
Private	PRICE JOHN
Private	PERRY DAVID
Private	PUMMELL SAMUEL
Private	PHILLIPS ISSAC
Private	PARTEN WM.
Private	RICHINS JOHN Col. Gaskells Sale May 1911
Private	READMORE JOSH.
Private	READMAN JOHN
Private	RODGERS JOHN
Private	ROSE HUGH
Private	RUMBOLD JOHN Died of his Wounds 5th July
Private	REEVES JOSH
Private	ROWE JOHN
Private	RIDLAR DAVID
Private	SWAIN THOS.
Private	SILDING SPENCER
Private	STUBBS JOHN
Private	SIDDINS JOHN
Private	SEATH DAVID
Private	STUMONEY JAMES
Private	SIMPSON BENJN.
Private	STEWART JOHN
Private	STEVENS NATHL. Dead
Private	STANLEY JOSHUA
Private	STEPPARD GEO.
Private	STEWART GEO.
Private	SHARP RUFAS
Private	SKIDMORE GEORGE
Private	SAPSTEAD THOS.
Private	STACEY THOS.
Private	TWYMAN JOHN
Private	TRIMB ELIJAH
Private	REWELL WM
Private	WILLIAMS JOSH.
Private	WILKINSON THOS.
Private	WILLIAMS WM.
Private	WILLISE WM.
Private	WOOD HENRY
Private	WAVER GEORGE
Private	WILLIAMS THOS.

Lt.Colonel Sir W. Burgh's Company

Lt.& Captain	LASCELLES CHAS.
Ensign	TIGHE DANIEL
S.Major	ALLEN WM.
Q.M.S.	LAWRENCE WM.
Drill Sjt.	MAIN CHAS.
Serjeant	HUTCHINS WM.
Serjeant	SHAW JNS. Discharged
Serjeant	CRANSHAW WM.
Serjeant	LEWIS WM.
Corporal	LEWES DANIEL Killed in Action 18th June
Corporal	BROWN BENJN.
Corporal	BACON JAMES Killed in Action
Corporal	LEWIS EDWD.
Corporal	PEGG JOHN
Corporal	ION THOS.
Drummer	BARRON WM.
Drummer	MERCER ROBT.
Private	ALLEN THOS. on sale at Baldwin's Feb. 1910
Private	AGER JOHN
Private	ALLEN WM.
Private	BURDOCK EDWD.
Private	BYRAM THOS.
Private	BARKER GEORGE
Private	BELL JAMES
Private	BOOTH JOHN
Private	BATTEY JAMES
Private	BEADLEY WM.
Private	BADHAM JOHN
Private	VLERK JOSH.
Private	COCKER RUBEN
Private	COX. WM.
Private	DICKENSON GEORGE
Private	DAVIS WALTER
Private	DAVIES DAVID
Private	DERRICK RICHD.
Private	ELLISON JAMES
Private	EDGE THOS.
Private	FORTH JOHN
Private	FRANCE ROBT.
Private	GREEN JAMES
Private	GREENWOOD JOSH.
Private	GRISTWOOD JOHN
Private	GILMAN STEPHEN
Private	GRIFFITHS OWEN
Private	GREEN WM.
Private	GOODLAND JAMES
Private	HALL WM.
Private	HUBBARD JOHN
Private	HUNTER JOHN Killed in Action 16th June 1815
Private	HARRIS THOS.
Private	HALLARD ROBT.

Private	HEWETT THOS.
Private	KICKEN THOS.
Private	HALT MATTW.
Private	HAZALHURST JOHN
Private	HANDSOM WM.
Private	ISTID THOS.
Private	JONES WM.
Private	JOSEPH THOS.
Private	JAMES SAML.
Private	JONES JOHN
Private	KIRTON JOHN Died of Wounds
Private	LOWE JOHN
Private	LEAVER JAMES
Private	LUDLOW GRIME
Private	MULCOCK JAMES
Private	MOYANTRAY SAML.
Private	MARTH JOHN
Private	McGREGOR JAMES
Private	MATTHEWS HENRY
Private	McDONALD PATT.
Private	NASH JOHN
Private	NUNN WM. Galway Foley Collection 1910
Private	OSBURN SAML.
Private	OLDHAM JOHN
Private	RISEBROOK RICHD.
Private	ROSS THOS.
Private	RAY GEORGE
Private	REESE DAVID
Private	ROSITER JOHN Died of Wounds
Private	STANISBY JAMES
Private	SMITH JOHN
Private	SHAW CHAS.
Private	STAINSBY SIMON
Private	THOMPSON DUGLAS
Private	TEMPEST JAMES
Private	TRESCATT WM.
Private	THRUSTON WM.
Private	TAYLOR HUMPY.
Private	TUCKER JACOB
Private	TANGE WM.
Private	TEW JOSH.
Private	WILD JOSEPH
Private	WYNN MATTW.
Private	WARMINGTON JAMES
Private	WHITE THOMAS
Private	WALKER JOSEPH
Private	WALTON JAMES
Private	WILLSON JOHN
Private	WOODALL JOHN
Private	YOUNG JOHN
Private	DIXON THOS.

* * *

LIGHT COMPANY 2nd Batt. Grenadier Guards

Lt.Colonel Pack's Company

Captain & Lt.Col.	MILNES W.H. Killed 18 June
Lt. & Captain	LUTTRELL FRANCES
Lt. & Captain	BROWN THOS. Killed 18 June
Ensign	GREVILLE ELGERNON
Serjeant	JONES JEPSEY
Serjeant	DRAFFEN JAMES Littledale sale Nov. 1910
Serjeant	CRACKNELL THOS.
Serjeant	GRIFFEN JAMES
Serjeant	HALL GEORGE
Corporal	HOGG PHILLIP
Corporal	MORGAN THOS.
Corporal	BAKER JOHN
Corporal	DOWNING GEORGE
Corporal	DICKENS GEORGE
Drummer	MARTIN STEPHENSON
Drummer	McKENZEY JOHN
Drummer	CLARK WM.
Private	AGER JOHN
Private	ALEXANDER THOS.
Private	ARISCOMB HENRY
Private	BOYTON BENJN.
Private	BISHOP JOHN
Private	BREEZE EDWD.
Private	BOTTRELL RICHD.
Private	BUCKLE ROBT.
Private	BUTCHER JOHN
Private	BAKER WM.
Private	BRYANT JOHN
Private	BARNES WM.
Private	BRIDGET JOHN
Private	COWELL JOHN
Private	COOPER JOHN
Private	CROFTS JAMES
Private	CREATON THOS.
Private	COOPER EDWD.
Private	DELBRIDGE THOS.
Private	DUDGEON EDWD.
Private	DAVIS THOS.
Private	EVANS MORGAN

Private	FEARN WM.
Private	FENCOTT WM.
Private	FORD JOHN
Private	GILES JOHN
Private	GILLETT JOSH.
Private	GOULD ISSAC
Private	GRUNER BENJN.
Private	GILBEY ROBT.
Private	HILL BENJN.
Private	HOOD JOHN
Private	HUGHES JOHN
Private	HOWARD THOS.
Private	HOLT ISSAC
Private	HORSLEY ROBT.
Private	HOLLINGSWORTH WM.
Private	HICKMAN THOS.
Private	HAMPTON GEORGE
Private	INGRHAM ROGER
Private	ISSAC JAMES
Private	JERVIS STEVEN
Private	JEPSON JOHN
Private	JONES THOS.
Private	KERSHAW JOHN
Private	KING GEORGE
Private	LUST CHAS.
Private	LEE RICHD.
Private	LONGFORD RICHD.
Private	MOORCROFT JAMES
Private	MIMMIC BERND.
Private	NAPIER WM.
Private	NEILD JOHN
Private	OSBORN ISSAC
Private	PYETT SAMUEL
Private	PERRINS SAML.
Private	PRING THOS.
Private	PATEMAN WM.
Private	POOLE JOSH.
Private	POYNTON JOHN
Private	PERRY GEORGE
Private	PERRITT JOHN
Private	RIDGEWAY WM.
Private	RALPH THOS.
Private	ROOKE JOHN
Private	ROGERS JOHN
Private	ROBERTS JOHN
Private	SHEPHERD JOHN
Private	SPINKS JOSH.
Private	SPEARS THOS.
Private	SMU JOHN
Private	SEATON THOS.
Private	SMITH JOHN
Private	SANDERS PETER
Private	SHAW WM.
Private	SMITH WM.
Private	TALBUTT WM.
Private	TERRY FRANCES
Private	TUNNICLIFFE WM.
Private	WRIGHT DANIEL
Private	WYNGATES CHRISTR.
Private	WILLIS THOS.
Private	WILLIAMS WM.
Private	WILLIAMS JACOB

Lt.Colonel Cooke's Company

Captain & Lt.Col.	COOKE R.H.
Lt & Captain	POWELL H.W.
Ensign	BATHURST Hon T.S.
Ensign	NORTON FLETCHER
S.Major	SMITH PHITHEON Discharged
Serjeant	BOOTH THOS Discharged
Serjeant	LEAKE THOS.
Serjeant	BROADMEAD RICHD.
Serjeant	BROWN WM.
Corporal	FOGG JOHN Killed in Action
Corporal	PASHEN ROBT.
Corporal	RILEY JOHN
Corporal	O'NEILL DANIEL
Corporal	LING JAMES
Corporal	HENDERSON JAMES
Drummer	MORTON JOHN
Drummer	ROGERS THOS.
Private	ADDIS WM.
Private	ANDREWS ROBT.
Private	BRANCH JAMES
Private	BLINKHORN RICHD.
Private	BESWICK RICHD.
Private	BRETT WM.
Private	BROWN ABRM.
Private	BAKES JOHN
Private	CHECK CHAS.
Private	CLARKE ROBT.
Private	CLULOW THOS.
Private	COX GEORGE
Private	DRAPER WM.
Private	DIXON JOHN
Private	DUNN ANTHONY
Private	DALTON JAMES

Private	DAKIN THOS. Discharged Sotheby's Sale March 1911
Private	DYSON JAMES
Private	DILWORTH THOS. Killed in Action
Private	DAWSON JAMES
Private	EATON BENJN.
Private	FOWELL GEORGE
Private	GATTENSBY WM.
Private	GRIMSHAW ISSAC
Private	GATON WM.
Private	GODFREY HENRY Gray Collection 1908
Private	GLADHILL WM.
Private	HARKILE JOHN
Private	HARRIS THOS.
Private	HATFIELD THOS.
Private	HURN WM.
Private	HELPS ISSAC
Private	HARFIELD WM.
Private	JONES WM.
Private	JONES JOHN
Private	KIRK THOS.
Private	KELLETT THOS. Killed in Action
Private	KEIGHLEY THOS.
Private	LEE THOS. DYSON
Private	MOORE JAMES
Private	McKEY JAMES
Private	McDONALD ROBT.
Private	MURRAY CHAS.
Private	MILLS WM.
Private	MOORHOUSE JOHN
Private	MAHON JOHN
Private	NORRIS JACOB
Private	NORTHAGE JOHN
Private	ORMROYDE JAMES
Private	OLDER JOHN
Private	OWENS OWEN
Private	PARKER ELIJAH On sale at Fenton's Nov. 1912
Private	PARSONS JOHN
Private	PILLBEAM CHAS.
Private	PEACHMAN WM. Died of Wounds
Private	RHODES WM.
Private	ROOME SAML.
Private	RAYNOR ROBERT
Private	REEVES JAMES
Private	ROGERS JOHN
Private	RUSHWORTH JAMES Killed in Action
Private	STEWART REUBEN
Private	STEWART GEORGE
Private	SMITH THOS.
Private	SANDERS WM.
Private	SMITH JOHN
Private	SPURGEON JAMES
Private	TAYLOR JAMES
Private	TUTTY THOS.
Private	TYSON CHAS.
Private	TAYLOR ALEXR.
Private	TROWER JOSEPH
Private	WHATMORE WM.
Private	WILLIS WM.
Private	WARD THOS.
Private	WILLIAMS JOHN
Private	WILLIAMS WATKIN
Private	WESTLAKE WM.
Private	WILLIAMS WM.
Private	WOOLSONCROFT JAMES
Private	WINPENNY EDWD. Killed in Action
Private	WEBB JAMES Killed in Action
Private	WALSH ROBERT

Lt.Colonel S.H. Bradford's Company

Lt. & Captain	BURGESS SOMERVILLE
Ensign	MURI GEORGE
Ensign	CROFT THOS. ELMSBY
Serjeant	GOLDSMITH SIMON
Serjeant	BIRD GEORGE
Serjeant	BRADLEY JAMES
Serjeant	BADHAM RICHD.
Corporal	HAWOOD GEORGE
Corporal	RILEY JOHN
Corporal	FLETCHER JOHN
Corporal	WARNER JOHN
Corporal	SCHOLES JOHN
Corporal	MABY JAMES
Drummer	WILLIAMS GEORGE
Private	ATKERSON JOHN
Private	ADDISON JOHN
Private	ABBOTT ELIJAH
Private	BURT RICHD.
Private	BOOTH THOS. on Sale at Spinks June 1910
Private	BAXTER ROBT.
Private	BROAD CHAS.
Private	BELLABY WM.
Private	BRIDFORD GEORGE
Private	BARNES JAMES

Private	BURKE WM.
Private	CRANE ROBERT
Private	CAUMP SAML.
Private	CLARKE JOHN
Private	COOPER AUSTIN
Private	CLARKE WM.
Private	EVANS ROGER
Private	EDWARDS JOHN
Private	EDWARDS ROBT.
Private	FISHER THOS.
Private	FROST JOHN
Private	FREEMAN HENRY
Private	GREAVES MATTW.
Private	GREAVES WM.
Private	GAND WM.
Private	GRAY JOHN
Private	GLAZIER GEORGE
Private	GREENHILL JAMES
Private	GISBOURNE THOS.
Private	GOPLING GEORGE
Private	HOWE JOSH.
Private	HULETT ABM.
Private	HUGHES JOHN
Private	HAWKINS JOHN
Private	HUNT WM.
Private	HAYWOOD THOS.
Private	HALL WM.
Private	HOY JOHN
Private	HARDING THOS.
Private	HOLDING WM.
Private	HORNEYGOLD ROBERT
Private	ISLEY THOS.
Private	JONES SAML.
Private	JAMES JAMES
Private	KENT THOS.
Private	LOCK JAMES
Private	LEE PATK.
Private	LEWIS THOS.
Private	LOWE PHILLIP
Private	MILLER JOHN
Private	MAYCOCK GEORGE
Private	MORRELL WM.
Private	NICE JOHN
Private	NEWTON JOHN
Private	OSBOURNE EDWD.
Private	OSBORNE FRANCES
Private	O'BRYAN MARTIN
Private	PAYNE JAMES
Private	PIMM WM.
Private	PEACOCK THOS.
Private	REED JOHN
Private	REED JOSEPH
Private	ROBSON CLEMENT
Private	ROOME JOSEPH
Private	ROUNDSLOW JESSE
Private	ROOKES JOHN
Private	RUMBALL THOS.
Private	SPICER EDWARD Cheylesmore Collection 1908
Private	SUTCLIFF JOHN
Private	STILLS JOHN
Private	SIMPKINS JOHN
Private	SWINDLE JOHN
Private	SPRIGGS WM.
Private	STRUSE JOHN
Private	SUTHERLAND THOS.
Private	TETLEY ROBT.
Private	THOMPSON JAMES
Private	TONGUE JAMES
Private	VAUGHAN JAMES
Private	WILLIAMS EDWD.
Private	WILLIAMS EDWD.
Private	WORSLEY WM.
Private	WRIGHT RICHD.
Private	WILSON SAML.
Private	WARD THOS.
Private	WORD THOS.
Private	WAY JAMES
Private	WATKINS THOS.
Private	WALTON GEORGE

<u>Lt.Colonel Colquett's Company</u>

Captain & Lt.Colonel	COLQUETT GOODWIN
Ensign	FLUDGER GEORGE
Ensign	FINLING W.F.
Serjeant	POXON PETER
Serjeant	JONES CHARLES
Serjeant	EDGE GEORGE
Serjeant	CHANDLER JOHN
Serjeant	HOLMES THOS.
Serjeant	JONES JOHN Discharged
Corporal	COATES GEORGE
Corporal	COURT THOS. Glendinnings sale Jan. 1911
Corporal	OAKES SAML.
Corporal	BOLENTINE ROBT. Died 20 June
Corporal	HALL JOHN
Drummer	PERRY JAMES

Drummer	SANDERSON THOS.
Private	ANETT SAML.
Private	BOLTON HENRY Killed in Action 18 June
Private	BOSWELL WM.
Private	BREWER WM.
Private	BEEK WM.
Private	BINNS JAMES
Private	BELL GEORGE
Private	BARLOW THOS.
Private	BUNGESS MATTW.
Private	BENTON WM.
Private	BERRY JOHN
Private	CRYER WM.
Private	CLARKSON JOHN
Private	CLARKE ELIJAH
Private	CANN EDWD. Discharged
Private	CATBULL ISSAC
Private	CARTMELL RICHD. Died 5th Aug.
Private	COOKE JOHN Died 1st Aug.
Private	DENNING FRANCIS
Private	DOW JOHN
Private	DEAN WM.
Private	DERRICK JAMES
Private	EDMONDS EDMON Killed in Action 16th June
Private	EXON JOHN
Private	FOOTER STEPHEN
Private	FRYER WM.
Private	FOULSTON JOHN
Private	GUTTRIDGE JOHN Killed in Action 18th June
Private	GREENAWAY JOHN
Private	HINES SAMUEL
Private	HASLER RICHD.
Private	HIBELL SAML.
Private	HUDSON JOHN
Private	HILL JAMES
Private	HAINES JOHN
Private	HEATH JOHN
Private	HARRIS GEORGE
Private	JONES JOHN
Private	JONES OWEN
Private	JINKS EDWD.
Private	JONES JAMES
Private	JONES JINKIN
Private	KNIGHTS DANIEL Watters Sale June 1913
Private	KING WM. Killed in Action 16th June
Private	KENNARDS WM.
Private	KING JAMES
Private	KERRIDGE WM.
Private	LANE JOHN
Private	LINLEY THOS.
Private	McJAMES JOHN
Private	MARTING HENRY
Private	MARSH JOHN
Private	MILLINGTON JOHN
Private	MOORE CHAS.
Private	MAXWELL WM.
Private	MACKETTS JAMES Discharged
Private	MARSHALL JAMES
Private	MARSON JOHN
Private	MORTIMORE WM.
Private	OWEN JOHN
Private	PURR JOHN
Private	PUMELL PETER
Private	PURSLOW JAMES
Private	PICKELLS BENJN.
Private	ROBINSON JONATHAN
Private	RIDING WM.
Private	RICH JOHN Killed in Action 18th June
Private	REYNOLDS JOHN
Private	RICHARDS RICHARD
Private	SPEAT JOHN
Private	SAILS WM.
Private	SHIPPARD FRANCIS Killed in Action 18th June
Private	SKELLY GEORGE
Private	SNAPE JOHN
Private	TOLLEY HUGH
Private	TOWNSEND LUKE
Private	TOWNSEND THOS Deserted
Private	TILLER HENRY
Private	WILD JOHN
Private	WAYNER HENRY
Private	WOOD PETER
Private	WILD WM.
Private	WILLES WM.
Private	WILLERBY JAMES
Private	WALLACE JAMES
Private	WILLIAMS JOHN
Private	WALKER JOHN

Lt.Colonel Sir Noel Hill's Company

Lt.& Captain	NIXON JAMES
Ensign	JACOB G.T.
Ensign	LASCELLES HENRY

Serjeant	CLARKE ISSAC
Serjeant	MACKAY NEIL
Serjeant	ADDISON JAMES
Serjeant	GREEN JOSEPH Wounded 18th June 1815
Serjeant	BRAMMAN WM.
Serjeant	BARRON JOHN
Corporal	ELLOITT JOHN Wounded 18th June 1815
Corporal	CROSSLEY JOHN Wounded 18th June 1815
Corporal	LOVELL WM. Curis Club Oct. 1908
Corporal	WELLS JOHN
Corporal	BOOTH JOHN
Corporal	HARTLEY EDWD. Wounded 18th June 1815
Drummer	PALMER JOHN Fife Major Wounded 18th June 1815
Drummer	FERGUSON JOHN
Private	BELSTON JOHN
Private	BURCHAM JOSEPH
Private	BRISTOW JAMES
Private	BUCK JOHN Wounded 18th June 1815
Private	BAILEY 1st JOHN
Private	BAILEY 2nd JOHN
Private	BULLOUGH ROBT.
Private	BUCHANNAN THOS. Wounded 18th June 1815
Private	BOWLING THOS.
Private	BARRINGTON DANIEL
Private	BLACKBURN JOHN
Private	BUTLER JOHN
Private	BROOKS RICHD.
Private	BANNISTER JOHN Dead 2nd Aug. 1815
Private	CLARKE DANIEL
Private	CARTWRIGHT GEORGE
Private	COLLETT JAMES Wounded 16th June
Private	CRIBB JOHN Wounded 16th June 1815
Private	COCKRANE PHILLIP
Private	CLANNER WM. Died of Wounds 29th June 1815
Private	DAVIS EDWD. Wounded 18th June 1815
Private	DANKS THOS.
Private	DUMBAR GEORGE
Private	DAVEY JAMES
Private	EDWARDS ROLAND Wounded 18th June 1815
Private	ELLWOOD JOHN
Private	FOSTER HENRY Killed in Action 16th June 1815
Private	GOODWIN JAMES
Private	GOODWIN WM.
Private	GRIFFIN THOS.
Private	GLADE WM.
Private	GREENWOOD WM.
Private	HINDLE NICHS.
Private	HAYTOR THOS.
Private	HUBBARD JAMES
Private	HULSE JNS. Wounded 18th June 1815
Private	HEATH JUNE Wounded 16th June 1815
Private	HASLUM JOHN
Private	HAWKSE GEORGE Wounded 18th June 1815
Private	HOOPER JOHN
Private	ISSACSON ROBT. Wounded 18th June 1815
Private	JONES THOS.
Private	JONES PETER Wounded 18th June 1815
Private	JONES ABEL
Private	JENKS THOS.
Private	KEATLEY JOHN
Private	LATHAM ROBT.
Private	LOWE THOS.
Private	LUCAS WM.
Private	LONE JOHN Wounded 18th June 1815
Private	LAMB WM.
Private	MOSS ROBT.
Private	McCUE BERND. Wounded 18th June 1815
Private	MAY JOHN
Private	MOXEY JOHN
Private	MUNRO JAMES
Private	MORGAN GEORGE
Private	NORMAN JOHN
Private	NORTON GEORGE Wounded 18th June 1815
Private	OSBOURNE RICHD. Wounded 16th June 1815
Private	PINHALL THOS.
Private	PERRY WM.
Private	WILSON ANDW.
Private	ROBERTS CHAS.
Private	REDGREAVES JAMES
Private	REDWOOD JAMES
Private	ROBERTSHAW JAMES

Private	SUGDEN BENJ.
Private	SMITH GEORGE
Private	SAWYERS WM.
Private	SUFFOLK WM. Payne Collection 1911
Private	STAINES JAMES
Private	SHOPTON WM.
Private	SHEPPARD GEORGE Killed in Action 18th June 1815
Private	THOMAS SETH
Private	THOMAS WM. Wounded 18th June 1815
Private	THOMAS EVAN Wounded 18th June 1815
Private	TANNER THOS. Wounded 16th June 1815
Private	TODD JOHN Wounded 18th June 1815
Private	VICKARS JOHN
Private	WRIGHT JOSEPH
Private	WHITEFOOT JAMES
Private	WELLING HENRY
Private	WOOTTON CHAS.
Private	WILLIAMS JAMES Killed in Action 1815
Private	WOODHAM JAMES

* * *

3rd BATTN. GRENADIER REGT.FOOT GUARDS

Lt.Colonel Jones Company

Captain	BOLDERS
Captain	DAVIES
Ensign	GRONOW
Serjeant	BACK JAMES
Serjeant	MIDDLEDITCH WM.
Serjeant	BROWN JERH.
Serjeant	HALL ROBT.
Serjeant	ROWLAN JOHN Whitaker Collection 1908
Corporal	EVANS THOS.
Corporal	IDLE CHAS.
Corporal	MURRY GEORGE
Corporal	LEIGHTON WM.
Corporal	SUTCLIFFE ROBT.
Drummer	GOWEN WM.
Private	ANCHORS JAMES
Private	ANDREWS JOHN
Private	ANDERSON JNS.
Private	BENTLEY ABRM.
Private	BLAKE JAMES Col.Murray's Collection
Private	BOWDLER JNS.
Private	BUXTON HENRY
Private	BOWKER WM.
Private	BARKER JNS. Wounded 18th June not heard of since.
Private	COLLINS RICHD.
Private	CLARKE JONAN.
Private	CHEDWICK THOS.
Private	CHEDWICK WM.
Private	CLOUGH STEVEN Wounded 18th June not heard of since
Private	CRIDDLE THOS.
Private	COOK NATHL.
Private	DUFTON JAMES
Private	DEAN STEVEN
Private	DERWIN ISSAC Wounded 18th June not heard of since
Private	DOWLING WM. Wounded 18th June not heard of since
Private	DAVIS SAML.
Private	DAVIS HENRY
Private	ELLEY JNS.
Private	FAX DAVID
Private	FLOWERS JOHN
Private	FISHER JOSEPH
Private	GORDON JAMES
Private	GIBBONS THOS.
Private	GREENSIDE GEO.
Private	GILL GEO.
Private	GREY WM.
Private	HORRAX JNS.
Private	HOLMS THOS.
Private	HILTON MOSES Wounded 18th June not heard of since
Private	HUGHES JOHN
Private	HUGHES GRIFFITHS
Private	HARVEY JAMES
Private	HURSTHOUSE EDWD.
Private	HURST SIMON
Private	JONES THOS.
Private	JONES DAVID
Private	JOHNSON RICHD.
Private	JOHNSON THOS.
Private	LONG JOHN
Private	LONGFORD JOHN
Private	LEWIS THOS.
Private	LLOYD SIMON
Private	MORLEY WM.
Private	MOORE JAMES
Private	MCEWEN EDWD.

Private	MORGAN JAMES
Private	MIDDAWS WM.
Private	MESSINGER WM.
Private	MASSEY ROBT.
Private	OGDEN JOHN
Private	OWEN THOS.
Private	NICHOLDS WM.
Private	PHITHAIN JAMES
Private	PATEFIELD SAML.
Private	PINK GEO.
Private	POLTON JOHN
Private	POLLMAN JOHN
Private	PATTERSON JOSEPH
Private	PICKLES JAMES Died 12th Dec. 1815
Private	ROBERTS ROBERT
Private	REAVES ISSAC
Private	RANDALL THOS.
Private	ROGERS JOSEPH
Private	SHEWARD THOS.
Private	SLATER JOHN
Private	SMITH WM.
Private	SMITH GEORGE
Private	SHUEMAN ANTHY.
Private	STACKWOOD WM. Wounded 18 June not heard of since
Private	SHEAD WM.
Private	SPECKMAN THOS.
Private	TRECKLEY THOS.
Private	TAYLOR JOHN
Private	TRUEMAN JOHN
Private	WHITACES JAMES
Private	WALTERS JAMES
Private	WALKER JOHN
Corporal	NICHOLD WM. Killed 18th June
Private	RULE THOS. Killed 18 June
Private	MUSGROVE ROBT. Killed 18th June
Private	HAMSON PETER Died of Wounds 24 June
Private	ROEBUCK BENJN. Died of Wounds 24 July
Private	YATES BENJN. Died of Wounds 27 July
Private	WOOD JNS Died of Wounds 3rd Aug.
Private	FORLING Orr.M. Died of Wounds 4th Aug.
Private	TURNER JOHN Belonged 1st Batt & att.to Genl.Lambert & has never been ret. until now
Private	BUCKLEY WM.

Lt.Colonel Edward Staples Company

Lt.Colonel	STABLES EDWD. Died of Wounds 19th June
Captain	ADAIR ROBT. Died of Wounds 19th June
Ensign	BATTY ROBT.
Ensign	DIRON J.P.
Serjeant	BELL JOHN
Serjeant	SLATER WM.
Serjeant	SANDROCK JOHN
Serjeant	CLARK PHILIP
Serjeant	THOMAS WM. Died 12 July
Corporal	VICKERS WM.
Corporal	THORNHILL WM. Killed in Action 18 June
Corporal	PERRY GRIFFITHS
Corporal	SMITH THOS.
Corporal	WORTHINGTON JOHN Glendinnings sale Jan. 1909 33/-
Drummer	FOX ANDW.
Drummer	KING LEWIS
Private	ADDIS FRANCIS
Private	ATKINSON JAMES
Private	ARTHUR WM.
Private	ALDING THOS.
Private	BUNN CHAS.
Private	BARRANCE WM.
Private	BROWN THOS.
Private	BUCK JAMES
Private	BRANDIDGE WM.
Private	BENNETT RICHD.
Private	BAUME JOHN
Private	BOYLE JOHN Killed in Action 18th June
Private	BUTTREY THOS.
Private	BURNE GEO.
Private	BULL JOHN
Private	BARNETT THOS. Killed in Action 18 June
Private	BURTON A.
Private	CARTER WM. Died 19 June 1815
Private	CURTIS GEO. Killed in Action 16th June
Private	CHRISTION THOS.
Private	COMPTON JOHN
Private	CRAWFORD WM.
Private	DAVIS PENSH.
Private	DENBY JOHN
Private	EDWARDS JOHN
Private	EVANS EDWD.
Private	FINLOW JAMES Died 24 July
Private	GELDING EDWD.

Private	GREEN THOS.
Private	GREEN DANIEL
Private	GOODHEAD LUKE
Private	GREY FRANCIS Died 19 June
Private	HOLEWELL WM.
Private	HYDE ROBT.
Private	HOGARTH JOHN
Private	HUNT WM.
Private	HERBERT THOS.
Private	HIBLE JOHN Killed in Action 18th June
Private	HARRISON EDWD.
Private	HERETAGE JOHN Killed in Action 18th June
Private	HOWARD ABRM.
Private	JONES THOS.
Private	JONES JOHN
Private	JINKINS MATTW. Died 26 Aug.
Private	JARSHAM THOS.
Private	KINCH JNS.
Private	LEWORTHY JOHN
Private	MORGAN THOS.
Private	MORGAN RICHD. Died 18 June of Wounds
Private	MITCHELL JOHN
Private	MAGALL JOHN
Private	MAHON FRANCIS Cheylesmore Collection 1908
Private	McCARRIS HENRY
Private	MAYFIELD JOHN
Private	MORLEY HENRY On sale at Speaks June 1910
Private	MOORE FRANCIS
Private	MADDOX THOS.
Private	McKINLEY JOHN
Private	NELSON WM.
Private	NELSON THOS.
Private	NEVETT JOHN
Private	OWENS THOS.
Private	PHILLIPS JOHN
Private	PENNEY THOS.
Private	PERNELL JOHN
Private	PRIDE ALEXR.
Private	PORTER EDWD.
Private	ROGERS SAML.
Private	RILEY TOBIAN
Private	ROBERTS ROBERT
Private	SIMMONDS JAMES
Private	SMITH SAML.
Private	SMITH PETER
Private	SAWFORD JOHN
Private	SWIFT JOHN
Private	SIMPSON HENRY
Private	STEVENS THOS. Died 23 July
Private	STEEL JOHN
Private	SHEPPARD THOS.
Private	SMIDLEY BENJN.
Private	SWINDALL SAML.
Private	SLATER SAML.
Private	STEWART DANL.
Private	STEVINSON BARNEY.
Private	TURVEY WM.
Private	THOMAS WM.
Private	TAYLOR JAS. Killed in Action 16th June
Private	WEST EDWD.
Private	WALKER JNS.
Private	WILLIAMS WM.
Private	REED WM.
Private	FOUNTON WM.
Private	DEWER ROBT. Killed in Action 18th June
Private	DAWSON WM. Killed in Action 18th June

<u>Lt.Colonel Miller's Company</u>

Lt.Colonel & Captain	MILLER W.
Lieutenant & Major	CLEMENTS Hon.ROBT.
Ensign	EDGECOMBE E.A.
Ensign	HAY L.J.
Serjeant	WOOD CHAS.
Serjeant	THEOBALD JOHN
Serjeant	McDONALD RONALD
Serjeant	ROUTLEDGE JOSH.
Serjeant	WILSON NATHL. Killed in Action 18 June
Corporal	HOYLES JOHN
Corporal	HARMOND WM.
Corporal	TURNER JOHN Killed 18 June
Corporal	DONNALLY THOS.
Corporal	GRANT CHAS.
Corporal	HAY PETER
Drummer	BLAKE WM.
Drummer	KINGHT JOHN
Private	ANTHONY EDWD.
Private	ABEL SAML.
Private	BRIERLY HENRY
Private	BURKE CHAS.
Private	BODMAN GEORGE Day Sale April 1910
Private	BROWN SAML.
Private	BATEMAN ROBT.

Private	BISSHOP THOS.
Private	BARBER JOHN
Private	COWLEY JOHN
Private	COLDRICK WM.
Private	CATCHPOLE JOHN
Private	CATTIMORE JAMES
Private	CLATRAM SAML.
Private	CORNWAITE JAMES Killed in Action 18 June
Private	CAMORAN JOHN
Private	CRUTCHLEY JOHN
Private	COWTHERN ROBT.
Private	CLARKE THOS.
Private	COLLINS SEVIL
Private	COBLEY ENCEBAS
Private	COLES JOHN
Private	DAVIES WM.
Private	DAVIES GEORGE
Private	DAVIES THOS.
Private	DIVAL WM.
Private	DAVIDSON ALEXR.
Private	DOGMORE THOS.
Private	DALLAS JOHN
Private	DALEY JAMES
Private	McDUGGLE JOHN
Private	DAWSON WM.
Private	HOORD SAML.
Private	GRIST WM.
Private	GOUKROGER MICHL.
Private	GRUNDY JOSH.
Private	GREEN WM.
Private	GREGORY RICHD.
Private	GRIFFITH JOHN
Private	GRAHAM WM. Watters sale June 1913
Private	HUNTLEY CHAS.
Private	HOYLE M.DUK.
Private	HOWARTH WM.
Private	HALL THOS.
Private	HAWKINS WM.
Private	HUTCHINSON JAMES
Private	HARTWELL THOS.
Private	HILL GEORGE
Private	JACKSON WM.
Private	JUBY THOS.
Private	JOHN WM.
Private	JONES THOS.
Private	JONES GEO. Killed in Action 18 June
Private	JENNINGS JOSH.
Private	JESSOP WALTER
Private	KATES SAML.
Private	KING THOS. Payne Collection 1911
Private	LATHWOOD RICHD. Killed 18 June
Private	LADDS THOS.
Private	LAWRENCE THOS.
Private	MORRIS WM.
Private	McINTOSH ALEXR.
Private	MARTIN WM.
Private	NEWLAND JOHN
Private	NEWLAND WM.
Private	OWEN EVAN
Private	PHILLIPS THOS.
Private	POTHERN JOHN
Private	PEARCE JOSH.
Private	PRITCHARD JOHN Killed 18 June
Private	PERRY HUGH
Private	RATCLIFF BART.
Private	ROBERTS HENRY
Private	ROBERTS JOHN
Private	RIPPINGALE WM. Killed 18 June
Private	REYLANCE WM.
Private	REECE JOSH.
Private	SMITH RICHD.
Private	SMITH JOSH.
Private	STAFFORD THOS.
Private	SADLER BARNY.
Private	SHEDDEN JOHN Killed 18 June
Private	STOCK GREGORY
Private	SWAN HENRY
Private	SCERSTON THOS.
Private	SHORE JOHN
Private	THOMAS BENJN. Killed 18 June
Private	TAYLOR SAML.
Private	TAYLOR WM.
Private	WILLIAMSON JOHN Died 10 Jan 1816
Private	WOOD JOHN
Private	WORMALD JOSH.
Private	WILSON GIDIAN
Private	WRIGHT JAMES
Private	YOUNG JAMES

Lt.Colonel Fead's Company

Lt.Colonel	FEAD GEORGE
Ensign	MASTERS RICHD. Valued for Ins.at NX for Stradling Cirencester 15/2/66
Ensign	BUTLER JAMES
Serjeant	RIPPIN JAMES

Serjeant	BAULCOTT JOSH.	Private	GOULD RAL.
Serjeant	MUNRO DANIEL	Private	HALL JOHN
Serjeant	CARTER JOHN	Private	HOSIE ROBT.
Serjeant	CREWS WM. Killed 16 June	Private	HEATH THOS. Killed 18 June
Corporal	MULLINER RALPH	Private	HEMSLEY WM. Wounded not since heard of.
Corporal	GREGORY PAUL Killed 16 June	Private	HANDFORD JAMES
Corporal	WALSH WM.	Private	HALES WM.
Corporal	NEWLAND JOHN	Private	HARRISON RICHD.
Corporal	MURRY WM. Killed 18 June	Private	HILL JNS.
Corporal	HAYWOOD THOS. Killed 18 June	Private	HURD JNS.
Drummer	HURTH WM.	Private	HOWE ROBT. Killed 18 June
Drummer	BEVINGTON WM.	Private	HILLIER JAMES
Private	ASHER WM. Killed 18 June	Private	HATFIELD WM.
Private	ASHTON JOSH.	Private	JENKINS JAMES
Private	ASHTON THOS.	Private	JENKINS THOS.
Private	BULLIMAN EDWD.	Private	JANNINGS ROBT.
Private	BRYANT JAS.	Private	JONES RICHD.
Private	BROADHURST THOS.	Private	KET RICHD. Wounded not since heard of.
Private	BUCKLEY WM.	Private	KIRK ROBT.
Private	BROWN SAML.	Private	KEYWORTH JAMES
Private	BENTLEY JAMES	Private	LEEPER JNS.
Private	BATHELOR JNS.	Private	LOYD WM.
Private	BYERS JAMES Died of Wounds	Private	LEES PETER
Private	BROADFOOT WM.	Private	LITTLE JAMES
Private	BUXTON JAS.	Private	LEE GEORGE
Private	BATRAM THOS.	Private	LAWS GEORGE
Private	BAGSHAW WM.	Private	LACEY JAMES
Private	COTTON JAMES	Private	MARTIN SAMUEL
Private	CARTER JOHN	Private	MITCHELL JNS.
Private	CANEY THOS.	Private	McCULLUM JNS.
Private	CLAY JNS.	Private	NUTTER JNS. Killed 18 June
Private	COPE JOSH. Wounded not since heard of.	Private	NETHERTON JNS.
Private	CARTWRIGHT JOHN	Private	OLIVER JNS.
Private	CHOWN THOS.	Private	OLDHAM WM. Killed 18 June
Private	DOILL BART. Killed 16 June	Private	PEGG JNS.
Private	DENHAM JAMES	Private	PAIR FREDK.
Private	DARBY ROBT.	Private	PRINCE EDWD.
Private	DAINTON JOHN	Private	PROUTE RICHD.
Private	DAVIS ANTHONY	Private	RHODES GEORGE
Private	DEDHAM JOHN	Private	ROBERTS JOSH.
Private	DALE GEORGE	Private	ROBERTS WM.
Private	EVENS THOS.	Private	ROYAL WM.
Private	EDWARDS JNS.	Private	RIGBY JNS.
Private	FRY JNS.	Private	STILES JOSH.
Private	FRANCHAM WM.	Private	SAWKINS JNS. Killed 18 June
Private	GROOM JOHN	Private	SUNDERLAND JNS Glendinnings Sale Oct. 1913 2-2-0
Private	GAYING STEPHEN	Private	STITT ANDREW
Private	GADSBY RICHD.		

Private	STANFIELD JNS.
Private	SMITH BEN. Wounded not since heard of
Private	STEVENSON JOHN
Private	SUFFOLK ROGER
Private	THOMAS DAVID
Private	WOODWARD JNS.
Private	WRIGHT JNS.
Private	WARREN WM.

Lt.Colonel Reeve's Company

Lt.Colonel	REEVES JNS.
Captain	HAY LORD JAMES
Lieutenant	SWINBURNE THOS.
Lieutenant	ERSKINE WM.
Serjeant	MAIN CHRISTR.
Serjeant	BROOKS JNS.
Serjeant	ROGERS WM.
Serjeant	PEARCE SAML.
Serjeant	FOORYAN JNS. on sale at Baldwins July 1912
Serjeant	WILLIAMSON JAS.
Corporal	HESKETH THOS.
Corporal	REEVES JAMES
Corporal	SNEAD JNS. Sick, Brussels
Corporal	ALSTON ALEXR Needes June 1908
Corporal	MOSS JOHN
Drummer	McCARTY JNS.
Drummer	CROOK WM.
Private	ANKLAND EDWD.
Private	ARNOLD WM.
Private	BAYNON HENRY
Private	BOON WM.
Private	BEAZLEY WM.
Private	BEARD JNS.
Private	BOARDMAN EDWD.
Private	BARTLETT JNS.
Private	BEEN RICHD.
Private	BONDEN WM.
Private	BRUZE SAML. Wounded 16 June not since heard of.
Private	BALL THOS.
Private	BRIDGE JNS.
Private	CLARK JNS.
Private	CUMMINS ALEXR.
Private	CADDOCK JOB.
Private	CONNACHER JNS.
Private	COURTNEY WM.
Private	CURTIS WM.
Private	DEAKIN JOHN
Private	DALE JNS.
Private	EVANS EVAN
Private	EMMETT BENJN.
Private	FORT JAMES
Private	FURNACE COATHS.
Private	GRIBBLE JAMES
Private	GRAVES JAMES
Private	GULLICK JOHN
Private	GREY JNS.
Private	GRIFFITHS RICHD.
Private	GOODWIN WM.
Private	HILDITCH WM.
Private	HAWES JNS.
Private	HAYE JAS.
Private	HUSCROFT JNS.
Private	HUGHES JAS.
Private	HUTCHINSON THOS.
Private	HARGRAVES WM.
Private	HILL HENRY
Private	ISRAELL DAVID
Private	ILETT GEORGE
Private	JOHNSON JOHN
Private	JONES ROBT. sick at Brussels
Private	JONES JNS.
Private	JONES WM.
Private	JOHNSON WM.
Private	KEEN GEO.
Private	KENDALL THOS.
Private	KIRK JAS.
Private	LUMLEY JAS.
Private	LANGSHAW JOSH.
Private	MITCHELL WM.SENR.
Private	MITCHELL WM. JUNR.
Private	MATES PETER
Private	MARSDEN SAML.
Private	MANSFIELD JAS.
Private	MAGGS SILAS
Private	MARSDEN BENJN.
Private	MITCHELL SAML.
Private	ORRY ROBT.
Private	PUGH HUGH
Private	PINCHBACK THOS.
Private	PICKLES JNS.
Private	PARROTT RICHD.
Private	PUZZEY JAMES
Private	RUSSELL WM.
Private	ROBINSON THOS.
Private	ROBERTS JNS.
Private	ROEBUCK GEO.
Private	ROTHWELL ROBT.
Private	SACKLEY JAMES

Private	SALTERS JNS. Puttick & Simpsons sale Feb. 1910
Private	STRUTTON THOS.
Private	SHARPELL JAMES
Private	SUMMERS ZEBIN. Sotheby's sale March 1911
Private	TATLER ABRM.
Private	TATLER GEORGE
Private	TURNER JNS. Glendinnings sale March 1912
Private	TOMLINSON JNS.
Private	TAYLOR JNS.
Private	WALTON THOS.
Private	WAKELAND CHAS.
Private	WALTERS SAML. Died 13 Nov. 1815
Private	WILLIAMSON WM.
Private	WILLSON WM.
Private	WINTERBOTHAM JNS.
Private	WITCRAFT JNS.
Private	WILLIAMS ROBT.
Private	WARBURTON PETER
Private	WATERFALL JAS.
Private	WIFFEN WM.
Private	YOXALL JNS.
Private	DUNN THOS. Killed 16 June
Private	LOCKWOOD JNS Wounded since dead
Private	GOODWIN THS. Wounded since dead

Lt.Colonel Charles Thomas's Company

Lt.Colonel	THONAS CHAS. Killed 18 June
Bde.Major	GUNTHORPE JAS.
Captain	CAMERON H.C.
Ensign	BRUCE ROBT.
Serjeant	WISEMAN WM.
Serjeant	BERLEY JOHN
Serjeant	BRADBURN THOS.
Serjeant	HODGEON THOS.
Serjeant	BARLOW SAML.
Corporal	BERTHENSHAW BENJN.
Corporal	WILSON DAVID
Corporal	SNELLING THOS.
Corporal	WRIGHT JNS.
Corporal	HUNTINGTON WM. Killed 16th June
Corporal	LOWTHER JNS. Killed 18th June
Drummer	MONTGOMERIE WM.
Drummer	TAYLOR CHAS.
Drummer	PEAD WM.
Drummer	LESTER JNS.
Private	ALLEN JAS. Phillips Sale
Private	ALLEN ROBT.
Private	ANDERTON WM. Galway Foley Collection 1910
Private	ASHTON THOS.
Private	ASHLEY JNS.
Private	BARTLETT WM.
Private	BROWN JOSH Died 26th Aug.1815
Private	BRAITHWAITE THOS.
Private	BULLEVENT JNS.
Private	BOWYER JAMES
Private	BROWN ANDREW
Private	BEATSON JEREH.
Private	BURBRIDGE PETER
Private	BOWER PAUL
Private	CARTER JNS.
Private	COOKE THOS.
Private	COOMBE WM.
Private	COCKETT THOS. Missing
Private	CHAPMAN JAS.
Private	CHRISTIE THOS.
Private	COOPER RICHD.
Private	CORDALL JAS.
Private	COLLIER WM. Missing
Private	DIXON GEORGE
Private	DANNIALS MORGAN Missing
Private	DAVIS DAVID
Private	DICKINSON STEPH.
Private	EVANS THOS.
Private	EVANS JNS.
Private	FARRELL JNS.
Private	FARDLEY ANDW.
Private	FEALLY JNS.
Private	GOTTS JAMES
Private	GREENWOOD RICHD.
Private	HUTLEY HENRY
Private	HODSKINSON THOS.
Private	HALW WM.
Private	HEATH THOS.
Private	HUBBARD WM.
Private	JENKINSON JNS.
Private	JONES DAVID
Private	JONES WM.
Private	JONES JOSA.
Private	JOHNSON BENJN.
Private	JOHNSON GEORGE
Private	KEALING JNS.

Private	KINGSTON RICHD.
Private	LEWIS WM.
Private	MITCHELL JNS.
Private	MESEER WM.
Private	MORTERUM THOS.
Private	MOORE WM.
Private	MARRIOTT WM.
Private	MORTEMORE JNS.
Private	MURREY JAS.
Private	NORTON JNS.
Private	NESBY WM.
Private	NEWTON EDWD.
Private	PAINTER DAVID
Private	PALMER SAML.
Private	PENNEY WM.
Private	RODGERS JAS.
Private	REECE JAS.
Private	RAMSDEN JAS.
Private	SHIPLEY JAS.
Private	SUTTON JNS.
Private	SMITH JOSH.
Private	SKELTON CHRISTR.
Private	SOUTHERN JAS.
Private	STOKES JOSH.
Private	TRIMMELL JAS.
Private	THOMAS SAML.
Private	WILSON DANIEL
Private	WILSON JEREH.
Private	WILLIAMS JNS.
Private	WALKER THOS.
Private	WHITE HENRY Missing
Private	WELLS JNS. Payne Collection 1911
Private	WRIGHT SAML.
Private	WYBURY WM.
Private	WEBSTER JOHN
Private	BRABLE ROBT. Killed 16th June
Private	ETHERINGTON EDWD. Killed 16th June
Private	CHRISTIAN SYMN. Killed 18th June
Private	FARRANCE JNS. Killed 18th June
Private	HICKS JNS. Killed 18th June
Private	JAMES THOS. Killed 18th June
Private	JOHNSON RICHD. Killed 18th June
Private	PEARSON WM. Killed 18th June
Private	PROTHERO JAS. Killed 18th June
Private	PAIN WM. Killed 18th June
Private	SMITH FRANS. Killed 18th June
Private	SWAFFORD DANIEL Died 16th July
Private	SMITH GEORGE Died 15th July
Private	SWEEPER JNS. Died 9th July
Private	PETTY JNS. Died 2nd July
Private	WALTERS JOSH Died 3rd Aug.

<u>Lt.Colonel Henry D. Oyly's Company</u>

Lt.Colonel	D.OYLY HENRY
Ensign	PARDOE EDWD Killed 18th July
Serjeant	TENNANT WM.
Serjeant	BOULEOTT WM. Wounded not since heard of.
Serjeant	PARSONS TIMY.
Serjeant	APPLETON PETER
Corporal	WORSICK JAMES
Corporal	MARSHAM ROBT.
Corporal	BALDWIN DANIEL
Corporal	BAYLIS PETER Glendinning's sale Oct.1913 1-1-0
Corporal	HARDY LUKE
Drummer	COLLINS MICHL.
Drummer	GOTTS JOHN
Drummer	SMITH WM.
Private	ABLE THOS. Wounded not since heard of.
Private	ALSOP JOHN
Private	BEADLE SAML.
Private	BRAGGINS JOSH.
Private	BARBER EDWD.
Private	BRIGHT JOHN
Private	BALES GEORGE
Private	BURTON JOSH.
Private	BERRY HENRY
Private	BROTHERS THOS.
Private	BURKE JOHN
Private	BELL JOHN
Private	BARRETT THOS. Died 28th June
Private	BANTLEY ELY.
Private	COWBURN JOSH.
Private	CLARKE WM.
Private	CHITTY WM.
Private	CORNICK WM.
Private	CHARLY JAMES
Private	COOKE JONA. Sotheby's sale Nov. 1909
Private	COCKRAM GEORGE
Private	CALWELL THOS.

Private	CLARKE JOHN
Private	CAMPBELL WM.
Private	CALLANHILL THOS.
Private	DAY WM.
Private	DAVIS JAMES
Private	DIVINE JOHN
Private	EVANS ROWLAND
Private	FRIMSHAW ROBT.
Private	FORTH JOSH.
Private	FLEMMING WM.
Private	GODFRE WM.
Private	GREEN SAML.
Private	GIBSON THOS.
Private	GRAVES JOSEPH
Private	HALLARD JOHN
Private	HUDSON JAMES
Private	HILL RICHD.
Private	HUGHEY THOS.
Private	HART WM.
Private	HARDIDGE JOHN
Private	HAYWOOD WM.
Private	HARVEY THOS.
Private	HUGHES WM.
Private	JONES EDWD.
Private	JACKSON SAML.
Private	JENNINGS LEWIS
Private	KEYFORD RICHD.
Private	LEECH GEORGE
Private	LAMB SAML.
Private	LUDHAM ROBT.
Private	MITTON GEORGE
Private	MOTT CHARLES
Private	MARTIN JNS.
Private	MUGG JNS.
Private	MILLER JNS.
Private	MORRIS RICHD.
Private	MARTIN SAML.
Private	MATTHEW RICHD.
Private	MELVIN ALEXR.
Private	MARKHAM JAMES
Private	NELSON JNS.
Private	NEALD JNS.
Private	OWEN JNS.
Private	OFFER ROBT. Col.R.T. Gascoigne's Collection March 1909
Private	PAINE JNS.
Private	PORTER WM. Wounded not since heard of.
Private	PORTER ROBT.
Private	ROGERSON WM.
Private	ROGERS STEPH.
Private	SCHOFIELD JNS.
Private	SCHOFIELD ROBT.
Private	SEYMOUR JNS.
Private	SMITH JAMES
Private	SULLIVAN HUMP.
Private	SWINNEY PATK.
Private	SALES JOHN
Private	TAYLOR ROBT.
Private	TAYLOR THOS.
Private	TURTON JOSH.
Private	THOMAS JOHN
Private	THOMPSON THOS.
Private	WALL JAMES
Private	WEIR ALLEN
Private	WILLIAMS RICHD.
Private	YOUNG JOSH. Wounded not since heard of.
Private	BATTY JOHN Killed 18th June
Private	HUTCHINS WM. Killed 16th June
Private	HORSLEY EDWD. Killed 18th June
Private	MOORE JAMES Killed 16th June
Private	OWEN JAMES Died 8th July
Private	THOMAS EDWD. Killed 18th June

Lt.Colonel the Hon. H.P. Townshend's Company

Lt.Colonel	TOWNSHEND Hon. H.P.
Captain	STREATFIELD THOS.
Ensign	VYNER CHAS.
Serjeant	COOPER THOS.
Serjeant	WOOD JNS. Died of Wounds 25th July
Serjeant	MAY JNS.
Serjeant	PIPER GEO.
Serjeant	MARCH JOHN
Corporal	LEWINGTON MICHL.
Corporal	JESSOP JNS.
Corporal	HOLT ADAM.
Corporal	PLAYLE WM.
Corporal	FAWCETT JAMES
Corporal	GRIFFITH JNS.
Drummer	ASHTON JAS.
Drummer	TAYLOR JAMES
Private	ARKLESS JNS.
Private	ANNETT WM.
Private	ALLEN EDWD.
Private	ALLEN JAS. Wounded not since heard of.
Private	ALLEN WM.

Private	ARDEN WM.
Private	BENTLEY THOS.
Private	BARKER EDWD.
Private	BRADFORD ISRAEL
Private	BROOKS ROBT.
Private	BURGESS ISSAC
Private	BROWN JNS.
Private	BADCOCK ROBT.
Private	BARKER WM.
Private	BENFIELD WM.
Private	BALL JNS.
Private	BARNFIELD JNS.
Private	BRUNT THOS.
Private	BISSHOP ROBT.THOS.
Private	CARR CHRISTR.
Private	CLARBOUN JNS.
Private	COLLOR JAMES Wounded not since heard of.
Private	CURTIS JAMES
Private	EVANS EDWD.
Private	FOSTER EDWD.
Private	FENLEY EDWD.
Private	FREEMAN JOHN
Private	FORWARD JOHN Glendinnings sale 17th June 1908
Private	FIRTH JAMES
Private	GRIST RICHD.
Private	GREENWOOD JNS.
Private	GAITER DANIEL
Private	GILES JNS.
Private	GILL DAVID
Private	HOLLOWAY AARON
Private	HENSHAW JAS.
Private	HUDSON SAML.
Private	HOPKINSON WM.
Private	HODGKINSON JAS.
Private	JONES DAVID
Private	JAMES DANIEL
Private	JOHNSON THOS.
Private	KNOWLES WM.
Private	LEWIS JNS.
Private	LEWICK ISRAEL
Private	McGOWEN NATHL.
Private	MILLBURN ROBT.
Private	MARSHALL JNS. Wounded not since heard of.
Private	McGREGOR JNS.
Private	MORRIS JNS.
Private	NEILD JOHN
Private	NEWBY JOSH.
Private	OWEN JOHN
Private	PIKE WM. Wounded not since heard of.
Private	POWELL EDWD.
Private	PRICHARD JNS. Wounded not since heard of.
Private	PHIPPS WM.
Private	PRINCE EDWD.
Private	PRICE GEORGE
Private	PRENTICE JOHN
Private	ROGERS ABRM.
Private	RICHARDSON CHAS.
Private	RICHARDSON JNS.
Private	SIMS GEORGE
Private	SMITH SION
Private	SHIELDS CHAS.
Private	SKIDMORE JOHN
Private	SMART JNS.
Private	SIMMONDS SAML.
Private	SAUNDERS WM.
Private	STRHORN HUGH
Private	SMITH WM.
Private	TRINGMORE GEORGE
Private	TOWNLEY JAMES
Private	THURSTON JAMES
Private	TITFORD JOSH.
Private	TALBOTT ROBT. Wounded not since heard of.
Private	TUMPENNY WM.
Private	THORN WM.
Private	VOWLES WM.
Private	WADSWORTH WM.
Private	WATMORE JAS.
Private	WYNN CHAS.
Private	WILLIAMS WM.
Private	WILDING GEORGE
Private	WORSLEY EDMD.
Private	WRIGHT JONAS
Private	WATERHOUSE JAS.
Private	WEBB JAS.
Private	WARD THOS. Glendinnings sale Oct. 1909
Private	WARREN JAS. Glendinnings sale 17th June 1908
Serjeant	VENETY BENJN. Killed in Action 16th June
Private	REDYARD JNS. Killed in Action 16th June
Private	CLARK JNS. Killed in Action 16th June
Private	THOMAS DANIEL Killed in Action 16th June

Private	JOHNSON BARTH. Died of Wounds 1st July 1815
Private	DOREY ROBT. Died of Wounds 1st July 1815

Lt.Colonel the Hon. J.H. Stanhope's Company

Lt.Colonel	STANHOPE Hon. J.H.
Captain	PHILLIMORE R.B.
Ensign	VERNON H.
Serjeant	MARTIN RICHD.
Serjeant	SMITH GEORGE
Serjeant	LOARING NATHL.
Serjeant	WHENN ROBT.
Serjeant	BENBOW JNS.
Corporal	GRANT JNS.
Corporal	LEE BENJN.
Corporal	COLQUHOUN ALLEN
Corporal	ALLISON ALEXR. Needes Collection 1908
Drummer	HERBERT JAMES
Drummer	McCARTY JAMES
Private	ALLEN WM.
Private	ANDREWS WM.
Private	BENDLE THOS.
Private	BRETT THOS.
Private	BLACKMAN WM.
Private	BRAUN JNS.
Private	BEANY HENRY
Private	BURNER JAMES
Private	BULL THOS.
Private	BARNETT JAS. Wounded 16 June not heard of since.
Private	CAMPBELL WM.
Private	COCKAYNE EDWD.
Private	CHALLIS PHILLIP
Private	CLARKE THOS.
Private	CROSS THOS.
Private	COOKE EDWD.
Private	COWBURN JOSEPH
Private	CALVER EDWD.
Private	DEAN CHAS.
Private	DAVIES WM.
Private	DAVIES BENJN.
Private	DICKINSON JAMES Wounded 18 June not heard of since.
Private	DAY JNS.
Private	DAVISON JNS.
Private	EVANS GRIFF.
Private	FARMER CHAS.
Private	FIELDING WM.
Private	FURNIFER RALPH
Private	FOXTON JNS.
Private	GREEN JOSEPH
Private	GELL PETER
Private	GASKIN LEWIS
Private	HARDY ISSAC
Private	HAINES MATTW.
Private	HORROX JAMES
Private	HARWOOD WM. Wounded 16 June not heard of since
Private	JONES SAML.
Private	JONES RALPH
Private	JENNINGS JNS.
Private	JOHNSON JOSEPH
Private	KELSEY JNS.
Private	LEWIS WM.
Private	LINFORD THOS.
Private	LEAKIN SAML.
Private	LANCASTER JONAN.
Private	LEAVER ISSAC
Private	MAYSFIELD MATTW.
Private	MARR GEORGE
Private	MARSHALL JOSEPH
Private	MORRIS JAMES
Private	MAXWELL JOHN
Private	MALLARD JNS.
Private	MAULE WM.
Private	NEWTON SAML.
Private	OGLE SAML.
Private	PRICE THOS.
Private	PARKER THOS.
Private	POOLE WM.
Private	PALMER JAMES
Private	ROGERS JAMES
Private	RANDALL SAML.
Private	ROBINSON JEREH.
Private	RATCLIFF RICHD.
Private	ROBERTS JNS.
Private	STANNER LEWIS
Private	SAINT JNS.
Private	SIMMONDS JAS.
Private	SHEIGHT BENJN. On sale at Baldwin's March 1909
Private	SHEFFIELD JNS.
Private	SINCE THOS.
Private	SWIFT JNS.
Private	SKEDMORE JNS.
Private	SINCLAIR SAML.
Private	SINNOCK THOS.
Private	SMITH JNS.
Private	SLAUGHTER HERBT.

Private	TURNER JAMES
Private	TUCKER WM.
Private	WILSON WM.
Private	WILSON JAS.
Private	WALKER JAS. Wounded 16th June not heard of since.
Private	WILLIAMS EDWD.
Private	WHITTON GEO.THOS.
Private	WATKINS GEO.
Private	WHITEHOUSE JNS.
Private	WALPOLE ROBT. Wounded 16th not heard of since.
Private	WILLIS THOS.
Private	WHEELER WM. Gray Collection 1908
Private	WATHALL RICHD.
Private	FOWLES THOS. Killed in Action 16th June
Private	FINCH DANIEL Killed in Action 18th June
Private	HARWOOD SAML. Killed in Action 18th June
Private	NICHOLLS THOS. Killed in Action 18th June
Private	REECE THOS. Killed in Action 16th June
Private	ROSE WM. Killed in Action 18th June
Private	REECE DAVID Killed in Action 18th June
Private	COLLIER CHAS. Retd.dead of Wounds, since heard of in London.
Corporal	SWANN WM. Killed 18th June in Action

LIGHT COMPANY GRENADIER GUARDS

Lt.Colonel Lord Saltourn's Company

Lt.Colonel	SALTOUN LORD.
Captain	GROSE EDWD. Killed
Captain	ELLISON ROBERT
Captain	ELLIS C.P. Wounded
Lieutenant	BARTON Wounded
S.Major	DIXON F.
Serjeant	SKERRATT JNS.
Serjeant	STEELE ROBT.
Serjeant	STONE JOHN Spinks List Dec. 1908
Serjeant	GREEN JAS.
Serjeant	NICHOLLS GEO.
Corporal	HOYLES WM.
Corporal	NIXON JAMES Wounded not since heard of.
Corporal	STABLES JOHN
Corporal	PINNINGTON THOS.
Drummer	SNELL EDWD. Killed 16 June 1815
Drummer	GREEN EDMUND
Private	ADDISON JOHN
Private	ANKROYDE JAMES
Private	ANNETT JOHN
Private	ASPINALL MOSES
Private	ASPINALL THOS.
Private	BLACKER ALEXR.
Private	BARLOW CHAS.
Private	BARDOLPH JOHN
Private	BEE WM.
Private	BEAUMONT WM.
Private	BYRAM HENRY
Private	BENNETT CHARLES
Private	BANNISTER JOSEPH
Private	BRYAN MICHL.
Private	CROFTS SAML.
Private	COLLEY WM.
Private	CROOK THOS.
Private	CARDEN STEP.
Private	COOPER GEORGE
Private	DIXON JNS.
Private	DANN THOS.
Private	DAVIS JAMES
Private	DAINSFORD ABRM.
Private	DUNK WM.
Private	EVANS JOHN
Private	EARLE JOHN
Private	FARRINGTON RICHD.
Private	FORSYTH ALEXR.
Private	FIELDING WM.
Private	FOGG JAMES
Private	FOWLER THOS.
Private	FOX DAVID
Private	GRAHAM JAMES
Private	GRAVES WM.
Private	GROVES WM.
Private	GRIFFITHS JOHN
Private	HOWARD JOHN
Private	HILL JOHN
Private	HUGHES JAMES
Private	HILLIER JOSEPH
Private	HOLDGATE WM.
Private	HYDE SAML.
Private	HUTCHINSON JOHN
Private	HOLLIS DANIEL
Private	HOUGHTON WM.
Private	HALL JONATHAN
Private	HOBBS WM.

Private	JONES THOS.
Private	JONES EVAN
Private	JAMES DAMIEL
Private	JOHNSTONE ISSAC
Private	JACKSON RICHD.
Private	JEPSON ROBT.
Private	KING THOS.
Private	KETTLE HENRY
Private	LEESE JAMES
Private	LEE JAMES
Private	MINCHELL THOS.
Private	MORRIS THOS.
Private	MARRIOTT JOHN
Private	MORSLEY THOS.
Private	MILLS PHILLIP
Private	MOORE ISSAC
Private	NAYLOR HENRY
Private	PROBIN JOHN
Private	REECE EDWD.
Private	ROBERTSHAW MATTW.
Private	ROGERS JAMES
Private	REED EDWD.
Private	ROBERTS EDWD.
Private	RICHARDS JOHN
Private	SWEENEY WM.
Private	SOUTHGATE THOS.
Private	SPAIN JNS.
Private	STENTON THOS.
Private	STAINES BENJN.
Private	SAYERS EDWD.
Private	STEWART GEORGE
Private	THOMPSON ABRM.
Private	THOMAS ROSSER
Private	THOMAS THOS.
Private	THRUSSLE WM.
Private	WALMSLEY JOHN
Private	WILLIAMS JOHN
Private	WILLCOX HENRY
Private	WOOD HENRY
Private	WARREN WM.
P-ivate	YETFORD JOS.
Private	BIGSWORTH JOHN
Private	BARTTAM AVERY
Private	CHAPPLE JOHN Killed 16th June 1815
Private	DETHICK ROBT. Killed 16th June 1815
Private	FAWCETT JONATHAN Killed 16th June 1815
Private	GOODY JOHN Killed 16th June 1815
Private	HARBER JAMES Killed 16th June 1815
Private	PEARSON JOHN Killed 16th June 1815
Private	PEGG ROBT. Killed 16th June 1815
Private	ROGERS SAML. Killed 16th June 1815
Private	LIVERSAGE DAVID Killed 16th June
Private	BROOMFIELD WM. Killed 26th June
Private	HATTON SAML. Wounded since dead
Private	HILL WM. Wounded since dead
Private	HALLIDAY WM. Wounded since dead
Private	ROGERS RD. Wounded since dead

3rd Battn. Grenadier Guards

Colonel	STUART Hon. WM.
Colonel	ASKEW 2nd Battn. Record Office
Captain	BOLDERO L. Acting Adjutant
Captain & Adjutant	ALLIX wnd Battn. Record Office
Pay Master	COLQUHOUN R.
Acting Qtr.Master	SMITH J.
Surgeon	WATSON W. H.Gaskell's Collection 1908
Ass.Surgeon	ARMSTRONG ANDW.
Ass.Surgeon	GILDER F.
Ass.Surgeon	GARDNER Record Office
Ass.Surgeon	HARRISON Record Office
2ndMaster	PAYNE Record Office

* * *

2nd BATTN. COLDSTREAM GUARDS

Lt.Colonel D. MacKinnon's Company

Lt.Colonel	MacKINNON D.
Ensign	GRIFFITHS H.F.
Ass.Surgeon	SMITH GEO.
Serjeant	SIMPSON JOHN
Serjeant	LEGG WM.
Serjeant	SLY THOS.
Serjeant	DAVIDSON ANDREW
Corporal	FERRIS JOHN
Corporal	BROWN JAMES
Corporal	VAUGHAN JOHN
Corporal	STRICKLAND JAMES
Drummer	RICE LUKE
Drummer	DARKIN EDWD.
Drummer	AIMS JOHN
Drummer	MILLAR JOHN

Private	AIKEN WM.
Private	ALLISON ROBT.
Private	BURBRIDGE WM.
Private	BEAZLEY AMOS
Private	BUSH WM.
Private	BUTLER JAMES
Private	BAKER JOSH
Private	BRADSHAW JOHN
Private	BRUCE ROBT.
Private	BABBAGE JOHN
Private	BISHOP WM.
Private	BONAS THOS.
Private	CORLEY JOHN
Private	CRAWFORD WM.
Private	CURRIE FRANCS.
Private	CHRISSOP THOS.
Private	COTTON WM.
Private	CARR JOHN
Private	COOKE JOHN
Private	CALLAGHAN DENNIS
Private	DEWAY WM.
Private	DARKIN JAMES
Private	FARRINGTON THOS.
Private	FLETCHER JAMES
Private	FRAZER ALEXR.
Private	FOSBERRY DANIEL
Private	GILL GEORGE
Private	GREEN WM.
Private	GORDON JOHN
Private	CARR JAMES Gray Collection 1908
Private	GRIST JAMES
Private	GRIFFITHS THOS.
Private	GALE CHAS.
Private	HOSKINS JAMES
Private	HEATH GEORGE
Private	HINWOOD CHAS.
Private	HARVEY SAML.
Private	HAWKINS SAML.
Private	JONES EDWD.
Private	KERBY JOHN
Private	LOWRIE GEORGE
Private	LUCIMORE EDMD.
Private	LINGHAM JAMES
Private	LINGHAM JOHN
Private	McMULLEN MATTW.
Private	MOORE JAMES
Private	McKAY WM.
Private	MANNING RICHD. Day Sale April 1910
Private	MATHER JOHN
Private	McCRACKING HUGH
Private	NEWBOLT JOSH.
Private	OWEN RICHD.
Private	PRICE RICHD.
Private	POOLE AMBROSE
Private	PINSER JAMES
Private	PARKIN JOSEPH
Private	PIKE JOHN
Private	ROFFEY JOHN
Private	ROSS FREDK.
Private	RAWLINS JAMES
Private	ROSE JOHN
Private	SHEPPARD WM. Phillips sale
Private	STROUD SAML.
Private	STACEY RICHD.
Private	SHRUBSHALL RICHD.
Private	STILES SAML.
Private	SHALE JOSH.
Private	SPARKS CHRISTMAS
Private	SANSON JAMES
Private	THORNHILL JOHN
Private	VINCENT NATTW.
Private	WRIGHT THOS.
Private	WOLSTENCROFT CHAS.
Private	WALTERS ROBT.
Private	BURT JAMES H.Gaskell's Collection 1908

Lt.Colonel MacDonnell's Company

Colonel	WOODFORD A.
Lt.Colonel	MacDONNELL JAS.
Captain	SOWERBY THOS.
Lieutenant	MONTAGUE T.
Surgeon	WHYMPER WM. Payne Collection 1911
Qr.Master	SELWAY R.
Serjeant Major	BUTLER THOS.
Q.M.S.	BLAMPFLOWER HENRY
Serjeant	CREIGHTON JOSH.
Serjeant	GANNAN CHRISTMAS
Serjeant	GREMIERS JOHN
Serjeant	DASENALL THOS.
Serjeant	FIDO JOHN
Serjeant	THERWELL JOHN
Serjeant	SAVAGE WM.
Serjeant	KNIGHT JOHN
Corporal	LINE EDWD.
Corporal	GLEAVES JAMES
Corporal	CARLISLE THOS.
Corporal	ROE RICHD.

Drummer	CONNOR JOHN
Drummer	SWEATMAN WM.
Private	ANDERTON DOCTOR
Private	ALSOP WM.
Private	ASPINALL RICHD.
Private	ALLCHURCH BENJN.
Private	BETTS JOHN
Private	BLIGH JOHN
Private	BUCKLAND HENRY
Private	BLAZEY WM.
Private	BETHILL JOSH.
Private	BECKETT JOHN
Private	BRADLEY THOS.
Private	CONSTANTINE ROBT.
Private	CRACKNALL ROBT.
Private	COURT THOS.
Private	CLARKE JOHN
Private	CARTER ABRM.
Private	COOPER WM.
Private	CLARKE ISSAC
Private	DOMMINCY WM.
Private	DORMER WM.
Private	DICKINSON WM.
Private	DEWSBURY JOHN
Private	EVANS WM.
Private	FOX ROBERT
Private	FINNEY GEORGE
Private	FLOWERS JOHN
Private	FEATHERSTONE GEORGE
Private	FARRINGTON WM.
Private	GRIFFITHS WM.
Private	GILBERT WM.
Private	GRINNING RICHD.
Private	HADLEY MARSDEN
Private	HEMMINGS RICHD.
Private	HASTIE GEORGE
Private	HARRISON JAMES
Private	HARRISON JOSEPH
Private	JONES CHARLES
Private	KILMURRAY PATK.
Private	KNELL JACOB
Private	LEWIS REES
Private	MUIR WM.
Private	MANN JOHN
Private	MORRIS THOS.
Private	MORGAN RICHD.
Private	MOAHAM HENRY
Private	NEWBY THOS.
Private	PAGELL WM.
Private	PHARE THOS. Whitaker Collection 1908
Private	PERKINS AMBROSE
Private	RUMBLE JOHN
Private	REYNARD WM.
Private	SAUNDERS JOHN
Private	SMITH JOHN
Private	STOTT ROBT.
Private	SCALLES JOHN
Private	SIMPSON WM.
Private	SEECH EDWD.
Private	SIMMONDS SAML.
Private	SOUTHWARD JOHN
Private	TINSEL JOHN
Private	TAYLOR EDWD.
Private	THOMPSON GILES
Private	TAYLOR RALPH
Private	WELDON JOHN
Private	WELBY ROBT.
Private	WOOD JOSEPH
Private	WALLER WM.
Private	WILSON WALTER
Private	WELLS W,.
Private	WILKINS WM.
Private	WHITEHEAD RICHD.
Private	WALKER JAMES
Private	WINGATE JOSH.

Colonel Hon.A.Abercromby's Company

Colonel	ABERCROMBY Hon.A.
Lieutenant	FORBES Hon. JAS.
Lieutenant	CAYLOR AUGT. Exatra A.D.C. to M.G. Cook
Serjeant	JAMES THOS.
Serjeant	BISHOP SAML.
Serjeant	NEWTON DAVID
Serjeant	GRASS HENRY
Serjeant	MAULE HENRY
Corporal	MILLAR WM.
Corporal	JEWITT ISSAC
Corporal	RICHLEY WM.
Corporal	ARMSTRONG ROBT.
Corporal	DUNFORD WM.
Drummer	MILLAR ARTHUR Galway Foley Collection 1910
Drummer	HOLLOWAY THOS.
Private	AMBROS EZEKIEL
Private	ALLBUT RICHD.
Private	AUST JOHN

Private	ALLEN JOHN
Private	ATKINSON JOHN
Private	BROWN SAMUEL
Private	BLIGH JOHN
Private	BREWER JOHN
Private	BIGGAR MATTW.
Private	BOSLEY ROBERT
Private	BROUGHTON CHAS.
Private	BAILEY JOSHUA
Private	BURROUGHS JOHN
Private	BINGHAM WM.
Private	BIRCH WM.
Private	BLAKE GEORGE
Private	BOLD JOSH.
Private	CHAMBERS CHRISTR.
Private	COLLEY GEORGE
Private	CARTLEDGE RALPH
Private	COX WM.
Private	CRAIGE WM. Glendinnings sale Oct.1913 2-10-0
Private	EMERY JEREH.
Private	EDE HENRY
Private	EWENS JAMES
Private	DAWSON SAML.
Private	DIGBY JOSH.
Private	FISHER JAMES
Private	FOXTON THOS.
Private	FOSTER JAMES
Private	FLOYD HENRY
Private	GIBBS JOHN
Private	GRAINGER THOS.
Private	GROSE THOS.
Private	GERTON ROBT.
Private	GROVES THOS.
Private	HENDERSON THOS.
Private	HOCKING WM.
Private	HAVINGHAM EDWD.
Private	HOCKING JAMES
Private	LEAVE EDWD.
Private	LAYCOCK JOSH.
Private	MORGAN JOHN
Private	MILLAR WM.
Private	MESSELDINE JAMES
Private	MAY GEORGE
Private	McCORMICK JOHN
Private	MORGAN EDWD.
Private	METCALF ALEXR.
Private	NASH RICHD.
Private	NOAD WM.
Private	O'NEILL FRANS.
Private	PARSONS THOS.
Private	PHILLIPS JAMES
Private	REECES THOS.
Private	RHODES GEORGE
Private	SANKEY JNS.
Private	SONE DAVID
Private	SHELL THOS.
Private	SHORE JAMES
Private	STEELE WM.
Private	SCOTT WM.
Private	SCOTTON WM.
Private	SIMMONDS RICHD.
Private	TROWELL JOHN
Private	TAYLOR JOHN
Private	TICLY WM.
Private	THURLEY THOS.
Private	THOMPSON CLAUDIUS
Private	WIND JOHN
Private	WEAVER CHAS.
Private	WARDLE JOHN
Private	WALDING WM.
Private	TRENCH JNS.
Private	BOND JNS.

Lt.Colonel Sir Wm. Gomm's Company

Lt.Colonel	GOMM Sir WM.
Captain	COWELL STEPNEY
Lieutenant	VANE HENRY
Lieutenant	FORBES Hon.WM.
Major	BENTINCK C.F. Adjutant
Serjeant	EVANS GRIFFITHS
Serjeant	JONES RICHD.
Serjeant	LOTT JAMES
Serjeant	CARTLAND JOHN
Serjeant	McAULEY JAMES
Serjeant	RICE JOHN
Corporal	CHAPPELL JAMES Glendinnings sale 17 June 1908
Corporal	HANNAH JOHN
Corporal	SIMMONDS JOSH.
Corporal	HAUGH EDWD.
Corporal	ATLEY HENRY
Drummer	WHITCOMBE ED.HENRY
Drummer	HAMMERSLEY WM.
Private	ASHWORTH JNS.
Private	ALLTIMES JOHN
Private	AYRES WM. Glendinnings sale 28 Feb. 1908
Private	BARLOW THOS.

Private	BOOTH HENRY
Private	BARNES JOHN
Private	BORROUGHS HENRY
Private	BLIGHT ROBT.
Private	BELSHAM ADAM
Private	BEAZLEY GEORGE
Private	BURTONWOOD PETER
Private	BUTLER THOS.
Private	BULLOCK JOHN
Private	BLACKBURN JOSH.
Private	CALLICOT PETER
Private	CORSAR THOS.
Private	CREWE ROBT.
Private	COPE GEORGE
Private	CRAIG ROBERT
Private	DUFFIELD SAML.
Private	DEAN GEORGE
Private	DIXON GEORGE
Private	DUNSCOMBE JOHN
Private	FINCHAM RICHD.
Private	FOSTER ARTHUR
Private	FREEMAN WM.
Private	GEE JAMES
Private	GILES JOHN
Private	HEAVEN ISSAC
Private	HOWARD JOHN
Private	HEDGES ROBT.
Private	HUDSON STEPHN.
Private	HEATH JOHN
Private	HUGHES EDWD.
Private	HICKMAN THOS.
Private	HEWEN EDWD.
Private	HILLARD WM.
Private	JOHNSON EDWD.
Private	INGLES JAMES
Private	JAYES GEORGE
Private	JEFFERY THOS.
Private	JONES THOS.
Private	KEMP ROBT.
Private	KIRKHAM JOHN
Private	KNOWLES EDWD.
Private	KEAN STEPHN.
Private	KELVIN JOHN
Private	LURWOOD SAML.
Private	LOWE THOS.
Private	LEIGH JAMES
Private	LAYCOCK JOSH.
Private	MOORHOUSE JOHN
Private	MOULD JOHN
Private	MACKLEY THOS.
Private	MAYHEW WM.
Private	MOORE JOHN
Private	MULVEY WM.
Private	NESBIT WM.
Private	NORRIS WM. Senr.
Private	NORRIS WM. Junr.
Private	NEAVE WM.
Private	PURCHEON THOS.
Private	POUND WM.
Private	PERFECT BARND.
Private	ROYDS SAML.
Private	SWANBOROUGH JOB Littledale sale Nov. 1910
Private	STIRLING ZACHS.
Private	SMITH LUKE
Private	TURNER THOS.
Private	TULLOCK JOHN
Private	WALKER WM.
Private	WHITING JOHN
Private	WRIGHT GEORGE
Private	WESTWOOD SAML.
Private	WATKINS JOHN
Private	WATSON WM.
Private	YOUNG JAMES

Lt.Colonel Hon. E. Acheson's Company

Ly.Colonel	ACKERSON Hon. E.
Lieutenant	GORDON ALEXR.
Serjeant	FOX WM.
Serjeant	JENT JOHN
Serjeant	MERRYMAN WM.
Serjeant	WORTHINGTON JOHN
Corporal	STAINER GEORGE
Corporal	DUNCAN JOHN
Corporal	DAVIDSON JAMES
Corporal	THOMPSON GEORGE
Corporal	HILL JAMES
Private	ASHTON RICHD.
Private	AITKENHEAD RICHD.
Private	AUSTIN ROBT.
Private	BROOKS JOHN
Private	BODINGHAM JAMES
Private	BOWEN JAMES
Private	BIGBY ADAM
Private	BONE ROBERT
Private	BATES MATTW.
Private	BELCANQUEL ROBT.

Private	BROWN WM.
Private	BORROUGHS STEPN.
Private	BROUGHTON ROBT.
Private	BANCROFT EDWD.
Private	BANKS ROBT.
Private	COLLINS HUMPY.
Private	COCKRAN JOHN
Private	COLLIER PETER
Private	CHARLTON SAML.
Private	COOKE WM.
Private	DENT JOSH. Glendinnings sale Jan. 1910
Private	DETRIDGE JOHN
Private	DAYLEY JOSH.
Private	DODD JOSEPH
Private	EVANS JAMES
Private	EVANS RICHD.
Private	FAULKNER JASPER
Private	FOREMAN THOS.
Private	GUEST GEORGE
Private	GLANWRIGHT WM.
Private	HILL WM.
Private	HAPLEY JOHN
Private	HARDING GEORGE
Private	HOLLOWELL JOB
Private	HALL JAMES
Private	HARPER GEORGE
Private	HERITAGE JAMES
Private	HEMMINGS WM.
Private	JONES WM.
Private	JEFFERY WM.
Private	LEWIS SHADWICK
Private	LEGGETT ROBT.
Private	LOWE THOS.
Private	MILLS JOHN
Private	MAYES HENRY
Private	MAYNE MUNGO
Private	METCALF WM.
Private	MUMFORD WM.
Private	NEWMAN ROBT.
Private	POOLE WM.
Private	POWELL JAMES
Private	RICHARDSON WM.
Private	SPRADBURY GEO.
Private	STAIR JNS.
Private	STANDLEY SAML.
Private	SHAKESPEARE JONAN.
Private	SMITH Senr. JNS.
Private	SELKIRK JOHN
Private	SPRATT JOHN
Private	SMITH Junr. JOHN
Private	STANDLEY EDWD.
Private	THOMAS THOS.
Private	WOODCOCK JOHN
Private	WOODING JOHN
Private	WALKLAND WM.
Private	WALL JOHN
Private	WRIGHT JAMES
Private	WALE THOS.
Private	WORTHINGTON THOS.
Private	WOODRUFF WM.
Private	WILLIAMSON THOS.
Private	WHITE THOS.
Private	TULLEDINE RICHD.

Lt.Colonel Hon. H.R. Pakenham's Company

Lieutenant	BOWEN ROBT.
Lieutenant	SHORT CHS.
Lieutenant	DOUGLAS F.J.
Serjeant	CHIBB NICHS. Payne Collection 1911
Serjeant	WILLIAMS THOS.
Serjeant	BURTON BENJN. Payne Collection 1911
Serjeant	TREHORNE STEPN.
Serjeant	MONKHOUSE WM.
Serjeant	HUGHES GEORGE
Corporal	CREATOUX JOSH.
Corporal	McCASIDAY ANDW.
Corporal	MATTHEWS ANDW.
Corporal	ELLIOTT ROBT.
Corporal	TERRY HUMPY.
Drummer	WADE BENJN.
Private	AMES ANTHONY
Private	AYLAND JOHN
Private	AGAR ROBT.
Private	BROWN WM.
Private	BOON JNS. Glendinnings sale Oct. 1913
Private	BATHGATE CHAS.
Private	BROWN BENJN.
Private	BROWN THOS.
Private	BELL JOHN
Private	COLEMAN NATHL.
Private	CHATWIN ELIJAH
Private	CHUBB GEORGE
Private	CLARKE WM.
Private	CORCORAN NATTW.
Private	CARPENTER JOHN

Private	COALES JAMES
Private	DEMAINE ANTHONY
Private	DUCKER JOHN
Private	DAWSHELL JOHN
Private	DEHAN PETER
Private	DICKINSON ROBT.
Private	EBRIEL THOS.
Private	ELLIS JNS.
Private	EYLES THOS.
Private	ELMS MESEKIAH
Private	FEW THOS.
Private	GOODWIN BENJN.
Private	GIBSON PETER
Private	GUY JOHN
Private	GILBERT JOHN
Private	HAMILTON GEORGE
Private	HEATH CHAS.
Private	HALL HENRY
Private	HUDSON WM.
Private	HAYDON JOHN
Private	HOWARTH JOHN
Private	HOLLAND EDWD.
Private	HAYDEN THOS.
Private	JOHNSON JOHN
Private	KELLOW EDWD.
Private	KIRKHAM MATTW.
Private	LINEHAM WM.
Private	LUKE JOHN
Private	MACKINTOSH JOHN
Private	MASTERS WM.
Private	MADGWICK RICHD.
Private	MORGAN GEORGE
Private	MOORE JOSEPH
Private	MANNING JNS.
Private	NOBBS JOSH.
Private	NABB WM.
Private	PUDDOCK EDWD.
Private	PESTON JOHN
Private	PORTER EDWD.
Private	PITMAN THOS.
Private	PURSEY RICHD.
Private	PARKER THOS.
Private	RUTLEY RICHD.
Private	RITCHIE WM.
Private	ROBERTSON JAMES
Private	RUBY FRANCIS
Private	SOWER JAMES
Private	STANTON GEORGE
Private	SPENCE ROBT.
Private	SPARROW RICHD.
Private	STOCKWELL RICHD. Puttick & Simpsons sale Feb. 1910
Private	SWANSBOROUGH MATTW.
Private	SODEN THOS.
Private	TRESLOVE JAMES
Private	WATTS JNS.
Private	WILKES CHAS.
Private	WHEELER WM.
Private	WEEKS SIMON
Private	WINDLE JOHN
Private	WADE WM.
Private	WILLIAMS CHAS.
Private	WATKINS JAMES

<u>Lt.Colonel Wyndham's Company</u>

Lt.Colonel	WYNDHAM HENRY
Captain	HOTHAM LORD
Serjeant	KING ABRM.
Serjeant	NOYCE JOHN
Serjeant	RING JONATHAN
Serjeant	STANDLEY JAMES
Serjeant	SMITH JOHN
Corporal	DRAPER JAMES
Corporal	SMITH JAMES
Corporal	FURPHY SAML.
Corporal	ROLLINS JOHN
Corporal	FARNELL JOHN
Corporal	BURKE WM.
Corporal	BUTLER THOS.
Drummer	REASON WM.
Private	AGGS SAML.
Private	BUSH WM.
Private	BENNET GEORGE
Private	BARSON JOHN
Private	BAILEY PAUL
Private	BRIDLE GEORGE
Private	BALL GEORGE
Private	BOND WM.
Private	CHAMPION THOS.
Private	CHADDERTON JOSH.
Private	CROUCH BENJN.
Private	CAMPBELL EDWD.
Private	CORDELL WM.
Private	CALAGHAN WM.
Private	DOBINSON THOS. Glendinnings sale Dec. 1913
Private	DOBSON THOS.
Private	DAWSON HENRY
Private	DAVIS EDWD.

Private	DAVIS EVAN
Private	EDWARDS THOS.
Private	EVANS DANIEL
Private	EVANS RICHD.
Private	ELTON JOHN
Private	FLINN JAMES
Private	FRANCIS JONAN.
Private	GREEWES JNS.
Private	GUBBITASS WM.
Private	GILLARD JNS.
Private	HEALEY JAMES
Private	HODGES JOHN
Private	HARGREAVES STEPN.
Private	HEYES JOSHUA
Private	HARRIS GILES
Private	INESON JAMES
Private	JENNINGS WM.
Private	JONES WM.
Private	JOHNSON GEORGE
Private	KELLY MICHL.
Private	KNIPER JAS.
Private	LEES WM.
Private	MERRIDELL EDWD.
Private	MUSSLEWHITE WM.
Private	MORRIS WM.
Private	McCLANE ALAN
Private	MAYERS ROBT.
Private	McANLEY JOHN
Private	PARKINGTON JOHN
Private	PRIOR JOHN
Private	PEARCE RICHD.
Private	PRATTON JNS.
Private	RAMSDALE JAMES
Private	REYNOLDS RICHD.
Private	SHUFFLEBOTTOM JOSH.
Private	SPEED WM.
Private	STEWARD DENIS
Private	STEER WM.
Private	SLANEY JOHN
Private	SMITH THOS.
Private	SMITH JAMES
Private	TOOMER WM.
Private	THOMPSON JNS.
Private	TRIMER GEO.
Private	WESTWELL GEO.
Private	WALTERS DAVID
Private	WOOD WM.
Private	WETTEN JAMES
Private	WHITTAKER KENDAL
Private	WILLIAMSON JAMES
Private	YOUNG THOMAS.

Lt.Colonel Sir. R. Arthbuthnots Company

Captain	BOWLES GEO.
Lieutenant	HARVEY JAS.
Serjeant	LANGDON SAML. Sotheby's sale 19 June 1908
Serjeant	WALKER JOHN
Serjeant	CLARKE ROBT.
Serjeant	LEWIS WM.
Serjeant	SELFE ROBT.
Corporal	DAWNEY JOSEPH
Corporal	BLAIR JAMES
Corporal	PROUD JOHN
Corporal	ROTHWELL EDWD.
Corporal	DUNFORD WM.
Corporal	GREENHALGH TIMY.
Private	ASLETT WM.
Private	BUSHTON JOHN
Private	BRENTON WM.
Private	BOWLER THOS.
Private	BULLEN EDWD.
Private	BULL JOHN
Private	BARTON JOHN
Private	BROWN THOS.
Private	BALL GEO.
Private	BAMBER EDWD.
Private	CLARKE GORDON
Private	CURTIS BENJN.
Private	CHAPMAN JAMES
Private	CRAWLEY THOS.
Private	COLLINS WM.
Private	CALLAIS JOHN
Private	DAFT STEPN.
Private	EVERATT JOHN
Private	GADSBY WM.
Private	GALT ROBT.
Private	GUY JOHN
Private	GUEST JOHN
Private	GIMBERT BASHAM
Private	GILLARD WM.
Private	HUMPHRIES JESSE
Private	HARDING JAMES
Private	HAWKINS WM.
Private	HEATLEY JAMES
Private	HAWKESWORTH THOS.
Private	HUNTER GEORGE

Private	HEYWOOD MOSES
Private	HOWELL JOHN
Private	JOHNSTONE WM.
Private	INWOOD JNS.
Private	IMPEY GEO.
Private	JENKINS PHILIP
Private	KENYON JAMES
Private	KEATES THOS.
Private	KEANE JAMES
Private	LARBY JAMES
Private	LINE JOHN
Private	LUCAS HENRY
Private	McCULLEN PATK.
Private	McGILL ROBT.
Private	MILLS JOHN
Private	MILLER RICHD.
Private	MORRIS WM.
Private	McLARIN JAMES
Private	MATHER JAMES
Private	MOORE WM.
Private	NEWTH ABRM.
Private	NEWMAN WM.
Private	NEWMAN JOHN
Private	POTTER JOHN
Private	PEGGS WM.
Private	PAPPS AMBROSE
Private	PERRIN WM.
Private	PONTEFRACT GAMIEL
Private	REEVES JOHN
Private	REYNOLDS GEO.
Private	PHILLIPS THOS.
Private	RAY PHILIP
Private	REEVES WM.
Private	STEELE JOHN
Private	STIRLING JAMES
Private	SURREY THOS.
Private	SMITH OBEDIAH
Private	SMITH PAUL
Private	SAVOURY CHAS.
Private	SENIOR GEORGE Glendinnings sale June 1912
Private	STANDING KEY
Private	SIMPSON JOSH.
Private	SUMMER JOHN
Private	STENDRICK JOHN
Private	STANDLEY WM.
Private	SHILLUM JAMES
Private	TRULOCK EDWD.
Private	THOMAS WM.
Private	TURNER SAML.
Private	URMSTONE JOSH.
Private	WADLEY STEPH.
Private	WAGSTAFF JOHN
Private	WILLIAMS ROBT.
Private	WEST WM.
Private	WEBB JAMES
Private	WHITE THOS.
Private	WATKINS THOS.

Lt.Colonel Dawkin's Company

Lt.Colonel	DAWKINS HENRY
Lieutenant	BEAUFOY MARK
Serjeant	MOORE JOHN
Serjeant	TERRY EDWD.
Serjeant	DOCKER THOS.
Serjeant	ROYLE JOHN
Serjeant	BEACON JOHN
Corporal	BELCHER GEORGE
Corporal	COREN WM.
Corporal	COOKING WM.
Corporal	GRACE WM.
Corporal	BOWER JOHN
Corporal	GRAINGER THOS.
Drummer	TURNER WM.
Drummer	BUSH WALTER
Private	ALLISON JAMES
Private	BARRETT JOHN
Private	BETTISON WM.
Private	BRUCE JOHN
Private	BROWN SAML.
Private	BENTLEY WM.
Private	BOYD JAMES
Private	BILLCOCK GEORGE
Private	CAMPBELL THOS.
Private	CUBIT THOS.
Private	CALLAND EDWD.
Private	DEWEY ROBT.
Private	DARCEY WM.
Private	DICKINSON JOHN
Private	DITCHFIELD HUGH
Private	DALE JESSE
Private	ETCHELLS BENJN.
Private	ELLIOTT ROBT.
Private	EVANS JOHN
Private	EDONSOR GODFREY
Private	FAWKENBRIDGE EDWD.
Private	FINCH DANIEL
Private	FALLOWS THOS.

Private	GOSLING WM.
Private	GOODALL JOHN
Private	GOSNEY WM.
Private	GREEN WM.
Private	GROCOTT THOS.
Private	GILL JAMES
Private	GUEST SAML.
Private	GREENHALGH WM.
Private	HERRITAGE WM.
Private	HAYWARD JOHN
Private	HITCHCOCK ROCHD. Glendinnings sale July 1913
Private	HUDSON RICHD.
Private	HARVEY JOHN
Private	HANDLEY JOHN
Private	HILL JOHN
Private	HATTERALL WM.
Private	IRELAND WM.
Private	IREMONGER MOSES
Private	JOHNSTONE THOS.
Private	JONES THOS.
Private	KELLY THOS.
Private	LANGSTON JOHN
Private	MATTHEWS JOHN
Private	MERRIATT WM.
Private	MEADOWS JOSH.
Private	MORELY GEORGE
Private	MIDDLETON WM.
Private	MACKINTOSH JAMES
Private	MATTHEWS WM.
Private	MARLOW JOHN
Private	PEARCE THOS.
Private	PEGDON PHILIP
Private	PHILIPS ROBT.
Private	PRESTON JAMES
Private	REVITT JAMES
Private	ROBINS THOS.
Private	SCOTT WM.
Private	SPEIGHT JNS. WM.
Private	STEELE THOS.
Private	SMITH JNS. Senr.
Private	SMITH JNS. Junr.
Private	STARKEY JAMES
Private	SPEIGHT BENJN.
Private	SIMPSON JAMES
Private	SAWKILL WM.
Private	STONE RICHD.
Private	THORP THOS.
Private	TURNER JAMES
Private	VICKERS THOS.
Private	WARBUTON JOHN
Private	WILSON HUMP.
Private	WALKER WM.
Private	YOUNG EDWD.
Private	RUFFLES WM.
Private	RAWSON SAINTLOW

* * *

COLDSTREAM GUARDS

Lt.Colonel Hon.J. Walople's Company (Light Company)

Captain	WALTON W.L.
Captain	MOORE Hon.R.
Lieutenant	GOOCH HENRY
Ass.Surgeon	HUNTER WM.
Serjeant	MILLAR DAVID
Serjeant	BIDDLE JOHN
Serjeant	BEALE RICHD.
Serjeant	LLOYD THOS.
Corporal	GRAHAM JAMES
Corporal	ROBINSON JAMES
Drummer	HINCHLEY GEO.
Private	ALLEN THOS.
Private	ANNING HENRY
Private	ATKINS EDWD.
Private	BURTON THOS.
Private	BELCHER RICHD.
Private	BAGANT JAMES
Private	BUTTERWORTH JAMES
Private	BAILLES GEORGE
Private	BELL JOHN
Private	BOWDEN PHILIP
Private	BRISLING EDWD.
Private	COTTON RICHD.
Private	COOPER WM.
Private	COOKE JOSH.
Private	CUGROVE JOHN
Private	CAMPBELL DAVIS
Private	CONNYBEAR THOS.
Private	COTTERILL GEORGE
Private	DAVIDSON JOHN
Private	DONOUGHY PATK.
Private	FULLER THOS.
Private	FREEMAN FRANS.
Private	GRIMSHAW JOHN
Private	GRIFFITHS JOHN
Private	GRIFFITHS EVAN
Private	GEORGE THOS.

Private	GIBBS JNS.
Private	HODSON HENRY
Private	HALE JNS.
Private	JONES THOS.
Private	JONES ROBT.
Private	JONES ISSAC
Private	KITE JAMES
Private	LLOYD JOHN
Private	LANGLEY BENJN.
Private	LAPLIN WM.
Private	LISHMAN WM.
Private	MILES NATHL.
Private	MACHIN JOSH.
Private	MUIRHEAD LEV.
Private	McCREE ALEXR.
Private	MORGAN DAVID Col.Murray's Collection
Private	McLAWRENACE RICHD.
Private	MOTHERLY ROBT.
Private	MALE RUBEN
Private	PEACE GEORGE
Private	RICHARDS JOHN
Private	ROBINSON JAMES
Private	SHERMAN RICHD.
Private	SUMMERLAND BENJN.
Private	STEPHENS WM.
Private	STAINER WM.
Private	SHELDON JOHN
Private	SMITH PETER
Private	SHERWIN ELISHA
Private	TAVLING THOS.
Private	TAYLOR JOHN
Private	TOLFREY BENJN.
Private	TURRANT JOHN
Private	THOMPSON JAMES
Private	TYSOM JOSEPH
Private	VALENTINE JOHN
Private	WILKINS RICHD.
Private	WEST JAMES
Private	WITHERS JOSH.
Private	WILBY SAML.
Private	WEBSTER JOHN
Private	WILLIAMS EDWD.
Private	WILD GEORGE
Private	WRIGHT JOHN
Private	WALKER EDWD.
Private	WILKINSON GEORGE
Private	WARMAN JOSH.
Private	WILD THOS.

2nd BATTN. 3rd REGT. OF FOOT GUARDS

Lt.Colonel Master's Company

Captain	EVELYN GEORGE
Captain	ELVINGTON JOHN
Serjeant	MACGREGGOR BRICE
Serjeant	COUZENS WM.
Serjeant	BOOTH GEORGE
Serjeant	TITTERTON JOHN
Serjeant	ASTON JOSH
Serjeant	WELCH COKER
Corporal	TRAVERS CHAS.
Corporal	FOX JONATHAN
Corporal	JOHN JOHN Glendinnings sale Oct. 1910
Corporal	JELLEY WM.
Corporal	WEBB ROBERT
Drummer	WILKINS CHAS.
Drummer	BRODIE JOHN
Private	AUSTIN EDWD.
Private	ARKINSTALL JOHN
Private	ALLEN JOSH.
Private	ALLEN JOHN
Private	ALLEN ADAM
Private	ALLWRIGHT GEORGE
Private	BRENNEN GEORGE
Private	BREMER JOHN
Private	BRENNER MATTW.
Private	BREWSTER CHAS.
Private	BIFFEN THOS.
Private	BOWSKILL CHAS.
Private	BENTLEY ISSAC
Private	BENFIELD THOS.
Private	BRUFF WM.
Private	BOOTH WM.
Private	BUCKLEY PHILIP
Private	BAILEY JAMES
Private	BROOKER ROBERT
Private	BARNFIELD HENRY
Private	BENNETT WM.
Private	BOWDEN JOHN
Private	BARNETT ROBERT
Private	BISCOE JAMES
Private	BROOKES THOS.
Private	COPE AARON
Private	CULLIS WM.
Private	CARTER WM.
Private	CLAY MATTW.
Private	CLEEVESLEY RICHD.

Private	CADDOCK JOHN
Private	CHEESEWORTH JOHN
Private	COUNSELL THOS.
Private	COPELAND JOHN
Private	DRING HENRY
Private	DRURY WM.
Private	DRURY JEREH.
Private	DAVENPORT JOHN
Private	DREW JOHN
Private	DARLING HENRY
Private	EDMONDS HENRY
Private	ECCLES WM.
Private	ECCLESTON CHRISTR.
Private	ELLIOTT MICHL. Glendinning sale Oct. 1912
Private	FOX SAML.
Private	FULLER WM.
Private	FORD THOS.
Private	GILBURN WM.
Private	GANN ROBT.
Private	GRIMSTONE JOHN
Private	GRAY EDWD.
Private	GREEN THOS.
Private	GARDINER GEORGE
Private	GRIMES THOS.
Private	HART JOHN
Private	HAMSON RICHD.
Private	HODGES JOHN
Private	HARCOURT WM.
Private	HOWSON THOS.
Private	JONES JAMES
Private	JONES JNS. 1st
Private	JONES JNS. 2nd
Private	JACKSON CHRISTR.
Private	KING JOHN
Private	LORD JAMES
Private	LOVITT GEORGE
Private	MORGAN THOS.
Private	MOTTRAM JAMES
Private	MANSELL THOS.
Private	MACDONALD JOHN
Private	MURRELL JAMES
Private	MURRAY WM.
Private	MARKHAM JOHN
Private	NUTTALL WM. Sotheby's Sale June 1913
Private	NESBITT ANDREW
Private	OWEN JOHN
Private	PROCTOR HENRY
Private	PERRY THOS.
Private	POULTNEY FRANCIS
Private	RYAN MICHL.
Private	RANN JAMES
Private	RYLIE HUGH
Private	SMART WM.
Private	SHAW ALEXR.
Private	SEARS JOSEPH
Private	SHORE SAMUEL
Private	STEEL CHAS.
Private	SIVITER JAMES
Private	TURNER ISSAC
Private	TWIGG BENJN.
Private	TAYLOR JOHN
Private	TAYLOR HENRY
Private	WEST WILLIAM
Private	WHEAT WM.
Private	WARREN EDWD.
Private	WALL ROBERT
Private	WHARTON EDWD.
Private	THOMAS THOS.
Private	TAYLOR MICHL.
Private	WILSON JOHN
Private	WAKELEY JOSEPH
Private	WOOD JOHN
Private	WILLIAMS WATKIN
Private	WARING THOS.
Private	SHAW HENRY
Private	STEEL JAMES
Private	FRITH DONALD
Private	BERRY WM.

Lt.Colonel C. Dashwood's Company

Lt.Coloenl	DASHWOOD CHAS.
Captain	FAIRFIELD E.B.
Ensign	JAMES WM.
Ensign	HAMILTON W.F.
Serjeant	PONSFORD JOHN
Serjeant	BRADBURNE TIMY.
Serjeant	PARKIN JAMES
Serjeant	MATTHEWS JAMES
Serjeant	ROSS HUNTER
Serjeant	LEATHER JAMES
Serjeant	BUCHAN DAVID
Corporal	MILLER GEORGE
Corporal	GRIFFITHS THOS.
Corporal	COX THOS.
Corporal	MORRIS JAMES
Corporal	DUFF ROBT.
Corporal	QUINTON JAMES
Drummer	STAFFORD WM.

Private	ALSOP ANTHY.
Private	ASHWORTH EDWD.
Private	ABBOTT THOS.
Private	ALLEN JOHN
Private	BENNEWORTH JOHN
Private	BENSLEY WM.
Private	BIRKIN JAMES
Private	BROUGHTON JOHN
Private	BAILEY WM.
Private	BULMORE URIAH
Private	BURRY GEORGE
Private	BILBEY DANIEL
Private	BARNES JAMES
Private	BURRAGE JOHN
Private	BLAKEY HENRY
Private	BURFORD THOS.
Private	BROWN ROBT.
Private	COX RICHD.
Private	CARPENTER JOHN
Private	COX JOSEPH
Private	CHAPMAN WM.
Private	CALLAND JOHN
Private	CUMMINGS WM.
Private	CULLEY JOHN
Private	CARMICHAEL JOHN
Private	DAVIS JAMES
Private	DICKENSON JOSH.
Private	DAVIS JOSH. Day Sale April 1910
Private	DYER THOMAS
Private	EDWARDS BENJN.
Private	FOWLER THOS.
Private	FISHER JOHN
Private	FENNICH RALPH
Private	FRYER WM.
Private	GREEN DONALD
Private	GALLAWAY THOS.
Private	GARDINER WM.
Private	GITTOE GEORGE
Private	HOLDHAM RICHD.
Private	HAWKINS RICHD.
Private	HOVER JOHN
Private	HORTON PAUL
Private	HOWELL THOS. Littledale Sale Nov. 1910
Private	HUMPHRIES HARRY
Private	HATTRALL DANIEL
Private	HOLLAND JOHN
Private	HATFIELD JOHN
Private	HESLOP ARCHD.
Private	IRELAND THOS.
Private	JOHNSTON HENRY
Private	JONES SAML.
Private	KIRKLAND MATTW.
Private	LEES SAMUEL
Private	McLOUD DANIEL
Private	MARSHALL STEPHEN
Private	MADDISON JOHN
Private	MANCUR WM.
Private	PICKARD JOHN
Private	POOL JAMES
Private	PLATT ROBERT
Private	PEARSON JOSH.
Private	PICKHAM WM.
Private	PATERSON WM.
Private	POWELL JEREH.
Private	REES WM.
Private	STRADLING JOHN
Private	SEAMAN ROBT.
Private	SMITH JAMES Col.Murray's Collection
Private	STUCKEY CHAS.
Private	SANDERS JAMES
Private	SCOTT ROBT.
Private	TAYLOR JOHN
Private	TOMLINSON JOHN
Private	THOMAS ROBT.
Private	WARD WM.
Private	WATTS ROBERT
Private	WIGGIN RICHD.
Private	WELLS WM.
Private	WELLS JAMES
Private	WILD NEGEY
Private	WOOL ROBT.
Private	WESTWOOD WM.
Private	WETHERALL ROBT.
Private	WYNE JEREH.
Private	WILMOTT ROBT.
Private	WRIGHT WM.
Private	WILLIAMS JOHN
Private	FINDLEY DANIEL
Private	EDGAR CHAS.
Private	McKENLEY MICHL.
Private	SHAW JOSH.
Private	WYNE JAMES
Private	RUDDOCK JOHN
Private	HOGGINS GEORGE
Private	SHORE JOSEPH

Private	RICHARDS GEORGE
Private	CASH WM.

Lt.Colonel Home's Company

Lt.Colonel	HOME FRANS. On sale at Baldwin's July 1912
Captain	HESKETH R.B.
Captain	HAWKINS HENRY
Captain	BARNETT CHAS. JNS.
Serjeant	HAINES BENJN.
Serjeant	BADDERLY JAMES
Serjeant	MILLER ALEXR.
Serjeant	BROOMHALL ABRM.
Serjeant	KING ALEXR.
Serjeant	DAVIDSON CHAS.
Corporal	TAYLOR WM.
Corporal	BLANKLEY ROBT.
Corporal	SCATTERGOOD JOHN
Corporal	HATTY EVAN
Corporal	HENDREY JOHN
Corporal	BAILEY JOHN
Corporal	DAVIS WM.
Corporal	VINCENT WM.
Drummer	STANIFORD GEORGE
Private	ASPINELL MATTW.
Private	ANDREWS JAMES
Private	ARTHUR PETER
Private	BAKER ENOCH
Private	BEER HENRY
Private	BAKEWELL MATTW.
Private	BROOKS JOHN
Private	BEARDSLEY SAML.
Private	BARROWCLIFFE EDMUND
Private	CALVERT WM.
Private	CRIBB ALEXR.
Private	CAFFREY MICHL.
Private	CUTHBERTSON THOS.
Private	CROSSIER ROBT.
Private	DAVIS WM.
Private	DIXON JOHN
Private	ELLIOTT THOS.
Private	FREEMAN WM.
Private	FRIEND SAML.
Private	FITZGIBBONS MORRIS
Private	FINDLAY ANDREW
Private	FROGGETT JOHN
Private	GREAR JAMES
Private	GEORGE DAVID
Private	GREEN ROBERT
Private	GENT WM.
Private	GOOBY WM.
Private	GREENWOOD WM.
Private	GIBSON THOS.
Private	GODFREY JOHN Glendinnings Sale Jan. 1910
Private	GOULDING JAMES
Private	HOLDER SAML.
Private	HARDICKER WM.
Private	HENDERSON ALEXR.
Private	HAMPSON SAMUEL
Private	HOPE THOS.
Private	HAGRAM THOS.
Private	HIXON WM.
Private	KIRBY JOHN
Private	LOWE CHAS.
Private	LAIDLER WM.
Private	LOWDEN GEORGE
Private	LOTT MATTW.
Private	LUMBER JOHN
Private	LEGG DAVID
Private	LIESTER JOSEPH
Private	LEACH GEORGE
Private	MELVILLE ANDREW
Private	MARSDEN GEORGE
Private	MOLINEAUX JAMES
Private	MEEK WM.
Private	MATTHEWS JAMES Glendinnings sale March 1912
Private	MANNING THOS.
Private	MERRICK BENJN.
Private	MILES EDWD.
Private	MASON JOHN
Private	MUTTER WM.
Private	MATTHEWS WM.
Private	MARSDEN FRANS.
Private	MILLER ANDREW
Private	NOTLEY OWEN
Private	POLLARD JOHN
Private	PRITCHARD SAML.
Private	PHILLPOTT JAMES
Private	PARBOTT JAMES
Private	PACKER JAMES
Private	RICHARDSON WM.
Private	ROY RICHD.
Private	SMITH JAMES
Private	SWANN JOSEPH
Private	STEPHENS JOHN
Private	SHERROCKS THOS.

Private	SUMMERS JAMES
Private	TINSLEY WM.
Private	THOMAS DAVID
Private	TURNER JOHN
Private	WOMBRIDGE RICHD.
Private	WYBOROUGH JAMES
Private	WHITTAKER THOS.
Private	WATT ROBERT
Private	WORTHING ROBT.
Private	WOOD JOHN
Private	TEAGUE JAMES

Lt.Colonel Henry Rooke's Company

Lt.Colonel	ROOKE H.W.
Wnsign	ANSON GEORGE
Serjeant	STEVENSON JOHN
Serjeant	STABLES JOHN
Serjeant	PAUL THOS.
Serjeant	MOSS THOS.
Corporal	GUNN ROBERT
Corporal	SHIPLEY JOHN
Corporal	FERRIER JOHN
Corporal	JAMIESON THOS.
Corporal	ANDERSON CHAS.
Corporal	RIDDLE ROBT.
Drummer	FOLLOWS JOHN
Private	ATTWOOD JOHN
Private	ABSOM WM.
Private	BURGESS WM.
Private	BRILEY RICHD.
Private	BROADHURST PETER
Private	BLAKE CHAS.
Private	BURGESS ALEXR.
Private	BISHOP NUGENT
Private	BOWYER ELIJAH
Private	BROOKS THOS.
Private	BIRCH WM.
Private	BRAIN MOSES
Private	COCKBURN JAMES
Private	CLEGG WM.
Private	COOMBES THOS.
Private	CHEESMAN JAMES
Private	COBLEY GEORGE
Private	DAY THOS.
Private	DYE SAMSON
Private	DOWNES JOSEPH
Private	DILKES WM.
Private	EVANS WM.
Private	EARNSHAW JOSEPH Glendinnings Sale April 1913
Private	EYRES WM.
Private	FLEET THOS.
Private	FISHER EDWD.
Private	FISHER DANIEL
Private	GARDINER WM.
Private	GEE WM.
Private	GOODWIN SAML.
Private	GRAY ROBT.
Private	GORDON ROBT.
Private	GREENWOOD ABRM.
Private	GRIFFITHS EDWD.
Private	GIBSON ROBT.
Private	HOLLIS BENJN.
Private	HITCHEN THOS.
Private	HUNT BENJN.
Private	HALE THOS.
Private	HOUGH GEO.
Private	HARRIS JOHN
Private	HINKES WM.
Private	IVES JOHN
Private	JUDGE GEORGE
Private	KENNERLY GEO. Glendinnings sale 21 July 1909
Private	KNIGHT JOHN
Private	LOCKHEAD JAMES
Private	LOYTH JAMES
Private	LENNOARD SAML.
Private	MOORE WM.
Private	MANLOVE GEO.
Private	MORRIS JOHN
Private	NASH ROBT.
Private	NATRESS ROBERT
Private	OLIVER THOS.
Private	PERRINS RICHD.
Private	PROCTOR WM.
Private	PAGE STEPHEN
Private	ROWSELL WM.
Private	ROSSINGTON WM.
Private	RAINE WM.
Private	ROLLINS DANIEL
Private	ROGERS JOSEPH
Private	RATTRAY JAMES
Private	SISLEY JAMES
Private	STEVENS JACOB
Private	STEVENSON JOHN
Private	SLOWMAN WM.
Private	THOMAS HENRY

Private	TATLER THOS.
Private	TUCKER GEO.
Private	TODSTELL THOS.
Private	TUCKER JOHN
Private	TOLHURST JOHN
Private	WILMOTT THOS.
Private	WHITE JOHN
Private	WITHERS JOHN
Private	WEARE EDWD.
Private	WOOD SAMUEL
Private	WEBB ROBT.
Private	WILSON ROBT.
Private	WALKER THOS.
Private	WELLER STEPHEN
Private	WHITEHEAD THEOPHILUS
Private	WILSON ARCHD.
Private	BLEAY JOSH.
Private	BRAMLEE WM.
Private	DAFT JOHN
Private	KIRK JOHN
Private	HUTCHINSON JOHN
Private	BATES THOS.
Private	LOCKYER LEONARD

Lt.Colonel Douglas Mercer's Company

Colonel	HEPBURN FRANS.
Lt.Colonel	MERCER DOUGLAS
Captain	MOORHOUSE WM.
Captain	STOTHURST WM.
Ensign	BUTLER WHIT.
Qr.Master	SKUCE JOHN
Surgeon	GOOD SAML.
Ass.Surgeon	HANROTT F.GEO.
S.Major	COX WM.
Q.M.S.	THOMPSON WM.
Ass.Serjeant	PARKS EDWD.
Serjeant	FRASER RALPH
Serjeant	SISON FRANS.
Serjeant	ROBERTS DANIEL
Serjeant	WILLIAMS THOS. 1st
Serjeant	JONES OWEN
Serjeant	WILLIAMS THOS. 2nd.
Serjeant	FOWLER ABRM.
Corporal	BLAKE JOHN
Corporal	MANSELL GEO.
Corporal	REYNOLDS GEO.
Corporal	BOYER WM.
Corporal	HOWIE DAVID
Corporal	DARKE EDWD.
Corporal	RAYNER JOHN
Corporal	ROSBOTTOM ABRM.
Drummer	STOTHURST ROBERT
Private	ALLEN GEORGE
Private	ALDRED THOS.
Private	ASHLEY SAML.
Private	BOND WM.
Private	BARRETT JOHN
Private	BARNS THOS.
Private	BRADLEY WM.
Private	BENFIELD BENJN.
Private	BOLTON ISSAC
Private	BOULD JOSH
Private	BRILEY JOHN
Private	BARBER WM.
Private	BROAD THOS.
Private	BURNESS DAVID
Private	BARRETT WM.
Private	COVENTRY THOS.
Private	CRUTCHLEY SAML.
Private	COLLIER WM.
Private	COCHRANE PHILIP
Private	CHADWICK CHAS.
Private	COLLEY THOS.
Private	DICK WM.
Private	DAVIS SAML.
Private	DAWS ISSAC
Private	ERLAM SAML.
Private	FARNISH CHAS.
Private	FROST THOS.
Private	FISHER CHRISTR.
Private	FUDGE JAMES
Private	FELTON JOHN
Private	FOMES JAMES
Private	GIMPSON THOS.
Private	GIRDLER JOHN
Private	GRIFFITHS THOS.
Private	GRAY JAMES
Private	GRINDRED JONATHAN
Private	HUNT STEPHEN
Private	HUGHES THOS.
Private	HULBERT THOS.
Private	HEFFORD SAML.
Private	JONES EVAN
Private	JONES JOHN
Private	JENNER JAMES
Private	KNIGHT BENJN.
Private	KIRK JOHN
Private	KIDD ROBT.

Private	LOCKHEAD WM.
Private	LINTRIDGE WM.
Private	LOMAS SAML.
Private	LANE JAMES
Private	McFADDEN JOHN
Private	MALLILEW GEO.
Private	MORRISON GEO.
Private	MOORE JOHN
Private	MORGAN THOS.
Private	NICHOLLS THOS.
Private	NASH JOHN
Private	NAILOR THOS.
Private	PHILLPOTT ISSAC
Private	PARTINGTON SAML.
Private	PERCE FRANCIS
Private	PILGRIM STEV.
Private	PENDLEBURY THOS.
Private	ROBERTS JOHN
Private	ROBERTS LEWIS
Private	RUSSELL JOHN
Private	REYNOLDS JOHN
Private	RICHARDSON JOHN
Private	READER RUBEN
Private	ROYAL JOSEPH
Private	ROSSER JOHN
Private	ROWLEY JOHN
Private	SCHOLES JAMES
Private	SWEETING GEORGE
Private	STANSFIELD JOHN
Private	THOMAS DAVID
Private	THOMAS JOHN
Private	TAYLOR WM.
Private	WAKELING SAML.
Private	WEBB JOHN
Private	WINTLE JAMES
Private	WERE DOUGLAS
Private	WILLIAMS WM.
Private	WETHERALL RICHD.
Private	DODSON WM.
Private	BONNEY THOS.
Private	CARR ROBT.

Lt.Colonel Keate's Company

Captain	DRUMMOND WM.
Ensign	STANDING G.D.
Serjeant	THOMPSON WM.
Serjeant	FERGUSON JOHN
Serjeant	WILSON ALEXR.
Serjeant	DAVIDSON JAMES
Corporal	WESTONS THOS.
Corporal	PEART JOHN
Corporal	COPELAND GEO.
Corporal	TAYLOR THOS.
Corporal	STONEHOUSE GEORGE
Corporal	PHILLIPS DAVID
Corporal	CONNACHER DONALD
Corporal	ALLEN JAMES
Drummer	DOYLE THOS.
Private	ASH JOSH
Private	ASHLEY RICHD.
Private	ALVEY WM.
Private	ADDICOT LUKE
Private	BIRCH JOHN
Private	BANKIER WM.
Private	BROWN WM.
Private	BISHOP WM.
Private	BENTLEY JOHN
Private	BAKER JAMES
Private	BARHAM JOHN
Private	BAIRD JOSH.
Private	BOXALL JOHN Col.R.T.Gascoigne's Collection March 1909
Private	BLACKHURST THOS.
Private	BRENNEN DENNIS
Private	COOKE JOSEPH
Private	CRABTREE JOSEPH
Private	CHEESMAN SOLOMON
Private	CHEATLEY WM.
Private	CHATHAM GEORGE
Private	DOUGALBY BRYAN
Private	DUNN FRANS.
Private	DUNCAN GEORGE
Private	DEWS NATHL.
Private	DAVIS THOS.
Private	ELLIS JOHN
Private	ELLIMENT WM.
Private	FULLER JOSEPH
Private	FISHER WM.
Private	FISHER THOS.
Private	FORSTER RICHD.
Private	FODEN JOSEPH
Private	GREENWOOD TITUS
Private	GOOCH WM.
Private	GARRETT JOSEPH
Private	HODGSON THOS.
Private	HILL PETER
Private	HUNTER HUGH
Private	HARDMAN ARTHUR

Private	HEARN DANIEL
Private	HADLER JAMES
Private	HAWKINS JOHN
Private	INGLES THOS.
Private	INGRAM HENRY Watters sale June 1913
Private	JONES GEORGE
Private	JACKSON RALPH
Private	KIDD JOHN
Private	LIVINGSTONE WM.
Private	LILLEY JAMES
Private	LARTER DANIEL
Private	MILLARD JOB
Private	MOSS AMOS
Private	McKENZIE WM.
Private	METCALF CHAS.
Private	MILLS EVAN
Private	MOXAM JOHN
Private	McCABLE HENRY
Private	MOORE WM.
Private	McDONALD WM.
Private	MANSTON WM.
Private	MILLS EDWD.
Private	PUDDIFORD SAML.
Private	PATRICK JOHN
Private	PRATT EDWD.
Private	PERRY WM.
Private	PALLANT WM.
Private	ROSSITER WM.
Private	ROOTS JOHN
Private	ROSSER THOS.
Private	RUSSELL GEORGE
Private	REYNOLDS THOS.
Private	SOMERVILLE THOS.
Private	SAUNDERSON JAMES
Private	STANLEY JAMES
Private	STOTT JOHN
Private	SANDFORD WM.
Private	SCATTERGOOD THOS.
Private	SWIFT JOSEPH
Private	SMITH THOS.
Private	TAPP THOS.
Private	TEAGUE WM.
Private	TYLIE JAMES
Private	WEBB HENRY
Private	WATTLEY GEORGE
Private	McGLAUHEN CHAS.

Lt.Colonel Canning's Company

Ensign	WEDGWOOD THOS.
Ensign	COCHRANE A.C.
Serjeant	PLUMTREE JOSH.
Serjeant	DAV.JOSH. A.A. Paynes Collection 1908
Serjeant	CHADWICK EDWD.
Serjeant	GIBSON ROBERT
Serjeant	GOULD RICHD.
Corporal	DONALD GEORGE
Corporal	McKENZIE DAVID
Corporal	STEPHENSON JOHN
Corporal	SHEPPARD WM.
Corporal	PHILLIPS JOHN
Corporal	BULLIS EDWD.
Corporal	BAILEY JAMES
Corporal	GEE BENJN.
Drummer	PEART THOS.
Private	ARKROIDE JOHN
Private	BAYLISS EDWD.
Private	BULL THOS.
Private	BARBER PAUL
Private	BRITTLE WM.
Private	BARNS STEPHN.
Private	BARRETT THOS.
Private	BRITTON WM.
Private	BEAMS JOHN
Private	BROWN JOHN
Private	BESWICK WM.
Private	BERRY MURDOCH
Private	BOOTH DANIEL on sale at Baldwin's July 1912
Private	CARKINGDALE WM.
Private	COWISON JAMES
Private	CARTER JOHN
Private	CHANDLER JOHN
Private	CHAMBERS JOHN
Private	CUMMINGS JOHN Glendinnings Sale Feb. 1911
Private	CHICK JOHN
Private	CARTER RICHD.
Private	CRESSWELL EDWD.
Private	CHINEY PETER
Private	CLIVE WM.
Private	COLLINS JOHN
Private	DIXON JOHN
Private	DAY JOHN
Private	DAVIS ISSAC
Private	DAVIS WM.

Private	DOBBS RICHD. Payne Collection 1911
Private	DUTTON MICHL.
Private	EVINSON WM.
Private	FAULKYER WM.
Private	FISHER WM.
Private	FAVICHILD PASHO
Private	GREEN THOS.
Private	GOVER THOS.
Private	GOWIN JOSHUA
Private	GREEN JAMES
Private	HIGHFIELD WM.
Private	HINCHLEY THOS.
Private	HARTON JAMES
Private	HUNT THOS.
Private	HODGSON JOHN
Private	HOUGH SAML.
Private	HUTTON WM.
Private	HACKETT WM.
Private	JONES WM.
Private	KNIBB JAMES
Private	KELLEY JOHN
Private	KILSAL RICHD.
Private	LIDDLE WM. 1st
Private	LOWDEN ROBT.
Private	LACKETT JOHN
Private	LEE JAMES
Private	LLOYD WM.
Private	MITCHELL SAML.
Private	MOREMON ROBT.
Private	McCALLY DANIEL
Private	MOORE HENRY
Private	NEWCOMBES JOHN Cheylesmore Collection 1908
Private	OLIVER NATHL.
Private	PORTER CHAS
Private	PATTERSON EDWD.
Private	PERKINS JAMES
Private	PULLIN JAMES
Private	PAINE RICHARD
Private	PRESTON JOHN
Private	RUSTON THOS.
Private	RANDLE WM.
Private	RAWBUCK GEORGE Gelndinnings sale Oct.1912
Private	RINGER JAMES
Private	SHERRIFF THOS.
Private	SANDS JOHN
Private	SMITH JAMES
Private	TAYLOR JOSEPH
Private	TUGDY ELIJA.
Private	UPTON MICHL.
Private	WICKHURST JOHN
Private	WHEELER JOHN
Private	WOODING JAMES
Private	WATSON THOS.
Private	WILDAY BENJN.
Private	WESTON RICHD.
Private	BOWEN EDWD.
Private	HARDING STEVEN
Private	CUTTER GEORGE
Private	FLANNAGIN WM.
Private	DEW WM.
Private	DUNSTON THOS.

Lt.Colonel Edwd. Bowater's Company

Lt.Colonel	BOWATER EDWD.
Ensign	DRUMMOND BIRKELEY
Ensign	BLAINE HUGH S.
Serjeant	GODDARD THOS.
Serjeant	DALLAWAY WM.
Serjeant	SELWYN THOS.
Serjeant	BUTLER JAMES
Serjeant	BOYD GEORGE
Serjeant	GILLING JOHN
Serjeant	ORDERS JAMES
Corporal	McBEAN ALEXR.
Corporal	MOSS RICHD.
Corporal	MORGAN THOS.
Corporal	OLDFIELD JOHN
Corporal	NEALE THOS.
Corporal	DORWARD WM.
Corporal	WHITEHEAD SAML.
Private	BAILEY JOHN
Private	BIRD WHISTLE HENRY
Private	BRADSHAW JOHN
Private	BLACKSHAW WM.
Private	BARROWCLIFFE EDMD.
Private	BURLY PRESTON
Private	CROSS WM.
Private	CANN THOS.
Private	DAWSON BENJN.
Private	DIMERY JOHN
Private	DOBER JOHN
Private	EWART DAVID
Private	FLETCHER WM.
Private	GRICE JOHN

Private	GEE ROBT.
Private	GODFREY JOHN
Private	HARRISON THOS.
Private	HARDWICK JOHN
Private	HOLLIS WM.
Private	HARDY GEORGE
Private	HODGE EDWD.
Private	HARPER MOSES
Private	HALL JAMES
Private	HARRIS JOSEPH
Private	HAMMOND THOS.
Private	HIPKISS WM.
Private	HOLDING CHAS.
Private	HANCOCK GILES
Private	HOGGINS THOS.
Private	ISSACS WM.
Private	JINKS JOHN
Private	JOLLY ROBT.
Private	LEAR WM.
Private	LEE BENJN.
Private	MAY THOS.
Private	McGREGOR DANIEL
Private	MILLER JOHN
Private	MARKWICK JAMES
Private	MASON NEWTON
Private	NICHOL JAMES
Private	NORTHORP GEORGE
Private	ORRELL THOM.
Private	OSBOURN GEORGE
Private	PAINTER WM.
Private	PARNELL WM.
Private	PRITCHARD WM.
Private	PLATTS JOHN
Private	PALMER JOHN
Private	ROSS LOCKET
Private	RUSSELL JOHN
Private	SWEET ROBT.
Private	SHENSTON JOSH.
Private	STEPHENSON EDWD.
Private	SMITH JOHN
Private	SANDERSON JOSEPH
Private	SYKES WM.
Private	SEXTON WM.
Private	SCOONS LEONARD
Private	SMITH WM.
Private	STANLEY GEORGE
Private	SINFIELD WM.
Private	STILLWELL THOS.
Private	TALBUTT EDWD.
Private	TAYLOR JOHN
Private	WALKER JOSEPH
Private	WILDGOOSE GEORGE
Private	WATMOUTH ROBT.
Private	WEAVER JAMES
Private	WORRELL JOHN
Private	WOODMAN WM.
Private	WHITE WM.
Private	WHITE JOHN
Private	WESTWOOD JOHN
Private	WILLIAMS CHAS.
Private	WHITEHEAD WM.
Private	WILLIAMS JOHN
Private	RAY THOS.
Private	BATHURST FRANS.
Private	SMITH THOS.

Lt.Colonel Hon.Sir Alexr. Gordon's Company

Lt.Colonel	GORDON Sir SLEXR.
Captain	WIGSTON RICH.HY.
Ensign	LAKE CHAS.
Ensign	BAIRD DAVID
Serjeant	MACROBERT WM.
Serjeant	SOUTHCOMBE THOS.
Serjeant	BARBER ANDREW
Serjeant	WHITTAKER WM.
Serjeant	SOMERVILLE WM.
Corporal	LILLEY ISSAC
Corporal	GREENSHIELDS WR.
Corporal	BAYNHAM WM.
Corporal	ROWSON JOHN
Corporal	GEAREY JOHN
Corporal	GREENWOOD JOSH.
Corporal	BALL WM.
Corporal	LEWIS THOS.
Drummer	ABBOTT CHAS.
Private	AGAR STEPHEN Galway Foley Collection 1910
Private	BARTLETT JOHN
Private	BRISCOE BENJN.
Private	BUCKLER WM.
Private	BATCHELOR RICHD.
Private	BLACK JOHN
Private	BARRAND JAMES
Private	BENSON JAMES
Private	BOYD JOHN
Private	BAINBRIDGE JOHN
Private	BATES WM.
Private	BROWN WM.
Private	CHAPPIN DANIEL

Private	COLLIER GEORGE
Private	CLARKE GEORGE
Private	CONNER DANIEL
Private	CRAWFORD WM. Glendinnings sale Oct.1913
Private	CARTER JOHN
Private	CARROUGH PETER
Private	EVANS ROBT.
Private	FULCHER CHAS.
Private	FERNLEY AZARIAH
Private	GILES ELIAS
Private	GREEN THURSTON Gray Collection 1908
Private	GRIFFEN RICHD.
Private	GREY JAMES
Private	GALLEY JOSHUA
Private	HORSEBOROUGH HUGH
Private	HAYSMAN JAMES
Private	HUDSON JOHN
Private	HURST GEORGE
Private	HOBSON JOHN
Private	HADDEN ALEXR.
Private	HOUSELANDER ISSAC
Private	INGLIS GEORGE
Private	KNIGHT JOHN
Private	KETTLEWELL JOHN
Private	KIDDY DAVID
Private	LOWANCE GEORGE
Private	LANGTON JAMES
Private	LAMB JOHN
Private	LOW DAVID
Private	LAKE EDWD.
Private	LEWIS THOS.
Private	LOYDFORD CHAS.
Private	LARGE GEORGE
Private	MILES WM.
Private	MORICE BENJN.
Private	MOODY JOHN
Private	NUTTALL JOSH
Private	NAILOR JOHN
Private	OSBOURNE GEORGE
Private	OULCOTT JOHN
Private	PORTER THOS.
Private	PUGH JAMES
Private	PRICE JOHN
Private	ROUCE RICHD.
Private	ROOKE WALTER
Private	RAYNER JOHN
Private	ROBERTS JAMES
Private	ROSE THOS.
Private	SMITH GEORGE
Private	SAXBY JAMES
Private	SYMINGTON JOHN
Private	THOMAS DAVID
Private	TRUNDLEY JOHN
Private	TAYLOR WM.
Private	TONKS WM.
Private	TUGNETT JAMES
Private	WOOD JOHN
Private	WALKER ROBERT on sale at Baldwins March 1909
Private	WINDSOR JOHN H.Gaskell's collection 1908
Private	WILCOCK RICHD.
Private	WEBB ISSAC
Private	WOOD THOMAS
Private	WORTHING JOHN
Private	YEALD WM.
Private	ASTLE THOS.
Private	LYON WM.
Private	LEWIS JOHN

<u>Lt.Colonel Charles West's Company</u>

Lt.Colonel	WEST CHAS.
Captain	MONTGOMERIE H.B.
Ensign	PRENDERGAST GEOFFRY
Ensign	MONTAGUE HENRY
Serjeant	JACQUES CHAS.
Serjeant	METCALF WM.
Serjeant	MURDOCK ALEXR.
Private	SUTHERLAND ALEXR.
Serjeant	LAWRENCE WM.
Corporal	MACLEAN ALEXR.
Corporal	ROWLEY MICHL.
Corporal	HAWES JAMES
Corporal	DONALDSON WM.
Corporal	HUGHES THOS.
Corporal	OWENS EUSTACE
Corporal	CRANTE JOHN
Corporal	HOWARTH JAMES
Drummer	BASSETT JAMES
Private	ALLEN JOHN
Private	BAKER JOSHUA
Private	BOYLE JOHN
Private	BYGATE THOS.
Private	BUTLER THOS.
Private	COOLEY WM.
Private	CARTWRIGHT WM.

Private	COOKE JOHN
Private	CLUTTERBUCK JOHN
Private	CLIFF SAML.
Private	CORDICK THOS.
Private	DOUGHTY JOHN
Private	DAUBIN ROBT.
Private	FOX JOHN Glendinnings sale 17 June 1908
Private	FOXALL FRANCIS
Private	FOLKES JOHN
Private	FISHER EUTHYCUS
Private	FULLER JOSIAS
Private	GREY GEORGE
Private	GREENSMITH GEORGE
Private	GRIFFITHS THOS.
Private	GOULDING GEORGE
Private	HILL JAMES
Private	HOBDAY MARK Whitaker Collection 1908
Private	HOOPER THOS.
Private	HEATHCOCK THOS.
Private	HUNT GEORGE
Private	HOLYLAND THOS.
Private	JONES JNS. 1st
Private	JONES JNS. 2nd
Private	JONES WM.
Private	JONES DAVID
Private	JONES EVAN
Private	JACKSON JOHN
Private	KIRKLAND ALEXR.
Private	KING WM.
Private	LOOSELEY JOHN
Private	LONG STEPHN.
Private	MALTBY CHRISTR.
Private	MAIN WM.
Private	MACGEORGE WM.
Private	MITCHELL RALPH
Private	MARTIN GEORGE
Private	NICKOLDS DAVID on sale at Spinks June 1910
Private	NOWLAND JOHN
Private	PERRY GEORGE
Private	PURDAY WM.
Private	PEACOCK DAVID
Private	PARKER THOS.
Private	PRIDE ALEXR.
Private	POPE JOSH.
Private	PETERS THOS.
Private	PEGG SIMON
Private	PLATFORD BENJN.
Private	PHIPPS THOS.
Private	RHODES THOS.
Private	RILEY EDWD.
Private	ROSS DONALD
Private	ROBINSON WM.
Private	ROBERTS JOHN
Private	SHEPHERD BENJN.
Private	SMITH JOHN
Private	SHERVILL HENRY
Private	SCUDDER RICHD.
Private	SMITH RICHD.
Private	SESSIONS THOS.
Private	SUMMER JOSH.
Private	SMITH BRYAN
Private	SCOTT WM.
Private	STOREY JOHN
Private	TOMKINSON JOHN
Private	TAYLOUR JOHN
Private	THOMPSON THOS.
Private	VARD SAML.
Private	WELLS ALEXR.
Private	WOODCOCK WM.
Private	WBSTER JACOB
Private	WICKS THOS.
Private	WALKER JOHN
Private	WRIGHT THOS.
Private	WELCH RICHD.
Private	NEWITT ROBT.
Private	CHAPMAN RICHD.
Private	WHITTAKER THOS.

* * *

3rd BATTALION ROYAL SCOTS

Major	CAMPBELL C. (Col)
Captain	ARGUIMBAU L. (Maj)
Captain	McDONALD R. (Maj)
Captain	MASSEY HUGH (Maj)
Captain	GORDON WM.
Captain	DUDGEON ROBT. Wounded at Quatre Bras
Lieutenant	MORRISON ARCHD.
Lieutenant	REA W.J. Promoted in 60th Foot
Lieutenant	INGRAM J.N. Glendinnings sale Nov. 1913
Lieutenant	CLARKE WM.
Lieutenant	GORDON THOS.
Lieutenant	STOYLE JOHN
Lieutenant	SCOTT R.H. In possession Col.R.C. Graeme late 51st L.I.
Lieutenant	LANE GEORGE

Lieutenant	SYMES JOSH.
Lieutenant	ALSTONE JAMES
Lieutenant	MANN JAMES
Lieutenant	DOBBS WM.
Lieutenant	MILLER J.F.W.
Lieutenant	STEWART GEORGE
Lieutenant	BLACK J.L.
Ensign	MUDIE CHAS.
Ensign	GRAHAM CHAS. H. Gaskell's collection 1908
Ensign	STEPHENS THOS.
Ensign	McKAY JOSH.
Ensign	COOPER LEONARD
Ensign	THOMAS WM.
Ensign	BLACKLIN RICHD. Then a volunteer
Pay.Master	THOMSON J.H. Payne Collection
Adjutant	CAMERON ALLAN
Qr.Master	GRIFFITH THOS.
Surgeon	GALLIERS WM.
Ass.Surgeon	FINNIE WM.
Ass.Surgeon	BOLTON THOS.

Captain James Cowell's Company No.1.

S.Major	KIDSON JOSH.
O.M.S.	OGILVIE JOHN
P.M.S.	GUM ALEXR.
Ar.Serjeant	FARNSWORTH DAVID
Serjeant	HARRISON MICHL.
Serjeant	RUSSELL GEORGE
Serjeant	STRONG GEORGE
Corporal	DODERY GEORGE
Corporal	KEEFE JAMES
Corporal	McHUGO RICHARD
Corporal	SEALEY RICHARD
Corporal	WILSON ROBT.
Drummer	EVANS THOS.
Drummer	MILLS ROBT.
Private	BEVIS JAMES
Private	BOUCHER WM.
Private	BULMER JOHN
Private	CARSON HILL
Private	COOPER ROBT.
Private	CRITCHLEY ROBT.
Private	CROCKER WM.
Private	CUTHBERT THOS. Dead
Private	DICKEY WM.
Private	DILLOW JAMES
Private	DIXON ROBT.
Private	DUNBOBIN HENRY
Private	EDWARDS PETER Walters sale June 1913
Private	GRAHAM ALEXR.
Private	GREEN THOS.
Private	GREENWOOD DAVID
Private	HALLETT ORLANDO
Private	HAMILL DANIEL
Private	HARVEY RICHD.
Private	HEALEY JOHN
Private	HIGGINSON PETER
Private	HINSHELWOOD JAMES Deserted
Private	HOBBS THOS.
Private	HOPE JOHN
Private	HURST WM. Deserted
Private	HYATT GILES
Private	IKIN EDWD.
Private	IRVINE HUGH
Private	KIRK JOHN
Private	LAMB RICHD.
Private	LOWES ABRAM.
Private	McGRADY JAMES
Private	McINTOSH JAMES
Private	McVEY JOHN
Private	MALLOW ISIAH
Private	MATTHEWS PATK.
Private	MATTHEWS THOS.
Private	MULLEN TERENCE
Private	OGLE WM.
Private	PARKES GEORGE
Private	QUARRY JAMES
Private	REID JOHN
Private	SMITH WM.
Private	STEWART CHAS.
Private	TAYLOR THOS.
Private	WALKER ALEXR. Deserted
Private	WILLIAMS JOSH.
Private	WILSON FRANS.

Captain W.L. Brereton's Company No.2.

Serjeant	CAMPBELL JAMES
Serjeant	HARRIS WM.
Serjeant	KENNEDY JOHN
Corporal	BENJAMIN BURTON
Corporal	CRAWFORD ALEXR.
Corporal	HEATH WM.
Corporal	MAGIN JOHN
Corporal	McEWWN ROBT.
Corporal	ODAM THOS.
Drummer	TUBBS JAMES
Private	ASPLINE JOHN

Private	BRYON THOS.
Private	BURNS EDWD.
Private	BUSHBY GEORGE
Private	CARROLL PATK.
Private	COLEMAN PATK.
Private	COOPER CHAS.
Private	COULSON GEORGE
Private	FISHER JAMES
Private	FULLER JOHN
Private	GALLAGHER MARTIN
Private	GLISSANE DAVID
Private	HATCHER JAMES
Private	HEAVY PATK.
Private	HODSON WM.
Private	JONES THOS.
Private	KIRDLING THOS.
Private	LINDSAY ALEXR.
Private	McDONALD JAMES
Private	McNANNY JOHN
Private	McSTRAVOCK JOHN
Private	MADDEN DENNIS
Private	MASON PATRICK Discharged
Private	MEDICOFT SAML.
Private	MOORE THOS.
Private	MULLEN SIMON
Private	MURRAY J.P.
Private	PETTIGREW JOHN
Private	POOK JOHN
Private	REED DAVID
Private	RITCHIE WM.
Private	ROWAN THOS.
Private	SWAFFIELD JOHN
Private	TEESDALE ROBT.
Private	THOMAS THOS.
Private	THOMPSON JOHN
Private	THOMPSON THOS.
Private	THOMPSON WM. Discharged
Private	WEBSTER JOHN
Private	YOUNG JAMES

Captain Thomas Moss's Company No.3.

Serjeant	DOWNS HUGH
Serjeant	ENWRIGHT MATTW.
Serjeant	HARVEY PATK.
Serjeant	McALPINE JOHN
Corporal	ANDO ROBT.
Corporal	CLYSDALE JAMES
Corporal	DENFORD WM.
Corporal	MAGHEE JAMES
Corporal	MARKS WM. Dead
Corporal	PRATT RALPH
Drummer	FRAZER ROBERT
Private	ALLEN JOHN
Private	BELL ISIAH
Private	BENSON JAMES
Private	CLARKE DANIEL
Private	CLAYHILL JOHN
Private	COFFIE MICHL.
Private	COOGAN OWEN
Private	COOLEY JOHN
Private	CORBETT JOHN
Private	CULBERT ELIAS
Private	CURRAN PATK.
Private	CURRAY DICKSON
Private	DALEY JEREH.
Private	ELLIOTT JOHN
Private	FARRELL ROBT.
Private	FULLERTY WM.
Private	GIBSON JAMES
Private	GREEN WM.
Private	GORDON JOHN
Private	GWYNN GEORGE
Private	HAGAN BERND.
Private	HALEY JOHN
Private	HILL JOHN
Private	JACKSON JAMES
Private	KANE WM.
Private	KELLY JOHN Discharged
Private	KERR EDWD.
Private	McFARLANE WM.
Private	McKAFFREY JAMES
Private	MILLS JAMES
Private	MONTGOMERY ROBT.
Private	MURRAY JOHN
Private	ORMROYDE THOS.
Private	PERRITT JAMES
Private	PERRY JOSH. Discharged
Private	PETRIE ROBT.
Private	QUIM THOS.
Private	ROGERS JAMES
Private	SCANLON PATK.
Private	SPRINGTHORPE JAMES
Private	TALBOT THOS.
Private	TURKENTON HAMILT.
Private	WAUGH JAMES
Private	WEBSTER JOHN Discharged
Private	WEBSTER JAMES
Private	WHITE SAMPSON

Private	WOOLSTENCROFT JOHN
Private	YOUNG WM.

Captain J. Mac Ra's Company No.4.

Serjeant	BADCOCK JOHN
Serjeant	CRAWFORD WM.
Serjeant	McCLUSKEY ANDREW
Serjeant	McDONALD ALEXR.
Serjeant	McMANUS MICHL. Galway Fo;ey Collection 1913
Serjeant	SMITH JAMES
Corporal	CLARKE FREK.
Corporal	DAVIS WM.
Corporal	GAUGHEGAN PATK.
Corporal	McSWEENEY MICHL.
Corporal	SLATTERY EDWARD
Drummer	LANG JAMES
Drummer	McCANN JAMES
Private	ALLEN JOHN
Private	ANDREWS JAMES
Private	ASTONS SAMUEL
Private	BOLAND JAMES
Private	BROWN WM.
Private	BURNS MATTW.
Private	CARRIGAN HUGH
Private	CURRAY JAMES
Private	DALTON ROBT. Gray Collection 1908
Private	DAVIDSON PETER
Private	DAVIS HOWELL
Private	DELANEY MICHL.
Private	DIXON ROBT.
Private	DIXON WM.
Private	DUGAN PATK.
Private	DUNCAN TIMY.
Private	FISHER JAMES
Private	FOYAR WALTER
Private	GRAHAM JOHN
Private	GRAY WM.
Private	GREEN THOS.
Private	GROVES REUBIN
Private	HAILES HENRY
Private	HANDY ROBT.
Private	HARRY DAVID Glendinnings sale 21st July 1909
Private	HEALY JAMES
Private	HENDERSON ALEXR.
Private	JOHNSTON SAML.
Private	JONES ANTHY.
Private	JONES DAVID
Private	IRELAND GEORGE
Private	IRVINE CHRISTN.
Private	IRVINE JOHN
Private	KANE JACKSON
Private	KIERMAN JAMES
Private	KELLY LUKE
Private	LAVERTY THOS.
Private	LEVINS JOHN Needes collection 1908
Private	LEWIS JAMES Whitaker collection 1908
Private	McCANN JOHN
Private	McCANNA WM.
Private	McCLUSKEY THOS.
Private	McDONALD MICHL.
Private	McELHAIR ROBT.
Private	McGOWAN ROGER
Private	McKAY ROBT.
Private	McLARNOW CHAS.
Private	McLAUGHLIN SAML.
Private	McLAUGHLIN WM.
Private	McSORLEY BERD.
Private	MOSS JAMES
Private	MURPHY JAMES
Private	PAISLEY JAMES
Private	PRIESTLEY JOHN
Private	REASIDE WM.
Private	REID FRANS.
Private	RIVETT JOHN
Private	RUSSELL JOHN
Private	SHERRATT CHAS.
Private	SMITH THOS.
Private	SUTCLIFFE STEPHEN
Private	THOMPSON THOS.
Private	TOOKEY ANTHY.
Private	WEIR PATK.

Captain H. Cowell's Company No.5.

Serjeant	BLOXHAM RICHD.
Serjeant	LEGG DAVID
Serjeant	McCLURE ANDREW
Serjeant	MIDLAM SAMPSON
Corporal	DOWNIE JOHN
Corporal	FRASER WM.
Corporal	HART MICHL.
Corporal	IRVINE GEORGE
Corporal	SHORTLEY JOSEPH
Drummer	McDONALD NORMAN
Private	BARNETT JAMES

Private	BELL HENRY
Private	BINDING SAML.
Private	BUCK JACOB
Private	BURGESS JOHN
Private	BURNS BARND.
Private	CALDER WM.
Private	CARTWRIGHT WM.
Private	COKER WM. Discharged
Private	CONWAY HUGH
Private	CRAIG JOHN
Private	CROGAN JOHN
Private	DONNALLY JOHN
Private	DOUGHERTY HUGH
Private	DUNCAN ALEXR.
Private	DYSERT ALEXR.
Private	FLYNN DENIS
Private	GARVEY PETER
Private	HAGAN JAMES
Private	HAMILL JOHN
Private	HARRISON ABEDO.
Private	HILL GEORGE
Private	HOGAN ROBT.
Private	JONES ANDW.
Private	KARR MURDK. Discharged
Private	KAY JOHN Discharged
Private	KNIGHT WM.
Private	McDERMOTT HUGH
Private	McINTOSH WM.
Private	McLEAN DAVID
Private	McNALLY FRANS.
Private	McQUADE THOS.
Private	PICKETT WM.
Private	SMITH DANIEL Discharged
Private	SQUANCE JAMES
Private	STRAWBRIDGE WM.
Private	TAYLOR WM.
Private	TEVELIN JAMES
Private	TINLEY PETER
Private	TURLEY PETER Discharged
Private	WALKER ANDRW.
Private	WILSON JOSEPH

Captain Geo.Marlay (Major's) Company No.6.

Serjeant	BUCHANAN ROBT.
Serjeant	CONWAY HUGH
Serjeant	McGEOUGH PATK.
Serjeant	OATS MICHL.
Serjeant	PENTON ISSAC
Serjeant	PURFIELD PATK.
Corporal	DRAYTON JOHN
Corporal	FAIR MICHL.
Corporal	LEARG TIMY.
Corporal	MARTIN PETER
Corporal	WOOD JOHN
Drummer	ARMAGER CHN.
Drummer	WHITE JOHN
Private	AUSTIN WM.
Private	BAKER AMARIAH Discharged
Private	BALL JOHN
Private	BRADLEY JAMES
Private	BROWN THOS. Discharged
Private	BURNS JAMES
Private	CARNELL RICHD.
Private	CARROLL EDWD.
Private	CARTER HENRY
Private	CHEW THOS.
Private	CLARKE JOHN
Private	CLEMIS JOHN
Private	COATS JOHN Discharged
Private	CURREN HENRY
Private	DAY JOSEPH
Private	DEVELIN WM.
Private	DEWART WM. Discharged
Private	DOUGHERTY NICHS.
Private	FARRELL JOHN
Private	FINLEY JAMES
Private	GOUGH JAMES
Private	HALL FRANS. Discharged
Private	HILL JOHN
Private	HILL THOS.
Private	HOGG GEORGE
Private	HORNEY JOHN
Private	JEPSON CHAS.
Private	JONES ISSAC
Private	LEARY PATK.
Private	LEE WM.
Private	LOWE JAMES
Private	McBRIDE JAMES
Private	McCABE JAMES
Private	McCAFFERY HUGH
Private	McCANN EDWD.
Private	McGEOUGH PATK.
Private	McNALLY CHAS.
Private	MOORE JOHN
Private	MURDOCK EDWD. Dead
Private	OAG WM.
Private	PENTON PHILIP
Private	SANGSTER WM.

Private	SCOTT FLETCHER
Private	SIMPSON WM.
Private	SLYE THOS.
Private	SMITH JOHN
Private	STOKER ROBT.
Private	TITTLE SAML.
Private	WALSH JOHN Day sale April 1910
Private	WINSTANLEY JOHN

Captain George Dods (Major's) Company No.7.

Serjeant	BENNEY JAMES
Serjeant	CALDERHEAD GAVIN
Serjeant	CANNING HUGH
Serjeant	HOBSON FRANS.
Serjeant	TIERNEY JOHN
Serjeant	WALLACE DAVID
Corporal	BRANAGAN MATTW.
Corporal	CLIMS GEORGE
Corporal	LLOYDE JOHN
Corporal	SMALL JOHN
Drummer	GRAY GEORGE
Private	BANNISTER NATHL.
Private	BEGG ALEXR.
Private	BOSTOCK THOS.
Private	BURRELL ANDW. Dead
Private	CHRISTIE ROBT.
Private	CREDDLE GEORGE
Private	CUMLEGE GEORGE
Private	DAVIS GEORGE
Private	DEAKIN JOHN
Private	FOY JAMES
Private	FOY ROBT.
Private	FRATSON DANIEL
Private	FROOD JAMES
Private	GALLOWAY WM.
Private	GAMBLYN GEORGE Payne Collection 1911
Private	GAVEN MICHL.
Private	GAWKROGERS JOSH.
Private	GORMLEY HUGH
Private	GRAY JOHN
Private	GRAY THOS.
Private	HOLIDAY JOHN
Private	HODSON JOHN
Private	JONES SAML.
Private	KELLEY JAMES
Private	KENNEDY HUGH Glendinnings sale 17th June 1908
Private	KERNS JOHN
Private	LAMONT JAMES
Private	McDONALD WM.
Private	McDOUGALL JOHN
Private	McPHERSON DOND.
Private	PAUL JOHN
Private	PAYNE WALTER
Private	PEARSON GEORGE DISCHARGED
Private	QUINN MICHL.
Private	REID ROBT.
Private	RIDGE JAMES
Private	SIMPSON FRANS.
Private	SMITH RICHD.
Private	TARZWELL JESSE
Private	TAYLOR DAVID
Private	VAUGHAN DAVID
Private	WALL WM.
Private	WATSON WM.
Private	WEEKES JAMES

Captain Robert Dudgeon's Company No.8.

Serjeant	DOUGLASS ROBT.
Serjeant	McLEARY JOSH.
Serjeant	MITCHELL ALEXR.
Serjeant	O'CONNER HENRY Discharged
Corporal	BOYDE ALEXR.
Corporal	DELAHUNTY THOS.
Corporal	MAHONEY JAS. Littledale sale November 1910
Corporal	SEAY ARTHUR
Corporal	WRIGHT CHAS.
Drummer	MALLIN MICHL.
Private	ALLEN JOHN
Private	ALLEN JAMES
Private	BARKER BENJN.
Private	BATLEY THOS.
Private	BIGWOOD JOHN
Private	CHUTER JOHN
Private	COLLOPY EDWD.
Private	DURHAM GEORGE
Private	EVANS THOS. Gray Collection 1908
Private	FULTON JOHN Discharged
Private	GALLINAGH DANIEL
Private	GORMAN WM.
Private	GRANT JAMES
Private	HALBOT JOHN
Private	HAMPSON JOHN
Private	HANSON JOSH.
Private	HARDIGE WM.
Private	HENDERSON SAML.

Private	HENESAY PATK.
Private	HESELTINE JEFFERY
Private	HOGG WM.
Private	HORSEBURGH WM.
Private	HUDSON ROBT.
Private	HUGHES RICHD. Col. N.T. Gascoignes collection March 1909
Private	JAMES NOAH Dead
Private	JONES THOS.
Private	KILPATRICK ROBT. Discharged
Private	KITCHEN WM. H. Gaskell's collection 1908
Private	LOBLEY JOHN
Private	McDONALD JOHN
Private	McKAY SAML.
Private	McLEAN JOHN
Private	McMULLEN JOHN
Private	McRONALD JOHN
Private	MANWELL WM.
Private	MILBURN ISSAC
Private	MULLEN PATK.
Private	O'CONNER PATK.
Private	O'HARA ROBT.
Private	PEATES NICHS. Discharged
Private	POTTS JOHN
Private	REESE HENRY
Private	REID ALEXR.
Private	ROSS JAMES
Private	ROURKE DANIEL
Private	SAMUEL JOHN
Private	SMITH JAMES
Private	SMITH LAWRE.
Private	STANLEY JOHN
Private	THOM ROBT.
Private	WATSON MICHL.
Private	WHITEHEAD THOS.
Private	YOUNG THOS.

Captain A. MacLachlan's Company No.9.

Serjeant	FLANAGAN JOHN
Serjeant	JOHNSTON JOHN Discharged
Serjeant	LLEWELLYN RICHD. Dead
Serjeant	TAITE DAVID
Serjeant	WHEATLEY DAVID Discharged
Corporal	BLOXHAM WM.
Corporal	BRYAN JOHN
Corporal	GILLESPIE DAVID
Corporal	HOGARTY JAMES Dead
Corporal	PETRIE GEORGE Sotheby's sale April 1911
Drummer	CRAMPTON DANIEL
Drummer	DONAGHOE MICHL.
Private	ADAMS THOS.
Private	BAKER JOHN
Private	BELDON NOAH
Private	BOATFIELD JAMES
Private	BRADREY JAMES Deserted
Private	BUCKLEY DENIS Discharged
Private	CLARKE CHAS.
Private	CHARLESWORTH GEORGE
Private	CRAWFORD ROBT.
Private	CUNNINGHAM JAMES
Private	DOWNIE BARTHW.
Private	ECCLESTON JOHN
Private	EVANS THOS. 1st
Private	EVANS Thos 2nd.
Private	GALLAGHER TERENCE
Private	GILLELAND ROBT.
Private	GILLESPIE ROBT.
Private	GILLESPIE SAML. Phillips sale
Private	HAKE ROBT.
Private	HAMILTON WM.
Private	HARKNESS JAMES
Private	HARRISON JAMES
Private	HASELDINE JAMES
Private	HURLEY WM.
Private	IBBETSON JOSH.
Private	JAMESON JOHN
Private	JONES WM.
Private	KENNEMOUTH PETER
Private	LATHIN THOS.
Private	McLAUGHLIN WM.
Private	MARSHALL JAMES
Private	MARTIN JOSH.
Private	OLDHAM JAMES
Private	PALMER THOS.
Private	POWELL JOHN Col.Murray's collection 1908
Private	SAVAGE JOHN
Private	SHIELDS JOHN
Private	STANTON AUSTIN
Private	TAYLOR ISSAC
Private	WALSH THOS.
Private	WHITEHEAD GEO.
Private	WILLIAMSON GEO.

Captain C.S. Hopkin's Company No.10.

Serjeant	BERTIE JOHN
Serjeant	FERRANS JAMES
Serjeant	GRANT PETER

Serjeant	MOORE THOS.
Corporal	DOUGLASS JOHN
Corporal	HUME WM.
Corporal	KING JOHN
Corporal	OLDAG JOHN
Corporal	QUIM JOHN
Drummer	COSGROVE PETER
Private	ANDREWS MATTW.
Private	BARTLEY JAMES
Private	BAUM WM.
Private	BROOMAN JAMES
Private	BROWN JAMES
Private	BROWN WM.
Private	BURNS ADAM
Private	DOUGHERTY HARRY Discharged
Private	DURICK FELIX
Private	FLYNN PATK.
Private	FORDYCE JOHN Cheylesmore Collection 1908
Private	GAFFREY JOHN
Private	GRIBBEN JOHN
Private	HALL ROBT.
Private	HAND JOHN
Private	HENERY JOHN
Private	HOWE WM.
Private	KING HENRY
Private	LAUGHLIN PATK.
Private	LOVERING WM.
Private	McCARROLL PETER
Private	McGAREY MALACHY
Private	McGAREY JAMES
Private	McGEE JAMES
Private	McKENZIE WM.
Private	McLEOD JOHN
Private	MARINER WM. Dead
Private	MARNEY GEORGE
Private	MAWHINEY DAVID Discharged
Private	MAYNE CHAS.
Private	MORRELL JOHN
Private	MURRAY JAMES
Private	PERRY JOHN Discharged
Private	QUIRE JAMES
Private	ROCK LAWR.
Private	RAYNER WM.
Private	SCOTT HUGH
Private	SHERIDAN PATK.
Private	SMITH WM.
Private	STANLEY MICHL.
Private	STEPHENSON THOS.
Private	WALMSLEY JOHN
Private	WALTON JOSEPH

* * *

1st BATTALION 4th (Or KINGS OWN) REGIMENT

Lt.Colonel	BROOKE FRANS. In possession Sir B. Brooke 1908 Commgd. 10th British Brigade
Captain	WILSON G.D. Commdg. The Battalion
Captain	EDGELL C.I.
Lieutenant	BROWN JMS.
Lieutenant	RICHARDSON GEO. Whitaker collection 1908
Lieutenant	BOULBY PETER
Lieutenant	HEARNE G.H. Gray collection 1908
Lieutenant	COLLINS B.M.
Lieutenant	BOYD HIGATT
Lieutenant	SQUIRE WM.
Lieutenant	BUSHELL JMS.
Lieutenant	MULHOLLAND RD.
Lieutenant	LONSDALE WM.
Lieutenant	BOULBY EDWD.
Lieutenant	CLARKE WM.
Lieutenant	FIELDE FRADK.
Lieutenant	GERARD ARTH.
Lieutenant	FERNANDEZ J.L.
Ensign	LEVINGE CHAS.
Ensign	TAYLOR W.S.
Ensign	MATTHEWS WM.
Ensign	HOLLAND J.E.H.
Ensign	SHIPTON H.N.
Adjutant	RICHARDSON W. (Lieutenant)
Surgeon	BURTON F. (Sd) Frans. Brooke Lt.Colonel
Ass.Surgeon	MORRAH W.
Pay.	LONSDALE T.
Lieutenant	BURY MARTIN

Captain Kippings Company Grenadiers

Serjeant	AGGAR JAMES
Serjeant	COPLEY BENJN.
Serjeant	McCRAW ALEXR.
Serjeant	RICHARDS JNS.
Serjeant	WOODRUFF GEO.
Corporal	HUMPHRIES JAMES
Corporal	MARTIN THOS.
Corporal	MILLINER SAML.
Corporal	TURNEY STEPN.
Drummer	HUDSON JOHN
Private	ANDREWS GEO.

Private	ARMOUR JAMES
Private	BAKER JNS.
Private	BELL THOS.
Private	BUTLER ROBT.
Private	CLEMENTS JNS.
Private	COLLIER JOSH.
Private	DURDON JOSH.
Private	EAGLE JNS.
Private	EVANS JNS.
Private	FRANCE JNS.
Private	GATFIELD JOSH.
Private	GILBORNE GEO.
Private	GITTINGS RICHD.
Private	GOOD SIMON
Private	GROSE JNS.
Private	HARMAN JNS.
Private	HAYES WM.
Private	HEPBURN CALEB
Private	HEAPLY THOS.
Private	HUBBARD JNS.
Private	KENNEDY WM.
Private	MARLOW JAMES
Private	McGAFFY HUGH
Private	MILLER WM. Needes Collection 1908
Private	MILLS JNS.
Private	MORGAN MORGAN
Private	MORGAN WM.
Private	PASCOE NICHS.
Private	PEACOCK JAMES
Private	RAMPLING JAMES
Private	RICHARDS WM.
Private	ROBINSON WM.
Private	ROPE CHAS
Private	SELSBY RICHD.
Private	SMITH JAMES
Private	SNELLING WM.
Private	STUBBS SIMON
Private	TOOLE CHAS.
Private	WOOLCOCK RICHD.
Private	YATES JNS.

Captain Shaw's Company No.1.

Serjeant	MARSHALL HENRY
Serjeant	McKELLAR (C.S.) ARCHD.
Corporal	CAFFEY PATK.
Corporal	JEFFERIES STEPHN.
Corporal	RICHARDSON DANL.
Corporal	THOMPSON JAMES
Drummer	DEVERS JAMES
Private	ASHEN THOS.
Private	BARTLETT JNS.
Private	BARTLETT HENRY
Private	BEDFORD STEPHN.
Private	BROWN JOSH.
Private	BUCKLE JNS.
Private	CATTON JAMES
Private	COLLINS JAMES
Private	CLARKE JOHN
Private	COOPER JAMES
Private	CORDELL JNS.
Private	DAWS RICHD.
Private	DAY PATK.
Private	DODD GEO.
Private	ELLAR JAMES
Private	EVANS SAML.
Private	GIBNEY LUKE
Private	HARDS WM.
Private	HAYES WM.
Private	MITCHELL WM.
Private	PARRY EDWD.
Private	RYAN THOS.
Private	SAVAGE ABM.
Private	SMART WM.
Private	SMITH SAML.
Private	SMITHY JNS.
Private	SPILSBURY THOS.
Private	STUBBINGS JNS.
Private	TUNNICLIFFE WM.
Private	WALKER JNS.
Private	WALKER RICHD.
Private	WEBB THOS.
Private	WHEATLEY ROBT.
Private	WILBEY JAMES
Private	WILLIAMS WM.
Private	WILLIS THOS.
Private	WYNN JNS.
Private	ROSEBLADE WM.

Captain Anwyls Company No.2.

Serjeant	GATES SIMON
Serjeant	HEATHER ROBT.
Serjeant	McCABE JAMES
Serjeant	NUNN JNS.
Corporal	EAKLEY GEO.
Corporal	CHAPPLE THOS.
Corporal	GREENFIELD GEO.
Corporal	LUCAS JAMES
Corporal	MORGAN THOS.
Drummer	ANDREWS ABRAM.

Drummer	HOULTON WM.
Private	ANDREWS THOS.
Private	ARNOLD JNS.
Private	BANYARD JAMES
Private	BARNES DAVID
Private	BRANCHETT THOS.
Private	BURNS FRANS.
Private	BURTON PETER
Private	BURTON ROBT.
Private	BUTLER THOS.
Private	CARD WM.
Private	CHAMBERLAIN WM.
Private	CHANDLER JAMES
Private	CHILDS JNS.
Private	COCKSEDGE M.
Private	COLE BENJ. Glendinnings sale 1909 29/-
Private	COLEMAN SOLN.
Private	COTTERELL ISSAC
Private	CONNELL MICHL.
Private	DAWES JOSH.
Private	DOWNEY ANDREW
Private	DREWITT JNO.
Private	FOLEY BRYAN
Private	GAME ROBT.
Private	GILLIGAN WM.
Private	GIRT JAMES
Private	HADAWAY JAMES
Private	HARRIS SAML.
Private	HEARLE JOHN
Private	HICKS CHAS.
Private	HOLLINGSHEAD BENJN.
Private	JORDAN JNS.
Private	KIDD GEO.
Private	LANGSTON JOHN
Private	MANNING WM.
Private	McGOVERN EDWD.
Private	MONTGOMERY GABL.
Private	MORRIS JNS.
Private	MUSGRAVE PETER
Private	NEWTON JNS.
Private	NORRIS RICHD.
Private	PERCIVAL ROBT.
Private	PLUMIN THOS.
Private	POVEY THOS.
Private	POWELL SAML.
Private	PRESLAND ROBT.
Private	ROBERTS THOS.
Private	ROSIER WM.
Private	SAGE SAML.
Private	SAVAGE JNS.
Private	SCERLE THOS.
Private	SINDEN JAMES H.Gaskell's collection 1908
Private	SMITH JESSE
Private	SMOOTHY JOHN
Private	TATTON JOSEPH
Private	WATSON JNS.
Private	WEBB GEO.
Private	WELLS MICHL.
Private	WILLIAMS JNS.

Captain Fletcher's Company No.3.

Serjeant	ARCHER JOHN
Serjeant	CASTLE (C.S.) WM.
Serjeant	MOON JOSH.
Drummer	DAVEY THOS.
Private	BAKER HARMAN
Private	BLUNT LAWRENCE
Private	BOND ROBT.
Private	BURKE JNS.
Private	BUTCHER MATTW.
Private	CALLAGAN JNS.
Private	CASTLE GEO.
Private	COOK MATTW. Glendinnings sale January 1910
Private	CORNWALL THOS.
Private	CORRIGAN BERND.
Private	DAWSON JNS.
Private	DEACON WM.
Private	DENNY JNS.
Private	FAGG GEO.
Private	FULCHER JAMES
Private	FULLER THOS.
Private	GARDINER GEO.
Private	GRAVELL SAML.
Private	HARBOURN THOS.
Private	HUNTLEY THOS.
Private	HUNTLEY EDWD.
Private	JONES WLATER
Private	KEMP LEOND.
Private	KENT THOS.
Private	KING RICHD.
Private	KNIGHTSMITH WM.
Private	LAMBOURN SAML.
Private	LAND JOHN
Private	LOFTS EDWD.
Private	MELKIN JAMES
Private	PAYNE THOS.

Private	PEARCE JOSH.
Private	QUIRK DANIEL
Private	ROSE DANIEL
Private	ROSE THOS.
Private	SARJENT THOS.
Private	SCATES DANIEL
Private	SIMMONDS JNS.
Private	SCANTLEBURY EDWD.
Private	SQUIRES WM.
Private	TAYLOR CHAS.
Private	THORNSLY THOS.
Private	WALSH JNS.
Private	WARD JNS.
Private	WATKINS EMMNL.
Private	WHITEHEAD STEPHN.
Private	WOOD WM.
Private	YATES WM.

Captain Erskine's Company No.4.

Q.M.S.	ROGERS JOHN
P.M.S.	HANNA WM.
Serjeant	ASHLEY JOHN
Serjeant	LEESON JAMES
Serjeant	RUSHTON RICHD.
Serjeant	STEAD JOSH.
Serjeant	YEARLDS (C.S.) EDWD.
Corporal	COWARD HENRY
Corporal	HAYDON WM.
Corporal	HUSSEY RICHD.
Corporal	JONES WM.
Corporal	MEDHURST JNS.
Drummer	BODLE MOSES
Drummer	FILER THOS.
Private	AVERY CHAS.
Private	BALL ANTHY.
Private	BAILEY EDWD.
Private	BAILEY WM.
Private	BANKS GEO.
Private	BILLS RICHD.
Private	BISHOP RODGR.
Private	BOSE WM.
Private	BRENDLE JNS.
Private	BULLOCK WM.
Private	BURKE WM.
Private	CHASTON JOHN
Private	CARMICHAEL JAMES
Private	COOK EDWD.
Private	CONNOR WM.
Private	CRANSHAW WM.
Private	CROTTY TIMY.
Private	ETHERINGTON GEO.
Private	GRIFFITHS EDWD.
Private	GRIGGS WM.
Private	GROVES JNS.
Private	HIGGINS MICHL.
Private	HISTEAD WM.
Private	HOGLEY FRANS.
Private	IGGLESDON EDWD.
Private	JEFFERIES WM.
Private	KENNEDY ARTHUR
Private	KING WM.
Private	LAST JAMES
Private	MARSH SAML.
Private	MATTHEWS WM.
Private	McCAFFERY PHILIP
Private	O'ROURKE PATK.
Private	PEAKE NOAH
Private	PRITCHARD SAML.
Private	ROBERTS JNS.
Private	RYAN JNS.
Private	STEPHENS ROBT.
Private	THOMAS JAMES
Private	THOMPSON SAML.
Private	TITTERSON JACOB
Private	TOWERS JAMES
Private	TUGNETT GEO
Private	WYTHE DENIS

Captain Craig's Company No.5.

Serjeant	CAMPBELL (C.S.) JOHN
Serjeant	JOHN EVAN
Serjeant	JONES WM. Cheylesmore collection 1908
Serjeant	COWARD JAMES
Corporal	ASHBY WM.
Corporal	FISHER JOSEPH Gray collection 1908
Corporal	HOSKINS WM.
Corporal	McCABE JAMES
Drummer	Nil
Private	BAGLEY JNS.
Private	BARRY WM.
Private	BASHFORD WM.
Private	BETTS WM.
Private	BORLEY JNS.
Private	BURGES JNS.
Private	BUSH JOSEPH
Private	BROWN WM.

Private	BONNEY PATK.
Private	CAREY THOS.
Private	CLAPSON WM.
Private	CLARKE ROBT.
Private	CLINNS JOHN
Private	COOK WM.
Private	EDWARDS JAMES
Private	GRAY GEO.
Private	HIGHAM THOS.
Private	HODGES JOHN
Private	HUDSON BENJN.
Private	INGLISH JOHN
Private	JOHNS JNS.
Private	JONES EDWD.
Private	JONES WARD
Private	JONES WM.
Private	KELLY PATK.
Private	LAMBKIN WM.
Private	LILLEY JNS.
Private	MENNELL JOSH.
Private	MASON SAML.
Private	MARSHALL THOS.
Private	MITCHAM JNS.
Private	MONTGOMERY WM.
Private	NIXON WM.
Private	NUNN JAMES Glendinnings sale 17th June 1908
Private	PRESTON WM.
Private	STACEY ROBT.
Private	SMITH SIMON
Private	SPEARS JAMES
Private	SKINNER JAMES
Private	THATCHER THOS.
Private	THROWER CHAS.
Private	THOMPSON JAMES
Private	WHITE JNS.
Private	WHITEMORE JAMES
Private	WILLIAMS DAVID

Captain Kirwan's Company No.6.

Serjeant	BALDCOCK WM.
Serjeant	HINKSMAN JNS.
Serjeant	JOHNSTONE JNS. Whitaker collection 1908
Serjeant	ROBERTS JNS.
Serjeant	SHANNON WM. Glendinnings sale 29th July 1908
Corporal	HARMER JAMES
Corporal	LEES SAML.
Corporal	ROBERTS RICHD.
Corporal	TAYLOR GABL.
Corporal	TOBIN JNS.
Drummer	SMITH ELLIS
Private	ABLE THOS.
Private	ADAMS WM.
Private	BIRCHALL DAVID
Private	BIRKIN RICHD.
Private	BRIMMER JNS.
Private	BURKE THOS.
Private	CHURCH JOSH.
Private	CLARKE EDWD.
Private	CURETON RICHD.
Private	DARBY WM.
Private	DAVIDSON ROBT.
Private	DAVIS EDWD.
Private	DAVIS JOHN
Private	DAVIS JOSH.
Private	DEWHURST THOS. Galway Foley collection 1910
Private	DIXON MARK
Private	FLOOD JOHN
Private	FORD WM.
Private	GALE JOHN
Private	HARMAN HENRY
Private	HARRISON THOS.
Private	HART CHAS.
Private	HEDGES JNS.
Private	HOOTON MICHL.
Private	HOPLEY HENRY
Private	IRELAND WM.
Private	JONES JNS.
Private	LINCOLN DAVID
Private	MAGRATH THOS.
Private	MAKELY JAMES
Private	MATTON WM.
Private	MITCHELL BENJN.
Private	MOON STEPHN.
Private	MORRIS JAMES
Private	NORMAN WM.
Private	OVENDEN WM.
Private	PEATLY THOS. Col.Murray's collection 1908
Private	PERCIVAL JACOB
Private	PIGGOTT JNS.
Private	POCOCK JNS.
Private	RATLEY THOS.
Private	REED JNS.
Private	RILEY EDWD.
Private	RICHARDSON THOS.

Private	ROBINSONJNS.
Private	ROOTE CHAS.
Private	SHIELDS RICHD.
Private	SHOEBRIDGE WM.
Private	SINFIELD THOS.
Private	SIRE CHAS.
Private	SMART JOSH.
Private	STONE JOSH.
Private	TACKABURY JAMES
Private	TOMKINSON CHAS.
Private	TROWELL THOS.
Private	TURNER JNS.
Private	WALKER SAML.
Private	WARD JNS.
Private	WHITEHEAD JAMES
Private	WRIGHT ROBT.

Captain Edgell's Company No.7.

Serjeant	BISHOP ROBT.
Serjeant	BODLE BENJN.
Serjeant	DEEKS (C.S.) JNS.
Serjeant	HARRIS JNS.
Serjeant	WADE JAMES
Corporal	BENNETT WM.
Corporal	COOPER JNS.
Corporal	LEONARD JAMES
Corporal	LOVE THOS.
Drummer	DIXON JOHN
Drummer	WALKER WM.
Private	ALLEN WM.
Private	ARMSTRONG JAMES
Private	BRED WM.
Private	BURN WM.
Private	CAMPBELL JAS.
Private	CHERRY JNS.
Private	CLARKE JOHN
Private	DARWIN JOHN
Private	DENMAN THOS.
Private	EDDY PHILIP
Private	EVANS JOHN
Private	FEGAN PATK.
Private	FINLEASON JOHN
Private	FLOYD WM.
Private	GIBBONS THOS.
Private	GILES GEO.
Private	GOODWIN JAMES
Private	HALLS CHAS.
Private	HARRIS THOS.
Private	HAWKINS JNS.
Private	HERBERT WM.
Private	HINES THOS.
Private	HOWE ISSAC
Private	KEMP EDWD.
Private	KERNHAM THOS.
Private	LAWRENCE JOHN
Private	LAWRENCE THOS.
Private	LOVEGROVE RICHD.
Private	MARSHALL GEO.
Private	MARTIN EMANL.
Private	MARSH WM.
Private	McCAFFRY JNS.
Private	MEES GEO.
Private	MINGAY GEO.
Private	MITCHELL JNS.
Private	MURPHY PATK.
Private	NORMAN OLIVER
Private	PASKINS PHILLIP
Private	RATCLIFFE FRANS.
Private	RAWSON JACOB
Private	REEVES JOHN
Private	RIGBY WATKIN
Private	ROWER THOS.
Private	STEVENS LAWRE.
Private	SWEENEY DENIS
Private	WALKER CHRIS.
Private	WATERS JNS.
Private	WILDING WM.
Private	WILLSON CHAS.
Private	WOODFORD DANIEL

Captain Wilson's Company No.8.

Serjeant	BALSDEN JAMES
Serjeant	COSE HENRY
Serjeant	JONES JOHN
Serjeant	REECE (C.S.) WM.
Serjeant	WRIGHT JOHN
Corporal	BENCROFT DANIEL
Corporal	CHAPMAN JAMES
Corporal	LIGHT WM.
Drummer	BERKSHIRE WM.
Private	BAILY JON.
Private	BARRETT JAMES
Private	BENNETT THOS.
Private	BUNN SAML.
Private	CHAMBERS THOS.
Private	CLEMENTS THOS.
Private	COBBLE JAS.
Private	COLEMAN JOB

Private	COADE JAMES
Private	COURT JNS.
Private	CROUCHER CHAS.
Private	CULLON WM.
Private	DAVIS THOS.
Private	EVANS THOS.
Private	GERENE BART.
Private	GROOM SAML.
Private	HAMMERSLY WM.
Private	HOWARD JAMES
Private	KEEN JOSH.
Private	KENT ROBT.
Private	KIRBY JNS. Walters sale June 1913
Private	KING RICHD.
Private	LEAR SAML.
Private	MARSDEN LUKE
Private	MALOY WM.
Private	MARTIN MICHL.
Private	MAY JAMES
Private	MILLIS EDWD.
Private	MITCHELL JNS.
Private	PERFECT CH.
Private	PICKRING GEO.
Private	POWELL JNS.
Private	RUSSELL ISSAC
Private	SNELGAR RICHD.
Private	SPENSWICK JAMES
Private	STEVENSON WM.
Private	STIFF JAMES
Private	THEOBALDS EDWD.
Private	THOMAS DANIEL
Private	WALKER JOHN
Private	WALLAR THOS.
Private	WEBB JNS.
Private	WEBB WM.
Private	WHITE THOS.
Private	YATES RICHD.

Captain Wood's Company Light Infantry

Serjeant	BOWEN (C.S.) HENRY to Ensign 1st West India Reg. 23rd June
Serjeant	COCKAYNE WM.
Serjeant	GOODMAN (C.S.) WM.
Serjeant	O'REGAN WM.
Corporal	BURNOP WM.
Corporal	SAGEMAN STEP.
Corporal	WOOD ISSAC
Drummer	COX WM.
Private	ALLEN JNS.
Private	ANDERSON JNS.
Private	ANDREWARTHA JNS.
Private	AYRES THOS.
Private	BAIRD STEP.
Private	BAMFORD ARNOLD
Private	BANHAM ROBT.
Private	BAMESTER JNS.
Private	BATH RICHD.
Private	BELL DANIEL
Private	BEVAN ELIAS
Private	BIGGS JAMES
Private	BILLINGS JOHN
Private	BOGGIS JNS.
Private	BRAZIER BENJ.
Private	BREWER WM.
Private	BROOKER SAML.
Private	BUCK THOS.
Private	BULLOWS JOSH.
Private	BIRCHALL SAML.
Private	CADWALLADN HUGH
Private	CAVEY THOS.
Private	COX THOS.
Private	DAVIS JAMES
Private	DAY JNS.
Private	DOUGHERTY CHR.
Private	EDMONSON JNS.
Private	EDWARDS JNS.
Private	FENN RICHD.
Private	GOLDSMITH JNS.
Private	GRAHAM WM.
Private	GRANT WM.
Private	GREEN WM.
Private	GREEN RICHD.
Private	HARRIS JOHN
Private	HARRIS JOSH.
Private	HARRISON JOHN
Private	HOWARD WM.
Private	HURCHATTON WM.
Private	JENKINS THOS.
Private	JONES DAVID
Private	JONES ISSAC
Private	JONES THOS.
Private	MALONEY JNS.
Private	MARSHALL WM.
Private	MAY JAMES
Private	MORRIS THOS.
Private	PARKER WM.
Private	PARRY S. - Day Sale April 1910

Private	PASK PETER
Private	PEAD WM.
Private	PUGMORE WM.
Private	RICHARDS WM.
Private	RIVETT JAMES
Private	ROBERTS JOHN
Private	ROBINSON JON.
Private	SADLER JAMES
Private	SAUNDERS JOHN
Private	SEYNOR WM.
Private	SHORT PATK.
Private	SIMPSON JOSH.
Private	SMITH JNS.
Private	SMOTHWAITE JNS.
Private	SOLLIS HENRY
Private	SHOUGHNESSY PATK.
Private	WARD WM.
Private	WARREN JOSH.
Private	WHITE LAWR.
Private	WINSON WM.
Private	WITHARS JNS.
Private	WOOD THOS.
Private	WOODGATE RICHD.

* * *

3rd BATTALION 14th REGIMENT OF FOOT

Major	TIDY F.S. Bt.Lt.Col.
Major	KEIGHTLY J.
Adjutant	BUCKLE W.H.
Qr.Master	ROSS ALEXR.
Ass.Surgeon	SHANNON ALEXR.
A.Serjeant	TERRY HENRY
Pay.Master	MITTON ROBT.
Captain	MARLAY G. Bt.Major

Captain Henry Morton's Company

Captain	RAMSAY THOS.
Ensign	NEWNHAM R.
Ensign	MATTHEWS J.P.
Sjt.Major	GRAHAM WM.
Qr.Master	GODDARD THOS A.A. Payne's Collection 1908
P.M.Serjeant	GRUNDLEY JOHN
Dr.Major	SUNDERLAND WM.
Sch.Mr.Sjt.	BOWER JAMES
Serjeant	CUNDLE WM.
Serjeant	SMITH (C.S.) I.
Serjeant	STRINGER THOS.
Corporal	FORD WM.
Corporal	LAMBERT JAMES Died of wounds 18th June
Corporal	WHEELER AMOS
Drummer	BAVINGTON JNS.
Drummer	NUTT JOSH.
Private	ABBOTT WM.
Private	ABRAHAM JNS.
Private	BAGGS JON.
Private	BAKER EDWD.
Private	BARNETT RICHD.
Private	BEAVER GEO.
Private	BORYER ROBT.
Private	BRADLEY HENRY
Private	BRIMLEY TAL.
Private	BROWN JAMES
Private	BURROWS SAML.
Private	CHAPLIN JNS.
Private	COLE JAMES
Private	COOPER ROBT.
Private	COWLAND WM.
Private	CUPID GEO.
Private	DAVIS JOHN Dead
Private	DAWSON FRANS.
Private	DELL WM.
Private	EDWARDS THOS.
Private	ELLIS GEO.
Private	ESTICK WM. On sale at Baldwin's Feb.1910
Private	FASSEY MOSES
Private	GIBBS WM.
Private	HARDY JNS.
Private	HARPER JNS.
Private	HERITAGE GEO. Dead
Private	HUCKLE PHILIP
Private	HUNT THOS.
Private	JUGGINS JOSH.
Private	KIMMS ROBT.
Private	LANE JNS.
Private	LYNCH JNS.
Private	LYFORD JNS.
Private	McLANE HENRY Fleming collection 1871
Private	MARKS WM. Dead
Private	NICHOLLS CHAS.
Private	PERRY JOHN
Private	POLDIN JNS. Day sale April 1910
Private	POPE JAMES
Private	SAUNDERS RICHD.
Private	SIMPKINS WM.
Private	TAYLOR JAMES
Private	THOROGOOD THOS.

Private	TITCOMB WM.
Private	VERE WM. Dead
Private	WELSBY HENRY Dead
Private	WHITBREAD JNS.
Private	WILKINS DAVID
Private	WILSON WM.
Private	WILLETT THOS.
Private	YEOMAN JOSH.

Captain William Turner's Company

Captain	TUNER WM.
Ensign	McKENZIE GEO.
Ensign	KEPPEL HOW.GEO.
Serjeant	HART JAMES
Serjeant	SCOTT (C.S.) JOHN Died of Wounds 18th June
Serjeant	WALLIS GEO.
Corporal	LEGGITT WM.
Corporal	PRATT DAVID
Corporal	ROBINSON JAMES
Drummer	DAVIS BENJ.
Drummer	HANDCOCK THOS.
Private	ABBOTT JNS.
Private	AYRES JOSH.
Private	BARBER THOS. Cheylesmore collection 1908
Private	BRITTON RICHD. Discharged
Private	BURGESS WM.
Private	BROND JNS.
Private	BURNETT JNS.
Private	CLARKE 2nd JAMES
Private	CRIMP ROBT.
Private	DANN WM.
Private	DAY HENRY Dead
Private	DICKER JAMES
Private	DUDLEY THOS.
Private	FAWCETT THOS.
Private	FRIEND SAML.
Private	FULLER JNS Discharged
Private	GARNER JAMES
Private	GILLESPIE ALEXR.
Private	GREY WM.
Private	GLEN RICHD.
Private	HAMMERTON JAMES
Private	HATCROFT JNS.
Private	JOHNSON JAMES
Private	KEEN JAMES
Private	KENT JOHN
Private	KIDMAN SIMON
Private	LANGFORD THOS.
Private	LOVERIDGE THOS. Sotheby's sale 18 June 1909
Private	MANN THOS.
Private	MARSHALL SAML.
Private	MARSHALL RICHD.
Private	MAYHEW THOS. Discharged
Private	MOLLES WM.
Private	MOORE JOHN
Private	MORGAN THOS.
Private	MOULDS CHAS.
Private	OVERHILL WM.
Private	PEARSON WM.
Private	PIGGOT WM.
Private	PILGRIM WM.
Private	PALFREMAN VAL.
Private	ROBERTS GEO.
Private	SAUNDERS RBT.
Private	SURRELL WM.
Private	SWANN THOS.
Private	TAYLOR JNS
Private	TILWORTH JAMES
Private	TIDBALL THOS.
Private	TOMLIN GEO.
Private	TRING WM.
Private	TURNER GEO.
Private	WILLIAMS WILL. Killed in Action
Private	WOODHAM RICHD.
Private	YATES JAMES
Boy	CAMPBELL GEO.

Captain Richard Adam's Company

Captain	ADAMS RICHD.
Ensign	REOWEN W.
Ensign	WOOD J.M. Payne Collection 1911
Serjeant	BENNETT THOS.
Serjeant	CATCHING JOHN
Serjeant	ROBINSON JON
Corporal	FOUNTAIN THOS.
Corporal	HOLDEN THOS.
Private	BAXTER GEO. Glendinnings sale Jan. 1910
Private	BETTY WM.
Private	BICHOP JNS.
Private	BREWER JNS.
Private	CANTRILL JAMES
Private	CARTER WM.
Private	CLEMENTS RICHD.
Private	COLLINS THOS.
Private	COOPER WM.
Private	COY JOSH

Private	EADEN JNS.
Private	EDWARDS JAMES
Private	FAIRCLOTH WM.
Private	FISHER THOS.
Private	FAGE RICHD.
Private	FAWCETT BENJ.
Private	GENTLE EDWD. Died of wounds rec. 18th June
Private	GENTLE JNS.
Private	GOODCHILD CHAS.
Private	HICKS WM.
Private	HAY WM.
Private	JACKSON WM.
Private	JOLLEY ROBT. Killed in Action
Private	JOHNSON JNS.
Private	JOHNSON WM.
Private	KEYS CHAS.
Private	LEACH JAMES Discharged
Private	LETTS GEO.A.
Private	MABBOTT THOS.
Private	MARLOW WM.
Private	MOBBS WM.
Private	MOORE JNS.
Private	MORRIN JAMES
Private	NEAL JNS.
Private	NEAD JNS.
Private	PERRIMAN JNS. Discharged
Private	PERRIMAN WM.
Private	PINCKNEY JAMES
Private	PLUMMER JERE.
Private	PULLEN THOS.
Private	REEVES JON.
Private	SHAW THOS.
Private	SIMPSON WM.
Private	SKINNER THOS.
Private	SMITH WM. Glendinnings sale Oct.1913 2-4-0
Private	TETLOW JNS.
Private	TODD CHAS.
Private	TURNER 1st JNS. Died of wounds rec. at Waterloo
Private	TUNER 2nd JNS.
Private	WARD MATTW.
Private	WARREN WM.
Private	WATSON JAMES Died of wounds rec. 18th June
Private	WOODS THOS.
Private	WORSLEY SAML.
Private	CAVANAGH CHAS.

Captain John Maxwell's Company

Lieutenant	AKENSIDE WM. Whitaker collection 1908
Serjeant	EGGBEAR JOSH.
Serjeant	WALSH (C.S.) WM.
Corporal	BUDDING JAMES
Corporal	BUFFITT WM. Discharged
Corporal	COLLIER THOS.
Corporal	MOORE WM.
Drummer	MILLARD JAMES
Private	BOWDEN WM.
Private	BRITTLE THOS.
Private	BURGESS HENRY
Private	BURLEY GEO.
Private	CARTER ROBT.
Private	CHURCH JNS. Dead
Private	CLAYTON DANIEL
Private	COOLEY STEP.
Private	COOPER WM.
Private	COOPER RICHD.
Private	DAWSON RICHD.
Private	DAY JOSH.
Private	DAY SAML.
Private	DEAN WM.
Private	DERRICK CHAS.
Private	DORMAN JOHN Killed in Action
Private	DUMAYNE WM.
Private	EASTAFF WM.
Private	ELLIOTT JAMES
Private	FRAKER JNS.
Private	GOODFELLOW JAMES
Private	GUDGEONN GEO.
Private	HAMBLING WM.
Private	HARNETT JNS.
Private	HARSTIN BENJ.
Private	HAWKINS WM.
Private	HILTON ROBT.
Private	HUNT EDWD.
Private	JONES THOS.
Private	KEYS JOHN
Private	KNIPTON TIM.
Private	LAMBOURNE JNS.
Private	LITTLE WM.
Private	MEACHEM WM.
Private	MOORE WM.
Private	MUMFORD THOS.
Private	PARSLEY WM.
Private	RUSSELL ROBT.
Private	SHIPPARD FRANS. Dead
Private	SIMPSON WM.

Private	STEEL REUB.
Private	SWIFT ISSAC
Private	TIMSON THOS.
Private	VOICE JOSH.
Private	WAKE THOS.
Private	WALSH WM.
Private	WHITE RICHD.
Private	WILKINSON JAMES
Private	WINDMILL JAMES
Boy	SWIFT ANDREW

Captain William Bett's Company

Lieutenant	BRAMAN C.W.
Lieutenant	HARTLEY J.C.
Ensign	HOLMES R.
Serjeant	GREEN THOS.
Serjeant	LYNES JOHN
Serjeant	MOORE GEO.
Corporal	HOYTE CHAS.
Corporal	MOULDING JNS.
Corporal	RASTRICK WM.
Private	ADAMS EDWD.
Private	BERRY WM.
Private	BOLTWOOD THOS.
Private	BRIARS THOS.
Private	BROWN CHAS.
Private	BURTON WM.
Private	CANNON JNS.
Private	CARTER GEO.
Private	CARTER THOS.
Private	CLARKE JOHN
Private	CLARKE JOSH.
Private	CLAYTON ROBT. Col. Gaskell's collection 1911
Private	CLOUGH THOS.
Private	COOPER THOS.
Private	DADD WM.
Private	DAVIS JAMES
Private	DICKERSON WM.
Private	FOSTER CHAS.
Private	GARDNER RICHD.
Private	GILBERT JNS.
Private	GILES FRAN.
Private	GLENISTER WM.
Private	GLOYNES FRANS.
Private	GOSS THOS.
Private	HAGGAR THOS.
Private	HILL JOHN
Private	HOLDING JAMES
Private	HORSFIELD SAML.
Private	HOY WM.
Private	JUNS JAMES
Private	JEFFS BENJN.
Private	KELK JERIAH
Private	LAMB JAMES
Private	LANGLEY RICHD.
Private	LARKINS ROBT. Discharged
Private	LEVER RICHD.
Private	LOVETT WM.
Private	LOWE JOSH.
Private	MITCHELL JNS.
Private	MUMFORD RICHD.
Private	NEWBURY JAMES Col.Murray's Collection 1908
Private	OTTAWAY LEVI
Private	OWEN GEO. Discharged
Private	PEARCE RICHD.
Private	PHILLIPS RICHD.
Private	RAMSLEY ROBT.
Private	ROBERTS JOHN
Private	ROWNEY JAMES
Private	SEAMAN JNS. Discharged
Private	SINGLETON JNS.
Private	SMITH WM.
Private	SOUTH JNS.
Private	TAYLOR BENJN.
Private	THOMPSON JAMES
Private	TIBBATH JAMES
Private	TIMMS WM.
Private	VAZEY WM.
Private	WHITE WM.
Private	YOUNG ISHMAEL

Captain Henry Hill's Company

Captain	HEWITT WM.
Lieutenant	BALDWIN GEO.
Ensign	ROWLBY J.
Ensign	COOPER A. Wounded
Serjeant	NUTCHER JOHN
Serjeant	STANNETT JOSH.
Corporal	BARBER JOHN
Corporal	HOLLAND RICHD.
Drummer	MATTHEWS GEO.
Drummer	BUTLER JNS.
Private	ARNOLD EDWD.
Private	BALDCOCK GEO.
Private	BASFORD JAMES
Private	BATES WM.
Private	BATEMAN WM.
Private	BEAVER GEO.

Private	BREED JAMES
Private	BROWN WM.
Private	BULLARD JNS.
Private	CASTLETON WM. Dead
Private	CHESHIRE GEO.
Private	COOPER JOHN Phillip's sale
Private	DEACON WM.
Private	DEAN SAML.
Private	EVERITT HENRY
Private	FRENCH JAMES
Private	GODFREY WM.
Private	HAYNES FRANS.
Private	HALFHEAD JNS.
Private	HAWLEY WM.
Private	HARMAN JNS.
Private	HICKSON WM.
Private	HEFFRISON JNS.
Private	HUNT GEO.
Private	HOWARD HENRY
Private	JEFFERY WM.
Private	JOHNSON JOSH.
Private	KNIGHT JOHN
Private	KNOWLES GEO.
Private	KENT WM.
Private	LAMBOURNE JAS.
Private	LANCASTER THOS.
Private	LEADER THOS.
Private	LIPSCOMBE JAMES
Private	LUCK MATTW.
Private	LANGLEY JAMES
Private	MILLARD WM. Dead
Private	NEWMAN THOS.
Private	NEAL FRANS.
Private	NORRIS WM. Dead
Private	PALMER THOS.
Private	PIZZEY CHAS.
Private	RANDALL WM. Gray collection 1908
Private	ROWTHORNE JOSH.
Private	RUSSELL WM.
Private	SELWOOD GEO.
Private	SLANEY WM.
Private	SMART THOS.
Private	STREETS WM. Discharged
Private	STAKES WM.
Private	TOCKFIELD GEO.
Private	TAYLOR THOS.
Private	WOND WM.
Private	WASHINGTON WM.
Private	WELLS WM.

Captain C. Wilson's Company

Captain	WILSON C.
Lieutenant	WESTWOOD L.
Ensign	STACKPOLE R.
Serjeant	BREARS JOHN
Serjeant	FISHER ROBT.
Serjeant	PALMER ROBT.
Corporal	BRADSHAW JAMES
Corporal	KEMP RICHD.
Corporal	SUMMERFIELD WM.
Drummer	MOORE JNS.
Drummer	WEDDLE JNS.
Private	ADAMS THOS.
Private	ALDRIDGE JAMES
Private	BROWN THOS.
Private	BUTLER WM.
Private	CLEMENTS JNS.
Private	COOPER BENJ.
Private	CROSS JNS.
Private	DAVIS THOS.
Private	DIVIS JOSH.
Private	DARBY WM.
Private	DAVIS WM.
Private	DENTON JNS.
Private	FAUKNER GEO.
Private	FOSTER FRANS.
Private	FOSTER DAVID
Private	FRANKLIN THOS.
Private	GIBBARDS THOS. Died of wounds rec. 18th June
Private	GODDARD WM.
Private	GRAY JNS.
Private	GROSVENOR EDWD.
Private	HARVEY ELLIS
Private	HAWKINS JNS.
Private	HILL JNS.
Private	HOPE THOS.
Private	HOPWELL SAML.
Private	HORNE THOS.
Private	HAUGH RICHD.
Private	HUNT THOS.
Private	IRONS WM.
Private	KEMP FREDK.
Private	KIRKMAN ADAM
Private	LAXTON JOSH
Private	LUNNON JNS.
Private	PHILLIPS JNS.
Private	RANDALL THOS.
Private	SMITH RICHD.
Private	SMITH EDWD.

Private	SMITH THOS.
Private	WARD SAML.
Private	WARD WM.
Private	WESTON WM.
Private	WIGGINS JNS.
Private	WILLCOX HENRY
Private	WINDMILL JNS.
Private	YATES SOLOMON

Captain J.L. White's Company

Captain	WHITE J.L.
Lieutenant	BOLDERS H.
Ensign	SMITH J.R.
Serjeant	GOSTELOW JOHN
Serjeant	NEWSON WM.
Serjeant	PARKER EDWD.
Corporal	CLIFTON CHAS.
Corporal	FENWICK WM.
Corporal	GAUNT JAMES
Drummer	MAYS JAMES
Private	ABBEY JAMES
Private	BAKER JNS.
Private	BARNES WM.
Private	BENNETT JAMES
Private	BOWDEN WM.
Private	BRIGGS JNS.
Private	BROOKS JAMES
Private	BUTTON EDWD. Glendinnings sale 17th June 1908
Private	CADD WM.
Private	CARTER WM.
Private	CAVESTIBS PHILIP
Private	CHAMBERLAIN THOS.
Private	CHAPPEL WM.
Private	CHESTNEY JNS.
Private	COMPTON P. Discharged
Private	CLAPSHAW WM. Glendinnings sale April 1912
Private	COOPER JAMES
Private	COVENTRY JOSH
Private	DOWLING HENRY
Private	EAGLE WM.
Private	EDDINGTON JAMES
Private	EDMONDS JAMES
Private	FLITCROFT MATTW.
Private	FOOT JAMES
Private	FOSTER WM.
Private	GEORGE JOSH.
Private	GRISWELL WM.
Private	GREGORY JOSH.
Private	HILL ROBT.
Private	JAKEMAN WM.
Private	LAMBSDON THOS.
Private	LYNE RICHD.
Private	MITCHELL WM.
Private	MORLEY JNS.
Private	OLIVER WM.
Private	PLESTEAD TIMY.
Private	RIDDLE GEO.
Private	RIMMINGTON WM.
Private	RAWKINS JAMES
Private	SUDBUROUGH JOSH
Private	SHERRIFF CHAS.
Private	TILL JOHN
Private	TURNER WM.
Private	WARD THOS.
Private	WARREN SAML.
Private	WELLS JOSH
Private	YATES BENJN.

Captain George Bolton's Company

Lieutenant	BEACHCROFT S.
Lieutenant	FRASER C. Joined 3rd Foot Guards
Ensign	BURROWS M. This Officer was Volunteer 18th June - H. Gaskell's Collection 1908
Serjeant	BRADSHAW WM.
Serjeant	CLARKE JNS.
Serjeant	JESSON THOS.
Serjeant	MANLEY (C.S.) JNS. On sale at Baldwin's March 1909
Corporal	FLETCHER JNS.
Corporal	SAVAGE JNS.
Corporal	WHYE RICHD.
Drummer	HANDCOCK THOS.
Private	BARRACK THOS.
Private	BRIDGEMENT JNS.
Private	BALLS JNS.
Private	BUTLER PAUL
Private	BULLIVANT THOS.
Private	BULL EDMD. Discharged
Private	CHARLTON WM.
Private	CHAMPION CHAS.
Private	COOK SAML.
Private	CRAWLEY WM.
Private	CRAMP DANL.
Private	CROSS JAMES
Private	DAVIS JOSH.
Private	DONNELLY WM.
Private	DORRELL JNS.
Private	DOVE HENRY
Private	DIFFIN GEO.

Private	EVERITT JAMES
Private	FIELD WM.
Private	FLOCKNEY SAML.
Private	FOWLER JON. Discharged
Private	GIBSON SAML.
Private	GOULD JAMES
Private	GILLING GEO.
Private	HARRIS WM.
Private	HAGUE JARVIS
Private	HOLT ISSAC
Private	HUGGINS WM.
Private	HUNT JAMES Killed in Action
Private	JACKSON BENJN.
Private	JEFFERY SAML.
Private	JONES HENRY
Private	JUST JOHN
Private	McDONALD JNS.
Private	MANN JNS.
Private	POPE JACOB Killed in Action
Private	POSTLEWAITE GEO.
Private	SMITH THOS.
Private	STEVENS WM.
Private	STEWART BENJN.
Private	SEALEY ROBT.
Private	THRIFT JAMES
Private	WINTER SAML.
Private	WHITHEAD THOS.
Private	WILLIAMS THOS. Killed in Action
Private	WILLIAMS JNS.

<u>Captain William Ross's Company</u>

Captain	ROSS WM.
Lieutenant	NICHOLSON J. Phillip's sale
Lieutenant	REED W.
Ensign	ORMSBY A. Sotheby's sale November 1911
Serjeant	DOUGLAS WM.
Serjeant	FRANCIS JOSH
Serjeant	GODDARD (C.S.) SAML.
Serjeant	NORTHWOOD FRANS.
Corporal	ELMER JAMES
Corporal	MOORE THOS.
Corporal	ROBINSON JNS.
Corporal	STEVENSON THOS.
Private	ABBOTT JNS.
Private	BAILEY ROBT.
Private	BARTON GEO.
Private	BANDY WM.
Private	BIGGS JAMES
Private	CHAWNER JOSH
Private	COLLIER GEO.
Private	DINSEY WM.
Private	DOWE JNS.
Private	DRING THOS.
Private	DUNDASS JNS.
Private	EASTAFF THOS.
Private	ELLIS JAMES
Private	GEORGE WM.
Private	GODFREY CHAS.
Private	HAMMOND GEO.
Private	HANDLEY JNS.
Private	HARLOW JNS. Galway Foley collection 1910
Private	HARRISON THOS.
Private	HOOK JNS.
Private	HOUSE GEO.
Private	JOTCE JNS.
Private	LAMBERT RICHD.
Private	LOVESAY JOHN
Private	LUDLOW JNS.
Private	MARCH ROBT.
Private	MOOD DANL.
Private	MARSDEN JNS.
Private	MARSH JNS.
Private	MILLARD WM.
Private	MILES JNS.
Private	MILLS THOS.
Private	MORLEY GEO.
Private	MUNN HENRY
Private	OVERTON JESSE
Private	POCOCK JNS.
Private	PURSER FRANS.
Private	QUICK ISSAC
Private	RADFORD THOS.
Private	ROWLAND ROBT.
Private	SALE JAMES
Private	SELBY TIMY.
Private	SLOAN WM. Died of Wounds 18th June
Private	SMITH BANJN.
Private	STANBURY WM. Dead
Private	STAPLETON THOS.
Private	STILES HENRY
Private	TIGGLE THOS.
Private	TRAES JNS.
Private	TREVISICH CHRIS.
Private	WALKER JNS.

Private	WATTS JAMES
Private	WELLS WM.
Private	WHEELER BENJN.
Private	WHITE THOS.
Private	WHITE JNS.
Private	WILSON THOS.
Private	WITNEY THOS.
Private	WRIGHT WADE
Private	SMITH WM.

* * *

23rd REGIMENT OF FOOT

Lt.Colonel	ELLIS Sir H.W. K.C.B. Died of wounds 20th June
Major	DALMER THOS. Lt.Col.
Major	HILL J.H.E. Lt.Col.
Adjutant	ENOCH JOHN
Qr.Master	SIDLEY GEO.
Surgeon	DUNN JOHN
Ass.Surgeon	SMITH THOS.
Ass.Surgeon	MONROE JOHN Payne Collection
Rec.Office , Lieutenant	FRYER CHAS.
Captain	BLANCKLY H.S. On the Staff D.A.A. General. H. Gaskell's collection 1908
Rec.Office Vol.	ELLIS ED. THOS.

Captain Hawtyn's (Major) Company Grenadiers

Captain	HAWTYN JOSH.
Lieutenant	BROWNE E.W.
Lieutenant	McDONALD JOHN
Lieutenant	GRIFFITHS W.A. Whitaker collection 1908
S. Major	MORRISSEY DENIS
Q.M.S.	MOORE GARRETT
P.M.S.	JESSON JOHN
Ar.Serjeant	CAVANAGH CHAS.
Dr.Major	GRIFFITHS THOS.
Dr.Major	LOVELL URIAH
Serjeant	DILLON RICHD.
Serjeant	INGHAM JAMES Sotheby's sale 19th June 1908
Serjeant	RIDGWAY WM.
Serjeant	WRIGHT GEO.
Corporal	BISHOP RICHD.
Corporal	GLOVER WM.
Corporal	ROBERTS ELLIS
Corporal	SMITH JOHN
Drummer	BENTICK RICHD.
Drummer	CONNELLY HENRY
Private	ANDREWS EDWD.
Private	BOND JOHN
Private	BURGESS HENRY
Private	DANIELLS SAML.
Private	DAVIS ROBT. Col.Murray's Collection
Private	DAVIS BENJN.
Private	ELSEGOOD JOSH.J.
Private	FARR RICHD.
Private	FARTHING WM.
Private	FOSTER WM.
Private	GLOVER JAMES
Private	GOLDSBERRY JOSH.
Private	GOULD JOHN
Private	GREYSON ROBT.
Private	GWYNNE THOS.
Private	HANNAH JAMES
Private	HARDY THOS.
Private	HOLLANDS RICHD.
Private	HOTCHKISS WM.
Private	HOWLETT THOS.
Private	HUBBARD JOHN
Private	HUGHS RICHD.
Private	JONES WM.
Private	JONES JON.
Private	JONES HUGH
Private	KEEFFE OWEN
Private	KENYON GEO.
Private	LUDGROVE THOS.
Private	MORGAN JOHN on sale at Baldwin's July 1912
Private	MORRIS ELISHA
Private	MOSELY SAML.
Private	MURPHY WM.
Private	NOBLE EDWD. Gray Collection 1908
Private	PRICE 1st THOS.
Private	PRICE 2nd THOS.
Private	PURCELL JAMES
Private	REES EVAN
Private	RICHARDS EDWD.
Private	ROBERTS JOHN
Private	ROBERTS RICHD.
Private	ROGERS ROBERT
Private	RUSHMORE DANL.
Private	SALT WM.
Private	SIMON DAVID
Private	WALKER ROBT.
Private	WILLIAMS JOHN

Private	WILLIAMS WM.
Private	WILLIAMS EVAN
Private	WILLIAMSON WM.
Private	WINNER WM.
Private	WOODS JOHN
Private	WOODS WM.

Captain Dalmer's (Major) Company No.1.

Captain	DALMER FRANCIS
Lieutenant	PALMER HARRY
Serjeant	BLEST THOS.
Serjeant	BOND THOS.
Serjeant	HUDSON JNS.
Corporal	ROBERTS RICHD.
Corporal	SUTTON WM.
Corporal	WRIGHT ROBT.
Drummer	LEEDS JOHN
Drummer	LYNN THOS.
Drummer	PARRY THOS.
Private	AINSWORTH THOS.
Private	BATES WM.
Private	BRADY MICHL.
Private	BRADLEY WM.
Private	BRITAIN JOHN
Private	BURROWS JAMES
Private	BYRON DAVID Killed 24th June
Private	CAMPBELL WM.
Private	CHEETHAM JOHN
Private	COLES SAML.
Private	CONATTY JAMES
Private	CONNICK JOHN
Private	DAVIS THOS. 2nd.
Private	DAVIS DAVID
Private	DIX JOHN
Private	EVANS WM.
Private	FARRAR JAMES
Private	GLAZEN WM.
Private	GOULD RICHD.
Private	GUMMOW GEO.
Private	HARRISON JOHN
Private	HEWLETT JOHN
Private	HOLDING OLIVER Day sale April 1910
Private	JENKINS JOHN
Private	JONES ROBT.
Private	LANCASHIRE JOSH.
Private	LEERWARD DANL.
Private	MATHER ISSAC.
Private	McALLISTER JOHN
Private	McCLUSKEY JAMES
Private	McGOWAN PETER
Private	McLAUGHLIN JOHN
Private	PARTINGTOM WM.
Private	PRICE EDWD.
Private	PRICE WM.
Private	REDFORD THOS.
Private	ROBERTS JNS. 1st
Private	ROBERTS JNS. 2nd
Private	ROSE JAMES
Private	ROYAL EDWD.
Private	RULE JOHN
Private	WALSH JOHN
Private	WEBB EDMD.
Private	WEBB JNS. 2nd
Private	WEBSTER WM.
Private	WHITTAKER JOHN
Private	WILLIAMS DAVID
Private	WILLIAMS WM.
Private	WINSTANLEY JAMES
Private	WINTERTON THOS.
Private	WRIGHT RICHD.
Private	YATES HENRY

Captain Strangeway's Company No.2.

Captain	STRANGWAY THOS.
Lieutenant	SMITH RALPH
Ensign	STAINFORTH GEO.
Serjeant	BRELSFORD SAML.
Serjeant	JENNETT JOHN
Serjeant	LEFEUER JAMES
Serjeant	OWLUS WM.
Corporal	AUSTIN EDWD.
Corporal	LOCKETT WM.
Corporal	MACKIE ALEXR.
Corporal	MASON SAML.
Corporal	WILLIAMS MORRIS
Drummer	BIRBECK THOS.
Drummer	PARSONS JOHN
Private	ABRAHAM WM. Glendinnings sale 17th June 1908
Private	BALDWIN SAML. Killed 18th June
Private	BUCKLEY JAMES
Private	CASTREE WM.
Private	CAWLINE JOSH
Private	COUSLEY JEREH.
Private	DAVIS DAVID 1st
Private	DAVIS DAVIS 2nd
Private	DAVIDSON HUGH
Private	DEVEY JOHN

Private	EDWARDS THOS.
Private	EVANS EVAN
Private	EVANS ROBT.
Private	EVANS WM.
Private	EVANS LEWIS
Private	FARTHING GEO.
Private	GAY WM.
Private	HASLEM DANIEL
Private	HEWITT THOS.
Private	HIGGINS JAMES
Private	HIGHAM JOSH.
Private	HOGG THOS.
Private	HOWARD GEO.
Private	HUGHES THOS.
Private	JANE DIGORY
Private	JONES RICHD.
Private	KNIGHT JOHN
Private	LAYTON RICHD.
Private	LEE GEO.
Private	LEWIS RICHD.
Private	LINDSAY THOS.
Private	LINE RICHD.
Private	LYNCH SILVESTER
Private	MARTIN JOHN
Private	MAYES JOHN
Private	MORGAN ROBT.
Private	MORGAN WM.
Private	PLUMB JAMES
Private	PRICE DAVID Spence collection 1914
Private	RIX ROBT.
Private	ROSS THOS.
Private	ROYLE JOHN
Private	SHEARMAN MICHL.
Private	SHEARMAN JOSHUA
Private	SIMPSON THOS.
Private	STRATTON WM.
Private	STRICKLETON THOS.
Private	TAYLOR JAMES
Private	THOMAS JOHN.
Private	WATTS ISSAC
Private	WEST JOHN
Private	WILLIAMS JOHN
Private	WILLIAMS ROBT.Glendinnings sale May 1909
Private	WILLIAMS WM.

Captain Harrison's Company No.3.

Lieutenant	CLYDE JOHN Died of wounds 3rd July
Ensign	FITZGIBBON GERALD
Serjeant	VIZARD JON.
Serjeant	YATES JOHN
Corporal	TITTON SAML.
Corporal	GAMESTER WM.
Corporal	MACE JOHN
Corporal	McKILLOP DAVID
Drummer	EDWARDS JOHN
Drummer	ETHELL THOS.
Private	ASHLEY PETER
Private	AUSTIN PETER
Private	BINGHAM RICHD.
Private	BRIGHTMAN ROBT.
Private	BROTHEROW EDWD.
Private	BROWN WM.
Private	CLARKE JOSH.
Private	COW BENJN.
Private	DERBYSHIRE THOS.
Private	DOYLE MICHL 1st Died 1st July
Private	DOYLE MICHL. 2nd
Private	EDWARDS EDWD.
Private	ELSON ASHTON
Private	EVANS JOHN
Private	FERRENCE JAMES
Private	GOLLAHER EDWD. Deserted 4th Sept.
Private	GATES THOS.
Private	GILSON BARNABY
Private	GOODWIN THOS.
Private	GRAVES JOSH.
Private	GREEN WM. Walter's sale June 1913
Private	GULLIVER SIMON
Private	HADDOCK THOS.
Private	HALL SAML. Littledale sale Nov. 1910
Private	HANDLEY WM.
Private	HAWKINS GEO.
Private	HISCOCK WM.
Private	HOGAN PATK.
Private	HOPLEY WM.
Private	HOWLETT HENRY
Private	HUGHES DANL.
Private	IRELAND WM.
Private	JONES EDWD.
Private	JONES JOHN
Private	JONES THOS.

Private	JONES WM.
Private	LAWRENCE EDWD.
Private	LAYWOOD GEORGE
Private	LEVERSEDGE JOHN
Private	LLOYD EDWD.
Private	LONG THOS.
Private	LOVE JOHN
Private	MARSH JOHN
Private	MASON THOS.
Private	MASON WM.
Private	MILLIGAN ROBT.
Private	MORGAN PHILIP
Private	NEWMAN JOHN
Private	PAGE JAMES
Private	PAIRPOINT JOHN
Private	PYKE MARK
Private	PROTHERS DAVID
Private	REAGAN MICHL.
Private	RHODES SAML.
Private	ROBERTS WM.
Private	SCHOFIELD JAMES
Private	SMITH HENRY
Private	STROUD RICHD.
Private	STYLES WM.
Private	WEAVERS THOS.
Private	WILLIAMS WM 1st
Private	WILLIAMS WM. -nd
Private	WILLIAMS THOS.
Private	YOUNG JOHN

Captain Brown's (Major) Company No.4.

Lieutenant	WALLEY WM.
Ensign	LEEBODY WM. Killed 24th June
Serjeant	FARRELL JOHN
Serjeant	PARRY OWEN
Serjeant	ROSTROW JOHN
Serjeant	SMITH JAMES
Serjeant	THATCHER THOS.
Corporal	BULLOCK JOHN
Corporal	CHILDS SAML. On sale at Baldwin's Feb. 1910
Corporal	MILLS THOS.
Corporal	MOULDING PHILIP
Corporal	TAYLOR JOSH.
Drummer	PHILLIPS JOHN
Private	BAKER JOHN
Private	BOOTH WM.
Private	BRIERLY JOHN
Private	CARLINE THOS.
Private	CLARKE JOSH.
Private	CLAYTON THOS.
Private	CUTTER THOS.
Private	DAVIS DAVID
Private	DAVIS JNS.
Private	DEVANNY JOHN
Private	DOUGALL JOS.
Private	EASTWOOD THOS.
Private	EDNEY JNS.
Private	FISH ROBT.
Private	FITZPATRICK THOS.
Private	FOULKS THOS.
Private	FRANCIS WM.
Private	GEE ELIAH
Private	HANDLEY JOSH.
Private	HANDSTOCK EDWD.
Private	HANMORE WM.
Private	HOOLE GEO.
Private	JAMES ISSAC
Private	JOHN BENJN.
Private	JONES ROBT.
Private	JONES EDWD.
Private	JONES 1st JNS.
Private	JONES RICHD.
Private	JONES DAVID
Private	JONES WM.
Private	LEWIS JOHN Galway Foley collection 1910
Private	MANNING CLARKE
Private	MANSFIELD ROBT.
Private	MARTINDALE JOSH.
Private	McDONOGH MICHL.
Private	MILLDENHALL ROBT.
Private	MORRIS JOHN
Private	MULLEN JOHN
Private	MYERS WM.
Private	NUNN JAMES
Private	O'CONNORS SAML.
Private	ORBLE JERE.
Private	PAIRPOINT WM.
Private	PITCHERS SAML.
Private	PITCHERS JAMES
Private	RICHARDSON PETER
Private	SALWAY SAML.
Private	SMITH ROBT.
Private	STEWART JOHN
Private	THOMAS DAVID
Private	THORN DANIEL
Private	WALLER JAMES

Private	WHITMORE HENRY
Private	WILLIAMS JOHN
Private	WILLSON WM.
Private	WRIGHT JAMES
Private	YEOMAN JOHN

Captain Campbell's (Major) Company No.5.

Captain	CAMPBELL WM. (M) on the Staff A.2.M. Genl.
Lieutenant	O'FLAHERTY FRANS.
Lieutenant	FIELDING GEO.
Serjeant	FOSTER GEO.
Corporal	NORTH WM.
Drummer	BOYLE ALEXR.
Drummer	DAVIS CAESOR
Private	ANDERTON WM.
Private	BARNETT ROBT.
Private	BRAGGER GEO.
Private	CALVER DANL. Davies collection 5-5-66
Private	CARR HENRY
Private	CARSON JOHN
Private	COOPER JAMES
Private	DARWIN JOHN Died 4th July
Private	DAVIS JOHN
Private	DAVIS ROBT.
Private	DAVIS THOS.
Private	DAVIS 2nd. WM.
Private	DOLLING PHILLIP
Private	EVANS JOHN
Private	EYNOW RICHD.
Private	FRANKS HENRY
Private	GRIFFEN THOS.
Private	GROSVENER MOSES
Private	HARPER CHAS.
Private	HIGGINS WM.
Private	HENLEY WM.
Private	HUGHES THOS.
Private	HULSE BARNABY
Private	HUMPHRIES ROBT.
Private	JEREMIAH JOHN
Private	JERVIS JOHN
Private	JONES LEWIS
Private	JONES RODERICK
Private	KENDRICK THOS. Deserted 28th July
Private	LARWOOD FRANS.
Private	LESTER THOS.
Private	LEWIS JOHN
Private	LUKE MORGAN
Private	MILLGATE PHILLIP
Private	MILLIGAN ROBT.
Private	MILLWARD JAMES
Private	MITCHELL GEO.
Private	MORLEY JAMES
Private	MORRIS THOS.
Private	MURPHY THOS.
Private	NEWELL JAMES
Private	NEWLAND ABRA.
Private	NORBURY THOS.
Private	OAKLEY HENRY
Private	OWENS JOHN
Private	PARRY EDWD.
Private	PHILLIPS THOS.
Private	POWELL JAMES
Private	PRITCHARD RICHD.
Private	PROSSER ROGER
Private	PROSSER WM.
Private	PROUT GEO.
Private	ROWLAND JNS.
Private	RICE JNS.
Private	RUDD JNS.
Private	RUSSELL JNS.
Private	SLAVIN THOS.
Private	SPENCER PETER
Private	TIDBURY DAVID
Private	TUCK JOHN
Private	VERNEY JOHN
Private	WARNER FRANS.
Private	WESTLY WM.
Private	WILLIAMS WM.
Private	WILLIAMS GEO.
Private	WILKINSON WM. Glendinnings sale 21st July 1909

Captain Johnson's Company No.6.

Captain	JOHNSON H.C.
Lieutenant	SIDLEY A.G.
Lieutenant	CLAYHILLS ALEXR.
Ensign	LILLE THOS.
Serjeant	BUTTERWORTH LUKE
Serjeant	GREGORY ROBT.
Serjeant	HAYES WM.
Serjeant	SHELLEY JOSH. Killed 18th June
Corporal	BARLOW JOHN
Corporal	JONES HUGH Died 19th July
Corporal	TINEWELL ROBT.
Corporal	WHITTAKER WM.

Drummer	CLARKE WM.
Drummer	WALKER MENDAMUS
Private	ASHTON HENRY
Private	BALDEROW JOHN
Private	BLAGBOROUGH SAML.
Private	BROOKS WM.
Private	CADE JOSH.
Private	CARMAN SAML.
Private	COOK JOHN
Private	CRABTREE SAML.
Private	EVANS LEWIS
Private	EVANS EDWD.
Private	EVANS JACOB
Private	FICKLING JOHN
Private	FELLOWES JAMES
Private	FRENCH JAMES
Private	GILLICE HUGH
Private	GREEN WM.
Private	GRIFFITHS JOHN
Private	HAGUE SAML.
Private	HEATH JOSH. Glendinnings sale Oct. 1913 3-10-0
Private	HETHERIDGE RICHD.
Private	HEWITT JAMES
Private	HUGHES EVAN
Private	HUGHES WM.
Private	JAMES RICHD.
Private	IRELAND WM.
Private	JENKINS JAMES
Private	JEREMIAH THOS.
Private	JONES ISRAEL
Private	JOSEPH THOS.
Private	LEMON JNS.
Private	LINCE JAMES
Private	MAYBURG OLIVER
Private	McEVAY WM.
Private	MERRIMAN JAMES
Private	MURRAY MICHL.
Private	MURRAY THOS. Deserted 21st July
Private	OWENS HUGH
Private	PALMER JOHN
Private	PEREGRINE JOHN
Private	PORKESS WM.
Private	PRICE JAMES
Private	PRICE 2nd JAMES
Private	PRICE JOHN
Private	PRITCHARD EDWD.
Private	PHILLIPS JAMES
Private	RABOULD JOHN
Private	REEL PATK.
Private	ROBERTS JNS. 1st
Private	ROBERTS JNS 2ns
Private	SEDDON HENRY
Private	SIMON THOS.
Private	SMITH JOHN
Private	SMITH SAML.
Private	SPEED JOSH. Died 25th Aug.
Private	STEPHENS BARNABY
Private	STEPHENSON JOHN
Private	THOMAS ENOS.
Private	VAUGHAN ROBT.
Private	WILLIAMS JNS. 1st
Private	WILLIAMS JNS. 2nd
Private	WILLIAMS JNS. 3rd
Private	WILLIAMS GEO.

<u>Captain Farmer's Company No.7.</u>

Captain	FARMER THOS.
Lieutenant	MILNE JAMES
Lieutenant	HARRIS J.W.
Serjeant	DAVIS THOS.
Serjeant	ELLIOTT WM.
Serjeant	SHARPLES WM.
Serjeant	WINSTANLY THOS.
Corporal	BOULT WM.
Corporal	ELIAS ELIAS.
Corporal	GODDEN THOS.
Corporal	LITTLEFORD WM. Died 21st June
Corporal	MORRIS JOHN Cheylesmore collection 1908
Corporal	ROSSITER RICHD.
Drummer	EDWARDS JOHN
Drummer	MATTHEWS JACOB
Private	ALLEN KEY
Private	ALLEN SAML.
Private	ALLSOP JOSH.
Private	BAKER RICHD.
Private	BENNETT SAML.
Private	BOUTLE WM.
Private	CLAYTON JACOB
Private	COCK JOHN Killed 18th June
Private	COCKSHOTT BRIGGS
Private	COOKE GEO.
Private	CREALY PETER
Private	CRISP JOSH.
Private	CROWE JOHN
Private	DAVIS GEO.

Private	DELAHAY THOS.
Private	EDWARDS JOSH.
Private	EDWARDS DAVID
Private	ELLIS REES
Private	FREDERICK ROBT.
Private	GRIFFITHS LEWIS
Private	HOLLIS JAMES
Private	HUGHS SETH
Private	JACKSON HUGH
Private	JOHN WM.
Private	JONES DAVID
Private	KELLY THOS.
Private	MACLETON JOHN
Private	MORGAN JOHN
Private	MORGAN REES
Private	NEWMAN JON.
Private	O'BRIEN TEAGUE
Private	ROWSALL THOS.
Private	SMITH GEO.
Private	SNELL JOSH.
Private	STEPHENS SAML.
Private	SWIFT WM.
Private	SYMMS HENRY
Private	TAYLOR JOHN Glendinnings sale 25 Oct. 1907
Private	THATCHER JAMES
Private	THOMAS DAVID
Private	THORN DANIEL
Private	TYRELL GEO.
Private	VICKERS WM.
Private	WORRELL JAMES
Private	WATSON JOSH.
Private	WEBSTER JOSH.
Private	WELLS SAML.
Private	WESTLER CHAS.
Private	WICKERS WM.
Private	WILLETTS SAML.
Private	WILLIAMS HENRY
Private	WILLIAMS THOS. 1st
Private	WILLIAMS THOS. 2nd
Private	WILLIAMS JOHN Killed 18th June
Private	WILLIAMSON WM.

Captain Jolliffe's Company No.8.

Captain	JOLLIFFE CHAS. Killed 18th June
Lieutenant	PHILLIPS GRISMOND
Lieutenant	HOLMES R.P.
Ensign	DUNN GEO.
Serjeant	HARDING HENRY
Serjeant	HUTCHINS RICHD.
Serjeant	QUERCHY JOSH.
Corporal	STANTON WM.
Drummer	BEADSLEY RICHD.
Drummer	MEW ROBT. Deserted 5th Aug.
Private	SOUTHALL WM.
Private	BELLINGHAM SAML.
Private	BLEE HENRY
Private	BROCKLESS JOHN Col.R.T. Gascoigne collection March 1909
Private	BROWN JOHN
Private	CURTIS EDWD.
Private	DOWNS JOHN
Private	DREW JOSH Deserted 23rd Aug.
Private	DAY RICHD.
Private	ENSER WM.
Private	FENTON WM.
Private	FISHER JNS.
Private	FOX WM.
Private	FRANCIS JNS. Killed 18th June
Private	GREEN THOS.
Private	GRINDED JAMES
Private	GRIFFITHS JNS.
Private	GRIFFITHS JAMES
Private	HALL GEO.
Private	HANSON THOS.
Private	HAWTHORN WM.
Private	HUGHES RICHD.
Private	HUGHES THOS.
Private	JAMES JOHN
Private	JERVIS WM.
Private	JONES REES
Private	JONES THOS. Killed 18th June
Private	JONES WM.
Private	KENDRICK JAMES
Private	KITCHEN LEXION
Private	LAYTON JNS.
Private	LEARY JNS. Died 30th June
Private	LUCAS JNS.
Private	LUCAS WM.
Private	MANSBRIDGE STEP.
Private	MORGAN RICHD.
Private	MORRIS JOHN
Private	MORRIS DAVID
Private	OLDHAM WM.
Private	PARRY WM.
Private	PEAKE JNS.
Private	PEARPOINT WM. Killed 18th June

Private	PEGG THOS.
Private	RUTTER CHAS.
Private	PYLEY WM.
Private	SHAKELADY SAML. Killed 18th June
Private	SHEPHERD JAMES
Private	STEWARDSON DANL.
Private	THOMAS JOHN
Private	THOMPSON WM.
Private	VILE JOHN
Private	WARRINGTON JOHN
Private	WILLIAMS ELIAS
Private	WILLIAMS WM.
Private	WILLIAMS THOS.
Private	WRIGHT GEO.

Captain Wynne's Company - Light Infantry

Lieutenant	FENSHAM GEO. Killed 18th June
Lieutenant	PRICE A.
Lieutenant	METHOLD EDWD.
Serjeant	HOWELL JOHN
Serjeant	MILLAR JAMES
Corporal	HUGHS JOHN
Corporal	LAUGHTON MARK
Corporal	ROBINSON THOS.
Corporal	WALLACE WM.
Drummer	MAWSON WM.
Drummer	WHITTINGHAM WM.
Private	ANDREWS JOSH.
Private	AUSTIN WM.
Private	BRADLEY BENJ.
Private	BARNES THOS.
Private	BAULCH JOSH.
Private	BAXTER JOSH
Private	BERRY TERENCE
Private	BLAZEY JAMES
Private	BROMLEY WM.
Private	BROWN CHAS.
Private	CALVER JAMES
Private	CASBOURNE THOS.
Private	CONNOLLY MICHL.
Private	COUSINS EDWD.
Private	CROSS JOHN
Private	DAVIS JAMES
Private	DAWSON JOSH.
Private	DONNE JAMES
Private	DYSON JAMES
Private	ELLIS JNS.
Private	EVANS JNS.
Private	GIBSON JOHN
Private	HALL ROBT.
Private	HUGHES GEO.
Private	JAMES DAVID
Private	JONES DAVID
Private	JONES THOS.
Private	JONES PETER
Private	JONES RICHD.
Private	JONES ROBT.
Private	LAYLAND PETER Glendinnings sale Jan. 1910
Private	McCOOEY PETER
Private	McCOOEY THOS.
Private	McDONALD JOHN
Private	MORRIS THOS.
Private	MORGAN WM.
Private	NEWITT AARON
Private	PEART JNS.
Private	PETERS JOSH.
Private	POMFRETT THOS.
Private	POMFRETT WM.
Private	SIMCO NICHS.
Private	SMITH JOHN
Private	SPENCER PETER
Private	STRONG H.W.
Private	SUTTON GEO.
Private	SYMMS WM.
Private	TAYLOR JNS.
Private	THOMAS JNS.
Private	THOMAS GEO.
Private	TOTTLE JONAS
Private	WARD THOS.
Private	WARING JOSH.
Private	WASSALL WM.
Private	WILKINSON EDWD.
Private	WILLIAMS REES

* * *

1st BATTALION OF THE 27th OF FOOT

Lt. Colonel	HARE JOHN
Captain	TUCKER JOHN
Lieutenant	McDONALD G.
Lieutenant	HENDERSON WM.
Lieutenant	HANDCOCK RICHD.
Lieutenant	FORTESCUE WM.
Lieutenant	CRADDOCK THOS.
Lieutenant	DREWE EDWD. Wounded
Lieutenant	MANLEY CHAS.
Lieutenant	MILLER JOHN

Lieutenant	BETTY JOHN
Ensign	KATER WM.
Ensign	DITMAS JOHN
Ensign	SMITH THOS.
Ensign	HANDCOCK THEO.
Qr.Master	TAYLOR T.
Ass.Surgeon	FITZGERALD G.
Ass.Surgeon	MOSTYN THOS.
Q.M.Sjt.	KENNEDY JOHN
Serjeant	PAPA FRANCIS.
Serjeant	DEVELIN MICHL.
Serjeant	LOCKE THOS. Discharged
Serjeant	McHUGH THOS.
Serjeant	O'HARA JAMES
Serjeant	STEWART JOHN
Serjeant	CROZIER RICHD.
Serjeant	KEEGAN JAMES
Serjeant	HUGH McCOY
Serjeant	MILLER ANTHY.
Serjeant	BLOWE WM.
Serjeant	FUTHEY JAMES
Serjeant	GARDNER JOHN
Serjeant	SHAWE JOHN
Serjeant	CAMPBELL JOHN
Serjeant	KELLY EDWD.
Serjeant	STANTON ULICK
Serjeant	TURNER WM.
Serjeant	THOMPSON THOS.
Serjeant	WALSH THOS.
Serjeant	EARLY EDWD.
Serjeant	McGOWAN JAMES
Serjeant	McDONALD DANIEL
Serjeant	SCOTT RICHD.
Serjeant	CONNELL LAWCE.
Serjeant	SUTHERLAND JOHN
Serjeant	TORPY HENRY
Serjeant	KERRIGAN THOS.
Serjeant	MULLINS JOHN
Corporal	CONWAY PATK.
Corporal	CAULFIELD EDWD.
Corporal	KENNEDY JOHN
Corporal	McCAFFRY LAWCE. Dead
Corporal	HARRIGAM JOHN
Corporal	LOUGHNY JOHN
Corporal	McCORMICK PATK.
Corporal	SHEA DAVID
Corporal	SULLIVAN JEREH.
Corporal	BRUCE JOHN
Corporal	HANCILL JAMES
Corporal	JOHNSTON THOS. Dead
Corporal	McCOURT JOHN Discharged Glendinnings sale Oct. 1910
Corporal	McVEETY WM.
Corporal	BROOKS THOS.
Corporal	BOWMAN JOHN
Corporal	COYLE EDWD.
Corporal	FALLIN JAMES
Corporal	MARTIN MICHL.
Corporal	SHORT FRANS.
Corporal	CAVANAGH ARTHUR Dead
Corporal	CARMIELE DUNCAN
Corporal	DEVINE BERND.
Corporal	DEANE THOS.
Corporal	HEYWOOD JOHN
Corporal	PACKER WM.
Corporal	SHANKS WM.
Corporal	COSGROVE JAMES
Corporal	FEGAN JAMES
Corporal	MOORE BENJN.
Corporal	STUDGEON ROBT.
Corporal	CODY JOHN Discharged
Corporal	JUDGE THOS.
Drummer	BUNTON JAMES
Drummer	ROBINSON JOHN
Drummer	KILLAN JOHN
Drummer	QUIM WM.
Drummer	MARTIN MICHL.
Drummer	MORGAN WILLM.
Drummer	STEWART CHAS.
Private	BOYLE THOS. Dead
Private	BROOKS JAMES Discharged
Private	BIRCH CHARLES
Private	CADDEN JOHN
Private	COLLINS JOHN
Private	CONWAY DENIS
Private	COLROY JOHN
Private	CONNER SAML.
Private	CRAY WM.
Private	CARBERRY JAMES
Private	CURNIAN PHILIP
Private	COWAN WM.
Private	DEVITT FRANS.
Private	DUFFEY OWEN
Private	DUNDAS JOHN
Private	DUNLOP ALEXR.
Private	DEMPSEY RODGER
Private	ENRIGHT JOHN
Private	FARNEY OWEN

Private FEENEY MICHL.
Private FULLARD PATK.
Private GOLLAGHER JAMES
Private GILBRIDGE OWEN
Private GOULDING BERND.
Private GUGGARTY CHRIS.
Private GRAHAM ARTH.
Private GOURLEY CHAS.
Private GRAY PETER
Private GREEN OWEN
Private HALL RICHD.
Private HART JOHN
Private HARE JAMES
Private HAMILTON JOHN
Private HEISSERMAN THOS.
Private HAMILTON WM.
Private HUGHES TERENCE
Private HUMPHRIES THOS.
Private JORDIN THOS.
Private JOHNSTON JOHN
Private KERRIGAN MATTW.
Private KEYS THOS.
Private KING JAMES
Private LAPPIN MICHL.
Private McCABE TERENCE
Private McCASHIN THOS.
Private McCRAKIN RICHD. Discharged
Private McCREADY JOHN
Private MOONEY JAMES
Private McCAY WM.
Private McDERMOTT PATK.
Private McGEE BERND.
Private McGUM FRANS.
Private MILLER JAMES
Private McHUGH NEILL
Private MOORE JAMES H.Gaskell's collection 1908
Private MOORE JOHN
Private O'BRYAN MICHL.
Private PETTY JOHN
Private QUINN JAMES
Private QUIGLEY CHRIS.
Private ROURKE JOHN
Private SOULTY DAVID
Private SHERKY MATTW.
Private SKILLEN DAVID
Private SMITH ROBT.
Private TONOR JAMES Discharged
Private TRAYNOR PATK.
Private WALSH PATK.
Private WALLACE THOS.
Private WEIR EDWD.
Private WEIR JAMES
Private WEIR WM.
Private WILLS MICHL.
Private WILSON ROBT.

Private AMPLE HUGH
Private ABBOTT WM.
Private ADAMS JAMES
Private BOYLE ROBT. Dead
Private BURNS MICHL 1st
Private BURNS MICHL. 2nd
Private BALL JAMES
Private BRAHENRY PATT. Discharged Payne collection 1911
Private BAIRD WM.
Private CAMERON CHAS.
Private CAMPBELL TERENCE
Private CLANCEY JOHN
Private COONSY JOHN
Private DRUM JOHN
Private DONNELLY JOS.
Private GAFFREY PATK.
Private GREMON JOHN
Private GRANT JOHN
Private GOODWIN RICHD.
Private HOLLIDAY DANL.
Private HIGGINS PETR.
Private HANNAH JAMES
Private HUGHES OWEN
Private HALLIMAN OWEN
Private HAMILTON JOHN
Private JOLLY JOHN
Private JOHNSTON NEILL
Private JOHNSTON PETER
Private KEARNS THOS.
Private KEARNS WM.
Private LAYDON DOMK.
Private McDONALD HENRY
Private McCONOY MICHL.
Private McKIBBON JOHN
Private MEEHAN ARTH.
Private MEDLEY SAML.
Private McSOURLY OWEN
Private McSOURLY WM.
Private McGIMETT FRAN.
Private McMAINS OLIVER
Private McGUIRE PHILIP

Private	McHUGH JAMES
Private	MURPHY JOHN
Private	McENTAGART CHAS.
Private	McLARNON JOHN
Private	MOONY WM.
Private	McGEE JOHN
Private	MURTAGH TIMY.
Private	MAHON WM.
Private	O'NEALE OWEN Discharged
Private	O'NEALE ALEXR.
Private	ORR DAVID
Private	PONSONBY GEO.
Private	PHILLIPS ROBT.
Private	SCOALE THOS.
Private	SMITH JAMES
Private	SMITH CHAS.
Private	STEWART ROBT.
Private	SWORDS BERND.
Private	STEVENSON SAML.
Private	SWARBRIG HENRY
Private	TACKERY JOSH
Private	TEMONY FRANS.
Private	THOMPSON JOHN
Private	WALSH EDWD.
Private	WALLACE NATH.
Private	WARD WM.
Private	WHITE THOS.
Private	ALLEN JAMES
Private	ALLEN DAVID
Private	BROWN JOHN
Private	BOYLE JAMES
Private	BOLES JOHN
Private	COUGHLAN CORN.
Private	COLLUM DAVID
Private	CAMPBELL JOHN
Private	CAMPBELL PATK. Dead
Private	COLVIN ANDW.
Private	CORRORAN JOHN
Private	CARSONS JOHN
Private	CONNELL JAMES
Private	CLANCEY PETER
Private	CURRAN HENRY
Private	DORAN HUGH
Private	DAILY PATK.
Private	DOUTHARD GEO.
Private	EAGAR SAML.
Private	FLYNN WM.
Private	FINNAN MARK

Private	GALLIMORE THOS.
Private	GAWEY EDWD.
Private	GALLAGHER THOS.
Private	HIGHERTY DANL.
Private	HANNAH DANL.
Private	HEWITT WM.
Private	HANNON THOS.
Private	HOWE WM.
Private	HUDDLESTON JOSH.
Private	JONES CHAS.
Private	KELLY WM.
Private	KELSTER PETER
Private	LUNEY HUGH
Private	LAPPIN HUGH Discharged
Private	LYONS THOS.
Private	LEONARD DENIS
Private	LEONARD JAMES
Private	LENNOX THOS.
Private	LAVEY JAMES
Private	LESLY JAMES
Private	McGAW JAMES
Private	McQUAID JNS.
Private	MAHONY WM.
Private	McKINWORTH BERND.
Private	McCOURT PATK.
Private	McCONNELL JNS.
Private	McGEE BERND.
Private	McGEE ARTHUR
Private	McLEECE DANIEL
Private	McGINNITY GEO.
Private	McANEEY DAVID Discharged
Private	McGINNIS PATK.
Private	MURDOCK JNS.
Private	McARDILL JOSH.
Private	McMULLEN PETER Glendinnings sale Feb. 1914
Private	MALONE JAMES
Private	NOWLAW JOHN
Private	O'DONNELL BENJN.
Private	QUINN JAMES
Private	REILLY CORNS.
Private	REILLY WM.
Private	ROURKE MICHL.
Private	RYAN WM.
Private	RODEN ANDREW
Private	RAFFERTY FRANS.
Private	SWORDS JAMES
Private	STEVINSON THOS. Discharged
Private	SMITH JOHN

Private	SUTHERLAND HENRY
Private	SKELLY JAMES
Private	TOOLE THOS.
Private	TAIPE DENIS
Private	TAYLOR PATK.
Private	VANE PATK.
Private	WADSWORTH GEO.
Private	WHITE GEO.
Private	WILLS RICHD.
Private	YORE THOS. Discharged
Private	LARKIN ARTHUR
Private	EUTAGART PETER
Private	ALEXANDER JAMES Col.Murray's collection 1908
Private	ARMSTRONG JAMES
Private	ANDERSON SAML.
Private	ABRAHAM THOS.
Private	BOYDE MATTW. Discharged
Private	BOWS BERND.
Private	BURKE PATK.
Private	CLARKE JOHN
Private	CONNELLY JOHN
Private	CREEGAN PETER
Private	COLEMAN LUKE
Private	CAMPBELL JOHN
Private	DEVELIN THOS.
Private	DENVER WM.
Private	DYER BERND.
Private	ELLIOTT ANDREW
Private	ELLIOTT JOHN
Private	EMERSON JOHN
Private	FLANIGAN THOS.
Private	FULLIN JOHN
Private	FARRELL THOS.
Private	FERGUSON THOS.
Private	FEARNS JOHN
Private	GREEN THOS.
Private	GORDON PATK.
Private	HUDSON JOEL
Private	HOLLIDAY JOSH
Private	HEWITT HUGH
Private	KELLY WM.
Private	KAIN MICHL.
Private	KEEGAN THOS.
Private	LYNCH JOHN
Private	LAHIFF DENIS
Private	LITTLE ROBT.
Private	LEWIS JOHN
Private	LACKEY WM.
Private	LOUGHLIN JNS.
Private	MARTIN JOHN
Private	MARTIN BERND. Whitaker collection
Private	McLOUGHLIN MICHL.
Private	MULDOON JOHN
Private	McCORMICK JEREH.
Private	MOORE WM.
Private	MOFFETT JOHN
Private	McKENNY JOHN
Private	McCABE JAMES
Private	McCABE THOS.
Private	McGUIRE PHILIP
Private	McARDILL EDWD.
Private	MULLINS JAMES
Private	McNULTY JAMES
Private	McCOLLOUGH JOHN
Private	McHAVILL HENRY
Private	MONAHAN HUGH
Private	McCARROW CHAS.
Private	McCAWLEY WM.
Private	McGINNIS EDWD.
Private	MULHEADY HENRY
Private	MAXWELL JAMES
Private	OWENS ALEXR.
Private	O'BOYLE PATK.
Private	PERRY JAMES
Private	PEABLES WM.
Private	ROONEY WM.
Private	ROONEY PATK.
Private	STEWART ROBT. Discharged
Private	STEWART SAML.
Private	SCOTT RICHD.
Private	THOMPSON JAMES
Private	WEATHERS JNS.
Private	LAWLER WM.
Private	SMITH THOS.
Private	SHORT ANDREW
Private	THOMPSON JOHN
Private	BRADLEY JAMES Dead
Private	BENNETT PHILIP
Private	BREADY PHILIP
Private	BURNS HENRY
Private	BRENNAN THOS.
Private	BRADLEY JAMES
Private	BRAMPTON CHAS.
Private	BOYLAN WM.
Private	COX TER.
Private	CORRIGAN THOS.
Private	COSTELLO GARRET

Private	CUNNINGHAM WM.
Private	CUNNIGHAM PATK.
Private	CORBETT WM.
Private	CAMPBELL JAMES
Private	CLARKE PETER
Private	CALLAGHAN JAMES
Private	CAULFIELD TIMY. Discharged
Private	CAULFIELD PETER
Private	COUGHRAN JOHN
Private	CONLAN THOS.
Private	CURRAN JAMES
Private	CARRAWAY JOHN
Private	COLLERY OWEN
Private	CASSIDY MATTW.
Private	DAY JAMES
Private	DONNELLY HUGH
Private	DAVIS NICHS.
Private	DOOLAN DANIEL
Private	DENSMERE WM.
Private	EVANS JOHN
Private	GAYNOR JOHN
Private	GUBBINS JOSH.
Private	HOPKINS WM.
Private	HARCOURT LUKE
Private	HARRISON WM.
Private	HAGAN JNS (Sr)
Private	HAGAN JNS (Jr)
Private	HERNAHAN WM.
Private	KENNY PATK.
Private	KENNEDY PATK.
Private	LANGIN PATK.
Private	McELVY MICHL.
Private	MAHONY DAVID
Private	McCONVILL JAMES Cheylesmore collection 1908
Private	MEYES-THOMAS
Private	McCANN PHILLIP
Private	MURRAY PATK.
Private	MORIARTY DANL.
Private	MASON JAMES
Private	MADDEN FERGUS
Private	McLELAND HAMILTON
Private	MAY JOHN
Private	McWILLIAMS JOHN
Private	MONTGOMERY PETER
Private	NICHOLSON MICHL.
Private	O'NEAL BERND. (Sr)
Private	O'NEAL BERND. (Jr)
Private	REILLY MICHL.
Private	READE PATK.
Private	RUTLEDGE ALEXR. in stock (approic 163 17-3-65) Badly rubbed
Private	SAVAGE JAMES
Private	SLATTERY ROBT.
Private	SMITH WM.
Private	SHERLOCK THOS.
Private	TYRELL JOHN
Private	WALSH THOS. (Sr)
Private	WALSH THOS. (Jr)
Private	WALSH CHAS.
Private	BOYDE JOHN
Private	CALLAHAN JOHN
Private	ARNETT JOHN
Private	BARNETT WM.
Private	BEGLEY EDWD.
Private	BELL CONWAY
Private	BURKE EDWD.
Private	CALLAHAN JAMES
Private	COLLINS THOS. Dead
Private	CLARKE FRANS. Col.Gascoignes collection March 1909
Private	DAVIS JOSH.
Private	DIEU JOHN
Private	DUNNIGAN PATK.
Private	DUNLEANY THOS.
Private	DORAN JAMES
Private	DUFFLY MICHL.
Private	DURNING JOHN
Private	ENNIS RICHD.
Private	GOULDING LEWIS
Private	GRAHAM THOS.
Private	COGGANS PATK.
Private	GILSON JAMES
Private	HENRY PARK.
Private	HENRY WM.
Private	HOGG MARTIN
Private	HUGHES WM.
Private	JOHNSTON WM.
Private	KELLY JOHN
Private	KILSO DAVID
Private	LAW CHAS.
Private	LAWN WM. Discharged
Private	LYNCH JAMES
Private	MACKIN PATK.
Private	McGUIRE JAMES
Private	MALONE PATK.
Private	MULLINS NETHL. Discharged

Private	McBRIDE JAMES
Private	McBRIDE SAML.
Private	McCLUSKEY DANL.
Private	McFARLANE WM.
Private	McGILL BERND.
Private	McCONNELL HUGH
Private	McCOLLOUGH CHAS.
Private	McGLONE JAMES
Private	McKEON THOS.
Private	McLEAN RICHD.
Private	McLOUGHLIN CORNS.
Private	McLOUGHLIN ARTHR.
Private	McMAHON FRANS.
Private	McMULLEN WM.
Private	MORTIMER MARK
Private	MURPHY JOHN
Private	NEWLAND JOHN
Private	O'HARA THOS.
Private	PURSLY WM.
Private	PRICE HENRY
Private	RICHMOND JAMES Discharged
Private	ROURKE PATK.
Private	RUSSELL MICHL.
Private	SAVAGE JNS.
Private	SEA JNS
Private	SCULLY BERND.
Private	STRUDGEON JNS Discharged
Private	TAGGART MOSES
Private	TIERNEY EDWD.
Private	WALLACE JAMES
Private	SPENCE WM.
Private	MATTHEWS WM.
Private	McLEAN JOHN
Private	FRAZER ALEXR.
Private	DALEY DANL.
Private	CUNNINGHAM JOHN
Private	CONNELL JEREH.
Private	CURRAN JOSH.
Private	CASSIDY JOHN
Private	DAILEY BERND.
Private	DIGON JOHN
Private	EAKINS JOHN
Private	GRAY ARTHUR
Private	GRAHAM FELIX
Private	GILLAN PATK.
Private	GOUHAN THOS.
Private	GORDON WM.
Private	HIGGINS PETER
Private	JONES JOSH.
Private	McDONNELL WM.
Private	McGUIRE PAT.
Private	McGUIRE JAMES
Private	McCRONEY PETER
Private	McMULLEN JOHN
Private	McANALLY HUGH
Private	McKNIGHT JAMES
Private	McGRATH MARK
Private	McGIVERAN JAMES
Private	McKINLEY PRICE
Private	MATTHEWS JAMES
Private	MULLINS JAMES
Private	OWENS BERND.
Private	SHERWOOD WM. Dead
Private	STEVSNS WM. Discharged
Private	SWIFT JOHN
Private	SHAW PAT Dead
Private	THOMPSON THOS.
Private	WILSON JOHN
Private	WALKER HENRY
Private	CASSIDY HUGH

* * *

28th REGIMENT OF FOOT

Lt.Colonel	BELSON C.P.
Major	NIXON ROBERT Needes collection 1908
Adjutant	BRIDGELAND THOS.
Qr.Master	REYNOLDS RICHARD Payne collection 1911
Ass.Surgeon	LAVANS P.H.
Ass.Surgeon	STEWART ALEXR.
Pay Master	DEWES JNS.

Captain and Bt.Major Irving's Company

Bt.Major	IRVING WM.
Lieutenant	MOUNSTEVEN WM.
Lieutenant	DEARS JNS.
S.Major	LYNCH PATK.
S.Major	IRWIN RICHD.
P.M.Sjt.	COOKE HUGH
Ar.Sjt.	OATES RICHD.
Dr.Major	BROWN ALEXR.
Serjeant	BIRDS JOSH.
Serjeant	KEATING JNS.
Serjeant	WATTS ROBT.
Corporal	FRANCIS WM.
Corporal	THORNE ROGER
Drummer	DONNELLY JAMES
Drummer	HANLEY JAMES

Drummer	HARRAPATH WM.
Private	BARTLEY JAMES
Private	BAILEY JOHN
Private	BLARNEY SOLOMON
Private	BRAKES WM.
Private	BRIDLE JOSH.
Private	BRIEN WM. Dead
Private	BURNETT JAMES
Private	BROOKS JOHN
Private	CARR HENRY
Private	CUNDY WM.
Private	CLARKE PATK.
Private	CLARKE ROBT.
Private	CHUBB WM.
Private	CUMMINGS WM.
Private	CUMMERFORD WM.
Private	DARLEY JOHN Deserted
Private	DIXON JAMES
Private	ELLIOTT WM.
Private	EVANS MICHL.
Private	FARMER DANL. Deserted
Private	FENNELL JAMES
Private	GILES JAMES
Private	HALSUP CHAS.
Private	HARDING JNS.
Private	HAWKER SAML.
Private	HAWKINS JNS.
Private	HUNT MICHL.
Private	JOHNSTONE JAMES
Private	LANE JNS.
Private	LAFFERTY JAMES
Private	MARKS WM.
Private	McSHAW DANL. Dead
Private	PETTER THOS.
Private	PRATT WM.
Private	QUINN PETER
Private	REYNOLDS WM.
Private	RYAN JAMES
Private	RYDER JAMES
Private	SMALLY JOSH.
Private	SHEEDY WM.
Private	TOOHEY PATK.
Private	WITHY JOSH
Private	WOODLEY EDWD.
Private	WRIGHT JNS.

Captain Henry Moriarty's Company

Captain	KELLY RICHD.
Lieutenant	WILKINSON J.F.
Ensign	SERGEANTSON WM.
Serjeant	O'CONNOR MICHL.
Serjeant	WILLIAMS HENRY
Corporal	BRENNON MICHL.
Corporal	ROBERTS JAMES
Corporal	WHEELER WALT.
Corporal	WHITE WM.
Drummer	DONNOLLY WM.
Drummer	HARRAPATH DANL.
Private	ADAMS JAMES
Private	BARNES JOSH.
Private	BOND JNS
Private	BOOTH RICHD
Private	BRIANT THOS.
Private	BRIGHT DAVIDSON
Private	CLARKE PETER
Private	CONNELL JAMES
Private	CONNELL JNS.
Private	CONNOLLY BARTW.
Private	CONNOLLY JNS Discharged
Private	CRUISE JNS Dead
Private	DAWE JAMES
Private	DOWNES WM.
Private	EDGE ROBT.
Private	EMERSON PETER
Private	FOGARTY MARTIN
Private	FOX PETER
Private	FRY GEO.
Private	GAYNOR WM.
Private	GAY JNS.
Private	HANDSBERRY JNS.
Private	HARDIMAN EDWD.
Private	HARRIS WM.
Private	HUXTON MARK
Private	KEENAN JNS.
Private	KEHERN PETER
Private	KETTERICK WALT. Dead
Private	LEE WM.
Private	LOUGHRANE VICAR
Private	McNULTY BRIAN Discharged
Private	McCURRY PATK.
Private	McGEE CHAS.
Private	MATTHEWS JNS.
Private	MORRIS JNS Glendinings February 1913
Private	NEEDHAM JAMES
Private	NEAL JAMES
Private	NICHOLSON RICHD.
Private	NUTWELL JOEL
Private	NUTT SAML.
Private	O'BRIEN JNS.

Private	PURRETT JNS
Private	PEARCE WM.
Private	PENNY SAML. Dead
Private	RIDER LUKE
Private	SANDFORD WM.
Private	SERWINS RICHD. Dead
Private	SHANNON PETER
Private	SHAW JON. Dead
Private	VICKERY TIMY.
Private	WARREN JNS.
Private	WILLIAMS THOS.
Private	WORLEY JNS.

Captain Chas. Cadell's Company

Captain	CADELL CHAS.
Lieutenant	HILLIARD HENRY
Lieutenant	IRWIN WM.
Lieutenant	CARROTHERS C.B.
Serjeant	DAVIS THOS.
Serjeant	FACEY PETER
Serjeant	MOLLOY WM.
Serjeant	REGAN JOHN
Corporal	BRESLAND WM.
Corporal	BRODEY PATK.
Corporal	HAMMER THOS.
Corporal	SWIFT HUGH
Drummer	CONNORS LAWRE.
Drummer	DOYLE DENIS
Drummer	HEAGUE JAMES
Drummer	JENTLE MATTW.
Private	ANDREWS JNS.
Private	ASH THOS.
Private	BAKER STEPHN.
Private	BOURKE WALT.
Private	BRAKEN THOS
Private	DEAN JNS.
Private	DOYLE JNS.
Private	DRENNON JNS.
Private	FAULKNER PATK.
Private	FLAHERTY TIMY.
Private	FOGARTY MICHL.
Private	FITZGIBBONS DANL.
Private	GREY WM.
Private	GREGORY WM.
Private	HAMMOND ALEXR.
Private	HIGGINS MICHL.
Private	HOBB CHAS.
Private	JACKSON MICHL.
Private	JEANES THOS.
Private	KINSMAN THOS.
Private	LENDLES RALPH
Private	LEONARD JNS Dead
Private	MARTIN MATTW.
Private	MARTIN PHILIP
Private	McENALLY THOS Deserted
Private	McCORMICK HENRY
Private	McKETTERICK JAMES
Private	METHERAL RICHD.
Private	MITCHELL EDWD.
Private	MONTGOMERY GEO.
Private	PARSONS JNS.
Private	PATTEN THOS.
Private	REAY JAMES
Private	ROBINS GEO.
Private	ROWE HENRY
Private	SMITH MICHL. Discharged
Private	TONKINS WM.
Private	WATTS JAMES
Private	WEBB WM.
Private	WILSON JAMES
Private	WITHERED ALEXR.
Private	WOODS GEO.

Captain & Bt.Major Richard Llewellyn's Company

Captain	LLEWELLYN RICHD.
Ensign	LYNAM WM.
Serjeant	BRITTAIN WM. Discharged Gray collection 1908
Serjeant	DAWLEY GEO.
Serjeant	KERR WM.
Serjeant	MASSEY EDWD
Corporal	EWENS CHAS.
Corporal	GRENHAM THOS. Dead
Corporal	LOCKHART SAML.
Corporal	PERHAM JOHN
Drummer	HICKEY JAMES
Drummer	McDEVITT NEILL
Private	BARRY MICHL
Private	CANAVAN MICHL.
Private	CLARKE THOS. Dead
Private	CHEW CHAS
Private	CHEDGEY RICHD Galway Foley collection 1910
Private	COTTLE MOSES Dead
Private	CONNOLLY CORNS.
Private	CONNORS MICHL.
Private	DANGER WM.
Private	DWYNE WM.
Private	ELLIOTT JAMES

Private	ELLIS THOS.
Private	EVORY JAMES
Private	EYERS EDWD
Private	FINNIGAN JAMES Dead
Private	GANNON JAMES Dead
Private	GORDON MICHL.
Private	GREEN JAMES
Private	GIBBS JOHN
Private	HANN THOS.
Private	HERVEY BERND
Private	HOBB JACOB
Private	HOSKINS WM.
Private	HUGHES PATK.
Private	JOHNSON JNS.
Private	JOINTS THOS
Private	KELLY DANL.
Private	KENNEDY JOSH Deserted
Private	KINFORD RICHD.
Private	LAVERY WM.
Private	LENNON JNS
Private	LOUGHRANE BERND.
Private	LUXHAM RICHD.
Private	MATTHEWS NATHL.
Private	McCABE PATK.
Private	McAWLEY JAMES
Private	McGUINESS JOHN
Private	McGWINN ROBT.
Private	McGUIRE FRANS. Dead
Private	MELLISH ROBT
Private	MILLS ISIAH
Private	MURRAY HUGH
Private	MURPHY T.
Private	MURPHY JOSH Discharged
Private	NEAL JNS
Private	NAUGHTON MICHL Dead
Private	NOWLAN THOS
Private	PEARCE RICHD
Private	QUIRKE JNS
Private	REILLY WALT.
Private	WATSON MICHL
Private	WHITE HENRY
Private	WOODWARD JAMES

<u>Captain Thomas English's Company</u>

Captain	ENGLISH THOS. Whitaker Collection 1908
Lieutenant	INGRAM GEO.
Ensign	SIMPKINS JAMES
Serjeant	GALE WM.
Serjeant	RUTHERFORD JUSTUS
Serjeant	TEESDALE JOHN
Serjeant	WHALEY GEO.
Corporal	ADAMS JNS
Corporal	DOHERTY CHAS.
Corporal	JERVIS JOHN
Drummer	ADAMS WM.
Drummer	WRIGHT WM.
Private	ALDBURY JAMES
Private	BICKLE JNS
Private	BOND JNS
Private	BRENNON THOS.
Private	CARROLL DENNIS
Private	CARTER WM.
Private	CASSIDY EDWD.
Private	DOBSON THOS.
Private	DOONAR PATK.
Private	FIELDING JAMES Discharged Col.R.T. Gascoigne's collection Mar. 1909
Private	FORSTER WM.
Private	FOGARTY PATK.
Private	GRANT JOHN
Private	HAGARTY THOS.
Private	HANOVER PHILIP
Private	HORE JNS.
Private	HORE RICHD
Private	HEWISH WM.
Private	INNIS WM.
Private	LEONARD ROBT.
Private	LYNDSAY JNS
Private	MARSHALL GEO.
Private	MARSHALL JNS.
Private	McGLONE HUGH
Private	McNAIR JAMES Dead
Private	MINERS WM.
Private	MOUNT JAMES
Private	NEAREY JOHN
Private	PEARCE ROBT.
Private	PERRIN WM.
Private	PUGSLEY JNS.
Private	QUINN EDWD.
Private	QUINN JAMES
Private	RICKETTS JAMES
Private	RYDER JNS.
Private	RUTLEY JNS.
Private	ROBINS HENRY
Private	SINON JEREH.
Private	SLUGG JAMES
Private	SMITH GEO. Dead
Private	SMITH PATK.

Private	SOABEY WM.
Private	TANK JAMES
Private	WALSH EDWD.
Private	WEBB MICHL.
Private	WHITE RICHD.
Private	WOODLAND THOS.

Captain Thomas Wilson's Company

Lieutenant	SEMPLE MATTW.
Lieutenant	PARRY JAMES
Ensign	MARTIN ROBT.
Serjeant	MASLIN THOS.
Serjeant	SULLIVAN JEREH.
Corporal	GLOWEN WM.
Corporal	HARVEY JAMES
Corporal	KING JOHN
Corporal	SHANNON ROBT.
Corporal	STREETS JOHN
Drummer	HICKSON JAMES
Private	CAMPBELL JNS.
Private	CROSSWELL ROBT. Col. Murray's Collection 1908
Private	CURRY JOSH.
Private	CHAPMAN JNS.
Private	CONDON THOS.
Private	COLLINS JNS.
Private	CONLAN JNS Dead
Private	CROZIER ARCH. Dead
Private	CARNEY JNS.
Private	FARRELL LUKE
Private	FAWCETT WM.
Private	FISHER JNS.
Private	FULLERTON ROBT.
Private	FOXWELL JNS.
Private	GATRAN BERND.
Private	HARTIGAN JNS.
Private	HARWOOD JNS.
Private	HAWKINS JAMES
Private	HAYSE JNS.
Private	HERRON WM.
Private	LEMMON JNS.
Private	LOUDS JAMES Dead
Private	MARSHALL DAVID
Private	McAWLEY DAVID
Private	McKENNA JAMES
Private	McGRATH EDWD.
Private	McVARLANE THOS.
Private	McWHA ROBT.
Private	MULHOLLAND PATK.
Private	MUTTON JAMES
Private	PENNY RICHD.
Private	PILLOW THOS.
Private	PLUNKETT JNS.
Private	RAFFERTY MICHL.
Private	ROBINS GEO.
Private	ROLLS THOS.
Private	RYAN THOS.
Private	SHEEHY MICHL.
Private	SIMMONDS WM.
Private	TSAMMING JOHN
Private	STUCKEY JOSH.
Private	TOMBS WM.
Private	WEBB ABRA.
Private	WRENN PHILIP

Captain John Bowie's Company

Captain	BOWLES JNS.
Lieutenant	EASON R.P. Cheylesmore collection 1908
Lieutenant	COEN JNS.
Ensign	STEWART ROBT.
Serjeant	ARMSTRONG JNS.
Serjeant	MATTHEWS PETER
Serjeant	CHARLESWORTH JNS.
Serjeant	RICHARDSON ROCHD.
Serjeant	TALBOT MATTW.
Drummer	DRYAN JNS.
Drummer	HILL JOSH.
Drummer	McGEE ANDREW
Private	ANDREWS CHRIS.
Private	ALLUMS DANL.
Private	AXFORD WM.
Private	BLACK ROGER Discharged
Private	BROWNING JNS. Dead
Private	CONNOLLY BRIAN
Private	CHAPMAN EDWD.
Private	CROSS SAML.
Private	CLARKE BENJN.
Private	DANIELS HUGH
Private	DAVEY EDWD.
Private	DUFFICEY WM.
Private	DENHAM THOS.
Private	DEVELLIN JAMES
Private	DURR THOS. Discharged
Private	FOY JNS.
Private	FLOWERS JNS.
Private	GRANT CHRIS
Private	GUINAN WM.

Private	HENDERSON ALEXR.
Private	HERRON HENRY
Private	HOLLIS JOS.
Private	KEMPLE MATTW
Private	KEARNES JNS.
Private	KERR PATK Dead
Private	LUMMING THOS.
Private	MALADY THOS.
Private	MAY WM.
Private	McDONALD ALEXR.
Private	MALLON JNS.
Private	McINTIRE JNS.
Private	MILLARD GILES
Private	MILLER JNS.
Private	McGAW DAVID
Private	MAJOR JNS. Dead
Private	MORGAN WM.
Private	MOORE EDWD. Dead
Private	PALMER ROBT.
Private	PEPPERAL CORNS
Private	PHILIPS JNS.
Private	PINKER THOS.
Private	QUICK ROBT.
Private	REYNOLDS MICHL.
Private	RUNDLE THOS Discharged
Private	SILVESTER EDWD.
Private	SUMMERS EDWD.
Private	STRINGER BARTW.
Private	TALBOT JNS.
Private	UNDERWOOD JNS.
Private	VILE JNS.
Private	WATERS WM.
Private	WINSTANLEY JAMES
Private	WILLIAMS SAML.

<u>Captain Richard Kelly's Company</u>

Captain & Batt.Major	MEACHAM W.P.
Lieutenant	GILBERT R.V.
Lieutenant	CLARKE J.T.
Lieutenant	SHELTON J.W.
Serjeant	COCKRANE SIMON Dead
Serjeant	CHARLESWORTH ROGER Discharged
Serjeant	LOCKE RICHD.
Serjeant	RYAN EDWD
Serjeant	TAYLOR JAMES
Corporal	BIRDS JOHN
Corporal	GRAHAM JAMES Discharged
Corporal	HOOPER JAMES
Corporal	JOHNSTONE ROBT. Dead
Corporal	RALSTON HENRY
Drummer	DONNOLLY EDWD.
Drummer	McCUDDEN JAMES
Private	AMOS JAMES
Private	BRENNON JNS.
Private	BROKENSHIRE JNS.
Private	CALLAGHAN JNS. Dead
Private	CAMPBELL HUGH
Private	CAMPBELL MICHL.
Private	COLLINS JAMES
Private	CANTWELL JNS.
Private	COLE JNS. Dead
Private	CONNORS JNS.
Private	DEAGAN LAWRE.
Private	DONALLAN WM.
Private	DONELLY PATK.
Private	FORD WM.
Private	GILES CHAS. H.Gaskell's collection 1908
Private	GREEN DAVID
Private	HOYLE WM.
Private	HOOPER PHILIP
Private	HAYWOOD THOS.
Private	JANNINGS WM. Dead
Private	JOHNSTONE IRWIN
Private	KILLION JNS.
Private	KINGSTON JNS.
Private	LAVIS GEO.
Private	McCARTHY PHILIP
Private	McFADDEN MICHL.
Private	MADDEN JAMES Dead
Private	MADDEN PETER
Private	MULCAHY THOS. Deserted
Private	MONTGOMERY ROBT.
Private	NEWCOMBE WM.
Private	O'NEAL JNS.
Private	PALMER CHAS.
Private	PERFECT ABRAM.
Private	SHILSTONE RICHD.
Private	SPRYCE WM.
Private	SWORDS DENIS
Private	TAYLOR WM.
Private	TOOGOOD THOS Dead
Private	URINE HENRY
Private	VICKERS WM.
Private	VIVIAN THOS.
Private	WEBBER RICHD.

Captain & Bt.Lt.Colonel Sir.FredK. Steven's Company

Lieutenant	CRUMMER J.H.
Lieutenant	HILL E.E.
Lieutenant	COLLETON T.W.
Serjeant	BAIRE JAMES Glendinings Sale 17th June 1908
Serjeant	GOODFELLOW WM.
Serjeant	PORTER ROBT.
Serjeant	WEST FRANS.
Corporal	BLIZARD JOHN Discharged
Corporal	DREWE ROBT.
Corporal	DILTON THOS.
Corporal	FINNIGAN JOHN
Corporal	MILTON WM.
Corporal	MORGAN JNS.
Drummer	CONDEAS JAMES
Drummer	GUILLEAM JOHN
Drummer	JEFFORD RICHD.
Drummer	SHIELDS PATK.
Private	ATWOOD EDWD.
Private	AXEWORTHY WM.
Private	BARBER JAMES
Private	BYNES JOHN
Private	CAMPBELL JNS. 1st
Private	CARBERRY THOS.
Private	CARROL MICHL.
Private	CAVANAGH JAMES
Private	COLE ANDW Dead
Private	CONNOLLY PATK Dead
Private	DAVIS GEO.
Private	DEACON RICHD.
Private	DILLON PHLIP
Private	FORWARD ISSAC
Private	GOGGERTY PATK Discharged
Private	HANDCOCK WM.
Private	HARROD SAML.
Private	HAWKINS GEO. Discharged
Private	HICKEY PATK.
Private	HOGAN MICHL. Dead
Private	HOLLAND GEO.
Private	HUGH THOS Discharged
Private	JEWSON ISSAC
Private	KENDLE THOS
Private	KERNEW RICHD.
Private	MANN DENNIS
Private	MASTERTON JAMES
Private	McCANN PATK.
Private	MILTON JNS.
Private	MINNICK MATTW.
Private	MITCHELL THOS.
Private	NAIREY MICHL.
Private	O'BEIRNE LUKE
Private	O'BRIEN THOS. Dead
Private	O'HARA JNS.
Private	POCOCK RICHD.
Private	ROGERS RICHD.
Private	SCOTT RICHD.
Private	SHEPPARD ISSAC
Private	SHIPCOTT WM.
Private	THOMPSON JNS.
Private	TULET THOS.

Captain Charles Tenlon's Company

Captain	TENLON CHAS.
Lieutenant	MOORE SAML.
Serjeant	PLUGNOTT WM.
Serjeant	SHEPPARD ISSAC Dead
Corporal	DARCH SAML.
Corporal	MORRIS JOHN Littledale Sale Nov. 1910 1-9-0
Corporal	SWEENEY BRIEN
Corporal	WALKER JAMES
Drummer	FINCH HENRY
Drummer	HOPKINS WM.
Corporal	RAWKINS HENRY
Drummer	THATCHER ISSAC
Private	ABERCROMBY HUGH
Private	AINSBOROUGH MATTW
Private	BARNES MARK
Private	BECJWITH JAMES Dead
Private	BELL RICHD. Discharged Walters sale 1913
Private	BLACKMORE WM. Dead
Private	BOLAND JAMES
Private	BRADBURN JAMES
Private	BRITTAIN EDWD.
Private	BUSH BENJN.
Private	CAVANAGH WM.
Private	DAVIS MICHL.
Private	DEVERS JAMES
Private	DOOLING ANDW.
Private	DUMMETT JNS.
Private	FISHER THOS.
Private	GALVIN JOHN
Private	GARRETT ROBT. Dead
Private	GLEESON DENNIS
Private	GLYNN JOHN
Private	GALLAGHER MICHL.

Private	HANRAHAN JAMES
Private	HIGGS DANL.
Private	HISCOX BENJN. Discharged
Private	HUGHES PETER
Private	HUMPHRIES JACOB Discharged
Private	INCLEDON WM.
Private	JEFFERIES WM.
Private	KELLY WM.
Private	LEE WM.
Private	LUDDEN TIMY.
Private	LYE RICHD.
Private	LYNCH JOSH
Private	MAUNDER THOS.
Private	McCANN CHAS.
Private	OLD WM. Discharged Day Sale April 1910
Private	PEGNUM EDWD. Discharged
Private	POWER JAMES
Private	QUINN JNS
Private	QUINN PATK.
Private	ROGERS WM.
Private	RYAN PHILIP
Private	SARAH WM.
Private	SPRIGGS WM.
Private	TOZER THOS
Private	UNDERHILL RICHD.
Private	WATKINS THOS.
Private	WEBBER THOS
Private	WHITESIDE JNS
Private	WITHYMAN THOS.

* * *

2nd BATTALION OF THE 30th REGIMENT OF FOOT

Lt.Colonel	HAMILTON ALEXR. Wounded seriously
Major	BAILEY W. Wounded seriously
Major	VIGOREUX E.A. Wounded seriously
Major	CHAMBERS F.W. Killed 18th June
Adjutant	ANDREWS M.
Qr.Master	WILLIAMSON JNS. Payne Collection 1911
Surgeon	ELKINGTON J.G.
Ass.Surgeon	EVANS JOHN
Ass.Surgeon	CLARKE PATK.
Pay.Master	WRAY H.B.

Captain Arthur Gore's Company

Captain	GOORE ARTHUR Wounded slightly
Captain	MACHELL RICHD.
Lieutenant	BAILLIE ANDW.
Lieutenant	LOCKWOOD P. Wounded severely
Lieutenant	BEERE HENRY Killed 18th June
S.Major	WOODS JAMES
Q.M.S.	HARRISON JOSH Discharged Glendinings sale Dec.1912
P.M.S.	CUTHBERT THOS.
Ar.Sjt.	ARTIS NATHL.
Dr.Major	POOLE THOS.
Serjeant	BARNWELL CHRIS. Wounded since dead
Serjeant	CAHILL JNS.
Serjeant	WARD WM.
Corporal	BAKER JNS.
Corporal	McDONALD HUGH
Drummer	BRIES JNS.
Private	ANGER JNS
Private	BIGGS PHILIP Discharged
Private	BRADY LAWRE Wounded
Private	BISHOP WM. Wounded
Private	BRENAN DANL. Wounded
Private	BRENNAN EDWD.
Private	BRANSOM RICHD.
Private	BURNLEY JNS
Private	BYRNE ANDRW.
Private	CHURCH SAML.
Private	CARPENTER MATTW.
Private	COYNE MARTIN
Private	DING ROBT. Wounded
Private	ELLINGS ROBT.
Private	FLINN DANL. Wounded
Private	FANNING JAMES
Private	FORBES ROBT. Wounded
Private	GALLEY JNS Glendinings sale 17 June 1908
Private	GALLANT ROBT.
Private	GRILISK PATK.
Private	HARRIS JAMES Discharged
Private	HAMILTON ALEXR.
Private	HARKER THOS. Wounded
Private	HUGHES WM. Killed 18th June
Private	JONES JAMES
Private	JONES THOS. Wounded since dead
Private	KINGSFORD CHAS.
Private	LAHEY MICHL. Wounded
Private	LYNCH PHILIP
Private	LAREY JNS

Private	MITCHELL PAUL
Private	McCARRION PETER Wounded
Private	McDONALD GEO.
Private	MAHON JAMES
Private	NOBLES JAMES
Private	NICE JNS
Private	OVENDEN WM. Wounded
Private	OVERTON THOS
Private	POWELL WM.
Private	ROCK JAMES Wounded
Private	ROWAN CHAS.
Private	RAWSON WM.
Private	SMITH HENRY
Private	SANXTER JNS Wounded
Private	TYERS SAML. Killed 18th June
Private	VIZER HUMPH. Wounded
Private	VIZER GARRETT Killed 18th June
Private	WHEATHERS JOSH.
Private	WOODS THOS.
Private	WALKER WM. Wounded
Private	WEBB RICHD. Wounded
Private	WINDUS JNS.
Private	WILSON THOS.
Private	WATERS JAMES Wounded
Private	WALTON JNS. Wounded
Private	STRAPPS WM.

Captain D. Sinclair's Company

Lieutenant	ELLIOTT R.C. H.Gascoigne's collection 1908 Payne 1911 Wounded slightly
Lieutenant	HUGHES R. Wounded slightly
Lieutenant	ROGERS R.N.
Serjeant	BRYAN NICHS
Serjeant	BALL SAML.
Serjeant	CART JON Wounded
Serjeant	SHERIDAN GEO.
Corporal	HANDLEY JNS.
Corporal	BROWN RICHD. Wounded, since died
Drummer	ASQUITH JAMES Cheylesmore collection 1908
Private	BELLAMY RICHD Wounded
Private	BANKER JAMES Wounded
Private	BAXTER JNS Wounded
Private	BARNES JOSH.
Private	BARNES THOS.
Private	BERRY CHRISPIN
Private	BURKE EDWD.
Private	CRANSWAY WM. Wounded, since died
Private	CLARKE RICHD.
Private	CONNER TIMY.
Private	CHAPMAN SAML.
Private	DWYER PHIP.
Private	DOWLING EDWD.
Private	DINGWELL JAMES Wounded
Private	DAVENPORTE SAML.
Private	GREEN RICHD. Wounded
Private	GOODHALL GEO.
Private	GREEN THOS. Discharged
Private	GRESSWALL JNS. Dead
Private	HOLLOWAY EDWD. Wounded
Private	HANLEY WM.
Private	HOPWOOD DAVID
Private	HAMMOND WM.
Private	JORDAN JOSH Wounded since dead
Private	ISSOTT WM.
Private	JENNINGS JOSH
Private	JONES THOS.
Private	LAMBERT WM. Wounded
Private	MAKEPEACE WM. Wounded
Private	MORGAN WM.
Private	McGUINNESS JNS
Private	MISKILL THOS Wounded
Private	MORRISEY RICHD Wounded
Private	MELBOURN JNS Killed 18th June
Private	McGINNIS HENRY
Private	NEIL JAMES
Private	NOWELL JNS.
Private	OAKMAN WM. Discharged
Private	PARKER JNS Killed in Action
Private	PATRICK JAMES Wounded
Private	PRYER WM. Wounded, since dead
Private	PYE ABRM.
Private	PITTS MATTW Discharged
Private	ROTHERS RICHD
Private	REED ADAM
Private	RYAN ROGER
Private	SENTANCE JNS.
Private	SMITH NATHL. Wounded
Private	SPARROW ROBT Wounded
Private	SYKES THOS.
Private	TAYLOR JAMES
Private	THOMPSON WM. Wounded
Private	TIDWELL JNS.
Private	WILSON STEPHN.
Private	WOOD JNS. Wounded

Captain Henry Cramer's Company

Captain	McNABB ALEXR. Killed 18th June
Lieutenant	TINCOMBE T.K.
Lieutenant	MONEYPENNY THOS. Wounded slightly
Ensign	NEVILLE P.P. Galway Foley Collection 1910
Serjeant	COSTELLO EDWD.
Serjeant	DITHERIDGE BENJN. Wounded
Serjeant	JACKSON JOSH Glendinings sale Oct. 1909
Corporal	HAMMOND ROBT.
Corporal	MURPHY PATK Wounded
Corporal	TAYLOR THOS.
Drummer	CORNALL JAMES
Drummer	JOHNSTON WM.
Private	ALLEN JAMES
Private	ADDY JNS Dead
Private	ASKEW THOS Wounded
Private	BRADLEY THOS.
Private	BRANDROUGH WM.
Private	BAILEY SAML.
Private	BROWN JOSH Wounded
Private	CAMPBELL JNS
Private	CLEMENTS BENJN.
Private	CARROLL PATK.
Private	DOUGHERTY OWEN
Private	DREWARY ROBT Wounded
Private	FULBECK THOS.
Private	FULBECK ROBT
Private	FAIRCLOTH ROBT.
Private	FISHER JOSH
Private	FEEHAN WM.
Private	GIRLING WM.
Private	GREY JOSH
Private	GREY THOS.
Private	GIBSON THOS.
Private	HEPWORTH JNS Wounded
Private	HILL JAMES Needes collection 1908
Private	HUSSEY PATK.
Private	JENKINS OWEN
Private	JACKSON THOS.
Private	KING JNS.
Private	KEY JOSH
Private	LOCKWOOD MATTW.
Private	LAUGHLIN THAD.
Private	LYNHAM JNS. Wounded
Private	LESLIE JNS Killed 18th June
Private	LONSDALE JNS.
Private	MULHOLLAND PATK.
Private	McPARTLAND PATK.
Private	NOWLAN CHRIS.
Private	NORMAN WM.
Private	NOWELL HENRY Wounded
Private	PLUMMER WM. Discharged
Private	ROSSITER THOS.
Private	ROPER MICHL.
Private	SCHOFIELD JAMES
Private	SCOTNEY HENRY
Private	THOMPSON JNS
Private	TAYLOR BENJN.
Private	TOWEY JNS Wounded
Private	TAYLOR WM Wounded
Private	WELTON WM.
Private	WHITEHEAD ELIJ. Wounded
Private	WARDLE JNS.

Captain & Bt.Major Ryan's Company

Captain	RYAN M.
Lieutenant	DANIELL R. Wounded slightly
Lieutenant	LATOUCHE D.
Ensign	BULLEN JAMES Killed 18th June
Serjeant	CARROLL JNS Wounded
Serjeant	DAVIS FRANS.
Corporal	BRADSHAW THOS. Walters sale 1913
Corporal	MORAN DENIS Wounded
Corporal	O'NEIL TERENCE
Drummer	GANNON JNS.
Private	ALLEN RICHD.
Private	BOSTON JNS Wounded
Private	BINNS CHAS Wounded
Private	BLOWES JAMES
Private	COULSTON JNS. Wounded
Private	CLEMMENTS EDWD Wounded
Private	CLANCEY JNS
Private	CONNELL WM.
Private	DYER MOSE
Private	DRAGE SAML.
Private	EDWARDS GEO Wounded
Private	FOLEY DANL. Dead
Private	FLINN MICHL.
Private	FREEMAN THOS Wounded
Private	GOODWIN WM.
Private	GILSHMAN PHILIP
Private	HILTON JNS
Private	HOLLIS AMOS
Private	HANTY JNS Wounded

Private	HALL JAMES
Private	JENKINSON JNS
Private	KILLERBY EPHRM.
Private	LAWLER MICHL Wounded
Private	McGRATH MICHL Wounded
Private	MUXLOW PETER Wounded
Private	MOULDER THOS.
Private	MORRELL EDWD
Private	MANNING JNS.
Private	McGLINN FRANS Killed 16th June
Private	MORRIS EDWD
Private	MANCHETT ROBT Discharged
Private	McGINNIS JNS
Private	O'BRIEN JNS Killed 16th June
Private	POWERS JAMES
Private	PAGE WM.
Private	PICKING WM.
Private	QUIGLEY DENIS
Private	RICE BENJN.
Private	RAWDING ROBT. Wounded
Private	RICHMOND JNS Wounded
Private	SMITH JOSH Wounded Littledale sale Nov. 1910
Private	SENIOR JNS. Wounded
Private	SHARP WM.
Private	SIMMS JOSH Wounded
Private	TAYLOR WM.
Private	TUITE JNS Wounded
Private	TOOLE WM
Private	UNCLE WM.
Private	WILKINSON JNS
Private	WEBB GEO Killed 18th June
Private	WINTON JNS.

Captain & Bt.Major Howard's Company

Captain	HOWARD ROBT Spinks List Dec 1908
Lieutenant	GOURAN JNS
Lieutenant	ROE 2nd JNS Wounded Slightly
Lieutenant	DRAKE EDWD.
Serjeant	O'NEIL MICHL.
Serjeant	KILLMARTIN CHAS Wounded since dead
Serjeant	WILKINSON JNS Killed 18th June
Corporal	COOKE CHAS Wounded
Corporal	GANLEY RICHD.
Corporal	GADBOROUGH JNS Killed 18th June
Corporal	McGUIRE THOS
Corporal	TAVILLE JOSH Wounded
Corporal	CARTER ROBT
Private	ATKINSON JOSH
Private	BRITTAIN SAML.
Private	BARNES THOS Wounded
Private	BURNS MICHL.
Private	BOWKER JNS.
Private	BOULTON EDWD Day Sale April 1910
Private	CAMPION THOS.
Private	CLINTON ARTH.
Private	CURNEAN MATTW.
Private	DOWLING THOS.
Private	DAWES WM. Wounded
Private	DEVOY JNS.
Private	ELMES JNS.
Private	FOGARTY JNS Dead
Private	HALLIDAY WM.
Private	HOLLAS SAMPSON
Private	HARTLEY JAMES Wounded
Private	HARVEY RICHD.
Private	HOLMES WM.
Private	HASLAM JAMES
Private	IRWIN WM.
Private	JUDSON JNS
Private	KIRBY BENJN.
Private	LOYD JONN.
Private	LAMB JAMES Wounded
Private	LEECH WM. Wounded
Private	MORAN PATK
Private	MILLS JAMES
Private	McCONE WM.
Private	NEARY JAMES
Private	OLOPHANT NICHLS.
Private	PLUCK JAMES
Private	PRINTY JAMES
Private	PEDLEY WM.
Private	PARKER THOS.
Private	RICE JAMES Wounded
Private	READING THOS. Wounded
Private	SAVAGE HUGH
Private	SELBY THOS.
Private	SIMONDS WM. Col.Gascoignes collection March 1909
Private	SIMMONDS ROBT.
Private	STUBBS JNS. Wounded
Private	SMITH JNS
Private	SMITH GEO Killed 17th June

Private	STEADMANS JNS.
Private	WHITE WM.
Private	CAMPBELL JAMES Killed 18th June

Captain James Skerrow's Company

Captain	FINUGANE J.
Lieutenant	TREEAR A.W.
Lieutenant	ROE 1st Jns.
Serjeant	CLYNE BERNARD
Serjeant	McCANN GEO.
Serjeant	WATKINS WM.
Serjeant	HILL WM.
Corporal	HILL JNS.
Corporal	DOYLE JAMES
Corporal	GEARING JAMES
Corporal	SMITH DAVID
Drummer	STEPHENS GEO.
Private	ALLUM THOS.
Private	ASHER DANL.
Private	APPLEYARD THOS. Wounded
Private	BENNETT JNS.
Private	BROWN LUKE Sotheby's Sale 19 June 1908
Private	BANKS EDWD.
Private	BARLEY EDWD Wounded
Private	BURGOYNE WM.
Private	BROGAN DENIS Wounded
Private	CANT RICHD.
Private	COLEMAN JACOB
Private	CONORAN THOS Wounded
Private	COYNE JNS.
Private	DAILEY PATK Wounded
Private	DAVIS JAMES Wounded
Private	DAWSON JOSH.
Private	DRIVER JNS. Wounded
Private	ENGLAND WM.
Private	GALLAGHER MICHL
Private	GARRETY JNS.
Private	HOLMES THOS.
Private	HAWES JNS.
Private	HALL HENRY
Private	HUNT STEPN Wounded
Private	JACKSON GEO.
Private	KEEGAN DANL. Wounded
Private	KELLY MICHL Wounded
Private	McQUON THOS Wounded
Private	McCABE JAMES Wounded
Private	McDONALD ALEXR.
Private	NASH THOS
Private	PAWLING JNS
Private	PATCKELL LUKE Wounded
Private	RUST SAML.
Private	REYNOLDS THOS.
Private	RIPTON EDWD Wounded
Private	RYAN WM. Wounded
Private	RYAN THOS.
Private	SHEARD JAMES
Private	SECRETT JOSH Wounded
Private	SELL JOSH
Private	SWAILS BENJN. Wounded
Private	WIRE PATK.
Private	WHITTAKER THOS.
Private	WALSH TIMY. Wounded
Private	WARDER WM. Wounded
Private	WARDE RICHD. Wounded
Private	MARLOW JOSH
Private	ROHAN DANL.
Private	JUDE JNS
Private	FOGARTY PATK.

Captain John Tongue's Company

Lieutenant	NICHOLSON B.W. Whitaker collection 1908
Lieutenant	HOLLORAN T.
Ensign	JAMES JNS Killed 18th June
Serjeant	BRYAN WM.
Serjeant	HARMAN ABRAM.
Serjeant	NICHOLSON ARMSTRONG
Serjeant	SWANN WM.
Corporal	ADDY JNS.
Corporal	KENDRICK GEO.
Corporal	LUMSDEN JNS.
Corporal	ROOKE JNS
Corporal	WILSON JNS Discharged
Drummer	WEAFER WM.
Private	BOURKE PETER
Private	BODYMORE MARSHALL Wounded
Private	CLARKE MICHL. Wounded
Private	CULLEN DAVID Wounded
Private	CONORAN PATK.
Private	CURTIS FRANS.
Private	CUNNINGHAM STEPHN.
Private	DOYNE WM.
Private	DENT JNS
Private	DING SAML.
Private	DAWES ROBT Wounded
Private	FURLONG WALTER

Private	FIELDSTONE BENJN Wounded
Private	GARRETY MICHL
Private	GILLEN PATK.
Private	GLEESON PATK
Private	GUMLEY JAMES Wounded
Private	HOTHERSALL THOS
Private	HARRIS DANL.
Private	HIRCHLIFF GEO.
Private	JERVIS WM.
Private	KERSHAW WM.
Private	LANGHAM THOS.
Private	LUMSDEN NICHLS. Wounded since Dead
Private	LOUGHMAN DENIS
Private	LANGHAM JOSH
Private	LEDDY THOS
Private	MIHAN ANDREW
Private	McDONALD WALTER
Private	MORAN SIMON Wounded
Private	MORAN WM
Private	MAUDE JNS
Private	McGUIRE GEO
Private	McGILLIGAN PATK.
Private	MANLEY THOS.
Private	PICK JAMES Wounded since dead
Private	PALMER ROBT Wounded since dead
Private	PRENDERVILL JAMES
Private	RICHARDSON JNS
Private	RONAN JAMES
Private	STANNETT JEREH.
Private	STORA CHAS Wounded
Private	SILKSTONE JOSH
Private	SIMPSON ELIAS Wounded
Private	SMITH FRANS. Killed 18 June
Private	SMITH GEO
Private	SPRINGALL JAMES
Private	SHERIDAN NICHS. Discharged
Private	TINSLEY WM. Wounded
Private	TINGHEY THOS
Private	WEAVER THOS
Private	WEETE JACOB
Private	BREHAN PATK. Wounded

Captain Robert Douglas's Company

Lieutenant	HEAVISIDE R. Payne Collection 1911
Lieutenant	HARRISON RICHD. Wounded
Lieutenant	WARREN W.O. Wounded dangerously
Serjeant	CONNELL CHAS
Serjeant	FORD WM.
Serjeant	KEATING THOS
Serjeant	SCOTTON JOSH Wounded
Serjeant	SUTTLE JNS Killed 16th June
Corporal	ANDREWS JOSH Wounded
Corporal	DOBBS THOS Wounded
Corporal	McGRATH THOS
Drummer	BRDSHAW WM.
Drummer	GAMMON LAWCE.
Private	BALL ROBT Wounded
Private	BECKETT JAMES Wounded
Private	BONSER JNS Wounded
Private	BURROWS GEO.
Private	BRYAN WM. Killed 16th June
Private	BAILEY THOS Wounded
Private	CULLEN JNS
Private	CONNELLY JAMES Wounded
Private	DANFORD HENRY
Private	DUNN JAMES
Private	DOWNEY PETER
Private	DOOGAN NICHS.
Private	DAVERY JNS Wounded
Private	FISHER BENJN.
Private	FOSTER THOS Wounded
Private	HANNON PATK. Wounded
Private	HOBBS THOS
Private	HALLIDAY EDWD Wounded
Private	HOGAN DANIEL
Private	HEAVEY BERND. Wounded
Private	HOLLAND BENJN.
Private	HARRISON JNS Wounded
Private	JOHNSTONE THOS Wounded
Private	KELLY MICHL.
Private	LOWE THOS
Private	LILLY JNS
Private	LYNCH HENRY Killed 18th June
Private	LOWE WM.
Private	MILLER HENRY Killed 18th June
Private	McGRATH PATK.
Private	MAYZE THOS
Private	MITCHELL JNS Wounded
Private	McLAUGHLIN OWEN Wounded
Private	MULDOON NEIL Wounded
Private	McCARTHY DANL.
Private	MARA JAMES Wounded
Private	McANDREWS JNS Wounded
Private	PACKER THOS
Private	RAGSDALE JOSH Killed 16th June

Private	ROBINSON PATK Wounded
Private	SMITH JNS
Private	SHANALAN JNS Wounded
Private	SHARP JNS Wounded
Private	SHEARMAN SAML Wounded
Private	SPENCER RICHD
Private	SKINNER JAMES Wounded
Private	TAYLOR JNS
Private	TRAYNOR EDWD Wounded
Private	THORNTON JNS
Private	TILLOTSON JNS Wounded
Private	WOODHAM ELA.
Private	WRIGHT EDWD Wounded
Private	WARD FRANS.

Captain John Powell's Company

Lieutenant	RUMLEY JNS Wounded severely
Lieutenant	PRATT JNS Wounded severely
Ensign	MACREADY EDWD
Serjeant	FROHOCK WM Wounded
Serjeant	PARKS JNS
Serjeant	BURROWS ISSAC
Serjeant	LANE EDWD
Corporal	DANIELLS RICHD.
Corporal	HOWARD ROBT.
Corporal	LUMSDEN SAML. Wounded Gray collection 1908
Drummer	ELLIOTT THOS Killed 18th June
Drummer	TURGOOSE ROBT.
Private	ASHBY JNS. Killed 18th June
Private	ANDERSON WM Wounded
Private	ABBOTT IS. Wounded
Private	BEMFORD HENRY Galway Foley collection 1910
Private	BONES JOSH Wounded
Private	BURKE ALEXR Wounded
Private	BEAUMONT THOS
Private	BARNACLE SAML. Wounded
Private	CLARKE THOS Wounded
Private	CAHILL DANIEL Wounded
Private	COLLEY BENJN. Wounded since dead
Private	CONNONGTON PATK. Wounded
Private	CARROLL LAWRCE. Wounded
Private	VOATES WM.
Private	DAY HENRY
Private	DUCKWORTH HENRY
Private	ELLIS WM.
Private	ELSEY WM.
Private	ELSOM ROBT
Private	ELWORTH JNS
Private	FOSTER JNS.
Private	GLEESON MICHL.
Private	GALLAGHER JAMES
Private	GAZEY THOS
Private	HENSON THOS.
Private	HORNBUCKER THOS.
Private	KENNEDY MICHL.
Private	KEYS RICHD Wounded,since dead
Private	LYNCH MICHL
Private	LACEY THOS
Private	LINNINGTON DARBY
Private	LEDGWAY THOS
Private	McCUNSTON EDWD.
Private	McLAIN JNS Wounded
Private	McDONALD MICHL.
Private	MOORE WM.
Private	MORTON PATK Killed 18 June
Private	MORRELL JNS
Private	MARSHALL WM Wounded
Private	NORFOLK CHAS Killed 18 June
Private	ORTON WM
Private	PRATT WM.
Private	REARDEN JNS
Private	SHEA JAS.
Private	SMITH RICHD.
Private	STONNY JNS Wounded
Private	SNODEN RICHD.
Private	SPARKES THOS
Private	SIDDONS BENJN.
Private	TOWEY THOS
Private	TAYLOR JOSH
Private	TRACEY THOS
Private	THORNTON PATK
Private	UPTON THOS
Private	WOODS EDWD
Private	WRIGHTON JAMES
Private	WEST JAS
Private	WORDEN RICHD.
Private	RAWSON EDWD.

* * *

32nd REGIMENT OF FOOT

Major	HICKS JNS.
Major	CLAVERT FELIX
Adjutant	DAVIES DAVID
Qr.Master	STEPHENS WM.

Suregon	BUCHANAN WM.
Ass.Surgeon	LAWDER RYND.
Ass.Surgeon	McCLINTOCK HUGH
Pay Master	HART THOS.

Captain H.W. Brook's Company

Captain	BROOKES H.W. H. Gaskell's collection 1908
Lieutenant	FITZGERALD JAMES
Ensign	BERTWISTLE JNS.
S. Major	PEPPERALL WM.
S. Major	OKE GEO.
Q.M.S.	MEDIMBER JNS
P.M.S.	BARTON JNS.
Sch.Master	BUKLEY GEO.
Ar.Serjeant	GLANVILLE WM.
Dr. Major	POLLARD SAML.
Serjeant	CLARKE JISH.
Serjeant	LESLIE JNS.
Corporal	DORE JAMES
Corporal	GRAHAM ROBT.
Corporal	RAMSAY WM. Killed in Action
Corporal	SUTTON WM. Littledale sale Nov. 1910
Corporal	WILLIAMS WM. Killed in Action
Private	ALLISON JNS.
Private	ASTIER JNS.
Private	BOTTOMLEY JOSH Whitaker collection 1908
Private	BRITTON JOSH.
Private	BROWNE JAMES
Private	BURKE JNS
Private	BURNS JAMES
Private	CARNES WM.
Private	COCKRAN JAMES
Private	CROZIER ROBT.
Private	DOHERTY JNS.
Private	DONAHUE EDWD.
Private	DONNELLY JAMES
Private	DUMPHY MICHL. Sotheby's Sale April 1911
Private	EASTMAN WM.
Private	FLEMMING WM.
Private	GILBERT THOS. Killed in Action
Private	GRIER PATK.
Private	GRIGG JOS.
Private	HAWES RICHD
Private	HARGROVES WM.
Private	HAWKES WM.
Private	HINDES JAMES
Private	HOLMES GEO.
Private	HUGHES JOS.
Private	HUNTLEY DAVID
Private	JAMES JAMES
Private	KINNON JOHN
Private	KIRBY JONN.
Private	KING ELIJ.
Private	LACEY WM.
Private	LAWLER DANL. Shown to us 8-4-65
Private	LITTLE JNS
Private	LOCKLEY JAMES
Private	McLELLAND ROBT.
Private	McKAY WM.
Private	MANLEY JNS.
Private	MORTIMER ALEDR.
Private	MURRAY JAMES Killed in Action
Private	MURRAY WM. Killed in Action
Private	NEILLY JNS.
Private	OLIVER JAMES
Private	PORTER HENRY
Private	PRITTING IS.
Private	PULLEN THOS.
Private	RAWLINGS WM.
Private	REDMOND HUGH
Private	REED JOSH
Private	REED SAML
Private	REYNOLDS JNS.
Private	RODGERS WM.
Private	SULLIVAN PATK
Private	THOMAS JOSH.
Private	TREGELGUS JNS
Private	WEBBER GEO
Private	WESTWOOD THOS.
Private	YOUNG JNS

Captain Charles Hawe's Company

Captain	HAWES CHAS.
Lieutenant	LUCAS JASP.
Ensign	BROWNE GEO.
Serjeant	BROAD SAML Killed in Action
Serjeant	BROWNE WM.
Serjeant	SEERY PATK.
Serjeant	SHEPPARD JNS
Corporal	CARPENTER JS.
Corporal	PRITCHARD RICHD.
Drummer	LOGDEN THOS
Private	ATKINS CAL.

Private	BARBER DREW
Private	BARRFIELD JNS
Private	BUTLER THOS.
Private	CAHILL JNS
Private	CARPENTER BENJN.
Private	COTTLE STEP.
Private	CROMPTON GEO.
Private	DOWNEY JAMES
Private	DUMHEATH JAMES
Private	GORDON THOS.
Private	GRIMES JNS
Private	HALL JNS.
Private	HOWES TIM.
Private	JAMES THOS Glendinings sale 17 June 1908
Private	JONAS JNS.
Private	KERR HENRY
Private	LAMSDEN WM.
Private	LEYTON WM.
Private	LOGAN JNS
Private	McAIRN W.
Private	McGURN MICHL. Killed in Action
Private	McKENRY PATK.
Private	McLAUGHLIN DAVID
Private	MAHON JAMES
Private	McQUARD JAMES
Private	MAGWOOD JNS
Private	MILLER THOS
Private	MILTON JAMES
Private	MOULTON THOS
Private	PEARVY THOS
Private	PHILLIPS JNS
Private	POWERS JNS
Private	PRUDOM JOS Glendinings sale 21st July 1909
Private	REA JAMES
Private	REILLY JOHN
Private	RODGERS JNS Baldwin's Feb. 1910
Private	ROONEY JNS
Private	SANDERSON GEO.
Private	SIMS GEO.
Private	SMITH JAMES
Private	SMITH THOS
Private	STANLEY RALPH
Private	THOMAS ROBT.
Private	TOMBINON FREDK.
Private	VEREKER DEN.
Private	WHITE BENJN.
Private	WILLIAMS JNS.
Private	WILLIS WM.
Private	YOUNG JOS.

Captain Stopford Cane's Company

Lieutenant	MEIGHAN M.W.
Lieutenant	QUILL HENRY
Ensign	DALLAS CHAS Payne collection 1911
Serjeant	BARNETT THOS
Serjeant	HILLS JAMES
Serjeant	JARRETT MAR.
Serjeant	LARKEN JNS
Serjeant	PIMLETT JNS
Corporal	BRYAN CHAS Gray collection 1908
Corporal	HANLAN JAMES
Corporal	MILLER HUGH
Corporal	SHANKLIN ANDW.
Drummer	DREW NICHS.
Drummer	DOWLING STEP.
Private	BAISELY WM.
Private	BARNETT TOBT.
Private	BINK HENRY
Private	BOTTEMLEY JOSH.
Private	BRYAN JNS
Private	BARNES JAMES
Private	COOPER STEP.
Private	CARNELL THOS
Private	CORCORAN JNS. Killed in Action
Private	DALTON RICHD.
Private	EAGAN GILBERT
Private	FITXSIMMONDS DANL.
Private	FORSTER THOS.
Private	GREENWOOD WM Killed in Action
Private	HALL CHAS Royal Hospital Kilinainham Feb. 1909
Private	HAMILTON FRANS.
Private	HANDS THOS
Private	HOLLANT JNS
Private	HUSTON BOYLE
Private	INGHAM JNS
Private	JONES THOS
Private	KENNEDY JNS
Private	LAMB THOS
Private	LANCASTER JNS
Private	LENNOX JAMES
Private	MASON GEO.
Private	MIGHAN JNS.
Private	MORRIS JNS
Private	MULLINS THOS.

Private	PHILIPS JNS
Private	PHILIPS THOS.
Private	PEWE JOHN
Private	PEARCE BENJN.
Private	REED WM.
Private	REYNOLDS JAMES
Private	RIDDLE JOS
Private	ROBERTS CHAS
Private	RODGERS FREDK.
Private	SCOTT WM.
Private	SHANNON SAML.
Private	SMITH JNS.
Private	SOLOMON ROBT.
Private	SWAIN JAMES
Private	THOMAS JNS
Private	THORNTON PATK.
Private	UPTON THOS.
Private	VAGUE ROBT.
Private	VALE THOS.
Private	WILLIAMS EDWD
Private	WILLIAMSON CHAS
Private	WORRALL THOS

Captain Robert Dillon's Company

Lieutenant	BOASE JOHN
Lieutenant	McCONCAY JAMES
Serjeant	COURTENAY THOS
Serjeant	GLYNN WM.
Serjeant	McGOWAN JOHN
Serjeant	NICHOLS JAMES
Corporal	BONNEY JNS.
Corporal	CANAKER JOHN
Corporal	HANDLEY ELIJ.
Corporal	WEBB RICHD
Corporal	WHITE JAMES
Drummer	CORNELIUS PETER
Private	ASTON JOHN
Private	BARRETT THOS.
Private	BARRY WM.
Private	BARTLE JAMES
Private	BARTLEY BENJN.
Private	BLACKWELL WM.
Private	BOWLES JOHN
Private	BRENNAN ANDREW
Private	BARNES PATK.
Private	CARSON SIMON Holloway sale Sotheby's May 1910
Private	CARTY OWEN
Private	COLRICK SAML.
Private	COLLIER RICHD.
Private	COSTELLO THOS.
Private	DONOVAN JEREH.
Private	DOVEY JOHN
Private	FARRELL FRANS.
Private	FLEMING JOHN
Private	GOLDING HENRY
Private	GREENSLADE WM.
Private	GREY RICHD.
Private	GWYNNE WM.
Private	HOLBERT WM.
Private	HOWELL ROBT.
Private	KIMBOE NATHL.
Private	LAWTON ROBT.
Private	LEONARD PATK.
Private	McCANOLL WM.
Private	MADDOX JOHN
Private	MILLER WM.
Private	MOORE JAMES
Private	MOORE ROBT.
Private	MORRIS CHAS.
Private	NOONAN TIMY.
Private	PAINTER SOL.
Private	PALMER WM.
Private	REEDMAN THOS
Private	REILLY MILES
Private	RORKE MICHL.
Private	ROWLEY JAMES
Private	SHERIDAN JOHN
Private	SKELLING WM.
Private	SHORT SAML.
Private	SMITH DANL.
Private	SMITH WM.
Private	SULLIVAN JAKE
Private	SUTTON JOSH.
Private	THOMAS 2nd GEO.
Private	THOMAS WM.
Private	TREWHELD HENRY
Private	TROTTER JOHN
Private	WALES THOS
Private	WEBB JNS.

Captain Charles Wallett's Company

Captain	WALLETT CHAS.
Lieutenant	LAWRENCE S.H. Day Sale April 1910
Ensign	STEWART ALEXR.
Serjeant	COLWELL WM.
Serjeant	DUFFEY JAMES
Serjeant	O'BRIEN PATK.
Corporal	COOPER WM.

Corporal	DUNBAR JOHN
Corporal	HENRY WM.
Corporal	WILLIAMS JOHN
Drummer	CULLEN ANDW.
Drummer	MAHON JAMES
Drummer	RODGERS JOHN Cheylesmore 1908
Private	BOWELL ROBT.
Private	BOYLE NEAL
Private	BRYAN DANL.
Private	CADELL JOS.
Private	COOPER JOHN
Private	COVE JON
Private	CRAIG WM.
Private	DANCER JOS.
Private	DIXON RICHD.
Private	DONNELLY JOHN
Private	DOYLE JAMES
Private	DUMHEATH DANL.
Private	EASTMAN THOS.
Private	ELLISON JNS Galway Foley collection 1910
Private	FLATLEY JOHN
Private	GARNER JOHN
Private	GRENFIELD JOHN
Private	HART THOS
Private	HOFLAND THOS
Private	HOOK WM. Killed in action
Private	JEFFERIES JOHN
Private	LINEGAR JOHN
Private	LOONEY WM.
Private	McCARROLL JAMES
Private	McCARTHY DAVID
Private	MILTON JAMES
Private	MORROW WM.
Private	MULHOLLAND ARTH.
Private	NESBITT JNS.
Private	ODGERS JNS
Private	PASCOE ROBT.
Private	PEYTON JOHN
Private	PILKINGTON JOHN
Private	PONGUE GEO.
Private	ROGERSON ROBT.
Private	SANDERS THOS
Private	SINNETT MOSE
Private	SKILLING GEO.
Private	SLADE JOHN
Private	SMITH BENJN.
Private	TAYLOR PETER
Private	TILEY JON.
Private	VUMDER BENJ.
Private	WARD DANL.
Private	WILKINSON JOHN
Private	WINTERS PATK
Boy	HEALE JACOB

Captain Henry Ross Lewin's Company

Captain	LEWIN H. ROSS
Lieutenant	BUTLER THEO.
Ensign	WM.
Serjeant	BINGHAM PETER
Serjeant	McCORMICK WM. Col.Murray's collection 1908
Serjeant	SPENCE JOHN
Serjeant	WARREN JOSH
Corporal	CLARKE JOSH.
Corporal	COLBECK JOHN
Corporal	HUNCHLIFFE THOS
Corporal	MOORE JAMES
Corporal	RAMSDEN JNS
Corporal	TURNER WM.
Drummer	REED JOHN
Private	BANFIELD WM.
Private	BANNISTER WM.
Private	BEAMISH JNS Col.Gascoigne's collection March 1909
Private	BRAY WM.
Private	BROWEN JOHN
Private	BRYAN EDWD
Private	CLUFF FRANS.
Private	CORNISH JOHN
Private	CRIPPS JOHN
Private	DAGG THOS
Private	DYER WM. SMALL
Private	EMSLEY BENJN. Payne collection 1911
Private	FOLEY TIM.
Private	FRANCIS CHAS.
Private	HANDCOCK WM.
Private	HANSON WM.
Private	HEAD WM.
Private	HOMES JAMES
Private	HUTCHINSON JAMES
Private	JOHNSTONE EDGAR
Private	KELLY DOM.
Private	LANSCOMBE WM.
Private	LUKES RICHD.
Private	McCARTHY HENRY
Private	McCREWER JAMES

Private	MACKLE CHAS
Private	McPHATRIDGE JOHN
Private	McMANUS EDWD
Private	MARLEY MILES Glendinings sale 1914 - Phillips Sale
Private	MARSHALL WM. Needes collection 1908
Private	MULLINS JAMES
Private	OATES JAMES
Private	PATRICK WM.
Private	PURSER IS.
Private	SADLER SAML.
Private	SAFEGUARD GEO.
Private	SALSBURY JOHN
Private	SANDERS WM.
Private	SANBROOK B.W.
Private	SLY THOS.
Private	SMITH LEWIS
Private	TONKS WM.
Private	WATLEY WM.
Private	WILLIAMS HUGH
Private	WOOLLEY JOHN
Private	LEDFORD WM.

Captain W.H. Toole's Company

Captain	TOOLE W.H. Gray collection 1908
Lieutenant	HORAN THOS.
Ensign	METCALFE MICHL.
Serjeant	HORFORD JNS.
Serjeant	MILLAR JNS.
Corporal	MURPHY PATK.
Corporal	BRETT PATK.
Corporal	ROCKELLY WM.
Drummer	BEATTY WM.
Private	BANNON DANL.
Private	BENNETT JNS.
Private	BINGHAM JNS
Private	BLIZZARD THOS
Private	BOYNTON GEO.
Private	BUNKWORTH ROBT.
Private	BROWNE JNS. Dead
Private	BROPHY JNS
Private	CADDEN MICHL.
Private	CLEAR PHIL.
Private	COBOURNE WM.
Private	COLLIER WM.
Private	CROWLEY WM.
Private	DELLAMORE THOS Killed in Action
Private	GODSON OLIV.
Private	GOULD IS.
Private	HARDING JNS.
Private	HOPE JNS
Private	HOSKINS THOS
Private	HOZIE PAUL
Private	HOOKWAY JNS
Private	HUGHES WM.
Private	JACKSON WM.
Private	JONES DANL.
Private	KIMBRE WM.
Private	LIDWELL JAMES
Private	McCANN TERENCE
Private	McHOOD EDWD.
Private	MITCHELL THOS.
Private	PALMER WM.
Private	PRITCHARD WM. Col.Murray's collection 1908
Private	PROBETT WM.
Private	PUGH WM.
Private	ROWDEN GEO.
Private	ROWEN STEP.
Private	RUDKIN HENRY
Private	SMITH VER.
Private	SLADE THOS
Private	SOMMERTON JNS
Private	STUART THOS.
Private	STRONG WM.
Private	SWEENEY JNS
Private	TOWNLEY GEO.
Private	UNDERWOOD BENJN.
Private	VINNARD JNS.
Private	WILKES GEO.
Private	WOODS PETER
Private	WHIMFREY WM.

Captain David Davie's Company

Captain	DAVIES DAVID
Lieutenant	BELCHER R.F.
Lieutenant	SMALL GEO.
Serjeant	FAGAN DAVID
Serjeant	SLATER JAMES Killed in Action
Serjeant	STEVENSON ROBT.
Serjeant	SWITZER CHRIS.
Serjeant	WEBSTER JNS. Discharged
Corporal	CROSKINS RICHD.
Corporal	PRIME JNS
Drummer	METCLAFE THOS
Private	ANNCAR WM.

Private	BEATTE THOS
Private	BENSON HENRY
Private	BOYD ROBT.
Private	CAIN JAMES Killed in Action
Private	CARSON GEO.
Private	CARR PETER
Private	CAVANAGH LAWRE.
Private	CLIFFORD ALEXR.
Private	CONHAM JNS
Private	COOKE JAMES
Private	DEVLIN HENRY
Private	FAGAN EDWD.
Private	GILDER MICHL.
Private	GORMLEY THOS Killed
Private	GRIMES SAML.
Private	HALLIGAN STEP.
Private	HAWE JAMES
Private	HENNESSY JNS.
Private	KENNEDY JAMES
Private	KNOWLES JAMES
Private	McCABE PETER
Private	McGOWEY THOS
Private	McHARRY JAMES
Private	McDOLE SMITH
Private	MARTIN ROBT.
Private	MILES MICHL.
Private	MILLS JOS.
Private	MITCHELL SILAS Killed in Action
Private	MONTGOMERY JAMES
Private	MOORE SAML.
Private	MULLAVEY MICHL.
Private	MURPHY MICHL.
Private	ONIONS WM.
Private	PLAMER ROGER
Private	PERKINS JOSH.
Private	PERRY JAMES
Private	PURNELL WM.
Private	SAVAGE RICHD.
Private	SOUTHALL JNS.
Private	STANBY THOS.
Private	STRIKE EDWD
Private	WALKER GEO.
Private	WEBBER WM.
Private	WILLIAMS JOSH.
Private	YAWLEY GEO.

Captain Hugh Harrison's Company

Captain	HARRISON HUGH
Lieutenant	BUTTERWORTH HENRY
Lieutenant	ROBINSON JMAES
Lieutenant	STEPHENS EDWD.
Serjeant	BATTERSBY JAMES
Serjeant	PRINGLE JNS.
Serjeant	WILSON CHAS.
Corporal	DAVEY WM. Killed in Action
Corporal	JENNETT JAMES
Corporal	REYNOLDS JNS.
Corporal	RICHARDSON GEO.
Drummer	MURRAY JAMES
Drummer	SPRY HENRY
Private	ANDREWS JOSH
Private	ARNOLD VAL.
Private	BEER WM.
Private	BRONKARD WM.
Private	BURNETT WM.
Private	BRYNE JAMES
Private	COLES DAVID
Private	COXON WM.
Private	DAVIES EDWD
Private	DAVIS JOHN
Private	DEVLIN JAMES
Private	DEVLIN JOHN Killed in action
Private	DOUGLAS GEO. Killed in action
Private	DUNNE LAWE.
Private	DUNNE WM.
Private	FREEMAN JAMES Officer's Mess D.C.L.I. 1909
Private	HANNON THOS
Private	HARFORD JNS.
Private	HEALEY THOS.
Private	HALLERON THOS.
Private	HOPKINS THOS. Whitaker Collection 1908
Private	HULSE JOSH.
Private	HUMPHERSON JOHN
Private	JOHN EVAN
Private	KNOX ANDW.
Private	LEE JOSH
Private	LAWTON THOS.
Private	McAFFEE JNS.
Private	McCARTHY JERH.
Private	McGUIRE JNS.
Private	MAYNE EMML.

Private	MATFIELD JOHN
Private	MITCHELL ROBT.
Private	MITCHELL THOS
Private	MORRIS MATTW.
Private	MURRAY MICHL.
Private	OLIVER JAMES
Private	OGDEN JAMES
Private	PARSONS RICHD.
Private	PEGLAR GEO.
Private	PERRY WM.
Private	PLANNER ANTHY.
Private	RICHARDS JNS.
Private	SHEA LUKE
Private	SHERRY WM.
Private	SMITH JAMES Killed in action
Private	SMITH JOHN
Private	SULLIVAN JAMES
Private	TOMLINSON JAMES
Private	TOOLE PATK.
Private	TRAVERS GEO.
Private	TREDWIN HENRY
Private	WHITHAM JAMES
Private	WRIGHT CHAS.

<u>Captain John Crowe's Company</u>

Captain	CROWE JNS.
Lieutenant	LEWIN THOS ROSS
Lieutenant	COLTHURST JAMES
Lieutenant	JAGOE JON.
Serjeant	ADWICKE JOHN
Serjeant	CLARKE FRANS.
Serjeant	DOBBLE WM.
Serjeant	VIRTUE JAMES
Corporal	JONES STEP.
Corporal	NOWLAND DENIS
Corporal	NOWLAND JAMES
Drummer	FISHER JOHN
Drummer	REED THOS
Private	AKERS JOSH.
Private	BARKER JAMES
Private	BARROW JOSH
Private	BATTYY JOHN
Private	BIBLE FRANS.
Private	BLAKE LEWIS
Private	BIRCH FRANS.
Private	BLUNN MOSES
Private	BROWNE JOS.
Private	CHALLIS THOS.
Private	COCK JAMES
Private	COLEMAN WM.
Private	DONLAN PATK. Discharged
Private	DOWNEY JOHN
Private	ECCLES THOS
Private	ELLIOTT GEO
Private	FAULKS GEO
Private	FRANCIS DAVID
Private	GARDNER THOS
Private	HAMILTON WM.
Private	HANDCOCK WM.
Private	HASLAM SAML.
Private	HEADY JOHN
Private	HERD GEO.
Private	HIGGS THOS
Private	HOLLAND JAMES
Private	HOY MICHL.
Private	IRELAND WM.
Private	JONES THOS.
Private	KIERNAN MICHL.
Private	KIRKWOOD WM.
Private	LANGLEY JOHN
Private	McDONALD TIMY.
Private	MARKS THE.
Private	McNAMARA JOHN
Private	MANIER SAML.
Private	MARTHARAN JOHN
Private	NOSELY THOS
Private	MORTIMORE JOSH.
Private	MURRAY JOHN
Private	PEARCE JAMES
Private	POXTON WM.
Private	RAWLINS WM. Killed in action
Private	ROECLIFFE JNS
Private	RUSDEN HENRY
Private	RUTHERFORD JOSH
Private	SERJEANT JNS.
Private	SHEPPARD NATL.
Private	SNEYD THOS.
Private	STANAWAY THOS.
Private	STANFIELD JAMES
Private	STUART JAMES
Private	TATLOCK MATTW.
Private	THORNTON WM.
Private	TRESCOTT GEO.
Private	WHARTON GEO.
Private	WOOD WM.

* * *

33rd REGIMENT OF FOOT

Lt. Col.	ELPHINSTONE W.K.
Major	PARKINSON EDWD. Wounded
Captain	MACINTYRE WM. Wounded
Captain	KNIGHT CHAS. Wounded
Captain	HARTY J.M. Wounded
Captain	GORE RALPH
Captain	LONGDON JOHN
Lieutenant	REID THOS Wounded
Lieutenant	BARRS GEO.
Lieutenant	TREVORS A.W.
Lieutenant	MURKLAND JAMES Wounded
Lieutenant	PATTISON J.M.
Lieutenant	WESTMORE RICHD. Wounded
Lieutenant	WHANNELL GEO.
Lieutenant	OGLE J.G. Wounded
Lieutenant	PAGAN T.A. Wounded
Lieutenant	CLABON EDWD.
Lieutenant	LYNAM JAMES
Lieutenant	ARCHIBALD JOHN
Lieutenant	FORLONG S. Wounded
Ensign	BAIN H. Whitaker collection 1908
Ensign	ALDERSON JNS. Wounded
Ensign	BAIN WM. Wounded
Ensign	HOWARD J.A. Wounded
Ensign	WATSON ANDREW
Ensign	SMITH CHAS. Oddy collc. Glendinings sale 1908
Ensign	HODSON WM.
Ensign	DRURY GEO. Wounded
Adjutant	THAIN WM. Wounded
Qr.Master	FAGACKERLY J.
Surgeon	LEAVER R.
Ass.Surgeon	FRY W.D.
Ass.Surgeon	FINLAYSON D.
Sjt.Major	COLBECK J. Wounded
Q.M.S.	GIBBONS GEO.
P.M.S.	PHILLIPS R.
Ar.Serjeant	SWAINSTONE EDWD.
Dr.Major	CRUTCHFIELD JNS. Wounded
Ar.Serjeant	EATON JAMES
Ar.Serjeant	GIBSON THOS Wounded
Ar.Serjeant	GREY JNS
Ar.Serjeant	ROBINSON B.
Ar.Serjeant	SNAWDEN J. Wounded
Ar.Serjeant	WOOD ANDW.
Serjeant	BAILEY DANL. Wounded
Serjeant	BEARDHALL MATTW. Died of wounds 31st July
Serjeant	BOLTON NATHL.
Serjeant	COLLINS JOS.
Serjeant	ENTWISTLE PETER
Serjeant	FERGUSON JNS Wounded
Serjeant	GIBSON JNS. Wounded
Serjeant	GOODWIN PETER
Serjeant	GRIEGSON JAMES Died of wounds 21st June
Serjeant	HAACKE CHAS
Serjeant	HANKISON THOS
Serjeant	HEARD ROBT Wounded
Serjeant	HINCHCLIFFE WM.
Serjeant	HANSTON ARTH. Died of wounds 21st June
Serjeant	INGRAM SAML.
Serjeant	LAUGHLIN ZACH.
Serjeant	LUPTON JOHN Wounded
Serjeant	PATRICK JOHN
Serjeant	ROBINSON JOSH
Serjeant	RUSHWORTH WM.
Corporal	AMBLER JOHN Wounded
Corporal	BLOXAM JOHN
Corporal	CHEETHAM JESSE
Corporal	CHRISTIE WM Wounded
Corporal	COCKING JAS Wounded
Corporal	DEARDING JNS Wounded
Corporal	DENT WM. Wounded
Corporal	DOZELL RICHD.
Corporal	DUNN JOS.
Corporal	ECCLESBY THOS Col.Murray's collection 1908
Corporal	GREENWOOD WM. Wounded
Corporal	HADLEY WM.
Corporal	HANDLEY JNS.
Corporal	HINCHCLIFFE JOS.
Corporal	HOLDSWORTH WM. Wounded
Corporal	HOLMES WM Wounded
Corporal	JEWITT THOS.
Corporal	LEE WM.
Corporal	LONSDALE HENRY
Corporal	MAIDEN GEO
Corporal	MANGISON FRANS Wounded
Corporal	MATTHEWS JNS
Corporal	POPPLETON JNS
Corporal	RAWSON WM.
Corporal	SHARPE WM.
Corporal	TWIGG JNS.
Corporal	VARLEY WM.
Corporal	WALBANK WALT
Corporal	WHITTAKER JOHN Wounded

Corporal	WIDDONS ABRA. Wounded
Drummer	ACKROYD JNS
Drummer	ALDRIDGE EDWD
Drummer	ALLEN THOS
Drummer	BOOTH JN.
Drummer	GAMROOD AMBROSE
Drummer	HEAPS JOHN
Drummer	HOLLEWELL JOHN Wounded
Drummer	LAWLEY THOS
Drummer	ODDY ABM.
Drummer	PASHLEY ROBT.
Drummer	PINDAR JOHN
Drummer	POWLSON ROBT
Drummer	ROBERTS B. Wounded
Drummer	THACKRAY THOS
Private	ADAMS WM. Wounded
Private	AKERS WM.
Private	ALLEN SAML.
Private	ALVEY JAMES
Private	ARTON THOS.
Private	ARMYTAGE GEO
Private	ARROW JAMES
Private	ASHTON JAMES Wounded
Private	ASKEW THOS Died of Wounds
Private	ATKINSON JAMES Died of wounds
Private	AUCKLAND THOS Died of wounds
Private	BAGSHAW JAMES Died of wounds
Private	BAGSHAW WM Died of wounds
Private	BALDWIN HENRY
Private	BALDWIN WM. Died of wounds
Private	BALME JNS.
Private	BALME JOSH Died of wounds
Private	BALMER SAML.
Private	BAMFORTH ADAM
Private	BARBER HENRY
Private	BARBER JNS
Private	BASTOWE JNS Wounded
Private	BATE WM.
Private	BAXTER JAMES
Private	BACON JAMES Wounded
Private	BEALE WM Wounded
Private	BEAUMONT ABRA.
Private	BEAUMONT JNS. Gray collection 1908
Private	BECK WM. Wounded
Private	BENT EDWD Died of wounds
Private	BENTLEY JNS.
Private	BERNARD JAMES
Private	BEST CHAS.
Private	BEVILL THOS.
Private	BIRCH JNS Wounded
Private	BLACKY DAVID Wounded
Private	BLAND MICHL
Private	BLAND JAMES
Private	BOLTON THOS.
Private	BOOTH THOS
Private	BOOTHROYD LUKE
Private	BOSWORTH GEO. Wounded
Private	BOTTOMLEY JOS. Wounded
Private	BOURNE JOS
Private	BOWERS AMOS
Private	BRADBURY THOS Wounded
Private	BRADLEY WM.
Private	BRADLEY JAMES
Private	BRIGGS WM.
Private	BRONSON BENJN. Wounded
Private	BROOK JOHN Wounded
Private	BROWNE THOS 1st Wounded
Private	BROWNE THOS 2nd
Private	BROWNRIDGE JOSH
Private	BUCKHAM JAMES
Private	BUCKLEY WM.
Private	BUCKLEY ROBT.
Private	BUCKLEY JAMES
Private	BUCKLEY JNS.
Private	BULLOCK WM.
Private	BUNNY WM. Wounded
Private	BURBRIDGE THOS.
Private	BURROW JOSH
Private	CALVERT GEO.
Private	CALVERT JOHN
Private	CARDING WM. Wounded
Private	CARTMAN JNS
Private	CARTMAN WM
Private	CARTY JNS Wounded
Private	CARVER WM Wounded
Private	CHADOCK CLARKE
Private	CHAPMAN JNS
Private	CHEETHAM JNS
Private	CHIVELY JAMES Wounded
Private	CLEGG ROBT
Private	COCKAYNE SAML.
Private	COKE RICHD. Wounded
Private	COLEY HENRY Wounded
Private	COWELL JAMES Wounded Day Sale April 1910
Private	COWLING WM.

Private	CRABTREE THOS Wounded
Private	CRAVEN THOS
Private	CROSSLEY DAVID Died of wounds 27th June
Private	CROWTHER JOSH
Private	CRYER JON. Wounded
Private	CUMMINS JOHN
Private	CUNDY THEO. Wounded
Private	DALTON JOHN
Private	DARLING FRANS.
Private	DEAKIN JOHN
Private	DEAN JOHN
Private	DIGHTON WM.
Private	DENBEIGH IS.
Private	DENTON JAMES 1st
Private	DENTON JAMES 2nd Wounded
Private	DENTON BENJN Galway Foley collection 1910
Private	DEWHURST THOS.
Private	DIXON JOHN
Private	DOCKER JAMES
Private	DODSON WM. Wounded
Private	DOLBY ROBT Wounded
Private	DOWNES THOS Wounded
Private	DOWNES WM
Private	DUCKWORTH THOS Wounded
Private	DRYDEN WM. Died of wounds
Private	DURANT NEAL
Private	EAGLES AARON
Private	EBOURNE JOSH
Private	ECCLES WM.
Private	ELLIS FREDK.
Private	EASTER EDWD
Private	EGGINTON JOSH
Private	EVERETT THOS
Private	FALLOWS JNS
Private	FARROW WM.
Private	FARRELL JNS Died of wounds 7th July
Private	FEARNICE THOS
Private	FEATHER ELIJ. Wounded Sotheby's sale Feb.1914
Private	FIDLER JOHN
Private	FIELD JOHN
Private	FIELDHOUSE THOS
Private	FIELDING GILES Wounded
Private	FIELDING JOSH.
Private	FIRTH IS. Wounded
Private	FISHER JAMES
Private	FISHER SAML. Wounded
Private	FLEMING JAMES
Private	FLINT G.P.
Private	FOSTER ROBT Wounded
Private	FOSTER ALLEN Wounded
Private	FOWLER WM. Wounded Walter's sale June 1913
Private	FOX FRANS. Wounded
Private	FRANCE JOHN
Private	FRIDAY JNS. L. Glendinings sale April 1911
Private	GARDINER JAMES Wounded
Private	GAY JAMES
Private	GOLDSBY MICHL Wounded
Private	GORDON WM
Private	GOULD JON. Wounded
Private	GOLDSMITH JON.
Private	GREEN WM. Wounded
Private	GREENWOOD JAMES Wounded
Private	GREIGSON THOS
Private	GRAY JOHN
Private	GRUNDY GEO
Private	GITSTONE THOS
Private	HAIGH EVAN
Private	HAIGH JON
Private	HAIGH JOSH Died of wounds
Private	HAIGH THOS.
Private	HAIGH RICHD
Private	HALL GEO Died of wounds H.Gaskell's coll. 1908
Private	HALLAS JOSH Wounded
Private	HALLICK JOSH
Private	HARRIS ROBERT
Private	HARRIS JNS
Private	HARRIS RICHD
Private	HARRIS SAML.
Private	HARRISON CHRIS. Wounded
Private	HARRISON JAMES
Private	HARRISON CHAS Wounded
Private	HARTLEY JNS
Private	HARTLEY THOS
Private	HATFIELD GEO
Private	HAYES JOSH
Private	HAYWARD WM.
Private	HAZELDENE JAMES Wounded
Private	HEALY JOSH Wounded
private	HEALEY ABRA.
Private	HEATOR RICHD.
Private	HEATOR JOSH
Private	HEATOR BENJN
Private	HERBERT THOS
Private	HILLS WM.
Private	HINCHLIFFE JON.

Private	HILL WM. Wounded
Private	HINDLE FLEM. Wounded
Private	HIRST ROBT.
Private	HODGKINSON WM.
Private	HODGSON DANL.
Private	HOHEIMA JOHN Wounded
Private	HOGGITT ROBT
Private	HOLDSWORTH JAMES
Private	HOLDSWORTH HERB.
Private	HOLDSWORTH SAML.
Private	HOLLAND MATTW Wounded
Private	HOLLINS THOS
Private	HOLLINSWORTH THOS
Private	HOLMES BENJN.
Private	HOLMES ROBT. Killed by accident 24th June
Private	HORSFALL JOHN
Private	HAUGHTON JOHN
Private	HOWARD CHAS.
Private	HOWARD WM.
Private	HOWSON WM.
Private	HOWSON JOHN
Privates	HUMPHRIES DANL.
Private	HEMMINGWAY GEO Wounded Glendinings sale Feb. 1909
Private	INGHAM JNS Wounded
Private	INSELE JNS
Private	JACKSON BARTW.
Private	JACKSON HENRY
Private	JACKSON JAMES
Private	JACKSON JOHN 1st Wounded Baldwin's 1912 Phillips
Private	JACKSON JOHN 2nd
Private	JACKSON THOS
Private	JEBSON JNS.
Private	JEFFERIES FRANS.
Private	JELLY WM.
Privates	JENNINGS WM. Wounded
Privates	JEWITT JERE.
Private	JOHNSON MATTW Wounded
Private	JORDAN WM.
Private	KAY AM.
Private	KAY JONAS Wounded
Private	KAY GEO. Wounded Glendinings sale 28-2-08
Private	KEHOE PATK Wounded
Private	KENDLE IS.
Private	KENNY EDWD. Wounded
Private	KENT JNS
Private	KENYON THOS Wounded
Private	KENSHAW JNS
Private	KILLINGBECK THOS. Wounded
Private	KIMBERLAND CHAS.
Private	KING JOSH
Private	KITSON SAML. Wounded
Private	KITON GEO
Private	KITSON DAVID
Private	LAMB THOS.
Private	LAMB JAMES
Private	LATTIMOW HENRY Wounded
Private	LEE THOS Wounded
Private	LINTON THOS.
Private	LORD JNS
Private	LOUN WM.
Private	LUMLEY WM. Wounded
Private	LUMLEY WM.
Private	McMONAUGHTY JNS.
Private	MACMAHON JNS
Private	McCOOLING SAML. Wounded
Private	McGUIRE HENRY Wounded
Private	MAKER JOSH Wounded Col.Gaskell's coll.May 1911
Private	MAKINGLEE ANDW.
Private	MANN JOHN Wounded
Private	MARTIN THOS Wounded
Private	MARTIN EDWD.
Private	MASSEY JOSH
Private	MAWLEY JOSH.
Private	MAWSON BENJN.
Private	MOULSON DAVID
Private	MAY THOS
Private	MILLARS SAML.
Private	MILLS CHAS.
Private	MITCHELL MATTW.
Private	MITCHELL SENIOR Wounded
Private	MITCHELL ABRA.
Private	MITCHELL IS.
Private	MITCHELL DANIEL Wounded
Private	MOULTON GEO.
Private	MURREN JOHN
Private	MORTIMORE WM Wounded
Private	MURGATROYD JNS.
Private	MURGATROYD THOS.
Private	MYERS JOSH
Private	NITTLES WM. Wounded
Private	NICHOLL DAVID Wounded
Private	NORBRAY DAVENPORT.
Private	NORTHROP JOHN
Privates	NOTENBORN ANDW.
Private	NOWELL MICHL.
Private	NOWLAND PETER

Private	O'HARA MICHL Wounded
Private	OGDEN JOSH
Privates	ORRELL JAMES
Privates	OSGAY CHAS
Private	OVEREND JOSH
Private	OXLEY WM. Died of wounds 5th July
Private	OVEREND WM.
Private	PARSONS WM.
Private	PEARSON HENRY Wounded
Private	PELE JAMES Died of wounds 4th July
Private	PERKINS WN.
Private	PERRY THOS Wounded
Private	PICKLE EDWD.
Private	PITTS JAMES
Privates	PLATTS JOHN
Private	POEWLL GEO.
Private	POWERS JOSH
Private	PRATT FRANS.
Private	PRECIANS JNS.
Private	PRIESTLEY GEO.
Private	PRUDENT WM.
Private	PYE GEO.
Private	RAMSDEN WM.
Private	RAWSON THOS
Private	RAYNOR EDWD Died of wounds 10th July
Private	REAKES ROBT. Died of wounds
Private	READER WM Died of wounds
Private	RICHARDS JAMES
Private	RIGLEY HENRY
Private	ROBERTS JOSH.
Private	ROBERTS JAMES
Private	ROBINSON THOS. Wounded
Private	ROBINSON JNS. Wounded
Private	ROBINSON JON.
Private	RODGERS JEREH.
Private	RODWELL THOS. Wounded
Private	ROLLINSON THOS.
Private	RESTHORN BENJN. Wounded
Private	RUSHWORTH THOS Wounded
Private	RYECROFT THOS
Private	SCHOFIELD THOS.
Private	SCHOOLEY WM.
Private	SELLWOOD WM.
Private	SEYMOUR GEO.
Private	SHAW GEO.
Private	SHAW JOSH.
Private	SHAW JOHN Wounded
Private	SHAW DAVID Wounded
Private	SHEPHARD THOS. Wounded
Private	SHIRES WM. Wounded
Private	SIMPSON PHILIP
Private	SINGLETON THOS. Wounded
Private	SKELLY WM. Wounded
Private	SKIDMAN HENRY
Private	SMALT JNS.
Private	SMITH JAMES
Private	SMITH JOSH Wounded Cheylesmore collection 1908
Private	SMITH JOHN Wounded
Private	SMITH JOSH. 1st Wounded
Private	SMITH JOSH. 2nd Wounded
Private	SMITH 1st Wm.
Private	SMITH 2nd Wm.
Private	SMITH 3rd WM. Wounded
Private	SMITH SAML.
Private	SMITHSOR DAVID
Private	SPENCER JON.
Private	SPENCER SAML.
Private	SPRIGGS JAMES Wounded
Private	STACEY JOHN
Private	STEELE JOHN
Private	STRANGE THOS.
Private	STROUDER SAML.
Private	STRINGER JNS
Private	STUBBS WM.
Private	SUGDEN JAMES
Private	SUNDERLAND TIMY.
Private	SUTCLIFFE JNS.
Private	SUTCLIFFE JAMES Wounded
Private	SUTCLIFFE WM Wounded
Private	SYKES JAMES 1st Wounded
Private	SYKES JAMES 2nd Wounded
Private	TAYLOR JOSH Wounded Sotheby's sale 1908
Private	TAYLOR WM. Wounded
Private	TAYLOR RICHD Wounded
Private	TAYLOR JNS. 1st
Private	TAYLOR JNS. 2nd
Private	TAYLOR THOS Wounded
Private	TEMPERLEY CHAS. Wounded
Private	TEMPEST SQUIRE
Private	THOMPSON RICHD.
Private	THOMPSON WM.
Private	THOMPSON THOS Wounded
Private	THORNTON BENJN.
Private	TIBBITTS DANL.
Private	TIPLING WM. Wounded
Private	TINDALE JAMES
Private	TINDALE JOHN

Private	TOMLINSON JOSH.
Private	TUCK JNS Wounded
Private	TURTON JAMES
Private	VAUGHAN AARON
Private	WADDINGTON CHAS.
Private	WADE THOS.
Private	WADE DANL.
Private	WAINMAN JAMES
Private	WALKER CHAS.
Private	WALKER JAMES Wounded
Private	WALMSLEY WM. Wounded
Private	WARBURTON JNS.
Private	WARREN JNS
Private	WATSON THOS.
Private	WEBSTER JNS.
Private	WELCH JOHN
Private	WESTLEY BENJN.
Private	WESTLEY WM.
Private	WHEATCROFT JNS.
Private	WHITTAKER GEO.
Private	WHITTAKER PHILP
Private	WHITE THOS.
Private	WHITEHEAD DAVID Wounded
Private	WHITEHEAD JOHN
Private	WHITEHEAD WM. Wounded
Private	WIDDOP JOHN Wounded
Private	WIGFALL JOHN Wounded
Private	WILKINS JOSH
Private	WILKINSON JONAS Wounded
Private	WILSON JAMES Wounded
Private	WILSON EDWD. Wounded
Private	WILSON WM. 1st
Private	WILSON WM. 2nd
Private	WILSON SIMEON
Private	WISE MOSES
Private	WORRELL ROBT.
Private	WOOD ABRA. Wounded
Private	WOOD BENJN. Wounded
Private	WOOD THOS. 1st
Private	WOOD THOS. 2nd
Private	WRIGHT WM. 1st
Private	WRIGHT WM. 2nd
Private	YALE CHAS Wounded
Private	ZAHA JOSH

* * *

2nd BATTALION. 35th REGIMENT OF FOOT

Major	MACALISTER CHAS.
Major	SLEESOR JNS.
Adjutant	BREARY C.S.
Qr.Master	FOOT ROBT.
Surgeon	DOYLE C.S.
Ass.Surgeon	KEOGHOE WM. Payne collc. 1911
Ass.Surgeon	PURCELL JOHN
Pay.Master	BURY WM.

Captain A. McDonald's Company

Lieutenant	SCARFE S.S.
Lieutenant	HEILDERBRAND J.
S.Major	HICKMAN BENJN.
Q.M.S.	PRICE JNS.
P.M.S.	HOWE WM.
Ar.Serjeant	BURGIN WM.
Serjeant	DANN JNS.
Serjeant	STOCKWELL ROBT.
Corporal	COOPER JNS. Whitaker collc.1908
Corporal	RICE JOSH.
Corporal	WILSON THOS.
Drummer	DIX JNS.
Private	BAGLIN CHAS.
Private	BIRD LAWCE.
Private	BITH JAMES
Private	BOULTER WM.
Private	BROOM JAMES
Private	BROWN THOS.
Private	BURROWS THOS.
Private	BUSSEY GEO.
Private	CHALLON ROBT.
Private	CROOM THOS.
Private	DAVIS JAMES
Private	DAVIS JNS.
Private	DAVIS ROBT.
Private	DOWLING CHAS.
Private	FARRELL LOUGHLIN
Private	FARRELL WM.
Private	FRY JOHN
Private	GAY JAMES
Private	GROUNSELL WM.
Private	HOLDER JAMES
Private	HUGGINS SAML.
Private	HURRY GEO.
Private	JAMES JOHN
Private	JONES THOS.
Private	KENEWAY JAMES
Private	KETCHLEY RICHD.
Private	LUCAS THOS.
Private	MANNING RICHD.
Private	MARTIN EDMD.
Private	McCORMICK ANDW.
Private	MOLLOY CHAS.

Private	MURPHY DANL.
Private	NEWMAN JOHN
Private	OKEY CHAS.
Private	PRIDEAUX JOHN
Private	QUINN JAMES
Private	SHEPPARD WM.
Private	STURT THOS.
Private	TALBUT STEP.
Private	WHITEAR JAMES
Private	MINGLE JUDD

Captain Cameron's Company

Lieutenant	McDONOUGH THOS.
Lieutenant	THOBURN ROBT.
Serjeant	BURNELL ROBT.
Serjeant	MONAGHAN PETER
Corporal	CALCUTT WM.
Corporal	HOAR JAMES
Corporal	HARRIS THOS.
Drummer	ANDERSON WM.
Drummer	SHUTER JOHN
Private	ANDERSON JOHN
Private	ATTWOOD JAMES Fenton's Oct. 1909
Private	BASSELL CHAS.
Private	BASSETT THOS Littledale Nov. 1910
Private	BASTIN JNS.
Private	BROWN JNS.
Private	BUSSEY IS.
Private	CLARKE JNS.
Private	DE FRANCE JOHN
Private	DE PUTRON JOHN
Private	DEWELL HUMP.
Private	DUNFORD FRANS.
Private	ESSEX EDWD.
Private	GARAYTHY BART.
Private	GIFFORD WM.
Private	GROGAN JNS.
Private	HARWOOD SAML.
Private	HILL SAML.
Private	HODGES CHAS.
Private	JACKSON HENRY
Private	JONES EDWD.
Private	KENNEDY OWEN
Private	McCUE TIMY.
Private	MIDDLETON JACOB
Private	MITCHELL ANDW.
Private	MITCHELL THOS.
Private	MULVEY WM.
Private	NEWMAN JAMES
Private	OLAND GEO.
Private	PAGE GEO.
Private	PARFITT JOHN
Private	PHILLPOTT ROBT.
Private	POULTON JOS.
Private	PRATTEN IS.
Private	RIPLEY GEO.
Private	ROBERTS PETER
Private	RUSSELL THOS.
Private	SANDLE STEV.
Private	SIMES CHAS.
Private	STAGG THOS.
Private	SUMMERS THOS.
Private	THOMAS JOSH.
Private	TYRRELL PETK.
Private	VEALE HENRY
Private	WELLBELOVED GEO.
Private	WILLOUGHBY GEO.
Private	WORRALL WM.

Captain Weare's Company

Lieutenant	FARRENT WM.
Lieutenant	MURDOCK PETER
Ensign	WYATT CHAS.
Serjeant	DAVIS CHAS.
Serjeant	SUMMERS FREDK.
Corporal	HUNT STEP.
Corporal	KETCHLEY JOSH
Corporal	SANSON THOS.
Drummer	McDONALD THOS.
Drummer	OSMON JOHN
Private	ALDRIDGE GEO.
Private	BENNION GEO.
Private	CADMAN JOHN
Private	CADMAN WM.
Private	CALDWELL WM.
Private	CANNON MATTW.
Private	COLLINS HUGH
Private	CONNER JAMES
Private	CARDIAL JAMES
Private	CUTCHLEY PETER
Private	DAMON SAML.
Private	DAVIS JAMES
Private	ELLFORD JAMES
Private	FRANDELL THOS.
Private	GLOVER THOS.
Private	GRANT JAMES
Private	HARDING JOHN
Private	HARRIS FRANS.
Private	HOLDER RICHD.
Private	HUMPHRIES THOS.

Private	HUNT JAMES
Private	HUTCHINGS HENRY
Private	KENNEDY BARND.
Private	KENNEDY PATK.
Private	KITELY THOS.
Private	LEAVEY HUGH
Private	LEAVEY WM.
Private	LONG WM.
Private	MARTIN FRANS.
Private	MEALEY FRANS.
Private	MERRETT WM.
Private	MURPHY MICHL.
Private	MURPHY PATK.
Private	PADON JOHN
Private	PAYNE JAMES
Private	PEGLER JOHN
Private	PENNYCOTT CHAS.
Private	POWELL JOHN
Private	PRESTON JACOB
Private	PHILLIPS HENRY
Private	PRICE JOHN
Private	PRITCHARD JOHN
Private	ROSSER ROBT.
Private	RUSSELL THOS.
Private	SANDELL THOS.
Private	SCOTT ALEXR.
Private	SMITH WM.
Private	STAPLES JOSH.
Private	TASKER DANL.
Private	TURNER WM.
Private	UNDERWOOD THOS.
Private	VETCH CHAS.
Private	WALTON HENRY
Private	WOOD WM.
Private	WORKMAN THOS.
Private	LESTER JAMES

<u>Captain Moulson's Company</u>

Captain	WALL C.W.
Lieutenant	WILKINS GEO.
Ensign	HEWETSON JOHN
Serjeant	BATES JOHN
Serjeant	KIRBY JOHN
Corporal	EDMUNDS CHAS
Corporal	HART CON. Glendinings sale July 1911
Corporal	PENNY THOS.
Corporal	BRICE WM.
Drummer	DAVIS JAMES
Drummer	LATTY JOHN
Private	ALLOWAY THOS.
Private	ARNOLD JNS%
Private	BROOM GEO.
Private	COSTELLO THOS.
Private	CONWAY MAURICE
Private	COOTE EDWD.
Private	CRAWFORD JOHN
Private	CREATON PATK.
Private	DAUGHTY GEO.
Private	DAY JAMES
Private	DONOUGH GEO.
Private	ELLIOTT GEO.
Private	ENWRIGHT JOHN
Private	FALLON PATK.
Private	FARLEY JAMES
Private	FELTHAM HENRY
Private	FLINN CHAS.
Private	GARDNER JOSH.
Private	GINN OWEN
Private	HARDING JOSH
Private	HARDING WM.
Private	HEATH ROBT.
Private	HIDE JAMES
Private	HISCOCK ANTHY.
Private	HISCOCK JOHN
Private	HOLLAND SAML. Walter's sale June 1913
Private	HOOLEY FRANS.
Private	JAMES JOHN
Private	JONES WM.
Private	KELLY MICHL.
Private	KING JOHN
Private	KINSMAN WM.
Private	MAYO THOS.
Private	O'NEAL JAMES
Private	PALMER JAMES
Private	POLLARD JOHN
Private	RHODES DAVID
Private	RIDLER GEO.
Private	RITCHINGS WM.
Private	SQUIRES WM.
Private	STRAW JOHN
Private	THOMAS CHAS.
Private	THOMPSON JOHN
Private	TIPPEN EDWD.
Private	WEBB JOHN
Private	WEST JOHN
Private	WICKS JAMES

Captain Newton's Company

Lieutenant	AMOS J.W.
Ensign	MACALISTER WM.
Ensign	McDONNELL A.
Serjeant	BROWN JAS. WM. Sotheby's July 1912
Serjeant	MOORE THOS
Serjeant	QUINN WM.
Corporal	BROWN WM.
Corporal	McNALLY WM.
Drummer	CASS JOSH.
Drummer	SMITH SAML.
Private	BAILEY WM.
Private	BARNES JOSH.
Private	BARTLETT ROBT.
Private	BELL JOHN
Private	CASS HENRY
Private	DANIELS HENRY
Private	DILLON PATK.
Private	FORD FRANS.
Private	FORD GEO.
Private	GILLARD RICHD.
Private	GLANNON JAMES
Private	HANSFORD SOLO.
Private	HOLT JOHN
Private	HULL JERH.
Private	JUPP FREDK.
Private	KINCHINGTON AMBROSE
Private	LAWRANCE ROBT.
Private	LEECH WM.
Private	McGEE BARND.
Private	MEADE WM.
Private	MOORE WM.
Private	NIXON GEO.
Private	NIXON JAMES
Private	PALMER THOS.
Private	PAYNE WM.
Private	PERKINS ARTH.
Private	PHILLIPS JAS 1st
Private	PHILLIPS JAS. 2nd
Private	PRITCHARD WM.
Private	QUINN JAMES
Private	RENFIELD HENRY
Private	ROACH JOHN
Private	RONDE JOSH
Private	SHERWOOD THOS.
Private	SWIFT JOHN
Private	SWORN SAML.
Private	TRAVERS JOHN
Private	TUNE JAMES
Private	WARNER THOS.
Private	WARTON SOLM
Private	WRENN WM.
Private	WILSON JAMES

Captain Rutherford's Company

Captain	RUTHERFORD HENRY	
Lieutenant	MIDDLETON J.	
Lieutenant	BARNWELL ROBT.	
Ensign	POTTENGER GEO.	
Serjeant	BENNETT GEO.	
Serjeant	SMEETON JAMES	
Serjeant	WATKINS JAMES	Discharged
Corporal	BAXTER JAMES	
Corporal	CRITCHLEY THOS.	
Drummer	GRAHAM NATHL.	
Private	ALEXANDER JNS.	
Private	AURTHER EVAN	
Private	BARNES SAML.	
Private	BASSETT MICHL.	
Private	BOND SAML.	
Private	BROWNING RICHD.	
Private	CARMICHAEL JOSH	
Private	DAVIS WM.	
Private	DOWLING JNS.	
Private	DUNSTON WM.	
Private	EGAN WM.	
Private	GALLOP JNS.	
Private	GEER THOS.	
Private	GIBBONS THOS.	
Private	GLANNEN DENIS	
Private	GOSLING THOS.	
Private	GURNEY JOHN	
Private	HAYES CORNS.	
Private	HAYLES JOHN	
Private	JONES CHAS.	
Private	JONES WM.	
Private	KEENAN JAMES	
Private	LOVELL GEO.	
Private	LOWER HENRY	
Private	LUCAS JOSH.	
Private	MANGEN JOHN	
Private	McCOMBS JOHN	
Private	NEW WM.	
Private	OATES JAMES	
Private	PARSON HENRY	
Private	PATCHING THOS.	
Private	POWELL JOHN	
Private	PUNCHON ROBT.	

Private	ROGERS TIMY.
Private	SEABRIGHT JOHN
Private	STEVENS DANL.
Private	TRIMM THOS.
Private	TURNER WM.
Private	TROWER JAMES
Private	WICKHAM GEO.
Private	COGGIN THOS.
Private	MASON THOS.

Captain McNiell's Company

Captain	McNEILL THOS.
Lieutenant	TOMKINS N.R.
Lieutenant	RAINSORTH WM.
Serjeant	BURT RICHD.
Serjeant	CASTLE THOS.
Serjeant	McLAUGHLIN FARRELL
Corporal	DAVIS WM.
Corporal	HEAD JOHN
Corporal	LAW JAMES
Drummer	CLISSOLD EDMD.
Drummer	DUICH JOSH.
Drummer	DEAMMER THOS.
Private	ALDER JOHN
Private	APPS CHAS.
Private	AYLING JAMES
Private	BAWN DANL.
Private	BAYLISS WM.
Private	BENNETT JOHN
Private	BERRY THOS.
Private	BIRCH STEP.
Private	BEXALL IRAM
Private	BRIANT JOB Discharged
Private	BROADLEY JNS
Private	BURRIDGE JNS
Private	BUSHROD JOHN
Private	BURT ROBT.
Private	COOPER WM.
Private	CRANFIELD JOHN
Private	DAVIS RICHD.
Private	DEEVEY CHAS.
Private	DOBSON THOS
Private	DRUM PATK.
Private	EDWARDS DAVID
Private	FARRELL THOS
Private	GREEN WM.
Private	GROVES JAMES
Private	GULLICK JAMES
Private	HARTLEY WI.
Private	HAWKINS JOHN
Private	HILLS BASCOM.
Private	HOLLOWAY WM.
Private	HUGHES JAMES
Private	ISSAC WM.
Private	JONES JAMES
Private	KEINEHAM HUGH
Private	KENNY MICHL.
Private	KENDRICK JOHN
Private	MINES JAMES
Private	MONCK WM.
Private	MODRY WM.
Private	MORGAN JOSH.
Private	OXENBRIDGE EDMD.
Private	PELLY THOS.
Private	PRITCHARD WM.
Private	STEVENS JOSH.
Private	STOCKER RICHD.
Private	THOMAS BENJN.
Private	THOMAS NATHL.
Private	WALTERS JOHN
Private	WEST PETER
Private	WILLS JOHN
Private	WALDRIDGE THOS
Private	PRICE WM.

Captain Gregory's Company

Lieutenant	OSBORN JOHN
Ensign	HEDDING W.L.
Serjeant	BENWELL WM.
Serjeant	HODGES WM.
Serjeant	STEEL SAML. Gray collc. 1908
Corporal	LAMB RICHD.
Corporal	TAYLOR WM.
Drummer	EDWARDS JOHN
Drummer	SMITH THOS.
Private	AUSTIN WM.
Private	AYRES GEO.
Private	BALLAM SAML.
Private	BARRY GEO.
Private	BROWN THOS.
Private	BROWN LUC.
Private	COOK WM.
Private	ELLOWAY DAVID
Private	FORD GEO.
Private	GEER JOSH.
Private	GOUGH JAMES Col.Gascoignes collection March 1909
Private	GRIFFIN HENRY
Private	HACKETT THOS.
Private	HARRIS RICHD

Private	HENDERSON WM.
Private	HEWETT SAM.
Private	HENDON WM.
Private	HOGG JOHN
Private	IDE WM.
Private	IVES HENRY
Private	KINGSTON JAMES
Private	LANE CHAS.
Private	LAWLER JAMES
Private	MALLEN JAMES
Private	MONCK JOSH.
Private	MONAGHAN PATK.
Private	MORAN THOS Day Sale April 1910 3-10-0
Private	ORCHARD RICHD.
Private	PERKISS JOSH.
Private	PRIGNELL ABRA.
Private	RUMERY WM.
Private	RUMBLE JOHN
Private	SANDERS ROBT.
Private	SERTIN JOHN
Private	SEARY BRIAN
Private	SHORT SOLON.
Private	SPENCE THOS.
Private	SPITTLE AMOS.
Private	TRIM JOHN
Private	TURNER JOHN
Private	WHITE MATTW.
Private	WINDERS GEO.
Private	WOODS CHAS.

Captain Drumgoole's Company

Captain	DRONGOOLE N.T. Gaskell collection 1908
Lieutenant	SHEWELL EDWD.
Ensign	NAMILTON A.D.
Serjeant	BROWN JAMES
Serjeant	PHILLIPS WM.
Serjeant	TULLY ALEXR.
Corporal	HEAD GEO.
Corporal	QUINN HENRY
Corporal	VIRGE WM.
Drummer	DOWN AARON
Drummer	WYMARK JOHN
Private	BAKER WM.
Private	BONNER RICHD.
Private	BULBECK WM.
Private	CHURCHER WM.
Private	CLARKE THOS.
Private	CLAYTON JAMES
Private	CLAYTON JOHN
Private	COLURN JOS.
Private	COOPER ROBT.
Private	DALEY PATK.
Private	DICKINSON WM.
Private	DOYLE PATK.
Private	EDMUNDS JOHN
Private	EVERRETT WM.
Private	FOGDEN WM.
Private	GALLINE ABRA.
Private	HERON JOHN
Private	HENDERSON JAMES
Private	HILL GEO.
Private	HILL WM.
Private	HOBBS JOHN
Private	IRWIN CHRIS.
Private	JOHNSTONE JAMES
Private	LOVEDORE GEO.
Private	McFADDEN EDWD.
Private	MAYLERD MATTW.
Private	MAPHAM EDWD. Col. Murray's collection 1908
Private	MURPHY JOHN
Private	PAYNE JOHN
Private	POOLE GEO.
Private	RUMBLE WM.
Private	SHEEVIN PATK.
Private	SIBLEY DANL.
Private	SIMPSON JOHN
Private	SMITH SAML.
Private	WATKINS WM.
Private	WEARE SAML.
Private	WEBB GEO.
Private	WEBLEY ROBT.
Private	WELLS JOHN
Private	WILLIAMS JOHN
Private	WOODS JOHN

Captain W. McDonald's Company

Captain	RAWSON WM.
Lieutenant	WILDER JAMES
Ensign	THOMAS JOHN
Serjeant	PEARCE JOHN Cheylesmore collection 1908
Serjeant	TERRELL JOHN
Serjeant	WILLIS ROWLAND
Corporal	HOLDER DANL.
Corporal	KING MERRICK
Corporal	SMITH ROBT.
Private	BELL JOHN
Private	BRUTON MARK
Private	BUCKWELL JAMES

Private	BULL HENRY
Private	BYRNES PATK.
Private	BERRY JOS.
Private	CLINCH WM.
Private	COLLINS JAMES
Private	DENNING JOHN
Private	EADE JAMES
Private	FRANKHAM THOS.
Private	HARRIS STEP.
Private	HAWTHRON JAMES
Private	HEATHCOT ROBT.
Private	HURLEY? OWEN
Private	JACKSON ROBT.
Private	KNOWLSON FREDK.
Private	KNOWLTON JASPER
Private	LANEWAY WM.
Private	LINES WM.
Private	LLOYD WM.
Private	MAGGS FRANS.
Private	McCLEAN JACOB
Private	McCLEAN JOHN
Private	MORGAN STEP.
Private	NEWBOLD JOHN
Private	ORHAM THOS.
Private	PITTMAN JAMES
Private	POSTONS JAMES
Private	PRATT JOHN
Private	SAMWAYS JOHN
Private	SMITH WM.
Private	SPARROW WM.
Private	STEER JAMES
Private	STOCKWELL SAML.
Private	THOMAS WM.
Private	TICK WM.
Private	TINDALL JOHN
Private	TURNER JOHN
Private	WARD GEO.
Private	WESTRIP THOS.
Private	WILLIS CHAS.

* * *

1st BATTALION 40th REGIMENT OF FOOT

Major	BROWNE F.
Adjutant	MANNING W.
Surgeon	JONES W.
Ass.Surgeon	BARRY W.
Ass.Surgeon	SCOTT G.

Captain J.H. Barnett's Company

Captain	BARNETT J.H. Wounded
Lieutenant	MOORE R. Wounded Whitaker collection 1908
Ensign	HEMSLEY H.
Ensign	MURPHY JAMES
S.Major	BRICE HENRY
Q.M.S.	WHEADON WM.
P.M.S.	SPENCER JNS. LEE
Ar.Serjeant	STOKES JOSH.
Dr.Major	SUTTON WM.
Serjeant	HODGES JAMES
Serjeant	BABY RICHD.
Serjeant	CLARE TIMY.
Serjeant	McGLOCHLAN IS.
Serjeant	LAWRENCE WM.
Corporal	BABY THOS.
Corporal	CHAPMAN JNS.
Corporal	OSBORNE CHAS.
Corporal	THEODY WM.
Corporal	WALKER JOHN
Corporal	WILLIS JOHN
Drummer	SIMBLETON THOS
Drummer	BISHOP GEO.
Private	BEAUMONT JNS.
Private	BRESLIN OWEN
Private	BLACKMORE WM.
Private	BRYSON WM.
Private	BRICE JNS.
Private	BOLWING HENRY
Private	CHEESEMAN HENRY Died 17.2.1816
Private	CURTIS RICHD. Died 18.6.1815
Private	COOKE WM.
Private	DAVIS WM.
Private	DAVIS HENRY
Private	DAVIS JNS.
Private	EDWARDS JNS.
Private	ENNIS GEO.
Private	EVANS HOWELL
Private	EWENS JNS.
Private	EXTON THOS.
Private	FAITHEN GEO.
Private	FAGAN JNS.
Private	FARRELL RICHD.
Private	FORD JNS.
Private	GILBERT JNS.
Private	GLEW JNS
Private	GORDON THOS.
Private	HALL WM.

Private	HASSAN MICHL.
Private	HEALEY BENJN.
Private	HANLY GEO.
Private	HORRELL RICHD.
Private	HAYDON JNS.
Private	JOHNSTONE JOSH
Private	JOHNS THOS.
Private	KINSELLA JAMES
Private	LEMMOND THOS.
Private	MORTIMORE JOSH.
Private	MOTE JAMES
Private	MOONEY JAMES
Private	NORTON ROBT.
Private	PHILLIPS DAVID
Private	PORTER EDWD. Gascoignes collection March 1909
Private	POOLE THOS.
Private	PALMER SAML.
Private	PYLE CHAS.
Private	QUIGLEY LAW. CHAS.
Private	POSE WM. Died 25th June 1815
Private	REED WM.
Private	REESE WM.
Private	RUTH JAMES Died 12th July 1815
Private	ROGAN HENRY
Private	SMITH HENRY
Private	SMITH GEO.
Private	THOMAS WM.
Private	TEIRNAN HUGH
Private	VILE WM.
Private	WALSH JNS.
Private	WHELAN GEO. Glendinings sale 17th June 1908
Private	WILLIAMSON JAMES

Captain E.C. Bowen's Company

Captain	BOWEN C.E.
Lieutenant	SANDWITH W.D.
Ensign	WALL J.L.
Serjeant	ROSE ROBT.
Serjeant	CONROY JNS.
Serjeant	MILES JAMES
Serjeant	REICKENBERG JOS.
Serjeant	SWEETLAND JAS.
Corporal	SEAGAR THOS.
Corporal	SEAL RICHD.
Corporal	PURLE JAMES
Corporal	STANNIFORD WM.
Drummer	PARDLES GEO.
Drummer	HILLMAN ALEXR.
Private	ADAMS MATTW.
Private	ATKINS JAMES
Private	ATKINS JAMES
Private	ABBOTT JOHN
Private	ASPLEY WM.
Private	BARBER JNS.
Private	BROWNE THOS.
Private	BONNING GEO.
Private	BENNETT SAML.
Private	BOYNE PATK.
Private	BROADRIBB JNS.
Private	CASSIDY THOS. Deserted 24th Aug. 1815
Private	CURRY WM.
Private	DAVIS ROBT.
Private	DEVERLAND ROBT.
Private	DAY JOHN
Private	DIXON JAMES
Private	EAKINS JOSH
Private	FRY SAML.
Private	FORSTER BENJN.
Private	FURLONG JAMES
Private	GARNER JOSH
Private	GOODWIN JAMES
Private	GROVES REUBEN
Private	GULLY SAML.
Private	HOOKWAY THOS.
Private	HOPKINS JENKIN
Private	HULCOMBE IS.
Private	HUSBAND HENRY Col.Murray's collection 1908
Private	JOHNS JNS.
Private	KENWORTHY WM.
Private	KING THOS.
Private	LEAVIONS HENRY
Private	LEWINGTON EDWD.
Private	LIDFORD WM.
Private	LANE JNS.
Private	MEALE WM.
Private	MORRIS JNS.
Private	MOORE THOS.
Private	MORGAN JAMES
Private	PAGE THOS.
Private	PEARSON GEO.
Private	PIKE DANL.
Private	PELLARD SAML.
Private	QUINN CHAS.
Private	QUINN DAVID
Private	RAINBOW CHAS.
Private	REED JOHN Glendinings sale April 1909
Private	SHARPE ROBT.
Private	SHAW THOS.
Private	SMITH JAMERS

Private	SMITH SAML.
Private	STEWART JAMES
Private	SQUANCE WM.
Private	SCOTT JNS. Died 10th Dec 1815
Private	SWEETMAN NICH.
Private	TAYLOR THOS.
Private	TRAER WM.
Private	TOWNS JNS.
Private	TROTTER ZACH.
Private	TATCHELL JOHN Died 27th August 1815
Private	VEAL BENJN.
Private	VICKERY JNS.
Private	WARREN JAMES
Private	WEBBER JAMES
Private	WEBBER JNS.
Private	WHITE JAMES

Captain S. Streton's Company

Captain	STRETTON S.
Lieutenant	WILKINSON H.
Lieutenant	CAMPBELL T. Wounded
Ensign	FORD F. Wounded
Serjeant	CHAPMAN FRANS.
Serjeant	TOOHEY LA.
Serjeant	BOWDEN JAMES
Serjeant	BUDBRIDGE JAMES
Corporal	HALL WM.
Corporal	BODDINGTON WM.
Corporal	EAGAN PATK
Corporal	HOOPER GEO.
Corporal	DYAGER ANDW.
Corporal	KNOTT JAMES
Drummer	ACHER THOS.
Drummer	DODGE JAMES
Private	ANDREWS THOS.
Private	BALE JNS.
Private	BARRINGTON JNS.
Private	BATES JAMES Died 7th Mar 1816
Private	BOOTH WM.
Private	BROWNE JNS.
Private	BERRY THOS.
Private	CHINNERLY HERB. H.Gaskell's collection 1908 Phillips sale
Private	CLARKE PHIL.
Private	COLBREATH BENJN.
Private	CHARLES JOS.
Private	DAVIS JOHN
Private	DAY JOHN
Private	DEIGHTON NATHL. Sotheby's sale 19th June 1908
Private	DUNIGAN CHRIS Died 29th June 1815
Private	EDWARDS JOSH Cheylesmore collection 1908
Private	ELLERMAN RICHD.
Private	EMMERY WM.
Private	FORWARD JOS.
Private	GAMBLE THOS.
Private	GREADY JAMES
Private	HADDON THOS.
Private	HAMMOND WM.
Private	HANKINS JOS.
Private	HARDIMAN WM.
Private	HAINS RICHD.
Private	HEMBERY CHAS.
Private	HURST WM.
Private	HUTCHFIELD CHAS.
Private	JACKSON JOS.
Private	JAMES JOS.
Private	JERVIS JAMES
Private	JORDAN JNS.
Private	JUST THOS.
Private	KING WM.
Private	LEAP SAML.
Private	LEGG ROBT.
Private	LEAVIONS THOS.
Private	LIDDON HENRY
Private	MATTHEWS WM.
Private	MALONEY JAMES
Private	MINNISEE ROBT.
Private	PHILLIPS WM.
Private	POET WALT.
Private	REED JNS.
Private	REED JAMES Died 18th June 1815
Private	REESE JOHN
Private	RILEY THOS.
Private	SMITH JAMES
Private	TIMMINS WM.
Private	TRISSELL THOS.
Private	TURNER WM.
Private	VERKER WM.
Private	WILKINSON SANDY
Private	WALCOCK DAVID
Private	WARREN THOS.
Private	WATTS GEO.
Private	WILSON THOS.
Private	WHITE JOHN Littledale sale Nov. 1910
Private	WILLIAMS ROBT.
Private	WOOLFE THOS.

Captain R. Turton's Company

Lieutenant	MILLS J. Wounded
Lieutenant	JONES R.
Ensign	HARLEY P.
Serjeant	GOLD JAMES
Serjeant	McMAHON JAMES
Serjeant	BABY JOSH
Serjeant	SPEARING WM.
Serjeant	HELLIER THOS.
Corporal	CROOK JAMES
Corporal	CROOK EDWD.
Corporal	WILLIAMS EDWD
Corporal	WILLEY WM.
Drummer	MARSCALL WM.
Private	ABRAMS WM.
Private	ANDERSON JOHN
Private	ALDRIDGE HENRY
Private	ASHTON WM.
Private	ACLAND WM.
Private	BABBS RICHD.
Private	BALLS BERND.
Private	BASS GEO. On sale at Fenton's Nov. 1912
Private	BARBER JNS
Private	BEST WM.
Private	BRAMLEY JNS.
Private	BROOM JNS.
Private	BULL JNS.
Private	BOND ARTH.
Private	BOSSACO ALEX.
Private	CALF WM.
Private	CHAPMAN THOS.
Private	CLIFFORD THOS.
Private	COLLINGS THOS.
Private	DINGLE JOSH.
Private	EDGAR JNS.
Private	FALLER MICHL.
Private	FRANKS WM.
Private	GARLAND THOS.
Private	GENTLE THOS.
Private	GRANGER LUKE
Private	GREEN JAMES
Private	GRIFFEN JAMES
Private	HAMMOND WM.
Private	HARVEY WM.
Private	HALE JAMES
Private	IRWIN JAMES
Private	INGRAM THOS.
Private	JONES JNS.
Private	JONES WM.
Private	KILPATRICK DANL.
Private	KINSELA PATK.
Private	LIKELY FRANS.
Private	MARTIN EDWD.
Private	MARSHALL WM.
Private	MONK CHAS.
Private	ODELL DANL.
Private	OWENS JNS.
Private	PERRY JNS.
Private	PETLEY WM.
Private	PITTMAN JAMES
Private	PRITCHARD THOS.
Private	QUIGLEY FRANS.
Private	REESE THOS.
Private	REVELL JNS.
Private	RICHARDS HENRY
Private	RODD SAML.
Private	RODGERS HENRY
Private	SLADE GEO.
Private	SMITH JOS.
Private	SPLEVIN JAMES
Private	STOCK JOS
Private	TILLMAN WM.
Private	TIBBOTT JOHN
Private	TOZER JOHN
Private	USHER JOHN
Private	VARNER JAMES
Private	WORRELL WM.
Private	WHEYBORN GEO.
Private	WILLMOTT JAMES
Private	WRIGHT JOSH.

Captain P. Bishop's Company

Captain	BISHOP P.
Lieutenant	RICHARDSON J.
Ensign	CLARKE W.A. Wounded
Serjeant	LEMON WM.
Serjeant	GOWING THOS.
Serjeant	McGEE DAVID
Serjeant	NORMAN JOHN
Corporal	TRENT BENJN. Galway Foley collection 1910
Corporal	DOWELL LOT
Corporal	HORNSEY JNS.
Corporal	MORGAN THOS.
Drummer	LOCKE JAMES
Private	BOARD JON.
Private	BOATS THOS.
Private	BURGAN WM.

Private	BURGE JAMES
Private	BRINELOW GEO.
Private	BARRETT JOHN
Private	BURROWS THOS
Private	BOWDEN WM.
Private	CHEENEY HENRY
Private	CHESTER THOS.
Private	COLES JNS.
Private	COVINGSTON SIMON
Private	CLARKE ROBT. Glendinings sale Feb. 1913 1-18-0
Private	CORDON GREGORY
Private	DAVIS WM.
Private	DOW WM. 1st
Private	DOW WM. 2nd
Private	DUKE JOS.
Private	DORAN PATK.
Private	FRY JOHN
Private	GREEN DANL.
Private	GREGORY THOS
Private	GOSLING SAML.
Private	HANNAGAN MICHL.
Private	HILL WALT.
Private	HIGGINS JOHN
Private	IRELAND JOHN
Private	JONES THOS.
Private	JENNINGS JAMES
Private	LEE JNS.
Private	LIGOURISH JNS.
Private	LANE HENRY
Private	MAHONY JAMES
Private	MAIN WM.
Private	MARTIN JNS. Died 24th June 1815
Private	MALLETT JNS.
Private	McCAWLEY MICHL.
Private	MUCKELROY ROBT.
Private	NOWAH THOS.
Private	NOWLAND ROBT.
Private	NORTON WM.
Private	OWENS JNS
Private	PYE JAMES
Private	PICKETT RICHD.
Private	REARDON JNS.
Private	RICHARDS JOS.
Private	RICHARDSON JOS.
Private	ROBINSON JNS.
Private	ROWE JNS
Private	RICKARDS PETER
Private	SPARROW JAMES
Private	SPENCER WM.
Private	THATCHER JNS.
Private	TEIRNEY JNS.
Private	TERINAN MICHL.
Private	TRUBY WM.
Private	THOMPSON JAMES
Private	VINCENT WM.
Private	WOODS STEP.
Private	WOOLLEY WM. Day Sale April 1918
Private	WRENN JNS
Private	YEOMAN JOSH

Captain G. Morrow's Company

Captain	FISHER WM. Killed
Lieutenant	WRAY H.
Ensign	McDONALD D.
Ensign	GLYNNE H.
Serjeant	THATCHER JNS.
Serjeant	BENSON PATK.
Serjeant	DELANY JNS
Serjeant	FORSTER JNS
Serjeant	HITCHCOCK WM.
Serjeant	McCABE JNS.
Corporal	BARRETT MICHL.
Corporal	CONN JNS.
Corporal	WRIGHT JNS.
Corporal	McGILL ROBT.
Drummer	BROWNE WM. TH.
Drummer	RIDLEY THOS.
Private	ARNOLD THOS
Private	ABBOTT JNS.
Private	ADAMS WM.
Private	BARKER JNS.
Private	BARRELL THOS.
Private	PYRNE PATK.
Private	BUTCHER GEO.
Private	BYNOR THOS.
Private	BROWNE RICHD.
Private	CARTY MARTIN
Private	CARBERRY JNS.
Private	COOKE JAMES
Private	DALY WM.
Private	ETHRIDGE ABRA.
Private	FRANKLYN JNS.
Private	FOSTER THOS.
Private	FACEY RICHD.
Private	GROVES WM.
Private	GODDARD JNS.
Private	GRIBBON SAML.
Private	GRAHAN JAMES
Private	GLEW ROBT.
Private	GRAY ARCH.

Private	HANLY PETER
Private	HANLY ANDW.
Private	HUNT SAML.
Private	HOULT RICHD.
Private	HOPPY JNS.
Private	JENKINS WAL.
Private	KINGHT JNS.
Private	LANE W. Died 18th June 1815
Private	LEE JNS.
Private	LYE JOSH.
Private	LODDEN JAMES
Private	MORIARTY WM.
Private	MANSFIELD JAMES
Private	MAINS MICHL.
Private	McGOURY DANL.
Private	MILLS ABRA.
Private	MURRAY EDMD.
Private	McGLOCKLAN BERND.
Private	McGLINN WM.
Private	MILLER JOHN
Private	PARKMAN GEO.
Private	PERRY ROBT.
Private	PHILLIPS WM.
Private	PHILLIPS JAMES
Private	PIKE JOHN
Private	RENNON EDWD.
Private	ROGAN MICHL.
Private	SWEET SAML.
Private	STOKESLY WM.
Private	STORER GEO.
Private	SIMS MOSES
Private	STEPHENS WM.
Private	THOMAS JNS.
Private	TURNER WM.
Private	UPHAM THOS.
Private	WATTS FRANS.
Private	WHITE STEP.
Private	WILTON DANL.
Private	WILSON HENRY
Private	WITCHELL JOB
Private	WINTER CHAS.

Captain R. Phillip's Company

Captain	PHILLIPS R.
Lieutenant	MILLAR H.
Ensign	RUDD R,
Serjeant	SIMMONDS JNS.
Serjeant	DAVAGE JOSH
Serjeant	CAHILL JOSH
Private	BURROWS ROBT
Private	CARDLE JAMES
Private	CLARKE JNS
Private	DAVIS SAML.
Private	MINNS IS.
Private	WALKER WM.
Drummer	AUNGER JNS.
Private	ANDREWS GEO.
Private	ARMSTRONG IRWIN
Private	ASPINALL THOS.
Private	BULLPITT ELIJ.
Private	BAILY DANL.
Private	CURRANT JNS
Private	CLARKE ROBT.
Private	CLARKE JOSH
Private	CLEMENTS WM.
Private	CONLY MICHL.
Private	DAVIS MORGAN
Private	DAVID GEO.
Private	DWYER EDWD.
Private	EDWARDS EDWD.
Private	EDMONDS THOS.
Private	FELTHAM THOS.
Private	FRANCIS FRAS.
Private	FUDGE JAMES
Private	FOWLER JNS.
Private	GREEN THOS
Private	GHERIN LEWIS
Private	HILL JNS.
Private	HILL BENJN.
Private	HOBBS WM.
Private	HOPPERS JNS
Private	HUTCHINS WM.
Private	HALL SQUIRES Died 28th Sept. 1815
Private	KENNEDY JAMES
Private	KELLSELL EDMD.
Private	LAFFERTY BERND.
Private	LUXTON WM.
Private	MACKENSON THOS.
Private	MORDELL FREDK.
Private	MORRIS DOM.
Private	McCLEAN PATK.
Private	McDONALD REYNOLD
Private	MURRY CHRIS.
Private	McGUIRE THOS.
Private	NEAL WM.
Private	POPE JNS.
Private	PRITCHARD ALEXR.
Private	PURLES WM.
Private	PAUL WM.

Private	QUINN JNS.
Private	RICH FRNAS.
Private	RICHARDSON THOS.
Private	SAVAGE JAMES
Private	SPEARING JOSH
Private	SEAGAR ROBT.
Private	SCORCE ROBT.
Private	SIMMONS RICHD.
Private	SCAMMELL EDWD.
Private	SPICER JNS.
Private	SERRELLS THOS.
Private	STEPHENS THOS.
Private	SWEENEY EDWD.
Private	SWEET WM.
Private	TABOR WM.
Private	TRACE JNS.
Private	VALLANCE JOSH
Private	WHITLEY JNS.
Private	WHATLEY JNS.
Private	WILLCOX JAMES
Private	WRIGHT WM.
Private	WALSH WM.
Private	WILSON SAML.
Private	WRIGHT JAMES

Captain R.P. Stewart's Company

Captain	STEWART R.P.
Captain	FRANKLIN T.D.
Lieutenant	HUDSON R.
Ensign	HIBBERT G.
Serjeant	WHITE WM.
Serjeant	BROWNE JERE.
Serjeant	JOY THOS
Serjeant	SNELION JOHN
Serjeant	SIMMONS JOHN
Corporal	FRANCIS WM.
Corporal	GILMORE JNS.
Corporal	HENDERSON JAMES
Corporal	MORGAN HENRY
Corporal	WILLCOX WM.
Drummer	WOOLFE JAMES
Drummer	WHITE THOS
Private	ANGELL THOS
Private	ALLEN CHAS.
Private	BARRETT GILES
Private	BOWDEN WM.
Private	BIRT JAMES
Private	BAKER JNS
Private	CARLTON BERND.
Private	COTES JAMES
Private	CONNOR TIMY.
Private	COOPER WM.
Private	COOPER MICHL.
Private	CEIDDLE RICHD.
Private	CURRY EBEN.
Private	CURTIS DESPARD
Private	CURTIS WM.
Private	COCKEROFT ROBT. On sale at Fenton's Oct. 1909
Private	DREDGE JOHN
Private	DOWNING JOS
Private	DUDDING WM.
Private	FOOD RICHD.
Private	FRANKLIN WM. Died 18th June 1815
Private	FRIDAY WM.
Private	FOLLARD JNS.
Private	GORMLEY REY.
Private	GREEN JNS.
Private	HARPER JNS.
Private	HILBURN BENJN.
Private	HEWLETT CHAS.
Private	HOSGROVE GEO.
Private	HOSKINS THOS.
Private	HYNES JNS.
Private	JOHNS JOS.
Private	LEONARD JAMES
Private	LAKE RICHD.
Private	McCARDLE HENRY
Private	McADAM THOS.
Private	MANLY THOS.
Private	MORGAN JNS.
Private	MITCHELL JOB
Private	MATHERS JNS.
Private	MOORE WM.
Private	MURPHY DANL.
Private	McBURNY JNS.
Private	PAINE THOS.
Private	PEARCE JOHN
Private	RICHARDS JAMES
Private	RADFORD GEO.
Private	RICHANS JAMES
Private	SPRIGGS JNS.
Private	SIMS EDWD.
Private	SANDY HENRY
Private	STEPHENS JNS.
Private	STURGESS SAML.
Private	STEERS JNS.
Private	TOOPE JOS.
Private	TUCKER HUGH
Private	TAYLOR EDWD.

Private	WATTS JAMES
Private	WARD JOHN
Private	WEBBER JAMES
Private	WHELAN EDWD.
Private	WILLIAMS DAVID
Private	WILLIS HENRY
Private	WOODS JNS.
Private	WRIGHT JNS
Private	WELLS GEO.
Private	WINN THOS.

Captain J. Lowry's Company

Lieutenant	THEREAN J.
Lieutenant	NEILLY WM.
Ensign	ATKINSON G. Payne collection 1911
Serjeant	HODGE JNS.
Serjeant	BAKER WM.
Serjeant	BROWNE SAML.
Serjeant	DYKE WM.
Serjeant	STEWART SAML.
Corporal	TROTT JNS.
Corporal	INGE WM. Glendinings sale 17th June 1908
Drummer	DOYLE JAMES
Private	ASHFORD DANIEL
Private	ATKINS WM.
Private	BEEMAN JNS. Glendinings sale Feb. 1909
Private	BELL ROBT.
Private	BOWDEN JNS.
Private	BROOKS ROBT.
Private	BURNS JAMES
Private	BROWNE JNS.
Private	BULLEN JOSH
Private	BAILEY BENJN.
Private	CASWELL JNS.
Private	CADE FRANS.
Private	COSTELLO JNS.
Private	COLTER JNS.
Private	CLARKE JNS.
Private	COAXLY GEO.
Private	CUMMINGS JNS.
Private	DEERE WM.
Private	DAY JOS.
Private	DONAGHY OWEN
Private	DUNN ANTHY.
Private	FARR WM.
Private	FOGHELL LEWIS
Private	FRENCH WM.
Private	FURBUR FRANS.
Private	GORE JAMES
Private	GREENFIELD JOHN
Private	HOBBS WM.
Private	HAWKINS WM.
Private	HOPWOOD WM.
Private	HEATH JOHN
Private	INKERSOLE JAMES
Private	JAMES EDWD.
Private	LYE CHAS.
Private	LARKINS JOS.
Private	MARTIN RICHD.
Private	McGUIRE JNS.
Private	McGOVERN MICHL.
Private	McCALLEN HUGH
Private	McNAMARA JNS.
Private	MORTIMORE JNS.
Private	MONKETTRICK ANDW.
Private	NEWMAN GEO.
Private	POCOCK ROBT. Gascoign's collection March 1909
Private	PICKFORD JERE
Private	PASCOE JNS.
Private	PRICE JOS.
Private	PURNELL SAML.
Private	SANSOM GEO.
Private	SMITH THOS.
Private	SMITH JOS.
Private	STROM JAMES
Private	SMITH OWEN
Private	STEPHENS JAMES
Private	STANNIFORD W.
Private	SWEET JAMES
Private	TOTTERSHELL PETER
Private	TONER PETER
Private	ULLINGHAM JNS
Private	WELLS THOS.
Private	WADE JAMES
Private	WISE THOS
Private	WOODHOUSE THOS.
Private	WOODROW RICHD.
Private	WHEELER WM.
Private	YEOMAN THOS. Gray collection 1908

Captain C. Ellis's Company

Captain	ELLIS C. Wounded
Lieutenant	ANTHONY J. Wounded
Lieutenant	GLYNNE A.E. H.Gaskell's collection 1908
Lieutenant	Hon.BROWNE M. Wounded
Ensign	THORNHILL R.

Serjeant	DUNSTER THOS.
Serjeant	BURFORD CHAS.
Serjeant	WALSH PATK.
Serjeant	SAVIOUR SAML.
Corporal	GARNER WM.
Corporal	HANSON RICHD.
Corporal	LEWIS WM.
Drummer	KEATON GEO.
Drummer	BENNETT JAMES
Private	APPLEBY ROBT.
Private	BARKER JNS. 1st
Private	BARHAM WM.
Private	BROWNE ROBT.
Private	BERRYMAN JAMES
Private	BILLINGTON CHAS.
Private	BUTLER JAMES
Private	BEATY ROBT
Private	CAREY JNS.
Private	CONNERS EDWD.
Private	DANIELLS WM.
Private	DAVIS WM.
Private	DORAN JNS.
Private	DICKSON GEO.
Private	EVANS HOPKIN
Private	FINLY PATK.
Private	GILL RICHD.
Private	GODFREY JAMES
Private	GRATTON SAML.
Private	GREGORY JAMES
Private	GALLWIN MICHL.
Private	GREEN DANL.
Private	HALL THOS.
Private	HARRIS JAMES
Private	HUGHES HENRY
Private	HICKS WM.
Private	HILSBURY JAMES
Private	JACKSON WM.
Private	KELLY THOS.
Private	KATES WM.
Private	KENNAN JAMES
Private	LEONARD JOHN
Private	MILLS WM.
Private	McCONNELL DAVID
Private	MARRIOTT JAMES
Private	MATTHEWS HENRY
Private	MADDEN JNS
Private	MURPHY SAML.
Private	McPHARLAN ARTHUR
Private	NEWBURY JNS.
Private	NOUNAN JOSH
Private	NORRIS WM.
Private	POTTER ROBT.
Private	PARKER JNS.
Private	PENNY JOS.
Private	PORTERS JAMES
Private	REED 1st JOS. Sotheby's sale 19th June 1908
Private	REED 2nd JOS.
Private	ROSS JNS.
Private	RAY WM.
Private	SPEARING GEO.
Private	SMITH DENIS
Private	SWANGER JAMES
Private	STEWART MATTHEW
Private	TRISTRIM JNS.
Private	TRACEY THOS.
Private	TOOZE JAMES
Private	WILTSHIRE JNS.
Private	WARREN JAMES
Private	WATTS THOS.
Private	WHEATLEY ROBT.

* * *

42nd REGIMENT OF FOOT

Lt.Colonel	DICK R.H. Wounded Quatre Bras.
Major	MENRIES ARCH. Wounded
Adjutant	YOUNG JAMES Wounded
Qr.Master	McINTOSH DONALD
Surgeon	McLEOD SWINTON
Ass.Surgeon	McPHERSON DONALD
Ass.Surgeon	STEWART JNS.
Ensign	CLARKE CHRISTOPHER Roll at Record Office. Vol.in 69th
Captain	STEWART DUNCAN
Lt.Colonel	MACARA Sir R. K.C.B. Killed at Quatre Bras. Whitaker Coll.1908. (Medal given to relatives)

Captain John Cambell's Company

Captain	CAMPBELL JNS. (Lt.Col)
Lieutenant	MALEVLIN JNS.
Lieutenant	FRASER A.L.
S.Major	KING FINLAY
Q.M.S.	GRANT ALEX.
P.M.S.	WATSON WM.
Ar.Serjeant	PATOUN EDWD.
Dr.Major	MARTIN HUGH
Serjeant	FORBES JNS.
Serjeant	JOHNSTON ANDREW
Serjeant	MORRIS GEORGE
Serjeant	ROSS DONALD
Corporal	CHISHOLM WM.

Corporal	HENDERSON MITCHELL
Corporal	MATHIESON DUNCAN
Corporal	McPHERSON DONALD
Private	CAMPBELL DUNCAN
Private	CAMPBELL KENNETH Discharged
Private	CLARKE WM.
Private	CONOLLY MICHL.
Private	CUNNINGHAM ARCH.
Private	CRUIKSHANK ANDW.
Private	DAVIDSON DONALD
Private	FERGUSON JAMES
Private	FRASER DONALD
Private	FRASER HUGH
Private	GRAY PETER
Private	GRANT PETER
Private	GAVINS JAMES
Private	HOLMES DONALD
Private	HOLMES WM.
Private	MELVILLE ALEX. 1st.
Private	MELVILLE ALEX. 2nd
Private	MOODIE JNS.
Private	McCANN JAMES
Private	McDONALD DONALD
Private	McDONALD JNS.
Private	McDONALD RHODERICK
Private	McGLASHON JNS.
Private	McGREGOR ALEXR.
Private	McGREGOR DONALD 1st.
Private	McGREGOR DONALD 2nd.
Private	McINTOSH JAMES Discharged
Private	McKAY ANGUS Died of Wounds
Private	McKAY GEORGE
Private	McKAY KENNETH
Private	McKAY ROBERT
Private	McLES ALEX.
Private	McLEAN JOHN
Private	McLINNAN MURDH.
Private	McPHILS NEILL
Private	NICHOLOS JOHN
Private	PATOUN ROBERT
Private	PALSON LEWIS
Private	PRINGLE JOHN
Private	RIDDELL CHAS. Discharged
Private	ROSS DAWSON
Private	ROSS FINLAY
Private	ROSS HUGH
Private	ROBERTSON JAMES
Private	ROY DONALD
Private	ROYCROSS ROBERT
Private	SMITH JOHN
Private	STEVENSON JAMES
Private	SWEENEY WM.
Private	WILSON JOSH.

Captain Murdoch McLaine's Company

Lieutenant	MACKENZIE DONALD
Ensign	CUMMING ALEX.
Serjeant	ANTON JNS.
Serjeant	MAY ROBT.
Serjeant	McCOLE JNS.
Serjeant	McGRIGOR DONALD
Corporal	BOWMAN WM.
Corporal	MURRAY DONALD
Corporal	McGRIGOR DUNCAN
Corporal	McLAUGHLIN LAUGHLIN
Corporal	SCOTT ALEX.
Drummer	MOONEY BARNEY
Drummer	McDONALD DONALD
Private	ADGE JOHN Invalided
Private	ANDERSON JOHN
Private	BEATTIE DUNCAN
Private	BENNETT JOHN
Private	BENNETT WM.
Private	CAMERON DUNCAN
Private	CARRY ROBT.
Private	CHISHOLM ALEX.
Private	CLACHER JNS.
Private	DAVIDSON JNS.
Private	EDOMS GEO.
Private	EDGAR ALEX.
Private	FRASER ALEX.
Private	GOURDIE ROBT.
Private	GRANT JAMES
Private	HOCKNELL WM.
Private	HILLIARD WM.
Private	INNES JOHN
Private	IRVINE JAMES
Private	KELLY PATT.
Private	KILGOUR ALEX.
Private	LEITH DONALD
Private	LOAG JAMES
Private	LUMSDEN ALEX.
Private	METCALF JNS.
Private	MUNRO JNS. Dis.Invalid.
Private	McDONALD JAMES Needes Coll.1908
Private	McDONALD JNS.
Private	McDONALD RONALD
Private	McDONALD WM.
Private	McTAVISH ALEX.
Private	McEWEN PETER
Private	McGRIGOR WM.
Private	McINTOSH JOHN

Private	McRAY JOHN
Private	McKEWELL WM.
Private	NOBLE ALEX.
Private	POOL WM.
Private	REID JAMES
Private	ROSS DONALD
Private	SMART DAVID
Private	SLARK ROBERT
Private	TANCH ARCH.
Private	TOUGH GEO.
Private	WATSON JOHN
Private	WHITELAW CHAS.
Private	WILSON JOHN

Captain Mungo McPherson's Company

Captain	McPHERSON MUNGO Wounded
Lieutenant	FRASER HUGH A. Wounded
Lieutenant	DUNBAR ALEX.
Lieutenant	INNES ALEX.
Serjeant	DUFF WM.
Serjeant	McGRIGOR JNS.
Serjeant	McCONACHIE JAMES
Serjeant	McLEOD ALEX.
Serjeant	ROBERTSON DONALD
Corporal	HUTCHINSON JNS.
Corporal	KAY DAVID
Corporal	McDONALD JOHN
Corporal	McPHERSON ANGUS
Corporal	REID JNS.
Drummer	McKENZIE JOHN
Drummer	SUTHERLAND SINCLAIR
Private	AFFLECK JAMES
Private	ANDERSON DONALD
Private	BEATTIE JNS. Invalided
Private	BENNETT PETER
Private	BURST GEO.
Private	CALDER WM.
Private	DALLAS JAMES
Private	DAVIDSON WM.
Private	FOSTER THOS. Glendining's sale Dec. 1912
Private	GWILLAM JAMES
Private	JESSIMAN GEO.
Private	MARTIN ALEX.
Private	MATHIESON WM.
Private	MILLER WM.
Private	MITCHELL WALTER
Private	MUCKLE ALEX.
Private	MILLREA DENIS
Private	MORTON JNS.
Private	MORRISON ALEX.
Private	McDONALD COLIN Discharged
Private	McDONALD RICHARD
Private	McKAY DONALD
Private	McINTOSH JAMES
Private	McKENZIE WALTER Died of Wounds
Private	McPHERSON DOUGAL Cheylesmore Collection 1908
Private	McMANUS EDWD.
Private	McKINNON ALEX.
Private	McLEAN JOHN
Private	ORE GEORGE
Private	PRIDE JAMES
Private	RUTTLEDGE JAMES Discharged
Private	ROSS GEORGE
Private	RUSSELL JAMES
Private	SMOLLETT JAMES Gray Collection 1908
Private	SIMSON KENNETH
Private	STEWART CHAS.
Private	STOBBS BART.
Private	SWEENEY PETER
Private	TAYLOR GEO.
Private	TURNER JAMES
Private	WARNOCK JOHN
Private	WAUGH JAMES
Private	WEBSTER ROBERT

Captain(Lt.Col) Thos. F. Wade's Company

Lieutenant	McDOUGALL KENNETH
Serjeant	FERRIE ROBT.
Serjeant	McIVER JAMES Sotheby's sale 19th June 1908
Serjeant	POLSON HUGH
Corporal	GRANT DUNCAN
Corporal	MARTIN JAMES
Drummer	DUFF JOHN
Drummer	McINNES MALC.
Private	BAGGRAY JNS.
Private	BANKS JNS.
Private	BARCLAY WM.
Private	BARKER JAMES
Private	BEGBIE ANDW.
Private	BLAINEY WM.
Private	CAMERON RODK.
Private	CAMPBELL ARCH.
Private	CONELLY JAMES

Private	DENT JNS. Capt. Stewarts Collection 1912
Private	DUFF HENRY
Private	GILMOUR ANDW.
Private	GAW NEIL
Private	HALLIDAY JAMES
Private	HARVEY ALEX.
Private	HUGHES JAMES
Private	JACK WM.
Private	KANE JOSH.
Private	LONDON JAMES
Private	MATHIESON RODK.
Private	MORRIS JOHN
Private	McALLISTER ALEX.
Private	McDONALD DOND.
Private	McGRIGOR JOHN
Private	McINTOSH JOHN
Private	McKAY DOND.
Private	McKILLOP ARCH.
Private	McLINNAN JOHN
Private	McMANUS HUGH
Private	McTAVISH HENRY
Private	PEARCE RICHD.
Private	RANDALL GEO.
Private	REID GEO. Invalided
Private	ROBERTSON DAVID
Private	ROSS ANDW.
Private	ROSS MATTHEW Discharged
Private	ROSS ROBERT
Private	SMITH JNS.
Private	STEWART ROBT.
Private	STEVENSON JAMES
Private	SUTHERLAND ARTHUR
Private	SUTHERLAND JAMES
Private	SUTHERLAND WM.
Private	TAYLOR CHAS.
Private	WARWICK JNS.
Private	WALTON WM.
Private	WILSON GILBERT

Captain Donald McDonald's Company

Captain	McDONALD DONALD Wounded H. Gaskells Coll. 1908 Payne 1911
Lieutenant	BRANDER JAMES
Lieutenant	STEWART ROGER
Lieutenant	GRANT JOHN
Serjeant	CHRISTIE JOHN
Serjeant	GRAHAM WM.
Serjeant	McDONALD GEORGE
Serjeant	ROSS WM.
Corporal	BETHUNE ALEX. Died of Wounds
Corporal	CAMPBELL ALEX.
Corporal	McKAY EDWD.
Drummer	AICHESON THOS.
Drummer	MURPHY WM. Cheylesmore Collection 1908
Drummer	MacKENZIE WM.
Private	ANDERSON CHAS.
Private	ANDERSON JAMES
Private	BAILLIE GEO.
Private	BAIN JNS.
Private	CAMERON DONALD
Private	CAMPBELL WM.
Private	CARROLL DAVID
Private	COGHILL WM.
Private	DELANEY JOHN
Private	DOUGLAS HUGH
Private	FRASER JOHN
Private	HAILBURTON JAMES
Private	HENDERSON DAVID
Private	MORRISON DAVID
Private	McARTHUR COLIN
Private	McCONNELL HUGH
Private	McDONALD DOND.
Private	McDONALD RONALD
Private	McDONALD THOS.
Private	McDOUGALL JOHN
Private	McKAY DOND.
Private	McKINLEY WM. Captain Stewart Collection 1912
Private	McRESSACK ARCH.
Private	McLEOD DOND.
Private	McLEAN ALEX.
Private	McLENNAN DUNCAN
Private	McLENNAN MURDOCH
Private	McPHERSON OWEN
Private	PATERSON JAMES
Private	RITCHIE JNS.
Private	ROBERTSON JAMES
Private	ROURKE JAMES
Private	ROSS ALEX. 1st.
Private	ROSS ALEX. 2nd.
Private	SHAW NEIL
Private	SHARPE GEO.
Private	STEDMAN WM.
Private	STERRATT DANIEL
Private	SUTHERLAND WM.
Private	SWANSON DONALD.
Private	SWEENEY JNS.
Private	TOUR JOHN

Private	TOWNS WM.
Private	TURNBULL JOHN
Private	WATERS JAMES
Private	WHITE WM.
Private	WEELEY ANDW.

Captain Daniel McIntosh's Company

Captain	McINTOSH DANIEL Wounded
Lieutenant	ROBERTSON JAMES
Serjeant	BANKIER WM.
Serjeant	EVANS THOS.
Serjeant	YOUNG JNS.
Corporal	MUNRO ALEX.
Corporal	McKENZIE COLIN
Corporal	SMITH JOHN
Private	ADAMS WM.
Private	ANDERSON ANGUS
Private	BARRIE JAMES
Private	BRANNON CHRISTR. Discharged
Private	CAMPBELL JOHN
Private	CATTNACH LEWIS
Private	CONDY GIBSON
Private	DUNCAN DAVID
Private	FERGUSON DONALD Col. Gaskell's sale May 1911
Private	FRASER ALEX.
Private	FRASER KENNETH
Private	GRANT JOHN
Private	GREEN JOHN
Private	HOLMES ARTHUR
Private	JACKSON DONALD
Private	JOHNSTON WM. Glendinings sale Feb. 1913
Private	KELLY CHAS.
Private	KENNEDY JAMES
Private	LEVACH DAVID
Private	MILNE JOHN
Private	MUNRO DUNCAN
Private	MUNRO HUGH
Private	McCULLOCK DONALD
Private	McDONALD ANGUS
Private	McDONALD HUGH
Private	McGRIGOR ALEX.
Private	McINTOSH JNS.
Private	McKAY JNS. 1st.
Private	McKAY JNS. 2nd.
Private	McKAY WM.
Private	McKENZIE DONALD
Private	McLAREN JAMES
Private	McLEOD JOHN
Private	McLEOD WM.
Private	NICOL WM.
Private	NICOL WM.
Private	PANTON JAMES Invalided
Private	ROBERTSON DAVID
Private	ROSS ALEX.
Private	ROSS DONALD
Private	ROSS WM. Phillips sale
Private	SMITH DONALD
Private	SYMONS JAMES
Private	WATSON JOHN
Private	WHITTLE JAMES
Private	WILSON WM. Galway Foley Collection 1910

Captain Robert Boyle's Company

Captain	BOYLE ROBT. Wounded Payne Collection 1911
Serjeant	SUTHERLAND DONALD
Serjeant	WHITE DONALD
Corporal	McKENZIE JOHN Discharged
Drummer	WATT JAMES
Private	AITKEN GEORGE
Private	CAMPBELL JAMES
Private	CAMPBELL WM.
Private	CHRUNCHIE JNS.
Private	CRAIB ALEX.
Private	CURTAIN THOS.
Private	DOWNIE JAMES
Private	DOWNIE JOHN
Private	FENNER JOHN
Private	FOWLER JOHN
Private	GRAHAM ALEX.
Private	HAMILTON HUGH
Private	HAMILTON JAMES
Private	HETHERINGTON THOS.
Private	LINDSAY THOS.
Private	LITTLE WALTER
Private	MARTIN MARTIN
Private	MERSON JOHN
Private	MUNRO DONALD
Private	MUNRO JOHN
Private	McARTHUR PETER
Private	McCALLUM DONALD
Private	McELLRAY GEO.
Private	McKAY ANGUS
Private	McKAY DONALD
Private	McKAY GEO.
Private	McKAY JAMES
Private	McRECHNIE JOHN
Private	McRECHNIE HUGH
Private	McKENZIE DAVID Discharged
Private	McKENZIE DONALD
Private	NICOLSON MURDOCH

Private	PARSONS DANIEL
Private	ROBERTSON PETER
Private	ROSS ALEX.
Private	ROSS JOHN
Private	RUSELL ARCH.
Private	RYRIE JAMES Invalided
Private	SMITH WM.
Private	STEWART ALEX.
Private	STEWART JOHN
Private	SUTHERLAND JOHN
Private	SUTHERLAND WM.
Private	THOMSON WM.
Private	TULLOCH GILBERT
Private	WALLACE MATTHEW
Private	YARDLEY SAML.

Captain James Stirling's Company

Lieutenant	MUNRO GEO. GUN. Wounded
Lieutenant	BROWN ALEX.
Serjeant	DUNN WM.
Serjeant	GOURLEY THOS.
Corporal	McINTOSH HUGH
Corporal	McEWAN ALEX.
Drummer	McLEOD ANGUS
Private	CAMERON EWAN
Private	CALDWELL WLATER
Private	CHAMBERS DUFF
Private	CHISHOLM RODK.
Private	DARE GEO.
Private	DONALD WM.
Private	DUNCAN WM.
Private	DRISCOLL TIMY.
Private	FRASER FONALD 1st
Private	FRASER DONALD 2nd
Private	GUNN JAMES
Private	MASON WM.
Private	MITCHELL WM. Discharged
Private	McCALLUM JOHN
Private	McDONALD ALEX.
Private	McDONALD ANGUS
Private	McDONALD RONALD Discharged
Private	McCAWAN JAMES
Private	McHARDY CHAS.
Private	McINTOSH DONALD
Private	McINTOSH JAMES
Private	McLEAN DONALD
Private	McLEAN JOHN
Private	McLAREN DONALD
Private	McLINNAN COLIN
Private	RANDALL JOHN
Private	RIDDELL ROBT.
Private	RITCHIE WM.
Private	ROBERTSON JAMES
Private	ROSS DONALD
Private	ROSS JOHN
Private	ROSS WM.
Private	SCOTT DUNCAN
Private	SHERRIFFS JAMES
Private	SMITH JAMES
Private	SMITH DONALD
Private	SMITH JOHN
Private	SMITH PETER
Private	SMITH ROBERT
Private	SMITH JAMES
Private	SUTHERLAND JOHN
Private	VINT BENJN.
Private	WYLIE JAMES 1st Discharged
Private	WYLIE JAMES 2nd

Captain Alexander Fraser's Company

Captain	FRASER ALEX.
Lieutenant	ORR JOHN Wounded
Lieutenant	FRASER WM.
Serjeant	SHAW DONALD
Serjeant	SHAW JOHN
Serjeant	THOMSON NINIAN
Serjeant	WATSON JAMES
Corporal	BAIN WM.
Corporal	HENDERSON RODK.
Corporal	SMITH JOHN
Drummer	McKENZIE LAUGHLIN
Drummer	STILL JOHN
Private	BAIN ALEX.
Private	BARKER CHAS.
Private	BARCLAY JOHN
Private	BARBER WM.
Private	BROWN DONALD
Private	BREMNER JOHN
Private	CAIE JAMES
Private	CAMERON ALEX.
Private	CAMERON JOHN
Private	DOGHERTY JOHN
Private	FYFE JAMES Col.Murray's collection 1908
Private	GEDDES FRANCIS WM.
Private	GILLIES ALEX.
Private	GOSNELL JAMES
Private	GRANT DUNCAN
Private	GUNN JAMES
Private	GRAHAM GEO.

Private HENDERSON ANDW.

Private HANILAN PATT.

Private HENDERSON PETER

Private JOHNSTON WM.

Private LONGSTAFF JOHN

Private MILLER WM.

Private MOIR JOHN

Private MUNRO DAVID

Private MUNRO WM.

Private McCALLIE JOSH.

Private McDONALD DONALD

Private McDONALD ROBERT

Private McKAY WM.

Private McKENZIE ALEX.

Private McKINLAY WM.

Private McLACHLAN JAMES

Private McLEAN DAVID

Private McLEOD DONALD

Private O'NEAL DANIEL

Private ROY DONALD

Private ROSS DONALD

Private SHUAN WM.

Private SINCLAIR WM.

Private SUTHERLAND JOHN

Private TAITT JAMES

Private THOMPSON JOSH.

Private VEITCH STEVEN

Private WALLACE THOS.

Private WILSON WM.

Captain Donald Chisholm's Company

Captain CHISHOLM DONALD Wounded

Lieutenant MacKAY DONALD Glendining's sale 17 June 1908

Serjeant BARLOW MICHL.

Serjeant BISSETT WM.

Serjeant PATTERSON WM.

Corporal ARNOTT JOHN

Corporal FORRESTER FREDK.

Corporal LESLIE ROBERT

Drummer PATTERSON WM.

Private BATCHELOR DOCTOR

Private CAIRNS JOHN

Private CAMPBELL WM.

Private DUNCAN JAMES Payne Collection 1911

Private EMMERSON JOHN

Private FIFE SMITH

Private FISHER DANIEL

Private FLEMING THOS.

Private GUNN WM.

Private HARPER ANDREW

Private HUTCHISON JOHN

Private JOHNSTON JAMES

Private KIRKWOOD ALEX.

Private KYLE ROBT.

Private LAMONT JAMES

Private LAWSON JOHN Died of Wounds

Private LAWSELL WM.

Private MILLAR MURRAY

Private MULLEN FRANS. Invalided

Private MUNRO JOHN

Private McCRAW ALEX.

Private McDONALD HECTOR

Private McDONALD HUGH

Private McDONALD JOHN

Private McINTOSH ALEX.

Private McKAY DONALD 1st

Private McKAY DONALD 2nd.

Private McLEOD JOHN

Private McPHERSON LACHLAN

Private ROBERTSON DUNCAN

Private ROSS HUGH

Private ROSS WALTER

Private SINCLAIR ARCH. Col.Murray's Collection 1908

Private SNEIDDON JAMES

Private SUTHERLAND GEO.

Private STEWART DAVID

Private TAYLOR JAMES

Private WATT GEO.

Private WATT JOHN

Private WISEMAN ANDREW

* * *

44th REGIMENT OF FOOT

Lt.Colonel HAMERTON J.M. Wounded

Lt.Major O'MALLEY GEO. (Lt.Col)

Adjutant McCANN THOS. Wounded

Surgeon HALPIN OLIVER

Ass.Surgeon COLLINS JOHN

Ass.Surgeon NEWTON WILLIAM

Captain David Power's Company

Captain POWER DAVID Wounded

Lieutenant RUSSELL ROBT. Wounded

S.Major CORCORAN JAMES

Q.M.S. ROSSITER JOHN Gray Collection 1908

Ar.Serjeant BOYDE HENRY

Serjeant	DUCKWORTH SAML.
Serjeant	GORDON JNS.
Serjeant	LYSTER FORBES
Serjeant	OWENS MICHL.
Serjeant	DICK ROBT. Died 19 Aug '15
Corporal	SMITH ROBT. Inv. Chelsea
Corporal	McKNIGHT FRANS.
Drummer	FENNELLY DAVID
Drummer	McCONNELL JOHN
Private	ADAM PATK.
Private	BAILEY JNS.
Private	BUTTERWORTH JAMES
Private	BROOKS JNS.
Private	BOGAN ROBT.
Private	CHAMBERLAIN ROBT. Died 4th Jan. '16
Private	COLLINS CHAS.
Private	COSTELLO MICHL. Deserted 20 Sept. 1815
Private	CAHILL ANTHY.
Private	CONNELLY WM. Invalided
Private	DOYLE JAMES
Private	EMONY WM.
Private	FURLONG GARRETT
Private	FAIR JAMES
Private	GILLMORE JNS
Private	GLEESON JAMES
Private	HARRIGAN PATT.
Private	HERALD EDWD.
Private	HAMILTON JAMES
Private	HIGGINS WM.
Private	JOHNSTONE HENRY Invalided
Private	JAMES BENJN.
Private	LANE JAMES Died July 1815
Private	LEE ALEX.
Private	McCONNELL JAMES
Private	McQUAIDE PATT.
Private	McDONALD DENIS Discharged
Private	NUTTALL GEO.
Private	PARRATT ELIJAH Died Jan 1816
Private	QUINN JNS.
Private	RAWLINSON WM. Died 17 July 1815
Private	WALLACE HENRY
Private	WHELAN FENTON
Private	WHITTAKER CHARLEY

Captain Thomas Mackrell's Company

Lieutenant	MARTIN HENRY
Lieutenant	HEARN WM.
Ensign	WHITNEY BENJN. Wounded
Serjeant	SCOTT THOS. Invalided. Col.R.T.Gascoignes collec.1909
Serjeant	STEELE RICHD.
Corporal	DAWBER THOS.
Corporal	FOLEY MICHL.
Corporal	SCOTT GEORGE
Drummer	GARWOOD SAMUEL Invalided
Private	AGNEW JOHN
Private	BRIEN JOHN
Private	BARLOW JOSHUA
Private	BLONG PETER
Private	BYRNE JOHN
Private	CULLEN JOHN Invalided
Private	COOPER THOS.
Private	HOWARD PETER
Private	HARRIS DANL.
Private	HAGERTY JAMES
Private	HANLEY PETER
Private	HORAN THOS.
Private	JEFFERS AMBS.
Private	KING JAMES
Private	LARKIN JOHN
Private	LEDDY JOHN
Private	LEWIS JOHN
Private	McCORMICK DAVID
Private	MEAGHER PATT.
Private	MacDONALD EDWD.
Private	MacDONALD WM.
Private	MORGAN PATT.
Private	MAURICE WM.
Private	MUNSAY THOS.
Private	MILLER WM. Invalided Chelsea
Private	McGRATH ANTHY. Invalided Chelsea
Private	McCABE THOS.
Private	O'BRIEN JAMES
Private	OWENS THOS.
Private	ORRELL ISSAC
Private	POWER JAMES Invalided Dublin
Private	PARKINSON CUTHT.
Private	PARNELL THOS.
Private	RAMSEY JNS. Discharged
Private	REARDON JNS.
Private	SULLIVAN PATT.
Private	WOOLSHAN JAMES Invalided
Private	WALL JOHN Invalided
Private	WILLER WM. Invalided

Captain W.A. Craig's Company

Serjeant	RADCLIFFE THOS. Invalided H.Gaskell's Collection 1908
Serjeant	McNAMARA JNS.

Serjeant	PARSLOW THOS.
Serjeant	PAYNE WM.
Corporal	GALLAGHER JNS. Invalided
Corporal	CUNNINGHAM JNS.
Corporal	OWENS THOS.
Drummer	MARTIN JAMES
Private	BRIEN JOHN
Private	BAKER GEO.
Private	BAILEY WM.
Private	BONHAM EDWD.
Private	CONROY PATT.
Private	DOGHERTY GARRETT
Private	DWYER FRANS. Cheylesmore Collection 1908
Private	ENNIS CHRISTR. Invalided
Private	FRENCH JOHN
Private	FRANCIS JOHN
Private	FARRELL MICHL.
Private	GREENE THOS.
Private	KENNY JAMES
Private	LINNEGAR HENRY
Private	McLEAN PATT.
Private	MAHON THOS. Sick in France
Private	MALLEN JAMES
Private	McGRATH MICHL.
Private	MOONEY DANL.
Private	McKERLEY SAML.
Private	MAHON WM.
Private	MADDELL MATTW. Invalided
Private	NOBLE JAMES
Private	O'NEILLE JAMES
Private	PARISH JOHN
Private	PLANT JOHN
Private	PRICE RICHD. Invalided
Private	POWELL FRANS.
Private	PHIPPS ROBT.
Private	ROBBINS WM. Sick in France
Private	SCOTT JNS.
Private	TURNER JNS.
Private	WHELAN GEO.

<u>Captain G.C. Hill's Company</u>

Lieutenant	TOMKINS WM. Killed 16th June 1815
Ensign	COOKE P. Killed 16th June 1815. Glendinings sale 1911
Serjeant	CLARKE THOS.
Serjeant	GREYDON RICHD.
Serjeant	O'NEIL JOHN
Serjeant	REDMOND HENRY
Corporal	BAUGH BENJN.
Corporal	DELANEY JAMES
Corporal	SIMPSOM PATT. Invalided
Corporal	WHELAN WARNER
Drummer	BRANNIGAN JOHN
Drummer	QUINN PATT.
Private	AUSTIN HENRY
Private	BURKE CHRISTR. Invalided
Private	BYRNES JOHN Sick in Dover
Private	BYRNES JAMES Sick in Dover
Private	CALLAGHAN JNS.
Private	CHAMBERLAIN SAM.
Private	CAMPBELL JNS.
Private	CONROY HUGH
Private	COLLISTER JAMES Invalided
Private	DUFLY PATT.
Private	DOWNEY JOHN
Private	DELANY PATT.
Private	ELPHIE JOHN
Private	FORSTER ALEX.
Private	GEARY MICHL. Died 29 Oct'15
Private	HARKINS PATT.
Private	HARDGRAVES ROBT.
Private	KELLY THADY.
Private	KNOWLES JOSEPH
Private	LYNHAM JAMES
Private	LYNHAM THOS.
Private	MEALY JAMES Invalided
Private	MURRAY THOS.
Private	McKEFFERTY DENIS
Private	MURPHY GEO.
Private	PANKHURST THOS.
Private	PEATTON JOHN
Private	ROBINSON HENRY
Private	SULLIVAN JOHN
Private	SULLIVAN CORNS.
Private	SPELLMAN JOHN
Private	WOODS HENRY Invalided
Private	WARREN GEORGE
Private	WINTERS CHAS.

<u>Captain Mildmay Fane's Company</u>

Captain	FANE MILDMAY Wounded
Lieutenant	TWINBERROW R.J.
Lieutenant	BURKE JAMES
Serjeant	SHEEHY EDWD.
Serjeant	AMOS JAMES
Serjeant	HART MICH. Died 6 Aug '15
Corporal	KENNY CHAS.
Corporal	DURNARS ADAM
Corporal	SMITH WM.

Drummer	MAGILL RICHD.
Drummer	MAGILL GREGORY
Private	ARKLE ALEX. Discharged
Private	BUTLER JAMES
Private	BANNISTER RICHD.
Private	BURKE JOSEPH Discharged
Private	COLLETT SAML. Invalided Col.Murray's Coll. 1908
Private	CROGHAN MICHL Discharged
Private	CANFIELD DARBY
Private	CONNELL JOHN
Private	CONNELLY JOHN
Private	DONNELLY EDWD.
Private	DELANY JAMES
Private	GORE THOS. Invalided
Private	HUMPHRIES HENRY
Private	HOLMES JAMES
Private	HEATTON JOHN
Private	KELLY PETER
Private	KORRIGAN DENIS
Private	KERRIGAN PATT. Sick in France
Private	KENEDY JAMES
Private	KEEFE THOS. Invalided
Private	LYONS JOHN
Private	MULCAHY DAVID
Private	MILLER JAMES
Private	McDERMOTT THOS.
Private	MURPHY DANL. Invalided
Private	MAGUIRE CHAS.
Private	MEREDITH JOSH.
Private	McMAHON JAMES Invalided
Private	NUNAN THOS.
Private	REYNOLDS RHODES Invalided
Private	ROBINSON JOHN
Private	STOTT JOSEPH
Private	SYMMS EDWD Invalided
Private	WHELAN JAMES
Private	DELANY WM. Dis.Chelsea

<u>Captain T.A. Dudie's Company</u>

Lieutenant	CAMPBELL JOHN Wounded
Ensign	CHRISTIE JOHN Wounded
Serjeant	WHELAN LAWRENCE Discharged but present with Reg.
Serjeant	TILER EDWD. Invalided
Serjeant	GLANDINNING JAMES Invalided
Serjeant	VHAIR JOHN
Serjeant	FLAXMAN WM. Invalided
Corporal	LEE JOHN
Corporal	MURRAY RICHD.
Corporal	LANE ANTHY. Discharged
Drummer	VARDOE CHAS.
Drummer	DONCHUE PATT.
Private	ALSOP JOHN Invalided
Private	BARTLY JOHN Invalided
Private	BYRNS MICHL.
Private	BARDSLEY JOHN
Private	BRAITHWAIT WM.
Private	CLENDINNING JOHN
Private	COTTLE WM.
Private	COGLAN JOHN
Private	DILLON ANDW.
Private	DILLON JOHN
Private	DAWSON WM.
Private	ELLIOTT ANDW.
Private	FERGUSON PATT.
Private	GALVIN TIMY.
Private	HAGUE THOS.
Private	HOWARD JOHN Discharged
Private	KENNY JOHN Sick in France
Private	KENNEDY JAMES
Private	KERLEY WALTER
Private	LEWIS THOS.
Private	McELROY CRNS.
Private	McELROY THOS.
Private	McCARTHY CHAS.
Private	MILLS THOS.
Private	NORTH FRANCIS
Private	OWENS THOS.
Private	PEARSON THOS. Invalided
Private	RENCHARD WM.
Private	REILLY ABRTW.
Private	SHEENAN PATT.
Private	SHARP JOHN
Private	TEELING THOS.
Private	TRACEY THOS. Invalided
Private	VINCENT WM.

<u>Captain William Burney's Company</u>

Captain	burney wm.
Lieutenant	STRONG W.B.
Serjeant	LITTLE COTTRELL
Serjeant	MOORE PETER
Drummer	SIMPTON SAML.
Private	BAXTER CHAS. Glendining's Sale Oct 1913 10-0-0
Private	BYRNE MARK Invalided
Private	BUCKLEY WALTER Invalided
Private	BROOKS THOS. Invalided

Private	BRODRICK GEO.
Private	CONNOR LAWRENCE
Private	CAMPBELL PATT. Discharged
Private	DELANY MICHL. Killed 16th June 1815
Private	DUFFY CHAS.
Private	FERGUSON ROBT.
Private	FARRELL ROGER
Private	GILMORE JOHN
Private	HORNSBY RICHD.
Private	HORRIGAN DANL.
Private	HAYES JAMES Invalided
Private	McGUIRE THOS.
Private	MANN ALEX.
Private	POWELL JAMES
Private	PHYLAN JOHN Invalided
Private	PARKS HUGH Invalided
Private	ROSSITER RICHD.
Private	REILLY JOHN Sick in France
Private	RYAN MICHL. Died 5 July '15
Private	STUART WM.
Private	SMITH WM. Invalided
Private	SCOTT CHAS.
Private	TYGHE JAMES Invalided
Private	TAYLOR THOS.
Private	WRIGHT JOSH. 2nd
Private	WARDLEY THOS.
Private	WALTERS JAMES
Private	WALSH JAMES

Captain Bostock Jacob's Company

Ensign	DUNLEVIS G.
Ensign	WEBSTER A. Wounded
Serjeant	HANNIGAN THOS.
Serjeant	HENNESSY EDWD.
Serjeant	HANNAGH JOSH.
Serjeant	KELLY DAVID
Corporal	JONES SAML.
Corporal	MYERS MICHL Discharged
Corporal	STANTON EDWD.
Drummer	O'MEARA MAURICE
Drummer	O'MEARA MATTW. Needes Collection 1911
Private	ADAMS GEO.
Private	BUGGY RICHD. Invalided
Private	BLICK JOB
Private	BUTLER WM. Invalided
Private	CONWAY WM.
Private	CLIFFORD JAMES
Private	CASEY DANIEL
Private	HORNER STEPN.
Private	HAMPSON GEO.
Private	HAYES WM. Invalided
Private	FLANNAGAN JOHN Invalided
Private	KENAGH THOS.
Private	LITTLE JOSH.
Private	McGAHAN HUGH
Private	MURPHY JAMES
Private	McCALL HUGH
Private	MAXWELL JOHN Invalided
Private	POWER PATT.
Private	PALMER THOS.
Private	RODGERS JAMES
Private	REEVES JOHN
Private	READY MAURICE
Private	REILLY PATT.
Private	STUART WM.
Private	STUARD ALEX.
Private	SCHOFIELD JAMES Sick in Dover
Private	SHEEDY WM.
Private	SHEEDY MICHL.
Private	SAUNDERS BENJN.
Private	STONE THOS. Sick in France
Private	TURNER ORMSBY
Private	TAYLOR JOHN
Private	WEBSTER JOHN
Private	WALSH JOHN

Captain George Crozier's Company

Lieutenant	KINGSLEY N.S.
Lieutenant	REDDOCK A.
Serjeant	LARKIN W.
Serjeant	WATERS PETER Invalided
Corporal	BURKE DENIS Invalided
Corporal	CONWAY JOHN Killed 16 June
Corporal	FITZPATRICK MARTIN
Corporal	MULLENS JAMES Invalided
Drummer	O'BRIEN DENIS
Private	ATKINS JOHN
Private	BEECE GEORGE
Private	BENSKIN JOHN
Private	BROWNE EDWD.
Private	BAMPTON RICHD.
Private	CARROLL TIMY.
Private	CASEY OWEN
Private	COLLINS THOS.
Private	CARNEY JAMES

Private	DONNELLY DANIEL
Private	FITZPATRICK PATT.
Private	FOY JOHN
Private	GREEN JOHN
Private	HAYE JOHN
Private	HADLON ROBT.
Private	HOUGH JOHN Whitaker Collection 1908
Private	JOHNSTON WM.
Private	JENKINSON JOHN Day Sale April 1910
Private	KEARNEY JOHN Died 24th June '15
Private	LAWLER JAMES Discharged
Private	MOTLEY JAMES
Private	McGRATH MICHL. Invalided
Private	NICHOLSON JNS.
Private	NOADE THOS.
Private	PAGETT ELIJAH Sick in Flanders
Private	PARKER JOHN Invalided
Private	QUINN MICHL. Invalided
Private	QUINN HUGH Invalided
Private	SMITH JNS.
Private	SIMMONS SAML. Invalided
Private	SOLOMON JNS.
Private	TOLLY JOSH.

Captain A. Brugh's Company

Captain	BRUGH ADAM Wounded
Lieutenant	GRIER ROBT.
Serjeant	GRIFFEN JOHN
Serjeant	KELLY JOHN
Serjeant	MOORE RICHARD
Corporal	CRONABERRY PHILLIP
Corporal	FINNELLY JOSHUA
Corporal	DODGE JOHN
Drummer	KEANE MICHL.
Private	BYRNES GEO.
Private	BRYAN FRANS.
Private	BOYLE JOHN
Private	BRYAN JOHN
Private	BERRY RICHD. Invalided
Private	BROOM JOHN Invalided Payne Collection 1911
Private	BARRY PATT. Sick in France
Private	CORE PATT.
Private	CARTHY MORGAN
Private	CONNOR JOHN
Private	CONNOR MICHL.
Private	CLEARY DENIS
Private	DONNELLY JAMES Invalided
Private	DONNELLY JOHN
Private	FAIRCLOUGH THOS.
Private	HAYES MICHL.
Private	HINDS JOHN
Private	HOLLAND JOHN Invalided
Private	HOLBRO SAML.
Private	JOHNSTONE TARLETON
Private	LYNCH PATT.
Private	MINNOCK JAMES
Private	MORAN PATT. Invalided
Private	McNAMARA PATT. Invalided
Private	NEVIN JAMES
Private	PRESTON EDWD.
Private	PENDLETON PETER Died 7th Jan.'16
Private	REILLY JOHN Died 7th Jan.'16
Private	RYAN PATT.
Private	REYNOLDS MARK
Private	RODD JOSH.
Private	SHERIDAN THOS.
Private	SHECHEY JOHN
Private	SUTTON PETER
Private	TOLLY THOS.
Private	WALKER JOHN
Private	WILLETTS NOAH Dead
Private	WILLIAMS WM.
Private	WILSON WM. Discharged
Private	YARRINGTON WM.

* * *

51st REGIMENT OF LIGHT INFANTRY

Lt. Colonel	MITCHELL H.H. (Col) Commd. 4th Brigade
Major	RICE SAML. (Lt.Col)
Major	THWAITES WM.
Adjutant	TONES WM.
Qr.Master	ASKEY THOS.
Surgeon	WEBSTER RICHD.
Ass.Surgeon	CLARKE J.F.
Ass.Surgeon	FITZPATRICK PERCY
Pay Master	GIBBS JOHN
Captain	MINCHIN FRANCIS

Captain J.T. Keyt's Company

Captain	KEYT J.T.
Lieutenant	HARE W.H.
Lieutenant	HAMANK JOHN
Lieutenant	ROBERTS H.H.
Ensign	JOHNSTON WM.
Sjt.Major	DAVID DAVID
Q.M.S.	VICKERMAN EDWD.
P.M.S.	BUSSIERE JOHN
Serjeant	FEGAN MICHL
Serjeant	McGRATH THOS.

Serjeant	STEPHENS JOHN
Corporal	BARRY ABRAM.
Drummer	FORD LAWRENCE
Private	ABERTON WM.
Private	ABBOTT JOHN
Private	ALLEN CHARLES
Private	ARDERLY DAVID
Private	BALL JOHN
Private	BOXALL THOS.
Private	BROWN ISSAC
Private	BRAMBLE WM.
Private	BENWELL THOS.
Private	CHARLWOOD WM.
Private	CROSSLEY FRANS.
Private	CHEETHAM HENRY
Private	DANIELS THOS. Whitaker Collection 1908
Private	DANIELS MATTW.
Private	DURNING GEO.
Private	DURRANT JOHN
Private	DEVINEY WM.
Private	DOUGLAS JOSH.
Private	DAVIS WM.
Private	DINGAY WM.
Private	ELLIS ISSAC
Private	FORFAY JOHN
Private	GILL ROBERT
Private	GUILDFORD GEO.
Private	HATFIELD GEO.
Private	HEATON GEO.
Private	HOYLE JOHN
Private	HUNSWORTH JOHN
Private	HUMPHRIES FREDK.
Private	JONES THOS.
Private	JUTSON CHAS.
Private	KILLICK JOHN
Private	LOCKWOOD GEO.
Private	McCONVILL CHRISTR.
Private	MITCHELL THOS.
Private	MORGAN RICHD.
Private	NAYLOR JAMES
Private	NUTTALL RICHD.
Private	PRICE WM.
Private	PETER RICHD.
Private	POWELL JAMES
Private	SMITH RICHD.
Private	SMITH JOSH.
Private	SYKES JOSH.
Private	THWAITES WM.
Private	WALSH MARTIN
Private	WILLIAMS JOHN
Private	WILLIAMSON THOS.
Private	WOOD WM.

Captain James Campbell's Company

Captain	CAMPBELL JAMES
Lieutenant	ELLIOTT W.H.
Lieutenant	LINTOTT JOHN
Ensign	LOCK HENRY
Serjeant	ADAMS JAMES
Serjeant	ELLICK JAMES
Serjeant	NORTHY MARTIN
Serjeant	LEES THOS.
Serjeant	WHEELER WM.
Corporal	BARRACLOUGH JOSH.
Corporal	MOORHOUSE JOHN
Corporal	RIDGMENT JOHN
Corporal	WHITTLE JAMES
Drummer	SKIN JOHN
Private	ARMITAGE GEORGE
Private	ASHWORTH EDWD.
Private	ATKINS JOHN
Private	BARNETT WM.
Private	BROWN GEORGE
Private	CAMP JOHN
Private	CHIPPING JAMES
Private	CHUDLEY THOS.
Private	COOPER WM.
Private	CLEMENTS JOHN
Private	DARCEY PHILIP
Private	DEXLY WM.
Private	DOYLE EDWD.
Private	EVANS WM.
Private	FARRANT JOHN
Private	FINNEY JOHN
Private	FOWLES GEORGE
Private	GROOM JOHN
Private	HOWARD JOHN
Private	HARMS THOS.
Private	HIGGINS MICHL.
Private	JOBBINS JAMES
Private	IRON ROBT.
Private	ISSACS ISSAC
Private	JACKSON WM.
Private	JOHNSTONE JOSH.
Private	JACKSON JOHN
Private	KERSHAW JOSH.
Private	LAMB GEORGE
Private	LAMPORT ROBT.
Private	LASHBROOK JOHN
Private	McDONALD CHAS.
Private	MACHIN JOHN

Private	MARSHALL JAMES
Private	MAUNDER ISRAEL
Private	MORRIS JAMES
Private	MOULD JOHN
Private	NURSE GEORGE Adamson Collection Jan. 1911
Private	POOLEY WM.
Private	RAPLEY STEPHN.
Private	RICHMOND THOS.
Private	SPURR MARK
Private	STEEL JOSH. Phillips sale
Private	THOMAS SAML.
Private	TUCKER JAMES
Private	WADLEY JOSH.
Private	WALSH MICHL.
Private	WILSON JOHN

Captain Edward Kelly's Company

Lieutenant	ISSACSON EGERTON H.Gaskell's Coll.1908. Payne 1911. Adamson 1913.
Ensign	BLAIR JOHN
Serjeant	GROVES CHARLES
Serjeant	HOLT NATHL. Adamson's Collection 1908
Serjeant	SMITH MICHL. On sale at Baldwin's March 1909.
Serjeant	WADDY JOHN A.
Serjeant	WOOD JOSEPH
Corporal	MAYBEY JOHN
Corporal	RUDGE JOSEPH
Corporal	THOMAS JOHN
Corporal	WARBURTON WM.
Drummer	WORROCKS THOS.
Drummer	WILKINSON JAMES
Private	ARMSHAW JOHN
Private	ARTHENS JOHN
Private	ASHWORTH WM.
Private	BALL WM.
Private	BETTISON WM.
Private	BEEN JOSHUA
Private	BIDDLE THOS.
Private	BRENNAN JOHN
Private	CAPLE JAMES
Private	CARTER JOSEPH
Private	CHEER JAMES 51st K.O. Yorkshire L.I. Coll.1908
Private	COX GEORGE
Private	DOUGLAS WM.
Private	FOSTER JAMES
Private	FRAZER SAMUEL
Private	GOODCHILD ISSAC
Private	GREGORY WM.
Private	GROOM FRANCIS
Private	HUGHES JAMES Col.Murray's Collection 1908
Private	INMAN GEORGE
Private	JORDAN JAMES
Private	KEANE WM.
Private	LUNN JAMES Payne Coll.1908
Private	McELWHAM JOHN
Private	McGUIRE JAMES
Private	MARSHALL FRANCIS
Private	MATTHEWS JOHN
Private	MURPHY PETER
Private	NEWTON RALPH
Private	OWENS RICHD.
Private	PARKER WM.
Private	PERKINS ROBT.
Private	PICKITT JOHN
Private	POWELL WM.
Private	QUINN PATK.
Private	REES THOS Adamson's Coll.1908
Private	ROBERTS RICHD.
Private	ROEBUCK RICHD.
Private	ROE WM.
Private	SCOTT JOHN
Private	SKEANE WM.
Private	SMITH THOS.
Private	SPEAR JOHN
Private	TALLIS BENJN.
Private	VICKERMAN JOSH.
Private	VINCENT ROBT.
Private	WIGGINTON THOS.
Private	WOOLER ROBT.
Private	WRAY CHAS.

Captain Richard Storer's Company

Captain	STORER RICHD.
Lieutenant	READ HENRY
Lieutenant	TROWARD THOS.
Serjeant	AKROYD HENRY
Serjeant	HORSEMAN RICHD.
Serjeant	KERSHAW THOS.
Corporal	HUTCHINGS JAMES
Corporal	PARKER JOHN
Corporal	WOODHEAD RICHD.
Drummer	PERKINS GEORGE
Drummer	SMITH JOHN
Private	BABINGTON WM.
Private	BENNETT THOS.
Private	BETSWORTH STEPHN.
Private	CALLOW GEORGE
Private	CARR THOS.
Private	CHALLIS JAMES

Private	CLARKE GEORGE
Private	CLEMENTS ANDREW
Private	CLUFF JONAS
Private	CULLEN THOS.
Private	DAVIS RICHD.
Private	DEANE GEORGE
Private	ELLIS JOHN
Private	FISHER WM.
Private	FLAHERTY JOHN
Private	FOX SIMON
Private	FRANCIS WM.
Private	FLETCHER THOS.
Private	GASKINS MICHL.
Private	HACKMAN JAMES
Private	HAMBLIN JOHN
Private	HARRIS WM.
Private	HOLLAND JAMES
Private	JONES HENRY
Private	KING NICHS.
Private	KINGS GEORGE
Private	LEAVEY OWEN
Private	McGUIRE MICHL.
Private	MARTIN NATHL.
Private	MEDLEY BENJN.
Private	NICHOLSON JOHN
Private	OAKES THOS.
Private	PALMER JOSEPH
Private	PARKER WM.
Private	REYNOLDS PATK.
Private	SHEPPARD THOS.
Private	SWIFT JOHN
Private	SIMPSON JOHN
Private	SLADE THOS.
Private	SLEDDING ABRM. On Sale at Baldwin's May 1910
Private	SMITH THOS.
Private	SMITH WM.
Private	SYKES GEORGE
Private	TAYLOR WM.
Private	TURNER THOS.
Private	UPPINGTON WM.
Private	WALKER WM.
Private	WALTERS JOHN
Private	WRAY JAMES

Captain James H. Phelps Company

Captain	PHELPS H.
Lieutenant	MAINWARING FRED. J.
Lieutenant	MARTIN HENRY
Serjeant	HACKMAN JOHN
Serjeant	HOLLINGWORTH JOHN
Serjeant	WEST SAML.
Corporal	CRIPPS WM.
Corporal	JACKSON JOHN Payne Coll. 1908 Adamson Collection 1913
Corporal	SANDERS STEPHN.
Corporal	WATKINS JAMES On Sale at Fenton's March 1910
Drummer	WESTLEY JAMES
Private	ANDERSON JAMES
Private	ANDERSON WM.
Private	BRIDGER WM.
Private	BROOM RICHD.
Private	BRIARLY ROBT.
Private	BELL JOHN
Private	BUDD GEORGE
Private	CHILDS THOS.
Private	CORNER JAMES
Private	COLLINS MICHL.
Private	CROKER WM.
Private	CULVERT WM.
Private	DELVES HUGH
Private	DAVIS WM.
Private	FALLEN JOHN
Private	GOODALL DAVID
Private	GOODWIN EDWD.
Private	HARVEY DAVID
Private	HARRIS WM.
Private	HAYTER JAMES
Private	HEMMINGS SAML.
Private	KERNAN PATK.
Private	LAWS THOS.
Private	LYONS THOS.
Private	LYONS JOHN
Private	LOWRY RICHD.
Private	McFARLAND JOHN
Private	MANN JOHN
Private	MATTHEWS JOHN
Private	MORTIMORE THOS.
Private	ROBERTS JOHN
Private	ROGERS SAML.
Private	STROUD STEPHN,
Private	SUMMERS NATHL.
Private	SWAINS JAMES
Private	STILWELL WM.
Private	THOMAS THOS.
Private	THOMAS WM.
Private	THOMAS JOHN
Private	TREZISE WM.
Private	VINE THOS.
Private	WHITE GEORGE
Private	WILLIAMSON JOHN
Private	WILLETT STEPHN.
Private	WINALL THOS.
Private	WOOD JOHN

Captain Peter Smellie's Company

Lieutenant	BROOK THOS.
Serjeant	BREEN MICHL.
Serjeant	HART JOHN
Serjeant	STANTON GEORGE
Serjeant	SPITTLE WM.
Corporal	FISHER THOS.
Corporal	KNOWLES WM.
Corporal	SYKES SAML.
Drummer	SINGLETON BENJN.
Private	ADAMS JOHN
Private	BAINES THOS.
Private	BAKER WM.
Private	BATTY WM. 51st K.O. Yorkshire. L.I. Collection 1908
Private	BEX JOHN
Private	BROOKS ADAM
Private	BOULT ROBT.
Private	CONNELLY PATK.
Private	COOPER ROBT.
Private	COWARD THOS.
Private	CROWTHER THOS.
Private	DAVIS JOHN
Private	FRENCH PATK.
Private	GARDNER WM.
Private	GILBERT ROBT.
Private	GRIFFEN JOHN
Private	HAIGH JOSHUA
Private	HART JOHN
Private	HARRIS JOHN
Private	HOLLERAN MICHL.
Private	HOWE JOHN
Private	HUGHES WM.
Private	INGHAM JOSPEH
Private	KAIM THOS.
Private	KIRK WM.
Private	LEWIS JOHN
Private	MAKER PHILIP
Private	MARTIN JOHN
Private	MORRIS PATK.
Private	NOWLAND FRANS.
Private	NICHOLSON MATTW.
Private	PALMER MOSES
Private	POWELL JOHN
Private	REGAN WM.
Private	REYNOLDS GEORGE
Private	ROSSER WM.
Private	SARGESON CORNS.
Private	SIMS JOHN
Private	SLEDDING RICHD.
Private	SMITH RICHD.
Private	SMITH JOHN
Private	WAINWRIGHT HUMY.
Private	WEBBER WM.
Private	WELLS THOS.
Private	WHITTINGTON THOS.
Private	WHITWORTH ABRM.

Captain James Ross's Company

Captain	ROSS JAMES
Lieutenant	AINSWORTH OLIVER
Ensign	FRASER ALEX.
Serjeant	CORMICK JOHN
Serjeant	LAMB JOHN
Serjeant	McKAY JOSH.
Serjeant	WATERS JOHN
Corporal	BASSETT SAML.
Corporal	BROWN ALEX.
Drummer	GREEN WM.
Drummer	MANION JOHN
Private	ANTHONY RICHD.
Private	BAINES PETER
Private	BENSON WM.
Private	BOSHER JAS. WM.
Private	BROWN WM.
Private	BURRELL JOHN
Private	COOPER WM.
Private	CORMICK SAML.
Private	CULLY SIMON
Private	DARWIN WM.
Private	DOLIVE JOHN
Private	GARRETT SOLOMON
Private	GRAHAM JOHN
Private	GREENAWAY GEORGE
Private	HAWKEM STEPN. 51st K.O. Yorkshire L.I. Collection 1908
Private	HAMPSON WM.
Private	HILL JOHN
Private	HOWEY WM.
Private	JAMES WM.
Private	JONES WM.
Private	KENNY THOS.
Private	KILLICK RICHD.
Private	LAMB THOS.
Private	LYTHER JAMES
Private	MIDDLETON WM.
Private	MITCHELL JOSH.
Private	McNEAL JAMES Cheylesmore Collection 1908
Private	MORGAN WM.
Private	NICHOLSON MICHL.

Private	NEWBERRY JOSH.
Private	OXNAM BENJN.
Private	POWERS JAMES
Private	RATCLIFF BENJN. Galway Foley Collection 1910
Private	ROGERS DANIEL
Private	SANDFORD MATTW,
Private	SHAW WM. Glendinings sale Feb. 1911
Private	SPEARS SAML.
Private	TIVENAN JOHN
Private	WADSWORTH WM.
Private	WATERHOUSE JAMES
Private	WESSON WM. Lt.Col.J.G. Adamson's Collection 1908
Private	WHITTAKER GEORGE
Private	WILLIAMS THOS.
Private	YEATES RICHD.

Captain John Ross's Company

Captain	ROSS JOHN
Lieutenant	MAHON WALTER
Lieutenant	SIMPSON W.D.
Lieutenant	KRANSE W.H.
Serjeant	THOMPSON WM.
Serjeant	THOMAS LEWILLIN
Serjeant	SERJEANT EDWD.
Serjeant	BURT JAMES
Corporal	GREENWOOD JOHN Cheylesmore Collection 1908
Corporal	GRUBB JOHN
Corporal	HAYMAN WM.
Corporal	KEARY MARK
Drummer	HISCOCK JOHN
Private	ALLEN WM.
Private	BAMFORTH THOS.
Private	BEDFORD JOHN
Private	BLAKE JOHN
Private	BLAKENY JOHN
Private	BLUETT PETER
Private	BURDEN RICHD.
Private	COLES WM.
Private	COPELY JOSH.
Private	CROWBETT NICHS.
Private	DAVIS LUKE
Private	DAVIS THOS.
Private	DAVIS RICHD.
Private	FLEET JAMES
Private	FOX JOHN
Private	GREEN EDWD.
Private	GREEN THOS.
Private	HAMILTON WM.
Private	HERBERT JOHN
Private	HOME JAMES
Private	HOWLETT THOS.
Private	JAMES THOS.
Private	JERRY RICHD. 51st K.O. Yorkshire. I. Collection 1908
Private	KING GEORGE
Private	LEE BART.
Private	LITTLE THOS.
Private	LIVERSEDGE SAML.
Private	LODGE GEORGE
Private	LYSHON ROBT.
Private	McCONNELL PATK.
Private	MATTHEWS JOHN
Private	MATTHEWS JAMES
Private	MOODY JOHN
Private	MORGAN WM.
Private	NURSE WM.
Private	PHILLIPS CHAS.
Private	PROSSER GEORGE
Private	REYNOLDS WM.
Private	ROBERTS JOHN
Private	ROBINSON EDWD.
Private	SPILLER WM.
Private	STEPHENS WM.
Private	TAYLOR WM.
Private	TREADMILL RICHD.
Private	WALSH JAMES
Private	WARNER WM.
Private	WOOD JOSH.
Private	WOODGER HENRY

Captain Samuel Beardly's Company

Captain	beardsley saml. 51st K.O. Yorkshire L.I. Collection 1908 Wounded.
Lieutenant	KENNEDY FRANCIS
Lieutenant	TYNDALE C.W. Lt.Col.J.G. Adamson's Collection 1910 Wounded
Ensign	ST.JOHN G.F.B.
Serjeant	MOSS CHAS.
Serjeant	PRODAM EDWD.
Serjeant	THURLEY WM.
Corporal	BAKER GEORGE
Corporal	BUCKLEY WM.
Corporal	HEFFER WM.
Corporal	WOOD FRANS.
Drummer	BERRYMAN JOHN 51st K.O. Yorkshire I. Collection 1908
drummer	DOUGLAS JOHN
Drummer	FORD MICHL.
Private	ASHWORTH JOHN

Private	BATLEY CHAS.
Private	BLIMMAN BENJN.
Private	COOPER JOHN
Private	DALE SAML.
Private	DAY JAMES
Private	ELLIOTT JOSH.
Private	GOLDING JAMES
Private	GUARD NICHS.
Private	GREADY MICHL.
Private	HARRIS THOS.
Private	HOOPER JOHN
Private	HOVELL THOS.
Private	HUGHES JOHN
Private	HIRST THOS.
Private	JENKINS DAVID
Private	JENNINGS MATTW.
Private	KAY DANIEL
Private	KEANE FRANS.
Private	KELLY CHAS.
Private	KILLEN JOHN
Private	KING SAMUEL
Private	McGLINCHY JOHN
Private	MALONE JOHN
Private	MARTIN FRANS.
Private	MAUNDER MICHL.
Private	NORTON JOHN
Private	PALMER THOS.
Private	PALMER WM.
Private	PARROTT JOHN
Private	PEARCE JONAN.
Private	PEARCY JAMES
Private	PEARSON JAMES
Private	PLUMMER MOSES
Private	POWELL JOHN
Private	REED DANIEL
Private	REYNOLDS JOHN
Private	RICHARDSON JAMES
Private	ROBSHAW JAMES
Private	SAVILL GEORGE
Private	SIMMONS CHRISR.
Private	TOLL SAMUEL
Private	TYRELL JOHN
Private	WALKER WM.
Private	WILSON WM.
Private	WRIGHT SAML.

<u>Captain Edward H. Frederick's Company</u>

Captain	FREDERICK E.H.
Lieutenant	DYAS JOSH.
Lieutenant	HAWLEY B.B.
Serjeant	BURROWS CHAS.
Serjeant	DANCER WM.
Serjeant	FIELD SAML.
Serjeant	LAMBERT JAMES
Corporal	COOK THOS.
Corporal	HART DANIEL
Corporal	LINTOTT JAMES
Drummer	WHITHAM WM.
Private	ALLEN JAMES
Private	BEESTON JOSEPH
Private	CHANDLER WM. 1st.
Private	CHANDLER WM. 2nd.
Private	CHEESEMAN JAMES
Private	CHOWLES THOS.
Private	COLES HENRY
Private	CRESWELL SAML. Col.R.T. Gascoigne's Collection 1908
Private	DOBB HENRY
Private	DIXON GEORGE Watters sale June 1913
Private	DYAS JEREH.
Private	FAULKNER JOSEPH
Private	GASKIS GEORGE
Private	HARRIS ANTHONY
Private	HARROWSMITH JOSEPH
Private	HARTLEY JOHN
Private	HAVERTY PATK.
Private	HEFFERMAN PATK. 51st K.O. Yorkshire. L.I. Collection 1908
Private	HERON SAMUEL
Private	HOCKING JOHN
Private	HUTTON WM.
Private	JONES JOHN Captain R.E. Boutton 1908
Private	JORDAN CROFTON
Private	JORDAN PATK.
Private	LANCELY THOS.
Private	LEWIS DAVID
Private	McBREDON JOHN
Private	McMURRY JOSH.
Private	MARCHANT WM.
Private	NORTH JAMES
Private	PENROSE MATTW.
Private	PICKLES WM.
Private	PINKETT WM.
Private	PETTS ROBT.
Private	REES THOS.
Private	REYNOLDS THOS.
Private	ROWLAND WM.
Private	SENIOR JOHN
Private	SANSON GILES

Private	SEABORN WM.
Private	SMITH MATTW.
Private	SPENCER JAMES
Private	SPICKETT JOHN
Private	SWIFT JOHN
Private	TAYLOR MATTW. Glendining's sale March 1909
Private	THOMAS RICHD. Gray Collection 1908. Col.Adamson 1909
Private	WATKINS THOS. On sale at Fenton's March 1910
Private	WILLIAMS EDWD.
Private	WHITNEY JOHN

* * *

1st Bn. 52nd REGIMENT OF FOOT

Colonel	COLBORNE Sir JOHN. United Service Institution 1909
Ltr.Colonel & Major	ROWAN CHARLES Wounded Slightly
Major & Capt.	CAMPBELL PATRICK
Lt.Colonel & Captain	CHALMERS WM.
Major & Capt.	ROWAN WM. Wounded
Captain	DIGGLE CHAS. Wounded severely
Captain	SHEDDEN JOHN
Major & Capt.	LOVE JAMES FREDK. Wounded severely
Captain	McNAIR JAMES
Captain	LANGTON EDWD.
Captain	CROSS JOHN
Major & Capt.	EARL de MARCH, CHAS.
Captain	YORKE CHAS.
Lt. & Ad.	WINTERBOTTOM JOHN Wounded Severely
Lieutenant	DAWSON CHAS. Wounded severely
Lieutenant	ANDERSON MATTW. Wounded severely left leg amputated
Lieutenant	KENNY CHAS.
Lieutenant	LOVE GEO. HARLY.
Lieutenant	RIPLEY WM.
Lieutenant	BARRATT J.C.
Lieutenant	CLERKE W.H.
Lieutenant	HALL GEORGE
Lieutenant	NIXON W.R. Dr.Payne's Collection 1909
Lieutenant	GAWLER GEORGE
Lieutenant	WHICHCOTE GEORGE
Lieutenant	OGILVIE WM.
Lieutenant	NORTHEY E.R.
Lieutenant	BROWN Hon. WM.
Ass.Surgeon	McCARTNEY WM.
Lieutenant	SCOONES EDWD.
Lieutenant	CAMPBELL GEORGE Wounded Severely
Lieutenant	AUSTIN WM.
Lieutenant	SNODGRASS J.J.
Lieutenant	CARGILL J.S. Whitaker Collection 1908
Lieutenant	YOUNGE W.C.
Lieutenant	COTTINGHAM THOS. Wounded severely. H.Gaskell's Collection 1908
Lieutenant	HOLMAR CHAS.
Lieutenant	MOORE GEORGE
Lieutenant	MITCHELL EDWD.
Lieutenant	SHAW CHAS.
Lieutenant	HART JOHN
Lieutenant	SCOTT G.E.
Lieutenant	OAKES H. THOS.
Lieutenant	GRIFFITHS JNS. ROGER
Lieutenant	BURNETT JNS.
Lieutenant	STEWART RONDAL
Lieutenant	ROBSON GEORGE
Lieutenant	LOVE FREDK. WM.
Ensign	JACKSON JOSEPH Payne Coll.1909 Adamson Collection 1913
Ensign	MASSIE THOS.
Ensign	McNAB DUNCAN
Ensign	MONTAGUE J.
Ensign	MAY JAMES FRERE
Ensign	MONINS EATON
Ensign	LEEKE WM.
Pay.Master	CLARKE JAMES
Qr.Master	SWEETEN BENJN.
Surgeon	GIBSON JOHN BUSHBY
Ass.Surgeon	JONES PRYCE

Captain D. Campbell's Company

Sjt.Major	DOWDALL JOHN
Q.M.S.	DOUGLASS WM. Watters sale June 1913
P.M.S.	CLARKE CHARLES
Ar.Serjeant	AMOS JOSEPH
Dr.Major	WINSTON MARTIN
Serjeant	DOAK JOHN
Serjeant	HENDERSON JAMES
Serjeant	JOHNSTON WM.
Serjeant	McALLISTER CHARLES
Serjeant	McCURRIE HUGH
Serjeant	WINUP ROBT.
Corporal	CLARK WM.
Corporal	DEAN JOHN
Corporal	O'HARA JOHN

Corporal	RICE DENIS Wounded
Corporal	RUTLEDGE MICHL. Wounded
Corporal	FROST GEORGE Gray Collection 1908
Drummer	JACKSON THOS.
Drummer	POPE CHAS.
Private	ALFORD MICHL.
Private	ANDREWS CHAS.
Private	ANDREWS WM.
Private	ASH DANIEL
Private	ASH THOS.
Private	AVIS JAMES
Private	BATES GEORGE
Private	BENBOW WM.
Private	BIRD CHARLES
Private	BLACKBOROUGH RICHD. Wounded
Private	BOTTLE JOHN
Private	BRIMSLEY JOHN
Private	BRAGG ROBT.
Private	BROAD JAMES Oddy Coll. Glendinings Sale 1908
Private	BURBLOW CLARK Wounded
Private	BURKE JAMES
Private	BURN ROBT.
Private	BUTLER JOHN Wounded
Private	CHEESEMAN CARPENTER Col. Murrays Collection 1908
Private	CLARK HENRY
Private	COLLOM JEREH.
Private	COLLICK WM.
Private	COVES GEORGE
Private	CROWLIE DANIEL
Private	CROKER WM.
Private	CROCKFORD JOHN
Private	CURRAN PATK.
Private	DAY JAMES Wounded
Private	DAYTON JAMES Wounded J.B.Gaskells Coll.1909
Private	DEMPSEY JAMES
Private	DONAGHOE PATK.
Private	DOWLING EDWD. Wounded
Private	DUNSTEAD JOHN
Private	DUTTON JOHN
Private	DYER ANTHONY Wounded
Private	ELSON JOHN
Private	FLANAGAN PATRICK Wounded
Private	FOSTER ROBERT Officer's Mess (52) Oxford L.I. May 1909
Private	GILL ELY Wounded
Private	GOULDING THOS. Wounded
Private	GREENWOOD ROBT.
Private	GRIFFIN MICHL.
Private	HADDING SAMUEL
Private	HADGES JAMES
Private	HILL ROBT.
Private	HOOLEY WM.
Private	HOLRANE MICHL.
Private	HOWARTH WM.
Private	HUNT WM.
Private	INKSTON THOS.
Private	JOHNSTON THOS. Wounded
Private	JONES ROBT.
Private	KINCHLEY PATK.
Private	LANE ROBT. Wounded
Private	LANSDOWNE NEBUCH.
Private	LILLEYWHITE JAMES
Private	LEWIS HENRY
Private	LOWE PATK.
Private	MALONEY BRIAN
Private	MERCHANT GEORGE
Private	McGINNIS FELIX
Private	McMAHON MICHL.
Private	McTAGUE THOS.
Private	MULLEN FRANS.
Private	NASH CHAS.
Private	OAKES JAMES
Private	O'DONALD DANIEL
Private	O'ROURK JOHN
Private	OWENS HUGH
Private	OWENS JOHN
Private	PALMERLY JOHN
Private	PARRINGTON JAMES
Private	PARRINGTON THOS.
Private	PENHORN CHARLES
Private	PRICE JAMES
Private	PURTON ROBT.
Private	ROBERTS JOSEPH
Private	ROUTHEN JOHN
Private	SEATON WM.
Private	SCATTERGOOD EDWD. Wounded
Private	SMITH ROBT.
Private	SMITHERMAN RICHD.
Private	STANLEY THOS.
Private	TOPPING SAML. Wounded
Private	WEBSTER THOS.
Private	WEATHERS EDWD.
Private	WILSON WM.
Private	WILSON RICHD.
Private	WILKINS SAML.
Private	WOOD THOS.
Private	WYNYARD GEORGE Wounded
Private	YOUNG GEORGE

Captain Robert Campbell's Company

Serjeant	GINN ROBT. Wounded
Serjeant	MAWBERY JOSH.
Serjeant	MILLS HENRY
Serjeant	RHODES JEREH.
Serjeant	STOKES PHILIP
Serjeant	WADSWORTH JOHN
Corporal	BROWN WM.
Corporal	COLEMAN THOS.
Corporal	LAND DAVID
Corporal	NASH WM.
Corporal	OWERS JOHN Wounded
Corporal	SMITH WM. Wounded
Corporal	WILLIAMS DAVID
Drummer	McMULLEN ENOCH
Drummer	SADLER SAML.
Private	ATHERTON JOHN
Private	AUSTIN JOHN
Private	BELLAMY WM. Wounded
Private	BLAYLOCK ROBT. Wounded
Private	BRICK WM.
Private	BLOXHAM ROBT.
Private	BOOTS HENRY
Private	BRADLEY GEORGE
Private	BRANT WM.
Private	BRIERLY HENRY Wounded
Private	BRODRICK THOS.
Private	CAREY THOS.
Private	CLARKE THOS.
Private	COOPER JOHN
Private	COOPER WM.
Private	COX JAMES
Private	COLES THOS.
Private	DEBENHAM JAMES Glendinings sale July 1909
Private	DAWSON FRANS.
Private	DIXON WM. Wounded
Private	FARRELL JAMES
Private	FITZPATRICK PATRICK
Private	FLEMING ANDREW
Private	FOWLER RICHARD
Private	GADDIS HUGH Wounded
Private	GARDNER DAVID
Private	GEE HENRY
Private	GARLIKE WM.
Private	GILLETT JAMES
Private	GOULD THOS.
Private	GURR GEORGE Wounded
Private	HAGAN JAMES Wounded
Private	HATTON JOHN
Private	HAYDON JOHN
Private	HOPWOOD THOS.
Private	HORE THOS.
Private	HINTON THOS. Glendinings sale May 1910
Private	JACKSON WM.
Private	JELL SANDERS
Private	JOHNSTONE JAMES
Private	JONES JOHN 1st.
Private	JONES JOHN 2nd.
Private	KEEP JOSH.
Private	KILKENNY JAMES
Private	KNOWLES PETER
Private	LEIR JAMES
Private	LENNOTT ROBT.
Private	LURMIE DANL.
Private	MADDON WM. Wounded
Private	MAYNE FRANS. Wounded
Private	MARTIN HUGH Wounded
Private	MATHEWS JOHN
Private	McGRATH PATK.
Private	McLAUGHLIN JOHN Wounded
Private	MILES THOS.
Private	MOORE WM. 1st.
Private	MOORE WM. 2nd.
Private	MORRIS JAMES
Private	MURPHY JAMES
Private	MURPHY MICHAEL
Private	OWENS JOHN
Private	PARKINSON PHILIP
Private	PATRICK ROBT.
Private	PEMBERTON WM.
Private	PERRY WM.
Private	POWELL WM.
Private	RAFFERTY EDWD.
Private	REEVES EDWD.
Private	ROBERTS ELLIS
Private	ROSS ALEX.
Private	SANDERS WM.
Private	SCULLY JOHN Wounded
Private	SNASHALL WM.
Private	SOUZA M. Gray Coll.1908
Private	STANAGE JNS.
Private	STOCKTON CHAS.
Private	SWEENEY JOHN
Private	TIMMS JOSH.
Private	TWYMAN RICHD.
Private	WEIGHTMAN THOS. Wounded
Private	WELCH GEORGE
Private	WHALING THOS.
Private	WILKINSON URIAH
Private	WILMORE JOHN Wounded
Private	WILSON SAMUEL

Private	WILLIS EPHRAIM
Private	WOOD MICHL. Wounded
Private	WOOLFE DANIEL
Private	YOUNG JOHN

Captain W. Chalmer's Company

Serjeant	ALTHROP JOHN
Serjeant	BOSSAM JAMES
Serjeant	CARTWRIGHT CHARLES
Serjeant	JACK DAVID
Serjeant	KILBANKS JOHN
Serjeant	MASKELL JOESPH
Serjeant	WILLOX JOHN
Corporal	WOOD ROBT. Wounded
Corporal	McPHERSON ALEX. Wounded
Corporal	KIMBER STEPN.
Corporal	SLATER JOHN Whitaker Collection 1908
Corporal	SENIOR PETER Wounded
Corporal	TAYLOR JOHN
Corporal	TOOTLE WM.
Drummer	HADDOCK JOHN
Drummer	ADEY THOS.
Private	ANTWISTLE RICHD.
Private	ARTHUR JOHN
Private	BARRETT JAMES
Private	BARNETT WM.
Private	BARTRIPP JOHN
Private	BELL GEORGE Wounded
Private	BASSOTT RICHD.
Private	BASTABLE PIERCE
Private	BLACKBURN HENRY
Private	BROWN GEORGE
Private	BURKE PATRICK Wounded
Private	BUXTON SAML.
Private	CAMPBELL JOHN
Private	CAMPBELL HENRY
Private	CHAPMAN WM.
Private	CHILD WM. Wounded
Private	CLARK WM. Wounded
Private	CLEMINGS WM.
Private	CLISBY WM.
Private	COOK THOS.
Private	CONNOLLY PATK.
Private	COUGHLAN MICHL.
Private	CURRAN ANDREW
Private	DALTON EDWD.
Private	DEMPSEY JOHN
Private	DILLON THOS.
Private	DIMOND HENRY
Private	ELLIOTT GEORGE
Private	ENDLE JOHN
Private	FINNER DAVID
Private	FREELAND THOS.
Private	FOSTER WM. Wounded
Private	FOSTER JOHN
Private	GADD RICHD. Wounded
Private	GALLAGHER JOHN
Private	GEE JOSH.
Private	GIBBS GEORGE
Private	GOLDSMITH WM.
Private	GOOD RICHD.
Private	GREEN ROBT.
Private	HAGAN JOHN
Private	HAMPSON JAMES
Private	HARDING HENRY Wounded
Private	HAZELL JAMES
Private	HAWOOD HENRY Wounded
Private	JENKINS JAMES
Private	JOHNSTON JOHN Wounded
Private	JONES WM.
Private	JONES. THOS. Wounded
Private	JONES RICHD.
Private	KINSEY THOS.
Private	LAWLER ANDREW
Private	LITTLE JAMES
Private	LONG JOHN Wounded
Private	LOWANDS THOS.
Private	MARGISON RICHD.
Private	MARTIN WM. Wounded
Private	MASTERS JOHN Wounded Cheylesmore Collection 1908
Private	McDERMOTT MICHL.
Private	McDONALD JOHN
Private	McGARR JOHN
Private	McSTOKER JAMES
Private	MEARS WM.
Private	MEDHURST ROBT.
Private	MILLER BENJN.
Private	MINTON GEORGE
Private	NORTON WM.
Private	PEARSON ALLEN Wounded. Glendinings sale 17 June 1908
Private	PHEASANT DAVID
Private	PITTS RICHD.
Private	PIKE JOSH.
Private	QUINBY AMOS
Private	RALPHS WM.
Private	RILEY JAMES Wounded
Private	ROBERTS ELY.
Private	RUSSELL RICHD.
Private	SAMMON GEORGE

Private	SMITH JOHN Day sale April 1910
Private	SMALLWOOD JAMES
Private	STAIRS HENRY
Private	SUTCLIFFE STEPHN.
Private	TASKER JAMES
Private	TANSEY JOHN
Private	VITTEY THOS. Wounded
Private	WOOD JOHN
Private	WALL WM.
Private	WHILMHURST WM.
Private	WHITAKER JOHN Wounded
Private	WILLIS ROBT.
Private	WILLIS WM.
Private	WORD JOSH. Wounded

Captain W. Rowan's Company

Serjeant	ALGOE JAMES
Serjeant	TREW JOHN
Serjeant	RILEY MARTIN
Serjeant	SLOSS DAVID
Serjeant	WILLIAMSON JOHN
Serjeant	WILLIAMS WM. Wounded
Corporal	BATTS RICHD.
Corporal	CLARK JAMES Wounded
Corporal	FARRELL JAMES
Corporal	HEATHESWICK DAVID
Corporal	MASKELL JAMES
Corporal	NEWBURN CHAS.
Corporal	STAFFORD PATK.
Drummer	HATTON PHILIP
Drummer	HEMMINGS WM.
Private	ALGOE ROBT.
Private	ALLEN PHILIP
Private	ANDERSON JOSH.
Private	APPER EDWD.
Private	ATKINS JOHN
Private	AUSTIN WM.
Private	ABBOTT WM.
Private	ALDRIDGE THOS.
Private	BOWMAN EDWD. Wounded
Private	BOXHALL HENRY Wounded
Private	BRADLEY JNS.
Private	BRAZIER WM.
Private	BROTHERS WM. Officer's Mess 52nd Oxford L.I. May 1909
Private	BRUNT JOSH.
Private	CADMAN JNS. Wounded
Private	CHARMAN FRANS.
Private	CHEWCRAFT JNS. Deserted
Private	CHRISTION ROBT.
Private	CLARK HENRY
Private	COFFILL FARRELL
Private	COFFILL FARRELL
Private	COPELAND JNS.
Private	CRABTREE JNS.
Private	COFFILL JNS.
Private	DELANEY JAMES
Private	DICKESON JOSH. Wounded
Private	EVANS JOHN
Private	FRANCISCE THOS.
Private	FRANCIS DAVID Wounded
Private	FUNNELL WM.
Private	GARSIDE JAMES Glendinings sale Feb. 1911
Private	GROGAN ANTHY.
Private	GREY ROBT.
Private	GREEN JOSH. Cheylesmore Collection 1908
Private	HAYES JARVIS
Private	HULWOOD WM.
Private	HARRIS WM.
Private	HEAP JOSH.
Private	HILL SAML. Wounded
Private	HOOK THOS.
Private	HOPEWELL ANDW.
Private	HUGHES JNS.
Private	KAIN EDWD.
Private	KELLY PATRICK
Private	LOCK JOHN
Private	MARKLAND SAML.
Private	MADDOX WM.
Private	MALONEY PATK.
Private	MATTHEWS THOS. Wounded
Private	MARSHAW WM. Wounded
Private	MacDERMOTT PETER
Private	McFARLANEJNS.
Private	McFARLANE JAS. Col.Murray's Collection 1908
Private	McLEAN JAS.
Private	McWIGAN STEPN.
Private	MEYERS JAMES Wounded
Private	MILLER GEORGE
Private	MORRISON BRYAN
Private	MOSS WM.
Private	NEWLAND WM.
Private	NEWNHAM ROBT.
Private	O'NEAL TERANCE Deserted
Private	PARKER DANL.
Private	PHIPPS THOS.
Private	REEVES THOS.
Private	ROGERS EDMD. Glendinings Sale July 1911
Private	ROGERS JNS. Deserted
Private	SAMMON BERND.
Private	SHERIDAN JNS.

Private	SIMMS WM. Deserted
Private	SLOSS THOS.
Private	SMITH WM.
Private	SMITH JNS.
Private	STONE JAMES
Private	TOOLEY HENRY
Private	SPLANE MICHL.
Private	THORP RICHD.
Private	TIPLADY ALEX.
Private	TUREY ABRM. Sold by Debenham Jan. 1910
Private	WALTER JAMES
Private	WARMINGHAM JOSH.
Private	WEBB PHILIP
Private	WILLIAMSON GEO.
Private	WILLIAMS JAMES Wounded
Private	WILLSON JNS.
Private	WILLSON THOS.
Private	WOODLAND HENRY
Private	WOODLAND WM.

Captain R. Brownrig's Company

Serjeant	DUFFEY MICHL.
Serjeant	KING JOHN Wounded
Serjeant	McCOLLA CHAS.
Serjeant	McLAUGHLIN JAMES
Serjeant	McCOY CHAS.
Serjeant	SHAW JOSHUA
Serjeant	WHITEHEAD JAMES Wounded
Corporal	CAMPBELL PATK.
Corporal	CONWELL CHAS.
Corporal	COLLIS SAML.
Corporal	DELICATE WM. Wounded Needes June 1908
Corporal	FARRELL JOHN
Corporal	NELSON ROBT.
Corporal	PINCHEN JOHN
Corporal	McKENZIE WM. Wounded
Corporal	McROBERTS WM.
Drummer	BLAKENEY RICHD.
Drummer	ROSS THOS.
Drummer	WESTWOOD BENJN.
Private	ABBOT MATTW.
Private	ALLEN WM. Wounded
Private	ATKINSON JOSH. Wounded
Private	BEDWORTH JOSH.
Private	BENCE RICHD Wounded
Private	BLISS HENRY
Private	BRENNON JOHN
Private	BENKRIDGE HENRY
Private	CHIDDLE GEORGE
Private	CROSS WM.
Private	CLANCEY JOHN
Private	DAWSON JAMES
Private	DAVIS WM. Wounded
Private	DAVIS JAMES Wounded
Private	DONAGHUE PATK.
Private	DORNING HUGH Wounded
Private	DUFFEY JAMES Wounded
Private	DUGGEN JOHN Wounded
Private	DUNSTER THOS.
Private	EAGON JOHN
Private	EVANS WM. On sale at Baldwin's March 1909
Private	EMMS JOSH.
Private	FALLON JOHN
Private	FAHEY THOS. Wounded
Private	FERGUSON WM.
Private	FITZGERALD JOHN Wounded
Private	FULLER CHAS. Wounded
Private	GAMMERY THOS.
Private	GANNON PATK.
Private	GALWIN JAMES
Private	GRAHAM JOHN Wounded
Private	GRIFFITHS OWEN
Private	GRANT JAMES
Private	GUNN ALEX.
Private	HIBBERT GEORGE
Private	HILTON THOS.
Private	HOLLIWELL WM.
Private	HORNE JOHN
Private	HOWE DAVID
Private	HOWARD WM. On sale at Baldwin's March 1909
Private	JACKSON JOHN
Private	KEATING EDWD.
Private	KEW RICHD.
Private	LAYDEN PATK. Wounded
Private	LEONARD JOHN Wounded
Private	LESTER JOHN Wounded
Private	LITTLE JOHN
Private	LILLYWHITE FRANS. Wounded
Private	LOWMAN THOS.
Private	McCOLLOM JOHN
Private	McLARNON DAVID
Private	MOORE JOHN
Private	MOTTRAM RALPH
Private	MURPHY CHAS. Wounded
Private	MULLEN CHAS.
Private	NICKLESON JAMES
Private	NORRIS MARTIN

Private	NOWLAND JOHN
Private	O'DONNELL OWEN
Private	POLLARD CHAS.
Private	POWELL JOHN
Private	PURKETT THOS.
Private	QUILTER WM.
Private	REYNOLDS JOHN
Private	ROBERTS THOS.
Private	ROBERTS JOHN
Private	SANDERS JAMES Wounded
Private	SANDERS DANIEL
Private	SEYMORE JOHN
Private	SHEPHERD THOS.
Private	SHERAN JAMES Wounded
Private	SAGE WM.
Private	SKINNER THOS.
Private	STEPHENSON JNS.
Private	STOKES SAML.
Private	SULLIVAN TIMY.
Private	TAYLOR JOSHUA
Private	TRIPP WM.
Private	TURNER JAMES
Private	THOMAS JAMES
Private	WALKER PHILIP
Private	WALKER SAML. Wounded
Private	WARD PATK. Wounded
Private	WHITHAM BERND.
Private	WILSON EDWD. Wounded St.J.Tombs Collection 1909
Private	WIGGENTON JOSH. Glendinings sale 29th July 1908
Private	WILDE JOSH.
Private	WRIGHT ELIAH

Captain Charles Diggle's Company

Serjeant	ARCHER THOS. Wounded
Serjeant	BUSWELL WM. Wounded
Serjeant	HIGGINS SIMON
Serjeant	INSALL THOS.
Serjeant	McKAY JOHN
Serjeant	SMART THOS.
Serjeant	WALTERS WM.
Corporal	COOPER JAMES
Corporal	DAWSON THOS.
Corporal	HONSLEY BENJN. Cheylesmore Coll. 1908
Corporal	HOVEY SAML.
Corporal	McCOMBE JOSH. Wounded
Corporal	SPENCER THOS.
Corporal	WELLS JOHN
Drummer	JOHNSTON ABRM.
Drummer	JONES GEORGE
Private	ATKINSON GEORGE
Private	BAKER JOHN
Private	BATTS THOS.
Private	BENNETT JOHN
Private	BLACK JOHN Wounded
Private	BLINCOE GEORGE
Private	BOND GEORGE
Private	BOSWORTH JOHN
Private	BRADDLE JAMES
Private	BURBRIDGE THOS.
Private	BUTCHER JOHN Officer's Mess (52nd)Oxford L.I.May 1909
Private	CALVERT HENRY
Private	CAWTE JAMES
Private	CHALMERS JOSH.
Private	CHARLES SAML.
Private	CLARKE JOHN
Private	COCKERTON HENRY Wounded
Private	COOK THOS.
Private	CRAIG THOS. Wounded
Private	CRATTER FREDK. Wounded
Private	DAVIS JOHN
Private	DAY CHAS.
Private	DEE EDWD.
Private	DOUGHERTY HUGH
Private	DOWDY WM. Glendinings sale Jan. 1910
Private	DOWLAND HUGH
Private	DOYLE SAML.
Private	DUNN LUKE
Private	ELLSWORTH JOSH.
Private	EMERY WM.
Private	EWELL THS.
Private	FRANCE WILLOWBY Wounded
Private	FREEL JOHN
Private	FROST THOS. Wounded
Private	GANLEY THOS. Wounded
Private	GOODMAN JOHN
Private	GOREY JOHN
Private	HAGUE MATTW. Wounded. Col.R.T. Gascoigne's Collection 1909
Private	HALL JOHN
Private	HEALEY JAMES
Private	HARDY SAML. Wounded
Private	HERON MARTIN
Private	HEGGERTY THOS.
Private	HODGINS GEORGE
Private	HOGG JOHN
Private	HOGDEN JOHN
Private	HORNER GEORGE Glendinings sale July 1911

Private	HOLDER DAVID
Private	INSCOW JAMES Wounded
Private	JOHNSTONE JOHN
Private	JONES WM.
Private	KAIN JOHN
Private	LECHER JOSH.
Private	LYONS MARTIN
Private	McGREW JOHN
Private	NAILOR JOHN
Private	NORTH ROBT. Wounded
Private	OLIVE WM.
Private	PAGE JAMES
Private	PAXTON GEORGE Wounded
Private	PECKS FREDK.
Private	PRESCOTT JOHN
Private	PRAY DANIEL Wounded
Private	PLUMBRIDGE JOSH.
Private	POWELL THOS.
Private	RADLEY THOS.
Private	RADLEY JOHN
Private	RATCLIFF ROBT. Wounded
Private	REGAN JOHN
Private	ROBERTS THOS. Wounded
Private	ROWE JOHN
Private	SEWELL ISSAC
Private	SHAW ABRM.
Private	SHORE KAMES Sold by Debenhams Jan. 1810
Private	SIDEN JONATHAN
Private	STONE JOHN
Private	SWAN WM.
Private	SOULLION NEAL
Private	TAYLOR THOS.
Private	THOMASON THOS.
Private	TURNER JOHN
Private	WRIGHT RICHD.
Private	WATERS EDWD.
Private	WATTS FRANCIS
Private	WARMSBY THOS.
Private	WHITE JAMES
Private	WHITMILL JOSEPH
Private	WHITHAM SAML.
Private	WHITHAM JOSH.
Private	WOOD JOHN
Private	WOODRUFF THOS.
Private	WOOTTAN JAMES Col.Murray's Collection 1908
Private	YATES JAMES

Captain John Shiddin's Company

Serjeant	DUGGIN MATTW.
Serjeant	INNIS GEORGE Wounded
Serjeant	LACEY MICHL.
Serjeant	QUINN ENEAS
Serjeant	SPORD JOHN
Serjeant	WEBB ADDISON
Corporal	BUSHELL THOS.
Corporal	FREEMAN THOS.
Corporal	HIND JAMES
Corporal	OPENSHAW ROBT.
Corporal	SMITH WM.
Corporal	VENABLE THOS. Wounded
Drummer	ALCORN SAML.
Drummer	McCOY JOHN
Private	AUSTIN JOHN
Private	BATT ELIAS
Private	BLACKLOCK WM. Wounded
Private	BOTHWELL JNS.
Private	BOWEN MICHL.
Private	BRADBURY RANDLE
Private	BULLIVANT MATTW.
Private	BURROWS JOSH.
Private	BUSHELL THOS.
Private	CAVANAGH DAVID
Private	CARDIFF THOS.
Private	CARTY JAMES
Private	CLEWS THOS.
Private	COBB SETH
Private	COLLINGS DENNIS 1st.
Private	COLLINGS DENNIS 2nd.
Private	COWLING JOSH.
Private	COX PATK. Wounded
Private	CUNNINGHAM MURTAGH
Private	DANIELS JOHN Needes Coll.1908
Private	DILLON ARTHUR Wounded
Private	DOWLING STEPN
Private	DRAY WM. Wounded
Private	EASTMAN WM.
Private	ELLIS JOHN
Private	FLETCHER HENRY
Private	GALLINAGH EDWD.
Private	GILMAN JOHN Wounded
Private	GORDAN WM.
Private	GREGORY WM.
Private	HAMMELL THOS.
Private	HAWES JAMES
Private	HEALING OWEN
Private	HENN MORRIS
Private	HICKMAN JAMES Wounded

Private	HINDS ALEX. Wounded
Private	IRONMONGER RICHD.
Private	JONES JNS. 1st. Wounded
Private	JONES JNS. 2nd. Wounded
Private	JONES THOS.
Private	JONES JOSH Littledale sale Nov. 1910
Private	JOHNSTONE THOS.
Private	KELK EDWD.
Private	LAFFORDY NEAL
Private	LEATHERBOROUGH JOSH.
Private	LINFORD WM.
Private	LONGWORTH JOHN
Private	LOMAS JAMES
Private	LOWE WM.
Private	MARLOW JAMES Wounded
Private	McCARTY PATK. Wounded
Private	McKENNA CLARK
Private	McKELVEY DAVID
Private	McEWEN LEWIS
Private	MELDRUM GEORGE
Private	MILLER CHARLES Wounded Officer's Mess 52bd Oxford L.I. 1909
Private	MOODEY JOHN
Private	MOYSTON JOHN
Private	MURRAY JOHN
Private	NAILOR JOHN
Private	NEAVES EZRA
Private	NUTTLE JAMES
Private	O'NEAL HUGH
Private	ORMSBY JAMES
Private	PAGE JOHN
Private	PIERCE RICHD. Wounded
Private	PLANT JAMES Wounded
Private	PLUMBER WM.
Private	PRITCHARD JOHN
Private	PURTON SHADRACK
Private	RANDLE HENRY
Private	RICHARDSON RICHD.
Private	ROBERTS ROBT.
Private	RUTH WM.
Private	SAWYER THOS.
Private	SIMMONDS JAMES
Private	SOONES CHAS.
Private	STANFIELD JOSH.
Private	STOPFORD JNS. Wounded
Private	STORN JNS,
Private	SUMMER JNS. Wounded
Private	VALE WM.
Private	VAUGHAN THOS. Wounded
Private	WASSALL JOHN
Private	WATSON THOS. Wounded
Private	WHITING THOS.
Private	WILSON JOHN Wounded
Private	WOOLLEY DANIEL
Private	WOODWARD JAMES
Private	YOUNG BENJN.

Captain Love's Company

Serjeant	ARCHER WM.
Serjeant	BASTABLE JOHN Wounded
Serjeant	CUNNINGHAM GEORGE
Serjeant	KEMPSTER SAMUEL
Serjeant	McDONALD DONALD
Corporal	GREGORY VALENTINE Wounded
Corporal	McMASTERS JAMES Wounded
Corporal	POWELL JOHN
Corporal	TAYNTON NATHL.
Drummer	BISHOP RICHD.
Drummer	BROOKS WM.
Private	ADLEY ELIAS Wounded
Private	ADDISON GEORGE
Private	BAKER STEPN.
Private	BARRON HUGH
Private	BAILEY JOHN
Private	BAILEY GEORGE
Private	BARRETT JAMES
Private	BELFOUR GEORGE
Private	BROTHERTON SAML.
Private	BROWN RICHD.
Private	BROWNSILL JOHN
Private	BULLEY JAMES
Private	BUTTONSHAW JOSH.
Private	BUTLER THOS. 1st
Private	BUTLER THOS. 2nd.
Private	BURNHAM JNS.
Private	CARTER WM.
Private	CONNOR MARTIN
Private	CROCKFORD ANTHY.
Private	DENNISON HUGH
Private	DAVIS JOHN Wounded
Private	DURROUGH HENRY
Private	EDGAR THOS.
Private	ELLIS ROBT.
Private	EVANS JOHN
Private	EVANS WM.
Private	EWENS WM.
Private	FISHER WM.
Private	FIELDS WM.
Private	GALLIER THOS.
Private	GRANGER WM.

Private	GRIFFEN DAVID
Private	GREENWOOD JAMES
Private	GINKEN JOHN
Private	HANLIN JAMES
Private	HARRISON JAMES
Private	HAIR JOHN
Private	HARE PATK.
Private	HODGES GEORGE
Private	HIGGANS WM.
Private	HICKS CHAS.
Private	HOLLAND JOHN
Private	HOLLAND HENRY
Private	HOLMES ADAM Wounded
Private	HUGHES JOHN
Private	JACKSON ROBT.
Private	INGHAM THOS.
Private	JONES WM. Wounded
Private	KAIN JOHN
Private	KEELEY MICHL.
Private	LEVELL JAMES Wounded
Private	LAWRENCE JOHN
Private	LEAMAN JOHN
Private	MARTIN JOSH.
Private	MARCHANT JAMES
Private	McEVOY JOHN
Private	McCANN EDWD. Wounded
Private	McDERMOTT JOHN Wounded
Private	McKENNA ARTHUR
Private	McCOY DENNIS
Private	McLAUGHLIN JAMES
Private	McLUNE WM.
Private	MASON WM.
Private	MILTON ANDREW Wounded
Private	MILLARD JOHN
Private	MORTIMER JAMES
Private	MULLEN JOHN
Private	NAILOR EDWD. Pair with M.G.S. (4Bars) E. Naylor
Private	NEILLSON WM.
Private	NOOM PATK.
Private	O'NEAL WM.
Private	PERROZO MANUEL
Private	POLLITT THOS.
Private	QUINN JOHN
Private	RAMKIN SAML.
Private	RATTERY JOHN
Private	ROYALS THOS.
Private	ROGERS JOHN
Private	RILEY THOS.
Private	SHORTLAND THOS.
Private	SHEHAN HENRY
Private	SHEALES JOHN
Private	SIMPSON SAML.
Private	SMITH JOHN 1st
Private	SMITH JOHN 2nd
Private	SMITH JAS. 1st
Private	SMITH JAS. 2nd
Private	SMALLWOOD PETER
Private	THOMPSON SAML.
Private	THOMAS DAVID
Private	WALTON JAMES
Private	WATSON THOS.
Private	WALKER WM.
Private	WILLIAMS THOS.
Private	WILLIAMS JOHN

Captain George Young's Company

Serjeant	BOND ISSAC
Serjeant	CLUFF EDWD.
Serjeant	MELVIN MOSES
Serjeant	NEWMAN JOHN
Serjeant	RAMSEY ALEX.
Corporal	BARTON CHAS.
Corporal	CLEWS THOS.
Corporal	DOYLE PETER
Corporal	FREEMAN ROBT.
Corporal	JACQUES WM.
Corporal	LOWE WM.
Corporal	WITHALL WM. Wounded
Drummer	ASHEN JNS.
Drummer	TORSELL WM.
Private	AYRES FRANCIS
Private	ASBILL JOHN
Private	AUDLEY JOHN
Private	BATES WM.
Private	BATTLE GEORGE
Private	BOOTH RALPH Wounded
Private	BOYES THOS.
Private	CALVERLY JAMES Wounded
Private	CARRINGTON JNS.
Private	CAVANAGH JAMES
Private	CHAPMAN JAMES Wounded
Private	CHEERS JOHN
Private	COLLINGS MICHL.
Private	CONNOR MATTW.
Private	CRAWFORD JAMES
Private	CUMMERFORD TITUS Wounded
Private	DEVLIN HUGH

Private	ELLIS RICE
Private	FALLON JAMES
Private	FARROW JOHN Deserted
Private	FITZGERALD JOHN
Private	FINDEY JAMES
Private	FOGERTY THOS. Wounded
Private	FROOME JOSEPH
Private	GORMAN SAML. Wounded
Private	HANLIN MICHL.
Private	HARES JOHN
Private	HORN WM.
Private	HUNT SAML.
Private	JACKSON THOS
Private	JAMES RICHD.
Private	JELLINGS WM.
Private	JONES WM.
Private	JONES CHARLES
Private	JONES GEORGE
Private	JOHNSTONE JNS.
Private	JOWETT BENJN.
Private	KAY JOHN Wounded
Private	KEOGH JOHN Wounded
Private	KELLY JOHN Wounded
Private	KELLY DENNIS
Private	KELK JOHN
Private	KENWORTHY EDWD.
Private	KNOTT JOHN
Private	LAY THOS.
Private	LEVELL ANDREW
Private	LOUGHRAN JOHN
Private	LOMAS NATHL.
Private	MANDERS THOS.
Private	McCARROLL PHILIP
Private	McCHESNEY WM.
Private	McDONALD WALTER
Private	McGRATH JAMES
Private	McNELLY JAMES
Private	McNEITH DAVID Whitaker Collection 1908
Private	McSORLEY DENIS
Private	MOLLOY PATK.
Private	MORELEY MICHL. Wounded
Private	MOWBEY JNS. Deserted
Private	MURPHY DANIEL
Private	MURPHY PATRICK
Private	NASH THOS.
Private	NELSON GEORGE Wounded
Private	NEAGLE JAMES Wounded
Private	NOBLETT JOHN
Private	NORRIS JOHN
Private	OAKES JAMES
Private	PAYTON JOHN
Private	PEMBER JAMES
Private	PRIEMORE WM.
Private	REDDY TEDDY
Private	RICE DANL.
Private	ROBINSON WM.
Private	SAVAGE THOS.
Private	SAVAGE GEORGE Wounded
Private	SCOTT WM.
Private	SEWELL WM. Wounded
Private	SWEENEY ANTHY.
Private	SPENCER JOHN
Private	TASKER JOHN
Private	TURLEY WM.
Private	TURNER JOHN
Private	WALL MICHL.
Private	WELLS EDWD.
Private	WHITE THOS.
Private	WILDSMITH JOHN
Private	WOODMAN JAMES Officer's Mess 52nd Oxford L.I. May 1909

Captain James McNair's Company

Serjeant	DEWIS WM.
Serjeant	HOLLIDAY JOHN
Serjeant	KING THOS.
Serjeant	MILLS JOHN
Serjeant	MENZIES ARCHD.
Serjeant	NEEDS THOS.
Serjeant	RIDDLER ARCHD.
Corporal	BARLOW WM.
Corporal	GILPIN HENRY Wounded
Corporal	MARTIN CHAS.
Corporal	ROBINSON JOHN
Corporal	TOWNSEND WM.
Corporal	WRIGHT JOHN
Corporal	WASMOND JAMES
Drummer	BOY JOSEPH
Drummer	HUNT NICHS.
Drummer	MORRISON ALEX.
Private	ALLEN WM.
Private	AXCELL NEMIAH
Private	AUSTIN GEORGE
Private	AYERS ROBT.
Private	BABY JAMES
Private	BACON JOHN
Private	BOTTOMS ROBT.

Private	BONE JOHN
Private	BRAND HENRY
Private	BLACKMAN THOS. Glendining's SALE Feb. 1911
Private	BROWN JAMES
Private	BRODRICK MICHL.
Private	CALLON JOHN
Private	CHEW WM. Glendining's SALE July 1911
Private	CLARKE ROBT.
Private	CLARK WM.
Private	COFFILL PATK.
Private	CONROY JOHN Wounded
Private	COLES GEORGE
Private	COCKLADE CHAS.
Private	COULTER SAML.
Private	COVENTRY WM.
Private	DIGHTON WM. Wounded Whitaker Collection 1908
Private	DUNN RICHD.
Private	EDWARDS JAMES
Private	EMMS JOHN
Private	EVANS WM.
Private	FAIRMAN WM.
Private	FRIEND ROBT.
Private	GIBBS BENJN.
Private	GELVIN DAVID
Private	GARLIKE SAML.
Private	GOULD JAMES Wounded
Private	GORRINGE THOS.
Private	GRIFFITHS ROBT.
Private	HARK CHARLES Wounded
Private	HARRIS WM.
Private	HILLIER GEORGE
Private	HIGGINS CARBRO.
Private	HUDD EDWD.
Private	HOOKAWAY JOHN
Private	HOLDING RICHD.
Private	HUGHES WM.
Private	HUNT RICHD. Wounded
Private	JONES ROBERT Wounded
Private	KINGSHIP CHAS.
Private	KEMPSEY ALEX.
Private	LYRNES TIMY.
Private	LANGFORD JNS.
Private	LUCAS THOS. Wounded
Private	MAHONEY MARTIN
Private	McDONAGH TIMY.
Private	McGEE HENRY
Private	McLAUGHLIN JAMES
Private	MOORE HENRY
Private	MORGAN WM.
Private	NEWING EDWD.
Private	NOWLAND JOHN
Private	ODDY WM.
Private	OVENDEN JOHN
Private	PAGE EDWD.
Private	POPE WM.
Private	PRATT ROBT.
Private	RICHENS WM.
Private	ROBINSON JOSH.
Private	SMITH WM. 1ST
Private	SMITH WM. 2nd
Private	SMITH STEPN Wounded
Private	SCONE GEORGE
Private	STANTON PETER
Private	THOMASON THOMAS
Private	WATERS THOS.
Private	WATT ROBT.
Private	WARD BERND.
Private	WHEELER SAML.
Private	WELLINGTON SAML. Wounded
Private	WIFFEN MICHL.
Private	WILLIAMS HUGH
Private	WILTSHIRE ROBT.
Private	WRIGLEY BENJN.
Private	WOOD CARNEY
Private	WOOD WM.
Private	WOONE WM.
Private	WINCH CHAS. Wounded

KILLED IN ACTION & DIED OF WOUNDS RECEIVED AT WATERLOO

Private	SIMMS WM.
Private	MATTHEWS THOS.
Private	GROGAN ANTHY.
Private	MARSHALL WM.
Private	DELANEY PATK.
Serjeant	WILLIAMS WM.
Private	CLEMMINGS WM.
Private	CHAPMAN JAMES
Private	DICKENSON JAMES
Private	WILLIAMS JAMES
Private	MEYERS JAMES
Private	WOODLAND HENRY
Private	ROGERS JOHN
Private	GOULD JAMES
Private	FAIRMAN WM.
Private	CONROY JOHN
Private	FLANAGHAN PATK.

Private	BATES GEORGE
Private	ASH THOS.
Private	TOPING SAML.
Private	BELL GEORGE
Private	COOK THOS.
Private	HARDING HENRY
Private	JONES THOS.
Private	VITTEY THOS.
Private	HODGES GEORGE
Private	MILTON ANDREW
Private	DORNING HUGH
Corporal	COLLIS SAML.
Private	BENCE RICHD.
Private	DUFFEY JAMES
Private	MURPHY CHAS.
Private	JONES JOHN 1st.
Private	McCARTY PATK.
Private	SUMMER JOHN
Private	PEARSE RICHD.
Private	WILSON JOHN
Private	JONES JOHN 2nd.
Private	PRAY DAVID
Private	NORTH ROBT.
Serjeant	BUSWELL WM.
Private	INSCOW JAMES
Corporal	WITHALL WM.
Private	NEAGLE JAMES
Private	HAGGERTY THOS.

* * *

54th REGIMENT OF FOOT

Lt.Colonel	WALDGRAVE JNS. Earl
Major	KELLY ALLEN
Qr.Master	COATES WM. Gray Coll.1908
Surgeon	REMOND GEO.
Ass.Surgeon	FINAN M.F.
Ass.Surgeon	LEACH GEORGE
Pay Master	IRWIN HENRY

Captain Leslie's Company

Captain	LESLIE JAMES
Lieutenant	POTTS J.H. Cheylesmore Collection 1908
Lieutenant	LEACROFT ROBERT
Lieutenant	CLAWS WM.
Serjeant	LONNON HENRY
Serjeant	CHAMBERS ROBT.
Serjeant	DEVELIN HUGH Galway Foley Collection 1910
Serjeant	GIBSON JNS.
Corporal	BLACK JAMES
Corporal	GIBSON ISSAC
Corporal	MUIR HENRY
Corporal	PRICE JOHN
Drummer	BRYANT WM.
Drummer	KEE JOHN
Drummer	WEST ROBT.
Private	ALLEN JNS.
Private	BETTS WM.
Private	BENSON WM.
Private	BOLTON JOHN
Private	BLEWER JOSH.
Private	BOND WM.
Private	BONNERS JAMES
Private	BOYLE ROBT.
Private	BROOKS GEO.
Private	BURTON JOHN
Private	BUTLER WM.
Private	CHILD THOS.
Private	COLLIN WM.
Private	COLLINGS CHAS.
Private	CRUISE MICHL.
Private	DELL JAMES
Private	DRAKE JAMES
Private	EARL THOS.
Private	FOSTER JOHN
Private	FOSTER DANL.
Private	GOOCH JAMES
Private	HENEDY BERND.
Private	HAMPTON WM.
Private	HOWES GEORGE
Private	HEDDON WM.
Private	JOHNSON SAML.
Private	JUDE WM.
Private	KARY ROGER
Private	LEWIS JNS.
Private	McMANNS JAS.
Private	MARRION PATT.
Private	McVIE WM.
Private	MOORE JAMES
Private	MURRY THOS.
Private	MURPHY PATK.
Private	NELSON HENRY Glendining's sale Oct. 1913
Private	OATES FRAMCIS
Private	PHILLIPS JOHN
Private	PHILLIPS JAMES
Private	PARISH WM.
Private	REVELL JAMES Glendining's sale 21 July 1909
Private	SCOTT STEPHEN

Private	SNEDDON JOHN
Private	SMITH EDWD.
Private	THOMAS JAMES
Private	TULLY JAMES
Private	WATERS WM.
Private	WALDRON JAS.
Private	WELDON CHRIS.
Private	WEBSTER WM. Died 29th July
Private	WOODS GEORGE

Captain Campbell's Company

Lieutenant	FRASER GEO.
Lieutenant	TAYLOR FRANS.
Ensign	CLARKE JNS.
S.Major	VITHETHLEY THOS.
Q.M.S.	ENWRIGHT MATTW.
P.M.S.	BORLAND WM.
Dr.Major	HOWE THOS.
Serjeant	FITZPATRICK JNS.
Serjeant	HORTON JAMES
Serjeant	MATTHEWS CHAS.
Serjeant	JONES THOS.
Corporal	ABBEY ROBT.
Corporal	BLOUT EDWD.
Corporal	HOWARD JNS.
Corporal	WALKINSHAW ROBT.
Drummer	CONNERS MICHL.
Private	BANFIELD JAMES
Private	BARRY PATRICK
Private	BEESON WM.
Private	BREADY BERND.
Private	BROWN WM.
Private	BULL JNS.
Private	BRUCE EDWD.
Private	BOYLE ANDW.
Private	CLINTON WM.
Private	COX JOSH.
Private	COOPER WM.
Private	COOTE WM.
Private	CUNNARDS WM.
Private	DEVELIN MICHL.
Private	ELMORE ABRM.
Private	GALLAGHER JNS
Private	GIBSON JOSH.
Private	GOOSE EDWD.
Private	GURNEY THOS.
Private	HAMMOND WM.
Private	HODGES JAMES
Private	HOWARD MICHL.
Private	KELLY PATT.
Private	KELLY MARK
Private	KIDD ROBT.
Private	LYNCH JAMES
Private	MANN JOHN
Private	McMANUS ROBT.
Private	McQUAID RODGER
Private	MILLS JOHN
Private	MITCHELL WM.
Private	NORTON ROBT.
Private	NORTON JOHN
Private	PETTITT EDWD.
Private	PEALE THOS.
Private	READING MATTW.
Private	RYAN JAMES
Private	SADLER JOHN
Private	SMITH RICHD.
Private	SMITH WM.
Private	SCASE WM.
Private	VOTIER WM.
Private	WARNES JAMES
Private	WILSON JOHN
Private	SIZELAND JAMES

Captain Blakeman's Company

Captain	BLAKEMAN RICHD.
Lieutenant	BURGESS FRANS.
Lieutenant	LLOYD M.S.H.
Ensign	NUGENT EDWD.
Serjeant	NEAL PATK.
Serjeant	BEADLE WM.
Serjeant	McCORMICK RODGER
Serjeant	PATTERSON JACK
Corporal	GRWADY TIMY.
Corporal	MvENNEY JAMES
Corporal	RICE JOHN
Corporal	ROWLAND WM.
Drummer	CHAMBERLAIN GEO.
Drummer	RICHMOND MATT.
Private	ALLCOCK WM.
Private	ANDREWS GEO.
Private	ASHLEY ROBT.
Private	BARKER WM.
Private	BELL WM.
Private	BELCHER GEO.
Private	CAMPION PATT.
Private	COUSINS RICHD.
Private	DALTON CHAS.
Private	DAILEY WM.
Private	DOWDE CORNS.
Private	DRAKE ROBT.

Private	EDWARDS ISSAC
Private	ELFLECT EDWD%
Private	ELLIOTT CHAS.
Private	FINCHAM ELFRED
Private	FISH BENJN.
Private	FOLEY PATT.
Private	FRENCH JAMES
Private	FUHES JOHN
Private	GORDON ROBT.
Private	GREEN MARTIN
Private	GRIEF HENRY
Private	GORRIVA MICHL.
Private	HOBAN EDWD.
Private	HUNTER JONTHN.
Private	KENNEDY THOS.
Private	MELLOWS GEORGE
Private	McQUILLAN JAMES
Private	NEAGLE THOS.
Private	O'NEALE MATTW.
Private	PVERAN JAMES
Private	PETTIS JOHN
Private	PIGSTONE GEO.
Private	FRENCH WM.
Private	PLUNKETT EDWD. On sale at Speaks June 1910
Private	PULLING WM.
Private	RICHES WM.
Private	RYAN JOHN
Private	SCHOCK JAMES
Private	SHELTHORPE THOS.
Private	STRUTT JOHN
Private	WEBB WM.
Private	WRIGHT WM.
Private	BETTS THOS.

<u>Captain Toppenden's Company</u>

Captain	TOPPENDEN G.J.
Lieutenant	GREY JOHN
Lieutenant	STACKPOLE RICHD.
Ensign	CLARKE PRYCE
Serjeant	NOBBS THOS.
Serjeant	PALMER EDWD.
Serjeant	PETTIGREW THOS.
Corporal	BARRY JAMES
Corporal	DARBY RICHD.
Corporal	DANE THOS.
Corporal	KETTLES ROBT.
Private	ASHWORTH JOHN
Private	ATKINS WALTER
Private	ALLEN THOS.
Private	ASHFIELD BENJN.
Private	BELL GEORGE
Private	BILMAN WM.
Private	BLAIN GEORGE
Private	CASSEDY JOHN
Private	DOWNEY JAMES
Private	DUNN HENRY
Private	ELEY JOHN
Private	FRENCH WM.
Private	GALL JOHN
Private	GLENNING PATK.
Private	GOSS WM.
Private	GOLDING THOS.
Private	HADLEY THOS.
Private	HIPWELL JOHN
Private	HERBERT NICHS.
Private	HOGG SAML.
Private	JOHNSTONE THOS.
Private	JONES JOHN
Private	KEOUGH PATT.
Private	KING CHAS.
Private	KITCHEN THOS.
Private	McCABE PATT.
Private	McCAFFERY PATT.
Private	MANNION PATT.
Private	MASON WM.
Private	METCALF MICHL.
Private	MERRIFIELD BENJN.
Private	MOORE PETER
Private	POPS JAMES
Private	PRICE THOS.
Private	PRIEST FRANS.
Private	REID JOHN
Private	SMITH HENRY
Private	SMITH THOS.
Private	SOUTHGATE JAMES
Private	TIGHE THOS.
Private	TOMPKINS JOHN
Private	WILKINSON WM.
Private	WILLIAMSON JOHN
Private	WRIGHT THOS.

<u>Captain Crofton's Company</u>

Captain	CROFTON WALTER Bde.Major Killed 18th June
Lieutenant	PILLON JOHN
Lieutenant	PERSE WM.
Ensign	FRASER THOS.
Serjeant	DONOGHUE BARTHW.
Serjeant	LAWLESS THOS.

Serjeant	LYNCH LAWRENCE
Serjeant	MARSHALL ANDREW
Corporal	HUGHES CHAS.
Corporal	OSBORNE THOS.
Corporal	WRIGHT DANL.
Drummer	BARNES JAMES
Drummer	CLARKE DANIEL
Private	BAXTER WM.
Private	BROCK JAMES
Private	BRUCE JAMES
Private	BURNES ANTHY.
Private	CAIN PAT.
Private	CLARY WM.
Private	COBB JAMES
Private	COKELY JOHN
Private	CROFTON JOHN
Private	CRANE ISSAC
Private	DEMPSEY ANTHY
Private	DIVINE JOHN
Private	DIGBY WM.
Private	DUNCAN THOS.
Private	DANI MERINIUS
Private	DEVLIN WM.
Private	ELVIDGE EDMD.
Private	GILBERT BENJN.
Private	GIDDY JOHN
Private	HEFFERON PAT.
Private	HILTON JOHN
Private	HART DOMK,
Private	HUGHES JOHN
Private	JOHNSTONE WM.
Private	LIVINGSTONE GEORGE Glendining's sale Dec.1909
Private	McCARTHY JOHN
Private	McGEE EPHRAIM
Private	McGAWLEY PETER
Private	MARTIN THOS.
Private	MOORE DANIEL
Private	NANE EDWD.
Private	PENTON RICHD.
Private	PETERS WM.
Private	RANDALL SOL.
Private	SAVAGE THOS.
Private	SCONCHING JEFFERY
Private	SMITH JOHN
Private	SPENCER EDWD.
Private	SPENCE JAMES
Private	STONE STEPHEN
Private	STANLEY ROBT.
Private	STUBBINGS DANIEL
Private	TORPY JOHN
Private	WATERS PAT.
Private	WENHAM WM.
Private	WISEMAN CLIFT.
Private	WARD JNS.
Private	YOUNG JAMES

Captain Chartre's Company

Captain	CHARTRES THOS.
Lieutenant	HUTCHINSON FRANS.
Lieutenant	DENHAM D.
Ensign	HILL CHAS.
Serjeant	BEATON PHILIP
Serjeant	CAVANAGH WM.
Corporal	THOMPSON JAMES
Corporal	KELLEHER WM.
Corporal	PALMER WM.
Corporal	DOOLAN JAMES
Drummer	JONES WM.
Drummer	ROBINSON JNS.
Private	BIZZY JOSUAH
Private	BLOCKWELL FRANS.
Private	BOYLE ROBT.
Private	BOOTH JONATHAN
Private	CASSADY GARRAD
Private	COOPER JNS.
Private	CUDMORE GEO.
Private	DALTON PAT.
Private	DAVIS JAS.
Private	FISH EDMD.
Private	FLAG CHRIST.
Private	FOLEY PATK.
Private	FUREY MICHL.
Private	GRANGER JAS.
Private	GREADY JAS.
Private	GRIFFEN MICHL.
Private	GLENNY PATK.
Private	HEMMINGWAY JOHN
Private	HOGAN JOHN
Private	HUMPHREYS JAS.
Private	IRWIN ARCHD.
Private	KEMP WM.
Private	KILLEALEA ANTHONY
Private	LACKEY DAVID
Private	LINDSEY JOHN
Private	LYNCH HENRY
Private	LYNCH JOHN
Private	McCORMICK JAMES
Private	MULLINS JOHN
Private	McCARTHY PETER
Private	McCAFFERY JAMES
Private	NOBBS HENRY

Private	O'NEALE PATK.
Private	O'DONNELL JOHN
Private	PRATT WM.
Private	PETMORE ROBT.
Private	RAISBROCK WM.
Private	SCOTTOE EDWD.
Private	SWAINE JAMES
Private	TAYLOR WM.
Private	VICKERS FREDK.
Private	WILLIAMSON DAVID
Private	WILLIAMSON ROBT.
Private	WAKE THOS.
Private	WELCH JAMES
Private	WRAY JAMES

<u>Captain Reeves Company</u>

Lieutenant	REID JOHN Whitaker Collection 1908
Ensign	MATTHEWSON ALEX.
Serjeant	CAHILL JAMES
Serjeant	CAHILL JOHN
Serjeant	HAND MICHL.
Serjeant	SLATERY WM.
Corporal	ALLEN THOS.
Corporal	GRAHAM WM.
Corporal	McNEIL NEIL
Corporal	REDMOND JOHN
Drummer	WHITELEY THOS.
Drummer	WHITE EDWD.
Private	ANTONY DAVID
Private	BENNETT JOHN
Private	BERRY JOHN
Private	BONNINGHAM JOHN
Private	BUTLER JOHN
Private	CARTER JAB.
Private	CLAYTON WM.
Private	CLITHEROE WM.
Private	COYNE JOHN
Private	COLLUM WM. Littledale sale Nov. 1910
Private	CULLY JAMES
Private	DAVERON JOHN
Private	DOGERTY MICHL.
Private	FLETCHER JAMES
Private	FLOOD PATK.
Private	FURY WM.
Private	GANNON DOM.
Private	HAZLEWOOD ROBT.
Private	HOARE EDWD.
Private	HOGAN MICHL.
Private	HOWARD THOS.
Private	HUGHES JAMES
Private	HUGHES MATTW.
Private	HUDSON HENRY
Private	KEIF JOHN
Private	KENNY JOHN
Private	LANDREGIN THOS.
Private	MALONE OWEN
Private	MANSEL JAS.
Private	McCABE JOHN
Private	McCONNELL JOSH.
Private	McNELLEN COUL.
Private	NAUGHTON PATK.
Private	ROBINSON STEPN.
Private	RUSH JAMES
Private	ROONEY CHRITR.
Private	SAUNDERS JNS.
Private	SELLARS RICHD.
Private	SMITH JNS.
Private	THOMAS ROBT.
Private	TIGHE JAMES
Private	WHITE JAMES

<u>Captain Pigot's Company</u>

Lieutenant	WOODGATE ROBT.
Lieutenant	PILKINGTON WM.
Ensign	McLACHLAN ARCH.
Serjeant	BURNES MICHL.
Serjeant	BROWN JOHN
Serjeant	GILLIGAN JAMES
Serjeant	HUBBARD JAMES
Corporal	HOWES WM.
Corporal	KENNEDY WM.
Corporal	RYAN THS.
Corporal	WALKER HENRY
Corporal	WILSON JOHN
Drummer	FLOWERS EDWD.
Drummer	TUNIPER ABS.
Private	ADDISON ROBT.
Private	BAILEY JAMES
Private	BASLBY THOS.
Private	BENWELL JOHN
Private	BEST JOHN
Private	BRIGGS ROBERT
Private	BROWN NATHL.
Private	BOND JAMES
Private	BOYLE CONNER
Private	BUTLER MICHL.
Private	COCKINGS JOSH.
Private	CONNORS DAVID
Private	COTNEY HUGH

Private	DAWSON THOS.
Private	DOWNING THOS.
Private	FISHER WM.
Private	FITZGERALD RICHD.
Private	GALLAGHER WLATER
Private	GODFREY THOS.
Private	GOSS JOHN
Private	HUDSON THOS.
Private	JACKS ROBT.
Private	KING CHAS.
Private	KENNY EDWIN
Private	KELF CHAS.
Private	LOURNE WM.
Private	LEE JAMES
Private	MARSH JAMES
Private	MEALEY EPTER
Private	MARTIN EDWD.
Private	NAVEN WM.
Private	PITCHELL THOS.
Private	REYNOLDS THOS.
Private	SMITH ROBT.
Private	STANTON BENJN.
Private	SYMONDS CHAS.
Private	TINLEY JOHN
Private	TACKABAY JOHN
Private	VEASEY JNS.
Private	WARD FRNS. Col.Murray's Collection 1908
Private	WALKER JOHN
Private	WEAVER WM.
Private	WESTLEY JOHN
Private	WHITE DANL.

Captain Black's Company

Captain	BLACK GEO.
Lieutenant	BROOMHEAD GONVILLE
Lieutenant	MANDILHON PHILIP
Ensign	THOMAS C.W.
Serjeant	HUSSER JOHN
Serjeant	SEXTON THOS.
Serjeant	MORGAN JOHN
Serjeant	SILK WM.
Corporal	BLACKMORE JAMES
Corporal	REDMOND MICHL.
Corporal	DENNIS THOS.
Corporal	ALLEN WM.
Drummer	HEMMINGWAY GEO.
Private	ADAMS MICHL.
Private	BALDWIN VAL.
Private	BALDWIN WM.
Private	BAXTER LUKE
Private	BLACKTOP JOSH.
Private	BOID JNS
Private	BOWERS THOS.
Private	BURKE JOHN
Private	BURKE PAT.
Private	BROGIN THOS.
Private	BLANNIN EDWD.
Private	BREADY ALEX.
Private	CURLEY JOHN
Private	DAVIS THOS.
Private	DEGUM MICHL.
Private	DENT ROBT.
Private	DONOHUE JOHN
Private	DUFF MICHL.
Private	EASTACE JON.
Private	FLANAGAN PATT.
Private	FOY OWEN
Private	FORSTER JAMES
Private	FREARNS HENRY
Private	GAYNER JAMES
Private	GRANGER EADY.
Private	HINDS GEO.
Private	HENDRY JNS.
Private	JACKSON JOHN
Private	JAMES THOMAS
Private	JADE JOHN
Private	LYONS FRANS.
Private	McLACHLIN JOHN
Private	MOORE PATT.
Private	O'BRIEN JOHN
Private	PERONE ROBT.
Private	RODGERS JAMES
Private	SAMPSON THOS.
Private	SCOTT JOHN
Private	SPARROW WM.
Private	SILK THOS.
Private	WADE MICHL.
Private	WANDS JOHN
Private	MITCHELL WM.

Captain Kirby's Company

Captain	KIRBY THOS.
Lieutenant	EVANSON E.A.
Lieutenant	KELLY RICHD. Gaskell Collection 1908. Payne Collection 1911
Lieutenant	MARCON EDWD.
Serjeant	LAURIE JOHN
Serjeant	STONEHAM ANDW

Serjeant	WATSON JAMES Gray Collection 1908
Serjeant	WILLCOCKS JAMES
Corporal	ANDERSON ANDREW
Corporal	CONWAY PATRICK
Corporal	GOLDBY THOS.
Corporal	SPRUCE DAVID
Drummer	CONROY PAT.
Drummer	WEBSTER JNS.
Private	BACON JOHN
Private	BECKETT GEO.
Private	BROWN ALLEN
Private	CARTER GEO.
Private	COX JOHN
Private	COLEBY JAMES
Private	CURTIS JAMES
Private	COOPER SAML.
Private	CUNNINGHAM THOS.
Private	DANN THOS.
Private	DARGIN JOHN
Private	DOWN ALLEN
Private	DOWNEY PATRICK
Private	EVATES EDWD.
Private	GEORGE ROBT.
Private	GOTTS ROBT.
Private	GREADY EDWD.
Private	HALL ROBT.
Private	HAGUE JOSUAH
Private	HAWES EDWD%
Private	HUBERD MILES
Private	HUSSEY PAT.
Private	JEFFERIES JOHN
Private	KEENAN JOHN
Private	KENNY JOHN
Private	KEDDINGTON THOS.
Private	KENNAN JOHN
Private	LADLEY BARTRAM
Private	LARKIN JOHN
Private	MANN ANTHY.
Private	MASON WM.
Private	MARSHALL JOHN
Private	MARGARAM JAMES
Private	MAYHEW JAMES
Private	MEASURES GEO.
Private	MILLER JAMES
Private	MOORE ROBT.
Private	NOBBS WM.
Private	OLLEY ROBT.
Private	PAYNE WM.
Private	QUIRK THOS.
Private	REEVES JOSH.
Private	ROBINSON JOHN
Private	SCALE JOHN Glendining's sale April 1911
Private	SCACE JOHN
Private	SERWELL FRANS.
Private	SMITH JOHN Killed 24th June
Private	SMITH ABRM.
Private	STOREY ROBT.
Private	UPTON WM.
Private	WADE SAML.
Private	WALKER SMAL.
Private	WICKHAM THOS.
Private	WICKHAM THOS.
Private	WIDOOWS JAMES
Private	WRIGHT THOS.

* * *

2nd Bn. 59th REGIMENT OF FOOT

Lt.Colonel	AUSTEN HENRY
Major	HOGSTED F.W. Bt.Lt.Col.
Major	DOUGLAS CHAS.
Adjutant	CAMPBELL ARCHD.
Qr.Master	BEARD WM.
Surgeon	HAGAN JAMES Gaskell Collec.1908
Ass.Surgeon	COLOIN ANDREW
Pay.Master	MARR CHAS.

Captain Pilkington's Company

Captain	PILKINGTON ABRM.
Lieutenant	O'HARA PATK.
Ensign	HILL R.F.
Sjt.Major	WATSON JAMES
Q.M.S.	ROBINSON JAMES
P.M.S.	McMANUS JOHN
Ar.Sjt.	HILL WM.
Dr.Major	KELSEY THOS.
Serjeant	CREIGHTON WM.
Serjeant	DOWLING PATT.
Serjeant	MURNO ANDREW
Corporal	ARNOTT WM.
Corporal	HANLON JOHN
Corporal	McQUIRK THOS.
Corporal	WINDSOR WM.
Drummer	McNALL WM.
Drummer	WATTS WM.
Private	ATKINSON WM.
Private	BAKER STEPN.
Private	BARRETT THOS.
Private	BEATTIE RICHD.
Private	BRADSHAW EPTER
Private	BROWN GEORGE
Private	BRYNE JOHN
Private	CHISHOLM JOHN

Private	CLAYTON JOSH.
Private	CLIFTON BENJN.
Private	CLOUGH JOSH.
Private	COLLINS THOS.
Private	COLVEA ROBT.
Private	COWPER SAML.
Private	CUDDEN PATT.
Private	CURTEN MICHL.
Private	DEBOE BENJN.
Private	DONAGAN EDWD.
Private	DOWLING THOS.
Private	EMMS JOHN
Private	EVANS RICHD.
Private	FITT WM.
Private	FLANAGAN EDWD.
Private	KEATLEY WM.
Private	KYLE JAMES
Private	MARSHALL JOSH.
Private	MORRIS JOHN
Private	PATE BEDFORD
Private	PERRY JOSEPH
Private	ROBINSON THOS.
Private	SMITH HUGH
Private	SPITTLE RICHD.
Private	SUTTON JOSH.
Private	SWEENEY MICHL.
Private	TAYLOR JOSH.
Private	THOMAS JOHN
Private	TREAVERS JOHN
Private	TURNER WM.

Captain Andrew Mancer's Company

Lieutenant	DENT ABRM.
Lieutenant	HILL W.H.
Lieutenant	ROBINSON GILMOUR
Serjeant	DEMPSEY JAMES
Serjeant	HOSSACK THOS.
Serjeant	MORGAN HENRY
Serjeant	WELLS RICHD. Cr.Sjt.
Corporal	BAGNELL JOHN
Corporal	CATOR JOHN
Corporal	KEARNEY BARND.
Corporal	KEENAN JOHN
Private	BRENNAN JAMES
Private	BROWN THOS.
Private	CLARKE THOS.
Private	CONNORS JOHN
Private	CROCKETT JAMES
Private	CROSTON JOHN
Private	DEMPSEY MARTIN Deserted 17th Aug. 1815
Private	DENHAM JOHN
Private	EATON JOHN
Private	FARRELL PATT.
Private	GREAY GEORGE
Private	GOOD WM.
Private	GRADY MARTIN
Private	GREEN THOS.
Private	HILL JOSEPH
Private	HOLE RICHD.
Private	JOHNSTON WM.
Private	KEATING PETER
Private	KELLY PATT.
Private	KELLY MATTW.
Private	KIRBY JOHN
Private	KIRBY PATT.
Private	LEE JOSH.
Private	LEAVER JNS.
Private	LENAGHAN JNS.
Private	McELMEEL EDWD.
Private	MAHAN JEREH.
Private	MURRELS SAMUEL
Private	OWINS MICHL.
Private	PICKSTON EDWD.
Private	RATH PATT.
Private	RICE PETER
Private	RYAN JAMES
Private	SALTER JOHN
Private	SHEERMAN JOHN
Private	SMITH JOHN
Private	SULLIVAN EDWD.
Private	SUTTLETON THOS.
Private	TAYLOR JOHN 1st.
Private	TAYLOR JOHN 2nd.
Private	TAYLOR JOHN 3rd.
Private	WARING JESSE
Private	WEBEN HENRY
Private	WHITBY JOHN
Private	WILSON THOS.

Captain James Macgregor's Company

Captain	MACGREGOR JAMES
Lieutenant	VEALL WM.
Ensign	MAKEPEACE GEORGE
Serjeant	CHEESEWRIOGHT WM.
Serjeant	DOWLING NICHS.

Serjeant	GORDON WM.
Serjeant	MURPHY JAMES
Corporal	BALL NICHS.
Corporal	WEBSTER JAMES
Drummer	HUMPHRIES WM.
Drummer	TAYLOR FRANS.
Drummer	TOMS JOSH.
Private	ARMSTRONG JOHN
Private	ATKINSON EDWD.
Private	BURROWS GEORGE
Private	BURNS THOS.
Private	CAIRNS DAVID
Private	CAWFIELD THOS.
Private	CLAYTON JAMES
Private	CORCORAN MICHL.
Private	CUNNINGHAM JAMES
Private	ENNES JOHN
Private	FITZGERALD THOS.
Private	GILLESPIE ALEX.
Private	GORMLEY PATT.
Private	HOPKINS WM.
Private	HURLEY DANIEL
Private	JEFFORD GEORGE
Private	JONES RICHD.
Private	KELLY JAMES
Private	KERSWELL WM.
Private	KIRBY JOHN
Private	LOONEY CORNS.
Private	LOUGHLAN ARTHUR
Private	McCORD JAMES
Private	McKENNA MICHL.
Private	McLERNAN HUGH
Private	McVEY HUGH
Private	MACK JAMES
Private	MALONE WM.
Private	MORAN BRIAN
Private	NURRAY MICHL.
Private	NURRAY NICHS.
Private	O'BRIEN DANIEL
Private	PAGE WM.
Private	READY THOS.
Private	RIORDEN JEREH.
Private	RICHARDSON ARTHUR
Private	ROSTON WM.
Private	SANDIFORD JAMES
Private	SULLIVAN JOHN
Private	TOOLE MICHL.
Private	WELSH JAMES
Private	WISE JAMES

Captain L.A. De Noe's Company

Lieutenant	PREEDY ROBT. Medal in coll.D. Matthews, 13 Hill St.Burnside S.Australia
Lieutenant	CHADWICK NICHS.
Ensign	PITMAN WM.
Serjeant	DOUGAN JAMES
Serjeant	HURFORD THOS. Gray Coll. 1908
Serjeant	McNALLY PETER
Corporal	BALL JOHN
Corporal	CANDISH MAURICE
Corporal	McLEERNAN JAMES
Corporal	WALLACE ISSAC
Drummer	BALL RICHD.
Drummer	HOUGHNEY JAMES
Private	BARBER JONATHAN
Private	BOWEN TIMY.
Private	BRENNAN LUKE
Private	BUTTERWORTH WM.
Private	CARVER JOSH.
Private	CHAMBERS JAMES
Private	CLARKE HUGH
Private	CLARKE THOS.
Private	DAVIS JOSEPH
Private	DONAGHY HENRY
Private	DONAGHY JOHN
Private	DONAVAN JAMES
Private	FOGG JOHN
Private	GAULLAGHER JOHN
Private	GENTLE WM.
Private	GORMLEY HUGH
Private	GRETT JOHN
Private	HALL JOHN
Private	HEAD WM.
Private	HOWELL THOS.
Private	LEARY RICHD.
Private	LEONARD FRANS.
Private	LLOYD CHAS.
Private	McGAVAGAN JAMES
Private	NICKLAN JERVICE
Private	O'BRIAN THOS.
Private	RABBITT THOS.
Private	SAVRAHAM or SORAGHAN SIMON Baldwin's List July 1912
Private	STEPHENSON CHRISTR.
Private	STEWART JAMES
Private	TATTERSALL GEORGE
Private	THOMPSON JOSH.
Private	WALLS JOSH. Absent from 18th June to 5th July 1815

Private	WHONAHON DENNIS Died of Wounds 27th June
Private	WOODLEY WM.

Captain Belche's Company

Lieutenant	MAYNE W.F.
Lieutenant	SCOTT ROBT.
Serjeant	BURBER JOHN
Serjeant	COURTIS THOS.
Serjeant	HAWSON WM.
Corporal	GANNON JAMES
Corporal	HOWARD LAWRENCE
Corporal	KEW THOS.
Corporal	SISSONS WM.
Private	BRAILY THOS.
Private	BRYAN JEREH.
Private	BUCHANNAN JOSH.
Private	BURKE JOHN
Private	CAHILL WM.
Private	CAMPBELL JAMES
Private	DANGER ARTHUR
Private	DAVY PETER
Private	DAVIS ROBT.
Private	DELFIELD WM.
Private	DOWNEY MICHL.
Private	EDGAR JOHN
Private	FITZGERALD EDMD.
Private	FITZGERALD JOHN
Private	HARRISON JOHN
Private	HEFFERNAN DAVID
Private	HENDERSON JOHN Col.Murray's Collection 1908
Private	HICKIN THOS.
Private	HONE RICHD.
Private	HORNER DAVID
Private	JEFFORD RICHD.
Private	KERSHAW JOHN
Private	KILDAY JOHN
Private	McDONALD JOHN
Private	MALONE JOHN
Private	MATTHEWS THOS.
Private	MOORE WM.
Private	NEWTON RICHD.
Private	PUGMORE WM.
Private	RAYNER JOSH.
Private	RICE JOHN
Private	RICHARDS FRANS.
Private	ROGERS THOS.
Private	SAMLL SAMUEL
Private	SUMMERS GEORGE
Private	THORLEY JOSH.
Private	THORNE HENRY
Private	TONE JOHN
Private	TOOL JAMES Absent from 18th June to 4th July 1815
Private	TURNER HENRY
Private	VARNEY ROBT.
Private	WHITNEY WM.
Private	WHITTON SAML.
Private	WOODWARD RICHD.

Lieutenant	McPHERSON ALEX Whitaker Collection 1908
Ensign	ROSS A.C.
Serjeant	FIELDING SAMPN.
Serjeant	MULLIMDER THOS.
Serjeant	McGORMICK GEORGE
Serjeant	NORRIS WM.
Corporal	McDOUGALL JAMES
Corporal	MURPHY JAMES
Drummer	TOWNSEND JOHN
Private	BRIDGE THOS.
Private	COATS WM.
Private	CONNELLY JAMES
Private	CURRY ROBT.
Private	DEVITT MARTIN
Private	DILLON PETER
Private	DOWLING THOS.
Private	DOYLE SIMON
Private	ENNES THOS.
Private	FALLON PATK.
Private	FARRELL FRANS.
Private	FINN EUSTICE
Private	GAHAGAN CHRISTR.
Private	GAHAN JOHN
Private	GREADY JOHN
Private	HARLEY PATT.
Private	HENDRY STEPHN.
Private	HOBBS ELIAS
Private	HOPEWELL ROBT.
Private	KELLY JAMES 1st.
Private	KELLY JAMES 2nd.
Private	KELLY OWEN
Private	KEOUGH JOHN
Private	LAWLESS JOHN Absent from 25th June to 3rd July 1815
Private	LOGAN HENRY
Private	LOGAN WM.
Private	MALONE PATT.
Private	MATTHEWS WM.

Private	O'HARA HUGH
Private	OLIVE JAMES
Private	PIEREY JOHN
Private	RUTLEDGE JOHN
Private	SEANTON THADY.
Private	SCOTT THOS.
Private	SEDGBEAU JAMES
Private	SMITH JOHN 1st.
Private	SMITH JOHN 2nd.
Private	TIERNEY LAWCE.
Private	TILL WM.
Private	THOMPSON EDWD.
Private	WILLES JOHN

Captain James Cockburn's Company

Captain	COCKBURN JAMES
Lieutenant	BROWN HENRY
Serjeant	CLARKE JOHN
Serjeant	FRASER JOHN
Serjeant	TAYLOR THOS.
Serjeant	TROY DENIS
Corporal	WELDON JOSH.
Corporal	MOORE WM.
Corporal	ROBINSON JOSH.
Corporal	SUTHERLAND JOSH.
Drummer	BAYNES JOSH.
Private	BALDWIN WM.
Private	BALL RICHD.
Private	BARBER THOS.
Private	BARKER JAMES
Private	BEDNELL RICHD.
Private	BOSHELL CHRISTR.
Private	BRIDGE RICHD. Deserted 8 July
Private	CAMPBELL JOHN
Private	CHAPMAN JAMES
Private	COOPER JOSH.
Private	CORCORAN MICHL.
Private	CRAGGS SAML.
Private	CRAWFORD SAMUEL Cheylesmore Collection 1908
Private	DAVIS HENRY
Private	DAWSON SAMUEL
Private	DENT GEORGE
Private	DONAGHY JAMES
Private	DOYLE JAMES
Private	GAVIN FRANS.
Private	GREY HUGH
Private	HAMILTON JOHN
Private	HUGHES PATT. Absent from 26th June to 6th July 1815
	LEAWORTHY JAMES

Captain John Fawson's Company

Captain	FAWSON JOHN
Lieutenant	HOVENDIN NICHS. Gaskells Collection 1908
Ensign	BLOOMFIELD H.K.
Serjeant	DALY STEPHN.
Serjeant	HARDY WM.
Corporal	BOLTON JAMES
Corporal	SPEIGHT THOS.
Corporal	SCOTT WM.
Drummer	MORRISON TERNECE
Private	BERGEN TIMY.
Private	CAIN MICHL.
Private	CARTLEDGE ROBT.
Private	DIGNAM JOHN
Private	DOYLE JOHN
Private	ELWELL WM.
Private	FARRELL DANIEL
Private	FLOOD CHRISTR.
Private	GARTHLANY JAMES
Private	GAUNT JOHN
Private	GOODMAN BENJN.
Private	GREEN JOHN
Private	HANLON PATT.
Private	HENSON WM.
Private	JONES JOHN
Private	KEENAN ANDW.
Private	KELSEY WM.
Private	McDANAUGHT RALPH
Private	McENNESSEY JOHN
Private	McKEON JOHN
Private	McLERNAN BARND.
Private	McLERNAN THOS.
Private	MADDEN JOHN
Private	MICK MICHL. Payne Coll.1911
Private	MOONEY GEORGE
Private	MORROW FRANS.
Private	PRICE JOSH
Private	RAY JAMES
Private	ROBINSON WM.
Private	ROOK CHAS.
Private	STENSON ROBT.
Private	TAPE EDWD.
Private	VALES SAML.
Private	WILSON MATTW.

Captain Francis Fuller's Company

Captain	FULLER FRANS.
Lieutenant	COWPER JOHN Payne Collection 1911
Lieutenant	DUNCAN EDWD.
Serjeant	BEDDIE ALEX.
Serjeant	HALLAM BENJN.
Serjeant	KEMP WM.
Serjeant	SMITH JOHN
Corporal	BAGNLEY ROBT.
Corporal	COUDLIFF JOHN
Corporal	LEWIS JAMES
Corporal	McKEE JOHN
Corporal	MORAN JOHN
Drummer	KNOX ALEX.
Drummer	THOMPSON JOHN
Drummer	WEST WM.
Private	ASH THOS.
Private	BEATTIE GEORGE
Private	BENNETT JOHN
Private	BROPHY MICHL.
Private	BULL ROBT.
Private	CALLAGHAM MICHL.
Private	CARTY THOS.
Private	COATS WM.
Private	CLAY JOSH.
Private	CROOKS JAMES
Private	CUTTLE THOS.
Private	DOYLE JOHN
Private	DOWNEY JOHN
Private	GRANT WM.
Private	GREEN JNS.
Private	KEATING CHRISTR.
Private	KYLE WM.
Private	LORD JOSHUA Cheylesmore Collection 1908
Private	McGEE FRANS.
Private	McGRATH GEORGE
Private	McGUIRE ROBT.
Private	McINTOSH JOHN
Private	MAKIN SAMUEL
Private	MILES WM.
Private	MONTKETTRICK ROBT.
Private	PEIRCE DANIEL
Private	PICOTT JOSH.
Private	RILEY JAMES
Private	ROBINSON JOHN
Private	SENIOR WM.
Private	SHANNANHOUSE JOHN
Private	SHIPSTON JOHN Littledale sale Nov. 1910
Private	SILKSTON HENRY
Private	SPRAY JAMES
Private	STAMP JOHN
Private	STEPHENS ROBT.
Private	STREIGHT NATHL.
Private	THOMPSON HENRY
Private	TIERNEY NICHS.
Private	TIERNEY HUGH
Private	TUFT WM.
Private	WALSH JOHN
Private	WHEATLEY JOHN
Private	WILSON WM.
Private	WOOD JOHN Glendining's sale Feb. 1911

Captain J.A. Crawford's Company

Captain	CRAWFORD J.A.
Lieutenant	CARMICHAEL LEWIS
Lieutenant	HARTFORD HENRY
Serjeant	BROTHERTON JOHN
Serjeant	CONNORS MICHL.
Serjeant	MURRAY ROBT.
Serjeant	SHIPSTON GEORGE
Corporal	CULLEN WM.
Corporal	DUNN MICHL.
Corporal	LODGE JACOB.
Corporal	MALONE MICHL.
Corporal	MURNO ARTHUR
Drummer	GANLEY WM.
Private	ATKINSON THOS.
Private	BRENNAN GEORGE
Private	CASSEDY MARTIN
Private	CASTLE JOHN
Private	CLEWS JAMES
Private	CONLAN JOHN
Private	COVINGTON EDWD.
Private	CROFT RICHD.
Private	CUNNINGHAM EDWD.
Private	DEGAIN DANIEL Deserted 21st July
Private	DIXON JOSH.
Private	DOLAN MARTIN
Private	DUNN PETER
Private	GAILY DAVID
Private	GRAY JOSH.
Private	HARDY WM.
Private	HAWKINS WM.
Private	HIGGINS JAMES
Private	HOPKINSON JOHN

Private	HUFFEN JAMES
Private	KELLY WM.
Private	KINGSMILL GEORGE
Private	LACEY JOHN
Private	McCABE JOHN
Private	McGILVRAY JOHN
Private	McKIBBIN ABRM.
Private	McLOUGHLIN JAMES
Private	MAKIN PATT.
Private	MALLON MARK
Private	MARRIOTT THOS.
Private	MARSHALL JAMES
Private	MAY RICHD.
Private	MULHOLLAND HUGH
Private	NEEDHAM WM.
Private	PEARSON WM.
Private	QUINN WM.
Private	ROACH DAVID
Private	ROBINSON RICHD.
Private	RUSSELL THOS.
Private	RUSSELL THOS.
Private	RYAN PATT.
Private	SHERIDAN JAMES
Private	SULLIVAN WM.
Private	SWANN WM.
Private	SWEENEY OWIN
Private	WHITTON DAVID
Private	WOODTHORPE EDWD.

* * *

2nd Bn. 69th REGIMENT OF FOOT

Major	MUTTLEBURY GEO. Bt.Lt.Col.
Captain	WATSON LEWIS Bt.Major
Xaptain	LINDSAY HENRY Bt.Major Wounded
Captain	COTTER G.S.
Captain	CUYLER CHAS.
Captain	BARLOW G.W.
Lieutenant	HARRISON W.H.
Lieutenant	FRANKLIN ROGER
Lieutenant	PARKER STEPN.
Lieutenant	PIGOTT BROOK Wounded
Lieutenant	BUSTED CHRISTR. Whitaker Collection.. Wounded
Lieutenant	ROY NEIL
Lieutenant	INGLE CHAS.W.
Lieutenant	HILL JOSH.
Lieutenant	DICKSON C.L.
Lieutenant	SYEWART JOHN Wounded
Lieutenant	ANDERSON HENRY Wounded
Ensign	HODDER EDWD. Wounded
Ensign	BARTLETT WM.
Ensign	SEWARD CHAS.
Ensign	KEITH E.D.
Adjutant	OLDERSHAW HENRY
Qr.Master	STEVEN MATTW.
Surgeon	BANCKS CLEMENT
Surgeon	BARTLETT JAMES

Captain Henry Cox's Company

S.Major	HASSELL WM.
Q.M.S.	BLYTHMAN WM.
Ar.Serjeant	PIERSON ISSAC
Dr.Major	LANGTHAN JAMES
Serjeant	FINIRAN FRANCIS
Serjeant	HOLLYHEAD JOHN
Serjeant	RIDDLE JAMES
Serjeant	TAPLADY CHRISTR.
Corporal	BENN WM. Gray Collection 1908
Corporal	DONHAVY FRANS.
Corporal	FLOME DENNIS
Corporal	SWEENEY PATK.
Drummer	GRAID WM.
Drummer	WILLIAMSON WM.
Private	ANDERSON WM. Invalided
Private	ARGENT GOULDING
Private	BAKER HENRY
Private	BEASHAM CORNS.
Private	BUTLER WM.
Private	BRIAN TIMY.
Private	BROOK THOS.
Private	BYFORD BENJN.
Private	CARPENTER THOS.
Private	CHADD WM.
Private	COLBY JOHN
Private	COTTER JOHN
Private	COWAN THOS.
Private	DAUBER WM.
Private	DELICATE JOHN Col.R.T. Gascoigne's Collec. March 1909
Private	EMBLAM CHAS.
Private	FOSTER CHAS.
Private	HART JAMES
Private	HEPERAN PATK.
Private	HYMAN JOHN
Private	JOHNSON JAMES
Private	KEARNEY ROGER
Private	KNIGHT JOSPEH
Private	LYNN SAML.
Private	McDONALD DANL.

Private	NEIL BRIAN
Private	O'DONALD ANDW.
Private	PRICE JOSH.
Private	PROSSER THOS.
Private	REDMOND PHILIP
Private	RYAN PATK.
Private	SHOOTER GEORGE
Private	STANNARD CHAS.
Private	STEPHENS WM.
Private	STOKES JOHN
Private	THOMPSON GEORGE

Captain Issac Downing's Company

Serjeant	CURRONS JOSH.
Serjeant	McMAHON WM.
Serjeant	SHILTON JOHN
Serjeant	KERR RICHD. Cheylesmore Collection 1908
Corporal	GEE THOS.
Drummer	TATE JOHN
Private	ASKEW JOSHUA
Private	BOLTON ELIAS Day sale April 1910
Private	CHRISTIE ALEX.
Private	CLARKSON FRANS.
Private	CLINTON ALEX.
Private	COE JOHN
Private	COE CHAS.
Private	COLLIS DANL.
Private	CUSHIE WM.
Private	DAVIS WM.
Private	GOODCHILD WM.
Private	GRENNAN JAMES
Private	HARRISON THOS.
Private	HARTY THOS.
Private	HAWKINS JOHN
Private	HEATH JOHN
Private	HICKEY MARTIN
Private	HURST SAML.
Private	IMPEY THOS.
Private	JOHNSON WM.
Private	LANDFORD WM.
Private	LARDER JAMES
Private	MARSHALL JOHN
Private	McCARTNEY WM.
Private	MOWSER JAMES
Private	O'BRIAN LAWRENCE
Private	PIGGS JOHN
Private	PHILLIPS JOHN
Private	PINHORN WM.
Private	POLLARD SAML.
Private	REGAN THOS.
Private	ROCHE WM.
Private	SAVERY JAMES
Private	SCROOB ROBT.
Private	SMITH THOS.
Private	STIDDARD JOHN
Private	THORNHILL WM.
Private	TAYLOR WM.
Private	THOMAS WM.
Private	TYLER JOHN
Private	WILSON GEORGE 1st
Private	WILSON GEORGE 2nd
Private	WRIGHT JOHN

Captain Charles Cuyler's Company

Serjeant	ROTTEN WM.
Serjeant	HENSON ZACH.
Corporal	PLUNKETT PETER
Corporal	KERR EDMUND
Corporal	BARROW JOSH.
Drummer	AKERS WM.
Private	BRAY MICHL.
Private	BROWN EDWD.
Private	BURKE PATK.
Private	BURKE WM.
Private	CLARKE WM.
Private	CORDWELL ROBT.
Private	COTTINGHAM THOS.
Private	CROFT ROBT.
Private	DONOGHUE THOS.
Private	EGHY THOS.
Private	FARQUHAR JOHN
Private	FORAN JOHN
Private	FORD PATK.
Private	GILLETT ELIJAH
Private	HOWLEY HUGH
Private	HUDSON JAMES
Private	HAUNSEY WM.
Private	McELHANNAN EDWD.
Private	McGIRL PETER
Private	McGRATH ANDW.
Private	MONAGHAN ARCHD.
Private	McDONALD JOHN
Private	MURRAY JOHN
Private	MALOY JOHN
Private	NEIL JAMES
Private	NEWTON THOS.
Private	ORMANDY ROBT.
Private	ORBRO PATK.

Private	PRITHERO JOHN Galway Foley Collection 1910
Private	ROTH JOHN
Private	STEPHENSON JOHN
Private	SHEPPARD LYNN
Private	SMIDLEY JAMES
Private	SOMERS THOS.
Private	SMITH ROBT.
Private	TRIVETT SAML.
Private	VAUGHT EDWD.
Private	WHITEHEAD JOHN
Private	WHITING JOHN
Private	WILKINSON JOHN
Private	WAGDALE GEORGE
Private	WALSH HENRY
Private	WARD THOS.

Captain Charles Lowrie's Company

Serjeant	DAWKINS JOHN
Serjeant	HACKETT LAW. Payne's Collection 1908
Corporal	CARROLL MICHL.
Corporal	VARLOW RICHD.
Corporal	LONG ALEX.
Drummer	FARROW JOHN Glendining's sale 17 June 1908
Drummer	BISHOP PETER
Drummer	COLLINGWOOD THOS.
Private	AMOS THOS.
Private	ANDERSON WM.
Private	CHAPMAN JAMES
Private	CHAPMAN WM.
Private	CONNELL JOHN
Private	COLLINS WM. Gray Collection 1908
Private	COOKE JOSEPH
Private	DEIGHTON WM.
Private	DONALDSON ANDREW
Private	DOWSCETT JOHN
Private	EWING CHAS.
Private	FAIRLEGS JAMES
Private	GREETHAM RICHD.
Private	HAWTHORN JOHN
Private	HAYALL RICHD.
Private	HOWARD THOS. Col.Murray's Collection 1908
Private	JOHNSON THOS.
Private	LOCKETT AARON
Private	MARTIN GEORGE
Private	MAITHLAND ALEX.
Private	MACKEY COLVIN
Private	NILSON JOHN
Private	NICKSON WM.
Private	OGLE TIMY.
Private	PHILLIPS JEREH.
Private	POTTER ROBT.
Private	PATCHETT ROBT.
Private	RYLANDS CHAS.
Private	SHERWIN EDWD.
Private	SMILEY JAMES
Private	SHUTTER JOHN
Private	SCOFFIN THOS.
Private	UTTING CHAS.
Private	WILLS JOHN
Private	WILDON THOS.
Private	WHIPHAM RICHD.
Private	WINSTANLEY RICHD.
Private	WOODSTOCK SIMON

Captain Mathew Jennour's Company

Serjeant	BROWM WM.
Serjeant	PRATT GEORGE
Corporal	LYNCH JOHN
Corporal	MURNEY ROBT.
Private	ALLEN CHAS.
Private	ALLEN WM.
Private	BARTON THOS.
Private	BROWN WM.
Private	BURRELL JONATHAN
Private	BYTHEWAY SAML.
Private	CLARKE THOS.
Private	CARTER JAMES
Private	DEALE JOSH.
Private	DRAKE SAML.
Private	ENOS JOHN
Private	FARRELL JOHN
Private	FERGUSON JOHN
Private	FISHER GEORGE
Private	HARADINE JAMES
Private	HARGREAVES JOHN
Private	HOGAN PATK.
Private	KENNEDY WM. 1st.
Private	KENNEDY WM. 2nd.
Private	LOCKHART ROBT.
Private	McLEAN JOHN
Private	MERRY WM.
Private	MORIER HENRY
Private	NEWSON SHADRACH.
Private	PEACOCK JOSH.
Private	RAREBY RICHD.

Private	TURNER JAMES
Private	WALKER GEORGE
Private	EGGINTON JNS.

Captain Peter Wallatt's Company

Serjeant	ABERNATHY JAMES
Serjeant	FLYNN MICHL.
Serjeant	HALL ARTHUR
Corporal	BERKIN JOHN
Corporal	BROWN HENRY
Corporal	EDWARDS SIMON
Corporal	WHITE WM.
Drummer	COOPER JOSEPH
Private	BAKER RICHD.
Private	BRINTON THOS.
Private	BEARD JOSH.
Private	CULLINGHAM JAMES
Private	CULLY JOHN
Private	CREANE THOS.
Private	COOPER WM.
Private	CARROLL JAMES
Private	CHRISTMAS WM.
Private	COYLE ROBT.
Private	DIXEY WM.
Private	DAVIS JAMES
Private	DOYLE MICHL.
Private	DAWKINS MARK
Private	DOBBS STEPHN.
Private	ELDRED ANDW. NEEDES Collection 1908
Private	FITZPATRICK THOS.
Private	GIDDIS JOHN
Private	HETHERINTON CORNS.
Private	HOLMES JOHN
Private	HEATON JOHN
Private	HALL MICHL.
Private	HAIGG PETER
Private	JONES WM.
Private	JORDAN JOHN
Private	KILLICK THOS.
Private	KELLY THOS. Puttick & Simpsons sale May 1913
Private	LUTTERHILL THOS.
Private	McGEE JAMES
Private	MICHAN JAMES
Private	MORIS EDMD.
Private	MORRIS RICHD.
Private	READ WM.
Private	SCARLOT ROBT.
Private	THORNTON SAML.
Private	THUSTON JOHN
Private	SUTTY THOS.
Private	VINERS JAMES
Private	WESTERLEY GEORGE
Private	WEST JOHN

Captain W.H. West's Company

Serjeant	GLEN FORBES
Serjeant	TAYLOR JAMES
Corporal	COATES WM.
Corporal	McNALLY HENRY
Corporal	KERR JOHN
Drummer	JACKSON CHAS.
Private	BELLINGHAM THOS.
Private	BELFORD DAVID
Private	BRIGHTON BENJN.
Private	BUNTING CHAS.
Private	BURGES JOHN
Private	BURKE WM.
Private	COBB DAVID
Private	COLVER RICHD.
Private	CORCORAN WM.
Private	CURTIS THOS.
Private	DEALE BENJN.
Private	FIFE THOS.
Private	FORAKISS THOS.
Private	FRYER RICHD.
Private	GALLANT JOSH.
Private	GANTE JNS.
Private	GRIFFITHS WM.
Private	HANLEY WM.
Private	HARBER SAML.
Private	HARRISON THOS.
Private	HOWARTH JOSH.
Private	JACQUES THOS.
Private	KERR MICHL.
Private	LOUTH WM.
Private	McGREGORY BERND. JOSH.
Private	McGINNIS LUKE
Private	MULCAHY TIMY.
Private	NICHOLS HAMMD.
Private	PERKS JAMES
Private	PHELAN GEORGE
Private	SKATES WM.
Private	SMITH JOHN
Private	SPENCER FRANS.
Private	SPOONER THOS.
Private	SUTTON JOSH.
Private	TURNER EDWD.

Private	WARNES GEORGE
Private	WOODWARD WM.

* * *

1st. Bn. 71st. REGIMENT OF LIGHT INFANTRY

Lt.Colonel	REYNOLLS THOS. Col. Wounded
Major	JONES ARTHUR Lt.Col. Wounded
Major	WALKER LESLIE
Captain	REED SAML.
Captain	PIDGEON F.
Captain	ARMSTRONG ARCHD.
Captain	CAMPBELL DOND. Wounded
Captain	GRANT W.A. Wounded
Captain	HENDERSON JAMES Wounded
Captain	McINTYRE A.J. H.Gaskell's Collection 1908
Captain	JOHNSTONE CHAS. Bt.Major Wounded
Captain	GRANT ALEX.
Lieutenant	BARRALLIER JOSH. Wounded
Lieutenant	RICHARDS LOFTUS
Lieutenant	ELMES JNS. R. Dead from Wounds.
Lieutenant	STEWART CHAS.
Lieutenant	BALDWIN ROBT.
Lieutenant	HANSON WM. C.
Lieutenant	LIND ROBT. Wounded
Lieutenant	ROBERTS JOHN Wounded
Lieutenant	COATES JAS. Wounded
Lieutenant	FRAZER JOHN Whitaker Collection 1909
Lieutenant	GILLCOURNE EDWD.
Lieutenant	WHITNEY JOHN H.Gaskell's Collection 1908
Lieutenant	LANG WM.
Lieutenant	LAWE ROBT. Wounded
Lieutenant	COX CHAS.
Lieutenant	LEEVIN CARIGUS Payne Collection Wounded
Lieutenant	WOOLLCOMBE WM.
Lieutenant	TORRIANO WM.
Lieutenant	HARTAN G.W.
Lieutenant	COOTE JNS. Wounded
Lieutenant	MOORHEAD CHAS.
Lieutenant	SOUTAR DRUMD.
Lieutenant	CAMPBELL N.
Ensign	MOFFATT ABRM.
Ensign	SMITH WM.
Ensign	THOMPSON H.W.
Ensign	BARNETT JOHN
Ensign	SPALDING JOHN
Ensign	HENDERSON A.M.
Ensign	IMPETT JOHN
Ensign	LESTRANGE A.R.
P.Master	McKENZIE H.
Adjutant	ANDERSON W. Lieut. Wounded
Qr.Master	GAVIN WM.
Surgeon	STEWART A.
Ass.Surgeon	WINTEROCKES JNS.
Ass.Surgeon	HILL SAML.
Volunteer	COELEY ROBT. Promoted to Ensign since.
Volunteer	MOORE THOS. Promoted to Ensign since.

Captain W.A. Grant's Company

Serjeant Major	BUCHAM JOHN
Q.M.S.	AGNEW JOHN
P.M.S.	SINCLAIR ALEX.
Ar.Serjeant	POWER WM.
Dr.Major	BURNETT WM.
Serjeant	ANDERSON THOS.
Serjeant	FOSTER WM.
Serjeant	SMITH JOSEPH
Serjeant	TOLLY THOS.
Serjeant	WHELAN JOHN
Corporal	FINLAYSON JOHN
Corporal	FRAZER RONT. Invalided
Corporal	McGRIGOR ANGUS
Corporal	McLENNAN GEORGE
Corporal	McNAIR WM.
Corporal	PATTERSON THOS.
Drummer	McFARLIM JOHN
Private	ANDERSON WM.
Private	AITKEN DAVID
Private	AIRD JOHN
Private	AVERILL WM.
Private	BOLTON JAMES
Private	BURGES ROBT.
Private	CAMERON JOHN
Private	CODDY MARTIN
Private	CALDWELL WM.
Private	CAMLESS JOHN
Private	CRAIG WM.
Private	DOUGHERTY JAMES Day Sale April 1910
Private	EGINTON JAMES
Private	FOREMAN JOHN
Private	GIBB JOHN

Private	GORDON ROBT. Invalided
Private	GRAHAM ALEX. Discharged Cheylesmore Collection 1908
Private	GRAY DAVID
Private	HARVILL HUGH
Private	HIGGINS WM.
Private	KICHIE JAMES
Private	KELLY MICHL.
Private	KELSO HUGH
Private	KEARNS JOHN
Private	KILLIN MICHL.
Private	McEWAN JOHN
Private	McLACHLIN MICHL.
Private	McLEAN HUGH
Private	McLEOD RODK.
Private	McLURE JOHN
Private	McNABB ALEX.
Private	McNAUGHT ROBT.
Private	McVEY DANL.
Private	MELLOW DANL.
Private	MATTHEWSON ARTHUR
Private	MAXWELL WALTER
Private	MULLIGAN ARTHUR
Private	MORRISON WM.
Private	NEIL HENRY
Private	NICHOLL HUGH Col.Murray's Collection 1908
Private	NICHOLL JAMES
Private	PAISTON WM.
Private	QUINN TERNECE
Private	RAMSAY JOHN
Private	RAMSAY ALEX.
Private	RAMSAY WM. Col.Gaskell's Sale May 1911
Private	ROBBIE ALEX.
Private	ROBERTSON JOHN
Private	ROSS JAMES
Private	RUSSELL WM. Invalided
Private	TALLY MICHL.
Private	TEABROOK JOHN
Private	SHORT JOSH.
Private	SYME THOS.
Private	SLAIN JOHN
Private	SLEVIN JAMES
Private	STEWART WM.
Private	SMITH THOS.
Private	SUTHERLAND HUGH
Private	SWAIN EDWD.
Private	TEMPLETON JAMES
Private	WILKINSHAW WM.
Private	WALLACE WM.
Private	WELLS LAWRCE.
Private	WILSON WM.
Private	YEALS JOHN
Private	BROWNBELL WM.

Captain Samuel Reed's Company

Serjeant	CREIGHTON THOS.
Serjeant	DRUMMOND JOHN
Serjeant	DURIE JOHN
Serjeant	MENZIES ALEX.
Serjeant	McKAY JOHN
Serjeant	SUTHERLAND JOHN
Corporal	CLEELAND ALEX. Invalided
Corporal	GRAHAM JAMES
Corporal	HOSSACK JAMES Discharged
Corporal	MILLER WM.
Drummer	LAMOND DANL.
Drummer	PETRIE JOHN
Drummer	STEWARDS ALEX.
Drummer	WEST JOHN
Private	AITKENHEAD JOHN
Private	ANDERSON ALEX. Discharged 10th Aug. 1815
Private	BENTON THOS.
Private	BEZLAND THOS.
Private	BLACKWOOD JAMES
Private	BURNETT JAMES
Private	CASSIDY JAMES
Private	CAMPBELL COLIN
Private	COLQUHOUN ADAM
Private	COLQUHOUN ROBT.
Private	COLLINS JOHN
Private	CRAIG JOHN
Private	CULLEN EDWD.
Private	DAKERS ALEX. Invalided
Private	DALZELL JOHN
Private	DEVLIN EDWD.
Private	DEVLIN DANL.
Private	DEWELL WM.
Private	DONALDSON ALEX.
Private	DONAGHUE FRANS.
Private	DUNCAN ROBT.
Private	FARMER ROBT.
Private	GIBSON ADAM
Private	GORDON WM.
Private	GRAIG ANDREW
Private	HUME GEORGE
Private	HALL AARON
Private	HARDIE PATK.
Private	HARVIE WM.
Private	HAUGHIE FELIX

Private	JACK ARCHD.
Private	JOHNSTON WM.
Private	KELLY MATTW.
Private	KING JOHN
Private	LAWLER MICHL.
Private	LAMOND HUGH
Private	LYNCH PATK.
Private	McKAY JAMES Discharged
Private	McNANNY JOHN Invalided
Private	MOFFAT EDWD.
Private	MORTON ANDW.
Private	ODEA THOS.
Private	PETTERSON JOHN
Private	PERRIE DAVID Invalided
Private	PHILLIPS JAMES
Private	RUSSELL JAMES
Private	SCOTT WM.
Private	SHEA EDWD.
Private	SMITH JAMES Discharged 10th Aug. 1815
Private	SMITH JOHN
Private	SHAW ANDW.
Private	WARSHAW THOS. Invalided
Private	WOOD JOHN
Private	WOOLFONDEN BUCKY Invalided
Private	WILSON JOHN Discharged 10th Aug. 1815

<u>Captain Archibald Armstrong's Company</u>

Serjeant	ANDERSON JOHN
Serjeant	COOKE ANGUS
Serjeant	GALLACHER NEIL
Serjeant	GRANT BERND.
Serjeant	KENNEDY ROBT.
Serjeant	MULLEN RICHD.
Corporal	FORBES GEORGE Discharged 10th Aug. 1815
Corporal	IRANS JOHN
Corporal	JAMISON JOHN
Drummer	WEST ROBT.
Private	ANDERSON ALEX.
Private	AHERN MICHL.
Private	BISSIT THOS.
Private	BRADY PHILIP
Private	BUCHAN JOHN
Private	CAMERON JOHN Discharged
Private	CAMPBELL JAMES
Private	CAMPBELL JNS. 1st
Private	CAMPBELL JNS. 2nd
Private	CAMPBELL WM.
Private	CARSE WM.
Private	FELLOWS THOS.
Private	FLEMING HUGH
Private	GIBSON ROBT. Gray Collec.1908
Private	GOLDRICK PATK.
Private	GOUGH JOHN
Private	GRIFFITHS JOHN
Private	HAYS WM.
Private	HENRY THOS.
Private	HUTCHINSON JAMES
Private	JACK JOHN
Private	KENNEDY PETER
Private	LAMBIE WM.
Private	LAVESTON JAMES
Private	LESINGSTONE DUNCAN Needes Collection 1908
Private	LOGUE ROBT.
Private	McALLUIN ALEX.
Private	McDONALD FRANS.
Private	McGOWAN WM.
Private	McINTYRE HAMILTON
Private	McINDOON ROBT.
Private	McINTYRE JAMES
Private	McINTYRE PETER
Private	McLEAN JAMES
Private	McLORRON DANL. Discharged
Private	McMASTER DAVID
Private	McMURRAY HUGH
Private	McPHEE DUNCAN
Private	MARLOW HUGH
Private	MARTIN MICHL.
Private	MENZIES GEORGE
Private	MORGAN THOS.
Private	MURRAY ANDREW
Private	NESMITH JAMES
Private	NICHOLL HUGH
Private	NICHOLL JOHN
Private	NEVEN JOHN
Private	RATCLIFF JAMES
Private	RIELLY GEORGE
Private	RITCHIE JAMES
Private	ROACH THOS.
Private	SHEERER JOHN
Private	SMITH DANL.
Private	SMITH JOHN
Private	SWINBURNE WM.
Private	TAYLOR JOHN

Private	TAYLOR JOSH.
Private	TACKSBERRY EDWD. Col. Gascoignes Coll.March 1909
Private	NEIL RICHD.
Private	PATTERSON WM.
Private	WALKER ALLEN
Private	WATERS JONAS
Private	WILMOT HENRY
Private	WEIR JOHN
Private	WILSON ADAM
Private	WILSON THOS.

Captain James Henderson's Company

Serjeant	CHAIN JOHN
Serjeant	HENNESSEY THOS.
Serjeant	MARSHALL JOHN
Serjeant	SOMERVILL WM.
Serjeant	TOLLY WM.
Corporal	McBAIN JAMES
Corporal	McLEA ANDW.
Corporal	TODD PETER
Corporal	TYLER JOHN Needes Collection 1908
Corporal	WILSON JOHN Invalided
Drummer	BOYLE JOHN
Drummer	YOUNG WM.
Private	BARR JAMES
Private	BARTON DANIEL
Private	CHALMERS ARCHD.
Private	CLARK MATTW.
Private	CHITTOCK CHRISTR.
Private	COOPER JNS. 1st
Private	COOPER JNS. 2nd
Private	CRONAN JOHN
Private	DEMPSEY JAMES
Private	DONALD JOHN
Private	EWINGTON WM.
Private	FRAZER JAMES
Private	FRENCH FREDK.
Private	GALLACHER DANL.
Private	GRANGER JOHN
Private	GRUNDAY THOS.
Private	GLEN JAMES
Private	GUN ALEX.
Private	HARVILL THOS.
Private	JOHNSTON ALEX.
Private	LENNIE JAMES
Private	LYLE ALEX.
Private	McDONALD ALEX Discharged
Private	McDOWELL JOHN Glendinings Sale May 1910
Private	McGURK FRANS.
Private	McLELLAND JOHN
Private	MILLER MATTW.
Private	MEAD PETER
Private	MOORE GEORGE
Private	MURTOCK BERND.
Private	MURRAY JOHN
Private	MURRAY THOS.
Private	MUSTARD JAMES
Private	NASSELL WM.
Private	NESBET JAMES
Private	NICHOLL SAML.
Private	NUTTLE JAMES
Private	ORR ANDREW Discharged
Private	QUIG JAMES
Private	REILLY MICHL.
Private	RAMSAY NICHS.
Private	ROBERTSON JOHN
Private	RUSSELL ADAM
Private	SCOTT ANDREW Discharged
Private	SEAGROVE THOS.
Private	SHERIDAN CHRISTR.
Private	STEWART MATTW.
Private	SUTHERLAND GEORGE
Private	TENNANT PETER
Private	THOMPSON WM.
Private	TODD ALEX. Discharged 10th August 1815
Private	WARDROPE RICHD.
Private	WHITE ARCHD.
Private	WOODS WM.
Private	WRIGHT JOHN
Private	ROGER YOUNG
Private	KEALE JOHN

Captain A.J. McIntyre's Company

Serjeant	ANDERSON JOHN
Serjeant	LESLIE GEORGE
Serjeant	LONIE JOHN Glendinings sale February 1911
Serjeant	RAMSAY ALEX. Discharged
Serjeant	ROSS GEORGE Discharged 14th September 1815
Serjeant	SAVIN EDWD.
Corporal	GAFFENY HENRY
Corporal	MEAGHER DENIS
Corporal	OLIVER JOHN
Corporal	REA NICHOLL
Corporal	ROBERTSON JAMES Discharged 10th Auguat 1815
Drummer	KEATING JAMES

Drummer	HILL JOHN
Private	AIDDIE MATTW. Invalided
Private	ALEXANDER WM.
Private	ARROLD JOHN
Private	BUCHANON THOS.
Private	BURNES PATK.
Private	BROWN WM.
Private	CONNELLY EDWD.
Private	CONOGHIE THOS.
Private	CUMMINGS THOS.
Private	DAVIS WM.
Private	DALZIEL JAMES
Private	DICKSON DAVID
Private	DUFF ALEX.
Private	DUNCAN ANDREW
Private	EDWARDS GEORGE
Private	FOREST THOS Discharged
Private	GORDON ARCHD.
Private	GILESAN JAMES
Private	GUNN JOHN Invalided
Private	GRANGER THOS.
Private	GRANT GEORGE
Private	HADDON WM. Invalided
Private	HOOD JAMES
Private	HOSIE GEORGE
Private	LIDDLE DANL.
Private	LIND JOHN
Private	NcDERMITT MICHL.
Private	McDONALD DUN.
Private	McDUGAT ALEX.
Private	McGILVERY DOND.
Private	McGREGOR JAMES Invalided
Private	McINTOSH JOHN
Private	McINTYRE JOHN
Private	McFARLANE JAMES
Private	McLENNAN PETER
Private	McKAY ANGUS
Private	McKEE WM.
Private	MAINS THOS.
Private	MATHEWSON WM.
Private	MEAGHER WM.
Private	MULLEN GEORGE Invalided
Private	MILLER WM.
Private	MILLER GEORGE Discharged
Private	MUNRO ALEX. Glendinings sale 25 Oct. 1907
Private	MURRAY DANL.
Private	PRATT BENJN.
Private	RAMSAY WM.
Private	REED WM.
Private	RIDDLE DANL.
Private	RENWICK GEORGE
Private	ROBERTSON WM.
Private	RUSSELL DAVID
Private	ROWAN JOHN
Private	SINCLAIR ARCHD.
Private	SMITH MALCOLM
Private	SUTHERLAND COLIN
Private	SMITH WM.
Private	THOMPSON ANDREW
Private	TOBINS JAMES
Private	TAMS WM.
Private	VAUGHAN JOHN
Private	WILLIS PETER
Private	WALKER ROBT.
Private	YEATS JOHN

Captain D. Campbell's Company

Serjeant	CADZOE JOHN
Serjeant	DOUGLAS WM.
Serjeant	McDONALD DONALD
Serjeant	ROSS JOHN
Serjeant	THOMPSON PETER
Corporal	HAMILTON FRANS.
Corporal	MILLEN JAMES Discharged
Corporal	RANDLE WM.
Drummer	IRVIN JAMES
Drummer	STEVENSON DAVID
Private	ANDERSON JOHN
Private	BLAIR JAMES Cheylesmore Collection 1908
Private	BROWN JAMES
Private	BROWN ROBT.
Private	BRICE WM.
Private	CAMERON JAMES
Private	CAMPBELL BRYAN
Private	CAMPBELL DONALD
Private	CONNERS DANIEL
Private	DOUGHERTY JAMES
Private	FLOOD JAMES
Private	FULTON WM.
Private	GILMORE JAMES
Private	GRAY JOHN
Private	GRUMLEY WM.
Private	HAY JOHN
Private	HOLINS RICHD.
Private	HOWIE THOS.
Private	HUTTAN JAMES
Private	KAIN ANTHY.

Private	KERR DANIEL Discharged	Corporal	SMITH CHARLIE
Private	LONG ROBT.	Corporal	WEST WM.
Private	LYNCH JAMES	Corporal	GARTHSIDE JOHN
Private	LENNON WM. Glendinings sale July 1911	Drummer	HARDIE JAMES
Private	McARDIE CHAS.	Drummer	McCULLOCH WM.
Private	McGRAIL JAMES	Private	BISHOP JOHN Invalided
Private	McLACHLIN DUNCAN	Private	BROPHY JOHN
Private	McLEOD ALEX.	Private	CAMPBELL ALEX. 1st.
Private	McLEAN DUNCAN Discharged	Private	CAMPBELL ALEX 2nd
Private	McLUSKIE THOS..	Private	CLARK ALEX.
Private	McMANNES THOS.	Private	COOK ADAM
Private	McNAB HUGH	Private	COYLE PATK.
Private	McVEY BART.	Private	CONNORA PATK.
Private	McVICKERS ALEX Discharged	Private	COX RICHD.
Private	MEASON WM.	Private	DALLYELL ALEX.
Private	MASKIE THOS. Invalided	Private	DAVIS ROBT.
Private	MURRAY THOS	Private	EWINGTON JAMES
Private	MURRAY DAVID	Private	FOSTER HENRY
Private	MURRAY ROBT.	Private	FOTHERINGHAM ANDW. Discharged
Private	MULVANY JOHN	Private	FRAZER JOHN
Private	McCORMICK MICHL.	Private	FRAZER THOS.
Private	ORMAND ROBT.	Private	FAIRLEY JAMES
Private	PATTERSON JOHN	Private	GORE SAML.
Private	PATTON JAMES	Private	GORMAN BRYAN
Private	PARK MOSES	Private	GLENNON CHRISTR.
Private	REYNOLDS MICHL.	Private	HARVIE WM.
Private	ROBERTSON ANTHY.	Private	HOSSACK WM. Discharged
Private	ROTHWELL JOSH.	Private	HUNTER WM.
Private	SHERIDAN PETER	Private	HALL ARCND.
Private	SINCLAIR JOHN	Private	KENNEDY JOHN
Private	THOMAS EDWD.	Private	KELT CHAS.
Private	TURLEY PETER	Private	LEES JAMES
Private	WINTERBOTTOM JOSH.	Private	LINDSAY WALTER
Private	WORTHINGTON JOHN	Private	LEWIS WM. Fleming Coll.1871
Private	MARSHALL ALEX.	Private	LEES ADAM
Private	McDONALD JAMES	Private	McCULLOCH JAMES
Private	ATHENCLOSE MATTW.	Private	McFARLIN JOHN
Private	BRONEN JOHN	Private	McLERRON DANIEL
Private	ROURK BERND.	Private	McLEOD ROBT. Depot.
Private	ANGHIE JOHN	Private	McKAY JAMES
Private	McCABE THOS.	Private	McLELLAND THOS.
Private	WEIGHTON JAMES	Private	McMULLEN ANTHY.
		Private	McINTOSH ROBT. Galway Foley Collection 1910

Captain A. Grant's Company

Serjeant	CLEMENTS GUS.	Private	McLACHLIN PATK.
Serjeant	DOWNS GILBERT	Private	McHARDIE ARCHD.
Serjeant	NESS JOHN Depot	Private	MAINES ALEX.
Serjeant	THOMPSON JAMES	Private	MARSAHLL GEORGE
Corporal	MATTHEWS ALEX.	Private	MILLER CHAS.
		Private	MILLS MICHL.

Private	ROBERTSON ALEX. Depot
Private	REED WM.
Private	PESTRICK WM.
Private	ROSS PETER Discharged
Private	ROACH THOS.
Private	RIGBEY HENRY
Private	STEVENSON THOS.
Private	SUTHERLAND DAVID
Private	SMITH JAMES
Private	STEWART JOHN
Private	SCOTT JOHN Discharged
Private	STANTON ANTHY.
Private	TAYLOR MAL.
Private	TAIT JAMES
Private	WATSON ROBT.
Private	WRIGHT NOBLE
Private	WHITE THOS.
Private	WELLS WM.
Private	YOUNG ANDW.
Private	DONNELLY THOS.
Private	HAY ROBT. Discharged 10th August 1815
Private	McCOMBE

<u>Captain C. Johnston's Company</u>

Serjeant	BISHOP ANDREW
Serjeant	DUFF JOHN
Serjeant	HALL JOHN
Serjeant	MILLER DAVID
Serjeant	MANCUR WM.
Serjeant	SMART CHARLES
Corporal	DONOGHIE GEORGE Invalided
Corporal	MAN ALEX.
Corporal	MOORE ANDW.
Corporal	THAIN JAMES
Drummer	COYLE WM.
Private	AIRD DAVID
Private	BANNING LAWRCE.
Private	BUTLER JOHN Invalided
Private	CUNNINGHAM ROBT.
Private	CLEGHORN MAXWELL
Private	CAMPBELL JOHN
Private	CALDWELL WM.
Private	CARNIE BRIAN
Private	CONNOR JAMES
Private	DAVIDSON ALEX.
Private	DAVIDSON RICHD.
Private	DYOTT HENRY
Private	DOUGLAS ROBT.
Private	DURNAN PATK.
Private	FARROW GEORGE
Private	FLANAGAN CORMICK
Private	FREW THOS.
Private	FRAZER JAMES
Private	GOURLEY DAVID
Private	GRAHAM EDWD.
Private	HALLIWOOD MICHL.
Private	HICKIE JOHN
Private	LENNORD JOHN
Private	LEWIS JOHN
Private	LIND WM.
Private	LIVINGSTONE ALLEN
Private	LAMB THOS.
Private	McDOWELL JOHN
Private	McFARLIN MALCOLM
Private	McINTOSH JOHN
Private	McKENZIE DUNCAN Discharged 10th August 1815
Private	McKENZIE ROBT.
Private	McPHEES JAMES
Private	McQUAIDE JAMES
Private	MENZIES JOHN
Private	MORRISON WM.
Private	McLEAN CHAS.
Private	McLEAN WM.
Private	McLUSKIE ROBT.
Private	QUIG THOS.
Private	RENNIE JAMES
Private	SHAW JAMES
Private	SIMPSON GEORGE Glendinings sale February 1911
Private	SPENCER WM.
Private	SPRATT MARK
Private	STEWART DUNCAN Discharged
Private	STEWART JAMES
Private	STEWART WM.
Private	TAWS ALEX.
Private	THOMPSON ROBT.
Private	TODD ANDW.
Private	TODD JAS. 1st
Private	TODD JAS. 2nd Discharged
Private	TODD JNS. 1st
Private	TODD JNS. 2nd
Private	WALKER GEORGE
Private	WATSON DANIEL
Private	WATSON THOS.

Private WILSON BENJN.
Private WILSON MATTW. Invalided
Private ROSS NATHL.
Private McNICHOLL DOND.
Private ROGERS ROBT.
Private GUNN JOHN

Captain J.F. Pidgeon's Company

Serjeant HANNAH JAMES
Serjeant McPHERSON GEORGE
Serjeant MUNRO ROBT.
Serjeant ROBERTSON ALEX.
Serjeant STEWART SAVID
Serjeant SCARTH JOHN
Corporal GALBREATH WM.
Corporal GLOVER WM.
Corporal HAMILTON WM.
Corporal McCULLOCH JAMES Invalided
Corporal MUNRO DONALD
Corporal ROSS WM.
Drummer MILLER JOHN
Drummer MURPHY HUGH
Private ADAMS ROBT.
Private BEETH JAMES
Private BERRY WM.
Private BOWIE WM.
Private BLYTHE WM.
Private BRANON MICHL.
Private BROWN JOHN
Private BROWN RALPH
Private BRISBANE JOHN
Private BRUCE JOHN Invalided
Private BURNS PATK.
Private CALLEEM JAMES Discharged 10th Aug. Sotheby's sale March 1908
Private CLARK WM.
Private COYLE MAINES Sotheby's sale December 1908
Private CRAIG THOS.
Private DAILLY JAMES
Private DICKIE THOS.
Private DOUGHERTY PETER
Private DRUMMOND ROBT.
Private DONEGAN JOHN
Private FITZPATRICK JOHN
Private FIELDING JOHN Invalided
Private FLOYDE EDWD.
Private FOWLER ANDW.
Private GLASFORD ARTHR.
Private GRIFFITHS ROBT.
Private HIGGINS TIMY.
Private HOUSTAN JOHN
Private HOWIE WM.
Private HUNTER ANDW.
Private JOHNSTON GEORGE Invalided
Private KENNEBRO WALTER
Private KYLE HENRY
Private LAWE JOHN Invalided
Private McDONALD ANDW.
Private McDONOGH THOS.
Private McEWAN MICHL.
Private McLEAN FURLEY
Private McPHERSON ALEX.
Private McSHERRY PATK.
Private McWILLIAMS HUGH
Private MORRISON LEWIS Watters sale June 1913
Private MALOOGE HUGH
Private NEWGENT CHAS.
Private PATTERSON JAMES
Private REILLY PHILIP Invalided
Private RIDDLE JOHN
Private ROBERTSON RICHD.
Private ROSS JAMES
Private SCOTT THOS.
Private SMITH WM.
Private STOBBO JAMES
Private STURROCK JAMES
Private URE JAMES
Private WILSON STEVEN
Private WISHART ANDREW
Private YOUNG GEORGE Discharged

Captain G.H. Gordon's Company

Serjeant AITTON JOHN
Serjeant CARMICHAEL WM.
Serjeant EALLS JAMES
Serjeant SUTHERLAND JOHN
Corporal CROSS ROBT.
Corporal GARLAND EDWD.
Corporal LAPPIN JAMES
Corporal MORRIS ADAM
Corporal STEWART SAML.
Corporal WILLIAMS JAMES
Drummer NEVILL WM.
Drummer SINCLAIR ANDW.
Private AITKERS THOS.
Private ANDERSON THOS.

Private	BAIN JAMES
Private	BEARDSWORTH WM.
Private	BENNERMAN ALEX. Invalided
Private	BENNETT DAVID
Private	BEVINS WM. Payne Coll.1911
Private	BROWN JOHN
Private	BURCH WM.
Private	BURGES THOS. Invalided
Private	BURNS JAMES
Private	CRAM PETER
Private	DEVLIN JAMES
Private	DONALDSON JOHN Whitaker Collection 1908
Private	DONNELLY JOHN
Private	DUNN WM. Discharged
Private	DURHAM JAMES
Private	FULLERTON JAMES Killed in Action 18th June 1815
Private	GAVIN ARCHD.
Private	GILCHRIST THOS.
Private	GOODFELLOW WM. Invalided
Private	HALFPENNY JAMES
Private	HAMILTON JOHN
Private	KELLY PHILIP
Private	KIRWIN DAVID
Private	LAMONT DAVID Glendinings sale 29 July 1908
Private	LONG JAMES
Private	LOTHIAN ROBERT
Private	McATHER PETER
Private	McBEATH THOS.
Private	McAVAY FENTON
Private	McDONALD DUN.
Private	McDONALD PETER 1st
Private	McDONALD PETER 2nd
Private	McFARLIN DAVID
Private	McKAY ANGUS
Private	McLEAN DUN. Discharged
Private	McLEOD ALEX.
Private	McQUAIDE FRANS.
Private	MADDEN EDWD.
Private	MANDLE JOHN
Private	MULLEN JAMES
Private	MULVANNY ALEX.
Private	NIXON JOSEPH
Private	NESS DANIEL
Private	OLIVER ROBT. Glendinings sale 17 June 1908
Private	PRENTICE ARCHD Discharged
Private	PETERS SAML.
Private	RICHARDSON JAMES
Private	RUSK THOS.
Private	SAMS WM.
Private	SCOTT JAMES
Private	SHIELDS JOHN Invalided
Private	SMITH JOHN
Private	SIMERSTON ARTHUR
Private	SPENCER JAMES
Private	SPRINGATE THOS.
Private	STEWART JOHN Discharged
Private	SUTHERLAND WM.
Private	TAYLOR GEORGE
Private	TENNANT JAMES
Private	WILSON HENRY
Private	WILSON JOHN
Private	WILSON WM.
Private	YOULE YOULE.

* * *

2nd Bn. 73rd REGIMENT OF FOOT

Lt.Col.	HARRIS Hon.W.G. Col. Wounded
Major	KELLY DAWSON Lt.Col. On Staff Employ
Adjutant	HAY PATRICK Wounded
Surgeon	McDERMID Dr. Whitaker Coll.1908
Ass.Surgeon	RIACH JOHN
Ass.Surgeon	WHITE F.B.
Py.Master	WILLIAMS JOHN
Captain	COANE HENRY Wounded
Lieutenant	LEYNE RICHD.
Lieutenant	McCONNELL JOHN Wounded
Ensign	E.HESELRIDGE R.C. Wounded
Ensign	McBEAN WM. Wounded
Ensign	DEACON THOS. Wounded
Ensign	EASTWOOD C.B. Wounded
Ensign	BRIDGE G.E. Wounded
Ensign	HUGHES GEORGE
Surgeon	COWAN H. Record Office

Captain Richard Drewe's Company

Lieutenant	REYNOLDS THOS. Wounded
Lieutenant	LLOYD J.Y. Wounded
Ar.Serjeant	TAYLOR JOHN
Serjeant	FENNING JAMES
Serjeant	SCARRETT THOS.
Serjeant	McLAUGHLIN LUKE
Corporal	BONSER THOS.
Corporal	EAGEN GARRATT
Corporal	JONES JOSH.
Corporal	WARD JOHN
Drummer	JOHNSON JMAES
Drummer	McNAUGHT DAVID

Private	BARNES WM.
Private	BELL PHINS Discharged
Private	BADGER JAMES
Private	BRUMWELL SAML.
Private	BROWN THOS.
Private	COLGAN LEWIS
Private	CONWAY JOHN
Private	CURRIN JAMES
Private	EATON RICHD.
Private	FEAGEN NATHL.
Private	FEELY JOHN
Private	GONNON MICHL.
Private	GOWENS DAVID
Private	GREY JOSEPH
Private	HOLTON HENRY
Private	HORAN MAURICE
Private	IZZARD HENRY
Private	LINDON PATK.
Private	LOWE JAMES
Private	LYNN WILLS
Private	McKNIGHT JON. Discharged
Private	McLAREN GEORGE
Private	McNAUGHT PETER
Private	MORRIS WM.
Private	MURPHY DANL.
Private	NAUGHTON JAMES
Private	PATTERSON JOHN
Private	RYAN JOHN
Private	SCARRETT WM.
Private	TAYLOR THOS.
Private	WALKER JAMES Dead
Private	WHYNN NICHS.
Private	YATES JOSH.

Captain John Pike's Company

Lieutenant	DOWLING JOSH.
Lieutenant	STEWART ROBT.
Serjeant	HORAN NICHS.
Serjeant	MEADE JOHN
Serjeant	QUINTON JOHN
Corporal	HORAN JOHN
Corporal	STREATTON JOHN
Drummer	BARBER JOHN
Drummer	FREEMAN THOS.
Private	BRAY WM.
Private	BARRON SAML.
Private	BRIAN JAMES
Private	BRYANT THOS.
Private	BROMLEY JOSEPH Glendining's sale September 1910
Private	BROOM JOHN
Private	CARR JAMES Littledale sale November 1910
Private	CARTER DANIEL
Private	CONNER MICHL.
Private	COUGHLAN JAMES
Private	CURTIS THOS.
Private	DICKSON ROBT.
Private	FITZGERALD PATK.
Private	FLANIGAN GEORGE
Private	FLANIGAN LAWCE. Dead
Private	GALOIN WM.
Private	HARRIS ABRM.
Private	HENDERSON WM.
Private	HOBLEY JOHN
Private	HOTT JOHN
Private	JONES HENRY
Private	KELLY JOHN
Private	LANDER JOHN
Private	LYNHAM CHRISTN.
Private	MANDUS THOS.
Private	McARTHUR ALEX.
Private	McGRANE THOS.
Private	McGREGOR EDWD.
Private	McLAREN ALEX. Discharged 12th November 1815
Private	MURRAY JOHN Dead
Private	NICHOLLS JOHN
Private	PARROTT JOHN
Private	PEARCE WM.
Private	SALMON ROBT.
Private	SMITH RICHD.
Private	SEAWARD THOS.
Private	SIMMONDS JOHN Cheylesmore Collection 1908
Private	SULLIVAN ANDW.
Private	TRACEY JOHN

Captain M. Carroll's Company

Serjeant	INGLIS DAVID
Serjeant	MURPHY JOHN
Serjeant	SMITH JOHN
Corporal	DUNLOP WM.
Corporal	EAGEN JOHN
Corporal	EATON JAMES
Drummer	BALL CHAS.
Drummer	VARLEY JAMES
Private	ALLEN GEORGE
Private	ATKINS THOS.
Private	BARNETT JOHN
Private	BATES JERH.

Private	BUNSTEAD BENJN.
Private	CLARK JOHN
Private	CONNERS PATK.
Private	COUNSELL HENRY
Private	COUNSELL WM.
Private	CROSS THOS.
Private	DURRANT MARTIN
Private	EVANS WM. Discharged
Private	FLUKE JOHN
Private	FORD JAMES
Private	GARDINER EDWD.
Private	HAWES EDWD.
Private	HEATON JOSH.
Private	HIFFORD JAMES
Private	HOGAN WM.
Private	HOPGOOD WM.
Private	HORAN EDWD.
Private	JACKSON WM.
Private	JOHNSON JOSH.
Private	KENNING WILLS
Private	KERRIGAN PATK.
Private	LACEY JOHN
Private	MARRIOTT WM.
Private	MASKERRY JOHN
Private	MASEY JOHN
Private	MASEY THOS.
Private	NICHOLLS HENRY
Private	OSTLER JAMES
Private	PARKER JOHN
Private	PLUNKETT JOHN
Private	PORTER JOSH.
Private	RICE JOHN
Private	SELLERS ANTHY.
Private	SHEPPARD GEORGE
Private	SIMPSON JOHN
Private	SMALLFIELD STEPHN. Discharged
Private	WOODS JOHN

Captain W. Wharton's Company

Captain	WHARTON WM. Wounded
Serjeant	CASSINS PATK.
Serjeant	KIRK WM.
Serjeant	MvNISH ROBT.
Corporal	MARSHALL WM.
Drummer	GORMON WM.
Drummer	WILSON JOHN
Private	ARGENT EDWD.
Private	ARNOLD JOHN
Private	BENFIELD JOHN Discharged
Private	BULLOCK SOLOM.
Private	CLEWES WM.
Private	CONWAY JAMES
Private	COWAN MICHL.
Private	DAVIDSON ANDW.
Private	DENT WM.
Private	ELY JAMES
Private	FITTER FREDK.
Private	FITZGERALD JEREH.
Private	GARDINER RICHD.
Private	HARRISON ROBT.
Private	JOHNS GEORGE
Private	LUCITT RICHD.
Private	MANSELL THOS.
Private	MANTLE JOSH.
Private	McGILSON HENRY
Private	McMAHON JAMES
Private	McNAUGHT THOS.
Private	MURRAY THOS. Galway Foley Collection 1910
Private	POOLE GEORGE
Private	PORTER GEORGE Discharged
Private	REYNOR JOSH.
Private	ROGERS WM.
Private	SALT JOHN
Private	SELLERS ROGER
Private	SMITH JOHN
Private	TAYLOR THOS.
Private	TERRY WM.
Private	THOROGOOD MOSES
Private	WAKEFIELD BENJN. Dead
Private	WESTON GEORGE
Private	WILKINSON THOS.
Private	WILSON JOHN
Private	WINTERBOURNE JOHN
Private	WHITE JOHN

Captain J. Garland's Company

Captain	GARLAND JOHN Wounded
Ensign	BLENNERHASSETT A.
Serjeant	EAVES WM.
Corporal	McCROHAN DANIEL
Corporal	REID JOHN
Drummer	HOAX THOS.
Drummer	LEWIS JOHN
Private	ALES DOURNIE
Private	BATES GEORGE
Private	BACON JAMES
Private	BROTHERTON WM.

Private	BROWN JAMES
Private	CHEADLE GEORGE
Private	CHEADLE JOSH. Gray Collection 1908
Private	CHIPMAN JOHN
Private	CANLAGHAN JAMES
Private	COURTES JOHN
Private	DICKSON ROBT.
Private	DOBSON MICHL.
Private	FLATTERY JOHN
Private	GODOLPHIN JOHN
Private	GRAHAM GEORGE Deserted 12th March
Private	HAMMOND WM.
Private	JAMES FRANS.
Private	JOHNSON JOHN
Private	KELLY MATTW.
Private	LANCASTER WM.
Private	McGRATH MATTW. Dead
Private	NEIGHBOUR DANIEL
Private	PARKINS JNS.
Private	PAYNE CHAS.
Private	PUDNEY JOSH.
Private	QUITLER JOSH
Private	REID JOSH.
Private	ROACH JAMES
Private	ROSE WM.
Private	RUDDEN JAMES Discharged Glendining's sale 17th June 1908
Private	SHEATH WM.
Private	SHEPPARD EDWD.
Private	SMALLEY ROBT.
Private	SMITH JOHN
Private	VICARS JOSH.
Private	VINCENT JAMES
Private	WADE JOHN

Captain R. Crawford's Company

Serjeant	COBBETT JOHN
Serjeant	McELROY EDWD.
Serjeant	O'LEARY PATK. Discharged
Corporal	CUMMINGS THOS. Dead
Corporal	SMITH WM.
Corporal	SUTHERLAND JOHN
Private	ASHFORD RICHD.
Private	AITKENS THOS.
Private	BEAGENT ROBT.
Private	BELL THOS.
Private	BELL ANTHY.
Private	BIRD WM.
Private	BRADWELL GEORGE
Private	CLARKE RICHD.
Private	COCHRANE JAMES
Private	COACHMAN WM.
Private	EDWARDS WM.
Private	ELLOITT ARCHD.
Private	FRISWELL JOHN
Private	GOODLETT WM.
Private	GRAHAM JOSH. Dead
Private	HULL JAMES
Private	ISSAC ALFRED
Private	JEVENS BENJN.
Private	LENHAM ROBT. Dead
Private	LEONARD PETER
Private	LINTON ANDW.MICHL.
Private	METCALF GEORGE
Private	McKENNY PATK.
Private	McKILLIGAN ALEX.
Private	McELROY JAMES
Private	MURRAY WALTER
Private	NAPIER WM.
Private	O'LEARY CHAS.
Private	PIERCE SAML.
Private	ROBERTSHAW PAUL
Private	RODBETT ISSAC
Private	ROLLINSON WM.
Private	SCRIVEN JOHN
Private	SIMPSON THOS.
Private	SMITH JOHN 1st
Private	SMITH JOHN 2nd
Private	SMITH WM.
Private	SHEARS CHAS.
Private	STEWART THOS.
Private	STOCKS BENJN.
Private	TINSLEY RICHD.
Private	UPTON RICHD.
Private	WALL RICHD.
Private	WOODALL JOHN
Private	YORK WM.

Captain W. Cheslyn's Company

Serjeant	VAN HUTTON JOHN
Serjeant	WESTON WM. Col.Gaskell's sale May 1911
Drummer	WILSON JNS.
Private	ALLEN WM.
Private	AITKENS THOS.
Private	BARCLAY JOHN
Private	BARTLE JOHN
Private	BEASLEY WM. Col.Murray's Coll.1908

Private	BIRMINGHAM PATK.	Discharged
Private	BOGGINS JAMES	
Private	BOWLES HENRY	
Private	BUGGINS WM.	
Private	BOROUGHS JOHN	
Private	CHAPLIN JAMES	on sale at Baldwin's March 1909
Private	COX WM.	
Private	DAWSON JAMES	
Private	DRAPER THOS.	
Private	DURBIN WM.	
Private	ELLIS THOS.	
Private	FROST JOHN	
Private	GORMON JOHN	
Private	GRIFFIN JOHN	Col.R.T. Gascoignes Coll.March 1909
Private	HARDING JUDD	Dead
Private	HANIFY PATK.	
Private	LAMBERT JAMES	
Private	LYNCH SIMON	Discharged
Private	McCOWEN WM.	Day sale April 1910
Private	MARTIN JOHN	
Private	McDONALD ARCHD.	
Private	MOORE ROBT.	
Private	PALMER BENJN.	
Private	REMMINGTON JAMES	
Private	REYNOLDS JAMES	
Private	SCARF BENJN.	Dead
Private	SMITH DAVID	
Private	TAYLOR SAML.	
Private	TYRRELL GEORGE	
Private	WAPLES WM.	
Private	WARRINGTON PATK.	
Private	WILKINSON THOS.	
Private	WOOD NOAH	
Private	WARMOUTH RICHD.	
Private	YOUNG RICHD.	

Captain H.B. Lynch's Company

Serjeant	DENBY ADAM	
Serjeant	GROOMBRIDGE JAMES	
Serjeant	LOWE SAML.	
Serjeant	McLEAN JOHN	
Serjeant	PICKETT RICHD.	
Corporal	ELLAM JOHN	
Corporal	WATTS THOS	
Drummer	ARGUE GEORGE	
Drummer	HUDSON SAML.	
Private	ALWRIGHT JOHN	
Private	ASHENDEN WM.	Col.Murray's Collection 1908
Private	BARTON RICHD	Dead
Private	BEVILLE JOHN	
Private	BINDER JAMES	
Private	BISHOP FRANS.	
Private	BROOKS GEORGE	
Private	BURRIDGE WM.	
Private	CREEKE CHAS.	
Private	CUTTON JOHN	
Private	DEEKS JOSH.	
Private	DUFF WM.	
Private	EABOURNE ISSAC	
Private	EAST GEORGE	
Private	EVANS MATTW.	
Private	EYLES CHAS.	
Private	FLEMING STOWELL	
Private	HANDFORTH JAMES	Discharged
Private	HINDES JAMES	
Private	HOBLEY JOHN	
Private	HOWE WM.	
Private	HURLEY JESSE	
Private	JOWERS WM.	
Private	KINNAIR JOHN	Deserted
Private	KENNOCK JOHN	
Private	LOWE JOHN	
Private	LOWER JOHN	
Private	MACKIN GEORGE	
Private	MILLER LUKE	
Private	MILLWOOD JOHN	
Private	MOORE JAMES	
Private	MORRIS HUGH	
Private	MURPHY EDWD.	
Private	PHILLIPS JOHN	
Private	ROSE GEORGE	
Private	RYAN MICHL.	
Private	SUNDELL PETER	
Private	TAYLOR JAMES	
Private	TYLER BENJN.	
Private	WEBSTER HENRY	
Private	WESTWOOD JAMES	
Private	WILLMOT DANIEL	Needes Collection 1908

Captain D. Dewer's Company

Serjeant	DUNN WM.	
Serjeant	BURTON JOHN	
Serjeant	McCORMICK PETER	
Corporal	ATKINSON HENRY	
Corporal	LONE MICHL.	
Drummer	STRETTON JOHN	
Private	ARNOLD JOHN	

Private	BANFORD THOS. Deserted 21st March
Private	BARLEY JOHN
Private	CAREY GEORGE
Private	COLE JOHN
Private	CONNER JOHN
Private	DANIELS THOS.
Private	DAVEY JNS.
Private	DOWNEY PATK.
Private	ELLWELL THOS.
Private	GEE JOHN
Private	GREENHAM BERND.
Private	HARMAN FRANS.
Private	HILL ELIAS
Private	HUNTER JNS. 1st
Private	HUNTER JNS. 2nd
Private	KIRTON SAML.
Private	MANNERLY JOHN
Private	MATTHEWS WM.
Private	McCABE JAMES
Private	MILSON JOHN
Private	MORICE THOS.
Private	MORRISON WM.
Private	MOTT JOHN
Private	PALMER EDWD.
Private	PARDOE WM.
Private	PATTERSON JOHN
Private	QUINN JAMES Dead
Private	RICE JOSH.
Private	ROBERTSON WM.
Private	SAXBY WM.
Private	SIVITER JAMES
Private	STANTON THOS.
Private	SURTIS RALPH
Private	STANLEY RICHD.
Private	TOLLY JOHN

(Late) Captain Kennedy's Company

Captain	KENNEDY JOHN M. H.Gaskell Collection 1908
Serjeant	AUSTIN GEORGE
Serjeant	BELL HENRY
Serjeant	FARRON JOHN
Corporal	EDWARDS THOS.
Corporal	FLUT JAMES
Corporal	RENNIE JOHN
Drummer	HOLLAND GEORGE
Drummer	HOLT GEORGE
Private	ABBIS DENIS
Private	ALDRIDGE EDWD.
Private	ALLEN JAMES
Private	ARMSTRONG MICJL. Dead
Private	ASHBY WM.
Private	BAKER BENJN. Dead
Private	BALL RICHD.
Private	BARRETT WM.
Private	BAYLEY J.L.
Private	BROXTON BENJN.
Private	CHANDLER THOS.
Private	CONNER PATRICK Discharged
Private	COOKE EDWD.
Private	COX WM.
Private	CROWSON THOS.
Private	DAILY WM.
Private	DONAHUE JOHN Discharged
Private	DOVE JOHN
Private	FOLEY JOHN
Private	GORMON JOHN Discharged
Private	HAMMOND ROCHD.
Private	HAWKES WM.
Private	HOCKADY CHAS.
Private	JONES JOSH.
Private	MATTHEWS RICHD.
Private	McGRATH MATTW.
Private	McMILLEN ALEX.
Private	MURRAY MICHL.
Private	O'NEIL JAMES
Private	OXLEY THOS.
Private	PARROTT JOSH.
Private	QUINLAN JAMES
Private	REID ALEX.
Private	REILLY PHILIP
Private	SCOTT ALEX.
Private	SHEA WM.
Private	SMITH ROBT.
Private	THOMPSON BENJN.
Private	TURTON GEORGE
Private	WALKER THOS. Dead
Private	WALTERFIELD JAMES
Private	WHITAKER MICHL.
Private	WILKINSON WM.
Private	WRIGHT DELEMER

* * *

DETACHMENT 2nd Bn 78th REGIMENT

Serjeant	MACKAY WM.
Private	MACHEAN LAUGHLIN Needes Collection 1908
Private	MACDONALD JOHN
Captain	FRASER JAMES Record Office

1st BATTN. 79th REGIMENT OF FOOT

Lt.Colonel	DOUGLAS NEIL
Major	BROWN ANDW. (Lt.Col)
Major	CAMERON DUN. (Lt.Col)
Adjutant	HARRISON GEO.
Qr.Master	CAMERON ANGUS
Surgeon	REDESDALE GEORGE
Ass.Surgeon	BURRELL W.G.
Ass.Surgeon	PERSTON DAVID
Pay.Master	McARTHUR JOHN

Captain A. McLean's Company - Grenadiers

Captain	CAMERON ALEX.
Lieutenant	LEAPER WM.
Sjt.Major	McINTOSH MASTERTON
Q.M.S.	HAY JAMES
P.M.S.	LANE WM. Glendining's sale Oct.1913
Sch.Mr.	GRAY WM.
Ar.Serjeant	MORRIS JOHN
Serjeant	CAMPBELL THOS.
Serjeant	COWIE GORDIN.
Serjeant	GUNN ALEX.
Serjeant	McDONALD COLIN
Corporal	CAMPBELL ROSE
Corporal	McNIE GEORGE
Corporal	WALTON JOHN
Private	ANDREW DONALD
Private	BECKIE GEORGE
Private	BLACK WM.
Private	BROWN EDENR.
Private	BUCKLEY DAVID
Private	BURNS HENRY
Private	CAMERON DONALD
Private	CAMPBELL DONALD
Private	CAMPBELL NEIL
Private	CLARKE MARK
Private	CORMICK WM.
Private	DILLON DANL.
Private	DUNBAR PETER
Private	FEWEL SAML.
Private	FRASER JOHN
Private	GALL JOHN Discharged 8th January 1816
Private	GOW ALEX.
Private	GREY ALEX.
Private	HAYTER JOHN
Private	HENDERSON DAVID
Private	HUTTON PETER
Private	HARVEY WM.
Private	KERR JAMES
Private	KIRKWOOD THOS.
Private	KENNEDY JOHN
Private	McARTHUR PETER
Private	McCASKHILL HUGH
Private	McCULLOCK PETER
Private	McDONALD JOHN
Private	McDONALD WM.
Private	McINTOSH DONALD
Private	McINTOSH CHAS.
Private	McINROY PETER
Private	McINNES ROBERT
Private	McGILVRAE DONALD
Private	McKAY KENNETH
Private	McKAY ROBERT 1st.
Private	McKAY ROBERT 2nd.
Private	McKECHNIE JOHN
Private	MvLEAN JOHN
Private	McLACHLIN ALLEN.
Private	McLARREN PETER
Private	McPHERSON JOHN
Private	McPHERSON NEIL
Private	McPHEE JOHN
Private	MANSON WM.
Private	MOOREHEAD ALEX. Discharged 8th January '16
Private	MOSS JOHN
Private	MOWART JOHN Died 5th Dec'15
Private	MURRAY THOS.
Private	NOBLE ANDREW
Private	NOBLE THOS.
Private	RAGGS JAMES
Private	REID JOHN
Private	RITCHIE ALEX.
Private	ROSS DAVID
Private	STEWART ALEX.
Private	SUTHERLAND DONALD
Private	SUTHERLAND JAMES
Private	SWANSON WM. Discharged 6th March
Private	TAYLOR ARCHD.
Private	WILLIAMSON WM.

Captain Wm.Bruce's Company No.1.

Captain	BRUCE WM.
Lieutenant	FORBES ALEX.
Lieutenant	McPHEE DONALD
Lieutenant	CRAWFORD A.T.
Serjeant	BANNERMAN HUGH Cheylesmore Collection 1908

Serjeant	McKENZIE EWAN
Serjeant	SINCLAIR GEORGE
Serjeant	SWANSON WM.
Serjeant	TAYLOR DAVID
Corporal	McLEEAN JOHN st.
Corporal	McLEEAN JOHN 2nd
Corporal	O'NEIL JOHN
Private	ADAMS WM.
Private	ALLEN WM.
Private	ANDERSON JAMES
Private	ARMSTRONG THOS.
Private	BOAG CHAS.
Private	BRIAN GEORGE
Private	BRUCE JOHN Died 21st June 1815
Private	CAMERON ALEX.
Private	CAMERON JOHN THOS.
Private	CAMPBELL ANGUS
Private	COGHILL GEORGE
Private	COLEMAN WM.
Private	COVENTRY JAMES
Private	DIVIR JAMES
Private	DIXON ANGUS
Private	GEVAN JAMES
Private	GRANT JOHN
Private	HAMILTON ARCHD.
Private	HENDERSON ARCHD.
Private	HUME JAMES
Private	HUNT STEPHN.
Private	JOHNSTONE WM.
Private	JEFFERY GEORGE
Private	KINNAIRD DAVID
Private	McBIRNIE HUGH
Private	McCETRIE JOHN
Private	McCREDIE WM.
Private	McINTOSH COLIN
Private	McKAY GEORGE 1st.
Private	McKAY GEORGE 2nd.
Private	McKAY NEIL
Private	McKENZIE GEORGE
Private	McLELLAN JAMES
Private	McLEOD ANGUS
Private	McLEOD HUGH
Private	McLEOD RODK.
Private	McLONGISH JOHN
Private	MARSHALL JAMES
Private	MARTIN WM.
Private	MITCHELL SAML. Died of Wounds 18th June'15
Private	MONRO HENRY
Private	MOORE THOS.
Private	NESBIT JAMES Col.R.T. Gascoignes Collection March 1909
Private	OWENS THOS.
Private	O'NEIL JOHN
Private	RAE JAMES
Private	ROBERTSON JAMES
Private	SCOTT JAMES
Private	SHEDDON ANDW.
Private	WEMYSS JOHN
Private	WHITSIDE THOS.

Captain J.S. Christie's Company No.2.

Lieutenant	POWLING JOHN Payne Coll.1911
Lieutenant	CAMERON JAMES
Serjeant	GRANT PETER
Serjeant	McLAUGHLAN LACHLAN
Serjeant	McCRUMMING GEORGE
Serjeant	McGOWN JAMES
Corporal	HENDERSON COLIN
Corporal	LOVE HUGH
Corporal	McLEOD JOHN
Corporal	ROSS ANGUS
Drummer	McKAY JAMES
Private	ATKINSON JAMES
Private	AYRE GILBERT
Private	BRECKINWRIDGE THOS.
Private	BRUCE ANGUS
Private	BURGES GEORGE
Private	CALDER ROBT.
Private	CAMPBELL ALEX.
Private	CAMPBELL JNS. 1st
Private	CAMPBELL JNS. 2nd
Private	CLOWE ALEX.
Private	CUMMINGS WM.
Private	EWART DANL.
Private	FAUWEATHER JAMES
Private	FISH DAVID
Private	FRASER ALEX.
Private	HARDEN DAVID
Private	HAYES JOHN
Private	HEATLEY CHAS.
Private	HAZLE JOHN
Private	KILLICK JAMES
Private	LAIRD DAVID
Private	LITHGOW WM.
Private	McBAIN DONALD
Private	McCULLOCH THOS. (1) Discharged 20th March'16
Private	McKAY DONALD

Private	McKAY WM.
Private	McKENZIE DONALD
Private	McKENZIE JAMES
Private	McLEOD JOHN Discharged 8th Jan.1816 Watters sale 1913
Private	McMILLEN ANGUS
Private	MORTON ALEX.
Private	McWHINNIE DAVID
Private	NEIL HENRY
Private	ROBERTS EDWD. Died of wounds 18th June
Private	ROBERTSON JAMES THOS.
Private	ROBERTSON JAMES 1st
Private	ROBERTSON JAMES 2nd
Private	SOUTHALL JOSH. Glendining's sale Oct.1930
Private	STARKE JOHN
Private	STEWART CHAS.
Private	SUTHERLAND DONALD
Private	VANNAN ROBT.
Private	WESTWOOD JOHN
Private	WEIR ALEX.

Captain T. Mylne's Company No.3.

Captain	MYLNE THOS. Gaskell Collection 1908
Lieutenant	MADDOCK WM.
Lieutenant	CAMERON EWEN
Lieutenant	McLEAN C.H.
Serjeant	CUMMINGS JOHN
Serjeant	GRAY JOHN
Serjeant	LAMONT ALEX.
Corporal	HORN ANDW.
Corporal	HOWART JAMES
Corporal	NEWBIGGIN WM.
Corporal	ROSS PETER
Drummer	BROUGALL JOHN
Drummer	CAMPBELL PETER
Private	ALLEN WM.
Private	ANDERSON ALEX.
Private	ANDERTON WM.
Private	BAIRD WM.
Private	BARR JAMES
Private	BLUNT JOHN
Private	BOYD MATTW.
Private	BRYSON THOS.
Private	BUIST DAVID
Private	CAMERON DUNCAN
Private	CAMPBELL WM.
Private	CONNEL RICHD.
Private	DRYSDALE GEO.
Private	EASTON JOHN
Private	FISHER JAMES
Private	GUILIER JOHN
Private	HAMILTON McBAIN
Private	HENDERSON THOS.
Private	HORTON WM.
Private	JOHNSTON JOHN
Private	KELLY EDWD.
Private	LESLIE NORMAN
Private	LUMSDEN JOHN
Private	McCOLL DONALD
Private	McCRAW MURK.
Private	McDONALD CHAS.
Private	McDONALD DOUGHALL Invalided
Private	McDONALD JOHN
Private	McDONALD MASTERTON
Private	McDONALD NORMAN
Private	McFARLIN MURDK.
Private	McGILVRAE HUGH
Private	McGRIGOR JNS. 1st
Private	McGRIGOR JNS 2nd
Private	McINTOSH PETER
Private	McCAIN DONALD
Private	McKAY JOHN
Private	McKENZIE JOHN
Private	McKENZIE WM.
Private	McKINNON JOHN
Private	McMILLAN ALEX.
Private	McNAUGHTON JOHN
Private	MARTIN ARCHD.
Private	MAY WM.
Private	MILLER JOHN
Private	MILLER WM. Died 28 Dec.1815
Private	MILLS JAMES
Private	MITCHELL THOS.
Private	O'DONNELLY HUGH
Private	PATTERSON JOHN
Private	PENMAN JAMES
Private	PETRIE ROBT.
Private	ROGERS JAMES
Private	SHAW JAMES
Private	SHAW JOHN
Private	SHAW NORMAN
Private	SMITH JOHN
Private	TAYLOR JOHN
Private	THOMPSON ANDW.
Private	WALSH JAMES

Captain R. Mackay's Company No.4.

Captain	McKAY ROBT.
Lieutenant	ROBERTSON JAMES
Serjeant	McKAY WM.
Serjeant	MALCOLM JOHN
Serjeant	MURRAY JOHN Sick Colchester
Serjeant	OWENS SAML.
Corporal	DONALD JOHN
Corporal	HAMILTON GAVIN
Corporal	McKAY ALEX.
Corporal	McPHERSON GEORGE
Private	ABERCROMBIE WM.
Private	ALEXANDER MICHL.
Private	ANGUS PETER
Private	BOGLE JOSH.
Private	BIRNIE JOHN
Private	BARTON JAMES
Private	BERGAM SAML.
Private	CAMERON DONALD
Private	CAMPBELL JAMES
Private	CAMPBELL WM. 1st
Private	CAMPBELL WM. 2nd
Private	COOPER WM.
Private	FITTON JOHN
Private	FLOCKART ANDW.
Private	FRASER RHODERICK
Private	GRAHAM JOHN
Private	GRAY ALEX.
Private	GLASGOW DAVID
Private	GRANT DONALD
Private	HAMILTON JOHN
Private	HATLEY WM.
Private	HARLEY WM.
Private	HEATH JAMES
Private	HENDERSON GEORGE
Private	HENDERSON WM.
Private	INNES JOHN
Private	JAMESON JAMES
Private	JOHNSON PETER
Private	KENNEDY JOHN
Private	KING JOHN
Private	LOFTUS MICHL.
Private	McCUNE SAML.
Private	McDONALD JOHN
Private	McDONALD THOS.
Private	McINTOSH JAMES
Private	McINTYRE WM.
Private	McKAY DONALD
Private	McKENZIE JAMES Discharged 24th March
Private	McKENZIE KENNETH
Private	McLEAN ANGUS Died 3rd Nov.1815
Private	McPHERSON JAMES
Private	MILLS ARCHD.
Private	PATTERSON ALEX.
Private	PATER JAMES
Private	PIRRIE JOHN
Private	PRINGLE PETER
Private	ROSS JOHN 1st
Private	ROSS JOHN 2nd
Private	RUSSELL ROBT.
Private	SHAW THOS.
Private	SINCLAIR DAVID
Private	SUTHERLAND JAS.
Private	SUTHERLAND WM.
Private	TAYLOR ARCHD.
Private	WARDROSS GEORGE
Private	YOUNG MATTW.

Captain P. Innes's Company No.5.

Captain	INNES PETER
Lieutenant	FRASER JAMES
Lieutenant	RIACH W.A.
Serjeant	GIBB JOHN
Serjeant	MANUEL GEORGE
Serjeant	WHITE JAMES
Serjeant	McINTOSH NEIL
Corporal	BARNET JOHN
Corporal	CLELLAND ARCHD.
Corporal	FRASER DONALD
Drummer	BALDWIN ROBT.
Drummer	MANNERS JOHN
Private	ALEXANDER ALEX. Died 30 Oct.1815
Private	ADAMS GEORGE
Private	ADAMS JOHN
Private	BAIN JOHN
Private	BANNERMAN ALEX.
Private	BENNIE WM.
Private	BLACK GEORGE
Private	BLAIR JOHN
Private	BROWN JAMES Glendining's sale 17 June 1908
Private	BROWN THOS.
Private	BRAND MATTW.
Private	CALDER WM.
Private	CAMERON DONALD Discharged 20th March 1816

Private	CAMERON GEORGE
Private	CLARKE WM. Died 8th April 1816
Private	COGHILL GEORGE
Private	DYKES JAMES
Private	FAIRLEY JAMES
Private	FALCONER ANDW.
Private	FARMS WM.
Private	FINNIE WM.
Private	FLETCHER ROBT.
Private	FERGUSON ANGUS
Private	GALLOWAY JAMES Discharged 5th March 1816
Private	GIBSON JOHN
Private	GUNN DONALD
Private	GRANT PETER
Private	HENRY ALEX.
Private	KELLY WM.
Private	LEE ANDW.
Private	LYALL WM.
Private	LAWRIE JOHN
Private	McDONALD ALEX.
Private	McDONALD JAMES
Private	McDONALD KENNETH Died 6 March 1816
Private	McGIBBON DUNCAN
Private	McGINNEGAR TIMY.
Private	McKAIL MICHL.
Private	McKAY ALEX.
Private	McKENZIE HOLT.
Private	McLEOD JOHN
Private	McLARREN JNS.
Private	MANGEL JNS.
Private	MALCOLM WM.
Private	MILLS DOUGLAS
Private	PATERSON JAMES
Private	REID JOHN
Private	REID WM.
Private	SCOTT NATHL.
Private	SHAW GEORGE
Private	STEWART WM.
Private	WATSON JNS.
Private	WARS ADAM
Private	WILDIE JOHN
Private	WINTON ROBT.

Captain James Campbell's Company No.6.

Captain	CAMPBELL JAMES
Lieutenant	THOMPSON JOHN
Lieutenant	CAMERON ARCHD.
Serjeant	BLACK JAMES
Serjeant	LAMBELL WM.
Serjeant	HENDERSON SINCLAIR
Serjeant	LEVER WM.
Corporal	GARDENER JOHN
Corporal	KENNEDY JOHN
Corporal	McGREGOR DUN.
Corporal	MARTIN ANGUS
Corporal	ROWEN JAMES
Corporal	TODD EDWD.
Drummer	McDONALD THOS.
Private	ARCHIBALD THOS.
Private	ATKINS JOHN
Private	BRANMER THOS.
Private	CAMPBELL ALEX. Died 11 Sept.1815
Private	CAMPBELL DAVID
Private	CAMPBELL WM.
Private	COWEN MATTW.
Private	FIFE JOHN
Private	FINLAY FREDK.
Private	FINLAYSON WM.
Private	FORSTER JOHN Galway Foley Collection 1910
Private	FRASER ALEX.
Private	GOLLAN DANL.
Private	GILLING THOS.
Private	GRANT DONALD
Private	GRAY JOHN
Private	GWILLIAM GEORGE
Private	GUNN WM.
Private	HARLEY JOHN
Private	HOGG JOHN
Private	HOUSTON JOHN
Private	HUMPHRIES WM.
Private	KERR WM.
Private	McCING DUNCAN
Private	McDONALD CHAS.
Private	McGINNERTY DAVID
Private	McGINNERTY DENNIS
Private	McKAY ALEX.
Private	McKAY ANGUS 1st
Private	McKAY ANGUS 2nd
Private	McKAY GEORGE
Private	McKENZIE DONALD
Private	McLEOD DONALD
Private	McPHERSON JOHN
Private	McQUATTIE DAVID Died 17 June 1815 of Wounds
Private	MOWAT JAMES

Private	MUNRO CHAS.
Private	MURRAY ANGUS Sick Colchester
Private	ROBERTSON JAMES
Private	SHAW ROBERT
Private	SMITH ARCHIBALD
Private	SMITH ALEX.
Private	SMITH WM.
Private	SPROWL NOBLE
Private	STEWART LACHLAN
Private	STEWART JOHN
Private	STRATTON JAMES
Private	STONE JAMES
Private	TAYLOR DONALD
Private	TRAVERS HENRY
Private	VALLENCE DIXON Discharged 6th March 1816
Private	WALTER WM.
Private	WATT DAVID
Private	WHITE ALEX.
Private	WILSON WM. Discharged 7th February 1816

Captain J. Campbell's Company No.7.

Lieutenant	McARTHUR CHAS.
Lieutenant	McKENZIE JOHN
Serjeant	McDONALD DUNCAN
Serjeant	McKENZIE DONALD
Serjeant	ROSE CHAS
Serjeant	SUTHERLAND JOHN Cheylesmore Collection 1908
Corporal	BARCLAY JAMES
Corporal	GRANT DUNCAN
Corporal	KERR DAVID
Corporal	McDONALD JOHN
Drummer	CHRISTMAS THOS.
Drummer	McCALL JAMES
Private	ANDERSON ROBT.
Private	BAILLIE FRANS.
Private	BARRIE ANDW.
Private	BIE Col.Murray's Coll.1908
Private	BROTHERS JOSH.
Private	BRUMAGE WM.
Private	CARRADICE WM.
Private	CHRYSTALL THOS.
Private	CULLROSS JAMES
Private	CRAIG CHAS.
Private	DEMPTER JOHN
Private	DONNELLY JOHN
Private	FLETCHER JOHN
Private	FRASER HUGH
Private	FULTON JESSE
Private	GOW CHAS.
Private	GORDON ADAM
Private	GREIG ANDW.
Private	HUGHES JOHN
Private	IRISON EDWD.
Private	JAMIESON JAMES
Private	KELLY EDWD.
Private	KENNEDY ANDW.
Private	KERR ANGUS
Private	KIRKBRIDGE THOS. Littledale sale Nov. 1910
Private	McBAIN JOHN
Private	McCOLL DONALD
Private	McFARLANE DUNCAN
Private	McGREGOR DAVID
Private	McINTOSH DAVID Discharged 25 Sept. 1815 Whitaker Coll.1908
Private	McINTYRE PETER Col.Murray's Collection 1908
Private	McIVER JOHN
Private	McKAY GEORGE
Private	McKAY HUGH
Private	McKENZIE EWEN
Private	McKERCHER DONALD
Private	McLARREN JAMES
Private	McLINNON HUGH
Private	McLEOD DONALD
Private	McPHERSON DONALD
Private	MUNOL PETER
Private	MITCHELL WM.
Private	MULLIGAN ALEX.
Private	PATTERSON CHAS.
Private	POLLOCK JAMES
Private	REID ALEX
Private	REID WM.
Private	SCOTT ALLEN
Private	SUTHERLAND WM. Discharged 25 Sept. '15
Private	SWANSON WM.
Private	WATSON JOHN Died 18 June 1815
Private	WHEELER HENRY

Captain M. Fraser's Company No.8.

Captain	FRASER MALCOLM
Lieutenant	LESLIE K.J.
Lieutenant	NASH JOHN
Serjeant	BAXTER WM.
Serjeant	McLACHLIN PETER Died 25 June 1815

Serjeant	SUTHERLAND DONALD
Serjeant	WRIGHT JOHN
Corporal	BIRCH THOS.
Corporal	CAMPBELL JAMES
Corporal	CLARKE ALEX.
Corporal	GODDARD JEFFERY
Drummer	FOGERBERRY HENRY
Private	ALLEN DAVID
Private	ATHOS WM.
Private	CALDER WM.
Private	CAMERON COLIN
Private	CAMPBELL DAVID Died 19 June 1815
Private	CLIFTON THOS.
Private	COOPER JAMES
Private	CUMMINGS ARCHD. Died 5th Sept. 1815
Private	DARGON HENRY
Private	DUNCAN DAVID
Private	ELLIOTT ROBT.
Private	FERGUSON ROBT.
Private	FINNIE THOS.
Private	GRANT RODK.
Private	HENNEY SAML.
Private	INGLIS JAMES
Private	IRONS ALLEN
Private	JACKSON THOS.
Private	KEIR JAMES
Private	LAMONT JOHN
Private	LIGHTBODY WM. Died of wounds 29 June 1815
Private	McDONALD JNS. 1st
Private	McDONALD JNS. 2nd
Private	McGILVRAE ROBT.
Private	McINDOE ROBT.
Private	McINTOSH WM. Discharged 6th March 1816
Private	McKAY JAMES
Private	McKECHNIE JOHN
Private	McKENZIE ISSAC
Private	McKENZIE JOHN
Private	McLACHLAN LACN. Died 28th June '15
Private	McLEOD JOHN
Private	McMILLEN NEIL
Private	McPHEE DOUGALL
Private	MULCHRIST JOHN
Private	NEIL JOHN Died 25th August 1815
Private	PAUL WM.
Private	ROSS DAVID
Private	SINCLAIR ROBT. Gray Coll.1908
Private	STEWART THOS.
Private	WALKER JOHN
Private	WANDS JOHN
Private	WEIR DONALD Died of wounds 18th June 1815
Private	WILLIAMSON DONALD
Private	WHITE WM.

Captain Wm. Marshall's Company Light

Captain	MARSHALL WM.
Captain	BROWN THOS.
Lieutenant	ROBERTSON FULTON
Serjeant	DEWAR WM.
Serjeant	McPHEE DONALD
Serjeant	McLEOD DONALD
Serjeant	ROBERTSON FINLAY
Serjeant	CAMPBELL CHAS.
Corporal	ATCHINSON JAMES
Corporal	BURNS JOHN Discharged 7th July 1816
Corporal	KENNEDY ANGUS
Corporal	LITHGOW MATTW.
Corporal	McKENZIE JOHN
Corporal	SUTHERLANB GEORGE
Drummer	BENTLEY THOS.
Private	ANDERSON JAMES
Private	BANNERMAN DAVID
Private	BROOKIE JOHN
Private	CAMPBELL ARCHD.
Private	CHALMERS ADAM
Private	CHALMERS WM.
Private	CLELLAND ROBT.
Private	CLUNES WM.
Private	CORMICK HENRY
Private	CARRICKSHANK ALEX. Needes Collection 1908
Private	COWIE GEORGE
Private	DAVIDSON BENJN.
Private	DICKIE MATTW.
Private	DUFFIE JAMES
Private	DOYLE JOHN
Private	DUNN JOHN
Private	GARDENER JAMES
Private	GARDENER THOS.
Private	GIBSON JOHN
Private	GUNN DONALD
Private	GUNN JOHN
Private	HAYES MATTW.
Private	HILL GEORGE

Private	JACK MURDOCH
Private	JOLLY HENRY
Private	LACHLAN JOHN
Private	LENNOX WM.
Private	LLOYD JOHN
Private	McCOLL CONNOR
Private	McDONALD DONALD 1st
Private	McDONALD DONALD 2nd
Private	McDONALD JAMES Died of Wounds 18 June'15
Private	McEWEN ANDW.
Private	McFARLANE DUNN.
Private	McGILVRAE ALLEN
Private	McINTOSH SWAIN
Private	McINTYRE NICOL.
Private	McKAY DONALD
Private	McKAY CHAS.
Private	McKAY WM. 1st
Private	McKAY WM. 2nd
Private	McKENZIE DONALD
Private	McKINNION LACHLAN
Private	McLEOD DONALD
Private	McLEOD DUNCAN Died of wounds 29 June 1815
Private	McLEOD JNS 1st
Private	McLEOD JNS 2nd
Private	McMILLAN WM.
Private	McPHERSON CHAS.
Private	McPHEATERS JAMES
Private	McTAVISH ALEX.
Private	MILLER JAMES
Private	MOORE GEORGE
Private	MUNGAY PETER
Private	NESMYTH ALLEN
Private	POCOCKE JAMES
Private	POOLE WM.
Private	ROSE WM.
Private	ROSS DONALD
Private	ROSS JOHN
Private	SCOTT DAVID
Private	SHERRATT WM.
Private	SMALLBROOK JOHN Discharged 24 March 1816
Private	SMITH JAMES
Private	SUTHERLAND JOHN
Private	THORBURN WM.
Private	WARDROP PETER
Private	WHITE DAVID
Private	YOUNG JAMES

* * *

1st BATTN. 91st REGIMENT OF FOOT

Lt.Colonel	DOUGLAS WM. Sir K.C.B. (Col)
Adjutant	SCOTT GEORGE (Lieut)
Qr.Master	STEWART JAMES
Surgeon	DOUGLAS ROBT.
Ass.Surgeon	McLACHLAN GEORGE
Ass.Surgeon	YOUNG WM.H.
Pay Master	CAMPBELL DUGALD Spinks list Dec.1909

Captain James Welch's Company

Captain	WALSH JAMES (Major)
Lieutenant	CATRHCART ANDW.
Lieutenant	McDOUGALL JOHN
Lieutenant	McDONALD JOHN
Sjt.Major	McLEAN ANDW.
Q.M.S.	McGREGOR DOND.
P.M.S.	MILLAR JAMES
Sch.Master	McPHERSON DAVID
Ar.Serjeant	GROVES EDWD.
Dr.Major	ALLEN ANDREW
Serjeant	CARMICHAIL ROBT. (C.S.)
Serjeant	CLARK HENRY
Serjeant	DEAR ROBT.
Serjeant	KENNEDY EDWD.
Serjeant	STALKER JOHN
Corporal	COLLINS ALEX.
Corporal	McDONALD ALLEN
Corporal	OGILVY ROBT.
Corporal	PATON THOS.
Drummer	BALLINTINE WM.
Drummer	LITTLE JOHN
Private	ALLEN JAMES
Private	BAILEY ROBT.
Private	BARNS JOHN Died 14 Oct.1815
Private	BEGGS LEWIS
Private	BOWRIE DAVID
Private	BURRELL JAMES
Private	CAMERON ANGUS Col.R.T. Gascoigne's Collection 1909
Private	CAMPBELL WM.
Private	CLARK JAMES
Private	COLLEY ALEX.
Private	CONNOLLY JOHN
Private	CRAIG CHAS.
Private	CUNNINGHAM JAMES
Private	DONALD ALEX.
Private	DONALDSON NATHL.
Private	EDGAR JOHN
Private	FAIRLEY GEORGE

Private	FLANNAGAN WM.
Private	GLEN JOHN
Private	GLOVER JOHN
Private	GREIGSON ROBT.
Private	GUNN GEORGE Volunteer
Private	HAMILTON THOS.
Private	HANLIN ANTHY
Private	HILL JAMES
Private	HUME DANL.
Private	JACK THOS
Private	KEW JOHN
Private	KEW MATTW.
Private	KEW WM.
Private	KING ALEX.
Private	KING JOHN
Private	LAWSON WM.
Private	LEES ALEX.
Private	LIDDLE JAMES
Private	LOCKHART THOS.
Private	LYSTER EDWD.
Private	McDERMID DOND.
Private	McDONALD JOHN
Private	McDONALD DUNN.
Private	McDOUGALL DONALD
Private	McGEE WM. Payne Collection 1911
Private	McLEAN HECTOR
Private	MANWILL ROBT.
Private	MARSHALL JOHN
Private	MILLAR JAMES
Private	MOFFAT THOS.
Private	MORROW JAMES Died 10th November 1815
Private	MORTON CHAS.
Private	NELSON JOHN
Private	PATERSON NEILL
Private	PATERSON GEORGE
Private	PHILLIPS JOHN
Private	RANKEN JOHN
Private	RADDLEY GEORGE
Private	ROBERTSON JAMES
Private	RODDICK JOHN
Private	RUTHERFORD WM.
Private	SCOTT JOHN
Private	SCOTT ROBERT
Private	SHAW JOHN
Private	SHEPPARD JOHN
Private	SIMSON ALEX.
Private	STEWART JOHN
Private	STEWART JOSH.
Private	THOMSON WM.
Private	TODD JAMES
Private	URQUHARD DOND.
Private	WALKER PETER
Private	WILKINSON JOHN
Private	WEIR WM.
Private	WRIGHT JOHN
Private	YOUNG JAMES

Captain Wm. Stewart's Company No.1.

Captain	STEWART WM.
Lieutenant	FENWICK J.L.
Lieutenant	BLACK JAMES
Ensign	TRIMMER WM. Gaskell Collection 1908
Serjeant	BURNS GEORGE (C.S.)
Serjeant	EATON ANDW.
Serjeant	McINTYRE JOHN
Serjeant	REID JOHN
Corporal	CHRISTIE BRUCE
Corporal	COWIE JOHN
Corporal	SANSOM JOHN
Corporal	WRIGHT JOHN
Drummer	ARCHER JOHN
Drummer	McMILLAN ANTHY.
Private	AFLECT JAMES Discharged 24 March 1816
Private	ANDREWS JOHN
Private	BALD JOHN
Private	BENNET JOHN
Private	BEAN JOHN
Private	BLACK WM.
Private	BOATH GRAHAM
Private	BRADBENT JOHN
Private	BROOKSBANK JOHN
Private	BRUMLEY JOHN
Private	CAHILL JAMES
Private	CAMERON DONALD
Private	CAMPBELL COLIN
Private	CAMPBELL DONALD
Private	CAMPBELL ANGUS
Private	CAMPSIE WM.
Private	COCKRAN ARCHD.
Private	CONNACHIE ALEX.
Private	CROLL JAMES
Private	DAVENEY THOS Died 24 Aug.1815
Private	DAVIDSON JOHN
Private	DINWOODIE JOHN

Private	DUNIASON THOS.
Private	EARDON JOHN
Private	ELDER WM.
Private	FENTON ALEX.
Private	GIFFENS JAMES
Private	GROVES JOSEPH
Private	HALLEY CHAS.
Private	JOHNSTON JOHN
Private	KEAN JOHN
Private	KELLY QWEN
Private	KILLGARE PATT.
Private	KNIGHT WM.
Private	LAIDLAW WM.
Private	LECKIE GEORGE
Private	McCUBBIN JOHN
Private	McDONALD JAMES
Private	McDONALD NEIL
Private	McDOUGALL PETER
Private	McKINNON DONALD
Private	McLAREN JAMES
Private	McLEAN JOHN
Private	McLEARY WM.
Private	McLURE JAMES
Private	McMILLAN JAMES
Private	McMILLAN JOHN
Private	McMILLAN PETER
Private	MAIR JOHN
Private	MARSHALL ABRM. Volunteer
Private	MARTIN JAMES
Private	MUNDAY JOHN
Private	MURROTT CHAS.
Private	MURCHY THOS.
Private	MURRAY PETER
Private	NEAL JOHN
Private	NUGENT CHAS.
Private	O'DONNELL WM.
Private	OGILVY GEORGE Needes Collection 1908
Private	PATTERSON ALLEN
Private	PROCTOR JOHN
Private	ROBERTSON GEORGE
Private	ROSS WALTER
Private	SHAFTON HENRY
Private	STEEL THOS.
Private	STEWARD JAMES
Private	SWANSON GEORGE
Private	TAYLOR FRANS.
Private	THOMPSON ALEX.
Private	VON DER WER, MICHL. CONRAD
Private	WALLACE WM.
Private	WANTON JAMES
Private	WHEGHAM ALEX.
Private	WILKINSON WM.
Private	WOOD WM. Col.Murray's Collection 1908

Captain A. Campbell's Company No.2.

Captain	CAMPBELL ARCHD.
Lieutenant	BROWNE EUGENE
Lieutenant	SWORD ALEX.
Ensign	SMITH ANDW.
Serjeant	MUIRHEAD ALEX. (C.S.) Glendining's sale April 1913
Serjeant	CAMERON JOHN
Serjeant	DALGETTIE JAMES
Serjeant	DODWORTH WM.
Corporal	FORREST WM.
Corporal	FULTON WM.
Corporal	HARLEY WM.
Corporal	McPHERSON GEORGE
Corporal	REED WALTER
Drummer	BROWN JOHN
Drummer	McNICHOLL DOND.
Private	ALLARDUE JOHN
Private	ANDREWS JOSH.
Private	BANNER ANDW.
Private	BROWN ROBERT
Private	BROWN WM.
Private	BUCHANAN ANDW.
Private	BUCHANAN ARCHD.
Private	BUCHANAN JOHN
Private	BURCH JOHN
Private	BUTLER JAMES
Private	CAMPBELL HUGH
Private	CARGILL THOS.
Private	CHAPMAN GEORGE
Private	CLARK CHAS.
Private	COLQUHOUN JOHN
Private	DAVIDSON ROBERT
Private	DICKIE MATTW.
Private	DOUGLAS WM.
Private	DOWNIE ANDREW
Private	DOWNIE ROBT.
Private	FORGAN WM.
Private	FRASER' ANGUS
Private	GIBSON JAMES
Private	GILHOOLY JOHN
Private	GLOVER ARCHD.

Private	GRAHAM JOHN
Private	GRANT ARCHD.
Private	HAROLD OWEN
Private	HILL CLARK
Private	HOUSTON JOHN
Private	HOWATSON ROBT.
Private	HOWE JOHN
Private	HUNTER MICHL.
Private	INGRAM WM.
Private	IRELOM WM.
Private	IRVING JOHN
Private	JOHNSTON GEORGE
Private	JOHNSTON ROBT.
Private	KILLPATRICK WM. Discharged 24 March 1816
Private	KIRLACHLAN JOHN
Private	KNOX ANDW.
Private	LAMBERT DAVID
Private	LESSLIE JOHN
Private	LINDSAY JOHN
Private	McCONNELL RICHD.
Private	McDONALD ALLEN
Private	McDONALD JOHN
Private	McFARLANE JAMES
Private	McGUISE JOHN
Private	McKAY JAMES
Private	McKENZIE KENNETH
Private	McLARDIE JAS.
Private	McLEAN HECTOR
Private	McMILLEN ALEX.
Private	MENZIES WM.
Private	MIDGLEY BANJN.WM.
Private	MONICUS STATIUS
Private	MOORE THOS.
Private	NEWTON JOHN
Private	PAUL SAML.
Private	PORTER JOHN
Private	PRIDE ROBERT
Private	RAE WM.
Private	ROSS JAMES
Private	SANDS PETER
Private	SCOTT JOHN
Private	SAMS JAMES
Private	SINCLAIR ROBT. Discharged 24 March 1815
Private	SMALL DAVID
Private	SPENCER HENRY
Private	SPENIE ALEX.
Private	STEEL JAMES
Private	TIVNIDALE WM.
Private	VENUS GEORGE
Private	WADDELL JAMES
Private	WALKER JOHN
Private	WATSON JAMES
Private	WEIR JAMES

Captain J.C. Murdoch's Company No.3.

Captain	MURDOCH J.C. Whitaker Coll.1908
Lieutenant	STEWART C.
Lieutenant	CAMPBELL A. (2)
Ensign	DUCAT DUGALL
Serjeant	ROLSTON ROBIN (C.S.)
Serjeant	FRASER JOHN
Serjeant	MELDRUM JOHN
Serjeant	O'NEILL JOHN
Serjeant	SIN WM.
Corporal	CAMERON JOHN
Corporal	DUKIE JAMES
Corporal	DRYDEN WALTER
Corporal	KING THOS.
Corporal	McKNIGHT JOHN Glendining's sale Jan. 1911
Drummer	CAMERON JOHN
Drummer	MORRISON GEO.
Private	ADDIE WM.
Private	ARCHER ALEX.
Private	BARCLAY JAMES
Private	BLACK JAMES
Private	BORTUMER CAROLUS FREDK.
Private	BROWN JAMES
Private	BURKE THOS.
Private	CAIRNS CHRISTY.
Private	CAMPBELL ANGUS
Private	CAMPBELL HUGH
Private	CAMPBELL JOHN
Private	CARMICHAEL JOHN
Private	CONNOR OWEN
Private	COUPER GEO. Discharged 24 March 1816
Private	CRAWFORD ROBT.
Private	DAVENPORT THOS.
Private	DEWAR DAVID Cheylesmore Collection 1908
Private	DOGHERTY PHIL.
Private	DONNELLY EDWD.
Private	DUNBAR JOHN
Private	ELLOR JAMES
Private	EWING JAMES Discharged 22 August 1815

Private	FAIRLAYS WM.
Private	FORD WM.
Private	GILMAN ROBT.
Private	GOOD JOHN
Private	GRAY HENRY
Private	HODGES KING
Private	HIGGINS JOHN
Private	HILL JAMES Killed 3rd July 1815
Private	HILL WALTER
Private	JAFFERY ALEX.
Private	JOHNSTON ROBT.
Private	JOPP GEO.
Private	JORDAN WM.
Private	JOSEPH JOHN
Private	KAY JOHN
Private	KELLY CHAS.
Private	LATTON JOHN
Private	LEPRACKE JAS.
Private	LINDSAY HECTOR
Private	McCALLUM DUNCAN Genl. Service 24 April 1816
Private	McDOUGALL JOHN
Private	McINNES DONALD
Private	McINTYRE ARCHD. Watters sale June 1913
Private	McLARDIE NEIL
Private	McLEAN ARCHD.
Private	McLEAN HUGH Discharged 22 August 1815
Private	McKNIGHT JOSH.
Private	MANNOX PAT.
Private	MAXWELL JAMES
Private	MAY JOHN
Private	MICHAL HUGH
Private	MORRISON WM.
Private	MOWAT FRANS.
Private	MURDOCH JAMES
Private	MURDOCH JOHN
Private	PITT WM.
Private	PROTZE FRANTZE
Private	RADCLIFFE JOHN
Private	RODDIE WM.
Private	ROGERS WM.
Private	SMITH PETER
Private	STEWART JAMES
Private	SWAN GEO.
Private	TEMPLETON JOHN
Private	TINLING ROBT.
Private	WALSH ROBT.
Private	WARDMAN JOSH.
Private	WATT JOHN
Private	WHITELOCH PETER
Private	WILSON JOHN
Private	YOUNG DAVID

Captain A.J. Callender's Company No.4.

Captain	CALLENDER A.J. (Major)
Lieutenant	EGAN CARBURY Col.Gaskell sale May 1911
Lieutenant	SMITH ALEX.
Serjeant	BROWN ARCHD. (C.S.)
Serjeant	HOLMES THOS.
Serjeant	MILLAR ADAM
Serjeant	STEWART FRANS.
Corporal	BROWN JOHN
Corporal	DOGHERTY GEO.
Corporal	EDWARDS JOHN
Corporal	GRAHAM DONALD
Corporal	McENTIE EDWD.
Drummer	McLEAN DUNCAN
Drummer	PATON DAVID
Private	AFLECT WM.
Private	ALLISON WM.
Private	ANDERSON GEO.
Private	BARR ALLEN
Private	BERNADINE ADOUS
Private	BURNIY WM.
Private	BRAID JOHN
Private	BRYCE JOSH.
Private	BURNS JAS.
Private	CAMERON JOHN
Private	CAMPBELL JOHN
Private	CAMPBELL JAMES
Private	CAMPBELL WM.
Private	CARROLL EDWD.
Private	CATTERNACH JOHN
Private	CHAPMAN MATTW.
Private	CRAIG JAMES
Private	CRAWFORD MATTW.
Private	DEWAR JAMES
Private	DICKSON ALEX.
Private	DOWNS WM.
Private	EDWARDS ROBT.
Private	FINLAY ROBT.
Private	FLANNERY CORN.
Private	GARDIN JAMES
Private	HENDRY DAVID
Private	HILTON JAMES

Private	HODGSON JOSH.
Private	JORDAN ANDW.
Private	KERR JOSH.
Private	LAMB RICHD.
Private	LONG THOS.
Private	LYON GEO.
Private	McALLISTER JOHN
Private	McCANN JOHN
Private	McGROWTHER JAMES
Private	McKENNON ARCHD.
Private	McLAREN ROBT.
Private	McNAIR ANDW.
Private	McNAIR WM. Discharged 24 March 1816
Private	McNAUGHTON ALLEN Spinks Collection 1914
Private	McNEILL JOHN
Private	McPHAILE JOHN
Private	McPHEE DOND.
Private	McQUEEN JOHN
Private	MANWELL WM.
Private	MARTIN PAT.
Private	MUNRO WM.
Private	NICOLL WM.
Private	NEILL SAML.
Private	OLIVER WALTER
Private	PATTERSON WM. Discharged 24 March 1816
Private	PEARCE ANTHY.
Private	PETERS THOS.
Private	QUEEN GEO.
Private	RADINS JACOBUS
Private	RESTON JAMES
Private	REYNOLDS JOHNSTON
Private	REYNOLDS THOS.
Private	ROBERTSON JOHN
Private	ROBERTSON THOS.
Private	ROGERS JOHN
Private	SHARP DANL.
Private	SIMSON ALEX.
Private	SMALL WM.
Private	SMITH JAMES
Private	SMITH WM.
Private	SOMERVILLE WM.
Private	STEEL WM.
Private	STEVENSON JOHN
Private	STEWART GEORGE
Private	THOMSON ARCHD.
Private	TINDALL WM.
Private	WALKER JOHN

Captain Robert McDonald's Company No.5.

Captain	McDONALD ROBT. A.A. Payne Collection 1908
Lieutenant	HOOD JAMES
Lieutenant	KNOX R.S.
Ensign	CAHILL PAT.
Serjeant	GOLDIE FRANS. (C.S.)
Serjeant	BLACK ANDREW
Serjeant	HENDERSON JOHN
Serjeant	McCONNELL JOHN
Serjeant	YOUNGER JAMES
Corporal	CREASER ALEX.
Corporal	DIGNEY JOHN
Corporal	HARVEY ROBT.
Corporal	RUTLEDGE JOHN
Corporal	SAMUEL MATTW.
Drummer	FERGUSON PETER
Drummer	GREEN WM.
Private	ADAMSON WM.
Private	ALEXANDER GEO.
Private	ANDREWS ROBT.
Private	ARMSTRONG JOHN
Private	BARRATT WM.
Private	BASSO HENRY
Private	BRUCE ALEX.
Private	CAMERON JOHN
Private	CAMERON WM. Discharged 24 March 1816
Private	CAMPBELL JOHN
Private	COCKBURNE THOS.
Private	COLLINSON THOS.
Private	CONNELLY DENIS
Private	COPLEN WM.
Private	CURRIE ANTHY.
Private	FAIRLEY JAMES
Private	FERGUS JAMES
Private	FORSYTH ROBT.
Private	GALLORHER TIM.
Private	GREAR ROBT.
Private	HAMILTON JAMES
Private	HARPER JOHN Discharged 24 March 1816
Private	HARVIE JAMES
Private	HILL ROBT.
Private	HOLMES WM.
Private	HOWARTH WM.
Private	HUNT JOHNN.
Private	JAFFERY JAMES
Private	KELLEY JOHN
Private	KELLEY ROBT.

Private	KENNEDY JOHN
Private	KEEYLER PHIL.
Private	KING JAMES
Private	KIRK JOHN
Private	LAMB ROBT.
Private	LAWSON ROBT.
Private	LEWIS JAMES
Private	LIDDELL JAMES
Private	McDONALD THOS.
Private	McLAREN JOHN
Private	McLEAN ANTHY.
Private	McMICHAEL JOHN
Private	MARSHALL JOHN
Private	MARTIN GEO.
Private	NELSON WM.
Private	NIVEN JOHN
Private	NORMAN JOHN
Private	POTT ROBT.
Private	PRINGLE JAMES
Private	QUIGLEY JOHN
Private	RANDLE PETER
Private	RENNIE JOHN
Private	RISH JAMES
Private	RENNIE ALEX.
Private	ROBBIE JOHN
Private	ROBERTSON JAMES
Private	SCOTT WM.
Private	SIMPLE JAMES
Private	SIMONS JOHN Deserted 19 July 1815
Private	SMEAL RICHD.
Private	SMITH JOHN
Private	SMITH WM.
Private	TALBOT WM.
Private	TAYLOR JOHN
Private	TEMPLETON HUGH
Private	VON DER WER JACOBUS Cheylesmore Collection 1908
Private	WARSAM JOHN
Private	WATKINS JOSH.
Private	WILLIAMSON WM.
Private	WILSON JAMES
Private	YOUNG ROBT.

Captain W. Gun's Company No.6.

Lieutenant	CAMPBELL JOHN
Lieutenant	McLACHLAN ANDW. Glendining's sale April 1912
Ensign	PATON JAMES
Serjeant	KENT HENRY (C.S.)
Serjeant	AIRD JAMES
Serjeant	HENDERSON JOHN
Serjeant	LOW GEO.
Serjeant	McGILIVNEY ALEX.
Corporal	CLARK JAMES
Corporal	HORNLEY JOHN
Corporal	INNES JAMES
Corporal	McKECHNIE DONALD
Drummer	RODGERS DOND.
Private	ADAMS JAMES
Private	BALD JAMES
Private	BARHAM ISSAC
Private	BEATTIE GEO.
Private	BOWIE ADAM
Private	BRADLEY JOSH.
Private	BRISNAHAN GEO.
Private	CALDERWOOD ISSAC
Private	CONNOR HUGH
Private	COWDEN JOHN
Private	DRYDEN ALEX.
Private	ELDER DAVID
Private	FAIRLEY GOVAN
Private	FLOCKARD DAVID
Private	FURFIE HUGH
Private	GILMOUR ROBT.
Private	GREENLIES JAMES
Private	GREIG ROBT.
Private	HAMILTON JAMES
Private	HARRIS EDWD. Galway Foley Collection 1910
Private	HENDERSON JAMES
Private	HENDERSON THOS.
Private	HORN JOHN
Private	HOUSTON JOHN
Private	HUNT DANL.
Private	IRVING JONATHAN
Private	JOHNSTONE JOHN
Private	KELLEY ANDW.
Private	KELLEY BERNARD
Private	KIRK JOSH.
Private	LAMBERT JAS.
Private	LOCKARD DAVID
Private	LOGGEN JAS.
Private	LOBBIE JAS.
Private	McGRATH BRYAN
Private	McGRIGOR ROND.
Private	McGUIRE JAS.
Private	McILLREATH DAVID
Private	McINDOE JOHN
Private	McKELLAR PETER
Private	McKEVAR PATT.

Private	McKINNON ANGUS
Private	McLEAN JOHN
Private	McMAHON ARTHUR
Private	McNISH THOS.
Private	McPARTLEN JOHN
Private	MITCHELL JNS 1st
Private	MITCHELL JNS 2nd
Private	MURRAY KENNETH
Private	MURRAY WM.
Private	PATERSON ROBT.
Private	PATERSON THOS 1st
Private	PATERSON THOS 2nd
Private	NORMAN COLIN
Private	OGILVY WM.
Private	PHILLIPS JOHN
Private	REID JOHN
Private	ROPE ROBT.
Private	SCOTT ROBT.
Private	SEXSMITH MICHL., Discharged 24 March 1816
Private	SHAW JOHN
Private	SINCLAIR ALEX.
Private	SLOAN JOHN
Private	SMITH THOS.
Private	SOMERVILLE WALTER
Private	TANSEY JOHN
Private	TENNANT ADAM
Private	TRACY PHILIP
Private	TURNBULL JAMES
Private	WARD WM.
Private	WOOD ANDW.
Private	WOOD WM.
Private	WYNNE EDWD.
Private	YOUART DAVID

Captain T.H. Blair's Company No.7.

Captain	BLAIR T.H. (Lt.Col.) Major of Brigade to 3rd Brigade
Captain	ANDERSON ROBT.
Lieutenant	MURRAY THOS.
Ensign	LIND L.
Serjeant	MARSHALL WM. (C.S.)
Serjeant	HERCULES NINEAN
Serjeant	KELLEY WM.
Serjeant	LYON JOHN
Serjeant	McGILLIVRAY ARTHUR Day Sale April 1910
Corporal	BUCHANAN ARCHD.
Corporal	HORN HENRY
Corporal	HUTCHISON JAMES
Corporal	McFARLANE WM. Discharged 24 March 1816
Drummer	ROCARDO ANTONIE
Drummer	WALKER ROBT.
Private	ADAMS HAMILTON
Private	ALLEN GEO.
Private	ALLISON THOS.
Private	ANGUS HUGH
Private	APPLEYARD JAMES
Private	BALD ALEX. Discharged 24 March 1816
Private	BEAN FRANS.
Private	BELL JOHN
Private	BISSETT WM.
Private	CAMERON ALEX.
Private	CAMEROM JOHN
Private	CARGILL JOHN
Private	CLARK DAVID
Private	CLEGHORN ALEX.
Private	COLLIER AARON Discharged 23 March 1816
Private	DONNELLY JAMES
Private	DOBBIE WM.
Private	DORAN RICHD.
Private	EDWARDS ROBT.
Private	ELLIS JOSH.
Private	EWING JAMES
Private	FARRINGTON GEO.
Private	FERGUSON JOHN
Private	FLEMING HUGH
Private	FORBES DONALD
Private	FULLERTON ALEX.
Private	GALLACHIE HUGH
Private	GASPARDS ANTONIO
Private	GIBSON HUGH
Private	GILCHRIST THOS.
Private	GILLIES EBEN.
Private	GRANGER ALEX.
Private	HAMILTON WM.
Private	HARPHAM WM.
Private	HILL JOHN
Private	JAMISON ROBT.
Private	KIRK WM.
Private	LAMBURNE JOHN
Private	LYON GRAHAM
Private	McARTHUR JOHN
Private	McCANN JOHN
Private	McDONALD DONALD
Private	McGARVIE WM.
Private	McINTYRE WM.

Private	McKENZIE ANDW.
Private	McKINLAY WM.
Private	McNABB JAMES
Private	McPAHIL JOHN
Private	MAGHAN DENNIS
Private	MALTMAN WM.
Private	MANNON MARTIN
Private	MATTHEWS THOS.
Private	MERCER JOHN
Private	MILLAR WM.
Private	MOORE THOS.
Private	MORRISON WM.
Private	RAE WM.
Private	RAMSAY ROBT. Discharged 24 March 1816
Private	REACH THOS.
Private	RICHARDSON GEO.
Private	STANFORD MAURICE
Private	SUTHERLAND ALEX.
Private	SPENCE WM.
Private	SWAN DAVID BELL
Private	TINNING JAMES
Private	WATTS WM. Gray Coll.1908
Private	WEIR JOHN
Private	WITSON JAMES
Private	WRAY ROBT.

Captain A. Ross's Company No.8.

Captain	CAMPBELL ARCH. (2)
Lieutenant	SMITH WM.
Ensign	LAMONT NORMAN
Serjeant	LYLE JOHN
Serjeant	ROY JOHN
Serjeant	SINCLAIR DUNCAN
Corporal	CARMICHAEL DANL.
Corporal	GENTLES THOS. Discharged 24 March 1816
Corporal	McWHINNIE JAMES
Drummer	HAMILTON JAMES
Drummer	KETTLE ALEX.
Private	ALLISON JOHN
Private	ANDREWS JOHN
Private	BARRIE JAMES
Private	BILL JAMES
Private	BROWN JAMES
Private	BRECHIN ROBT.
Private	CAMPBELL DAVID
Private	CAMPBELL JAMES
Private	CAMPBELL JOHN
Private	CAMPBELL WM.
Private	COSGROVES WM.
Private	DUNHARS JOHN
Private	DOGHERTY CHAS.
Private	DOW PETER
Private	DOWNS RICHD.
Private	DUNN ANDW.
Private	FITZGERALD THOS
Private	FLEMING ROBT.
Private	FRASER WM.
Private	FULTON WM.
Private	GOW DONALD
Private	GRAHAM JOHN
Private	GROVES JOHN
Private	GREIGSON WM.
Private	HAINS WM.
Private	HARLEY WM.
Private	HENDERSON ROBT. Discharged 24 March 1816
Private	HEPBURNE DAVID
Private	HEWET HENRY
Private	HONEYMAN WM.
Private	KERR THOS.
Private	LATTIMORE JOHN
Private	LITHGOW SAML.
Private	McALLISTER HENRY
Private	McARTHUR JOHN 1st
Private	McARTHUR JOHN 2nd
Private	McCLEMONT ABRM.
Private	McCOWAT WM.
Private	McCULLOCH WM.
Private	McDOUGALL DUNCAN
Private	McDEED CHAS.
Private	McFAYDIN THOS.
Private	McGILL JAMES
Private	McGILLIVRAY HUGH
Private	McGEE THOS.
Private	McINTOSH ALLEN
Private	McINTYRE PETER
Private	McKERTH WM.
Private	McKINLEY HUGH
Private	McLEAN ARCHD.
Private	McMILLAN JAMES
Private	McNEE PETER
Private	MANWELL GEO.
Private	MULLIGAN ROBT.
Private	MILLS WALTER
Private	MURPHY BERNARD
Private	NIEVISON ROBT.
Private	PATTELO THOS.

Private	PEACOCK FRANS.
Private	ROBERTSON THOS. 1st
Private	ROBERTSON THOS 2nd
Private	RUTLEDGE THOS.
Private	SIMSON JOHN
Private	SOWERBY HENRY
Private	STEWART JAMES
Private	STEWART WM.SHAW
Private	SUTHERLAND ROBT.
Private	SWINDLES JOSH.
Private	TAYLOR THOS.
Private	WHITE ALEX.
Private	WHITE ANDW.
Private	WOOD JAMES

Captain D. Campbell's Company Light

Captain	CAMPBELL DUGALD
Lieutenant	RUSSELL JOHN
Lieutenant	CAMPBELL ALEX. Col.Murray's Collection 1908
Lieutenant	STEWART ROBT.
Serjeant	HENDERSON ROBT. (C.S.)
Serjeant	DUNN ANDW.
Serjeant	DUNN BENJN.
Serjeant	HAMILTON JOHN Col.Murray's Collection 1908
Serjeant	WATSON CHAS.
Corporal	BAIRD ROBT.
Corporal	CLARKSON ANDW.
Corporal	BOYD JAMES
Corporal	GRADY PAT.
Drummer	BROWN DAVID
Drummer	LIVINGSTON JAMES
Private	AFLECT JOSH.
Private	ALLEN JAMES
Private	ASHLEY CHAS.
Private	BALFOUR WM.
Private	BARRIE JOHN
Private	BENSON FRANS.
Private	BLACK DONALD
Private	BLACK JOHN Discharged 24 March 1816
Private	BREARLY EDWD.
Private	BROWN DAVID
Private	BURGOS JOSH.
Private	CAMERON JOHN
Private	CANNON WM.
Private	CARLOW JOHN
Private	CASWELL SAML.
Private	CHRISTIE JOHN
Private	CHRISTIE WM. Deserted 30 Oct. 1815
Private	DAVIDSON DONALD
Private	DARVILLA WM.
Private	DUNCAN JAMES
Private	FALCONER WALTER
Private	FLEMING DONALD
Private	FERBY JAMES
Private	GRAHAM JOHN
Private	GRAY GEO.
Private	GRAY JOHN
Private	HAMILTON ALEX.
Private	HAMILTON DAVID Discharged 24 March 1816
Private	HAMILTON DOUGLAS
Private	HARVIE DAVID
Private	HARROW JOHN
Private	HILL WM.
Private	HOBBS JAMES
Private	HUTCHINSON DAVID
Private	INGLES JAMES
Private	JOHNSTON THOS. Killed 1st July 1815
Private	JOHNSTON WM.
Private	KESSON JOHN
Private	LAMBER WM.
Private	LAWSON LAWRENCE
Private	LOGGAN JOHN
Private	LOWRIE WALTER
Private	McBEAN WM.FORBES
Private	McDONELL JOHN
Private	McKAY JOHN
Private	McLEAN ARHCD.
Private	McLEAN DONALD 1st Littledale sale Nov.1910
Private	McLEAN DONALD 2nd
Private	McLEAN JAMES
Private	McMILLAN JOHN
Private	McLONG WM.
Private	MITCHELL JAS.
Private	MOONLIGHT JOHN
Private	NICOLL JOHN
Private	PARKER JOHN
Private	PARK JOHN
Private	PEST WM.
Private	REID JAMES
Private	ROSS ANDW.
Private	RUTLEDGE PAT.
Private	SANDS GEOP.
Private	SHARP PETER

Private	SIMSON THOS Discharged 24 March 1816
Private	SMITH THOS.
Private	SOUTIE JOHN
Private	STEWART ROBT.
Private	THOMSON JAMES
Private	WALKER ALEX.
Private	WATSON WM.
Private	WEBSTER JOHN
Private	WILKIE ALEX.
Private	WILSON JAS. 1st
Private	WILSON JAS, 2nd
Private	YOUNG JOHN

* * *

92nd REGIMENT OF HIGHLANDERS

Lt.Colonel	MITCHELL JAMES
Major	McDONALD DONALD
Major	HOLMES GEO.W.
Surgeon	HICKS GEORGE
Ass.Surgeon	STEWART JNS.
PayMaster	GORDON JAMES

Captain Dougald Campbell's Company

Captain	CAMPBELL DUGD.
Lieutenant	McDONALD RONALD
Lieutenant	GORDON THOS.
Q.M.S.	BRYCE ROBERT
Q.M.S.	McCOMBIE JOHN
P.M.S.	FRASER JAMES
Ar.Serjeant	GIBB GEORGE
Dr.Major	McGEE JAMES Payne Coll.1911
Serjeant	CAMERON ALEX.
Serjeant	CUMMINGS ALEX.
Serjeant	FRASER JOHN
Serjeant	GORDON JOHN
Serjeant	TAYLOR GEORGE
Serjeant	WATSON WALTER
Corporal	FRASER JOHN
Corporal	McEWEN JOHN
Corporal	MURRAY ALEX.
Corporal	SMILLIE JAMES
Corporal	RENTON JOHN
Drummer	SMITH DUNCAN
Private	AMAND ADAM
Private	APPLETON WM. Dead
Private	BACKIE JOHN
Private	BAIN WM.
Private	BAXTER WM. Dead
Private	BRENNER ANDW.
Private	CAMERON JOHN
Private	CLARK ARCHD.
Private	CHRISTIE THOS.
Private	DAVIDSON ANDW.
Private	DIXON THOS.
Private	FRASER JAMES
Private	GORDON DAVID
Private	GUNN PETER
Private	HIGGINS CHAS. Dead
Private	HEALEY MICHL.
Private	HUNTER WM.
Private	INNES ALEX.
Private	INNES JOHN Discharged
Private	INGRAM ALEX.
Private	INGRAM DANL.
Private	KEITH WM.
Private	LEMON ALEX.
Private	LODGE JOSH.
Private	LOGIE JOHN
Private	McCARTHEN JNS.
Private	McCONACHIE SAML.
Private	McCRAW DONALD
Private	McDONALD ARCHD. Discharged
Private	McDONALD DONALD Cheylesmore Collection 1908
Private	McGILVRAY BENJN.
Private	McINNES JOHN
Private	McKENZIE DUNCAN
Private	McLEAY DOUG.
Private	McLEOD WM.
Private	McLORE WM.
Private	McMILLAN EWEN Discharged
Private	McPHERSON ANGUS
Private	MILNE WM.
Private	MOORE JOHN
Private	O'DONNELL JEREMH.
Private	PIPER JOHN Dead
Private	ROSS JOHN
Private	ROSS HUGH
Private	ROSS NEIL
Private	ROSS OSWALD
Private	RUSSELL DAVID
Private	SHAND ALEX. Discharged
Private	SMART ALEX.
Private	SMITH DUNCAN
Private	SIMPSON ALEX.
Private	SOMERVILLE WALTER

Captain Archd. Ferrier's Company

Captain	FERRIER ARCHD. C.
Lieutenant	ROSS JAS. K.
Ensign	McPHERSON DUN.
Serjeant	ROBERTSON DAVID
Serjeant	STOOL JOHN
Corporal	BARNETT WM.
Corporal	CAMPBELL WM.
Corporal	KILPATRICK ARTH. Discharged
Corporal	MOORE JNS.
Corporal	McPHERSON ANGUS
Drummer	GILES NORMAN Col.R.T. Gascoignes Collection March 1909
Private	ANDERSON JAMES
Private	BREMNER JOHN Dead
Private	BUCHANAN GEO.
Private	CABLE JAMES
Private	CAMPBELL DAVID
Private	CAMPBELL JOHN
Private	CAMPBELL KENNETH
Private	CRAIG MOSES Discharged
Private	DAVIDSON ALEX.
Private	DALY PETER
Private	DODDS ANDW.
Private	DUSTON PETER Ddead
Private	FITZPATRICK JOHN Dead
Private	GLASS ROBT.
Private	GLEN JOHN
Private	GRANT LEWIS Dead
Private	GRIFFIN TIMY.
Private	HUTHERSTALL JOHN
Private	McDONALD DUNCAN
Private	McGEE EDWD.
Private	McLARIN JOHN
Private	McLEOD ALEX.
Private	McPHERSON WM. Discharged
Private	McRAE JNS.
Private	MACHER JNS.
Private	MATTHERS WM.
Private	MURRAY JOHN
Private	NEILSON ROGER
Private	NICHOLSON ALEX.
Private	PETERS WM.
Private	POTTS JOSH
Private	ROSS ALEX.
Private	ROSS CHAS.
Private	ROSS DAVID 2nd
Private	ROSS DONALD
Private	ROSS HUGH
Private	SELBIE PETER
Private	SMITH GEORGE Phillips sale
Private	SUTHERLAND ANGUS
Private	SUTHERLAND PETER
Private	THORNTON DAVID
Private	WILSON JAMES

Captain Claud Alexander's Company

Captain	ALEXANDER CLAUD.
Lieutenant	McINNES HECTOR
Ensign	McDONALD ANGUS
Serjeant	FRASER JAMES
Serjeant	HENDERSON ANGUS
Serjeant	MALCOMSON LAWCE. Littledale Sale Nov.1910
Serjeant	NOBLE WM. Meedes Collec.1908
Corporal	CONNELL JAMES
Corporal	NIVEN ALEX.
Corporal	STOVE JNS. ROBT.
Drummer	BARTIE JOHN
Drummer	McKENZIE THOS.
Private	ANDERSON ALEX.
Private	BEATON DONALD
Private	BEAUCOCK SAML.
Private	BEGG WM.
Private	BIRRELL JOHN
Private	BLACK WM. Dead
Private	BRUCE JAMES
Private	BUDGE HENRY
Private	CAMERON JAMES
Private	CAMERON SIMON
Private	CHRISTIE JOHN Discharged
Private	CONNELL JOHN
Private	CRUIKSHANKS WM.
Private	DALLAS JAMES
Private	GILL WM.
Private	GILLES JOHN
Private	GLASHAM ALEX.
Private	GRAY GEORGE
Private	HOPPER WHITEFIELD
Private	HUNTER WM.
Private	McCONNELL JAMES
Private	McCULLUM JOHN Dead
Private	McDERMOT ALEX.
Private	McDONALD RONALD Discharged
Private	McINTYRE JOHN

Private	McKAY DONALD	Discharged
Private	McLEAN JOHN	
Private	MAY JAMES	
Private	MELVILLE JOHN	
Private	NELSON JOSH.	
Private	NIMMO ALEX.	
Private	PROCTOR WM.	
Private	REID JAMES	
Private	ROGERS HENRY	
Private	ROSS DAVID	
Private	SHERIDAN JAMES	
Private	STRACTRAN JOHN	
Private	STEWART ALEX.	
Private	SOUTTIE JOHN	
Private	TALBERT JOHN	
Private	TAYLOR JOHN	
Private	THAIN JOHN	
Private	WILSON JOHN	
Private	WILSON WM.	

Captain Robert Winchester's Company

Captain	WINCHESTER ROBT.	
Lieutenant	WILL ANDW.	
Lieutenant	BRAMWELL JOHN	
Ensign	HEWITT ROBT.	
Serjeant	McBAIN WM.	
Serjeant	McKAY WM.	
Serjeant	RAINNIE ALEX.	
Serjeant	YOUNGSON JOHN	
Corporal	DALACHY JOHN	
Corporal	DORARD ANDW.	
Drummer	BEATTIE ROBT.	
Private	ALLEN JOHN	
Private	ANDERSON JOHN	
Private	ARCHER REUBEN	
Private	BAIN ARCHD.	
Private	BOWIE JOHN	
Private	BROWN DAVID	
Private	BUCHANAN JOHN	
Private	CAMERON ALEX. 2nd.	Discharged
Private	CAMERON DOND. 2nd.	
Private	CATTANACH DOND.	
Private	CONNOR WM.	
Private	DOUGAN JOHN	
Private	DONNELLY MICHL.	
Private	FLETCHER ADAM	
Private	FOWLER KENNETH	
Private	FRASER WM.	
Private	GAVIN PATT.	
Private	HARRYGARY JAMES	
Private	INNES PETER	
Private	LINDSAY WM.	
Private	McDONALD EWWN	Discharged
Private	McGAWRAN JAMES	
Private	McGRIGGAN PETER	
Private	McGUIRE THOS.	
Private	McKAY RODK.	
Private	McKENZIE DOND.	
Private	McKENZIE JAMES	
Private	McLACHLAN DUNCAN	
Private	McLACHLAN JOHN	
Private	McLEOD DONALD	
Private	McPHERSON JAMES	
Private	MITCHELL WM.	
Private	MUNRO DONALD	
Private	MUNRO HARRY	
Private	MUNRO JAMES	
Private	MUNRO JOHN	
Private	MUNRO SIMON	
Private	MURDOCH JOHN	
Private	RATCLIFF JOHN	
Private	REILLY HUGH	
Private	ROSS ALEX.	
Private	SMITH ALEX.	
Private	SMITH JAMES	
Private	STEWART JAMES	
Private	STEWART PETER	
Private	THORN JAMES	
Private	THOMSON WM.	
Private	THORNSBERRY THOS.	

Captain John Warren's Company

Captain	HOBB THOS.	
Lieutenant	LOGAN GEORGE	
Lieutenant	LOGAN ROBT.	
Serjeant	GRANT WM.	
Serjeant	SETH JOSEPH	
Drummer	SHARP THOS.	
Private	ALLARDYCE WM.	
Private	ANDERSON DAVID	
Private	BATCHEN JAMES	
Private	BORLAND WM.	
Private	BROWN JOHN	Littledale sale Nov.1910
Private	CATTANACH DOND.	Left at Brussells Wounded
Private	CRUIKSHANK JNS.	
Private	CUMMINGS DUNCAN	
Private	CUMMINGS GEORGE	

Private	DIVELIN MICHL.
Private	DIXON JOHN
Private	DOSY GEORGE
Private	DUNCAN ROBT. Dead
Private	ELDER WM.
Private	FISHER DOND. Dead
Private	FORBES JOHN
Private	GOSLING WM.
Private	GRANT WM.
Private	HAXTON THOS.
Private	HOLMES JOHN
Private	INNES GEORGE
Private	INGRAM ALEX.
Private	INGRAM WM.
Private	KING JAMES Glendining's sale 17 June 1908 Galway Foley 1910
Private	McDONALD FINLAY
Private	McEWEN JOSHUA
Private	McGRIGOR ALEX.
Private	McINNES JOHN
Private	McKAY ANGUS
Private	MACKAY DONALD
Private	McLEAN ARCHD.
Private	McLEVINE JNS. Dead
Private	McRAE ROBT.
Private	MILNE DAVID
Private	MOORE ALEX.
Private	NICOLSON DONALD
Private	REED WM. Dead
Private	ROSS DOND. 2nd
Private	ROSS JOHN
Private	THORNWOOD ALEX.
Private	TORN WM.
Private	WATSON JAMES
Private	WEBSTER ALEX.

Captain Angus Fraser's Company

Lieutenant	MACKINLAY JOHN
Lieutenant	MACKIE GEORGE
Serjeant	BAIN BENJN.
Serjeant	McKILLIGAN WM.
Serjeant	ROBB JAMES
Corporal	ANDERSON JAMES
Corporal	McLEAN ANGUS
Drummer	McLEAN ALLEN
Private	ALLEN JOHN
Private	ANDERSON CHAS.
Private	ANDERSON WM.
Private	BRADY HENRY
Private	BROWN JAMES Discharged
Private	CARLTON JAMES
Private	CARLTON PAT.
Private	CONNELLY JOHN
Private	CRUIKSHANKS JAMES
Private	DUFF PETER
Private	DUNN DAVID
Private	DIVER ANDW.
Private	EDDIES THOS.
Private	FINLAY JAMES
Private	FITZPATRICK WM.
Private	FRASER ANDW. Discharged
Private	FRASER DONALD
Private	FRASER WM.
Private	GOODBRAN JOHN
Private	KEITH GEORGE
Private	KEITH ALEX.
Private	KEY JOHN
Private	LAING JAMES
Private	LAWRENCE JOHN Discharged
Private	McGRIGOR WALTER Discharged
Private	McINTOSH JOHN
Private	MACKAY WM. 1st
Private	MACKAY WM. 2nd
Private	McLEAN MURDOCH
Private	McLEOD ALEX.
Private	McLEOD DONALD
Private	McLEOD RONALD
Private	MATHIESON DONALD Dead
Private	MUNRO GEORGE
Private	MURRAY DAVID
Private	NISBETT GILBERT
Private	OGILVIE JOHN
Private	RANNAY WM.
Private	PETRIE ALEX. Dead
Private	REID ROBT.
Private	ROBERTSON CHAS.
Private	ROSS RODK.
Private	ROY JAMES
Private	SCOTT SAML.
Private	SHEEN JAMES
Private	SOUTTAR JAMES
Private	TOVRIE JAMES
Private	TWIRLIE BERND.
Private	VICARS CHRISTR.
Private	WALSH MICHL.

Captain R. McDonald's Company

Lieutenant	McDONALD DOND.
Lieutenant	HOPE JAMES
Serjeant	BROWSTER DAVID
Serjeant	MacINTOSH JOHN
Serjeant	WYLIE WILSON Discharged
Corporal	DALGETTY JAMES
Corporal	MacINTOSH ALEX.
Corporal	MacPHERSON WM.
Corporal	SUTHERLAND DOND.
Private	AULD WM. Discharged
Private	BISSETT ALEX.
Private	BISSETT WM.
Private	BURKE JOHN
Private	CAMERON ALEX.
Private	CAMPBELL COLIN Dead
Private	CROSS DAVID
Private	DOWNIE JAMES
Private	DOWNIE JOHN
Private	DUNCAN LACHLAN Dead
Private	FERGUSON PETER
Private	GILLETLY NEIL
Private	GRANT ALEX Dead
Private	HAGGERT THOS.
Private	HAY JAMES
Private	JINKENS ALEX.
Private	McDONALD ALEX.
Private	McDONALD DUNCAN
Private	McDONALD GEORGE
Private	McDONALD JAMES 2nd
Private	McDONALD LEWIS
Private	McDONALD PETER
Private	MacKAY RODK. Dead
Private	McKENZIE JNS.
Private	McKINLAY WM.
Private	McLEGGAN PETER
Private	McLEAN DONALD
Private	McLEAN JOHN
Private	McRAE HUGH
Private	MADDEN JOHN
Private	MILLAR ROBT.
Private	MILNE ALEX.
Private	MILNE ROBT.
Private	MURDOCH DAVID
Private	MURRAY THOS.
Private	RHIND JOHN Gaskell Collection 1908
Private	ROSS DAVID
Private	ROSS GILBERT
Private	ROY JAMES
Private	SHAND JAMES
Private	SMITH DONALD
Private	SUTHERLAND JOHN
Private	WALKER GEORGE
Private	WILSON WM.
Private	YOUNG JOHN

Captain S.Maxwell's Company

Lieutenant	McINTOSH THOS.
Lieutenant	McPHERSON ALEX.
Serjeant	GORDON WM.
Serjeant	IRVINE JAMES
Serjeant	MYLES GEORGE
Serjeant	ROSS JOHN
Corporal	EWING PETER
Corporal	GIBB JAMES Dead
Corporal	GRANT JAMES
Corporal	JOHNSTON ALEX.
Corporal	PRIMROSE JOHN
Drummer	BROWN ALLAN
Drummer	McDONALD ARCHD.
Drummer	WEBB JOSH.
Private	ARCHINADUE ALEX.
Private	BONNIMAN JAMES
Private	BREMNER JAMES
Private	BROWN HECTOR
Private	BUCHAN ALEX.
Private	BURNET GEORGE
Private	BURNET JAMES
Private	BURNET WM. Dead
Private	BURNET JOHN Dead
Private	CAMERON MALCOM
Private	CAMPBELL HUGH
Private	CAMPBELL ROBT.
Private	CROWELL WM.
Private	CLARK WM.
Private	DINGWALL JOHN
Private	DONALD JOHN
Private	DINGWELL WM.
Private	DONALDSON GEORGE
Private	DONALDSON ALEX. Gray Coll.1908
Private	FARQUHAR WM.
Private	GALWAY GEORGE
Private	GARWICK JOHN
Private	GRANT GORDON
Private	GRANT JAMES

Private	GRANT JOHN
Private	GRANT ROBT.
Private	HARPER FRANS.
Private	HUNTER ALEX.
Private	HUNTER GEORGE
Private	JACK ALEX.
Private	LIDDLE WM.
Private	McDONALD ALEX.
Private	McDONALD DONALD 1st
Private	McDONALD DONALD 2nd
Private	McDONALD JOHN
Private	McGEE WM. Discharged
Private	McINTOSH JAMES
Private	McCACHIE ROGER
Private	McLACHLAN DUNCAN
Private	McKENZIE DONALD
Private	McPHAIL JOHN
Private	McSIVINE PETER
Private	MUIRE JAMES
Private	POLSON GEORGE
Private	PORTER GEORGE
Private	RANKEN BRUCE
Private	RAE THOS.
Private	READFORD ANDW.
Private	ROSS DONALD Dead
Private	REILLY LEWIS
Private	SPARK ARCHD.
Private	WATSON JOHN Discharged
Private	WILLIAMS THOS.

Captain George Couper's Company

Lieutenant	CAMPBELL EWEN
Lieutenant	CLARKE JOHN
Serjeant	CAMERON ANGUS
Serjeant	CHRISTIE JOHN
Serjeant	GORDON JOHN Discharged
Serjeant	McKENZIE WM.
Corporal	McARDIE JAMES
Corporal	McKENZIE GEORGE
Corporal	SHARP ARCHD.
Drummer	McLEOD HUGH
Private	ANDERSON GEORGE
Private	BROOKLESS DAVID
Private	BORLAND JOHN
Private	BORTHWICK JOHN
Private	CARMICHAEL HENRY Discharged
Private	CHEYNE JAMES
Private	CHRISTIE WM.
Private	CLARK JOHN
Private	CLARIHUE JAMES
Private	CRAIG JOHN
Private	DONALDSON JAMES
Private	DOWNIE JAMES Discharged
Private	DRUMMOND ALEX.
Private	FORBES JOHN
Private	FRASER ALEX.
Private	FRASER JOHN
Private	GALBREATH ROBT.
Private	GIBB WM.
Private	GILLAN WM.
Private	GRANT WM.
Private	HAMPTON WM.
Private	IRVINE JOSH.
Private	JACK COOTS
Private	JINKINS JAMES
Private	LAVEY JOHN
Private	McCONACHIE JOSH. Discharged
Private	McGILVRAY ALEX.
Private	McINTYRE MURDK.
Private	McKAY THOS.
Private	McKENZIE JOHN
Private	McLEAN DUNCAN
Private	McLEOD MALCOLM Dead
Private	McPHERSON ANGUS
Private	McCREA THOS.
Private	MANDERSTON WM.
Private	MATHIESON DONALD
Private	MATHIESON HUGH
Private	MUNRO ALEX.
Private	RAFFERTY ROBT.
Private	REILLY JAMES Discharged
Private	ROBSON GEORGE
Private	ROSS JOHN
Private	ROSS WM.
Private	SOPPET MARK
Private	STEWART WM.
Private	STRATH ROBT. Glendining's sale March 1911
Private	SUTHERLAND ALEX.
Private	THOMSON JAMES
Private	WATT ALEX. Col.Murrays Collection 1908
Private	WATT ROBT.
Private	WILKIE STEWART
Private	YATES SAML.

Captain Peter Wilkie's Company

Captain	WILKIE PETER
Lieutenant	McDONNELL RICHD.
Lieutenant	ROSS OWEN
Lieutenant	PEAT RICH.J.
Serjeant	DUNCAN GEORGE
Serjeant	GRAY JAMES
Serjeant	RAE DAVID
Corporal	COLLIE JOHN
Corporal	LESLIE ROBT.
Corporal	McBAIN PETER
Private	THOMAS JOHN
Corporal	WOOD ALEX.
Private	ALLEN JOHN
Private	ANDERSON JAMES
Private	BARR ROBT.
Private	BLACK DAVID Discharged
Private	BLACK JOHN
Private	BORLAND WM.
Private	CAMERON DAVID
Private	CAMERON DUNCAN
Private	CAMPBELL DONALD
Private	CHISHOLM HAROLD
Private	CLARK GEORGE
Private	DAVIDSON NATHL.
Private	DUNCAN ROSE.
Private	FRASER DAVID
Private	FRASER DONALD
Private	GILLINGHAM MATTW.
Private	GOWANS JOHN
Private	GRANT JAMES
Private	HAMILTON ROBT.
Private	HARPER THOS. Glendining's Sale April 1913
Private	HATTRICK JOHN
Private	HENDERSON ALEX. Glendining's Sale January 1910
Private	KIRKWOOD THOS.
Private	LEE PETER
Private	McBAIN ANDW.
Private	McDONALD DONALD Dead
Private	McDONALD HUGH
Private	McDOUGALD DONALD
Private	McEWEN JOHN
Private	McINTOSH DAVID
Private	MACKAY GEORGE
Private	McKENZIE GEORGE Whitaker Collection 1908
Private	MILNE ALEX.
Private	MILLS WM.
Private	MITCHELL JOHN
Private	MUNRO FINLAY WM.
Private	NEWRIE JOHN
Private	NEWLANDS JAMES
Private	RATTRAY DAVID
Private	ROBERTSON JOHN
Private	ROSS JAMES 1st
Private	ROSS JAMES 2nd
Private	ROSS JOHN
Private	ROSS KENNETH
Private	ROSS PHILLIP Day Sale April 1910
Private	SKINNER DONALD
Private	SMITH JAMES
Private	STEWART JAMES
Private	TOWNSEND DAVID
Private	WATT JAMES

* * *

1st Battn. 95th REGIMENT OF FOOT

Lt.Colonel	BARNARD Sir A.F. K.C.B.
Major	CAMERON A.
Adjutant	KINCAID J.
Qr.Master	BAGSHAW J.
Surgeon	BURKE J.
Ass.Surgeon	ROBSON J.
Ass.Surgeon	HETT R.H.
Pay Master	McKENZIE J.
Captain	SMYTH H.G. (Bt.Lt.Col.) Deputy Asst.Qr.Mr.General
Captain	SMYTH C. Bde.Major Killed 16 June
Captain	ECLES C. Bde.Major Killed 16 June

Captain J. Leach's Company

Captain	LEACH J. Bt.Lt.Col.
Lieutenant	COX J.
Lieutenant	GARDENER J.P.
Lieutenant	FITZMORRIS J.G.
S.Major	SHINE WM.
P.M.S.	FRASER JAMES
Ar.Serjeant	ANDERSON JOHN
Serjeant	GILBERT THOS.
Serjeant	KENNEDY DANL.
Serjeant	MASLING CHAS.
Serjeant	WHITHAM JOSH.
Serjeant	CROWTHERS THOS. Killed in Action 18th June
Corporal	KELLUM WM.

Corporal	MARSHALL JOHN
Corporal	RIDDINGS JAMES
Corporal	SHANAGHAN THOS.
Corporal	TONKISON EDWD.
Drummer	CANHAM JOHN
Drummer	LEES HENERY
Private	ABLE THOS.
Private	ATWOOD RICHD.
Private	BAGNELL THOS.
Private	BANDLE RICHD.
Private	BANDLE THOS.
Private	BARMAN JAMES
Private	BRADBURN THOS. Deceased
Private	BROWN GEORGE
Private	BURNET WM.
Private	CALLANS JOHN
Private	CASTLES JOHN
Private	CAVANAGH PATK.
Private	CHARITY THOS.
Private	COOPER THOS.
Private	CONNOR JOHN Invalided
Private	COSTELLOW EDWD.
Private	DAVIS WM.
Private	DAVIS JOHN
Private	DEACON ROBT.
Private	DONEVAN JOHN
Private	DUFTY GEORGE
Private	ESTWOOD THOS.
Private	FLETCHER GEO.
Private	GASCOIGN CHAS.
Private	GREHAM WM.
Private	GREEN GEO.
Private	GREENSDALE WM.
Private	GIBBON PATK.
Private	GRIFFITHS JOHN Invalided
Private	HAGUE THOS.
Private	HARVEY ISERAL Discharged
Private	HOWARD JOHN
Private	KELLY DANL.
Private	KITCHEN GEORGE
Private	LOVEKING GEO.
Private	LAIKEN CHAS.
Private	LOCK THOS.
Private	McRAE ALEX.
Private	MINNIKIN JAMES
Private	MURPHY JOHN
Private	ORMOND CHAS.
Private	PAGE JOHN
Private	PARKER WM.
Private	PARKER WM.
Private	PARSONS THOS. Glendining's sale 25th October 1908
Private	PASKETT JOHN
Private	RAMKIN THOS.
Private	RABB JAMES Invalided
Private	ROBERTS ROBT.
Private	RYAN PHILIP
Private	SIMMONS WM.
Private	SMITH JNS. Discharged
Private	STOCK SAML.
Private	SUTHERLAND EDWD.
Private	THOMAS DAVID
Private	TROUTER THOS.
Private	TURNER PETER
Private	UNDERHILL CHAS.
Private	WAGHORN THOS.
Private	WALTERS JOHN
Private	WINHAND JAMES
Private	WESTON WM. Chadwick sale Nov 1912
Private	WILLIAMS WM.
Private	WILKISON WM.
Private	WILSON GEO.
Private	WILSON HENRY
Private	WRIGHT WM.
Private	YOUNGER JAMES
Private	SMITH JOHN Killed in Action 18th June
Private	DAVEY WM. Killed in Action 18th June

Captain E. Chawner's Company

Captain	CHAWNER E.
1st Lieutenant	STEWART ARCHD.
Lieutenant	LESTER WM. Killed in Action 18th June
Lieutenant	GARDINER J.
Ensign	STEWART ALLAN
Volunteer	KELLETT R.J.
Serjeant	NEVIN WM.
Serjeant	ANTHONY MICHL.
Serjeant	DIGBY TOBIAN
Serjeant	MATTHEWS WM.
Corporal	DILLON MAICHL.
Corporal	EVENS RICHD. Invalided
Corporal	JONES JOHN
Corporal	MASTERSON ALEX.
Corporal	NAUGHTON JOHN
Drummer	PLUMB JOHN
Drummer	ALLEN THOS.
Private	ALLEN THOS. Invalided

Private	ALLUM WM.
Private	BATH CHRISTIE
Private	BOOTY NATHL. Putticks sale June 1912
Private	BOTT JAMES
Private	CAVANAGH WM.
Private	CHAWKLY JOHN
Private	CHITTY ANTHY. Invalided
Private	CLARK ANDW.
Private	COGGS RICHD.
Private	CORNER THOS.
Private	CAUGHLIN JAMES Discharged
Private	COWARD JOHN
Private	COX 2nd JOHN
Private	CRAWLEY THOS.
Private	CUMMINGS THOS.
Private	DAVIS JOHN
Private	DRAWBRIDGE EDWD Deceased
Private	DUFF JAMES
Private	EATON THOS.
Private	EDWARDS THOS. Invalided
Private	FAIRBRASS HENRY Invalided
Private	FISHER JOHN
Private	FRANK JOHN Deceased
Private	HARGREAVES THOS.
Private	HARLING ROBT.
Private	HARRY WM.
Private	HART JAMES
Private	HAUGHTON CHAS.
Private	HEELS JOSHUA
Private	HICKIE JAMES
Private	HOLLIDAY MATTW.
Private	JACKSON THOS.
Private	JACOBS THOS.
Private	JENKINS THOS.
Private	JOYCE MICHL.
Private	KELLEAGHER WM.
Private	KENNY THOS.
Private	McGUGAN ARCH.
Private	MILLER ALEX.
Private	MILLER ISSAC Invalided
Private	MILLER SAML.
Private	MURPHY BERND.
Private	O'NAILE THOS.
Private	PAIGN JAMES
Private	PRINCE GEO.
Private	RANOLD JOHN
Private	ROBINSON THOS.
Private	ROBSON MATTW.
Private	ROONEY JOHN
Private	ROWE GEO.
Private	RUSSELL JAMES
Private	SAVELL CHAS.
Private	SMITH JAMES
Private	SMITH JOHN
Private	SMITH PETER
Private	SPARROW ARCH.
Private	STACEY WM. Invalided Day sale April 1910
Private	STANTON PATK.
Private	STEVENS JOHN
Private	STORRY THOS.
Private	SWINGLER JOHN
Private	THOMPSON THOS.
Private	TOOTH CHAS. Payne Coll.1911
Private	TOWN ISSAC Chadwick sale Nov 1912
Private	TOWNSEND WN.
Private	VIRGO WM.
Private	USHER WM. Invalided
Private	WHETSTONE THOS.
Private	WIFFEN EDWD.
Private	WIGLEY WM.
Private	WILLIAMS JOHN
Private	WOOLLEY JOHN
Private	WAYNE JAMES
Private	YEATHERS JOSH.
Private	BATTERSBY JAMES Killed in Action 16th June
Private	MATSON HENRY Killed in Action 18th June

Captain Wm. Johnston's Company

Captain	JOHNSTON WM. Gaskell Coll.1908
Lieutenant	CHAPMAN W.
Lieutenant	TREERE R.B. Whitaker Coll.1908
Lieutenant	STILWELL J. Died of wounds 20th June
Serjeant	GRIFFITHS THOS.
Serjeant	CUNNINGHAM WM.
Serjeant	JACKSON ESAU
Serjeant	RICKS JOHN
Serjeant	SPINKS DAVID
Serjeant	WALSH DAVID Killed in Action 18th June
Serjeant	McBAIN JOHN Killed in Action 16th June
Corporal	HALL JOHN
Corporal	HOWIE DAVID

Corporal	LONGHURST EDWD.	Private	SHELLETS JOSH. Deceased
Corporal	McCUSKIE PAT. Invalided	Private	SLAYN JOHN
Corporal	PORTER JAMES	Private	SMILLEY WM.
Drummer	PALMER JOANTHAN	Private	SMITH GEORGE Invalided
Private	ALLEN HUMP.	Private	SMITH THOS.
Private	ASHTON JOHN	Private	SMALLY THOS.
Private	BALDWIN WM.	Private	SPRAGS WM.
Private	BEETIE MARK	Private	STEDHAM WM.
Private	BEDWELL WM.	Private	STEWART GEORGE
Private	BAWE ANDW.	Private	STERLING THOS.
Private	BOOTH HENRY	Private	SHARPLY THOS.
Private	BROWN JOSH	Private	SWALWELL MATTW.
Private	BUCKLER JAMES Glendining's sale 22nd May 1908 Galway Foley 1910	Private	TUNICLIFFE GEO.
Private	BURGESS ABRM Gray Coll.1908	Private	TUTT GEO.
Private	CONNELLY OWEN	Private	TURNER HENRY
Private	DENT ZACH.	Private	TWINER STEPHN.
Private	DONNELLY HUGH	Private	WADE FRANCIS Deceased
Private	DILKS WM. Discharged	Private	WATTS JAMES
Private	EDWARD WM.	Private	WATNIFF JOSH.
Private	FORTUNE DANL.	Private	WALKER JAMES Phillips sale
Private	FREEMAN WM. Not entitled	Private	WHITTINGHAM JOHN
Private	GARVEY PATK.	Private	WHEALON OLIVER
Private	GISBURN WM. Deceased	Private	WHEELER WM.
Private	GOLDING WM. Invalided	Private	WILSON JOHN
Private	GREENFIELD THOS.	Private	WILSON THOS.
Private	GREENFIELD CHAS.	Private	WILTSHIRE GEO.
Private	HANKIN DAVID Not entitled	Private	BURTON JAMES Killed in Action 18th June
Private	HOBBS PETER	Private	KING JOSH. Killed in Action 18th June
Private	HOLMES THOS. Invalided	Private	McREA JOHN Killed in Action 18th June
Private	HORNER JOHN	Private	BURNES WM. Killed in Action 18th June
Private	HUNT THOS.	Private	BANKS JOHN Killed in Action 18th June
Private	KAINE JAS.	Private	LINDSAY ALEX. Killed in Action 18th June
Private	KAINE JNS.		
Private	LINTON JAMES		
Private	LAVETT SAMUEL		
Private	McKAY WM.		
Private	MALLOCK JOHN		
Private	MASSON JOHN Invalided		
Private	MAIDEN WM. Discharged		
Private	MURRAY NICHS.		
Private	PAGE PETER		
Private	PARKER HENRY Deceased		
Private	PIPER GEORGE		
Private	PITT WM.		
Private	RHODES WM. Invalided		
Private	ROACH JOHN		
Private	REECE JOHN Deceased		
Private	SERES RICHD.		

Captain H. Lee's Company

Captain	LEE HENRY
Lieutenant	MOLLOY J.
Lieutenant	HAGGUP J.
Lieutenant	JOHNSTONE E.D. Killed in Action 18th June
2nd Lieutenant	CHURCH J.
Serjeant	FAIRFOOT ROBT.
Serjeant	CHAMBERS THOS.
Serjeant	HENDERSON JOHN
Serjeant	SHARPLESS ROBT.
Serjeant	MORGAN THOS. Killed in Action 18th June

Serjeant	KITCHEN WM.
Corporal	BROWN JOHN
Corporal	GRIFFITHS THOS. Glendining's sale Dec.1910
Corporal	McGEE JOHN
Corporal	McDERMOD SAML.
Corporal	PETERS SAML.
Corporal	STREET SAML.
Drummer	McKAY GEO.
Drummer	WEST HENRY
Private	ANDSELL THOS
Private	ALLEN CHAS
Private	ALLEN WM.
Private	ARMS.JOSH.
Private	ALTON JAMES
Private	BABLISH JOHN
Private	BURGE ROBT.
Private	BELLINGS JOSH.
Private	BROWN THOS.
Private	BULCOCK JAMES
Private	BAKER SAML.
Private	BUCKLEY JOHN
Private	BURROWS JOHN
Private	CARTER THOS.
Private	COUTHERON JOHN
Private	COLEMAN CHAS.
Private	CUMMINGS RENOLD
Private	DINICLOW WM.
Private	DODD JOSH.
Private	DUCKWITH ROGER
Private	EABURN WM.
Private	EDMUNDS WM.
Private	EGINTON JAS.
Private	EGINTON THOS.
Private	FITZGERALD JOHN
Private	GILLESPIE JOHN
Private	GLEW WM.
Private	GRAY DAVID
Private	GREENWOOD JOHN
Private	HAWKINS JOSH.
Private	HART MARTIN
Private	HEWETT JOSH.
Private	HUGHES DAVID
Private	JACTELL JOHN
Private	JOYNS JOSH.
Private	JUDE WM.
Private	KEELING WM.
Private	LESTON ROBERT
Private	McKELLY JOHN
Private	McCUBBY JOHN
Private	MARCH JOHN
Private	MILES or MILLS JAMES Col. Gascoignes Coll.March 1909
Private	MORRIS JOHN
Private	MURPHY JOHN
Private	MURRAY DENIS
Private	NORTON MICHL.
Private	O'CONNER WM.
Private	O'NAILE JAMES
Private	PAISLY HUGH
Private	PARRY ROBT.
Private	POOLE WM.
Private	POWLE JOHN
Private	PRATT JOHN
Private	PRICE WM.
Private	PRING BENJN.
Private	ROBINSON SAML.
Private	ROOT JOSH.
Private	RODGERS HUGH
Private	ROSS ADAM
Private	SIMPSON WM.
Private	SHOEBRIDGE JAMES
Private	SMITH JOHN
Private	SMITH THOS.
Private	THOMAS THOS.
Private	WARREN JAS.
Private	WARBURTON JAS.
Private	WATKINS WM.
Private	WILLIAMS ELIAS
Private	CROOKSHANKS GEO. Killed in Action 18th June
Private	McCONNELL BERNARD Killed in Action 16th June
Private	MAIDS WM. Killed in Action 18th June
Private	SULLEVAN DANL. Killed in Action 16th June
Private	WAINE JOHN Killed in Action 18th June
Private	SMITH JAMES Killed in Action 18th June

Captain F. Glass's Company

Lieutenant	SHINLEY W.
Lieutenant	DRUMMOND GEORGE
Ensign	WRIGHT WM.
Serjeant	BALLER GEO.
Serjeant	CROSBY CHAS.
Serjeant	SMITH JOSEPH Invalided Watters sale June 1913
Serjeant	PLATTS JOHN

Serjeant	TWINER WM.
Serjeant	WAGER SAML.
Serjeant	HUFTON ANTHY. Killed in Action 18th June
Corporal	CHAMBERS JAMES Invalided
Corporal	COLLUM JOHN
Corporal	JOHNSTONE SAML.
Corporal	SANDY JOHN
Corporal	SWANSON DANL.
Corporal	BLANFORD THOS. Killed in Action 18th June
Drummer	ALLEN WM. Deceased
Drummer	DOYLE EDWD.
Private	BARRETT JAMES
Private	BARNETT JOSH.
Private	BAYLIS JOHN
Private	BLINKIN WM.
Private	BRICE JAMES
Private	BRIGHT JAMES
Private	BROTHERTON ROBT.
Private	BRYAN JOHN
Private	CAHILL JOSEPH
Private	CLARK JOSH.
Private	CROKETT JOHN
Private	COLLIS JOSHUA
Private	DAVIS EDWD.
Private	DEVAREAUX EDWD.
Private	FORD JOHN
Private	FRAM JAMES
Private	HARLE GEO. Deceased
Private	HARROLD WM.
Private	HARRIS JOHN
Private	HARRIS ROBT.
Private	HATFIELD JOSH. Deserted
Private	HAWKINS THOS.
Private	HUMPHRESS HENRY
Private	HURST JOHN
Private	JINKS JOHN Invalided
Private	JERRAM WM.
Private	JONES JOHN
Private	KENNEDY DENIS Invalided
Private	LAMB NICHS.
Private	LAWRENCE JOHN
Private	LINDSELL JOHN
Private	LINTNER JOHN
Private	LOLLE SAML. Needes Collection 1903
Private	McINTIRE PATK.
Private	MATTHEWS PETER
Private	MEADOWCROFT RALPH
Private	MERREDEATH JOHN
Private	MIDHURST JOHN
Private	MILLER WM.
Private	MERRITT WM. Deceased
Private	MOLLOY MICHL.
Private	MORRISS PETER
Private	McNABLE WM.
Private	MOONEY WM.
Private	MURNAN JOHN
Private	OUTREAM SOLON.
Private	PERRY RICHD.
Private	PRICE JOSH.
Private	RHODES JOSH.
Private	RHODES THOS. Deceased
Private	ROBERTS THOS.
Private	ROWE SAML.
Private	SALSBERRY BENJN.
Private	SKETCHLEY ROBT.
Private	SMITH JOHN
Private	THOMAS JOSH.
Private	TRACEY THOS.
Private	UNDERWOOD THOS.
Private	WALKER ABRM.
Private	WALKER JNS.
Private	WALTER JNS.
Private	WALTER WM.
Private	WATERS JNS.
Private	WILKS WM.
Private	WILLIAMS JAS.
Private	WRIGHT WM.
Private	BLYTHEN MOSES Killed in Action 16th June
Private	COWDRY JNS. Killed in Action 18th June
Private	GREEN JNS. Killed in Action 18th June

Captain C. Beckwith's Company

Captain	BECKWITH C. (Bt.Lt.Col.) Ass.Qr. Mr.Genl. on the Staff
Lieutenant	LAYTON J.
Lieutenant	SIMMONE G.
Lieutenant	FELIX O.
Volunteer	SMYTH C.
Serjeant	HILL WM.
Serjeant	ALLISON MATTW. Killed in Action 18th June
Serjeant	DANCER JOHN
Serjeant	EEDSON ALEX.
Serjeant	LEE EDWD.
Serjeant	MORRISON WM.

Serjeant	UNDERWOOD DANL.
Corporal	BURBRIDGE RICHD.
Corporal	EWART JAMES Invalided
Corporal	LAW GEO.
Corporal	MORAN JNS.
Corporal	SHAW WM. Killed in Action 18th June
Corporal	THORNTON WM.
Drummer	JENNISON JNS
Drummer	TIERNEY BRIEN
Private	ANDERSON THOS.
Private	BASFORD JOSH.
Private	BECK JNS.
Private	BEECHY WM.
Private	BROWN JOHN
Private	BURTON MATTHIAS
Private	BINDLEY JOSH.
Private	BURBRIDGE ROBT.
Private	BURR JOHN
Private	BURNELL WM.
Private	BRION WM.
Private	CARDY ZACH.
Private	CLARK WM.
Private	CONNELLY THOS. Killed in Action 18th June
Private	COLMAN JAMES
Private	CURRAN JAMES
Private	COOPER GEORGE
Private	DAVIS JNS. 1st Invalided
Private	DAVIS JNS. 2nd
Private	DONAHAUGH FELIX
Private	DOWNS JAMES
Private	DIXON JOHN
Private	ELLISS EVAN
Private	EWING ROBT.
Private	FORSTER EDWD.
Private	GIFFIN WM.
Private	GRIMES CHRIST.
Private	GRIFFITHS WM.
Private	HARVEY WM.
Private	HALL WM.
Private	HUSBAND JNS.
Private	HUCOURT JAMES
Private	HARSELL DAVID Deceased
Private	HUSSAY PATK.
Private	HARDING THOS.
Private	HUDSON ROBT.
Private	INGHAM CHRISTR.
Private	KARNEY JAMES
Private	LACKIE ARCHD.
Private	LEE WITHERINGTON
Private	LORRISON THOS.
Private	MESSOR ANDW.
Private	McCANN JOHN
Private	MASTERS JOHN
Private	MAHANY PATK. Deceased
Private	McINTOSH DONALD
Private	MOORE ALEX.
Private	MOORE JOHN
Private	MOUNT JOSH.
Private	MULLINGS JOHN
Private	MAHONEY WM.
Private	McDONOUGH JNS.
Private	MORRIS WM. Deceased
Private	NORMAN JAMES
Private	OVERDEN THOS. Glendining's sale Feb.1911
Private	PITCHFORTH JAMES Deceased
Private	PRITCHARD JAMES
Private	PASKINS WM.
Private	PAULE JAMES
Private	PETERS JOHN
Private	POULTER WM. Deceased
Private	PITT GEO.
Private	RIVERS CHAS.
Private	REYNOLDS HENRY
Private	ROTHERHAM WILLIBY
Private	ROUSE JOHN Col.Murray's Collection 1908
Private	STOKES WM.
Private	STUBBS THOS. Deceased
Private	STEEL JAMES
Private	SNOW HENRY
Private	SMART MICHL.
Private	SIMPSON ROBT.
Private	SLAUGHTER BENJN. Cheylesmore Collection 1908
Private	SEWELL SAML.
Private	THOMAS JOHN
Private	TURNBULL THOS.
Private	TOWNSEND HENRY Invalided
Private	TILBROOK SAML. Invalided
Private	TAYLOR WM.
Private	TALL THOS.
Private	WATTS JOSH. Deceased
Private	WILDING JOHN
Private	WILES JAMES

* * *

2nd BATTN. 95th REGIMENT OF FOOT

Major	NORCOTT A.G.
Major	WILKINS G.
Adjutant	SMITH THOS. In possession Mrs.Lambert(Daughter) January 1909
Surgeon	SCOTT F.
Ass.Surgeon	ARMSTRONG J.
Ass.Surgeon	SCOTT R.
Pay.Master	MACDONALD A.
Qr.Master	ROSS DONALD
Volunteer	POE GEORGE Record Office

Captain G.Miller's Company

Captain	MILLER GEO.
Lieutenant	COCHRANE THOS.
Lieutenant	FRY JOHN
Lieutenant	URQUHART CHAS.
2nd Lieutenant	SHEAN J.B.
2nd Lieutenant	HARRISS ELIAS
P.M.S.	GRAHAM ROBT.
A.S.	ODLUER DAVID
Dr.Major	MITCHELL JAMES
Serjeant	LAWRENCE JOHN
Serjeant	BRUTON RICHD.
Serjeant	DAVIDSON ALEX.
Serjeant	JONES JOB.
Serjeant	RUTLEDGE JOHN
Serjeant	STANLEY JAMES
Corporal	BURROWS JOHN
Corporal	COCKER JOHN
Corporal	DAY WM.
Corporal	KILLAN DANL.
Corporal	MURREY JAMES
Corporal	McDONALD DAVID
Corporal	McCHRISTOL JAMES
Corporal	NAGLES MICHL. Killed 18th June
Corporal	PERRY GEO.
Corporal	STEVENSON FRANS.
Corporal	WATT ALEX.
Drummer	JOHNSON WM.
Drummer	PERRY CHAS.
Drummer	WALLACE THOS.
Private	ALLDRIDGE WM.
Private	BROCKENBROW WM.
Private	BENTON LUKE
Private	BENNETT JAMES
Private	BEVON HOWEL
Private	BUSHMILL THOS.
Private	COLBURNE GEO.
Private	CONQUEST THOS.
Private	CHILD BENJN.
Private	CHEATHAM SAML.
Private	COOKE WM.
Private	COLUMBINE GEO.
Private	DIGNAM PATK.
Private	DULLIA CHAS.
Private	DANIELS JOHN
Private	DOGGETT SAML.
Private	EDWARDS WM.
Private	ELLIS RICHD.
Private	EVANS JOHN
Private	ELLIOTT JOSH.
Private	FOSTER JOSH.
Private	FULTON ROBT.
Private	FREER STEPHN.
Private	FRANCIS JOHN
Private	GILES ZACH.
Private	GREYSON WM.
Private	GIFF JAMES
Private	GARDINER DANL.
Private	GARDINER THOS.
Private	HART JOHN Col.Gascoigne's Collection March 1909
Private	HAGUE DAVID
Private	HEMBURY JOHN Col.Murray's Collection 1908
Private	HARDY SAML. On sale at Baldwin's March 1909
Private	HOPKINS GEO.
Private	HUFF DENNIS
Private	HURST WM. Glendining's sale 17 June 1908
Private	HALFPENNY WM.
Private	JONES THOS.
Private	JONES WM.
Private	JORDAN RICHD.
Private	JORDAN THOS.
Private	JOHNSON THOS.
Private	KNIGHT THOS.
Private	KEARY JOHN
Private	KELLY PATK.
Private	KEMP JOSH.
Private	KINCH JOHN
Private	KING JAMES
Private	LAWRENOW THOS.
Private	LUSCOMB JOSH.
Private	LEWIS JOHN

Private	MITCHELL JOHN
Private	MARRIOTT EDWD.
Private	O'NEILL GEO.
Private	O'CONNOR CORNS.
Private	PERRY JOHN
Private	PERRY WM.
Private	PIERS JOSH.
Private	PEARCE JOHN
Private	PAXTON SAML.
Private	POLLARD HENRY
Private	PLUNKETT THOS.
Private	POWELL GEO.
Private	SAUNDERS JAMES
Private	SELL JAMES
Private	SMITH ALEX.
Private	SMITH THOS.
Private	SMITH JAMES
Private	SMITH WM.
Private	STAMP WM.
Private	SPATFIELD RICHD. Glendining's sale Feb.1911
Private	STREET PETER
Private	SUTHERS WM.
Private	SPENCER JAMES
Private	SULLIVAN OWEN
Private	SULLIVAN JOHN
Private	TIFFILY THOS.
Private	TURNBULL GEO.
Private	UNDERHILL RICHD.
Private	VOSS RICHD.
Private	WESTBERY THOS.
Private	WELLS WM.
Private	WINHANN JOHN
Private	WELLINGTON WM.
Private	WOOD NATHL.
Private	WALSH JAMES
Private	YOUNG WM.

Captain J. Logan's Company

Captain	LOGAN JOSH. Gaskell Collection 1908
Lieutenant	BUDGEN J.R. Littledale sale Nov.1910
Lieutenant	COREN E.
Lieutenant	MADDEN E.
2nd Lieutenant	WALSH J.
Serjeant	WALKER GEO. (Colour)
Serjeant	BAKER JOHN
Serjeant	FARREN RICHD.
Serjeant	JOHNSTON JAMES
Serjeant	McKAY ANGUS
Serjeant	MORAN JOHN
Corporal	NROWN JOHN
Corporal	BEDFORD STEPN.
Corporal	HARPER BENJN. Severely Wounded since dead
Corporal	HENDERSON JOHN
Corporal	JONES THOS.
Corporal	IRDLE GEO.
Corporal	McLEOD ALEX.
Corporal	McCURRY WM.
Corporal	MORRIS THOS.
Corporal	MUXLOW JAMES
Corporal	NORTH GEO.
Corporal	PRIMROSE NEIL
Corporal	SPENCER JOHN
Corporal	WEEKS JOHN Killed 18th June
Drummer	BEEBS JOHN
Drummer	HOWE GEORGE
Drummer	KENNEDY JOHN
Private	ABERFIELD WM. Sotheby's sale Nov.1909
Private	BADICOTT JOHN
Private	BAGNALL SAML.
Private	BENSTEAD JOHN
Private	BARRETT JOHN
Private	BATES JOSH.
Private	BAGE JOHN
Private	BAILEY MARK
Private	BALDWIN WM.
Private	BROWN ZACH.
Private	BURNS EDWD. Killed 18th June
Private	CONNEL TIMY.
Private	COUSINS JOHN
Private	CORTLOW BARND.
Private	CHANDLER MOSES
Private	CHEDLE FRANS.
Private	CROSSLEY JOHN
Private	DAY ZACH.
Private	DAVIES DAVID
Private	DILLAN TERRCE.
Private	DARKEN THOS.
Private	DRAKE FRANS.
Private	DODD JOHN
Private	DOOMSDAY GEO.
Private	DONAHUE EDWD.
Private	DOWNE JOHN
Private	FINCH WM.
Private	FOX RICHD.
Private	GIBBS FRANS.
Private	GILLETT PHILIP

Private	GREAVES THOS. 1st
Private	GREAVES THOS. 2nd
Private	GREGG THOS. Galway Foley Collection 1910
Private	HEED THOS.
Private	HEAD JAMES
Private	HAWKS JAMES Killed 18th June
Private	HARGREAVES JAMES
Private	HAYS JOHN
Private	HACKETT JOSH.
Private	HILTON THOS.
Private	HORROWS JAMES
Private	HUGHES THOS.
Private	JOHNSON ZOBT.
Private	JONES EVAN Col.Murray's Collection 1908
Private	JONES THOS.
Private	LANE ROBT.
Private	McGLINZEY FRANS.
Private	MAIDEN THOS.
Private	MILES EDWD.
Private	MOULDS JOHN
Private	MARTIN STEPN.
Private	McGENNIS JAMES
Private	OLDKNOW JOSH. Killed 18th June
Private	OLDKNOW CHIRSTR.
Private	PETTEWAY WM.
Private	PLOWMAN HENRY Killed 18th June
Private	PURSER WM.
Private	RIDDLE JOHN
Private	RATHBURN JAMES
Private	ROBINSON THOS.
Private	RODGERS THOS.
Private	SOPP HENRY
Private	STAMERS JOSH.
Private	STEPHENSON JOHN
Private	STEPHENS JOHN
Private	SMITH RICHD.
Private	SIMPKINS JOHN
Private	SHEPHERD JAMES
Private	TAYLOR ROBT.
Private	TAYLOR JNS.
Private	TAREY JOHN
Private	WYLETT HENRY
Private	WORRELL JOSEPH
Private	WILKINSON JOHN
Private	WRIGHT BENJN.
Private	WHONE BENJN.
Private	WALSH JOHN

Captain J. McNemara's Company

Captain	McNEMARA J.
Lieutenant	DIXON F.
Lieutenant	CAMERON D.
Ensign	DRUMMOND G.
Serjeant	EASTHAM JOHN (Colour)
Serjeant	McGIBBON WM. (Colour)
Serjeant	GRANT JOHN
Serjeant	MALONE NICHS.
Serjeant	PILLING THOS. Killed 18th June
Serjeant	SAWYER WM.
Serjeant	TRESHAM JOHN
Corporal	ANDERSON GEORGE
Corporal	ANDERSON JAMES
Corporal	BIGGS MARTIN
Corporal	COURTMAN WM.
Corporal	DENBY THOS.
Corporal	GILLES WM.
Corporal	HENDERSON WM.
Corporal	HOPGOOD JNS. Severely Wounded since dead
Corporal	KENEDY NEIL
Corporal	LAWE WM.
Corporal	McPHERSON NEIL
Corporal	NEWTON SAML.
Corporal	SAMPSON JOS.
Corporal	WILE WM. Severely Wounded since dead
Corporal	WISEMAN ROBT.
Drummer	COLLINS WM. Killed 18th June
Drummer	CROFT WM.
Drummer	ROPER JOHN
Private	ADDY RICHD.
Private	ATKINS RICHD.
Private	AUSTIN WM.
Private	HOOK JOSEPH
Private	HUMPHERSON WM.
Private	JONES THOS.
Private	LOWRY ROBT.
Private	LOMAS GEO.
Private	LEWIS JOHN
Private	McANLY JAMES
Private	McGOWAN PATK.
Private	McNULTY THOS.
Private	MARSDEN GEO.
Private	MILLER JNS. 1st

Private	MILLER JNS. 2nd
Private	OBOURN JAMES
Private	OLLIVER WM.
Private	RAWSON ROBT.
Private	ROBERTS BENJN.
Private	ROWLAND JAMES
Private	ROWLAND JOHN Cheylesmore Collection 1908
Private	RYAN DANIEL
Private	RUSSELL WM.
Private	SCANLAN MICHL.
Private	SIMONS JOHN
Private	SHEPHERD JAMES Killed 18th June
Private	SMALLY DANIEL
Private	SHERROX JOHN
Private	SYKES JAMES
Private	SPERRY JOHN
Private	STAINES WM.
Private	TELL WM.
Private	THATCHER JAMES
Private	TOMLINSON JAMES
Private	UNDERHILL THOS.
Private	WEST NATHAN.
Private	WILKES WM.
Private	WEAVER EDWD.
Private	WILLSHAW WM.
Private	WILLIAMSON JOHN
Private	WINMARK ISSAC
Private	WOODS WM.
Private	WOODS JOHN
Private	WINTERBOTTOM JAMES
Private	WORMALD HENRY
Private	WHITEHEAD WM.
Private	WRIGHT JOHN

<u>Captain J.G. McCollough's Company</u>

Captain	McCOLLOUGH J.G.
Lieutenant	COCHRAN R.
Lieutenant	WEBB N.
Ensign	ROCHFORD C.
Serjeant	GRANT JAMES
Serjeant	WHITE JAMES
Serjeant	McCAUL CHAS. Killed 18th June
Serjeant	ROCHFORD EDWD.
Serjeant	WELSH THOS.
Serjeant	GRANT WM.
Corporal	BARLOW JOHN
Corporal	CROZIER DANIEL
Corporal	HARRIS JOHN
Corporal	HOLLAND SAML.
Corporal	KEARNEY PETER
Corporal	SCOTT WM.
Drummer	GREGSON WM.
Private	ARTHUR AARON
Private	ASHWORTH CHAS.
Private	AYNES JOHN
Private	BAKER EDWD.
Private	BAKER JOHN
Private	BALDWIN JOHN
Private	BIRD HUGH
Private	BOUNCER JAMES
Private	BROOKES GEORGE
Private	BRADLEY GEO.
Private	BREEDS JOSH.
Private	BRUMFITT WM.
Private	BUCKLAND JOSH.
Private	BENBRIDGE FREDK.
Private	CAST JOHN
Private	CASSIDY JOHN
Private	CARR THOS.
Private	CLARK SAML.
Private	CONNER JAMES
Private	CONNER PATK.
Private	COX WM.
Private	CAUSER JOHN
Private	CROWE JOHN Died of Poison 18th June
Private	DEADMAN THOS.
Private	DICKENSON WM.
Private	DRURY JAMES
Private	DUFFY JAMES
Private	EXELBY ROBT.
Private	EVANS WM.
Private	FARMER JOHN
Private	FALLAN MATTW.
Private	FIDDIMAN BURTON Killed 18 June
Private	FINNERTY JAMES
Private	FLOOD JAMES
Private	FUTTER JAMES
Private	GUNNING WM.
Private	GREEN SAML.
Private	HAYES JOHN
Private	HAYES THOS.
Private	HORSEMAN JOHN
Private	HAMILTON THOS. Killed 18 June
Private	HAYNER JOHN
Private	JONES THOS. 1st
Private	JONES THOS. 2nd

Private	JONES ROBT.
Private	JONES WM.
Private	JONES JNS.
Private	KERRIGHAN WM.
Private	KEMP WM.
Private	KNIGHT EDWD. Severely Wounded since dead
Private	LANCASTER RICHD.
Private	LEADBEATER HENRY
Private	LEVINGSTONE DUN.
Private	LAWS LEOND.
Private	LEE WM. Killed in Action
Private	LEVER JAMES
Private	LEWIS DANL.Killed in Action 18th June
Private	LOCK WM.
Private	McMORROW PATK.
Private	McGUIRE PETER
Private	MASON JAMES
Private	MEREDITH THOS.
Private	NEIL JOSEPH Killed in Action 18th June
Private	NEWSTEAD THOS.
Private	NORTON WM.
Private	NOUCH WM.
Private	O'BRIEN CHAS.
Private	PAINTER THOS.
Private	PENSION THOS.
Private	PETTLE WM.
Private	PRATT THOS.
Private	PRICE WM.
Private	PRITCHARD WM.
Private	RUSSELL HENRY
Private	RYAN PATK. on sale at Baldwin's March 1909
Private	SKELTON ISSAC
Private	SMITH WM.
Private	SPENDER WM.
Private	STAPLES JOHN
Private	STOKES JAMES Killed in Action 18th June
Private	STOKES JOHN
Private	STRINGER JAMES
Private	THOMPSON JAMES
Private	THOMAS ROBT.
Private	TINGUE JNS.
Private	TOPPIN JNS.
Private	TROW JNS.
Private	WALTON GEORGE
Private	WEBSTER JOHN
Private	WHITMORE JOHN
Private	WILLIAMS EVAN
Private	WILLIAMS JOSH.
Private	YOUNG JOHN

Captain C. Eaton's Company

Captain	EATON C. Payne Collection 1911
Lieutenant	BENNETT F.W.
Lieutenant	RIDGWAY J.A.
Ensign	FOWLER R.
Serjeant	CROW WM.
Serjeant	DAY THOS.
Serjeant	DOULAN TERR.
Serjeant	HAINES RICHD.
Serjeant	JOHNSON JOSEPH
Serjeant	RAND JAMES Killed in Action 18th June
Corporal	COPE EDWD.
Corporal	DIXON WM.
Corporal	HAINES WM.
Corporal	KEYS ROBT.
Corporal	LUCAS JOHN
Corporal	MORRIS ROBT. Gray Collection 1908
Corporal	SMITH GEORGE
Corporal	WILSON SMITH
Drummer	CONNOLLY THOS.
Drummer	TAYLOR WM. 1st
Drummer	TAYLOR WM. 2nd
Private	ALLEN WM.
Private	ALLENSON THOS.
Private	BILLS THOS.
Private	BORE HUGH
Private	BRIGHT HENRY
Private	BOOTH GEORGE
Private	BROOKS WM.
Private	BROWN JOHN
Private	BURNS RICHD.
Private	CHAMBERLAIN WM. Glendining's sale Jan. 1910
Private	CLERK WM.
Private	COLLINS RICHD.
Private	COOPER JAMES
Private	COUSINS JOHN
Private	COX GEORGE
Private	COX WM.
Private	CRANSON RALPH
Private	CROUCHER THOS.
Private	DOYLE MORRIS
Private	EDWARDS THOS.
Private	ENGHAM EDWD.
Private	EVANS RICHD.

Private	FLINT ALEX.
Private	GAMMOND JAMES
Private	GIDDENS WM.
Private	GILLETT JOSH.
Private	GRANT JAMES
Private	GRADDAGE RICHD.
Private	GRIMSTEAD ABRM.
Private	GRINDLEY JOSH.
Private	HAIRLEM RICHD.
Private	HARBOUR WM.
Private	HART JOHN
Private	HART MICHL.
Private	HAVERLEY JOHN
Private	HOBBS THOS.
Private	HORROUX PETER
Private	HUMPHRIES WM. 2nd
Private	HUNT JAMES
Private	HUNT JOSIAH
Private	HYDES PETER
Private	JAMES JON.
Private	JONES JOHN
Private	KEARNY DANL.
Private	KITCHLOW BERND.
Private	LAPPING PETER
Private	LOVETT THOS.
Private	LUXTON WM.
Private	McCANN THOS.
Private	McPHERSON NEIL
Private	MAGHAN PATK.
Private	MORRAN MARK
Private	MULLEN STEWART
Private	MURRAY JOHN
Private	NEIL JOHN
Private	NEIL JAMES
Private	POINTING WM.
Private	PRICE THOS. Glendining's sale Dec.1910
Private	PRIVETT MICHL.
Private	PILTON JOHN Killed in Action 18th June
Private	RHODES JAMES
Private	RIDDLES REILLY
Private	RODGERS GEORGE
Private	SANKEY EDWD.
Private	SCRAGG RICHD.
Private	SEEDEN HUGH
Private	SERVILL WM. Sotheby's sale July 1912
Private	SHEPPERD JAMES
Private	SHELDRICK RICHD.
Private	SHAUGNESSEY WM.
Private	SIMMS EDWD.
Private	SMITH HARRY Sotheby's sale 19th June 1903
Private	SMITH WM.
Private	STARR JOSEPH
Private	STATWOOD WM.
Private	STRINGFELLOW JOHN
Private	STROUD JOHN
Private	STRICKEN JOHN
Private	SWAINE THOS.
Private	TAYLOR BENJN. Glendining's sale 21 July 1909
Private	TAYLOR JOSHUA
Private	WARNER JAMES
Private	WHITLEY JOHN
Private	WILLIAMS EDWD.
Private	WILLIAMS JAMES
Private	WILLIAMS RICHD.
Private	WINTERTON JOHN
Private	WOOLLER RICHD.

<u>Captain F. Le Blanc's Company</u>

Captain	LeBLANC F.
Lieutenant	HUMBLY WM.
Lieutenant	LYNHAM J. Payne Coll.1911
Ensign	EYRE R.
Serjeant	BELL JOSH. Glendining's sale December 1910
Serjeant	CAVENAGH JAS.
Serjeant	GOOCH WM.
Serjeant	McGROTTY HENRY
Serjeant	PEACOCK JOHN
Serjeant	SPENCER RICHD.
Corporal	BLINCE JOHN
Corporal	CARR GEORGE
Corporal	DINNAGE SAML.
Corporal	DIVINE PATK.
Corporal	DUNN DENNIS
Corporal	LOWE JOHN
Corporal	SANDERS DANL.
Drummer	FARMER RICHD.
Drummer	JONES EDWD.
Drummer	WILDES MORRIS
Drummer	PRESTRIDGE WM.
Private	ADAMS JOHN
Private	BALL JOHN
Private	BACK WM.

Private	BARRON JOHN
Private	BAIRD WM.
Private	BLACK THOS.
Private	BLACKMAN WM.
Private	CAVE JOHN
Private	CHAPMAN THOS.
Private	CLARKE WM.
Private	CLAYTON THOS.
Private	COOPER THOS
Private	CORBETT THOS.
Private	DAWN EDWD.
Private	DEACON WM.
Private	DAVIS JOHN Killed in Action 18th June
Private	DOWNES JOHN
Private	DUTTON JOSH.
Private	ELLIS HENRY
Private	ELLING WM.
Private	ECKELS ROBT.
Private	EVERITT ANTHY.
Private	GAUGE JOHN
Private	GAME SAML.
Private	GOODMAN ROBT.
Private	HARLEY JOHN
Private	HARPER THOS.
Private	HART JAMES
Private	HENNILL N.
Private	HOWISON ROBT.
Private	HIGGINS PATK.
Private	HODGKINS JOSH
Private	HORBIN MORN.
Private	HOLLINGS WM.
Private	JACKSON JOHN
Private	JACKSON JOSH.
Private	JUDD HENRY
Private	KENNEDY DAVID
Private	KENNEDY JOHN
Private	KITCHLOVE EDWD.
Private	KNIGHT GEORGE
Private	LARKIN DAVID
Private	LOTHERN JOHN
Private	LUXTON JOHN
Private	LECK JOSH.
Private	LENNOX JAMES
Private	LEMMOW WM.
Private	LEWIN JOHN
Private	McLENNON ALEX.
Private	McNIFF JOHN
Private	MAY WM.
Private	MARTIN WM.
Private	MILLER JOHN
Private	MALLON JOHN
Private	MILTON DANIEL
Private	MOORE WM.
Private	MORAN JOHN
Private	NEAL WM.
Private	OLDERSHAW THOS.
Private	PALMER SAML.
Private	PRIESTLEY JOSH.
Private	PRYKE SAML.
Private	REYNOLDS PATK.
Private	REDDY PATK.
Private	REILLY FRANS.
Private	RODGERS BART.
Private	ROBINSON JAMES
Private	ROBINSON WM.
Private	ROSTRIN JOHN
Private	SCANLAN MICHL.
Private	SHORLACK MATTW.
Private	SAUNDERS DAVID
Private	SHAW GEORGE
Private	SHIPLEY WM.
Private	SPRINGLE JOHN
Private	STREETING ROBT.
Private	SWEENEY OWEN
Private	SMITH JOHN
Private	TEAM WM.
Private	TUCKER ROBT.
Private	TWO WM.
Private	WATERS THOS.
Private	WESTCOTT WM.
Private	WHITING WM.
Private	WILSON JOSH.
Private	WRIGHT HENRY
Private	YOUNG FREDK.

* * *

<u>3rd BATTN. 95th REGIMENT OF FOOT</u>

Major	ROSS T. (Lt.Col.)
Captain	FULLERTON J. (Lt.Col.)
Captain	EELES WM. (Major)
1st Lieutenant	VICKERS G.
1st Lieutenant	WORSLEY T.T.
1st Lieutenant	SHENLEY G.H.
1st Lieutenant	McFARLANE D.
1st Lieutenant	HOPE J.C. 2nd Bn.Served with 3rd. Whitaker Collection
2nd Lieutenant	MILLIGAN A.

2nd Lieutenant	PROBART C.
Ass.Surgeon	McCABE THOMAS

Captain J. Fullertons Company

Serjeant	COLLIER SAML. Discharged 10th April 1816
Serjeant	KENSTOCK JASPER Died 28th September 1815
Serjeant	PERCIVALE THOS.
Serjeant	SHEARMAN WM. Discharged 15th April 1816
Serjeant	SHARP JAMES
Corporal	GRIFFITHS HENRY
Corporal	HAYSMORE EDWD.
Corporal	LORD WM.
Corporal	WHITNEY WM. Col.R.T. Gascoigne's Collection March 1909
Drummer	KENEDY PATK.
Drummer	DAWSON THOS.
Drummer	HUNT SAML.
Private	ADAMS JOHN
Private	ANGELL JAMES
Private	ALLOTT GEORGE
Private	BALL JOHN
Private	BEEATTON WM.
Private	BROOMLEY WM.
Private	BORDIN WM.
Private	BRADLEY JOSH.
Private	BOLTON JAS.
Private	BOOTH MICHL.
Private	BUSS GEORGE
Private	BILLIS JOHN
Private	BAMFORTH RICHD.
Private	BUCHANAN DANL.
Private	CLARKE JNS. 1st Glendining's sale 17th June 1903
Private	CLARKE JNS. 2nd
Private	CARBREW JAMES
Private	CARSON FRANS.
Private	CLEMENTS EDWD.
Private	CROUCH WM.
Private	COWARD JOHN Discharged 10th April 1816
Private	DOWE THOS.
Private	DAWSON ELISHA
Private	DAWSON WM.
Private	EDWARDS EDWD. Died 25th October 1815
Private	ELDRIDGE THOS.
Private	FRENCH JAMES
Private	FREERE CHAS.
Private	FINCH SAML.
Private	FOX WM.
Private	GORMAN THOS.
Private	GREEN SAML.
Private	GALE DANL.
Private	GREENWOOD WM. Col.Murray's Collection 1908
Private	GREEN TOBIAS Gaskell Coll.1908
Private	GILL JAMES
Private	GASTRILL JOHN
Private	GOLDUP JOHN
Private	HALL JOSH Killed in Action 18th June 1815
Private	HAND TIMY.
Private	HANDLEY ROBT.
Private	HENSON JAMES
Private	HAMMOND HENRY
Private	HALL WM.
Private	HINDS THOS.
Private	HICKS ROBT.
Private	HYDES WM.
Private	ISHERWOOD JOHN
Private	JACKSON ROBT. Discharged 4th April 1816. Cheylesmore Coll.1908
Private	JONES PAUL
Private	JOHN WM.
Private	KILBY JAMES
Private	KNIGHT THOS.
Private	LANE WM. Discharged 1st April 1816. Gray Collection 1908
Private	LOWE JAMES
Private	LEWIS WM.
Private	LAIGHT RICHD.
Private	MESHAM MICHL.
Private	MARSH BENJN,.
Private	MARSHALL WM.
Private	MIDDLETON WM.
Private	NAGGS JNS.
Private	NEWNE JNS.
Private	NEWTON GEO.
Private	OLIVER JOS.
Private	PENTON JAMES
Private	PETTY JAMES
Private	RHODES BENJN.
Private	RIDGWAY WM.
Private	STUBBLEY ROBT. Died 4th Aug.1815
Private	SMITH BENJN.
Private	SWEENEY ROBT.
Private	SADLER JAMES

Private	THOMPSON DAVID
Private	TOWN FRANS.
Private	WHITE ARTHUR
Private	WRIGHT PETER
Private	WRIGHT WM.
Private	WESTON JNS.
Private	WILSON HENRY
Private	WHEATLEY WM.
Private	WHITE JOHN
Private	YEATS CHAS.
Private	YOUNG JOSH.

Captain Eele's Company

Serjeant	GAMBLE DAVID
Serjeant	HALL WM. 1st
Serjeant	HALL WM. 2nd
Serjeant	STAPLES SAML.
Serjeant	TRAFFORD ROBT.
Serjeant	WILLIAMS THOS. Discharged 10th April 1816
Corporal	CAWTHORN JOSEPH CHAS. In possession Mrs. Russell 1910 also M.G.D. Medal
Corporal	NORRIS JAMES
Corporal	WARD JNS.
Corporal	WILSON JNS.
Private	WARD PETER
Corporal	WOODLEY JAMES
Drummer	CRITTLE JOHN
Drummer	SWEENEY JOHN
Drummer	SWEENEY JAMES
Private	ASHFORTH HENRY
Private	AULD JOHN
Private	BARTHRAM WM.
Private	BAKER GEO.
Private	BAYLEY THOS. Died 5th Dec. 1815
Private	BAYNE WM.
Private	BEYMONT THOS. Died of Wounds 18th June 1815
Private	BICHERTON RICH.
Private	BIGGS WM.
Private	BIRCH JOHN
Private	BLAKE JAMES
Private	BLYTHMAN ANGUS
Private	BOWLES JOSH.
Private	BROWN WM.
Private	BUNGALL EDWD.
Private	BYATT THOS.
Private	CARLEY JOHN
Private	CHAPMAN THOS.
Private	CHAPMAN WM.
Private	CHILMAN BENJN. Sotheby's sale June 1911
Private	CLARKE THOS.
Private	COLES THOS.
Private	COLLINGHAM JAMES
Private	COOMBS NICHS.
Private	DIABBLE GEORGE
Private	EDWARDS WM.
Private	EGGLETON WM.
Private	ELLIS JAMES
Private	EVANS CHAS.
Private	EVANS EVAN
Private	FIELD JOSEPH Needes Coll.1908
Private	FLETCHER GEO.
Private	FOMPSON RICHD.
Private	FOULKS JAMES
Private	FRENCH JOHN
Private	GILPIN JAMES
Private	GOODMAN WM.
Private	GOSEEMLEE THOS.
Private	GREENSTREET JAMES
Private	GREEN CHAS.
Private	HALL JOHN
Private	HOPKINS GEO.
Private	HUTCHINS WM.
Private	JENKINS THOS.
Private	JENKS ROBT.
Private	JONES RICHD. Whitaker Coll.1908
Private	KEIGHTLY GEORGE
Private	KING GEORGE Killed in Action 18th June 1815
Private	KIRKMAN WM.
Private	KNOWLES WM.
Private	LARVILL DAVID Galway Foley Collection 1910
Private	LANGUM JAMES
Private	LIVINGS CHAS.
Private	LONG JAMES
Private	LONG SAML.
Private	MACHIN JAMES
Private	McCARLY CHAS.
Private	McDOUGAL JNS.
Private	MIPHAM JAS.
Private	MILLINER JOHN
Private	MILLS WM.
Private	MOORE GEORGE
Private	MORIS BEN.

Private	NASH JAMES
Private	NEVIN HENRY
Private	O'BRIAN PATK.
Private	OLDFIELD JOHN Day sale April 1910
Private	POWELL THOS. Payne Collection 1911
Private	PRICE EDWD.
Private	PRICE JAMES
Private	REARDON JOHN
Private	RIX CHAS.
Private	ROBBINS PETER
Private	ROWLAND GEO.
Private	SADDINGTON GEORGE
Private	SMITH THOS.
Private	SNOW RICHD.
Private	STATESMAN THOS.
Private	SLYTES WM.
Private	THOMPSON WM.
Private	THORNTON JOHN
Private	WELLS JNS.
Private	WILSON WM.

* * *

ROYAL STAFF CORPS.

Colonel	NICOLAY WM. Gaskell Collection 1903
Major	STAVELEY WM.
Captain	WRIGHT THOS.
Lieutenant	HALL G.D.
Lieutenant	JACKSON BASIL
Lieutenant	BRAUNS A.C.G.
Ensign	SEDLEY J.S.
Ensign	MILLIKIN JOHN
Private	GRANGER WM. Whitaker Collection 1908
Private	HILLIER WM.
Lieutenant	TAIT Payne Coll.1911

* * *

3rd GARRISON BATTALION

Private	ANDREWS JNS. 3rd Battn. Royals
Private	LAMB RICHD. 3rd Battn. Royals
Private	OVENROD THOS. 3rd Battn. Royals
Private	TOWERS JAMES 1st Battn. 4th
Serjeant	HARDING HENRY 1st Battn. 23rd
Private	GROSVENOR MOSES 1st Battn. 23rd
Private	BALL JAMES 1st Battn. 27th
Private	WADSWORTH GEORGE 1st Battn. 27th
Private	FRANKS GEORGE 1st Battn. 28th
Private	QUINN PATK. 1st Battn. 28th
Private	CHURCHILL JAMES 1st Battn. 28th
Private	CAVANAGH WM. 1st Battn. 28th
Private	SNEAD THOS. 1st Battn. 32nd
Private	WOODS ABRM. 1st Battn. 33rd
Corporal	KNOTT JAMES 1st Battn. 40th
Private	COLLITT SAML. 2nd Battn. 44th
Private	CONNOLLY WM. 2nd Battn. 44th
Private	BRAY WM. 2nd Battn. 73rd
Private	HONEYFOY PATK. 2nd Battn. 73rd
Private	MANSELL THOS. 2nd Battn. 73rd
Private	HUGHES JOHN 2nd Battn. 79yh
Private	McCLURE WM. 2nd Battn. 79th
Private	DAVIDSON ALEX. 1st Battn. 92nd
Private	CROOKSHANKS THOS. 1st Battn. 92nd
Private	PETERS WM. 1st Battn. 92nd
Private	BOWIE JNS. 1st Battn. 92nd

* * *

1st REGIMENT OF LIGHT DRAGOONS K.G.L.

Colonel	DORNBERG Sir WM. Severely Wounded
Lt.Colonel	BULOW JOHN Severely Wounded
Major	REIZEUSTEIN AUGUST. Severely Wounded
Adjutant	FRICKE WM. Severely Wounded
Surgeon	GROSSHOPF FREDERIC
Ass.Surgeon	MEYER DANIEL Payne Collection
Ass.Surgeon	FRIDERIN HENRY
Vty.Surgeon	FLEUER LUDOLPUS
Qr.Master	KRANZ HENRY

Captain George Hattorff's Troop

Captain	HATTORFF GEORGE Severely Wounded
Lieutenant	FISCHER AUGUST
Trp.Sjt.Major	SCHWAGERMANN ANDW.
Rgt.Sjt.Major	SCHUMASHER CHARLES
P.M.S.	LEE MATTW.
A.Serjeant	SCHELLER DANIEL
Sad.Serjeant	SCHMIEDT FRDRIC.
Serjeant	BOSSE LEWIS
Serjeant	DOHMEYER CHRISTOPH.

Serjeant	NATHAURFF HURGEN
Serjeant	SCHAMBACH HENRY
Corporal	FREYRE ERNEST Wounded since dead
Corporal	GRABOW FERDINAND Wounded lost one arm
Corporal	MARKS HENRY Wounded
Corporal	WALTER JOSEPH Littledale sale Nov. 1910
Trumpeter	CANZELEUEIER DEDREE Wounded
Private	ADRIAN NICHOLAUS
Private	BANNIER CHRISTOPH. Killed 18th June
Private	BEMKE FREDREC
Private	BORSHERS CHRISTIAN
Private	BOSIKE HENRY
Private	BAULEMANN HENRY
Private	BRAND GEORGE Wounded
Private	BAUERMEISTER HENRY
Private	BRENNEIKE ANDW.
Private	BOSIHKY PETER Wounded
Private	BAUERMEISTER GODFRY
Private	CLAREN WM.
Private	DARJES CHRISTIAN
Private	DAHL JOHN
Private	FELDMAN CONRAD
Private	GRIECE CHRISTIAN
Private	GRAMUSH CHRISTOPH.
Private	GOTZE FREDRECK
Private	GRANE HENRY
Private	GRUSSENDORFT CHRISTIAN
Private	HELIUS HENRY
Private	HOMEYER FREDRECK
Private	HUNZLEMANN HENRY
Private	HINZE DAVID Wounded
Private	KOSH JOHN
Private	KRANGE HENRY Wounded
Private	KOTHE HENRY
Private	KUCHMANN FREDRECK
Private	KALENBERG JOHN
Private	LANE AUGUST
Private	LUTTERMANN CHRISTIAN
Private	LUBBERS CHRISTOPH.
Private	MEYER FREDRECK
Private	MEYER DOMINIS
Private	MEINHEYET FREDRECK
Private	OHLSCHAGER CONRAD Discharged 25th Aug.1815 OLDERSHAUSEN
Private	PREIK CHRISTOPH.
Private	PENTZ JOHN Killed 18th June 1815
Private	SCHAFFER FREDRECK
Private	SCHRODER CHRISTIAN
Private	STOBER FREDRECK
Private	STORK CONRAD Discharged 25th Aug.1815
Private	SCHLEMME FREDRECK
Private	SPANGENBERG THOS.
Private	STRUCK HENRY
Private	THRAN HENRY Killed 18 June
Private	VANDERBON HERMAN Wounded
Private	WEHLER FREDRECK
Private	WALTER CLAUS
Private	WIEYMANN CONRAD
Private	WITTE ERNEST Wounded
Private	WEIDEMANN AUGUST
Private	ZIEBERG FRANCIS
Private	ZELLER GODFRY

Captain B. Bothmer's Company No.2.

Captain	BOTHMER BERND. Wounded R.Leg amputated
Lieutenant	LINDES CHARLES
Cornet	NANNE HENRY Severely Wounded
T.Sjt.Major	BAARS HENRY
Serjeant	MATTHIAS JOHN
Serjeant	RABBLE ERNEST
Serjeant	TAPSUNDER HENRY Killed 18 June
Serjeant	WIELE HENRY Discharged 25th August 1815
Corporal	ALTEN LEWIS Wounded
Corporal	BUHRMANN WM. Wounded
Corporal	HANNING CHRISTIAN
Trumpeter	BACKER JOHN
Private	ANSHELM HENRY Wounded
Private	BOIE AUGUST Wounded
Private	BUHRMANN HENRY Killed 17 June
Private	BENSEMANN CHRISTIAN
Private	BORMAN JOHN
Private	BLAZS FRANCIS Wounded
Private	BARTELS LAMBERTUS
Private	BOCK ERNEST
Private	BEHNE JURGEN Wounded
Private	BRUNS ROLF
Private	COHRS LEWIS
Private	COHRS HERMAN
Private	COUVELIER WM.
Private	DILLE JUSTERS Wounded
Private	DEDENGEN JOSEPH
Private	EGGARS CHRISTPH.
Private	EICKHOFF JOHN

Private	FUCKER FRANZ
Private	GRIMSCHL HENRY
Private	GEERKE CHRISTIAN
Private	HOVENER CHRISTOPH
Private	HIETHE CHRISTIAN
Private	HELLER GEDFREY
Private	HETTERICK ANDREW
Private	HENBROCK IGNATY
Private	INTONDT FRANCIS Taken Prisoner
Private	KOCKEMIELLER FREDRECK
Private	KIRCHHOFF HENRY Wounded
Private	KUSTREBE JOHN
Private	KRETH HENRY
Private	KERLL LEWIS
Private	KNIEP FREDK.
Private	KRACKE FREDRECK Wounded since dead
Private	KROSCHE JOHN
Private	KUSTER HENRY
Private	MATTHIAS CHRISTIAN Wounded
Private	MULLER DANIEL
Private	NERO JOHN Taken prisoner
Private	OPPERMANN CHRISTOPH
Private	PIPPINGHAM JOSEPH
Private	PRUMPEL JURGEN
Private	SCHOPMANN HENRY
Private	SCHAPER WM.
Private	STIER HENRY
Private	SPRONAGEL TOBIAS
Private	TIMPNER ALBERT
Private	TIMME HENRY
Private	VANGESDELL IGNATIUS Taken prisoner
Private	WINKELMANN HENRY Wounded
Private	WILDER FREDRECK Wounded
Private	ZELLMAN HENRY

Captain Hans Hattorf's Company No.3.

Captain	HATTORFF HANS
Lieutenant	LEFTREW HENRY
Cornet	BREYMANN FREDRECK
T.S.M.	MEYER LEOPOLD Discharged 25 August 1815
Serjeant	KOHNE HENRY
Serjeant	MATTHIAS JOHN Killed 18 June
Serjeant	MEYER JOHN Gray Coll.1908
Serjeant	STANGE FREDRECK Wounded
Corporal	RICKENBERG LUDOLPH
Corporal	ROGGE HENRY Killed 18 June
Corporal	SCHLIEPER CHRISTOPH
Trumpeter	HARSTRISH HENRY
Private	BENECKE FREDRECK Wounded
Private	BEHNE WM.
Private	BEILKE AUGUST
Private	BRUNS CHRISTOPH
Private	BRACKHAHN CONRAD
Private	DENECKE CHRISTIAN
Private	DETTMER CHRISTIAN Wounded
Private	DREYER JOHN
Private	DENNIS GEORGE Wounded
Private	FORST LEONHARD
Private	GOTTE HENRY Watters sale June 1913
Private	GROSS CHARLES
Private	HARMS ANDREW
Private	HAACE LORENTZ
Private	HILDEBRAND HENRY Wounded
Private	HORSTMANN HENRY
Private	HAACKE FREDRECK Wounded
Private	HUSAR PHILIP
Private	HUBENER HENRY
Private	HIESING HENRY
Private	KLINGE CHRISTIAN
Private	KRESSMANN HENRY
Private	LOHRBERG HENRY Wounded since dead
Private	LEAR CHRISTOPH Wounded since dead
Private	LENECKE VICTOR Wounded since dead
Private	MEYER JOHN Killed 18 June
Private	MEYER CASPER Discharged 25 August 1815
Private	MERZ PETER
Private	MEYER GEORGE
Private	NEUSINGER JACOB
Private	PAPE CONRAD Wounded
Private	PELARSKY WITIENNE
Private	SCHAMELS ALBERT
Private	SCHLEISHER CHRISTIAN
Private	SCHNEHAGE CHRISTIAN Discharged 25 Augist 1815
Private	SCKELLER JOHN Wounded
Private	SCHMALE HENRY
Private	SCHNITZLER PETER
Private	SCHAFFER MATTEW Wounded
Private	SPANHACKE GERHARD Wounded
Private	SCHROT HENRY
Private	SCHENKEL DAVID
Private	SIEGFRIED JOSEPH Wounded
Private	STEINMANN HENRY Discharged 25 August 1815
Private	STITZEL JACOB

Private	STILLE GEORGE
Private	THIEFS JOHN
Private	TIMKE HENRY Wounded
Private	TRONIER GODFRY
Private	ULRICH CHRISTIAN
Private	WINDHORST HENRY Killed 18 June
Private	WEELDERN WM.

Captain Witzendorff's Troop No.4.

Lieutenant	MACKENZIE WM. Wounded
Cornet	MILLER LEWIS
T.S.M.	DUHRKOP CHRISTOPH
Serjeant	AHRENS HENRY
Serjeant	BARTELS CHRISTOPH
Serjeant	GOTTING HENRY
Corporal	HAGEHORN ANDW.
Corporal	JONS WM.
Corporal	LINDE LEWIS
Corporal	WERNER JOHN
Trumpeter	SEYFARTH CHARLES
Private	AHRENBERG MATTW.
Private	ARENS ERNEST
Private	ACKER JOHANNES Gaskell Collection 1908
Private	BORNEMANN CHRISTIAN
Private	BORNEMANN JOHN Wounded
Private	BRAND WM.
Private	BEYER HENRY
Private	BEHRENS CHRISTIAN
Private	BODENSTAL ANTON
Private	CHRISTOPHELS CONRAD
Private	CLARIEN GEORGE
Private	DEESELS FREDRECK
Private	DEDECKING HENRY
Private	DORFFMUND HENRY Wounded
Private	DUFORT JOSEPH
Private	DRISCH HENRY
Private	ECKEL JOHN
Private	EULENTRUP THEODOR
Private	GRANKE HENRY
Private	GRIM GERHARD
Private	HOLTZHAUSEN CHRISTIAN
Private	HALLER LEWIS
Private	HOLTE ERNEST
Private	HEYDEMEYER CASPER
Private	KONERDING JOHN Killed 18th June
Private	KOLLMANN GEORGE
Private	KASCHOLLY CASPER
Private	MEYER JURGEN
Private	MEYER FREDRECK
Private	MEINECKE HENRY
Private	OELBE JOHN Wounded
Private	PRETHMEYER HENRY
Private	PROHLKE PHILIP
Private	SCHULTZE GODFRY Killed 18 June
Private	SCHEELE HENRY
Private	SCHONBERG HENRY
Private	THIES HENRY
Private	VANDERMEULEN HENRY Wounded Since dead
Private	WAGENER JOS.
Private	WERTER HENRY Killed 18 June
Private	WOHLING HENRY
Private	WEHRMANN JOHN
Private	WAITER CASIMIR
Private	WEYKOPF JOHN

Captain Philip Sichart's Troop No.5.

Captain	SICHART PHILIP Wounded
Cornet	FRITTAN EDWD. Wounded
T.S.M.	SCHUMACHER JOHN
Serjeant	COHRS JOHN
Serjeant	LANGREHER HENRY
Serjeant	MEYNE HENRY Wounded & Discharged 23 August 1815
Serjeant	OLFLECKE HENRY Wounded
Corporal	HABERT PETER
Corporal	KIRCHNER JULIUS Wounded
Corporal	SENKLER HENRY Killed 18 June
Corporal	SCHORLING HENRY
Corporal	HEINECKE HENRY
Private	ARBE FREDRECK
Private	BEHRENS HENRY
Private	BOIKER CHRISTIAN
Private	BODE CHRISTIAN
Private	BETHE FREDRECK
Private	BREMER CONRAD
Private	BRISTAC ANDREW
Private	CORELES HERMAN Discharged 25 August 1815
Private	DONEKEL DIDRECK
Private	DERO AUGUSTIN
Private	ENGELKE CHRISTOPH
Private	ENGELKINH CHRISTIAN
Private	FREICKE HENRY
Private	FLOTER FREDRECK

Private	FILGES CHRISTOPH
Private	GRANE HENRY
Private	de GROEF PETER
Private	HOBERMANN HENRY
Private	HOFFMEISTER HENRY
Private	HARTLE PABTIST
Private	KOOH DEARECK
Private	KONHERDING FREDRECK
Private	LEON PETER
Private	LEWEN VINCENT
Private	LUMPE JOHN
Private	MEYER FREDRECK
Private	MEYER ERENRICK
Private	MEYER V CTOR
Private	NEUHAUSEN JACOB
Private	OFFENEY CHARLES Deserted
Private	POTT JOHN
Private	SCHNELLE FRANTZ
Private	SCHULTZE HENRY
Private	SCHMIDT JULIUS Killed 18 June
Private	SCHELLER ERNEST
Private	SERBLET HENRY
Private	SCHANER MICHEL
Private	SCHREIBER ALBERT
Private	STEYMANN CHRISTIAN
Private	STEINMITZ HENRY Wounded
Private	WOOLH DEARECK
Private	WEBER GODLIB Wounded
Private	WILLING JOHN
Private	WAGLINGER FREDRECK
Private	WAHLER JOHN
Private	WYND PHILIP

Captain Fredreck Uslar's Troop No.6.

Captain	USLAR FREDRECK
Lieutenant	KUHLMANN OTTE Killed 18th June
T.S.M.	FEHRENSON JOHN
Serjeant	HOFFMEISTER WM.
Serjeant	HEFSE CHRISTOPH
Serjeant	THOMHOFE HENRY Wounded
Serjeant	UTERMARK LUDOLPH
Corporal	ALTEN HENRY
Corporal	BISCHLOFF JOHN
Corporal	FELDMANN HENRY Wounded
Corporal	JUNEMANN CHRISTOPH Wounded
Trumpeter	BARTEL JACOB
Private	ANSLIENE MARTIN
Private	BARNDES WM. Wounded
Private	BRUGER FREDRECK
Private	BROOCKMANN LEWIS
Private	BAUER HENRY
Private	BRADEN JACOB
Private	BARKHAN CHARLES
Private	BAGGEL CASPER
Private	DAULE FREDRECK Wounded
Private	DEDERS GEORGE
Private	DIEDERICKS LEWIS
Private	DETTMER LUDOLPH
Private	DREWES GEORGE
Private	FLESSONER JULIUS
Private	FLAER HERMAN
Private	FRISCH JOHN Wounded
Private	HARTELS JOHN
Private	KRAMER CONRAD
Private	KURTY GODFRY Col.Gaskell's sale May 1911
Private	KNODE FREDRECK
Private	KASSEBAUM LEWIS Wounded lost one arm.
Private	LAUNERT GODFRY
Private	MULLER WM.
Private	MEYER CONRAD
Private	MEYER HENRY
Private	NIEBUHR HENRY
Private	OLINKE HENRY Wounded
Private	SCHRODER CHRISTOPH
Private	SCHLUTER HENRY Killed 18 June
Private	SCHONBERG HENRY
Private	SCHUTZ FREDRECK
Private	THIES WM.
Private	THOLKE HENRY
Private	ULRISH WM.
Private	VERSORRY MARTIN
Private	WIEBE HENRY
Private	WINKELMANN HENRY
Private	WELLMANN FREDRECK
Private	WINKELMANN PETER
Private	WALTER ANTON
Private	WEEKE CONRAD Wounded
Private	WREDA HENRY

Captain C. Elderhorst's Troop No.7.

Captain	ELDERHORST CHAS.
Lieutenant	LEVETZOW FREDRECK Killed 18 June
T.S.M.	KIELPENNIG AUGUST
Serjeant	RATHKAMP HENRY
Serjeant	SCHEIKER RUDOLPH
Serjeant	WOLBER NICLAS

Corporal	DIEDERICKS CHRISTOPH
Corporal	FUILLE JOHN Wounded
Corporal	FREDRECKS CHRISTOPH Killed 18 June
Corporal	PEHRAN HENRY
Trumpeter	KERLL LEWIS
Private	ANTHONY FRANS. Discharged 25 August 1815
Private	ABELING CHRISTIAN
Private	BODEN JOHN
Private	BUSCHMANN FREDRECK
Private	BAILLIS PETER
Private	BREMAN JOSEPH Killed 18 June
Private	CAPPE CHARLES
Private	DEFATTER JOHN
Private	DERING PETER Wounded
Private	FRANKE JACOB
Private	FUCHS PETER
Private	FUNKE ARNHOLD
Private	HAMMER MICHEL
Private	HENKEN NICLAS
Private	JANSEN PETER
Private	KUNTZ CHRISTIAN
Private	LOHRENGEL GEORGE
Private	LUBKE HENRY
Private	MALDECKEN FERDINAND
Private	MEINE ULRICH
Private	MEYER DAVID
Private	MEYER HENRY
Private	PICKER PETER
Private	PIROT LEWIS
Private	RADIKA HENRY
Private	RENTZ PETER
Private	SCHAMEL WM.
Private	SCHUTTE CHRISTOPH Day Sale April 1910
Private	SEN JOHN
Private	SIEGER JOHN
Private	SURMONT JAMES
Private	VERBECKENS JOHN
Private	WEIGAND JOHN
Private	ZIMMERMANN CONRAD

Captain B. Decken's Troop No.8.

Captain	DECKEN BENEDIX
Lieutenant	BOSSE HENRY Wounded
Cornet	PATEN CONRAD
T.Q.M.	TITTMANN CHARLES
Serjeant	HOFMEISTER JOHN Wounded
Serjeant	JABELMANN HENRY Wounded Day Sale April 1910
Corporal	BODE LEWIS
Corporal	LEFSMANN AUGUST
Corporal	MERZ JACOB
Trumpeter	NOSS ANDRW.
Private	BASCH CHARLES
Private	BORCHERDING CHRISTIAN
Private	BRANDES HENRY
Private	BRILL JAMES
Private	BUNTE HENRY
Private	BURCKHART JOHANNES
Private	CHIESHAWSKY IGNATZ
Private	EHLERS HENRY
Private	GERING JOHN
Private	GOTIE HENRY Wounded
Private	GRAHLE FREDRECK
Private	JAHNS BARTOLD
Private	LAMOTH MICHEL
Private	MARYUSARD HENRY
Private	MISOMER MICHEL
Private	MONTH CHRISTOPH
Private	NARJES FREDRECK
Private	PEITER JOHN Wounded
Private	PENDORFF GEORGE Taken prisoner
Private	PAKEMANN JOHN
Private	SIHIMANSKY PAUL Wounded
Private	SOHNS CONRAD Wounded
Private	VANHAUFF FERDINAND
Private	VANTHIEL HENRY
Private	VENANDY MICHEL Wounded since dead
Private	WOOLFF FREDRECK Taken prisoner
Private	SMITH PETER
Private	ZIESENEFS HENRY

Captain Ramdohr's Troop No.9.

Captain	RAMDOHRS GEORGE
Cornet	KERSHNER LEWIS Whitaker Collection 1908
T.S.M.	STUKE DEDNES
Serjeant	BARKING LUDO PH Killed 18 June
Serjeant	BEOHTEL WM.
Serjeant	HIMMELSTOFS CHRISTIAN
Serjeant	LINNE HENRY Sotheby's sale Feb.1914
Corporal	KRUCE HENRY
Corporal	SCHONBORN CHARLES
Corporal	WUST LEWIS Wounded
Trumpeter	BODECKER HENRY Killed 18 June
Private	AHRENS JOHN Killed 18 June
Private	AHRENS CHRISTOPH
Private	de BOCK HERMAN
Private	BREDA JOSEPH

Private	BRUST PETER
Private	BAHRENBURG HENRY
Private	DEDIR JOSEPH
Private	FESSE CASPER
Private	FURSLEY PHILIP Glendining's sale Nov.1913
Private	FLUTH JACOB Wounded
Private	GARDINER WM.
Private	GROUDMANN GODLIEB
Private	HAHN JOSEPH
Private	HEILY JOSEPH
Private	HUMBERT CASPER
Private	JASPER NICHOLAUS Taken prisoner
Private	KREIPE LEWIS
Private	LEISTEN JACOB
Private	LOBLEIN VALENTINE
Private	MOERSCH WM.
Private	PANGELS LEONHARD Deserted
Private	PIANTKOWSKY ALBERT
Private	SCHAFFER CHRISTIAN
Private	SCHUF JOHN
Private	SMIDT PETER
Private	SCHNEIDER IMBERTUS
Private	SCHRODER HENRY Wounded
Private	SIEBERT ALBERT Discharged 25 August 1815
Private	HOLSTE JOHN
Private	STORMS FRANTZ
Private	THEIS JOHN
Private	UHRIG JOHN
Private	ULMER JOHN
Private	VIETMEYER HENRY
Private	WEBER CASPER
Private	WINTER CHRISTIAN

Captain Leftrew's Troop No.10

Captain	PETER FREDRICK Killed 18 June
Lieutenant	HAMMERSTEIN OTTE Wounded
Cornet	LESHEN HONNACH
T.S.M.	FREYTAG DANIEL
Serjeant	MALUVINS HENRY
Serjeant	SCHRODER FREDRECK
Serjeant	RITTER HENRY
Corporal	DEICKE CONRAD
Corporal	RATTMANN ANTON
Corporal	SCHWENKHOFF HENRY
Corporal	SCHMANN PETER Wounded
Trumpeter	SIEMERS GEORGE
Private	AUGUSTINE PETER
Private	BAUER NATHL.
Private	BOHL JOHN Wounded
Private	CONRAD JOHN
Private	CORDEMANN PETER
Private	DIEPHOLD ANTON Wounded
Private	DUGARDIN JOHN
Private	EGGERS JACOB
Private	EICKHOFF HENRY
Private	FETTERLING HENRY
Private	GEYSER IGNATZ
Private	GORBENZIE GEORGE
Private	GRABER JOHN Wounded
Private	HUGO HENRY Wounded
Private	JAGER JAMES Discharged 25 August 1815
Private	LORASS JOHN
Private	LISSENS JOHN
Private	MAWINKEL HENRY Discharged 25 August 1815
Private	V.d.NESTE ANTON Deserted 19 August 1815
Private	NOSEN LEWIS Wounded
Private	RABITSCH ALLOIS
Private	RENTZ ANTON
Private	SCHAFER BALTHASER
Private	SCHNARNTEZ FRANS Killed 18 June
Private	SCHEELE HENRY
Private	SCHUH JAMES
Private	SCHWEIFS PHILIP
Private	SPINRATH PETER Wounded
Private	STEDLEY JOSEPH
Private	VERGOSSEN PETER
Private	WELSHINGER JOSEPH
Private	WILLEMS LEWIS
Private	WEHNERT HENRY
Private	ZEIGER GEORGE
Private	ZINDE PETER

* * *

2nd LIGHT DRAGOONS K.G.L.

Lt. Colonel	de TINQUIERES CHAS.
Lt.Colonel	MAYDELL C.B.
Major	FRIEDRICKS AUGUSTUS
Captain	WILLMERDING LEWIS
Captain	AUHAGEN GEORGE Gaskell Coll.1908 Payne 1911
Captain	THIELE LEWIS
Captain	MARSCHALCK C.B.
Captain	LUDERITZ LEWIS

Captain	QUENTIN WM.
Captain	SEEGER WM.
Captain	de HARLING THEODOR
Captain	BULOW F.B.
Lieutenant	BRANN GEO.
Lieutenant	POTEN AUGUST
Lieutenant	BERGMANN FREDK.
Lieutenant	HUGO LUDOLPH
Lieutenant	FUMETTE AUGUSTUS
Lieutenant	SCHAFFER CHARLES
Lieutenant	RITTER H.H.C.
Lieutenant	MEIER ERNEST
Lieutenant	CLESSELER JNS
Cornet	POCOCK C.M.
Cornet	KUSTER FERDINAND
Cornet	BULOW OTTO BARND.
Cornet	NIESS AUGUSTUS
Cornet	LORENZ FERDINAND
Surgeon	DETTMER FREDRICK
Ass.Surgeon	LANGE JOHN D.
Ass.Surgeon	THALACKER B.
Qr.Master	GROPP HENRY
Vty.Surgeon	HOGREFE HENRY
R.S.M.	HOLTY CHAS.
T.S.M.	FRETER CHRISTIAN
T.S.M.	KLINKER JOHN
T.S.M.	RODEMANN HENRY
T.S.M.	SCHMAHLFELD LEWIS
T.S.M.	SCHOLTE HENRY
T.S.M.	WEISER BERND.
Serjeant	BENTZE JASPER
Serjeant	BOHLE HENRY
Serjeant	BROCKHOFF FREDRICK
Serjeant	BRACKMAN FREDRICK
Serjeant	COOGAN MATTW.
Serjeant	ERDFELDER HENRY
Serjeant	HARMS CHAS.
Serjeant	KOCH HENRY
Serjeant	KOLLE HENRY
Serjeant	KIPP PHILLIP
Serjeant	KAHLE ERNEST
Serjeant	LUEDERS HENRY
Serjeant	MEYER GODLIB
Serjeant	MEYER DEDRICK
Serjeant	MUHLENBERG CHRISTOPH
Serjeant	NESEMAN HENRY Discharged 24th August
Serjeant	PANKUCHEN HENRY Discharged 24th August
Serjeant	RICKE HENRY
Serjeant	ROMER CONRAD
Serjeant	SIELING JOHN
Serjeant	SCHWENKE HENRY
Serjeant	SCHMIDT HENRY
Serjeant	WUSTER LEWIS
T.Major	LUHMANN DEDRICK
Trumpeter	BEHRENS WM.
Trumpeter	GIESE HENRY
Trumpeter	HENNACKE JUSTUS
Trumpeter	KRUSE RUDOLP
Trumpeter	RUHKOPH ERNESR
Trumpeter	RUDDOLF CARL
Trumpeter	WESCH ERNEST
Trumpeter	ZIETZ LEWIS
Corporal	AHRENS JOHN
Corporal	BODE CHRISTIAN
Corporal	BIDEWALD GEORGE
Corporal	BARTELS CHARLES
Corporal	BEHRENS HENRY
Corporal	BECKER FREDRICK
Corporal	BRUNING CHRISTOPH
Corporal	FUCKS GEORGE
Corporal	GERKE HENRY
Corporal	GRETHE HENRY
Corporal	HERZOG CHARLES
Corporal	HILLERT CHARLES
Corporal	KUCKUK CHRISTOPH
Corporal	KIRCHNER LEWIS
Corporal	MEYER HENRY Discharged 24 Aug.
Corporal	MARTENS THEODOR
Corporal	MUNKEL CHRISTIAN
Corporal	OHLMANN JULIUS
Corporal	POTTHOFF ARNOLD
Corporal	SCHOPPE FREDRICK
Corporal	SCHRADER HENRY
Corporal	SPANHOFF CHRISTOPH
Corporal	SPILNER HENRY
Corporal	SPREINE HENRY
Corporal	STIEG LEWIS
Corporal	TRENHEISER PETER
Corporal	TRAPHAGEN HENRY
Corporal	VOLGER FREDRICK Discharged 24th August
Private	ASHLAND CHRISTOPH Discharged 24th August
Private	ARNEMANN FREDRICK
Private	ABELMANN FREDRICK
Private	ALPACH GEORGE Deserted 24 Aug.
Private	ALBERS CASPER
Private	AMES BAPTIST

Private	BICKMAN LEWIS
Private	BRUGER LEWIS
Private	BUFSE JUSTUS
Private	BRUNS CONRAD Discharged 24th August
Private	BRUMMER CHARLES
Private	BARRAN JOHN
Private	BAUER FREDRICK
Private	BERLIN ANDREW
Private	BODENBERG LEWIS Discharged 24th August
Private	BOVENTZ BASTIAN
Private	BORKELMANN CHARLES Discharged 24th August
Private	BANSEN CHRISTOPH
Private	BERGHAHN HENRY
Private	BRETHORST CHRISTIAN
Private	BRINKHOFF JOHN
Private	BUDDE LEWIS
Private	BODENSTAEDT REN.HENRY
Private	BERNHAUSEN PETER
Private	BLOCK JOHN
Private	BECK HENRY
Private	BEHLTE JOHN
Private	BORMANN HENRY
Private	BUCHOLZ JOHN
Private	BADE FREDRICK
Private	BECK GEORGE
Private	BICKER HENRY
Private	BOCK HENRY Col.Murray's Collection 1908
Private	BODE LEWIS
Private	BRENNACKE CASPER
Private	BIELE HENRY
Farrier	BANCK HENRY
Private	BORCHERS CONRAD
Private	BEHRENS WM.
Private	BARTELS CHRISTOPH Discharged 24th August
Private	BRUGGEMANN HENRY
Private	BELLER FREDRICK
Private	BAGGENBERG FREDRICK
Private	BORCHERS SAMUEL Discharged 24th August
Private	BORGHOLTZ CHRISTOPH Discharged 24th August
Private	BIERMANN HNRY.
Private	BLOCK MATHEW
Private	BARTELS FREDRICK
Private	van BEGIN PHILIP
Private	BEHLTE CONRAD
Private	BUNKE HENRY
Private	BUNKE CORD
Private	BEHNE FREDRICK
Private	BARTH ADAM
Private	BLACKMANN HENRY
Private	BAUERMEISTER CHRISTOPH
Private	BRIER FRANZ
Private	BRAUN STEPHEN
Private	CRAMER JOSEPH
Private	CREGELBERG HENRY Deserted 2nd Sept.'15
Private	CANUVE JOHN
Private	CONRADY FREDRICK Discharged 24th August
Private	CARLS BARTHOFF
Private	CRAMER HENRY
Private	CARTUSCH JOHN
Private	CRANKEN ANDW
Private	CORNER PHILIP Deserted 17 Aug
Private	CALLANDER FRANZ
Private	DANKER JOHN
Private	DEVOS FRANCIS
Private	DUNTE CHRISTIAN
Private	DEFREN JACOB
Private	DAES JOHN
Private	DANNETTCH HERMAN
Private	DESTROM JOHN
Private	DURLES JOHN
Private	DORNWIND GEORGE
Private	DAMBROWSKY JOHN
Private	DRUHMANN WM.
Private	DALLAMNN HENRY
Private	DENECKE HENRY
Private	DEBLE JOSEPH
Private	DEFSY HENRY
Private	DACHSIN ANDREW
Private	DEGENT FRANCIS
Private	EFFERS WM.
Private	ENGELKE FREDRICK Discharged 24th August
Private	EHIENSTEIN JACOB
Private	EHLING ALLEXANDER
Private	EICKE HENRY
Private	ENGEL WM.
Private	EICKSTAEDT NICOLAUS
Private	EICKEWROTH·ANDERSON
Private	EBRECHT WM.
Private	EDEL MATHEW
Private	EGOTT BONIFAS
Private	EGOTT FRANCIS

Private EHRENBERG HENRY
Private FAUST JACOB
Private FINKE MATHEW
Privaté FOSTEN HENRY
Private FREVEL HENRY
Private FIEGON FRANCIS Deserted 21st August
Private FORSTER MATHIAS
Private FREDE CONRAD
Private FLECKE LEWIS
Private FRICKE HENRY
Private FRANK JOHN
Private FRANZ JOSEPH
Private FUNK PETER
Private FLICK JOHN
Private FRANKEN PETER
Private FAESCHE HENRY
Private GIESE JOHN
Private GEGITTERS FRANS.
Private GREWY JOHN
Private GIESE SURGEN
Private GRUBE CHRISTOPH
Private GALSKA ANTON
Private GARTNER HENRY
Private GERLING FERDINAND
Private GAUDROFF JOHN
Private GELLMAN HENRY
Private GING ADAM
Private GRUWE CHRISTOPH
Private GRUWE LEWIS
Private GABEL PETER
Private GNEDIG ARMOND
Private GODECKE CHRISTIAN Discharged 24th Aug.
Private GEWE JOHN
Private FRIESHEIMER VANENTIN
Private GERKE CHRISTOPH
Private GRUBE FREDRICK
Private GILLES LEWIS Watter's sale June 1913
Private GORTZ CASPER
Private GROFF HENRY
Private GERRITZ PETER
Private GRIESHEIMER JOHN
Private HAMANN CONRAD
Private HORST HENRY
Private HARTZE HERM.CONRAD
Private HALBFAS JUSTUS
Private HENNECKE HENRY
Private HEINS PETER

Private HELBERG ERNEST Glendining's sale Dec. 1909
Private HOMANN FREDRICK
Private HERBST CHRISTOPH
Private HUSMANN JOHN Whitaker coll.1908
Private HERZBERG HENRY
Private HELMS WM.
Private HORMAN CONRAD
Private HERRIES BERND. Deserted 21 Aug.
Private HEINRICH JOHN
Private HARTLER CHAS.
Private HAUCH JACOB
Private HESIER CHRISTIAN
Private HABENICHT HENRY
Private HOFFMEYER FREDRICK Discharged 24th August
Private HEITMULLER DANIEL Discharged 24th Aug. Gray Collection 1908
Private HILLEBRECHT HENRY
Private HENKER JOHN
Private HEMING JOHN
Private HABENICHT CHRISTOPH
Private HAASE FREDRICK
Private HARTUNG CASPER
Private HEISTER HENRY
Private HEIDELBERG FREDRICK
Private HILLEN CHRISTOPH
Private HAVIGKOST HENRY
Private HEYER HENRY
Private HANTZEL ANTON
Private HOMEYER CHRISTIAN Discharged 24th August
Private ISERNHAGER FREDRICK
Private JUNG JOSEPH Deserted 7th Aug.
Private INWIDE HENRY
Private KLOCKIMANN CONRAD
Private KRAGE GEORGE
Private KITTLER GEORGE Discharged 24th August
Private KLINGENHAGEN JOHN
Private KUKEN HENRY Discharged
Private KLIMER JOHN
Private KNOBELAUCH HENRY
Private KNOLLE CONRAD
Private KOCKEMOHR FREDRICK
Private KRUMMEL LEWIS
Private KRUMMEL CHRISTOPH Discharged 24th August
Private KAHLE HENRY
Private KAHLE CHRISTIAN Discharged
Private KLEINE ADAM

Private	KUNST HENRY
Private	KRUGER FREDRICK
Private	KLOEBING VINCENT
Private	KERMER JACOB Day sale April 1910
Private	KUHLE ANTHONY
Private	KAUFFMANN GREGORY
Private	KEBEL HENRY
Private	KRAUFS CHARLES
Private	KEYSER CONRAD
Private	KNOP LEWIS
Private	KNOCKE FREDRICK
Private	KONECKE HENRY
Private	KRITZ JOHANNES
Private	KUSTER NICOLAUS
Private	KNOCK CHARLES
Private	KYVERIN MARTIN
Private	KLEMME CHARLES
Private	KEMPSTER CASPER Gr.y Collection 1908
Private	LINNEMANN FREDRICK
Private	LINDEMANN HENRY
Private	LAMPE HENRY Discharged 24th August
Private	LINDHORST WM.
Private	LILJE HENRY
Private	LENZ SERVAS
Private	LONGFIND JOSEPH
Private	LURIG FREDRICK
Private	LEMKE ANDREW
Private	LURING LEWIS
Private	LEDER ANTON
Private	LUTYENS HENRY
Private	LUHRSEN HENRY
Private	LAGSON ANDREW
Private	LEPPERS LEWIS
Private	LIPPEL FREDRICK Discharged 24th August
Private	LEMARS FRANZ
Private	MANHARD JOSEPH
Private	MAY ADAM
Private	MEYER JOHN
Private	MUHLENBERG HENRY
Private	MEYER HENRY
Private	MOHRING CHRISTIAN
Private	MONKEMEYER CONRAD
Private	MEYER CRISTOPH
Private	MEYER DEDRICKS Discharged 24th August
Private	MEYER MATHIAS
Private	MULLER CHRISTOPH
Private	MULLER CHARLES
Private	MEYER ANTON
Private	MEINECKE HENRY
Private	MEYER CHRISTIAN
Private	MULLER HENRY
Private	MULLER FREDRICK Discharged 24th August
Private	MEYER JOHN
Private	MELDAN WM.
Private	NAGEL HENRY
Private	NETTELROTH HENRY
Private	NICKERKE AUGUST
Private	NURNBERG CLEMENS
Private	NIEBUHR HENRY
Private	NOLL PETER
Private	NOSBAUM FRANCIS
Private	NYSSON JACOB
Private	NIEMEYER CONRAD
Private	OSTFELD HENRY Discharged 24 Aug.
Private	OBSTATEN CORNELIUS
Private	OLHMANN CHRISTOPH
Private	OPPERMANN FREDRICK Discharged 24th August
Private	OTERS HENRY
Private	OPPERMANN FREDRICK (Junr)
Private	OSTWALD JOHN
Private	PITZ JOHN
Private	PECHTELOFF VALENTIN
Private	PIEPENBRING HENRY
Private	PUDER FREDRICK
Private	PIEPER LEWIS
Private	PESCH JOHN Deserted 29th Aug.
Private	PIMMING JOHN
Private	PAESELER FREDRICK
Private	PURQUAIN FRANCIS
Private	RATHMANN WM.
Private	REHSER HERMANN
Private	RUBLES JOHN
Private	RODE CHRISTIAN
Private	RIEMENSCHNIEDER FREDK.
Private	RENDORFF HENRY
Private	RICKE ERNEST Discharged 24th Aug.
Private	RITTER JOHN
Private	RUNGE HENRY Discharged
Private	ROTTA BALTERS
Private	RUPRECHT SEBASTIAN
Private	REINECKE JOHN
Private	RIECHERS LEWIS

Private	RATH HENRY Discharged 24th August
Private	RAHLS HENRY
Private	RUHE FREDRICK
Private	REGNERY PETER
Private	RENNIER ROWES
Private	RUWERE JOHN
Private	RATHANS ANTHONY
Private	SCHAPER CHRISTOPH
Private	STUDE LIBORIUS
Private	SCHAPER GEORGE
Private	SCHMIDT CONRAD
Private	SCHREIBER JUSTUS
Private	SCHWARTZ FREDRICK
Private	SEEBERGER HENRY
Private	STEIGHOFFER CONRAD Discharged 24th August
Private	SPANACHE CLAUS HENRY
Private	SPORLEDER HENRY
Private	STALLMEISTER GERHARD
Private	STERRE CHRISTIAN
Private	STILLE CHRISTOPH
Private	SCHWAN CHARLES
Private	STURM LEWIS
Private	SCHRODER PHILIP
Private	SOLTER HENRY
Private	SERTON PETER
Private	SENGER HENRY
Private	SCHULTZE GODFRY Deserted 1st Sept.
Private	STUDIEUS GERHARD
Private	SCHNEHAGEN JURGEN
Private	SAAST SIMON
Private	STAUNCH MICHEL
Private	STUBER HENRY
Private	SEFE HENRY
Private	STEINBERG JOHN
Private	SCHNEIDER FREDRICK
Private	SCHOMBERG FREDRICK
Private	SCHMIDT BERNHARDT
Private	SCHELKE FREDRICK
Private	SCHOLT JOHN
Private	STOLLE HENRY
Private	SUFFER FREDK.
Private	SABEL GEORGE
Private	SCHAPER HENRY Discharged 24th August
Private	SCHLE JURGEN
Private	SCHLE JOHN

Private	LEISNER JOSEPH
Private	SUERMANN CHRISTOPH
Private	SETEN HENRY
Private	SKOTT LEWIS
Private	SCHRADER HENRY
Private	SIESS FRANS
Private	SERWINSKY CHARLES
Private	SIESS HERMAN Deserted 10 July
Private	SCHMIDT LEONARD
Private	TAR JOHN
Private	TONJER CHRISTIAN
Private	TAMPMANN JOSEPH
Private	URLAB JOHN Discharged 24 Aug.
Private	VANVORDE ANTHY.
Private	VANDERSMISSELL JOSH.
Private	VANHERMERD PETER
Private	VANRAULT MATHIAS
Private	VANDERHORST HENRY
Private	VANDERWEHR MATTW Deserted 26 Aug
Private	VANCKE JAMES
Private	VANWERK FREDRICK
Private	VARENDOFF LEWIS
Private	VANDERWUNDLE JOSH.
Private	VANDEREAS JOHN
Private	VOLLMER CONRAD Discharged 24 Aug
Private	WALTER JOHN
Private	WEDEKIND HENRY
Private	WICKENBERG CHRISTOPH
Private	WEIGMANN ERNEST
Private	WILHELMS GODFREY
Private	WISSELL JOHN
Private	WEDEKIND JOHN
Private	WALHEINKE HENRY
Private	WEBER GODLIEB
Private	WEDEKIND FRANZ
Private	WICKMANN DIEDRICK
Private	WELBRECHT ERNEST
Private	WENDT HENRY
Private	WILLMANN BENEDICTUS Deserted 21 Aug.
Private	WELF CHARLES Deserted 1 Sept.
Private	DE WOLF JOHN
Private	WEIPGEN JOHN
Private	WIEGMAN DANIEL
Private	WALTEMATE FREDRICK
Private	WERNER GEORGE Cheylesmore Collection 1908
Private	WAGENER JOSEPH
Private	WERMETCH PIERE

Private	WIEDENROTH HENRY Discharged 24th August
Private	WACHENDORFF FREDRICK
Private	WEBER JOHN
Private	WEISSENSTEIN GEORGE
Private	WINKLER ABRM.
Private	WOLSCHLAGER FRANZ
Private	WINZENBERG HENRY
Private	ZUFALL CHRISTOPH
Private	ZINN JOHN
Private	ZUFALL HENRY Discharged 24th August
Private	OSTERHAUSEN JOHN

* * *

1st HUSSARS K.G.L.

Lt.Colonel	de WISSELL AUGUST
Major	VON GRUBEN PHILIP
Captain	DECKEN, BARON GEORGE
Captain	POTEN ERNEST
Captain	DECKEN BARON FREDK.
Captain	KRAUCHENBERG LEWIS
Captain	CORDEMANN ERNEST
Captain	SHAUMANN GUSTAV
Captain	BAERTLING GEORGE (alias Fredk.)
Captain	WISCH BARON HIERONIMUS
Captain	TEUTS BERNARD
Lieutenant	BARING GEORGE
Lieutenant	POTEN CONRAD
Lieutenant	de ZILTEN ADOLPH
Lieutenant	SCHULZE LEOPALD Payne Collection 1911
Lieutenant	FREDENTHAL SIGISMD.Adjut.
Lieutenant	BEHRENS HENRY
Lieutenant	GUNBORN A.C. WALLMODEN
Lieutenant	TRITTAM WM.
Lieutenant	BLUEMEN HAGEN FREDK.
Lieutenant	LEONHARDT GEORGE
Cornet	VERSTENNE LEWIS Galway Foley Collection 1910
Cornet	HEISE OTTO
Cornet	CONZE G.L.
Cornet	KIELMANSEGGE LEWIS CT.
Cornet	OLDHAUSEN FREDK. B.
Cornet	GEBSER THEODOR
Cornet	RAHLEVES FREDK.
Cornet	HAZSELL WM. BON.
Pay.Master	LONGMAN J.WM.
Qr.Master	COHRS HENRY
Surgeon	FIORILLO FREDK.
Ass.Surgeon	DEPPE FREDK.
Ass.Surgeon	MEYER G.C.
Vty.Surgeon	POWER THOS. Cheylesmore Coll.1908

* * *

3rd REGIMENT OF HUSSARS K.G.L.

Captain Gaeben's Troop

Captain	GOEBEN GUIN BARON
Lieutenant	FREDRICKS EBERHARD
Cornet	de DASSELL CONRAD
T.S.M.	WALTERS HERMAN
P.M.S.	KERKE HENRY
A.S.	SCHELLER GEORGE
Sad.S.	GEIERSBACH HENRY
T. Major	NEUBERT VALENTIN
Serjeant	KOBERT CHRISTIAN
Serjeant	KRUGER LEOPOLD
Serjeant	TIPPE HENRY
Serjeant	WORTMANN HENRY
Corporal	BANEY AUGUST
Corporal	HEYDORN FREDK.
Corporal	KRUGER JOHN
Corporal	TROLLER PHILIP
Private	ABELING HENRY
Private	AHN CHRISTIAN
Private	ARNEMANN JOHN
Private	BARENTRAGER CARL
Private	BARTELS JOHN
Private	BRUNS JUSTUS
Private	BERTHEYER HENRY
Private	BAGENER GEORGE
Private	BELTRAM JOHN
Private	BERGMANN MARTIN
Private	DIETMERING HENRY
Private	DIERKING HENRY
Private	DIETMERS CHRISTIAN
Private	EGGERS HENRY
Private	FLUGGE HERMAN
Private	FISCHER JACOB
Private	FRANKE PETER
Private	GRAMUSCH JNS.HY.
Private	GRIMMAU GEORGE
Private	GORRESSEN JACOB
Private	GRAMUSCH FREDK.
Private	HELMS FREDK.

Private	HEITMANN HENRY
Private	HEIDE V.D. HENRY
Private	HINTZE JNS. FRDK.
Private	HEINS LEWIS
Private	JURGENS JOHN
Private	JACOBY HENRY
Private	JACOBY JOHN
Private	KRUGER MINKE
Private	KAMMER V.D. L.C.
Private	KUSTTER GOTTFRIED
Private	KELLER CARL
Private	LUCAS WM.
Private	MICHELMAN WM.
Private	MAGER ANTONY
Private	MELYER JOHN
Private	PAULIN JACOB
Private	RIPPE ALBERT
Private	RODEWALD FREDK.
Private	RATHMAN FREDK.
Private	RODE HENRY
Private	REDELHAMMER FREDK.
Private	SCHURMANN HARM
Private	SCHULZE HENRY
Private	SCHLIORERING JOHN
Private	SCHAEFER CARL
Private	STEINWAG FRANZ
Private	SEIB JOHN
Private	SCHULZ JOHN
Private	STARKE JOHN
Private	SCHNADER HENRY
Private	THIESFELD HENRY
Private	VERBAUM AUGUST
Private	WIEBE DIEDRICK
Private	WITTE RUDOLPH
Private	WINDHORST WM.
Private	WIEGMANN CONRAD
Private	ZORN HENRY

<u>Captain George Meyer's Troop</u>

Captain	MEYER GEORGE
Lieutenant	OEHLKERS CHRISTIAN
T.S.M.	KATER HENRY
Serjeant	GEHRKE CHRISTIAN
Serjeant	REMMERS FREDK.
Serjeant	SCHRODER ERNEST
Corporal	CALLMEYER LEWIS
Corporal	KRAPP WM.
Corporal	PAGELS HENRY
Trumpeter	WINLELMANN PETER
Private	BARENBUSCH HERMANN
Private	BENECKE FREDK.
Private	BENECKE HENRY
Private	BULTMANN DIEDRICK
Private	BLANKE JNS.HY.
Private	BALLANDS HERMANN
Private	BALLWIG HENRY
Private	BRUBESCHECK FRANZ
Private	BUCHHALZ JOHN
Private	BARTELS HENRY
Private	CASTENS JOHN
Private	DRUISH WM.
Private	FURST ADAM
Private	FEIFFER JOHN
Private	FROBUSCH HENRY
Private	FLUGGE WM.
Private	HANNOVER HENRY
Private	HALLER LEWIS
Private	HAMBROK FREDK.
Private	HALLER FREDK.
Private	HART CLEMENTS
Private	HERPORT LEOPOLD
Private	HATTENDORFF HENRY
Private	HARMS GEORGE
Private	HAMPKE CHRISTIAN
Private	ISERMANN NICOLAUS
Private	IMIGBLUTH HENRY
Private	KOSHICK JOSEPH
Private	KOCH FREDK. Cheylesmore Coll.1908
Private	KRONE LEIDWIG
Private	LEHR FREDK.
Private	LOVANG GEORGE
Private	LUTYENS DIEDRICK
Private	MATHIAS HENRY
Private	MEYWORK GEORGE
Private	MENKING WM.
Private	MEYER DIEDRICK
Private	MINOU HENRY
Private	MORITZ HERMANN
Private	NULLE PHILIP
Private	PAHL JURGEN
Private	RANKE DIEDRICK
Private	RUST CHRISTIAN
Private	REESING FREDK.
Private	REBENDISCH DANIEL
Private	ROTTGER WM.
Private	STOFFELMANN CONRAD
Private	SCHRODER JOHN
Private	SIEGMANN CHRISTIAN

Private	SCHULZ CHRISTIAN
Private	THENT HENRY
Private	UPBRAIK HENRY
Private	WILLMSEN HENRY
Private	WINSEMANN CHRISTOPH
Private	WANDEIK MARTIN
Private	WENDT FREDK.
Private	WAKENER GEORGE
Private	WILLHELMS FREDK.

Captain A. de Harling's Troop

Captain	HARLING AUGUST
Lieutenant	TRUE HERMANN
Cornet	HODENBERG AUGUST
T.S.M.	BULLANELT FREDK.
Serjeant	FISCHER CARL
Serjeant	NERVA JOHN
Serjeant	SCHARLMANN HENRY
Serjeant	SCHRADER HENRY
Corporal	BUGENSTOCK GEORGE Gray Collection 1908
Corporal	DECKEN FREDK.
Corporal	MANSFIELD HENRY
Trumpeter	WARNECKE HENRY
Private	ADELUNG JOHN
Private	BOHNSEYER HENRY
Private	BERGMANN HENRY
Private	BACK CHRISTIAN
Private	BOHNSTAL FREDK.
Private	BORCHERS CONRAD
Private	BECKMANN AUGUST
Private	DAVEKAN HENRY
Private	ELMENDORFF THEODOR
Private	ENGHAUSEN ADOLPH
Private	FORDE FREDK.THOS.
Private	FETTE FREDK.
Private	FRUCHT HENRY
Private	FISCHER HENRY
Private	FISCHER JOSEPH
Private	GROSSHEIM HENRY
Private	GLEUE JURGEN
Private	GRAEBER FREDK.
Private	GRIMPE CHRISTIAN
Private	GALLER SUMON
Private	HADLER DIEDK.
Private	HAAKE HENRY
Private	KUSTER CHRISTIAN
Private	KRAMER ANTON
Private	KRATH WM.
Private	KOHLER CHARLES
Private	LERPS LEWIS
Private	LORENZ HENRY
Private	LEGER CARL
Private	LAURITZ SERVATIUS
Private	MEYER ALBERT
Private	MULLER JNS.(Snr)
Private	MULLER JNS.(Junr)
Private	MATHIAS WM.
Private	MURKFIELD HENRY
Private	NIEMANN CONRAD Whitaker Coll.1908
Private	NATIS JACOB
Private	OPPERMANN FREDK.
Private	PRATTE JUSTUS
Private	PAUERT ANTON
Private	PFENNING FREDK.
Private	RASEN PETER
Private	RIEBESCHL CLAUS
Private	RATHING LEWIS
Private	ROBER DIEDK.
Private	RANTERBERG LEWIS
Private	ROSEMEYER CORD.
Private	STUMPEL HENRY
Private	STUMPEL DIEDK.
Private	SCHMIDT NICOLAUS
Private	THIEJE HENRY
Private	THIES WM.
Private	VOLKERS FREDK.
Private	WISMAR HENRY
Private	WINTERBERG HENRY
Private	WEDE CONRAD

Captain Wm. Hellin's Troop

Captain	KELLIN WM.
Lieutenant	ZIMMERMANN FREDK.
Cornet	HAMMERSTEIN ALEX.
T.S.M.	KUSTER LEWIS
Serjeant	BUHRDORFF HENRY
Serjeant	HILLMER HENRY
Serjeant	RAMPENTHAL HENRY
Corporal	BECKMANN HENRY
Corporal	FAST HENRY
Corporal	KRAGE CHRISTOPH
Trumpeter	WICKENBERG GATTLIEB
Private	BENTHE JNS.HY.
Private	BACKHAUS CHRISTIAN
Private	BUHRE CHRISTIAN
Private	BAHM JOHN G.
Private	BARKHAUSEN HENRY

Private	BLATHE DIEDK.
Private	BODE FREDK.
Private	BARTLING FREDK.
Private	CORS CHRISTIAN
Private	DORMANN FREDK.
Private	DEWIS MICHEL
Private	DUNKELL WM.
Private	ENGEL DIEDK.
Private	EGGERLING JNS.FREDK.
Private	EBERT LEWIS
Private	FAST JURGEN
Private	FABER JOHN
Private	HIMSTEDT DIEDK.
Private	HACKMANN FREDK.
Private	HAUSMANN LEVY
Private	HAAKER FRANZ
Private	KILMER HANS WM.
Private	JACOBS CONRAD
Private	KASTENS CHRISTH.
Private	KASTERMANN JNS.HY.
Private	KRATH CONRAD
Private	KELLER CONRAD
Private	KUTSCHER GEORGE
Private	KANIG CHRISTH.
Private	KANTER THOS.
Private	KRANTZ CONRAD
Private	LUCKE CHRISTH.
Private	LUHRS LEWIS
Private	LUNIG PETER
Private	LINDERT CHRISTN.
Private	MEYER CONRAD
Private	MEYER JNS.FK.
Private	MAUBACH THOS.
Private	MEYER JNS ALBERT
Private	MANSCHEWSKY JOHN
Private	MINI NICOLAUS
Private	OHLE HENRY
Private	OLDENBUTTEL DIEDK.
Private	PUTJENTER HENRY
Private	PRANGE HENRY
Private	PETERS CHRISTH.
Private	ROLFS FREDK.
Private	RIESCH FREDK.
Private	REIMERS DIEDK.
Private	SCHONEBERG FREDK.
Private	STREITHORST JOHN
Private	SCHONTROP JOHN
Private	SPEYER JOHN
Private	SCHONEBERG CARL
Private	TUERBURG FREDK.
Private	TACKE HENRY
Private	VANDEISS REGNIER[
Private	WIEBRECHT FREDK.
Private	WATJE HENRY
Private	WEBER FREDK.
Private	WUHRMANN HENRY
Private	WIEGMANN HENRY
Private	ZIEMS JOHN
Lieutenant	PAWER FRANS.
Cornet	KAGER ANTON FK.
T.S.M.	LUDEMANN FREDK.
Serjeant	AMMANN JOSEPH
Serjeant	KRANSHAGEN HENRY
Serjeant	SCHAPER FREDK.
Serjeant	SCHWARTZ CHRISTN.
Corporal	LOHRBERG CHRISTN.
Corporal	PIENER FREDK.
Corporal	RUBRECHT FRANS.
Corporal	WRISBERG FREDK.
Trumpeter	ZIERNAN JOHN
Private	BRANDES JNS.HY.
Private	BRECHT DIEDK.
Private	BARNBALD HENRY
Private	BATTERMANN JAACHIM
Private	BASEDAN OTTO
Private	BRUNSWICK JAACHIM
Private	BRAND CASTEN
Private	BAHRE JOHN
Private	CASTENS CHRISTH,
Private	DIERECKS FRANZ
Private	DIEDRICK HENRY
Private	ENGELMANN LEWIS
Private	EWERS FREDK.
Private	FRANCIS WM.
Private	FORTMULLER WM.
Private	FRANKE AUGUST
Private	FOCK WM.
Private	GRATE HENRY
Private	HOMEYER HENRY
Private	'AAKE JOSEPH
Private	HELM FRANZ
Private	HAASE CHARLES
Private	HARNEY LEWIS
Private	HALLER FRIEDK.
Private	KOSTERMANN HENRY

Private	KUPER JACOB
Private	KOHNEMANN LEWIS
Private	KRANS HENRY
Private	KUHNE FREDK.
Private	LINDEWEY LEWIS
Private	LEITZEN CASPER
Private	LERSCHENFELD FRIEDK.
Private	LABAHN JURGEN
Private	LETZMANN CHRISTN.
Private	MULLER JNS.FK.
Private	MEYER PHILIP
Private	MEYER CHRISTIAN
Private	MEYER HENRY
Private	MINKS JOHN
Private	MINTON CARL
Private	NEDDERMEYER FREDK.
Private	PIEPER FREDK.
Private	QUAL JNS.PETER
Private	RIERSCH BERNHARDT
Private	REESING EBARHARD
Private	RETTIG CARL
Private	SCHOMBERG JOHN
Private	SCHUMACHER DIEDK.
Private	SCHULTER CONRAD
Private	SPONNAGEL HANS
Private	STAHLHUTH ANTON
Private	SEMISCH JOSEPH
Private	SSHWENKE CHRISTH.
Private	SCHMIDT JNS.FK.
Private	STRUCKMANN JOHN
Private	STRUBE CARL
Private	THIES CHRISTIAN
Private	THATER CHRISTOPH
Private	WICHEL HENRY
Private	WILLE PETER
Private	WOLFF HENRY
Private	WEBER WM.
Lieutenant	REINECKE AUGUST
Lieutenant	GERSTLACHER EBRHARD
Cornet	FRIEDRICKS RUDOLPH
T.S.M.	RUGSEMEYER CHRISTN.
Serjeant	BADE JOHN
Serjeant	DOPKE DIEDRICK
Serjeant	HOPKE HENRY
Serjeant	MUHLENBRINK DIEDK.
Corporal	KRAMER CHRISTIAN
Corporal	MEYER GEORGE
Trumpeter	GADE GUTTLIEB

Private	ASPELOH CHRISTN.
Private	BALLAND ANDREAS
Private	BIERFISCHER HENRY
Private	BRUNJES CHRISTN
Private	BRANDT HENRY
Private	BREYHAN PETER
Private	BRUNJES HENRY
Private	BRIEL CHARLES
Private	BUFSE HENRY
Private	DOHMEYER HENRY
Private	EBERHARD CHRISTN.
Private	FLEISCHMANN FREDK.
Private	GRATE FREDK.
Private	GARTNER JOHN
Private	HANENSCHILDT FRIEDK.
Private	HENNIGS CHRISTOPH
Private	HILDEBRAND GOTTLIEB
Private	HORMANN JACOB
Private	HINTZE JAACHIM
Private	HUNIG FREDK.
Private	JURGENS LEWIS
Private	KLENKE CONRAD
Private	KNOPEL ARNOLD
Private	KRATH WM.
Private	KEMMADE FREDK.
Private	LANGHEIM FREDK.
Private	LIBERTY FREDK.
Private	MEYER FREDK.(Senr)
Private	MENKE JNS.FK.
Private	MOLIN JOHN
Private	MEYER FREDK.(Jnr)
Private	MEYER WM
Private	MEYER CHRISTOPH
Private	NESTOR JOHN
Private	PUFKE FREDK.
Private	PAULMANN LEWIS
Private	PLESEY ANDREW
Private	RAMSTON FREDK.
Private	RESCHEOK JOHN
Private	RELY RICHD.
Private	RADEWALD AUGUST
Private	SCHNEMANN HENRY
Private	SCHARNHORST WM.
Private	SCHMALKAKE FREDK.
Private	SCHMIDT FREDK.
Private	SCHLEY JACOB
Private	THIELE ERNEST
Private	VANDALIANT FREDK.
Private	WUNDERLISH HENRY

Private	WEISS JOHN
Private	WALDSCHALK ANDREW
Private	WACSIHER THADEUS
Private	WELLER GEORGE
Private	WEDEMEYER CHRISTOPH
Private	WESTHOFF JOHN

Captain Uriah Hayer's Troop

Captain	HAYER URIAH
Lieutenant	THUMANN JAACHIM
Cornet	DU FRESNAY FREDK.
T.S.M.	DIERKING CHRISTIAN
Serjeant	BUHLMAHN HENRY
Serjeant	BERGHEIM CHRISTIAN
Serjeant	EHLERS JNS.FREDK.
Corporal	EGGERS NICOLAUS
Corporal	KAMMERT CHAS.
Corporal	MOHLE GEO. WM
Corporal	WIDEKING CHRN.LUDN.
Private	ALBERT JOHN
Private	NEHR CONRAD
Private	BUERMESTER JND.FDK.
Private	BASCHE CHRISTN
Private	BEHRENS CHRISTN.
Private	BOSSEWITZ JAMES
Private	BREUNICK PETER
Private	BUERMESTER JNS.CHRN.
Private	BUERMESTER CARL
Private	BARTELS FREDK.
Private	BIERMANN HENRY
Private	CUSTACHER GERHARD
Private	CALLMEYER HENRY
Private	DEGENER FREDK.
Private	DIEDRICKS FREDK.
Private	DORING ANDREW
Private	DANEY STEPHAN
Private	DANNENBERG DIEDK.
Private	ENKE FREDK.
Private	EGGERS JNS.FK.
Private	ENGEL ANTON
Private	FINDORFF NICOLAUS
Private	FEHLHABER FREDK.
Private	FUSH JURGEN HY. Littledale Sale Nov.1910
Private	FRABOSE WM.
Private	GEHRKE FREDK.
Private	GARBE DANIEL
Private	HOWE V.THOMAS
Private	HERBERMANN JURGEN HY.
Private	HAMMELMANN JURGEN
Private	KLEMME JNS.CHRN.
Private	KOHLER FREDK.
Private	KRANSE JOHN
Private	KOHLER HENRY
Private	LEHNE CHS.FK.
Private	LANLY MATHIAS
Private	METHE CHRISTIAN
Private	MULLER ANTONY
Private	MAUER PETER
Private	MOHWINKEL HENRY
Private	PAUL VALENTIN
Private	RADENBURG FREDK.
Private	RIEKE ANDREW
Private	REHREN CHRISTIAN
Private	SCHULTZ CHRISTIAN
Private	SCHAPER CHRISTIAN
Private	SCHACHT LEWIS
Private	SCHULZE FREDK.
Private	SCHUCHMANN GEORGE
Private	SCHRODER CARL
Private	SCHURMANN CHRISTIAN
Private	SCHUFT HENRY
Private	SCHMIDT ANTONY
Private	SCHLEISNER FREDK.
Private	VOORHEN V.D. LEONHARD
Private	VALKER FREDK.
Private	WISSE CHRISTIAN
Private	WESCHER HENRY
Private	WASELOWSKY JOHN

Captain Charles Bremer's Troop

Lieutenant	HUMBALD HENRY de
Cornet	DECKEN V.D. ERNEST
T.S.M.	RUDOLPH HENRY
Serjeant	HUSTEDT HENRY
Serjeant	SCHUMACHER GEORGE
Serjeant	SIEBERS HENRY
Corporal	ENGELKE HENRY
Corporal	LEUNIG GABRIEL
Corporal	STENZIG JNS.HY.
Corporal	GUNTHER JNS.
Trumpeter	FREISE FREDK.
Private	ASSMUS HENRY
Private	BODE JUSTUS
Private	BRUGGEMANN JOHN
Private	BODECKER FK.(Snr)
Private	BRANDER HENRY
Private	BORM JOHN

Private	CALENSCE HY.W.
Private	ECKEL JACOB
Private	FISCHER LEWIS
Private	FLESSEL FREDINAND
Private	GRATE CHRISTIAN
Private	GOHMANN FREDK.
Private	HEPE FREDK.
Private	HUSIG HY.WM.
Private	HEMMINGS CHRISTOPH
Private	HEITMANN GEORGE
Private	HUTOFF JOHN
Private	JUNG PAUL
Private	KAUFMANN HY.LEVY
Private	KERSEBOOM FREDK. de
Private	LANGE FREDK. (Senr)
Private	LUBECK JNS.FEDK.
Private	LAMPE FREDK.
Private	LUHRING HENRY
Private	LEHR GOTTLIEB
Private	LANGE CHRISTIAN
Private	LANGE CARL
Private	LANGE FREDK.(Junr)
Private	LUBBERS FREDK.
Private	MEYER JNS.HY.
Private	MIEDE DANIEL
Private	MOSKE GOLTHELF
Private	MULLER FREDK.
Private	MEYER HY.CONRAD
Private	MEYER FREDK
Private	MEYER HENRY (Junr)
Private	NEURE HENRY
Private	NIESCHLAG CONRAD
Private	PAPENDORFF CHRISTIAN
Private	POTTGER HENRY
Private	ROBE JAMES
Private	SCHELLER JOHN
Private	SCHULZE GUTTLIEB
Private	SCHALTE FREDK
Private	STRUBER FREDK.
Private	STARKE WM.
Private	STEPHAN FREDK.
Private	SANTELMANN FREDK.
Private	SARTORTY FREDK.
Private	SCHRADER HENRY
Private	TAIKEL CASPEL
Private	THONE CHRISTIAN
Private	WEIDERS GUTTLIEB
Private	WOLPER FREDK.
Private	WISMAR CHRISTN.
Private	ZIESENTIZ CONRAD

Captain Frederick Paten's Troop

Captain	SCHNEHERS WM.
Lieutenant	NANNE FREDK.
Cornet	HODENBERG HANS de
T.S.M.	THIELHE ANDREAS
Serjeant	BORNEMANN FREDK.
Serjeant	RUNGE CHRISTIAN
Serjeant	SCHLABOHM CHRISTIAN
Serjeant	WEDEMEYER ANDREAS
Corporal	BEHR CHRISTOPH
Corporal	BADE HENRY
Corporal	HISCHE HENRY
Corporal	WENDT FREDINAND
Private	AHREN FREDK.
Private	BOLTZE PETER
Private	BEHRENS HENRY
Private	BENTHE GEORGE
Private	BUSING HENRY
Private	DICKMANN JOHN
Private	FLECHTMANN JOHN
Private	GESTERLING CHRISTIAN
Private	GITZ PETER
Private	GADECKE FREDK.
Private	GONETZ JYNAZ
Private	HELMKE FREDK.
Private	HINRICHS LUDOLPH
Private	HUFFMANN JOHN
Private	HUTHMACHER HENRY
Private	HARMS HENRY
Private	HAPKE HENRY
Private	HALLER LEWIS
Private	HEYDORN AUGUST
Private	HEIMBERG ERNEST
Private	HOCH LEWIS
Private	JUNNERMANN CHRISTIAN
Private	JUNG HENRY
Private	JATHO WM.
Private	KIPPER JOHN
Private	KLAGES ERNST
Private	KHULMANN HENRY
Private	KAYSER AUGUST
Private	KRUSE HENRY
Private	LUTJENS FREDK.
Private	MATZKER ABRM.
Private	MEULMASTER JOHN
Private	MEYER PETER
Private	MARIONE PETER
Private	MULLER ANDREAS

Private	MUHLENBECK FREDK.
Private	MEYER HENRY
Private	MARKWARD JOHN
Private	MENSING CHRISTIAN
Private	NARJES HENRY
Private	OPFERGELD MATTHIAS
Private	PETERS FREDK.
Private	PRELLENBERG ERNST
Private	PILLERT MATTHIAS
Private	ROBERT JAMES
Private	ROLANDS HENRY
Private	RUMLANDS JOSEPH
Private	SCHWIERING FREDK.
Private	SCHWARM PETER
Private	SCHAEFER LEWIS WM.
Private	SCHADT HENRY
Private	STEINHOFF CHRISTOPH
Private	STOESANDT ERNST
Private	SCHRADER HENRY
Private	THIELBERGER LEWIS
Private	THONBAHN HENRY
Private	VOLBRECHT ZACHARIAS
Private	VANOTHEN THEODOR
Private	WREDE HENRY
Private	WREDE CASPER
Private	WREDE GEORGE
Private	WEISSENBOM FERDINAND

<u>Captain Christian Heisin's Troop</u>

Captain	HEISE CHRISTIAN
Lieutenant	KRANSE LEWIS
T.S.M.	BREKERBAUM HENRY
Serjeant	BASTEL JOHN
Serjeant	BIELEFELD HENRY
Serjeant	WIEGAND AUGUST
Corporal	MEYER FREDK.
Corporal	MEYER DAVID
Corporal	SCHRADER WM.
Trumpeter	LUTZ LEWIS
Private	AHLEFELDS FREDK.
Private	ADOLPH CARL
Private	ANGEMANN HENRY Gaskell Collection 1908
Private	ANE HENRY
Private	ANTON BAUER
Private	BORCHERS JUSTUS
Private	BARTELLS HENRY
Private	BARTLING HENRY
Private	BREMER HENRY
Private	BALKE FREDK.
Private	BEHRENS AUGUST
Private	CASTECHER JOSEPH
Private	DECKEL HENRY
Private	ECK ERNST
Private	FUNKE HENRY
Private	FREISE CONRAD
Private	FALKE HENRY
Private	GEWECKE CONRAD
Private	GEWECKE WM.
Private	GRAFT HENRY
Private	HESPAR HERMANN
Private	HONRATH CARL
Private	HELMS HENRY
Private	HEINSATH HENRY
Private	NARJES BRONJE
Private	LEHLHAUSEN JOHN
Private	LANE HENRY
Private	KRUGER HENRY
Private	KNIGGE AUGUST
Private	MURMONY JOHN
Private	MEYER HENRY
Private	MIERLENBURG CHRISTIAN
Private	MULLER JOHN
Private	MARKS HENRY
Private	NIEBUHR ERNST
Private	PALMEN GERHARD
Private	ROSE CHRISTIAN
Private	ROSE FREDK.
Private	SCHARWENSKY JOSH.
Private	SCHMIDT ANDREAS
Private	SCHULZE JAACHIM
Private	SCHRADER GEORGE
Private	SANDER CARL
Private	STÊCKMANN HENRY
Private	SCHULTZE HENRY
Private	THONTER FRANCIS
Private	WIERING JOHN
Private	WERDER HENRY
Private	WEPPE JOHN
Private	WALDING GEORGE
Private	WILLE HENRY
Private	WISCHMANN HENRY
Private	WESTERMANN FREDK.
Private	WARNECKE JAACHIM

Colonel	ARENTSCHILDS SIR W.
Major	KRANCHENBERG GEORGE
Surgeon	RIPKING GEORGE
Ass.Surgeon	BAURMEISTER GEORGE Payne Collection 1911
Vty.Surgeon	EIDMANN FREDK.
Qr.Master	HOPPE J.W.
Pay Master	WIELER J.W.
Ass.Surgeon	BRUGGEMANN HENRY Attached to this Regiment from the 7th Line Battalion K.G.L.

* * *

1st LIGHT BATTALION K.G.L.

Lt.Colonel	BUSSCHE LEWIS
Major	STARTWIG FREDK.
Major	BUMKES HANS
Captain	HULSEMAN FREDK.
Captain	HUDORFF GEORGE
Captain	GILSA FREDK.
Captain	WYNCKEN CHRISTIAN
Captain	HOTZERMANN PHILIP Killed 18th June 1815
Captain	MARSCHALK HENRY Killed 18th June 1815
Captain	GOEBEN ALEX. Killed 18th June 1815
Lieutenant	BOTH FREDK.
Lieutenant	SCHADLER FERDINAND
Lieutenant	ALBERT ANTHONY Killed 18th June 1815
Lieutenant	WAHRENDORFF AUGUST
Lieutenant	HARTWIG FREDK.
Lieutenant	HEISE CHRISTOPHER
Lieutenant	FINCKE FREDK.
Lieutenant	BREYMAN GEORGE
Lieutenant	WOLRABE HERMAN
Lieutenant	HENGEL WM.
Lieutenant	BAUMGARTEN JOHN
Lieutenant	KESSVER CHAS.
Lieutenant	MININFSER NICKOLAUS
Lieutenant	KOESTER ADDOLPHUS
Lieutenant	LEONHART HARRY
Lieutenant	GIBSON EDGAR
Lieutenant	MACDONALD STEPHAN Payne Collection 1911
Lieutenant	KUNZE FREDK.
Ensign	RUBING WM.
Ensign	BEST GUSTAV
Ensign	REDEN LEWIS
Ensign	GENTZKOW ADOLPH
Ensign	HEISE FREDK.
Ensign	WILLING HENRY
Ensign	BEHNE CHARLES
Ensign	MARSCHALCK OTTO
Ensign	HEISE ADOLP
Pay Master	NAGEL ADOLPHUS
Adjutant	BUHSE WM.
Qr.Master	HUPEDIN RUDOLPH
Surgeon	GRUPE JOHN
Ass.Surgeon	FEHLAND DANIEL
Ass.Surgeon	DUVEL HENRY
Captain	MARSCHALCK GUSTAV

Staff

S.Major	HEINE FREDK.
Q.M.S.	BLANCKE GEORGE
P.M.S.	BEHR HENRY
Ar.Serjeant	SANDER CHRISTN. Discharged 24 Aug.
Bde.Major	SCHMALSTICH DANL.

1st Company

C.Serjeant	HINTZE CHAS.
Serjeant	DENICKE CHRISTN
Serjeant	GRIMME LEWIS Discharged 24 Aug.
Serjeant	KEITHEL CHAS.
Corporal	ALBRECHT HENRY
Corporal	HOCKER FREDK.
Corporal	LUDUCKE EBERHARD
Corporal	SANDER CONRAD
Corporal	TOLLE CHRISTOPHER
Corporal	UHRHAN CHRITSN.
Bugleman	DANNENBERG BERND.
Bugleman	HOFF WM.
Bugleman	MERKEN CHARLES
Private	ADAM JOHN
Private	ARNEMAN CONRAD
Private	BARTRAM WM.
Private	BECKEN PETER
Private	BEULE GERHARD
Private	BLANCKE HENRY
Private	BOLTE FREDK.
Private	BORCHERS FREDK.
Private	BRANDT FREDK.
Private	COHRS FREDK.
Private	CORTY ANTONY
Private	DERWIG FREDK.
Private	DEPPE ZACH. Dead of wounds 24th June 1815
Private	DREYER HENRY
Private	EIMLER GODFRIED Killed 18th June 1815

Private	FIHLING JOHN Killed 18th June 1815
Private	FOERSTERMANN FREDK.
Private	GOEDECKE HENRY
Private	GOTTHARD CHAS. Discharged 24th August
Private	GOTTHARD LORENZ
Private	GRANSTEIN MATTW.
Private	GROTTWOLF HENRY Discharged 24th August
Private	GUNTER JOHN
Private	HARARDUS PHILIP
Private	HELNUKE HENRY
Private	HISSE CHRISTIAN Gray Collection 1908
Private	HOTICO HENRY
Private	HOLWEDEL HENRY Discharged 24th August
Private	HORSTMAN JOHN
Private	HUYSDENS JOHN Whitaker Collection
Private	JURGENS HENRY Killed 10th July
Private	KIMMERER FREDK. Killed 10th July
Private	KIBBLER SEBASTIAN
Private	KIRCH PAUL
Private	KNITTEL ADOLPH
Private	KNUST WM. Killed 18 June
Private	KOCH CHRISTIAN
Private	KOLTER LESJE Killed 18 June
Private	KRIMMLER ANDREW
Private	KRUSE HENRY
Private	LISSERING CHARLES
Private	LUDERS JOHN
Private	LUFT FREDK.
Private	MEYER HENRY Discharged 24th August
Private	MEYER JOHN
Private	MEYER MATTW.
Private	MISSLING HENRY
Private	MORITZ CHRISTIAN
Private	NICOLES JOHN
Private	NITINS FREDK.
Private	OSTERMEYER ERNEST
Private	POTTGER WM.
Private	RASCH AUGUST
Private	RIMKINS HENRY
Private	RIGAWITZ MATTW.
Private	ROHLING FREDK.
Private	SASSE MATTW.
Private	SCHALCK ANTHONY
Private	SCHWEERS HENRY Discharged 24 Aug.
Private	SEIDENTOPF CONRAD
Private	STAHLSMIDT HENRY
Private	STUCHER WM. Discharged 24 Aug.
Private	TRUPOLT EMERICK Killed 18 June
Private	WALTER MARTIN Killed 18 June
Private	WITTEKING ANDREW
Private	WOLKENHAUSER FREDK.
Private	WYBROCK AHREND Killed 18 June

<u>2nd Company</u>

C.Serjeant	WINTER ERNEST
Serjeant	DAMMEYER HENRY
Serjeant	LINDEMAN PHILIP
Serjeant	MEYER FREDK.
Corporal	DORJE FREDK.
Corporal	ETTINGER CHARLES
Corporal	GUMMER CHRISTIAN
Corporal	HARTJE FREDK.
Corporal	HOLSTE CHAS.
Corporal	KEITEL GEORGE Killed 18 June
Corporal	MEYER LEWIS
Bugleman	FRANTZ MARTIN
Bugleman	HOLLE WM.
Private	AHRENS JOHN
Private	ALSTROP CHRISTIAN
Private	BAUCHBACH FREDK.
Private	BERNER CHARLES
Private	BUDE EMERICK
Private	BUHL ANTHONY
Private	COHRS LUTZE
Private	DEHLE GODFRIED
Private	DEMPMER HENRY Killed 18 June
Private	DINING HENRY Killed 18 June
Private	EICKE HENRY Discharged 24 Aug.
Private	ERNST FREDK. Killed 18 June
Private	FELLMAN WM.
Private	FLACKE ERNEST Discharged 24 Aug.
Private	FRESCHEN HENRY Discharged 24 Aug.
Private	GASSER JAMES
Private	GLATT MARTIN
Private	GOTTING CHRISTIAN
Private	GRUVINCKEL WM.
Private	HAAS PETER Dead of wounds 6 July 1815
Private	HAN de WM.
Private	KASTEN LEWIS
Private	KNOPP JOHN
Private	KOPPELSMEYER HENRY
Private	KRAUSE CHRISTN.
Private	KREYENBERG FREDK.

Private	KUHNEMAN HENRY
Private	LAMBACH LEWIS
Private	LANGILLOTZ JOHN
Private	MARCKWARD FREDK. Killed 18th June
Private	MARGOSKY MICHAL
Private	MARTINS ANTONY
Private	MOHRMAN HENRY
Private	MOHWINS JOHN
Private	MULLER JOHN
Private	MULLER WM.
Private	OHLERSHAUSEN CONRAD Discharged 24 August Cheylesmore Collection
Private	NEWMAN JOHN
Private	OLBERG JOSEPH
Private	PIERRE LEWIS
Private	RIEMAN JOHN
Private	ROHR WM. Died of wounds 5th July 1815
Private	RUHL CONRAD
Private	RUHLAND JACOB
Private	SACHER DANIEL
Private	SAUER ERNEST Discharged 24th August
Private	SCHEHU CHRISTOPH
Private	SCHENOWITZ JOHN Killed 18th June
Private	SCHLACHT AUGUST Killed 18th June
Private	SCHLUTER HENRY
Private	SCHUSSTER JACOB
Private	SCHWERDFIGER WM.
Private	SIEGNAB CHRISTOPH
Private	SPIEGEL JOHN
Private	STEINFELD JOHN Killed 18th June
Private	STEINWORTH JOHN
Private	STEER JOHN
Private	STINDT JOHN
Private	VOIGT FREDK.
Private	WILDNER CHARLES
Private	WEYRCHE CHRISTOPHER

<u>3rd Company</u>

C.Serjeant	VICTOR CHARLES
Corporal	ADAM WM.
Corporal	ARMBRECHT FREDK.
Corporal	KAUFMANN LEWIS
Corporal	BODERKER WM.
Corporal	MULLER HENRY
Corporal	DERWIG CHAS.
Corporal	DORMAN HENRY
Private	GARMS HENRY
Private	HERTZOG LEWIS
Bugleman	SCHULTZ CHAS.
Private	BATTHUS BARTW.
Private	BAUER PHILIP
Private	BERNING CHAS.
Private	BEYMUNER FREDK.
Private	BOHMEN HENRY Killed 18 June
Private	BOHNE FREDK.
Private	BRANDING FREDK.
Private	BRITTENS ANTON
Private	BUDE FREDK.
Private	DESMEL CHARLES
Private	DORJE DETLEF Boy
Private	FLASHILL FRANS.
Private	GEISSEL HENRY
Private	GILIN PHILIP
Private	GRAFT DAMIT
Private	HAASE WM.
Private	HUNIG JOHN
Private	HOLTZHAUSEN CONRAD
Private	HURST (ran) HENRY
Private	KAHLE WM.
Private	KIRCHNER HERMAN
Private	KORNEMAN EBERT Dead of wounds 25th July 1815
Private	LABLONSKY JOHN
Private	LOSE CHRISTIAN
Private	LUCAS MATTW.
Private	MAY D.V. JOSEPH
Private	MEYER FREDK.
Private	MOHLENBERG FRANS.
Private	NAGEL JOSEPH
Private	NOACK JOHN
Private	PANTZER ANTHONY Dead of wounds 3rd July 1815
Private	POSCH JOHN Killed 18 June
Private	RAGEWSKY PETER
Private	RAUBER ANDREW
Private	REINECKE CHRISTOPH
Private	REISS MARTIN
Private	RITTIG GEORGE
Private	RIBARZ CHARLES
Private	RUBEN LORENZ
Private	RUSTMAN CHRISTR.
Private	SCHADE MARTIN
Private	SCHAEFER JOHN
Private	SCHALL FREDK. Deserted 12 Aug 1815

Private	SCHENY ANTHONY
Private	SCHLIER JOHN
Private	SCHLUSSELBURG HENRY
Private	SCHOBER ADAM Killed 18 June
Private	SCHOLERMAN LEWIS
Private	STINT JOHN
Private	STOBER FRANS.
Private	STOLTZEL CHRISTIAN
Private	STRUEL HENRY
Private	TOLLE CHRISTIAN
Private	TONNICO FREDK.
Private	UNGER CHRISTOPH
Private	WANDERLE FREDK. Killed 18th June
Private	WEISSHUHN GEORGE Killed 18th June
Private	WERLING FREDK.
Private	WERRACK ANDW.

<u>4th Company</u>

C.Serjeant	DIECK CHARLES Gaskell Collection 1908
Serjeant	SAIGER FREDK.
Serjeant	MARCH CHRISTOPH
Serjeant	STUMKEL HENRY
Corporal	BORCHERS FREDK.
Corporal	ELVERS HENRY
Corporal	KIMRODT CHRISTIAN
Corporal	SPANNAGEL AUGUST Killed 18th June
Corporal	WINTER ANDW.
Corporal	WUSSLOW ALBERT
Bugleman	MEYER CONRAD
Bugleman	VASEL WM. Discharged 24th August
Private	AHLHORN CHARLES
Private	ANTERMAN CONRAD
Private	BAHLHORN HENRY
Private	BALDINGER JOHN
Private	BEHNE HENRY
Private	BONG FRANCIS
Private	BORJES CONRAD
Private	BOX ADRIAN
Private	BURCKHARD JOHN
Private	ERNST HENRY
Private	FASSBINDER ANTHONY
Private	FAUST HENRY
Private	FRANTZ BENJN.
Private	GEHMAN HENRY
Private	GOLLNITZ HANS
Private	GREHA HENRY
Private	GUNTHER FREDK.
Private	HATRIG JAMES
Private	HAMM FREDK.
Private	HENNERS HENRY Discharged 24 Aug.
Private	HOFFMAN JOHN
Private	HOVERMAN HENRY
Private	JANATZ JOSEPH
Private	JOURNEICK JURGEN
Private	JUNG HENRY
Private	JUNGHOLTER NICKOLUS
Private	IVANOW JOHN
Private	KOHLER CHARLES
Private	KOLHE FREDK.
Private	KOENIG ANTON
Private	KISCHNE CHRISTIAN
Private	KULLA CASIMIR
Private	LANGE GODLIEF
Private	LUHRSEN CONRAD Discharged 24 Aug.
Private	LUWING HENRY Killed 18 June
Private	MARTZ JOHN
Private	MILIUS JOHN
Private	MOHR JOHN
Private	MUHLHAUSEN GODLIEB
Private	MULLER WM.
Private	NESEMAN FREDK.
Private	NEUDORFF JOHN
Private	NORDEMAN HENRY Killed 18 June
Private	OCLIG FREDK. Boy
Private	RAHRIG HENRY
Private	RIESING LEWIS
Private	REINFELD PETER
Private	REINHOLZ JUSTUS
Private	RIBERAN PETER Galway Foley Collection 1910
Private	RICHEY WM.
Private	RITZE HENRY
Private	ROPER HENRY Discharged 24 Aug.
Private	SANDER CONRAD
Private	SANDER HELMUTH
Private	SCHAEFER JOHN
Private	SCHELHASE HENRY
Private	SCHMALSTICH VANENTIN
Private	SCHMIDT ANTHONY
Private	SCHULTZE HENRY
Private	SCHWARTZ JOHN
Private	SETTEPASS PETER
Private	SONTAG JOSEPH
Private	STADTLER CONRAD
Private	STAHLBERG ANDREW
Private	STUMKEL LEWIS
Private	WESTRANDT JOHN
Private	WILCKENS CHRISTOPH

5th Company

Cr.Serjeant	NOLTE LEWIS
Serjeant	TRAMMER JOHN Killed 18 June
Serjeant	KLINGE DANIEL Died of Wounds 5th July 1815
Serjeant	REINECKE FREDK.
Serjeant	RIGOLY ANDREW Died of Wounds 24th June 1815
Corporal	ANDREAS DAVID
Corporal	ENGELHARDT WM.
Corporal	FISCHER JAMES
Corporal	REIHBEN HENRY
Corporal	SCHMIDT WM.
Corporal	VOGEL JAMES
Corporal	WHITTEL CHRISTR. Killed 18th June 1815
Bugleman	BURGDORFF JOHN
Bugleman	MAN CHARLES
Private	AHLERS HENRY
Private	ANE FREDK.
Private	BEHNECKE CHRITSN
Private	BERG CHARLES
Private	BEYER JACOB
Private	BRODRICK CASPER
Private	BUDOSKY FRANCIS
Private	CARLSON ADAM
Private	COHRS GEORGE
Private	CROME JOHN
Private	DONECKE CHRISTN Killed 18th June
Private	DORING FREDK.
Private	DREISS JOHN
Private	EICKEMEYER JULIUS
Private	ENGELHARD DIETERICH
Private	FAHRENHOLTZ HENRY
Private	FEHLER FREDK.
Private	FEHZENSEN ERNST
Private	FERMER FRANS.
Private	FISCHER JURGEN
Private	GANNZ JOHN
Private	GEISSELMAN HENRY
Private	GORTLER ANDREW
Private	GUTTACHER PHILIP
Private	HELLBERG JOHN
Private	HEUR HENRY Killed in Action 18th June
Private	HILLMAN HENRY Cheylesmore Collection 1908
Private	JACGER FREDK.
Private	JINCKER HENRY
Private	KLEINING CONRAD
Private	KLENGENBERG GERARD
Private	KOHNE FREDK.
Private	KRIEG ADOLPHUS
Private	KRUGER HENRY
Private	LANGOSHE FREDK.
Private	LEHMAN SIMON Dead od wounds 6th July 1815
Private	LEHMACKE WM. Discharged 24 Aug.
Private	LEOPOLD CHRISTOPH
Private	LOBEDANZ HENRY
Private	LUNING CHARLES Discharged 24 Aug.
Private	MESSESICK PAUL
Private	MULLER CHRISTIAN
Private	PALADINE JOSEPH
Private	RASSIER WM.
Private	REINECKE HENRY
Private	RINSKA HENRY
Private	ROSETER BENJN.
Private	SCHAFER GEORGE Dead of wounds 24th June 1815
Private	SCHLEMM DIETERICH
Private	SCHNEIDERS CONRAD Killed 18 June
Private	SCHNER DAVID
Private	SCHRITZ FREDK.
Private	SEELEGER CHARLES
Private	SPENT JOHN
Private	STARCKE CHRISTN.
Private	STEEN VAN DER LEANDER
Private	STOFFREGEN FREDK.
Private	THIMAN CHRISTOPH Killed 18 June
Private	VANVIVAR FRANS.
Private	WEITNER JOSH.
Private	WELAR JOHN
Private	WIDDERS ANTHONY
Private	WIEGAND FREDK.RICHD.
Private	WRONOFT PETER

6th Company

C.Serjeant	SEINKE GEORGE
Serjeant	HERRE HENRY
Serjeant	REINECKE CONRAD
Serjeant	ROH CONRAD
Corporal	ETTINGER EDWD.
Corporal	GEROSWITZ MICHAEL
Corporal	GRUPE HENRY
Corporal	KLEINHANS HENRY
Corporal	RUMENAP LORENZ
Corporal	SCHWABE HENRY
Corporal	WAGENER GEORGE
Bugleman	KNAUFF FREDK. Discharged 24th August

Private	AELDERS THEODOR
Private	AMENDE FREDK.
Private	ANTON GEORGE
Private	APFET MATHEW
Private	BAUER CHRISTIAN
Private	BEHRENS JURGENS
Private	BODE HENRY
Private	BOTTSHER ANTHONY
Private	BROMON SIMON
Private	BUROSE HENRY
Private	BUSCH CHRISTOPHER
Private	BUSCH LEWIS
Private	CLAUS CHRISTIAN
Private	DANNENBERG HENRY
Private	DAUM PETER
Private	DICHL JOHN
Private	DIRTRICH HENRY
Private	EBERT WM.
Private	ENGELBURG AUGUST
Private	FOERHER CHRISTIAN
Private	FRISCH JULIUS
Private	GEISER DOMINICK
Private	GRAEGER CHRISTIAN
Private	GREBE LEWIS
Private	HARMS CHRISTOPH
Private	HEINRICH JOHN
Private	HOPER HENRY
Private	HULCKE WM.
Private	ISRAEL JOHN
Private	KAUFMANN JOSEPH Killed 18th June
Private	KICHNE ANDREW
Private	KLINGE WM.
Private	KLUSSMAN JOHN
Private	KOHLER FREDK.
Private	KOENECKE HENRY
Private	KORBER HENRY
Private	LARBEMANN JOHN
Private	LEHR PETER
Private	LINDE FREDK.
Private	LINNEMANN CHRISTIAN Killed 18 June
Private	MAGALINE JOHN
Private	MEYER ANTHONY
Private	MEYER CLAUS
Private	MORROW FRANCIS
Private	OPPE FREDK.
Private	OTTENS GODLIEB
Private	PETERSON FREDK. Killed 18th June
Private	RUCKMAN CHRISTH.
Private	SANDER CHRISTIAN
Private	SCHADT VALENTIN Killed 18 June
Private	SCHULTZE FREDK.
Private	SCHULTZE GEO.HY.
Private	SCHULTZE HENRY Discharged 24 Aug.
Private	STADELMANN CONRAD
Private	STAUB GEORGE Boy
Private	STEGE LEWIS Discharged 24 Aug.
Private	WACHTEL CHRISTIAN
Private	WEIDEMAN CHRISTIAN
Private	WESSELL JOHN

<u>7th Company</u>

C.Serjeant	SCHULTZE WM. Discharged 24 Aug.
Serjeant	HEISE FREDK.
Serjeant	SAEP FREDK.
Serjeant	WASSMAN FREDK. Discharged 24th August

<u>8th Company</u>

C.Serjeant	LOLLEMAN FREDK.
Serjeant	BEHRENS GEORGE
Serjeant	KAHLE LEWIS
Serjeant	LAMPE LEWIS
Serjeant	WIERNER CHRISTR.

<u>9th Company</u>

C.Serjeant	BLANCKE FREDK.
Serjeant	BRANDT CHRISTIAN
Serjeant	HAGEN HENRY
Serjeant	SAUSTMAN FREDK.
Serjeant	SCHROEDER FREDK.

<u>10th Company</u>

C.Serjeant	FEISE GEORGE
Serjeant	BUNNENBERG GENRY
Serjeant	SCHWENCKE CHRISTIAN

* * *

<u>2nd LIGHT BATTALION K.G.L.</u>

Colonel	Sir HALKETT COLIN K.C.B.
Major	BARING GEORGE
Captain	BOSEWIEL ADOLPHUS
Captain	HEISE AUGUSTUS
Captain	HAASMANN GEORGE Cheylesmore Collection 1908
Captain	STOTTE WM.
Captain	WIGMANN HENRY Killed 18 June
Captain	HOLZERMANN ERNEST
Captain	SCHAUMANN WM. Killed 18 June
Captain	HOME ALEX. Whitaker Coll.1908
Lieutenant	KESSTER FREDK.
Lieutenant	MEYER GEORGE

Lieutenant	MEYER CHARLES
Lieutenant	McGLASHAM JAMES
Lieutenant	LINDAM OLE
Lieutenant	RIEFKUGEL BERND.
Lieutenant	JABIN MARIUS
Lieutenant	D'MERWEDE CHARLES
Lieutenant	CAREY THOS.
Lieutenant	BIEDERMANN EMANUEL
Lieutenant	D'MEURON FRIDK.
Lieutenant	D'GRAME GEORGE
Lieutenant	INGERSTEBEN LEOPOLD
Lieutenant	EARL SOLOMON
Lieutenant	HURTZIG RUDOLPH
Lieutenant	DORING WM.
Ensign	ROBERTSON FREDK. Killed 18th June
Ensign	FRIDERECKS AUGUST
Ensign	FRANCK GEORGE
Ensign	KNOP AUGUST
Ensign	SMITH WM.
Ensign	BARING LUER
Ensign	MEYER CHARLES
Pay Master	KNIGHT JOHN
Lt.Adjutant	TIMMANN D.WM. Gaskell Collection 1908
Qr.Master	PALMER JAMES Payne Collection 1911
Surgeon	HEISE GEORGE
Ass.Surgeon	MULLER FREDK.
Ass.Surgeon	GEHSE HENRY
<u>Staff Serjeants</u>	
S.Major	WIEPKING GEORGE
Q.M.S.	MULLER THEODOR
P.M.S.	SCHULZE EDWARD
<u>1st Company</u>	
C.Serjeant	SCHMIDT LEWIS
C.Serjeant	MENTZ WM.
Serjeant	COURCELLES LEWIS
Serjeant	EGGERS HENRY
Serjeant	FROHNE HENRY
Serjeant	REGENTHAL FREDK.
Serjeant	ZIMMANN VALENTIN Killed 18th June
Corporal	EICHLER DIEDK. Discharged 24th August
Corporal	HOLTZE HENRY
Corporal	KIPP FREDK. Discharged 24th August
Corporal	METZ ANDREW
Corporal	SCHINPF ZACHS.
Corporal	WEISLEDER HENRY
Budleman	VAN DYCK ARY.
Bugleman	FRICKE FREDK.
Private	BANGEMANN CHRISTIAN
Private	BATARD ALEXIS
Private	BEHRENS CHARLES
Private	BENOFSKY VINVENT
Private	BLEYER HENRY
Private	TERNESS PETER Killed 18 June
Private	TIEFER GABRIAL Killed 18 June
Private	WEBER BERND.
Private	WELLERSCHEID CHRISTIAN
Private	WEINHARDT CHRISTN.
Private	ZENS GOTTFREID
Boy	SEDELMEYER FREDK.
<u>2nd Company</u>	
Serjeant	BERNACK HENRY
Serjeant	FORSTERMANN FREDK.
Serjeant	HOLLAMN LEWIS
Serjeant	HOFFMEISTER HENRY
Serjeant	KUMMER FREDK.
Serjeant	MATHIAS SIMON
Serjeant	SCHABE JOHN
Serjeant	ZENS ANDREAS
Bugleman	BOHN JOHN
Bugleman	HENNING CHARLES
Private	ABRAHAM HENRY
Private	ALBRANDT JOHN
Private	BARTRAM CHRISTIAN Discharged 24th August
Private	BARTZ MARTIN
Private	BECKER WM.
Private	BERGMANN JOHN
Private	BEUMER NICOLAUS
Private	BISCHOFF JOSH.
Private	BOSSELMANN CONRADT
Private	BOUFFELJON PETER
Private	DIETERS HENRY
Private	EGGERS HENRY
Private	FAHRENHOLTZ JOHN
Private	GOEDERTIER JOHN
Private	GREGOR CHRISTIAN
Private	HARBERS JOHN Killed 18 June
Private	HAUPT JOSEPH
Private	HEIDORN HENRY
Private	HENKING FREDK.
Private	HOPPE ALBERT Killed 18 June
Private	HORST JOHN
Private	HUBERT LEWIS
Private	JANTZEN ELZICH

Private	JANTZEN JOHN
Private	JOHNSEN JOHN
Private	KESTNER MARTIN Gray Collection 1908
Private	KIRSCHNER MICHAEL
Private	KNOLLE JOHN
Private	KRAUSE DANIEL Discharged 24th August
Private	LUDECKE JOHN
Private	LUHRING FREDK.
Private	MELGES FREDK.
Private	NOWACK PAUL Killed 18 June
Private	OBERDICK GEORGE
Private	PETERS CHARLES
Private	PETROWITZ ANDREAS
Private	RICKS DIEDK.
Private	ROLFS PHILIP
Private	SCHAMME PETER
Private	SCHAULZE JOHN
Private	SCHUB GEORGE
Private	SCHUMANN FREDK.
Private	SIATZ CHRISTIAN
Private	SIEVERS MORITZ
Private	SOLTTHALE FREDK.
Private	STOCKMAN GEORGE
Private	VANTILLBURG JOHN
Private	WAGENER CASPER
Private	WOTTERSDORFF HENRY Discharged 24 Aug.
Private	ZERRE GETTFREID
<u>3rd Company</u>	
C.Serjeant	KEINERT LEWIS
C.Serjeant	WEISS CHRISTIAN
Serjeant	BARONTZ PETER
Serjeant	BORNEMANN WM.
Serjeant	FELGE CHRISTIAN
Serjeant	MEYER HENRY Killed 18 June
Corporal	BEUTE CHRISTIAN
Corporal	DUBE FRANTZ Killed 18 June
Corporal	ERNEST FREDK.
Corporal	GOSEWISCH WM.
Corporal	HEMMINGSEN HENRY Killed 18th June
Corporal	KNAUF CHRISTIAN
Corporal	KURK HENRY
Bugleman	HARTING JOHN
Private	BARTELS JOHN
Private	BERGMANN JOHN
Private	BERICKE FREDK.
Private	BRITENCIAK THOMAS
Private	BUSSE HERMANN
Private	CONRAD FREDK.
Private	DAMMER PETER
Private	DEICHMULLER FREDK.
Private	DEKMET PETER
Private	DOBRITZKY ALEX Killed 18 June
Private	FISCHER HENRY
Private	FOCKEN HERTE
Private	FOSTYN JOHN
Private	HAGENADE GRATES
Private	HAUFF ADAM
Private	HEINE GOTTFRIED
Private	HEINE ULRICH Discharged 24 Aug.
Private	HEINBERG HENRY
Private	HELBERG PETER
Private	HOFFMANN CHRISTN. Killed 18 June
Private	HULSEWIG STEPHAN
Private	KEMPE CHAS.
Private	KERTMACHER MICHAEL
Private	KIRST JOHN
Private	KUSTER HENRY
Private	LACROIX LEWIS ANTON
Private	MALITZKY ANTON
Private	MEYER CHRISTIAN Killed 18 June 1815
Private	MULLER GEORGE
Private	NEENGARDT DANIEL Killed 18 June
Private	OHMS CHAS.
Private	OTTE DIEDK.
Private	PERTZ JOHN
Private	REINECKING WM.
Private	RENZELMANN GERRARD
Private	RUNGE HENRY Discharged 24 Aug.
Private	RYE PETER
Private	SANDVOFS PHILIP
Private	SANGERE MATHIAS
Private	SCHMEERS MATHIAS
Private	SCHRAMM DIEDK. Discharged 24 Aug.
Private	SCHURMANN HENRY
Private	SIEVERS HENRY
Private	STEMPEL HENRY
Private	THIELKE HENRY
Private	TIESTE FREDK.
Private	TIEMANN FREDK.
Private	TURNAN FREDK.
Private	VOGELSANG JAMES
Private	VOIGHT FREDK.
Private	WIGHT ANTON
Private	ZIMMERMANN GEORGE

4th Company

Cr.Serjeant	AHRENS HENRY
Cr.Serjeant	SUBKE JAACHIM Discharged 24th August
Serjeant	BUCHER CASPAR Killed 18th June
Serjeant	REIFFER FREDK.
Serjeant	SPAHN ADAM Discharged 24th August
Serjeant	SCHWABE DAVID
Serjeant	STEUERNAGEL HENRY Killed 18th June
Corporal	FABRIAN LEWIS
Corporal	HUBLITZ CHRISTIAN
Corporal	KLOCKE JOHN
Corporal	KRUGER THEODOR
Corporal	LUTTERLOH JURGEN
Bugleman	DIEDRICK ANDREW
Bugleman	PAREN FRANTZ
Bugleman	STEIRLANG CORNELIUS
Private	AHLERS CONRADT
Private	ALVERS HENRY
Private	BARTH CHARLES
Private	BRANDT HENRY
Private	CAPELLE HENRY
Private	DEWOLFF JOHN
Private	DEWOST JOHN
Private	DREYER GOTTLIEB Discharged 24th August
Private	EINHAUS GERHARD
Private	GARBY JOSEPH
Private	GENELCKE HENRY
Private	GERBOTH CHRISTIAN
Private	HAGEN HENRY
Private	HAN CHARLES Died of wounds
Private	HAUSEN HENRY
Private	HEGENER FREDK.
Private	HENRY MICHL. Killed 18 June
Private	Heintz MENTZ ANDREAS Gray Coll.1908
Private	HOPPE CHRISTIAN
Private	JURGENS MARTIN
Private	KIEBUSCH JOHN
Private	KELLAR JOHN
Private	KOCK CHRISTIAN
Private	KRAMER NICOLAUS
Private	KOPKY FRANTZ
Private	KUNBELL HENRY
Private	LINDEMANN FREDK. Discharged 24th August
Private	LINDNER GEORGE
Private	LUTTERTOH HENRY
Private	MAULMEISTER PHILIP
Private	MARSCHMANN HENRY
Private	MULLER ANDREAS
Private	MUNDFROM DANIEL
Private	MUNN JOHN
Private	OTTE CHRISTIAN
Private	PHILLIP ANTON
Private	ROCK MANNO
Private	ROVE BERND.
Private	ROBKE WM.
Private	ROMMERMAN HENRY Killed 18 June
Private	RUHR FREDK.
Private	SHONGAN GOTTFREID
Private	SOKOWALSKY WM.
Private	SCHANCHTEBECK HENRY
Private	SCHAPER JOHN
Private	SCHLENTZ GOTTFREID
Private	SCHMIDT FREDK.
Private	SCHRADE FREDK. Killed 18 June
Private	SCLANCE JOHN
Private	SPERT JOHN
Private	SCHUTZER ANDREW
Private	VANDERBECK JOHN
Private	WACSCH PETER
Private	WERNER ANDREAS
Boy	VAN DYCK WM.
Boy	RICKS FREDK.
Boy	SCHNGEN CHARLES

5th Company

Cr.Serjeant	MEVINS LEWIS
Serjeant	BOHLING CONRAD
Serjeant	KOHNE FREDK.
Serjeant	LASCHE HENRY
Serjeant	KOUTJER LEWIS
Serjeant	WIEBE WM.
Corporal	BEYER AUGUST
Corporal	KRAMER HENRY
Corporal	MEYER ANDREAS
Corporal	NOLKE CHRISTIAN
Corporal	RUSSO FREDK.
Corporal	STEINHOFF CHARLES
Bugleman	SCHUMACHER JOHN
Bugleman	TROCKELMANN HENRY
Private	BENECKE CHRISTN.
Private	BEDA BAPTIST
Private	BIDLA FRANCIS
Private	BIEGER WM.

Private	BURCHARD CHRISTN.
Private	BLUM JOHN Killed 18 June
Private	BOHNE FREDK.
Private	BRYNE CORNELIUS
Private	CHARLES BAPTIST Killed 18th June
Private	CONRAD IGNATZ
Private	CAUSSAT GEORGE
Private	DAHRENDORFF LEWIS Invalided
Private	FOURIER FRANCIS
Private	GANTER FREDK.
Private	GRUNHAGEN CHRISTIAN
Private	GUSTAV CHRISTIAN
Private	GOLLOGOSKY JOHN
Private	HERTMANN HENRY Discharged 24th August
Private	HEINEMANN CHRISTN.
Private	HOLLMANN FREDK.
Private	HAGELSTROM PETER Died of Wounds
Private	IKERIT PETER Missing
Private	JONKIER PTR.
Private	KUNARD JOSEPH
Private	LAMBSTER CHRISTN.
Private	LINDHORST ERNEST
Private	MACKENSTEADT JOHN
Private	MENSHEIM HENRY
Private	MULLER ANTON
Private	MAHRING JOHN
Private	MUTHERS FREDK. Col.Gaskell's Sale May 1911
Private	PULSEN PETER
Private	PRUMHOFF HENRY
Private	RANWALD JOHN Killed 18 June
Private	REIMERS CLAUS
Private	REIMSTEADT CONRADT Died of wounds
Private	SCHMIDT NICOLAUS
Private	SCHWUZER FREDK.
Private	SCHONNEMANN JOHN
Private	UCHTOFF JOHN
Private	VAESSEN NICOLAUS
Private	VANBENEDEN BAPTISTE
Private	VERKERT CORNELIUS
Private	WAGNER JOHN
Private	WIESE WM.
Private	WOUTHERS JOHN

6th Company

C.Serjeant	EGERSDORFF CHRISTIAN Discharged 24 Aug.
C.Serjeant	GRETE HENRY
Serjeant	EBERT JOHN Killed 18 June
Serjeant	HARMS HENRY
Serjeant	KLOCKE HERMANN
Serjeant	MUNDHENCK ERNEST
Serjeant	MEYER DIEDK.
Serjeant	NIECKELS HENRY
Serjeant	POPPE CHRISTIAN Killed 18 June
Corporal	HALBERT CHRISTIAN
Corporal	HEISE HENRY
Corporal	LEURS HENRY killed 18 June
Corporal	MUND CHRISTIAN
Corporal	D'REUTER ARNOLD
Bugleman	BOSSER PETER
Bugleman	BUCHMULLER JOHN
Private	AHRENS LEWIS
Private	AUHAGEN WM.
Private	BECK ANTON
Private	BLIDING CHARLES
Private	BOLAND FREDK. Killed 18 June
Private	BRINKMANN GOTTFREID
Private	BUCHER NICOLAUS
Private	EICHORN HENRY Discharged 24 Aug.
Private	GABU ANTON
Private	GELWEDRISCH PAUL
Private	HAHN CHARLES Discharged 24 Aug.
Private	HERALD HENRY
Private	HOBERG CHRISTN.
Private	HUPPE FREDK. Killed 18 June
Private	ISERMANN SIMON
Private	KEPPENHAUSEN HENRY
Private	KIESTING GOTTFRIED
Private	KODDELBAUER JOHN
Private	KOTWITSCH GOTTFRIED
Private	KRAMER JAMES
Private	LUTTERMANN LEWIS
Private	LIPITZKY THOS.
Private	LOVEKING GISTAV
Private	MEINECKE HENRY
Private	MORGENSTERN GOTTFRIED
Private	MULLER HENRY
Private	NEILSEN KNUT
Private	PRUSINSKY CHARLES
Private	REINHOLD GOTTLIEB Killed 18 June
Private	REINHOLZ HENRY

Private	ROWAY JOSEPH
Private	RICHARD JOHN
Private	RITZAN HENRY
Private	SCHOULLY THOS.
Private	SCHULTZE GOTTFRIED
Private	SCHUM JULIUS
Private	STOFFER MATHIAS
Private	STEINBACH WM.
Private	VENTO JOHN
Private	VOSS HENRY
Private	WEURDEMANN HENRY
Private	WILKENS HENRY
Private	ZETTENBAUR JOHN
Private	MESS JOHN 3rd Co.

* * *

1st LINE BATTALION K.G.L.

Major	ROBERTSON WM.
Captain	GOEBEN FREDK.
Captain	GEOBEN GEORGE
Captain	SCHLUTTER ANDREAS
Captain	SAFFE AUGUST Killed in Action 18th June
Captain	SCHLUTTER GERHARD
Captain	HOLLE CHAS. Killed in Action 18th June
Captain	RETTBERG LEOPOLD VON Gaskell Collection 1908
Lieutenant	HOLLE LEWIS
Lieutenant	ROSSING FREDK.
Lieutenant	DURING HENRY
Lieutenant	KUMME LUDOLPH
Lieutenant	ALLEN THOS.
Lieutenant	BEST CHAS.
Lieutenant	EINEM DIEDRICH
Lieutenant	WUHMANN GEORGE
Lieutenant	WYHE CHAS.
Lieutenant	FELLOWS BENJN.
Lieutenant	WOLFE WM. Whitaker Collection 1908
Lieutenant	ARENTSCHILD ADOLPHUS
Lieutenant	DRYSDALE WM. Gaskell Collection 1908
Lieutenant	MULLER AUGUST
Lieutenant	BEST WM.
Lieutenant	WILDING HENRY
Lieutenant	CARMICKEL ALEX.
Ensign	LESLIE FRANS.
Ensign	LEFORTH AUGUST
Ensign	BRANDIS AUGUST
Ensign	HEISE WM.
Ensign	LUCKEN HARTWIG Killed in Action 18th June
Ensign	KENTING FREDK.
Ensign	LODEMANN GEORGE
Ensign	REICHE AUGUST
Ensign	HELLEN CHAS.
Pay Master	TEIGHE THIMAS
Adjutant	SCHNATH FREDERIC Payne Coll.1911
Qr.Master	CAROLIN JOHN
Surgeon	WETZIG GOTTLIEB
Ass.Surgeon	LANGENHEINECKEN PHILIP
Hosp.Mate	MEYER JOHN Attd.as Ass.Surgeon
S.Major	GOTTSCHALK ERNEST Died of wounds
Q.M.S.	WEGENER JOHN
Serjeant	BAHR JOHN
Serjeant	BAUMER PETER
Serjeant	BECKMANN HENRY
Serjeant	BEUERMANN CHRISTIAN
Serjeant	BODE JOHN
Serjeant	BRANDT ANDREAS
Serjeant	BREITENBACK LEWIS
Serjeant	REINECKE GEORGE Discharged 4 Aug.
Serjeant	DAMBKE HENRY
Serjeant	DROGER FREDK.
Serjeant	SANDER AUGUST
Serjeant	EVERS FREDK.
Serjeant	SANGER GEORGE
Serjeant	FISCHER AUGUST
Serjeant	FLEDERMANN CHRISTOPH
Serjeant	SCHAPER HENRY
Serjeant	GEVEN WM.
Serjeant	GLASTADTER PHILIP
Serjeant	SCHMIDT HENRY
Serjeant	HEINE HENRY
Serjeant	HEINEMEYER LEWIS
Serjeant	HELD LEWIS
Serjeant	HUTTERSON ENRIG
Serjeant	SCHREIBER HENRY
Serjeant	JASPER FICT.
Private	SCHREIBER ENGELH.
Private	KNENERT HENRY Killed 18 June
Private	KOCH WM.
Private	LOCHERS ALEX.
Private	MEYER LEWIS
Private	MOLL WM.
Private	MOLZ HENRY
Private	MECH OTTO
Private	SCWAM ANTHONY

Private	OTTENFIELD
Private	SCHWATZE CHRISTOPH
Private	SEWRIN CHRISTN.
Private	STEINMITZ CHRISTN.
Private	STRAUB LEWIS
Private	THIELEMANN HENRY
Corporal	ALTEN FREDK.
Corporal	BAUMANN FREDK. Discharged 4th August
Corporal	BECKER CHRISTN.
Corporal	BECKMANN JOHN
Corporal	BIEDENWEG JOHN
Corporal	BIELEFELDT HENRY
Corporal	BORSUM HENRY Discharged 4th August
Corporal	BOWK FREDK.
Corporal	BRECKEL JOHN
Corporal	DEBUS WENTZEL
Corporal	DESARTORY JOSEPH Watters Sale June 1913
Corporal	GLADIS JOHN
Corporal	HOPPE HENRY Killed 18 June
Corporal	HOPPE GOTTLIEB
Corporal	LINDEMANN CHRISTOPH Discharged 4th Aug.
Corporal	LIPPEN MARTIN
Corporal	MEINHARDT JOHN
Corporal	MULDER HERRMAN
Corporal	NOHRMANN JOHN
Corporal	PAPE JOHN
Corporal	RICK WM.
Corporal	RUSCH JOSEPH
Corporal	SCHAFFER HENRY Discharged 4th August
Corporal	SCHRADER CHRISTN.
Corporal	SCHWARZE HENRY
Corporal	SPRUTE GEORGE
Corporal	STALIGIVE CHRISTIAN Died of Wounds 11 July 1815
Corporal	TEYTONBERG LEONHARD
Corporal	WEDE HENRY
Corporal	WIECHERT HENRY
Corporal	WIECHERS HENRY
Corporal	WINKELMANN HENRY
Drummer	APPELSTADT ANTHONY Cheylesmore Collection 1908
Drummer	BERGER PETER
Drummer	CLUOO JOHN
Drummer	DORNSEIF HENRY
Drummer	FREY AUGUST
Drummer	HEISE PHILIP Killed 18 June
Drummer	HELLM CHAS
Drummer	TEGER CASPER
Drummer	KUHLS CONRAD
Drummer	KIESELER AUGUST
Drummer	REINECKE FREDK.
Private	ADAMANTYIAK MARTIN
Private	ALBRECHT W.
Private	ALEXANDER ADAM
Private	ALMAN PETER
Private	ANDREAD MARTIN
Private	BADEN RICHD.
Private	BARTELS HENRY
Private	BECKER LEWIS
Private	BECKMANN L.WM.
Private	BEHRING HENRY
Private	BENNING ANDREW
Private	BERGEL GODFRY
Private	BERGMANN HENRY
Private	BERNHARD CHRISTIAN
Private	BERTHONIUS JOHN
Private	BINDER JOHN
Private	BISCHOFF ANTHONY
Private	BLATTER JOHN
Private	BOOKER FREDK.
Private	BORMANN LEONHARDT
Private	BORNER AUGUST
Private	BRADAT JOHN
Private	BRANDT CONRAD Discharged 4 Aug.
Private	BRAUMANN CHRISTH.
Private	BRAUN MICHL.
Private	BRUNS CHRISTN.
Private	BREIZOWSKY BASIL
Private	BRINKET JOHN
Private	BROOKMEYER ALBRECHT
Private	BRUNSKEL ANTHY.
Private	BRUM JOHN
Private	BURMANN FREDK.
Private	BRISINSKY GERHARD
Private	BUSSE GEORGE
Private	BUTKOSSKY FRANS.
Private	CARLEY JOHN
Private	CHIKORSKY JOSH.
Private	CHNIBOWSKY JOSH.
Private	CLAUS BERND
Private	COMBROWSKY THEODOR
Private	CONRAD HENRY
Private	CONRADES LEWIS
Private	CORNET CHRISTN.
Private	CROSSA MICHL.

Private	DOMBROWSKY IGNATZ
Private	DARTO FRANS.
Private	DAUL LORENZ
Private	DECK HENRY
Private	DECKER JOSEPH
Private	DELY JOHN Killed 18 June
Private	DEMULE WM.
Private	DETERDING FREDK.
Private	DITTMER CHRISTN. Discharged 4th August
Private	DECKER MARTIN
Private	DORGER ANDREAS
Private	DORGER THOS.
Private	DRINSKA VALENTIN Col. Gaskell's sale May 1911
Private	DUFTS FRANS.
Private	EUKHOFF CORD.
Private	ELBERT ANTHY.
Private	ELSENER FRANS.
Private	ELWEDY JOSEPH
Private	EMME FREDK.
Private	ENGEL GODFRY
Private	ERLIN CH.
Private	EVERS HENRY
Private	FALKE HENRY
Private	FINK HENRY
Private	FISCHER HENRY
Private	FISCHER FREDK.
Private	FLASCHLY HERRHAM
Private	FLEISCH CREATUS
Private	FLARIAN FREDK.
Private	FREY GEORGE
Private	FREISE JOHN
Private	FRICKE MARTIN
Private	FROHSTADT ANTHY. Killed 18th June
Private	GABRIEL FREDK.
Private	GARTNER CHRISTN. Discharged 4th August
Private	GASELY DOMINIGUED
Private	GEFFERT JURGEN
Private	GEORGENSEN PETER
Private	GESOND PETER
Private	GIER FREDK.
Private	GLADOWSKY SREPN.
Private	GOEBEL JOSEPH
Private	GUHR FREDK.
Private	GRAIN HENRY Discharged 4 Aug.
Private	GREBEIN CHRISTN.
Private	GRUPE CHRISTN.
Private	GUNTHER CHAS. Discharged 4 Aug.
Private	GUNTHER FREDK
Private	HAACKE CONRAD
Private	HABICH FREDK.
Private	HAGEDORN HENRY
Private	HAMMELMANN HENRY
Private	HARTE CHRISTN. Killed 18 June
Private	HAUER HENRY
Private	HEINTZE GEORGE
Private	HARTJE FREDK. Killed 18 June
Private	HEISE JURGEN
Private	HELLMERSCH FORSTER
Private	HELMBRECHT FREDK.
Private	HENNEICKE WM.
Private	HINSING HENRY
Private	HEPTA ANTHY.
Private	HERRMANN MARTIN
Private	HERRMAN JOHN
Private	HERTZ GEORGE
Private	HEUER LEWIS
Private	HEYSTER CHRISTN.
Private	HENZE FREDK. Discharged 4th Aug.
Private	HUHOO PAULINS
Private	HOLZWITTER HENRY
Private	HONIG CONRAD
Private	HORN MATHIAS
Private	HUG FREDK. Discharged 4 Aug.
Private	HUMMEL FERDINAND
Private	JACOB JOHN
Private	JAN JOHN
Private	JANKSACK LUCAS
Private	JAININSKY JOHN
Private	JANTIZ JOHN
Private	JANOTTE JOSEPH
Private	JANOWSKY BLASINS
Private	JANSEN ANDREW
Private	JARITZ PETER
Private	JACK FRANZ
Private	JERRAVA LEWAS
Private	IGNATS DANIEL
Private	JOHANNES FREDK.
Private	JONSARK THOS.
Private	JUNG PETER
Private	JUNGMEISTER JOHN
Private	JUNGEMANN HENRY Discharged 4 Aug.
Private	KATZMIOCK WOITZCOK
Private	KAH:E JOHN
Private	KASIMETZO STANILAUS
Private	KAUFMANN FREDK. Discharged 4 Aug.

Private KEISER LEWIS
Private KHUN ADAM
Private KIDELSKY CASIMIER
Private KIESELER AUGUST
Private KIRSCH PETER
Private KIRSCHNER WM.
Private KIRSCHNER MARTIN Discharged 4th August
Private KLENDRICK FREDK. Discharged 4th August
Private KLEMENS MICHL.
Private KLINGLY JOSEPH
Private KLOPS ANDREW
Private KLOTZ FREDK.
Private KNAPP GEORGE
Private KNUPLOST ANDREW
Private KNUPPEL CONRAD
Private KOHLER DANIEL
Private KOGE MICHL.
Private KOLESERN JOSEPH
Private KOMENS DAVID
Private KOWALSKY ANTY.
Private KRABON PETER
Private KRESSING CHRISTN. Discharged 4th August
Private KRESER JOSEPH
Private KREMER NICOLAUS
Private KREYBOHN AUGUST Died of Wounds 19 June 1815
Private KNIETER HENRY KRIETER
Private KROMER JACOB
Private KRUVKE WM. Discharged 4 Aug.
Private KRUGER JOHN Killed 18 June
Private KRUGER LEWIS Killed 18 June
Private KRUSE CHAS.
Private KUHLEN JOHN
Private KUMMER THEOPHILUS
Private KUNTZE CONRAD
Private KUTSCHE GOTTLIEB
Private KUVAR CHRISTN.
Private LANGERBEIN HENRY
Private LANGENES FREDK.
Private LASSOWY STEPN.
Private LEHMANN ANDREW
Private LEIFERMANN HENRY
Private LENECKE HENRY
Private LEONHARD HENRY Discharged 4th August
Private LIDA JAMES
Private LINGEMANN PETER
Private LINNEMANN PETER
Private LOCKEMANN HENRY
Private LONDT PETER
Private LUBBERT CHRISTOPH
Private LUNDT FREDK.
Private LUNGRY JOSEPH
Private LUPKE JOHN
Private LUTTICH JOHN
Private LEIVER PAUL
Private MACK FRANZ
Private MANNO PHILIP
Private MARCKOFF CHRISTN.
Private MARSECK THEODOR
Private MARTIN GODFRY
Private MATERS RUDH Sotheby's sale 1908
Private MATHENS JOHN
Private MATHZACK PETER
Private MATSCHINECK JOHN
Private MATSCHINECK PETER
Private MATTHEW FRANS.
Private MAUER JOHN
Private MEAMEL ADOLPHUS
Private MEHRING JOHN
Private MELIUS CONRAD
Private MERCK CHRISTN.
Private MESSENBRINK HENRY
Private MEYER GEORGE Discharged 4 Aug.
Private MEYER ANTHY. Killed 18 June
Private MEYER MICHL.
Private MILBRA CHRISTN.
Private MINATZCOK ADAM
Private MELITORS FRANZ
Private MONNECKEL ANTHY.
Private MULLER CHRISTN.
Private MULLER CH.
Private MULLER CHRSITN.
Private MULLER MATTW.
Private MULLER HENRY
Private MUNDEG JOHN
Private NAGATSKY IVAN
Private NAVARRA JOSEPH
Private NEUMANN GEDFREY
Private NEUTEL JOHN
Private NEUTH JOHN
Private NIEDER BERND.
Private NIEDERPELL JACOB
Private NIEMANN CHRISTN. Killed 18 June
Private NIZELSKY PEDRO

Private	NOCADIS MARTIN
Private	NOLS JOSEPH
Private	NORKSWITZ LORENZ
Private	NOVELASKY PETER Discharged 4th August
Private	OFZERAT PETER
Private	OLSEN PETER
Private	PENECKE FREDK.
Private	PERMITZSKY ANTHY.
Private	PETER GEORGE
Private	PIONOWSKY MICHL.
Private	PITZACH PETER
Private	PLATE HENRY
Private	POLACHOFSKY ANDREW Killed 18 June
Private	POLATUSH IGNATZ
Private	POLEY FREDK.
Private	POLOFSKY MATHIES
Private	PRUSS GODFRY
Private	QUADEL ENGELBRECHT
Private	RAKOF JOHN
Private	RASCH ERNEST Discharged 4th August
Private	REDLER GERHARD
Private	REESH HENRY
Private	REIMERT LEWIS
Private	REINECKE HENRY
Private	RIGGS ANDREW
Private	RINGE FREDK.
Private	RINTELMANN CONRAD Killed 18th June
Private	RODLER ANTHY.
Private	ROHRMAN FREDK.
Private	ROSENBERG CHRISTN.
Private	ROSENBERGER JOHN
Private	ROSKFSKY GREGOR
Private	ROSETT FREDK. Gray Coll.1908
Private	ROSSWALD DIEDK.
Private	RUBERTS GERHARD
Private	RUDOLPH JOSEPH
Private	RUDOLPH HENRY
Private	RUTHLICH JOSEPH
Private	RUSHKA ANDREW
Private	SACKENDAN JOHN
Private	SACKEL HENRY
Private	SACKMANN JOSEPH
Private	SAYOSKY JEAN
Private	SALEMENN LEWIS
Private	SCHAPER HENRY
Private	SCHELLHAUER JOHN
Private	SCHLAEGER CHRISTN.
Private	SCHMEDECKE CHRISTN.
Private	SCHMIDT JOHN
Private	SCHMIDT JOSEPH
Private	SCHOFER BATHW.
Private	SHOOS PHILLIPH
Private	SCHRADER CHRISTN.
Private	SCHRADER LEWIS
Private	SCHARDER FREDK.
Private	SCHARDER ANDREW
Private	SCHREIBER JOSEPH Discharged 4 Aug
Private	SCHREIBER FREDK. Killed 18 June
Private	SCHRODER DANIEL Discharged 4 Aug
Private	SCHULER GEORGE Died of wounds 22nd June 1815
Private	SCHULTZ JOHN
Private	SCHULZE FREDK.
Private	SCHULZE CHRISTIAN
Private	SCHULZE JAACHIM
Private	SCHULZE GODFRY
Private	SCHURE SEBATIAN Died of wounds 6th July 1815
Private	SCHULTE ANTHY.
Private	SCHWERTZEL FREDL. Discharged 4th August
Private	SCHWARTZ HERMAN
Private	SEITZ GEORGE
Private	SERWATSWICK ADAM
Private	SEVERIN FREDK.
Private	SEYPNICKY JOHN
Private	SIDON CHRISTN.
Private	SITZER JOHN Died of wounds 28th June 1815
Private	SOBADATSCH MICHAEL
Private	SONNTAG HENRY Discharged 4 Aug.
Private	STAHLBAUM HENRY
Private	STEINWEDEL ERNEST
Private	STENZEL JURGEN
Private	STEPHAN JOHN
Private	STEPHAN ANTHY.
Private	STEMINSKY JOHN
Private	STURZENBERGER MICHAEL
Private	TORNAGROTSKY STANILAUS
Private	TASCHOCK THOS.
Private	TERTZIE PHILLIPH
Private	THIELE JAMES Discharged 4 Aug.
Private	THIELEBEULE FREDK. Discharged 4th August
Private	THIES PHILLIPH

Private	THOMANN GEORGE
Private	THOMAS HENRY
Private	TOLLE CHRISTN.
Private	TOMASCHOFSKY SEBASTIAN
Private	TOMATE THOS.
Private	TONIEGER THOS.
Private	TOPF CHAS.
Private	TOYKA THOMAS
Private	TRUMPER FREDK. Discharged 4th August 1815
Private	UHRIG NICOLAUS
Private	ULMS HENRY Discharged 4 Aug.
Private	ULRICH JNS.(Snr)
Private	ULRICH JNS (Jnr)
Private	VANDERBUSCH JOHN
Private	VANDERKEHLE FREDK.
Private	VANDERLAHN HENRY
Private	VIRTELHAUSFN CH. Discharged 4th August
Private	VOLLMER HERMAN
Private	VOLMERDNIG CHRISTOPH
Private	VANBARLOW HENRY
Private	WACHORSKY PETER
Private	WAHLMANN HENRY Discharged 4th August
Private	WASKOWITZ JOHN
Private	WASSILLER STEPHAN
Private	WANISDEIN JOHN
Private	WATSCHKOFSKY JACOB
Private	WEBER GOTTLIEB
Private	WEBER CHAS.
Private	WEGEUER HENRY Discharged 4th August
Private	WEISS JOHN
Private	WEGEUER CHAS.
Private	WOITZIG PAUL
Private	WELLHAUSER JOHN
Private	WERNEBERG CHRISTN.
Private	WIDDEL DANIEL
Private	WIECHERS JOHN
Private	WIEGMANN CHRISTOPH
Private	WEISEMEYER HENRY
Private	WILKE CONRAD
Private	WILLEOFSKY JOSEPH
Private	WILLOVENSKY WIVINZ
Private	WITTESCHORK SIMON
Private	WOCATSCHEG FRANS.
Private	WOITSCHECK NICOLAUS
Private	WOLTERS CHRISTN.
Private	WORETZSKY MICHAEL
Private	WORESCHAULK IVAN
Private	ZIMMERMANN CHAS.
Private	ZIMMERMANN JOSH.

* * *

2nd LINE BATTALION K.G.L.

Major	MULLER GEORGE
Captain	DECKEN WM.
Captain	HARTMANN AUGUST
Captain	PURGOLD FREDK.
Captain	TILCE GEORGE Died of wounds 19th June 1815
Captain	BEURMANN CHARLES
Captain	WYNECKEN CLAUS
Captain	HENCKSTERN FREDK.
Captain	WOOLKENAAR GEORGE
Lieutenant	DECKEN CLAUS
Lieutenant	KULEMANN WM.
Lieutenant	TIENSCH GODFRY
Lieutenant	FLEISCH ERNEST
Lieutenant	HESSE ADOLPHUS (Adjut)
Lieutenant	BILLEB CHAS.
Lieutenant	MEYER GEORGE
Lieutenant	KATHMANN AUGUST
Lieutenant	PASCHAL FREDK.
Lieutenant	KESSLER ADOLPHUS
Lieutenant	DAWSON WM. Whitaker Coll.1908
Lieutenant	HAMILTON JAMES
Lieutenant	GAIRDNER PATK.
Lieutenant	FISCHER CHARLES
Lieutenant	LA ROCHE FRANCIS
Lieutenant	LOWSON GEORGE
Lieutenant	ZIEL AUGUST
Lieutenant	SICHART HENRY
Ensign	SICHART LEWIS
Ensign	STEGLITZ ADOLPHUS
Ensign	LYNSH ADOLPHUS
Ensign	DISELHORST FREDK.
Ensign	HARTMANN GUSTAV
Ensign	BERGMANN HENRY
Private	GARVENS HENRY
Private	USLAR TILO V.
Private	LUNING AUGUST
Surgeon	THOMPSON CHAS.
Ass.Surgeon	RATHJE HENRY
Ass.Surgeon	SCHCHART HENRY
Qr.Master	SCHILVESTER JOHN
Sjt.Major	SEMROTH HENRY
Q.M.S.	SCHIDEMANN CHARLES

Ar.Serjeant	REINBOLD FREDK.
Dr.Major	STURM FREDK.
Serjeant	ALBRECHT NICOLAUS
Serjeant	BERKHAUSEN GODLAY
Serjeant	BERTRAM FREDK.
Serjeant	BEGGE LOUIS
Serjeant	BRUNOTTE CONRAD
Serjeant	DAMMAN GEORGE
Serjeant	DOGGENFUSS WM.
Serjeant	ECKERT AUGUST
Serjeant	ELERHAGEN WM.
Serjeant	ENGELBRECHT HENRY
Serjeant	FETTE CHRISTOPH
Serjeant	FISCHER CONRAD
Serjeant	FISCHER CHRISTIAN
Serjeant	FLORKE LEWIS
Serjeant	GERCKE GEORGE
Serjeant	GRIMPE HENRY
Serjeant	GUNDLACH CONRAD Killed 18th June
Serjeant	HENCKEL LEWIS
Serjeant	HOCKSTEIN WM.
Serjeant	KLUNDER FREDK.
Serjeant	LINDE LEWIS
Serjeant	LIPPMANN GEORGE
Serjeant	LOUIS JOHN
Serjeant	LUTJENS HENRY
Serjeant	MARTENS FREDK.
Serjeant	MUHLERT HENRY
Serjeant	MULLER CHRISTOPH
Serjeant	MULLER JOHN
Serjeant	OLDELAND ERNST
Serjeant	RUHMANN HENRY
Serjeant	SCHMECK FREDK. Cheylesmore Collection 1908
Serjeant	SCHNEIDER JOHN
Serjeant	SCHWEIGHART GEORGE
Serjeant	SIMPSON JOHN Col.Murray's Collection 1908
Serjeant	STEINECKE JOHN
Serjeant	THIELE HENRY
Serjeant	THIELEMANN ERNST
Serjeant	FROST SIGISMUND
Serjeant	TUBBE FREDK.
Serjeant	TWIETMEYER ANTHY
Serjeant	VEIT HENRY
Serjeant	WIETZEL MICHL.
Corporal	ALEXANDER WM.
Corporal	BENING LEWIS
Corporal	BERKENPIEL FRANS. Died of Wounds 3rd August 1815
Corporal	BUSCH FREDK.
Corporal	DREYER HENRY
Corporal	EDLER JOHN
Corporal	EICHE ERICK
Corporal	FELTON CHRISTIAN
Corporal	GERBERDING DIEDRICK
Corporal	GOLISCH LEWIS
Corporal	GREENEWALD FRANCIS
Corporal	GULLET JOHN
Corporal	HESSE CASPER
Corporal	HOFFMANN HENRY
Corporal	JACOB CHAS.
Corporal	JACOBY JOHN
Corporal	KASTAN HENRY
Corporal	KIECKER FREDK. Killed 18 June
Corporal	KULTZE HENRY
Corporal	MEYER CONRAD
Corporal	MUSCHLER FREDK.
Corporal	OBLADEN ANTHONY
Corporal	PAETZMANN AUGUST
Corporal	REIMERS PETER
Corporal	SCHAFFER FREDK.
Corporal	SCLIEPER CHRISTN.
Corporal	SCHNEIDER FRANCIS Killed 18 June
Corporal	SCHNEIDER MICHAEL
Corporal	SCHULTZE AUGUST
Corporal	TEUTEBERG FREDERICK
Corporal	WARNECKE FREDK.
Corporal	ZAHN AUGUST
Drummer	BENTIZ DANIEL
Drummer	BULGER CHARLES
Drummer	HAGEMANN DANIEL
Drummer	HELMS LEWIS
Drummer	HEFS JOHN
Drummer	KREBS JOHN
Drummer	PAPE FREDK.
Drummer	PAPPE JOHN
Drummer	PETERSEN WM.
Drummer	SEITZ DANIEL
Drummer	TOTT HERY
Private	ACHILLES GODFRY
Private	AHLY GEORGE
Private	AHREND ANDREW
Private	AHRENHOLD DIEDRICK
Private	AHRENS HERMANN
Private	AHRENSHEDT CONRAD
Private	AHRIA JOSEPH Killed 18 June
Private	ALBINSKY CASIMIR
Private	ALEITA CASPER

Private	ANDERSON EDWD.
Private	ANITY CASPER
Private	ANTHONY PETER
Private	ANTONOWEA THOS.
Private	AUSSEN VINCENT
Private	BABEROTSKY ALBERT
Private	BACKHAUS HENRY
Private	BADER CHARLES
Private	BALSBERGER JOHN
Private	BANN FRANS.
Private	BARRICO GEORGE
Private	BARTELS PETER
Private	BATTEL JAMES
Private	BAUER CONRAD
Private	BAUM GEORGE
Private	BAUM HENRY
Private	BEHREN BERND.
Private	BINDENER WOITSCH
Private	BINZE ANTHONY
Private	BISCHOFF JOHN
Private	BLAUSCHUTZ DANIEL
Private	BOCK NICOLAUS
Private	BODE GODFRY
Private	BOHNE ANDREW
Private	BOLLIES NICOLAUS
Private	BOLTE CHRISTOPH
Private	BONN ROHMAN
Private	BOTTGER ANDREW
Private	BRAND DIDRICK
Private	BRAND FREDK. Killed 18th June 1815
Private	BRANDT FREDK.
Private	BRANSE JOHN
Private	BRAUN GODLIEB
Private	BROBECK JAMES
Private	BROCKMULLER AUGUST
Private	BROZOSKY JOHN
Private	BUSCHBECK THOS.
Private	BUTCHOLZ CASTEN
Private	BOKOSKY ANDREW
Private	BUTKOSKY VALENTIN
Private	BUTTERWORTH WM.
Private	BREY JOHN
Private	CANT PETER
Private	CAROLWITZ ANTHONY
Private	CASPER ABRM. Killed 18 June
Private	CASSAN HENRY
Private	CHEER IGNATZ
Private	CORDES JOHN

Private	COWATSCH FREDK. Killed 18 June
Private	CREMER THEODOR
Private	CROAN HENRY
Private	DANNECKE JOSEPH
Private	DANNENFELDT JURGEN
Private	DAVID CHARLES
Private	DEBRUN FRANS.
Private	DEDOBBLER LAMBERT
Private	DELAMINSKY JOSEPH
Private	DEMUTH WM.
Private	DEPART JAMES
Private	DERUDDER PETER
Private	DIDERICH HENRY
Private	DISMER GEORGE
Private	DOMANSKY JOHN
Private	DOMBROSKY SIMON
Private	DONNINGER SEBATIAN
Private	DOTTE JOSEPH
Private	DREPKA PAUL
Private	DRUCKE CHRISTIAN
Private	DUDECK THOS.
Private	DUHM PETER
Private	DUNCKAKE HENRY
Private	DURMONT JOSEPH
Private	DUMARCK HENRY
Private	DRIANOSKY WAIECK
Private	EDLER FREDK.
Private	EHRENBERG NATHAN
Private	ELSNER JOSEPH
Private	ENGEL CONRADE
Private	ERNSTBERGER JAMES
Private	FAHRENBERG DANIEL
Private	FERBETZAK GEORGE
Private	FERRIOR IGNATZ
Private	FINGER GEORGE
Private	FISCHER HENRY
Private	FISCHER LEWIS
Private	FITZ ANDREW
Private	FLADING FREDK.
Private	FLORY BLASY
Private	FRANCISKO ANTHY.
Private	FREYFOGEL JAMES
Private	FRICKE PHILLIP
Private	FRIEDERICHS ANTHY.
Private	FUHRENBERG HENRY
Private	FUHRHOP DAVID
Private	GANRIEL CHRISTIAN
Private	GAIDOMAWITZ ANTHONY
Private	GAYDUSCH JOSEPH

Private	GEORGE GODFRY
Private	GERHARD FREDK.
Private	GILLES PHILLIP
Private	GLABACH JOHN Killed 18 June
Private	GLUCK DANIEL
Private	GOROWSKY MARTIN
Private	GRADIG ANDREW
Private	GRAULICH DANIEL
Private	GRONAN DIDRIK
Private	GROSS HENRY
Private	GUNTHER HENRY Killed 18 June
Private	GUNTHER WM.
Private	HALLEGO CHRISTN.
Private	HANSON LAAS
Private	HAMUSKA CHARLES
Private	HARTMANN FREDK.
Private	HARTZMEYER DIEDK.
Private	HAVENSCHILDT JAMES
Private	HEIDE HENRY
Private	HEINE HENRY
Private	HEISE HENRY
Private	HEISTER FREDK.
Private	HELMKER CHRISTN.
Private	HENKE JOHN
Private	HENNIGES CHRISTN.
Private	HERMAN ANDREW
Private	HESSE ANDREW
Private	HESSE CHRISTIAN
Private	HESSE DAVID
Private	HESSE FREDK.
Private	HESSE HENRY
Private	HINTZE CHARLES
Private	HUSSING WM.
Private	HOFFMANN ADAM
Private	HOFFMANN HENRY
Private	HOFFMEISTER PHILIP
Private	HOLZDERBER JOHN
Private	HOLZMANN HENRY
Private	HUMBURG PETER
Private	HUTH JOHN
Private	JACONET CHRISTOPH
Private	JAANDEHEER FRANCIS
Private	JANEZACK SIMON
Private	IDANER GEORGE
Private	INMICH PETER
Private	JURKA THOMAS
Private	JUSEZACK VALENTIN
Private	KABISCHECK MARTIN
Private	KOROFSKY THOMAS
Private	KAGURA MICHL.
Private	KALL JOHN
Private	KAMINSKY ANDREW
Private	KAMINSKY PETER
Private	KAMP JOHN
Private	KANNENBERG PETER
Private	KARNEBOH CHARLES
Private	KASTEN COBRAD
Private	KAUFFMANN ERNEST Killed 18 June
Private	KECKER HENRY
Private	KEELING JOSEPH
Private	KELLENARD JOHN
Private	KELLNER FREDK.
Private	KIMMENA CHRISTIAN
Private	KILMAUNS MICHL.
Private	KILMARDT JOSEPH
Private	KIRCHNER WM.
Private	KLAGES FREDK.
Private	KLEMAN CHRISTIAN
Private	KLOSTER FRANCIS
Private	KNEBAL JOSEPH
Private	KNOLLE FREDK.
Private	KOBURG CHRISTN.
Private	KOLBE FREDK.
Private	KOLLMANN HENRY
Private	KOLLMEYER CONRAD
Private	KONECKE CHARLES
Private	KONIG WM.
Private	KOPPELMEYER JOHN
Private	KORABY ALEX.
Private	KORING GODFRY
Private	KORTES WM.
Private	KOSS GEORGE
Private	KOSSMINER FRANS.
Private	KOSSMINSKY JOHN
Private	KRAḰOBITZSKY MARTIN
Private	KRANZ WM.
Private	KRAUSS LEOPOLD
Private	KRECH GEORGE
Private	KRIPSKY ROOHAN
Private	KUHNE JOHN
Private	KULZE EDMUND
Private	KUNZ JOSEPH
Private	KUROSSKY JOHN
Private	LAAS CHRISTIAN
Private	LANGE WM.
Private	LAUMANN CHAS.
Private	LEGANSKY ANTHONY
Private	LEHNE WM.

Private	LEONHARDT GODRAY
Private	LEPP ANTHONY
Private	LERECKE BENDIC.
Private	LEWANDOSSKY JOSEPH
Private	LINDENSCHMIDT CHRISTOPH
Private	LINDER GEORGE
Private	LORCH FREDK.
Private	LUNZMANN GERHARD
Private	LUOS CHRISTIAN
Private	LUPKE MICHL.
Private	MAARS JOHN Gaskell Collection 1908
Private	MANDELICK JOSEPH
Private	MARTCHINS ANTHONY
Private	MARTIN PHILIP
Private	MARTINS BENEDICT
Private	MAN JOHN
Private	MECHLER CHARLES
Private	MENDON ADOLPH
Private	MEYER ANTHONY
Private	MEYER FREDK.
Private	MEYER HENRY
Private	MEYER JOHN
Private	MEYER LEWIS
Private	MEYER PETER
Private	MICHEL PHILIP
Private	MULBACH VINCENT
Private	MULLER CHAS.
Private	MULLER FREDK.
Private	MULLER JAMES
Private	MULLER NICOLAUS
Private	MULLER FREDK.
Private	NAGEL JOHN
Private	NAUHARDT ADAM
Private	NEHRLICH HENRY
Private	NELLY THOS.
Private	NERJES LEWIS
Private	NEUMANN JOHN
Private	NEWMANN FREDK.
Private	NEUMANN HENRY
Private	NIEMEYER WM.
Private	NIERSCAK JOHN Killed 18 June
Private	NOLTE WM.
Private	OPPERMANN LORENZ
Private	PARROW JOHN
Private	PATTEROCK NICOLAUS
Private	PETERMANNS JAMES
Private	PETRUS JOHN
Private	PFEFFERLEE PILLARY
Private	PFENNIG CHRISTIAN
Private	PLIANECK JOSEPH Galway Coll.1910
Private	PINPEL PETER
Private	PAVELOT BARTHW.
Private	PURTNER LEOPOLD
Private	RACKE CHRISTIAN
Private	RADOW ABRM.
Private	RAUSCH CHRISTIAN
Private	RAUSCHENBACH GODFRY
Private	RAUTH SEBASTIAN
Private	REHLANDER CONRAD
Private	REICHERT HENRY Gray Coll.1908
Private	REIMANN HENRY
Private	REINERS HENRY
Private	REINHARD JOHN
Private	REITTEMEYER CHRISTIAN
Private	REISSINGER NICOLAUS
Private	REIMER ANTHONY
Private	RINSCH JOHN
Private	REPIATER JOHN
Private	REISHERS WM.
Private	RICKE CHRISTIAN
Private	RICKE HENRY
Private	RODEMUNDE FREDK.
Private	ROHLEDER AUGUST
Private	RONSCHKOFSKY MARTIN
Private	ROSENLACHER CHRISTIAN
Private	ROTH GODLIEB
Private	ROTHE CHRISTIAN
Private	ROUTSCH PETER
Private	RUFF JOHN
Private	RUHNE DIDRICK
Private	RUST FREDK.
Private	ROSEMOD JOHN
Private	SABO JOSEPH
Private	SABOLSACH JOHN Killed 18 June
Private	SALOMON JOHN
Private	SAMUEL JOSEPH
Private	SANDER ANDREW
Private	SATTLER FREDK.
Private	SCHAEFER CHAS.
Private	SCHAFFER HENRY
Private	SCHARMAN DAVID
Private	SCHIFFER JOSEPH
Private	SCHIVELTZ MARTIN
Private	SCHLEBACH HENRY
Private	SCHOLESING JOHN
Private	SCHMIDT GEORGE
Private	SCHMIDT JOHN

Private	SCHMIDT PETER
Private	SCHNEIDER GEORGE
Private	SCHNEIDER HENRY
Private	SCHNELL CHRISTIAN
Private	SCHNARK JOHN
Private	SCHROT JOHN
Private	SCHULZ CHRISTIAN
Private	SCHULZ CHRISTIAN
Private	SCHULZ JOHN
Private	SCHULZE HENRY
Private	SCHULTZE JOHN
Private	SCHURENDORSKY MARTIN
Private	SCHWACHHEIM HENRY
Private	SCHWARTZ HUBERT
Private	SCHWEBLE JOSEPH
Private	SCHWEIGHARDT GEORGE Littledale sale Nov.1910
Private	SCHWIDALSKY JAMES
Private	SCHWIENNIG HENRY
Private	SEELE HENRY
Private	SEIBERT GEORGE
Private	SEIFFERT CHAS.
Private	SEITZECK JOSEPH
Private	SEITLER JOHN
Private	SIEBURG LEWIS
Private	SIGNALEE MICHL.
Private	SINGSHEIM JACOB
Private	SINN PETER
Private	SKUPIN MARTIN
Private	SOBOLOSKY CASIMIR
Private	SPINDLER ERNEST
Private	SPIES FREDK.
Private	STEINWAY JOHN
Private	STEPHAN WM.
Private	STEYERS CHAS. Killed 18 June
Private	STIEGHAN LOUIS
Private	STILLENGRASS FREDK.
Private	STOBESAND CHRISTIAN
Private	STRUBE HENRY
Private	SCHEDING HENRY
Private	THUNPONT JOSEPH
Private	THIMAVEC KUSMA
Private	TIETJE CHRISTIAN
Private	TOKUTS JOHN
Private	TOMJACK JOSEPH
Private	TRAWSCHOCK JAMES
Private	TREYLE NICOLAUS Killed 18 June
Private	TRETTKISKY STANISLAUS

Private	ULLEMANN BERND.
Private	ULMIS CLEMANT
Private	UWARY MARTIN
Private	VALEUCKER ANTHONY
Private	VANCART CHAS.
Private	VANDERWERF WM.
Private	VANIFENBURG JOSEPH
Private	VANMEALKORPF PETER
Private	VANDERBERG PETER Payne Coll.1911
Private	VELGER SEBASTIAN
Private	VOGEL ANTHONY
Private	VOGELSANG CHRISTIAN
Private	VOLOKER HENRY
Private	VOLMER CHRISTIAN
Private	VONS ANDREW
Private	WACHENHEIM VALENTIN
Private	WAGENER ADAM
Private	WAGENER CHAS.
Private	WANNOWITZ JOHN
Private	WEBER FREDK.
Private	WECHTER HENRY
Private	WEDEKIND HENRY
Private	WEDEMANN HENRY
Private	WAGERICH CHRISTIAN
Private	WAGENER CONRAD
Private	WEISSMANTEL JOHN
Private	WIMARSKY FLORIA
Private	WARLE PHILIP
Private	WERNER HENRY
Private	WESSLING WM.
Private	WETZEL ANTHONY
Private	WEGERICH NICOLAUS
Private	WICKERS DIDRICK
Private	WIEGAND CHRISTIAN
Private	WILL CONRAD
Private	WILL JOHN
Private	WILLERS GEORGE
Private	WINDHOLZ ANDREW
Private	WINCKLER FREDK.
Private	WITTACHOCK STANILAUS
Private	WITTMER FREDK.
Private	WOLFF HENRY
Private	WOUTRIGANT JOSEPH
Private	WUNSCH JOHN
Private	WUNDERLICH CHAS.
Private	WOESTENFELD WM.
Private	ZUNERT CHRISTIAN
Private	ZIGELER FREDK.

Private	ZELINSKY VALENTIN
Private	ZINECKE JOHN
Private	FREYSE HENRY From 7th Line Battalion
Private	MEYER ANTHONY From 6th Line Battn. Killed 18 June

* * *

3rd LINE BATTALION K.G.L.

Lt.Colonel	de WESSELL FREDK.
Major	de LUTTERMANN FREDK.
Major	BOD en ANTHONY
Captain	de HOHNHORST GEORGE
Captain	de DREVES LEWIS Whitaker Collection 1908
Captain	CURREN AUGUSTUS
Captain	LUEDER EWERARD
Captain	LESCHEN FREDK.
Captain	de SCHLEICHER WM.
Captain	PRIDEL FREDK. Killed 18 June
Captain	CORDEMANN ALBERT
Lieutenant	TERNIM JUSTUS
Lieutenant	de USLAR HANS Gaskell Collection 1908 Payne 1911
Lieutenant	APPUHN GEORGE
Lieutenant	de HEINBURG FREDK.
Lieutenant	BRAUNS CHAS.
Lieutenant	de TEINSEN FREDK. Died of Wounds
Lieutenant	de SODEN CHRISTAIN
Lieutenant	SCHNEIDER BERND. (Adjut)
Lieutenant	de LAFFERT WEYPART
Lieutenant	KUCKUCK AUGUSTUS
Lieutenant	BRINKMANN JULIUS
Lieutenant	DEHNEL HENRY
Lieutenant	le BACHELLE LEWIS
Lieutenant	LESCHEN FREDK. Died of Wounds
Lieutenant	KUCKUCK EDWD.
Ensign	de STORREN FREDK.
Ensign	de SCHLUTTER FREDK.
Ensign	de SADE AUGUSTUS
Ensign	KUCK AUGUSTUS WM.
Ensign	HUCEDEN RICHARD Glendining's sale Dec.1909
Ensign	BODEWALD ERNSET
Ensign	BREYMANN FREDK.
Ensign	de RONNE FREDK.
Ensign	BEUERMANN ERNEST
Ensign	de USLAR ADOLPHUS
Qr.Master	LEVIEN FREDK.
Surgeon	STUNZ LEWIS
Ass.Surgeon	SCHUNTERMANN CHAS.
Ass.Surgeon	DEGENHARD FRANS.
Sjt.Major	BENDROT LUDOLPHUS Discharged
Q.M.S.	BUGSING FREDK.
P.M.S.	ASCHENLAMP LEWIS
Ar.Serjeant	WIEGERS AUGUSTUS
Dr.Major	BERTRAM CONRAD
Serjeant	BORNEMAN CONRADE
Serjeant	DECKER CHAS.
Serjeant	DIEDERICKS CHRISTIAN
Serjeant	EMSHOFF HENRY
Serjeant	GOTTING JOHN
Serjeant	GRETHE CHRISTOPH
Serjeant	GRIESBACH FREDK.
Serjeant	GROBE FREDK. Discharged
Serjeant	HECKER CHRISTIAN Discharged
Serjeant	HOLZE GEORGE
Serjeant	HOPPSTEDT FREDK.
Serjeant	KLEINSCHMIDT LEWIS
Serjeant	KNOLLE HENRY
Serjeant	KONECKE FREDK.
Serjeant	LANZ HERMANN
Serjeant	LERCHE CONRADE
Serjeant	LULLE ANDREW
Serjeant	MEYER FREDK.
Serjeant	MEYER HENRY
Serjeant	MULLER GEORGE
Serjeant	PLINCKE HENRY
Serjeant	PLOITZE HENRY
Serjeant	PROFFEN ERNEST
Serjeant	REINDLE CHAS. Discharged
Serjeant	REINESHE FREDK.
Serjeant	RICKMANN HENRY
Serjeant	RUGSE HENRY
Serjeant	SCHUERBREY CHRISTIAN
Serjeant	SCHAPER HENRY Glendining's Sale March 1912
Serjeant	SCRODER CHRISTIAN
Serjeant	SIEVERS CHRISTIAN
Serjeant	STERNBERG LUDOLPHUS
Serjeant	ULRICH LEWIS Killed 18 June
Serjeant	VOLLMANN CHRISTIAN
Serjeant	WERCKMEISTER ALBERT Discharged
Corporal	BAHR CHAS.
Corporal	BAUMGART HENRY Discharged
Corporal	BELLER CHRISTIAN Died of Wounds

Corporal	BIERMANN JUSTUS Discharged
Corporal	BRICKNER CHRISTIAN
Corporal	BRINCKMANN CHRISTIAN
Corporal	COLONIUS WM.
Corporal	DAMMANN WM.
Corporal	DEMPEWOLF CHAS.
Corporal	DIEHLE AUHUSTUS Discharged
Corporal	DRAHMANN JOHN
Corporal	ENGELBRECHT HENRY
Corporal	GROTE FREDK.
Corporal	HENCKEL HENRY
Corporal	HESS JOHN
Corporal	HILFER CHAS.
Corporal	KOHLEWAY JOHN
Corporal	KOLLE FERDINAND Discharged
Corporal	KREIG FREDK.
Corporal	KUSTER HENRY
Corporal	MEYER FREDK.
Corporal	MUNTE HENRY
Corporal	NORTEMANN CHRISTIAN Killed 18 June
Corporal	PAULSEN GEORGE
Corporal	RIEFKOHLL CHRISTIAN Killed 18 June
Corporal	RIPPE GEORGE Discharged
Corporal	SCHULZE FREDK.
Corporal	SENGEWALD FREDK.
Corporal	SIEVERS LEWIS
Corporal	VIERKE JOHN
Corporal	WEISE THEOPHILUS
Corporal	WESTPHAL FREDK.
Corporal	WITTHUHN JOHN
Drummer	BEHNE HENRY
Drummer	BIERMANN FREDK.
Drummer	BOTTGER AUGUSTUS
Drummer	COLONIUS HENRY
Drummer	FEDEL WM.
Drummer	GREVE CHRISTIAN
Drummer	GUNDLACH FREDK. Discharged
Drummer	LICHTENBURG HENRY
Drummer	MOURTZEN FREDK.
Drummer	SEHEN NICOLAUS
Drummer	WALDHAUSEN AUGUSTUS
Drummer	WERBA ALBERT
Private	ABEL JAMES Discharged
Private	ADAM MATHEW
Private	AHRENS ERNEST Discharged
Private	AHRENS WM. Discharged
Private	ALBERS HENRY

Private	ALLMACHER FREDK.
Private	ANDERSON NICLS.
Private	ANDREAS RALPH
Private	ANNECKE FREDK.
Private	APELMANN FERDK.
Private	BAARS HENRY
Private	BACHMANN FREDK. Discharged
Private	BACHR HY.FREDK.
Private	BAHN FREDK.
Private	BANCO JOHN
Private	BARTELS GEORGE
Private	BASITZYKY ANTHONY
Private	BAUER FREDK.
Private	BAYER HENRY
Private	BEAU CONRAD
Private	BECKER CONRAD Discharged
Private	BECKER FREDK.
Private	BECKER HENRY
Private	BECKER JOHN
Private	BEHNSEN OTTO
Private	BEHRENS WM.
Private	BERCKE HENRY Killed 18 June
Private	BERGFELD CHAS.
Private	BERGES WM.
Private	BERGHAUSEN HENRY
Private	BERNKAMP HENRY
Private	BIERMANN FREDK.(Senr)
Private	BIERMANN FREDK.(Junr) Discharged
Private	BITTERBERG LEWIS
Private	BLANCKE ERNEST Discharged
Private	BLUME LEOPOLD
Private	BODE CONRADE Killed 18 June
Private	BODE GEORGE
Private	BODE HENRY Killed 18 June
Private	BODENSTEIN HENRY
Private	BOEGERS ANTHONY
Private	BOECKER CONRADE
Private	BOLTE HENRY Discharged
Private	BONICOFKY JOHN
Private	BORCHERS HENRY
Private	BORGER HENRY
Private	BRANDES LEWIS
Private	BRANDES GEORGE
Private	BRANNING LEWIS Discharged
Private	BRUNS CHAS.
Private	BUDDE HERMANN
Private	BUHRDORP WM. Discharged
Private	BUNDING HENRY

Private	CARL GEORGE
Private	CARL HENRY
Private	CELLE HENRY
Private	CLEWE HENRY Killed 18 June
Private	COLONIUS LEWIS
Private	CONRADE JOHN
Private	DELION HENRY Discharged
Private	DEMASKY THOS.
Private	DENECKE HENRY
Private	DEPPE HENRY
Private	DETMERING LEWIS
Private	DERBINOF ANDREW
Private	DEZ SIEMON
Private	DICKER HENRY
Private	DIEDERICKS CHARLES
Private	DIERSON CHRISTIAN
Private	DIERSEN FREDK.
Private	DEISTEL CHRISTOPH
Private	DOBBERKY CHRISTIAN
Private	DOCKENFUS HENRY
Private	DOHRMANN HENRY
Private	DOHRSCHENKA MATRY.
Private	DORENWEND LUDOLPHUS Discharged
Private	DRESSING HENRY
Private	DREYER FREDK. Discharged
Private	DUEWELL JOHN Discharged
Private	DUREMECK STEPHAN
Private	EICKHOFF FREDK. Discharged Col.Gaskells sale May 1911
Private	EICKHOFF HENRY Discharged
Private	EISENSTADT JOSEPHUS
Private	ECHSTEIN JOHN
Private	ECHSTEIN MATTHEW
Private	ELDERMEYER CHARLES
Private	ELLSMANN HENRY
Private	ENCKHAUSEN ERNEST
Private	FANT ANOLD
Private	FEDEROSS JOHN Died of Wounds
Private	FENCKER DIEDERICK
Private	FERDINAND GEORGE
Private	FERGOTT JOHN
Private	FETTKOTHER CHRISTIAN
Private	FIGRETTO JOHN
Private	FILTER JOHN
Private	FISCHER CONRADE Discharged
Private	FISCHER JAMES
Private	FISCHER FREDK. Discharged
Private	FLEISCHMANN CHRISTIAN
Private	FLORETT PETER
Private	FOLTIMAN JOHN
Private	FREREK FREDK.
Private	FRICKE CHRISTIAN
Private	FUCHS ADAM
Private	GASTEL THEOPHILUS
Private	GAVRILLO PIETOS
Private	GIBE HENRY
Private	GEBECKE LEWIS
Private	GEHBAUER FREDK.
Private	GEHRKE WM.
Private	GEIGE CONRADE
Private	GELW LARS
Private	GENGE JOHN
Private	GERITZ REINHARD
Private	GERZ AUGUSTUS
Private	GEWECKE HENRY
Private	GIFFHORN CHRISTIAN Discharged
Private	GILDEHAUS HERMAN
Private	GLISMANN CONRADE
Private	GOHS LEWIS
Private	GOSLAR MICHL.
Private	GOTTENFELS JOHN
Private	GRAF CHAS.
Private	GREVE FREDK.
Private	GROB FREDK.
Private	GROHMEMEYER JOHN
Private	GROTE GEORGE
Private	GROTE PHILIP
Private	GRUHNE CHRISTOPHER
Private	GUILLIUS JOSEPHUS
Private	GUNTHER AUGUSTUS
Private	HALEEIGHT CONRADE
Private	HASPE LEWIS
Private	HAGEMANN ADAM
Private	HALLE XAVER Discharged
Private	HAMMERSCHMIDT HENRY
Private	HAMPE FREDK. Discharged
Private	HAMPE HENRY
Private	HARTMANN ADOLPHUS
Private	HARTMANN WM. Discharged
Private	HARTJE LAW WM.
Private	HARTING CONRADE Discharged
Private	HASTERFF JOHN
Private	HOTOPP FREDK.
Private	HOTOPP CHRISTR. Boy
Private	HEIDEMANN DANIEL
Private	HEILIGENSTADT JUSTUS
Private	HEINSOTH GEORGE

Private	HEINECKE CHAS. Discharged
Private	HEINMEYER CHRISTIAN
Private	HEINMEYER FREDK.
Private	HEINMEYER GEORGE
Private	HEINRICH BALTHASER
Private	HIETMAN HENRY
Private	HELLE HENRY
Private	HELLENBRECHT GEORGE Discharged
Private	HELMBALD JOHN
Private	HINCKELMANN CHAS.
Private	HENDRICKSON SAML.
Private	HENNE FREDK.
Private	HENNIGES FREDK. Killed 18th June
Private	HENNIGES HENRY Discharged
Private	HENIGSEN FREDK. Discharged Baldwins List July 1912
Private	HENNING CHRISTIAN
Private	HENZE CONRAD
Private	HEGUE HENRY
Private	HERRMANN WM.
Private	HILDEBRAND JOHN
Private	HILDEBRAND JOSEPHUS
Private	HILDEBRECHT ERNEST
Private	HILLMANN GEORGE Discharged
Private	HINZE CHAS. Discharged
Private	HIRSCHFELD HENRY Discharged
Private	HOBACH NICOLAS
Private	HOCHM PETER
Private	HOER ANDREW
Private	HOFFARTH SIMON
Private	HOMANN FREDK.
Private	HOMEYER HENRY
Private	HOPER HENRY
Private	HOPFELD JOHN Died of Wounds
Private	HORACK FRANCIS
Private	HOTHAN CHRISTIAN Discharged
Private	HUCBE CONRADE
Private	JACKEL FRANCIS
Private	JAEGER HENRY
Private	JAGESCHULTZ CHRISTIAN
Private	JANISON WM.
Private	IBANO ALEX.
Private	IBURG BERND. Killed 18 June
Private	IENISCH CHRISTIAN
Private	IETELE ANDREW Discharged
Private	IGNAS PETER
Private	JOHANNSEN NIELS

Private	JURGENS JOHN
Private	KANNACHER JOHN
Private	KANTISKY JOSEPHUS
Private	KEBEL WM.
Private	KEGELER GEORGE
Private	KEGEL JOHN
Private	KERNERT BERND.
Private	KESEMEYER CONRAD
Private	KESSLER JOHN
Private	KIEFERT ADAM
Private	KIENE JOHN Discharged
Private	KIRSCH LEWIS
Private	KLAGES CHRISTR.
Private	KLAPROTH HENRY
Private	KLANSEN HERMANN Discharged
Private	KLEIN GEORGE Discharged
Private	KLEINE DIEDERICK
Private	KLEINE LEVIEN
Private	KLEINSTAUBER LAW.
Private	KLEITCH CHRISTR.
Private	KLIND DAVID
Private	KNORRE HENRY
Private	KNUTZEN NICOLAUS
Private	KOBBE FREDK.
Private	KOCH HENRY
Private	KOCH HERMANN
Private	KOCHNE HENRY
Private	KOHLHAUS FREDK.
Private	KOHLER DIEDK. Discharged
Private	KOHLER HENRY Discharged
Private	KONIG FREDK. Discharged
Private	KORBER CONRADE
Private	KORTENKAMP FREDK. Cheylesmore Collection 1908
Private	KOTHER WM.
Private	KOTUSH HENRY
Private	KRAAS HENRY
Private	KREBS GEORGE Discharged
Private	KRUSE JURGEN
Private	KUCKUCK GEORGE
Private	KUHNE ANDREW
Private	KUHNE ERNEST
Private	KULITZ LUDOLPHUS
Private	KUNCKEL FREDK.
Private	KUNE HENRY
Private	KURPINSKY MICHER
Private	KUTMANN HENRY Discharged
Private	LAMPE CHRISTIAN
Private	LANDLER SIMON

Private	LANGE CASTEN	Private	MULLER PHILIP
Private	LASINS JAMES	Private	MUSCHINSKY JOSEPHUS
Private	LANDY HENRY	Private	NATHER JOHN
Private	LICHTENBERG HENRY Discharged	Private	NAWE WM.
Private	LIEDMANN HENRY	Private	NEISE CHRISTN. Discharged
Private	LIEFELD JOHN	Private	NELLES FRANCIS
Private	LINDERMANN DIEDK. Discharged	Private	NIEBUHR CHRSITR.
Private	LINNEMANN LEWIS	Private	NIEMEYER JOHN
Private	LOEBGER JOHN	Private	NISSOM JUSTUS
Private	LOHRBERG ANDREW Discharged	Private	OBERG DANIEL
Private	LOTT FREDK.	Private	OCKLERKING CHRISTR.
Private	LUHRING PHILLIP	Private	OELSNER FREDK.
Private	MALMSTEIN CHRISTR.	Private	OLSEN GRIMMER Discharged
Private	MAINZ JOHN	Private	ORTHE PETER
Private	MANZIER MICHL.	Private	OTTE HENRY
Private	MARROCK HENRY	Private	PANNIER JOHN Glendining's sale 21st July 1909
Private	MARTINI JOHN	Private	PETERS DIEDRICK
Private	MATHIES JURGEN	Private	PETERS GEORGE
Private	MEICKLING ANTHONY Killed 18 June	Private	PETERSEN BENT
Private	MEINECKE FREDK.	Private	PETERSEN CHRISTN.
Private	MERLIER ANTHY.	Private	PFANNKUCH WM. Killed 18 June
Private	MEYER ANDREW Discharged	Private	PFEIFER GEORGE
Private	MEYER CHRISTN.	Private	PLINCKE HENRY
Private	MEYER CONRAD	Private	POCORNY POWL
Private	MEYER ERNEST Discharged	Private	POLLE LEWIS
Private	MEYER HENRY (Snr)	Private	POTT FREDK.
Private	MEYER HENRY (Junr)	Private	POTTBERG HENRY
Private	MEYER LAWRENCE	Private	PRECHT GEORGE
Private	MEYNS HARM Discharged	Private	RATHMANN AUGUSTUS
Private	MINDERMANN LEWIS Discharged	Private	RECHBEIN JAMES
Private	MONTAG GEORGE	Private	REINHARD CHRISTN. Died of Wounds
Private	MOOSES CHRISTN.	Private	REINHARD FREDK. Discharged
Private	MORDFELD GEORGE Discharged	Private	REIPER CHRISTN.
Private	MORRITZ JURGEN	Private	RETTIG CHAS.
Private	MORRO JOSEPHUS	Private	REUTER WM. Discharged
Private	MOWINKEL HENRY Killed 18th June	Private	RINGEL MICHL.
Private	MUCKENHAUPT CHRISTN.	Private	RINNE WM.(Snr)
Private	MULLER CHRISTN. Discharged	Private	RINNE WM. (Jnr) Discharged
Private	MULLER CHRISTR. Discharged	Private	RISCHMULLER HENRY
Private	MULLER DIEDK.	Private	ROHCKE CHAS.
Private	MULLER FREDK.	Private	ROHLFS HENRY
Private	MULLER GODFRY(Snr) Discharged	Private	ROHRS FREDK.
Private	MULLER GODFRY (Jnr)	Private	ROMER IGNATIUS
Private	MULLER HY (Snr) Watters Sale June 1913	Private	ROHMEYER FREDK.
Private	MULLER HY. (jr)	Private	ROSENQUIST HANS Discharged
Private	MULLER JAMES	Private	RUHE HENRY
		Private	RUPRECHT MARTIN
		Private	SANDER JOSEPHUS

Private	SAVADAR MARTIN
Private	SCHAFER WM.
Private	SCHAFER HENRY Discharged
Private	SCHARAPER HENRY
Private	SCHARLACH JOHN
Private	SCHARNESKY JOHN
Private	SCHEBEN LEONHARD
Private	SCHELLE PETER Killed 18 June
Private	SCHIEBER CHAS. Discharged
Private	SCHLACKE FREDK. Discharged
Private	SCHMIDT ADAM
Private	SCHMIDT HENRY
Private	SCHMIDT JOHN
Private	SCHMIDT PETER
Private	SCHMIDT THEODOR
Private	SCHMIDT WERNER
Private	SCHMIDT MEYER HENRY Discharged
Private	SCHMINCKE MELCHIOR Discharged
Private	SCHNEIDER JOHN
Private	SCHNEMANN GEORGE
Private	SCHOLLE JUSTUS
Private	SCHOMBERG CGRISTR.
Private	SCHONFELD CHRISTN.
Private	SCHORMANN HENRY
Private	SCHOTTLER FERDINAND
Private	SCHRADER HENRY
Private	SCHRAGE FREDK.
Private	SCHUBACH LEWIS Discharged
Private	SCHULTZE JURGEN
Private	SCHULZE ANDREW Discharged
Private	SCHULZE DANIEL
Private	SCHULZE HENRY Discharged
Private	SCHULZE JAACHIM
Private	SCHULZE JOHN
Private	SCHUMACHER FREDK. Discharged
Private	SCHUTTE JOHN Boy
Private	SCHWANENFUGEL CHAS.
Private	SELL ADAM
Private	SEMSROTH HENRY
Private	SIEBER JOHN
Private	SIETAS HENRY
Private	SIEVER JOHN
Private	SIEVERS CHRISTR.
Private	SINDEL NICS.
Private	SCHL HENRY
Private	SOLTER HENRY
Private	SPANGENBERG FREDK.
Private	SPELLING GEORGE
Private	STAAKE FREDK.
Private	STANISOLF JOHN
Private	STANDINGER WM.
Private	STEIN HENRY Discharged
Private	STEINBERG ANDREW Killed 18 June
Private	STEINHOFF CHRISTR. Discharged
Private	STEINMEYER CONRAD
Private	STOBENER JOHN
Private	STOCKSEN HENRY
Private	STORRE GODFRY
Private	STROBEL HENRY
Private	STROMEYER DIEDK.
Private	STRUCKMAN WM. Discharged
Private	STUBNER GEORGE
Private	SUERLAND FREDK.
Private	SUFT LEWIS
Private	TASSER VALENTIN
Private	TEGTHOFF HENRY
Private	TEGMEYER HENRY
Private	THEISMEYER JOHN
Private	TIESING HENRY Discharged
Private	TIETGEN CHRISTN.
Private	TOLLE JOHN
Private	TANSFELD HENRY
Private	TIETGAN FREDK.
Private	UDERSTADT CHAS.
Private	VALLANTEWTICH ANDREW
Private	VIERENZ LAURENCE
Private	VIERKE HENRY
Private	VOLCK HENRY Died of wounds
Private	VOLLMER FREDK. Discharged
Private	VONAN HENRY
Private	WACHTER LEWIS Discharged
Private	WAGENER WM.
Private	WARNECKE DIEDK.
Private	WARNECKE FREDK.
Private	WARNECKE WM.
Private	WEBER FRANS.
Private	WEDEMEYER FREDK.
Private	WEGENER AUGUSTUS
Private	WEINART LEWIS
Private	WEISS JOHN
Private	WENIGER HENRY
Private	WENTRUM FREDK.
Private	WERNER CHRISTIAN
Private	WESELEY JOSEPHUS
Private	WESSLING FREDK.
Private	WETTIG JURGEN

Private	WEY KALLUS
Private	WIECHERS HENRY
Private	WIEPKING GEORGE
Private	WIESE WM.
Private	WIEZORECK VINCENT
Private	WILLBAUER JOHN
Private	WILKENING ANTHONY
Private	WINDHORN DIEDK.
Private	WITTHOEFT JOHN
Private	WITTHORN AUGUSTUS
Private	WITTHORN AUGUSTUS
Private	WITTE HENRY
Private	WICKENHAUSER HENRY
Private	WIMER JOHN
Private	WLAZIESCH STEPHAN
Private	WOLLFARTH CHRISTIAN
Private	WORTMANN HENRY
Private	ZAHL GODFRY
Private	ZIMMELHAKE FREDK.
Private	ZURICK CHRISTN.
Private	ZWICKER DANIEL

* * *

4th LINE BATTALION K.G.L.

Lt.Colonel	du PEAT CHAS. (Bt.Col.) Died of Wounds
Major	REH FREDK.
Major	CHUDEN GEORGE Died of Wounds
Captain	MEYER PHILIP (Bt.Maj.)
Captain	LANE GEORGE Died of Wounds
Captain	HEYDENREICH WM.
Captain	LEEDONWIG GEORGE
Captain	RUMANN AUGUSTUS
Captain	BRANDS AUGUSTUS
Captain	HEISE FREDK. Died of Wounds
Captain	HOTZEN FREDK.
Captain	SCHLICHTHORST CONRAD
Lieutenant	OTTO FREDK.
Lieutenant	KEOZLER FREDK. Col.Gaskell sale May 1911
Lieutenant	PAPE WM.
Lieutenant	BOTH CASPER Col.Gaskell Collection 1908
Lieutenant	RANTZEN WM. Major of Brigade
Lieutenant	FEUDENTHADT AUGUSTUS
Lieutenant	KRIETSCH FREDK.WM.
Lieutenant	SICHTENBERGER CHRISTIAN
Lieutenant	SASPERG CHAS.
Lieutenant	YEINSON CHAS.
Lieutenant	RUMANN THEODOR
Lieutenant	LONGWORTH ADOLPHUS
Lieutenant	SUDEWIG ADOLPHUS
Lieutenant	WITTE HENRY
Lieutenant	SIEBOLD GEORGE
Lieutenant	FARGUE WM.LEWIS Whitaker Coll.1908
Lieutenant	BRANKMANN ERNESTIUS
Lieutenant	LASHPERG FREDK.
Lieutenant	SHEA WM.
Ensign	LUNING WM.
Ensign	BRANDES FREDK.
Ensign	MANNSBACH JAMES
Ensign	SCHAEFER WM.
Ensign	USLAR FERDINAND Payne Coll.1911
Ensign	APPISTON ARNOLD
Ensign	CRONHELM THEODOR Killed in Action
Ensign	FRENDENTHAL FREDK.
Ensign	SODEN LEWIS
Adjutant	HARTWIG ADOLPHUS
Qr.Master	BECKER AUGUSTUS
Surgeon	GUNTHER GEORGE
Ass.Surgeon	MATTHIAS J. DANIEL
Ass.Surgeon	WICKE J. HENRY
Sjt.Major	KRACKE LEWIS
Q.M.S.	ROUSSIT HENRY Discharged
P.M.S.	MITTERBACHER GERHARD Discharged
Ar.Serjeant	DENCKER WM.
Dr.Major	HUFSCHMIDT PETER
Cr.Serjeant	GROTE HENRY
Cr.Serjeant	KOCK JNS. DIEDK.
Cr.Serjeant	LINDE GEORGE
Cr.Serjeant	MASTIEN FREDK.
Cr.Serjeant	REUTER BURCHARD
Cr.Serjeant	RICHTER GEORGE
Cr.Serjeant	SCHWARTZE FREDK. Discharged
Cr.Serjeant	WIEBKING WM.
Serjeant	ALBRECHT JNS.FREDK.
Serjeant	BRANDT CHRISTR.
Serjeant	BRAUN JULIUS
Serjeant	BUSSE HENRY
Serjeant	DEGENHARDT HENRY
Serjeant	FASCHER HENRY
Serjeant	FRETER CHRISTN.
Serjeant	FURCHTENICHT WM.
Serjeant	HAGENAU JOACHIM
Serjeant	HARTGEN CHRISTIAN Discharged
Serjeant	HERMANN JOHN
Serjeant	HEYLAND HENRY
Serjeant	KOCK FREDK. Discharged Gray Collection 1908

Serjeant	KRACKE CHAS.
Serjeant	KRAMER HENRY
Serjeant	KRATSCH GEORGE
Serjeant	KUNZMANN JOHN
Serjeant	LIEBECKE FREDK.
Serjeant	LINSING DEDERICK
Serjeant	MULLER EBERHARD
Serjeant	NOTH G. HENRY
Serjeant	NORDMANN GEORGE
Serjeant	PIEPER AUGUSTUS
Serjeant	PLAT DEDERICK
Serjeant	RIEMER DEDERICK Killed in Action
Serjeant	ROHDE JOHN
Serjeant	SCHMIDT THEOPHILUS
Serjeant	SCHMIDT FREDK.
Serjeant	SPIESS WM.
Serjeant	WILLERS JACOB
Corporal	AHRENS HENRY
Corporal	BAUMGARTEN DANL.
Corporal	BERGMANN J. GODLOVE Discharged
Corporal	BERGMANN JOHN
Corporal	BEUERMANN DANL. Discharged
Corporal	BIERKAMPF FREDK.
Corporal	BLOCK FREDK.
Corporal	BODE FRED.
Corporal	BORSHAUSEN ANDREW
Corporal	BRINCKMANN WM. Discharged
Corporal	BUNCKE HENRY Killed in Action
Corporal	CHRISTOPH DANL. Discharged
Corporal	DEGENGARDT CHRISTN.
Corporal	DORGIS FREDK.
Corporal	DREYER HENRY
Corporal	HOTTJE CHRISTN.
Corporal	EGGERS CHRISTN. Discharged
Corporal	ENGEHAUSEN LEWIS Discharged Cheylesmore Collection 1908
Corporal	ERDMANN WM.
Corporal	EVERS HENRY
Corporal	HEINE HENRY
Corporal	GIEBEL WM.
Corporal	HEINE HENRY
Corporal	HOHNBOLM HENRY Discharged
Corporal	KERSTING JOHN
Corporal	KRUSE HENRY
Corporal	MULLER AUGUSTUS
Corporal	NETTERMEYER GEORGE
Corporal	PLATE JOHN
Corporal	RAABE DEDK.HY.
Corporal	SCHNOOR HENRY Killed in Action
Corporal	STERN CHRISTN.
Corporal	FEWERHOLZ ANDREW
Corporal	THOMAS JOHN
Corporal	VOGE HENRY Discharged
Corporal	WELLMANN CHRISTN.
Corporal	WENTZER PHILIP
Corporal	WIEDA FREDK. Discharged
Corporal	WINKELMANN HENRY
Corporal	WINTERBERG CHAS.
Drummer	BODENSUCK FREDK.
Drummer	FLOREKE FREDK.
Drummer	GRAM HENRY
Drummer	HUNE WM.
Drummer	KRUGER JOHN
Drummer	MEYER JOHN Discharged
Drummer	NIERODT CHRISTN.
Drummer	OHSEN HENRY
Drummer	ZIPPEL FREDK.
Private	ADDERKIRCHEN HENRY
Private	AHRENS FREDK.
Private	ALBRECHT FREDK.
Private	ATTMANN HENRY
Private	ANDERMANN GERT.
Private	ANDREAS PETER
Private	APPEL ANTHONY Discharged
Private	APPEL JOHN
Private	AHRENDORF GEORGE
Private	ARMBRECHT GEORGE
Private	ASCHEN CHRISTN. Discharged
Private	BARKHAUSEN HENRY
Private	BARTELS RUDOLPH
Private	BARTRAM HENRY Discharged
Private	BECKMANN H.FK.
Private	BENNEMANN HENRY
Private	BERNHARDT FRANS.
Private	BENS WM.
Private	BICKMEYER HENRY
Private	BEERING FREDK. Discharged
Private	BLIDON HENRY
Private	BLUMENHAGEN JOHN
Private	BODE CHRISTN.
Private	BODENBERG LEWIS
Private	BODENSTAL FREDK. Discharged
Private	BORANOW FREDK.
Private	BORMANN CONRAD
Private	BOSHAUSEN HENRY
Private	BOTMANN JOHN
Private	BOTTCHER ERNEST

Private	BRANDIS CHRISTN. Discharged
Private	BRENNECKE CHRISTN.
Private	BRINKS HENRY Discharged
Private	BROTHER JOHN
Private	BRUNS HENRY
Private	BUCKS GEORGE
Private	BUHRE HENRY Killed in Action
Private	BURGHARD HENRY
Private	BUSLAUF PETER Discharged
Private	BUTTNER JOHN
Private	CHILNOWSKY THOS.
Private	CLAUSMEYER JNS.GERT. Discharged
Private	COHRS FREDK.
Private	CORRUNA ALBERT
Private	DAMS FREDK.
Private	DANIEL JOHN
Private	DANNENBERG HENRY
Private	DENECKER HENRY Discharged
Private	DENECKE HENRY
Private	DIERS HERMANN
Private	DOHLKE HENRY
Private	DOLLACK FRANCIS
Private	DOLLE CHRISTOPHER
Private	DONMEYER WM.
Private	DREBUS ANTHONY Died of Wounds
Private	DREYER HENRY
Private	DUNCKER HENRY
Private	EBELING FERDINAND
Private	EGGERS CHRISTN Discharged
Private	ERNST LUDOLPH
Private	FAHRONHOTT HENRY
Private	FECK AMBROSIUS
Private	FECKERT WM.
Private	FENCK JOHN
Private	FEUERHACKE CONRAD Killed in Action
Private	FICKE HENRY
Private	FINCKE CHAS.
Private	FINGERHUTH FREDK.
Private	FISCHER JAMES
Private	FLACKMEYER CONRAD
Private	FLEBE HENRY
Private	FLEISCHACKER CHRISTR. Died of Wounds
Private	FLORCKE LEWIS
Private	FRICKE ENGELBATUS
Private	FRICKE HENRY
Private	FRICKE JURGEN
Private	FRIEDRICHS HENRY
Private	FUCHS HENRY
Private	FUNDLE GEORGE Discharged
Private	FUSS GEORGE Discharged
Private	FUSSY ALEX.
Private	GALLANT DOMINIOUS
Private	GARBE GEORGE
Private	GARVENS GOTTLIEB Discharged
Private	GEBHARD HENRY
Private	GEIGER IGNATIUS
Private	GERKE FREDK. Killed in Action
Private	GLABATZ JOHN
Private	GLOSEWALD FREDK. Killed in Action
Private	GOPPER HENRY
Private	GOTSCHALK HENRY
Private	GOTZ HENRY
Private	GRAF JOSEPH
Private	GRETHE FREDK.
Private	GRONAN LENZS
Private	GRONEN JOHN
Private	GROTE CHRISTN.
Private	GRUMME DANIEL Discharged
Private	GRUNHAGEN HENRY
Private	GUNDLACH HENRY
Private	GUTGESELL JOHN
Private	GUTTERMANN JACOB
Private	HAGEDORN WM.
Private	HAHBERLACH FREDK.
Private	HANHORST GODFREY
Private	HANNE FREDK.
Private	HANSEL CHRISTN.
Private	HAROKE FREDK.
Private	HARENKEMPF CHAS.
Private	HARTMANN FREDK.
Private	HARTMANN CHAS.
Private	HASSELBACH AUGUSTUS
Private	HASTONG CHRISTN.
Private	HEDENHAUSEN FRANCIS Discharged
Private	HEYDER GODFRY
Private	HEINE CHRISTN.
Private	HEINECKE JOACHIM
Private	HELLMANN HENRY Discharged
Private	HELM BATHASER
Private	HENCKE LUDOLPH
Private	HENZE LEWIS
Private	HERBTZE WM. Discharged
Private	HEROLD CHAS.
Private	HERZOG FREDK.
Private	HESS CHRISTN.

Private	HEYDORN CONRAD
Private	HILLEBRECHT HENRY
Private	HILLMAN ANDREW
Private	HISCHE ANTHONY
Private	HLOWACK LUCAS
Private	HOLSCHER MORITZ
Private	HOLTZER WM.
Private	HOOFT HENRY
Private	HUBSCHER ANDREW Killed in Action
Private	HUGEMEYER DEDRICH
Private	JACOB CONRAD
Private	JEGER LEWIS
Private	ILSE JNS. CHRISTN. Discharged
Private	INNICH FRANCIS
Private	IRLING CONRAD
Private	KANDENHARD HENRY Discharged
Private	KANEWURF ERNEST
Private	KATZMANN JOHN
Private	KAUFMANN HENRY
Private	KAUFMANN FERDINAND
Private	KAYSER FREDK.
Private	KEITHAN FREDK.
Private	KENNER PETER
Private	KLINCKE FREDK.
Private	KNORR CHRISTN.
Private	KNORR PETER
Private	KNUST HENRY
Private	KOBELKE ANDREW
Private	KOCH GEORGE
Private	KOECKER CHRISTN.
Private	KOCHLER JOHN
Private	KOCHLER LEWS.
Private	KOENHARDT FREDK.
Private	KOENEMANN FREDK.
Private	KONIG CHAS. Discharged
Private	KORF HENRY Discharged
Private	KORNRUMPF CHRISTN. Discharged
Private	KOTHE JNS. AHREND
Private	KRAMSEWITSCH CASIMIR
Private	KRAUSCHECK LAWRENCE
Private	KRAUSE ANDREW
Private	KRECKLER FREDK.
Private	KRON ANDREW
Private	KRONBERGER CHAS.
Private	KRONE JNS. JUSTUS
Private	KRUGER WM.
Private	KRUSE HENRY
Private	KRUSE CHRISTN.
Private	KUNRICH FREDK.
Private	KUSTER HENRY Discharged
Private	LAGES JNS.CHAS. Discharged
Private	LAHMSON CONRAD
Private	LANGE FREDK.
Private	LANGE GEORGE
Private	LASCHUCK IVAN
Private	LEHMANN ANDREW
Private	LEHNER FLORIAN
Private	LINDERMANN FREDK.
Private	LINDERMANN PETER
Private	LINNE HENRY Discharged
Private	LOHMEYER WM.
Private	LORG JOSEPH
Private	LUDECKE HENRY
Private	LUSTHOFT DIEDERICK
Private	LUTTER HENRY
Private	MARKWARD FREDK. Discharged
Private	MARM PETER
Private	MARTONS DIEDERICK
Private	MATTECKA THOS.
Private	MATTERT DANL.
Private	MATTHIAS JOHN
Private	MELITZ JOACHIM Died of Sickness
Private	MENNE HENRY
Private	MESECKE LEWIS
Private	MESSERSCHMIDT JNS.CASPAR
Private	MEYER FREDK.
Private	MEYER CHAS.CHRN. Killed in Action
Private	MEYER FRANCIS
Private	MEYER CORT.
Private	MEYER ERNEST
Private	MEYER CHRISTN. Discharged
Private	MEYER JOHN
Private	MEYER HENRY
Private	MEYER DIEDERICK
Private	MICHAEL HENRY
Private	MICHAEL JACOB
Private	MINATZKY ANDREW
Private	MINNER HENRY
Private	MOHRING CHRISTN.
Private	MONNECKAMEYER LEWIS
Private	MULLER DIEDERICK Discharged
Private	MULLER FREDK. Discharged
Private	MULLER FREDK. Discharged
Private	MULLER FREDK. Discharged
Private	MULLER CHRISTN.
Private	MULLER JOHN
Private	MUNSTER J.HENRY

Private	MUNSTERMANN FREDK.
Private	MURICH PETER
Private	MUSSMANN FREDK.
Private	NEWHEUSTER JOHN
Private	NEWMANN JOHN
Private	NICOLE DOMINICO
Private	NOHASKY SUMON
Private	NOTTE LEWIS
Private	NOTTE NICHOLAS
Private	OIGRIG JOSEPH
Private	OPPERMANN GEORGE
Private	OTTELEBEN CHRISTN.
Private	OTHEUER HENRY
Private	PANTROLZER CHRISTN. Died of Wounds
Private	PAUL CHAS.
Private	PAUL HENRY
Private	PAULING JNS.HY.
Private	PETER CONRAD
Private	PETER DAVID
Private	PFEFFER CHRISTN.
Private	PFEFFER ADAM
Private	PFINGSTON HENRY Discharged
Private	PLAAGE HENRY
Private	POETZCH JNS.CHAS. Discharged
Private	POLITZ CASIMIR
Private	POTHAST CHAS. Discharged
Private	PRACKMANN LEWIS Discharged
Private	RACKEBRANDT HENRY Discharged
Private	RADEMACHER PETER
Private	RAMPENTHAL HENRY Discharged
Private	RAMUSCH CASPAR
Private	RAPCKE CONRAD
Private	RASINSKY IGNATIUS
Private	RATHKAMP HERMANN Discharged
Private	REDEL GREGORY
Private	REINECKE LEWIS
Private	REININGER JOHN
Private	RENNEMULLER CHAS.
Private	RICHERS GEORGE Discharged
Private	RIECKE HENRY Discharged
Private	ROBER ANDREW
Private	ROCKAR FREDK.
Private	RODE DIEDK.
Private	RODE HENRY
Private	RODEWALD FREDK. Killed in Action
Private	ROHLFS HENRY
Private	ROHMANN CHAS. Died of Wounds
Private	ROHRIG FREDK.
Private	ROLLEN JOSEPH
Private	ROMER JOHN
Private	ROSE HENRY
Private	ROSESCHEFSKY BATHASER
Private	ROTH HENRY
Private	RUMENAP WM.
Private	RUMENAP HENRY
Private	SACK JOHN
Private	SANDER ERNEST
Private	SANDER HERMANN
Private	SAPERS PETER
Private	SCHACHTEL CHAS. Discharged
Private	SCHAUGELLES
Private	SCHELLER CONRAD
Private	SCHIEF LAURENZ Discharged
Private	SCHLEGEL MARTIN
Private	SCHOLOTTE FREDK. Discharged
Private	SCHMIEDING JOHN
Private	SCHMIDT GODFRY
Private	SCHMIDT HENRY
Private	SCHNEIDER CHRISTN.
Private	SCHRADER JOHN
Private	SCHRADER CHRISTN.
Private	SCHRODER HENRY Discharged
Private	SCHRODER HERMANN
Private	SCHULTZ HENRY
Private	SCHULTZE CHRISTN.
Private	SCHULTZE CHRISTN.
Private	SHULTZE CHRISTN. Discharged
Private	SCHULTZE WM.
Private	SCHULTZE JNS.HY.
Private	SCHUWORD ANDREW
Private	SCHWARTZE CHRISTN.
Private	SCHWARTZ MARTIN
Private	SCHWEDHELM CHAS. Died of wounds
Private	SCHWEINING ERNEST Discharged
Private	SENGE WM. Discharged
Private	SIEMERS CHRISTN. Discharged
Private	SIEVERS JOHN
Private	SIEVERT CHRISTN. Discharged
Private	SOBISKY ADAMKilled in Action
Private	SOCKER HENRY
Private	SOMMER JNS.ERNEST
Private	SOMMER CHAS.
Private	SONDMACHER HENRY Discharged
Private	SPECHT HENRY
Private	SPIEFS LEWIS Discharged

Private	STAHLMANN HENRY Killed in Action
Private	STANAU HENRY Discharged
Private	STEINECKE HENRY
Private	STEINKOSKY JOHN
Private	STENDER NICHOLAS
Private	STOCKMANN SIEMON Discharged
Private	STOTTE FREDK.
Private	STRAMANN JNS.FREDK.
Private	STRAUSS JOHN
Private	STREITHORT HENRY
Private	STUCKE FREDK.
Private	STURM GEORGE Discharged
Private	SUCHERT CHRISTN.
Private	SUCHERT FREDK.
Private	TEMPEL PAUL
Private	TERISER NICH.
Private	THEDA ERNEST
Private	THIMANN HENRY Discharged
Private	TORRIS HENRY Discharged
Private	TRAUT JOHN
Private	TRELENRITZ VALENTIN
Private	TURNEY JOSEPH Discharged
Private	UCKER FREDK.
Private	ULMER LEWIS
Private	VEST CHRISTN.
Private	VOGELER JNS.HY.
Private	VOIGHTS FREDK.
Private	WAHLE CHRISTN.
Private	WALLBAUM HENRY
Private	WALLKOWENICK NIC.
Private	WARGE JOHN
Private	WARNECKE HENRY
Private	WASSMATH JOHN Discharged
Private	WEDEMEYER DANL. Discharged
Private	WISLAND ANDREW
Private	WEISE JOHN
Private	WENDEL CONRAD
Private	WERFELMANN DIEDK. Discharged
Private	WERHAN AUGUSTUS
Private	WESTERHAUSEN HENRY
Private	WIEDENROTH JOHN
Private	WIEGMANN WM.
Private	WIENECKE JOHN Discharged
Private	WIESE FERDINAND Discharged
Private	WINTER ERNEST
Private	WIRTHS JOSEPH
Private	WITTE HENRY
Private	WITTLER HENRY
Private	WITZOUCK MICHL.
Private	WOHLBOLD HENRY
Private	WOTTERS JOACHIM Discharged
Private	ZIENECK ANTHONY
Private	ZIESE GODFREY
Private	ZIESENITZ HENRY
Private	KOING CHAS.FRED.

* * *

7th LINE BATTALION K.G.L. DETACHMENT

Lieutenant	BACHALLE WM.
Lieutenant	POTEN CHAS.
Lieutenant	FELMRICH CHAS.
Ensign	LOESCEKE WM.
Ensign	BACKHAUS EHRIG Gaskell Coll.1908
Ensign	LUCKON GOTTLIEB
Ensign	NEUSCHAFER CHAS.JOHN
Ensign	BACKHAUS FREDK.
Ensign	MARTIN CHAS.
Ass.Surgeon	BRUGGEMANN HENRY
Ass.Surgeon	SCHUCHARD FREDK.
Serjeant	ALBERS CHAS.
Serjeant	MULLER CHRISTIAN
Private	AHREND JOHN
Private	APPEL HENRY
Private	BACHUTZKY WATJE
Private	BERGMANN FREDK.
Private	BUNGER HENRY
Private	HAGEDERN F.DAVID Killed in Action
Private	HITTLING DANIEL Discharged
Private	METZE HENRY Discharged
Private	POETZ DAVID Discharged
Private	STANRICK JOHN Discharged
Private	VANIG HENRY
Private	WIEGREVE FREDK.

* * *

5th LINE BATTALION K.G.L.

Colonel	OWPTEDA BARON CHRISTN. Killed in Action
Lt.Colonel	LISINGEN BARON WM.
Captain	WURMB BARON CHRISTIAN Killed in Action
Captain	SANDER FREDK. Whitaker Coll.1908
Captain	NOTTING GEORGE
Captain	DURING ERNEST
Lieutenant	BOTHMER CHAS.
Lieutenant	BRANDIS EBERHARD
Lieutenant	BERGER CHAS.

Lieutenant	MEJER AUGUSTUS
Lieutenant	BUHSE GEORGE
Lieutenant	SCHAWROTH GEORGE
Lieutenant	WITTE CHAS.
Lieutenant	WINCKLER AUGUSTUS
Lieutenant	SCHLAGER CHAS.
Lieutenant	KLINGSOHR GEORGE
Lieutenant	GUSMANN LEWIS
Lieutenant	WHEATLEY EDMUND
Lieutenant	VASSMER HENRY
Lieutenant	OWYVTEDA LEWIS
Lieutenant	WISCHMANN GEORGE
Lieutenant	PROON BERNHARD
Lieutenant	WEISS CHAS.
Ensign	SXHARNHORST FERDINAND
Ensign	FLEISCHMANN A.
Ensign	REINBOLD JULIUS
Ensign	WLATHER WM.
Ensign	WRINKLER CHAS.
Ensign	KLINGSOHR LEWIS
Ensign	OWYVTEDA A.
Ensign	BARING ERNEST
Ensign	SCHARNHORST ADOLPHUS
Ensign	CARSTENS RUDOLPHUS
Pay Master	KNIGHT HENRY
Surgeon	DEPPEN HERMANN
Adjutant	SCHUCK LEWIS Killed in Action
Ass.Surgeon	KOHRS JULIUS Glendining's sale Feb.1913
Ass.Surgeon	GERSON GEORGE

<u>Staff</u>

S.Major	RODWALD FREDK.
Q.M.S.	GOEBEL CHRISTIAN App.Ensign 15th August 1815
P.M.S.	RODEWALD GEORGE
Ar.Serjeant	KONSING FREDK.

<u>Grenadier Company</u>

Serjeant	ARANTE HERMANN
Serjeant	GROTHEGUTH HENRY
Serjeant	HOPPE HENRY
Serjeant	UHLE WM.
Corporal	HEIL ANTHONY
Corporal	HERMANN FREDK.
Corporal	THOELCKE ANDREW
Corporal	WALTKINGER BATH.
Drummer	BOHNE JACOB
Drummer	HEMME HENRY
Drummer	SCHOMBERG EMANUEL
Drummer	THOLESKE LEWIS
Private	CONVREE CHAS. Killed in Action
Private	HORNEY AUGUSTUS Killed in Action
Private	PETERSON JOHN Killed in Action
Private	ACKERMANN JOHN Deserted
Private	BARTMANN JOSEPH
Private	BATTISTE STEPHAN
Private	BERCKMANN PETER
Private	BLUME JOHN
Private	BRENE ANDREW Discharged
Private	BRODMANN HENRY Discharged
Private	BRON JOSEPH Deserted
Private	BUSSE FRANZ
Private	BUSSMANN FREDK.
Private	DAMBKO STEPHAN
Private	DEJACK NICOLAS
Private	DIEDRICK ANTHONY
Private	EIB JOSEPH
Private	ENGEL JOHN
Private	FUST GOTTLIEB
Private	FLOHR FREDK.
Private	GOLICK FLORIAN
Private	HAAFS CHRISTIAN Deserted
Private	HAUSCHILDT JOSEPH
Private	HEUSER JOHN
Private	KAMINSKY GEORGE
Private	KERMEEL JOHN
Private	KNOOR NICOLAS
Private	LATTER JOHN
Private	LEBERINS JOHN
Private	MAAFS JACOB
Private	MARCKS ADOLPHUS
Private	MARWEGE FREDK.
Private	MILOFSKY PETER
Private	MEYER ULRICH Deserted
Private	MONK JOHN
Private	MULLER FREDK.
Private	MULLER JOSEPH
Private	NUVENDORFF HENRY
Private	OSTEN HENRY
Private	OTZMANN HENRY Discharged
Private	REDY URBANS.
Private	RODE LEWIS
Private	ROHL FREDK.
Private	ROHLFER BERNARD
Private	ROLLIEN FRANZ
Private	SAFS PAUL
Private	SCHLIVENSKY JOSEPH
Private	SEHOENWISNA AUGUSTUS
Private	SCHOSTA ALBERT
Private	THEIR MATHIAS

Private	TREYE VEIT
Private	TOGES HENRY
Private	WEIGENER JOHN
Private	WARNEST GODFRY Discharged
Private	WIMBERGER HENRY
Private	ZAROMBA JOSEPH

1st Company

Serjeant	GERLACH FREDK.
Serjeant	JOHN HENRY
Serjeant	KNOCHE FREDK. Discharged
Serjeant	KUNTZE FREDK.
Corporal	HEINE CHRISTN.
Drummer	HILDEBRECHT CHRISTN.
Drummer	WITMANN PETER
Private	BACHERET JOSEPH Killed in Action
Private	OSTMANN CHRISTN. Killed in Action
Private	SABOLESKY THOS. Killed in Action
Private	TURZIN ANDW. Killed in Action
Private	WINEKEL GODFRY Killed in Action
Private	ALBRECHT FREDK.
Private	APPENROTH HENRY
Private	ARNEMANN AUGUSTUS
Private	BLOCKE THEOBALD
Private	BOCKELMANN BERND.
Private	BROCKMEYER FREDK.
Private	BRUM JOHN
Private	BUHR PETER
Private	BUSING CONRADE
Private	DAKOSKY MATHS.
Private	DROK JOHN
Private	DUTCH HENRY Discharged
Private	EGERT HENRY
Private	FREDERICKS AUGUST
Private	FRONEZACK DOMINIC
Private	GESTROWITSCH PAUL
Private	HAGELSTANGE IGNATZ
Private	HEINEFEDER FREDK.
Private	HISTAND LORENZ
Private	HOMANN JUSTUS
Private	JAEGER MICHL.
Private	JANITZSKY ANDW.
Private	KAISER GEORGE
Private	KAMPHUYSEN DANIEL Cheylesmore Collection 1908
Private	KELLE HENRY
Private	KLINCKE JOS.
Private	KOHRS HENRY Died of Wounds
Private	KOSCHEN MIDRE
Private	LEHMANN CHAS.
Private	LIESMANN JOSEPH
Private	LON FRIELOLIN
Private	METJE JOHN
Private	MICHALOFSKY JAMES
Private	MICHALOVSKY THOS.
Private	MULLER FREDK.
Private	MULLER HENRY
Private	MULLER OTTO
Private	MUSBACK PETER
Private	POPPE JURGEN
Private	RUSTING FREDK. Discharged
Private	SABLONSKY MARTIN
Private	SABLONSKY STANISL.
Private	SCHELM WM.
Private	SCHIMANSKY JOSEPH
Private	SCHOMBERG HENRY
Private	SERJESCHISKY JOHN
Private	SIEDES STEPHAN
Private	STAHLY JOSEPH
Private	STEMPIN ANTHONY
Private	VANDERLINDE BERND.
Private	VANVARRA JOSEPH
Private	VOIGHT LEWIS
Private	WALLENTON ANTON
Private	WASCHELLY ANDREW
Private	ZINGREVE LEWS Discharged

2nd Company

Serjeant	BAUMANN JOSEPH Gaskell Coll.1908
Serjeant	BLAGE FREDK.
Serjeant	GIMBEL JOHN
Corporal	ERNST CHRISTN.
Corporal	HOFFMANN MICHL.
Corporal	KNOLLMANN FREDK.
Corporal	OPPERMANN JOHN
Drummer	MULLER CHRISTN.
Private	ALBRECHT PETER Killed in Action
Private	NAGEL FRANZ Killed in Action
Private	WARNECKE FREDK. Killed in Action
Private	WEGARTH LEWIS Killed in Action
Private	BERENTER FREDK. Payne Coll.1911
Private	BLATTER ANDREW
Private	CALLEES CHAS.
Private	CANFIN JOHN
Private	CARRAN VALENTIN
Private	DEMULL BONIFUSE
Private	DERICLER FRANCIS
Private	DILLIG ANTHONY Deserted

Private	FRANSRICH CHAS.
Private	FRAU CHRISTR.
Private	FRONIZEZACK JOSEPH Died of wounds
Private	GILLARD FRANZ
Private	GOLONBOWSKY PHILIP
Private	GOETZE FREDK.
Private	GRODNIACK SIMON
Private	GUERSON VINCENT
Private	GUIREENTZSKY WOITSCHECK
Private	HANEBUT CHAS.
Private	HAFS CHRISTIAN
Private	ISCHE FREDK. Discharged
Private	KABONIACK JOHN
Private	KAFS LEWIS
Private	KAZMEREZACK JOHN
Private	KAWOSKY JAMES
Private	KRAUSS PETER
Private	KUMMIT DANIEL
Private	LANG LORENZ
Private	MEYER LEWES
Private	MUGGE HENRY Discharged
Private	MULLER CHRISTN.
Private	MUNELHENKE HENRY
Private	NEULAND JOHN
Private	NOWACK JOHN
Private	OBERFELD JOHN
Private	PETERS HAGEN
Private	POPPE ZACHS. Discharged
Private	PROHL PETER Discharged
Private	PUNGE HENRY
Private	RONANOW JOHN
Private	SCHAFER CHRISTN.
Private	SCHILLING JOHN
Private	SCHULTZE HENRY
Private	SOBIRALSKY ADAM
Private	SPEER FREDK.
Private	STORM HENRY
Private	THOTE LEWES
Private	VANGLOS THOS.
Private	VOLLMER ANDREW
Private	WIECHELS HENRY
Private	WINCHSEKY JACOB
Private	WODE CONRADE
Private	WOHEFF HENRY

<u>3rd Company</u>

Serjeant	BRANDT CONRAD Discharged
Serjeant	EBERWEIN CHRISTN.
Serjeant	SCHARSBIER WM.
Serjeant	SCHAFER LEWES
Serjeant	STEINERT FREDK.
Corporal	BECKER DERRIK Killed in Action
Corporal	ACKERMANN FREDK.
Corporal	BIERWIRTH GEORGE
Drummer	SCHULTZ CHRISTN.
Drummer	VORKE ANTHONY
Private	BLASY ANDREW Killed in Action
Private	BONSKOWITZ JOSEPH Killed in Action
Private	FRITZ JOHN Killed in Action
Private	GILTICKA JOSEPH Killed in Action
Private	HILLEMANN ADAM Killed in Action
Private	KONETSKY JOHN Killed in Action
Private	KEUSCH JOSEPH Killed in Action
Private	KIRRA JOSEPH Killed in Action
Private	PROSINZKY LUCAS Killed in Action
Private	SCHIFFLER JOHN Killed in Action
Private	ARMBRUSTER URBAN
Private	BARANISKY JOSEPH
Private	BAYER MICHAEL
Private	BERMEFS PETER
Private	BIERBOHM HENRY
Private	BIERMANN JAMES
Private	BLAU NICOLAS
Private	BLECHER PETER
Private	BØRKER CHRISTR.
Private	BONY LEWES
Private	BUKA ANDREAS
Private	DEBER CHRISTN.
Private	DEIAMP TEASOR
Private	FINECK DOMINIC
Private	FISCHNEBATT HENRY
Private	GEBHART CHRISTN.
Private	GEIGER JOHN
Private	GIESECKE JACOB
Private	HERBST CHRISTN.
Private	HONIGBAUM HENRY
Private	KELLOSCK GREGORS.
Private	KIRALL MICHL.
Private	KUHNE ERNEST
Private	LISIACK VALENTIN
Private	MANNS CASPAR
Private	MARWANSKY STANISL.
Private	MELLERD MICHEL
Private	NERZ GEORGE
Private	MULLER AUGUSTUS
Private	MULLER WM.
Private	PAPILIER PETER
Private	PETRO MARTIN
Private	RANGONINI DOMINIC
Private	REINHARD CHRISTR.

Private	ROUSANO PETER
Private	SATOR IGNATZ
Private	SCHAFER WM. Discharged
Private	SCHOINSKY ANTHONY
Private	SCHULTZ NICOLAS
Private	SCHWENELNER MICHAEL
Private	SECK JOHN
Private	SIMANSKY JOHN
Private	STUTEKER JOHN
Private	TILLE FREDK.
Private	WISCHNOFSKY DASIMIR
Private	WOLELMANN CHRISTR. Discharged
Private	ZIGLER JOHN
Private	ZIMMERMANN GEORGE Discharged
<u>4th Company</u>	
Serjeant	RAMMEYER JOHN Killed in Action
Serjeant	HUSCHE CHAS.
Serjeant	JORELEMANN CHAS.
Serjeant	REINECKE JOHN
Corporal	MEYER HENRY
Corporal	ROSOSKY JACOB
Corporal	SCHMIDT FREDK.
Drummer	KUHNE AUGUSTUS
Drummer	SEIDEL GODFREY
Private	BONELDT JOHN Killed in Action
Private	CARPENTHIER FRANS. Killed in Action
Private	ENGELMANN JOHN Killed in Action
Private	JOHANNECK JACOB Killed in Action
Private	MATFELD JOHN Killed in Action
Private	BILER PETER
Private	BLUMERGARTEN LEWES
Private	BOCKER AREND
Private	BUCHOLZ CHRISTN.
Private	DEKREMER PETER
Private	DIETZ JOHN
Private	DORRE HENRY
Private	ETWERS WM.
Private	EVART FREDK.
Private	FLIEGER JAMES
Private	HAHNS JOHN
Private	HARENBOSTEL JURGEN Discharged
Private	HERMANN JOSEPH
Private	HONIG HENRY
Private	HONIGBAUM HENRY
Private	HUARDT FRANCIS
Private	HUBERTH JOHN

Private	HUMBERG GEORGE Discharged
Private	JANIOWSKY JOHN
Private	KOHLER CHAS.
Private	LAMPE HENRY Discharged
Private	LAWRIGS FRANCIS
Private	LUKENER JOHN
Private	MACKE FREDK.
Private	MALLAND HENRY
Private	MEYER CHRISTR. Discharged
Private	MIETH HENRY Deserted
Private	MINT JACOB
Private	MULLER CONRAD Discharged
Private	MULLER JACOB
Private	MULLER JOHN
Private	NOLLE JOHN Discharged
Private	OLTHARFS HENRY Discharged
Private	PROSTLER AMBROS.
Private	REDSCHORK JOHN
Private	REINECKE HENRY
Private	RENCK JOHN
Private	ROSHMEYER JOHN
Private	SXHMIDT JOHN
Private	SCHEIDER FRANCIS
Private	SCHUTTE CHRISTN. Sotheby's sale March 1911
Private	STENZEL THEOPHUS.
Private	STOPPENHAGEN JOHN
Private	TEPEL HENRY Discharged
Private	VANDAMME JOHN
Private	VANWETTER JOHN
Private	WEISS FREDK.
Private	WOLFH HENRY Discharged
Private	JAEGER JURGEN Discharged
<u>5th Company</u>	
Serjeant	BAUER HENRY
Serjeant	EINEM WM.
Serjeant	FREHREKING HENRY
Serjeant	KLEEMEYER CHRISTN.
Corporal	DAUBE FREDK. Killed in Action
Corporal	GEHRIKE HENRY
Corporal	HEISE HENRY
<u>6th Company</u>	
Serjeant	BUERMANN HENRY Discharged
Serjeant	JURGENS GEORGE Discharged
Serjeant	STRUBE LEWES
Corporal	NOSHSTEIN JACOB Killed in Action
<u>7th Company</u>	
Serjeant	MAXEN CHAS. Discharged Glendining's sale May 1909
Serjeant	SCHMIDT FRANCIS Discharged

Serjeant	TRAHN JOHN
Corporal	BOSHMANN FREDK.

8th Company

Serjeant	BOCK CHRISTR.
Serjeant	KOCH CHRISTN.
Serjeant	MULLER ERNEST Discharged
Corporal	ASCHENBACH JOHN
Corporal	PEPER JAMES Discharged
Corporal	VOGEL LEOPOLD Discharged
Corporal	WOLFF FREDK.
Drummer	NICOLAS WM.

Light Company

Serjeant	FETTE FREDK. Discharged
Serjeant	HENNE GEORGE
Serjeant	KEHR ANTHONY
Serjeant	STEGE WM.
Serjeant	VAHLE CONRADE.
Corporal	BEUCHLIER JAMES
Corporal	DRAGER JOHN
Corporal	LAMPE JOHN
Corporal	PALSHOFF LEWES
Corporal	PFINGSTEN THEOPH.
Drummer	MULLER DAVID
Drummer	SURKAMP DERRIK Discharged
Private	ENCHOWSKY MATTW. Killed in Action
Private	HAUSMANN ADOLPHUS. Killed in Action
Private	HORN CONRADE Killed in Action
Private	REIKERT CONRADE Killed in Action
Private	SANFS LEWIS Killed in Action
Private	SCHREIDER GODLIEB Killed in Action
Private	WAIHE CONRADE Killed in Action
Private	AMONTH JOSEPH
Private	AUC ANDREW
Private	BANDE LEWIS
Private	BARTE HENRY
Private	BELLE HENRY
Private	BELLOF CASPER
Private	BERLNIECKE HENRY
Private	BLASSKE GEORGE
Private	BLESS DANIEL
Private	BOCK HENRY
Private	BNEITHAUPT FRED.
Private	BUDDELMANN HENRY
Private	CHARLY JOHN
Private	COLUMBUS JOHN
Private	DEMIELDER HENRY
Private	DIBO GEORGE
Private	EBERHARD JOHN
Private	FURKER JOSEPH
Private	FRISCHMUTH LORENZ
Private	GLATZ JOHN
Private	GRONEMANN HENRY Discharged
Private	GROSSHEIM HENRY
Private	HIBAEZACK JOHN
Private	HOLZHAUSEN LUDOLPH
Private	JACZESCHIN JOHN
Private	JIENSEE WM.
Private	KAUSCH HENRY
Private	KLEE JOHN Deserted
Private	KOFFE HENRY
Private	LANFEST GUSTAV
Private	LEBOFSKY WENZEL Died from accident
Private	LINDICH GODLIEB
Private	MACKOWITZ GODLIEB
Private	MACKE HENRY Discharged
Private	MEDLER LEWES
Private	MEYER WM.
Private	MITTLESTADT CHRISTN.
Private	MUNCK CONRADE
Private	NOLECKE JOHN
Private	PFLUGER JUSTUS
Private	POPPERT PHILLIP
Private	POSTELBAUER JOHN
Private	PUPPE FREDK.
Private	ROSH SIMON
Private	SANDER HENRY
Private	SCHIER CARL Gray Coll.1908
Private	SCHMITZ PETER
Private	SCHULZE CHRISTR.
Private	SORKA BERND.
Private	STITZIG AUGUSTUS
Private	THOMAT JOHN
Private	VOLKEMANN FRED.
Private	WEDEL LEWES
Private	WITTROCK CHAS. Discharged
Private	WITZ PETER

* * *

8th LINE BATTALION K.G.L.

Lt.Colonel	BEST CHARLES Payne Coll.1911
Major	PETERSDORFF CHARLES
Major	BREYMANN FREDK. Ass.Adjt.General
Captain	BRINCKMANN JULIUS
Captain	BRAUNS SIGIMUND
Captain	VOIGHT AUGUSTUS Killed in Action

Captain	JEHNE HENRY
Captain	MARBURG FREDK.
Captain	ROUGEMONT CHAS.
Captain	WESTERNHAGEN THILO. Killed in Action
Captain	DELINS GEORGE
Captain	MOTZEN GEORGE
Captain	LEIDERITZ FREDK.
Lieutenant	POTEN CHAS.
Lieutenant	MODENBERG LEWIS
Lieutenant	MARENHOLZ WM. Killed in Action
Lieutenant	WEYHE FERDINAND
Lieutenant	WILKENS HENRY
Lieutenant	PATTLER CHRISTN.
Lieutenant	ZIERMANN FREDK.
Lieutenant	GRAHN ERNEST
Lieutenant	SCHMIDTS FRANCIS
Lieutenant	BRUEL OTTO
Lieutenant	BERTRAM BERNARD Gaskell Collection 1908
Lieutenant	SCHLICHTING HENRY
Lieutenant	MULLER FREDK.
Lieutenant	MELMICH AUGUSTUS
Ensign	KUNOTH GODLOVE
Ensign	MOREAU WM.
Ensign	STANLEY EDWARD
Ensign	SPIEL AUGUSTUS
Ensign	MULLER FREDK.
Ensign	SEFFERS HENRY
Ensign	LUNDE FREDK. Galway Foley Collection 1910
Adjutant	BRINCKMANN FREDK.
Qr.Master	TOBING CHRISTN.
Surgeon	ZIERMANN AUGUSTUS
Ass.Surgeon	SANDER ERNET.
Ass.Surgeon	ZIERMANN LEWIS
Sjt.Major	KREBS MAXIMILLIAN
Q.M.S.	SCHMIDT HENRY
Serjeant	ADAM TRANGOTT Killed in Action
Serjeant	WALDMANN CHRISTN. Killed in Action
Serjeant	MITCHELL FREDK.
Serjeant	SCHLIEMANN WM.
Serjeant	HARMS HENRY
Serjeant	ALBRUCK HENRY
Serjeant	BORNER HENRY
Serjeant	HOOHEL CHRISTN.
Serjeant	KOEMELING CHRISTN.
Serjeant	SCHULTZ FREDK.
Serjeant	ADOLPH FRANCIS
Serjeant	PAPE CHAS.
Serjeant	STUART FERDINAND
Serjeant	VINCENTZ CHAS. Discharged
Serjeant	SPANGENBERG AUGUSTUS
Serjeant	BRILL HENRY
Serjeant	FREE JAMES
Serjeant	SCHIMPF CHRISTOPH
Serjeant	DIEDRICKS CHRISTN.
Serjeant	SCHULZ CHAS.
Serjeant	SCHNEIDER CHRISTN.
Serjeant	BAGER JOSEPH Discharged
Serjeant	KEHR LORENZ Discharged
Serjeant	VOLLMER FREDK.
Serjeant	WEISS FREDK.
Serjeant	SCHULZE ERNST.
Serjeant	WERNER ADAM Missing since 18 June
Serjeant	WECKER GODLOVE
Serjeant	KLOSE JOHN
Serjeant	PLEHNE CHAS.
Serjeant	PAMEYER CHRISTN.
Serjeant	KABERKORN JAMES
Serjeant	WOLFF DERK. Discharged
Serjeant	HOPPE HENRY
Corporal	SCHEIDER CHRISTN. Killed in Action
Corporal	BOOK GODLOVE DDischarged
Corporal	BERNUM HENRY
Corporal	HASENJAEGER LEWIS
Corporal	HESTERIN MATHEW
Corporal	MOSER JAMES
Corporal	WUNSCH HENRY
Corporal	BECKER LEWIS
Corporal	GRONOCKE CHRISTOPH Discharged
Corporal	MANSON ANTON
Corporal	STARKE WM.
Corporal	WOLLENHAUPT CASPAR
Corporal	FREY FRANCIS
Corporal	GROLL SAML.
Corporal	MEYER LEWIS
Corporal	SEMPF CHRISTN.
Corporal	SCHULZ FREDK.
Corporal	ARENT IGNAZ
Corporal	BERTRAM CHRISTIAN
Corporal	BERIFAN JOSEPH
Corporal	DETERDING FREDK.
Corporal	LISSENER JOSEPH
Corporal	UHLENDORFF FREDK.
Corporal	HARTUNG FREDK.
Corporal	HUTHMANN AUGUSTUS

Corporal	KOLLING CHRISTN.	Private	BERGMANN JOHN Killed in Action
Corporal	KAHRS JOACHIM	Private	ENGEL CHAS. Killed in Action
Corporal	WEBER FRANCIS	Private	HERMANN CHAS. Killed in Action
Corporal	BATTMER JOHN	Private	KETZNER ADAM. Killed in Action
Corporal	HETTING JOSEPH	Private	ORNE JOHN Killed in Action
Corporal	MINDE CONRAD	Private	SPANOWITZ PHILIP Killed in Action
Corporal	MULLER JOSEPH Discharged	Private	LIEBERGELD GEORGE Killed in Action
Corporal	RICHTER JOHN Discharged	Private	WERNER GEORGE Killed in Action
Drummer	HENTZE CHRISTN. Killed in Action	Private	WERNER DERK.
Drummer	DOWROWOLSKY DOMINIC	Private	GEGEL MARTIN
Drummer	HOFSMANN JOSEPH	Private	BECKMEYER CHRISTN.
Drummer	DOROSNEF ANTHONY	Private	BECKER CONRAD
Drummer	GROCHE FREDK.	Private	BOHNHORST HENRY Discharged
Drummer	MOHLE CHAS.	Private	BRUSSMANN FREDK.
Drummer	PLATTE AUGUSTUS	Private	BENNE HENRY Discharged
Drummer	MULLER CORN.	Private	BANDERER VALENTIN
Drummer	FISCHER JOHN	Private	CAMBRY JOSEPH
Drummer	HELJE FREDK. Discharged	Private	DOROCH ALEX.
Drummer	KUHL CHRISTN.	Private	DENOT JOHN
Drummer	SCHWARZ CHAS.	Private	DOMME PETER
Drummer	ISTERHOFF MICHL.	Private	FITTGER JOHN Discharged
Drummer	SCHNELLHARD CHRISTN. Discharged	Private	FERRENS ANTHONY
Private	SCHOPER PETER Killed in Action	Private	GRUNEWALD JOSEPH
Private	SCARLIAN JOHN Killed in Action	Private	GRAEFKE JURGEN Discharged
Private	SCHWARTZ FREDK. Killed in Action	Private	HAAK HENRY
Private	TENGER ANTHONY Killed in Action	Private	HORNBOSTEL HENRY Discharged
Private	DEMETER JOSEPH Killed in Action	Private	HASELOP CHRISTN.
Private	PAUL FREDK. Killed in Action	Private	HARSLINGER LORENZ
Private	IWANOF JOACHIM Killed in Action	Private	HOFFMANN WM.
Private	HAUSKNECHT MATTW. Killed in Action	Private	HIRSCHFELD LEVIN
Private	TOLOSKY FRANCIS Killed in Action	Private	IOSTEN JOHN
Private	ROLHER BERND. Killed in Action	Private	KESTMACHER GODLOVE
Private	AUGUSTIN CHRISTN. Killed in Action	Private	KANGEL PETER
Private	PETRASH JOHN Killed in Action	Private	KROWBINSKY SAMSON
Private	BOSCHLING DERK. Killed in Action	Private	KRUBER JAMES
Private	TARNESKY ANTHONY Killed in Action	Private	KEFSMEYER FREDK.
Private	FLOCK NICOLAUS Killed in Action	Private	KIMZE FREDK.
Private	LUDWIG FREDK. Killed in Action	Private	LINGOTSKY JOHN
Private	MAURER MARTIN Killed in Action	Private	LASSOCK MARTIN
Private	ZERNEZKY JOSEPH Killed in Action	Private	LINGE JOSEPH Watters sale June 1913
		Private	LUCAS JOSEPH
		Private	LANSE ANTHONY
		Private	LEITNER LUCAS
		Private	LINSTOW WM. Discharged
		Private	MUMBRAUER HENRY Discharged
		Private	MEYER FREDK.
		Private	NASKE HENRY
		Private	NOWARSKY VINCENT
		Private	REHBEIN HENRY

Private	SCHUH JOHN
Private	SEYGANZ MATTHEW
Private	STANDER JNS Whitaker Collection 1908
Private	STANDER PETER
Private	SALGE HENRY
Private	SCHMIDT FREDK.
Private	TOLLE GEORGE
Private	TRIBIAN LEWIS
Private	THIELE WM.
Private	TEGTMEYER CHRISTN .
Private	VOLCKER MICHAEL
Private	WOSCHICK JOSEPH
Private	WILAUTHY JOHN
Private	WAGENER HENRY
Private	ZANKOSKY ANTHY.
Private	BUTJACK ANTHY.
Private	BLUMBERG HENRY
Private	BELL JOHN
Private	BODENSTEIN LEOPOLD
Private	DOBLAR FRANCIS
Private	DELVAAN WM.
Private	DEOLERK FRANCIS
Private	CUDLICK ADAM
Private	CEASAR HENRY
Private	EGGERS GEORGE
Private	ENGEL GODLOVE
Private	FRITZ JAMES
Private	FERNSKY GARDA
Private	GERMANSTEDT HENRY Discharged
Private	GROBE CONRAD
Private	GOLDMANN THADEUS
Private	HELMICH WM.
Private	HANSER ANTHY. Discharged
Private	HOFFMANN FREDK.
Private	HETZ JOHN
Private	HOCHMUTH JOHN Discharged
Private	IGES PETER
Private	IWANO JOHN
Private	KREBS HENRY
Private	KEMNER DAVID
Private	KIPPENBERG FREDK.
Private	KERL JOHN
Private	KOCH FREDK.
Private	KAMPE HENRY
Private	KOSTER JOHN
Private	KONWITZSKY JOSEPH
Private	MUGGE CHARLES
Private	MEGGES JOHN

Private	METZLOFF PETER
Private	NICOLAY ANDREW
Private	NAGEL HENRY Discharged
Private	NAFSARWITZ THOS.
Private	ORBAN JOHN
Private	PRAER HENRY
Private	ROWER CLAUS
Private	SIEMON PETER
Private	SCHABACK JOHN
Private	STRASSER MATTW.
Private	SCHMIDT FRANCIS
Private	SPORLANDER FREDK.
Private	STAERMICKEL JOHN
Private	SCHNEIDER LORENZ
Private	THOMAS THEODOR
Private	UNIE MICHL.
Private	VOIGT HENRY
Private	WENDT CHRISTN.
Private	ZABOE JOSEPH
Private	AHRENDS FREDK.
Private	ARMBRECHT HENRY
Private	ARMBRECHT FREDK.
Private	ANTON FRANCIS
Private	BOSS HENRY
Private	BALLACH JOSEPH
Private	BLUMENHAGEN JOHN
Private	ERDMANN JOHN
Private	EHLERS HENRY Discharged
Private	FEISELER BERND. Discharged
Private	FRISCH HENRY
Private	FELBER BARTHW.
Private	FREDERACK FREDK.
Private	FUCHS HENRY
Private	GUNTHER FRANCIS
Private	HAAKE CHRISTN.
Private	HOFFMANN MICHL.
Private	HEIGAN MATTW.
Private	HENER HENRY
Private	JACOB JAMES
Private	KININSKY JOSEPH
Private	KLAUS GODLOVE
Private	KREGMEYER JOHN
Private	KANNE JOSEPH
Private	KOBARSKY JOHN
Private	LINNEMANN FRANCIS
Private	LAUBE MICHL.
Private	MASKANITSCH PAUL
Private	MEYER CHRISTN.
Private	MIERK JOHN

Private	MEYER PETER	Private	PABSH CONRAD
Private	NOAK GODHELF	Private	PLACE JAMES
Private	NEUMANN JOHN Discharged	Private	POSS ANTHY.
Private	OTTO GODFRIED	Private	POACE JOSEPH
Private	PEYMANN HENRY	Private	ROTHMANN JOHN
Private	SCHRADER CHAS.	Private	ROSCHESKY THOMAS
Private	SCHUMANN FREDK.	Private	SCHNEIDER JAMES
Private	STEINING WM.	Private	SCHEIT WM. Gray Coll.1908
Private	SCHULZ GEORGE	Private	STEINBERG WM. Discharged
Private	THALMANN JAMES	Private	SCHACHT CONRAD Discharged
Private	THIEL HENRY	Private	STAMMEL MICHL.
Private	THOMAS ENOAS	Private	SCHMIDT CHRISTN. Discharged
Private	WILLMER FREDK. Discharged	Private	SCHAFERER JOHN
Private	WIERACK JOSEPH	Private	SUSKOSKY IWAN
Private	WOITSCHER JAMES	Private	SCHULZ LEWIS
Private	WEITH CHRISTOP	Private	TELLITT FREDK.
Private	WENZEL MATTW.	Private	TASTOW HENRY
Private	ZIGELLO JAMES	Private	VOLK FRANCIS
Private	ZINZOLL VALENTIN	Private	WAGENER HENRY
Private	ANGERS MICHL.	Private	WELLER CONRAD Discharged
Private	BREMEKE CHRISTN.	Private	WARNECKE AUGUSTUS
Private	BOGINSKY JAMES	Private	WENHOLZ HENRY
Private	BITZER GODLOVE	Private	WEYER WM.
Private	BORNFRAGER CHRISTN.	Private	ZINGER JOHN
Private	CROSCHINSKY JOSEPH	Private	ZIEGENBAUER JOSEPH
Private	DANNLO ABRM.	Private	AHRENS HENRY
Private	FEDRO PETER	Private	BACH FRANCIS
Private	FLORIN GEORGE	Private	BOSCHOOK ALEX.
Private	GEFFERT JOHN	Private	BLUME GODFREE
Private	GROMMOFF IWAN	Private	BECKER FREDK.
Private	GROTHE WM.	Private	BADER HENRY
Private	GRUPE HENRY	Private	BECK ADAM Col.Murray's Coll.1908
Private	HABERER FREDK.	Private	BOOKEL JAMES
Private	HAUSER ANTHY.	Private	ECKHARDT MICHL.
Private	HANSEN ARTHUR Discharged	Private	EBELING ANDREW
Private	HASENJAEGER CONRAD	Private	ENDLICH JOHN
Private	KARRAS GERICK	Private	EIRICH ADAM
Private	KUSDAY HENRY Discharged	Private	ERNEST JOHN
Private	KONECKE CHRISTN.	Private	ELBES FREDK.
Private	LEOPOLD HENRY	Private	ESCH WM.
Private	LOHMANN JOSEPH	Private	FLEISCHER GEORGE
Private	LANGE HENRY	Private	FOREMANN FRANCIS
Private	LORENZ CHRISTN.	Private	FLORGA PAUL
Private	MENGER LEWIS	Private	FRESSDORFF DANIEL
Private	MULLER FREDK.	Private	FLARZOOK ALBERT
Private	MANSACK MICHL.	Private	FONTAIN GEORGE
Private	NEUKIRCH JOHN Discharged	Private	FISCHER CHAS
Private	NOLLAND ANTHY. Discharged	Private	GITTO FREDK.
Private	PALUMBE JOSEPH	Private	GOERS ENGELBRECHT

Private	GRASS JAMES
Private	GILBERT CHAS.
Private	HOPPE HENRY
Private	HIRSCHEN JOHN
Private	HERTZ JOHN
Private	KOCH JOHN
Private	KLAPROTH WM.
Private	KAHLENBERG JOHN
Private	KEGEL JOSEPH
Private	KENER JOHN
Private	KNOBLOCCH LEWIS
Private	KITOR ANTHY.
Private	KAWALLE MICHL.
Private	KREISELER GODFREE
Private	LEFSMANN JOHN
Private	MAEDLER HENRY
Private	MORSCH SEBASTIAN
Private	MEYER CHRISTIAN
Private	OTTENBERG CHRISTN.
Private	RATH FREDK.
Private	ROSKOSKY JOSEPH
Private	RITZAN CHRISTN.
Private	REINHARD GODLOVE
Private	SCHULZ ANTHY.
Private	SAY ANDREW
Private	SCHONEWALD JOSEPH
Private	SCHULZ MARTIN
Private	STEYER JOHN
Private	SCHITTAS JAMES
Private	SCHAFER JOHN Discharged
Private	SCHEFEUCK JOSEPH
Private	VOIGT JOHN
Private	VOIGT JOSEPH
Private	WAUFSMANN GEORGE
Private	WENTEL FREDK.
Private	WITZEL FREDK.
Private	BODE HENRY Discharged
Private	BRESSLER CHAS.
Private	BEHRINS JOHN Discharged
Private	BREMER WM.
Private	BACH JOSEPH
Private	CUTELOCH NICOLAS
Private	DREMMER FREDK.
Private	EBBRECHT CHRISTN.
Private	EHMANN JOSEPH
Private	ERIS PETER
Private	FAULBRUCK CHAS.
Private	FEISEL CONRAD Discharged
Private	FORTH PETER
Private	GREWY LEWIS Discharged
Private	GOTZLING CHAS. Discharged
Private	GAERTZER JOHN Discharged
Private	GENSCH MARTIN
Private	GARTES CHAS.
Private	HAMMELMANN ANTHY. Discharged
Private	HUBER HENRY
Private	HARTMANN CHRISTN. Discharged
Private	HANDEL JOHN
Private	HOLZHAUSEN JOHN
Private	JAEGER MICHL.
Private	JEFINSF IWAN
Private	KRIEGSFELD JOSEPH
Private	KEGELER MICHL.
Private	KEMBER JOHN
Private	KUNNERT JOHN
Private	KAMINSKY MICHL
Private	KRUGER HENRY
Private	LEINGANG FRANCIS
Private	LENNING FRANCIS
Private	LANGE JOHN
Private	MULLER GEORGE
Private	MULLER ABRM.
Private	MEBK DERK
Private	MAY GERHARD
Private	MARTIN JOHN
Private	MEYER GODFREE Discharged
Private	NACHTMANN FRANCIS Discharged
Private	NEMETZ JAMES
Private	NOWITZSKY GREGORIC
Private	OTTO MARONS
Private	OTTO JAMES
Private	RESSMEYER FREDK.
Private	RULLAN FRANCIS
Private	RENTE CHAS. Littledale sale November 1910
Private	RINGE CHAS.
Private	RIEL GEORGE
Private	ROHN GODLOVE
Private	SCHONEMEYER GEORGE
Private	SCHMIDT WM.
Private	SCHAPER FREDK.
Private	SCHUBKEGEL CONRAD
Private	SILBER MARTIN
Private	SMOLICK THOS.
Private	SPOSSY ANTHY.
Private	SCHRAGGE BERNHARD Cheylesmore Collection 1908
Private	SCHAD ALEX.
Private	STADELER JOSEPH

Private	WEGENER JOHN
Private	WOLFARTH CHRISTN.
Private	WASSILOFF JOHN
Private	WEGENER HENRY
Private	WOLTERSDORFF FREDK.
Private	WIEDMANN SAML.

* * *

KINGS GERMAN ARTILLERY

Staff

Major & Bt. Lt.Colonel	HARTMANN GEO. JULIUS
Ass.Surgeon	RENZHAUSEN ADOLPHUS
Ass.Surgeon	BEYER WM.

1st Troop

Captain	SYMPHER AUGUSTUS
2nd Captain	BRANN WM.
Lieutenant	STOCKMANN LEWIS
Lieutenant	GOEBEN V. WM.
Lieutenant	SCHORNHORST V. WM.
Ass.Surgeon	KRONE GEORGE
Q.M.S.	SCHRADER CONRAD
Serjeant	GERLING CHRISTN.
Serjeant	BRUKS FREDK.
Serjeant	ENZEHAUSON GEORGE
Corporal	TOLLE CONRAD
Corporal	MORTFELD LEWIS
Corporal	HEYNE CHAS.
Bomber	HEINRICKE FREDK.
Bombr.	KIENE HENRY
Bombr.	DENECKE FREDK.
Bomber	PINKWOFS JOHN
Bombr.	QUITMEYER HENRY
Bomber	NIEMEYER HENRY
Farrier	GELIS AUGUSTUS
Smith	BOLTE FREDK.
Smith	FLAGE CHAS.
Smith	OHLERKING JURGEN
Coll.Maker	HARTMANN HENRY
Coll.Maker	MERTEN AUGUSTUS
Wheeler	MULLER GABRIEL
Gunners	HELMHOLD CHRISTR.
Gunner	BIERMANN JOHN
Gunner	TATJE CHRISTN.
Gunner	DOPKE ANTHY.
Gunner	EGGERS FREDK.
Gunners	MULLER JOHN
Gunner	SEELMEYER FRANCIS
Gunner	MEYER WM.
Gunner	MEERHEIMB ERNEST
Gunner	PECK JAMES
Gunner	DEGENER HENRY
Gunner	BONNYARTIN CHRISTN.
Gunner	GUDEHUT GEORGE
Gunner	GOHNT FREDK.
Gunner	KAMLAH HENRY
Gunner	KRAGE FREDK.
Gunner	LEHNE DEDK.
Gunner	DRAGE FREDK.
Gunner	GAPEL HENRY
Gunner	STEHRMANN WM.
Gunner	SCHONFELD CHRISTN.
Gunner	HOPPE CHRISTR.
Gunner	LUDE MANN JOHN
Gunner	HULSE FREDK.
Gunner	HOBEIN HENRY
Gunner	SCHAFER GEORGE
Gunner	STELLING GEORGE
Gunner	ADAM HENRY
Gunner	BECKMANN HENRY
Gunner	MUHRENBERG HENRY
Gunner	BAUMGARTE HENRY
Gunner	HACHMEISTER HENRY
Gunner	MUHLKE CHAS.
Gunner	BONNEY FREDK.
Gunner	FETTE LEWIS
Gunner	MUNSTERMANN HENRY
Gunner	PFINGSTEN FREDK.
Gunner	BOHNHAUS FREDK.
Gunner	MEYER JUSTUS
Gunner	DUSCHE JOHN
Gunner	MUNKEL LEWIS
Gunner	SCHARENBERG WM.
Gunner	MARWITZ LEWIS
Gunner	BOHNHAUS HENRY
Gunner	BEHREN CONRAD
Gunner	KOHLER CHAS.
Gunner	BIERWIRTH CHAS.
Gunner	HEMME HENRY
Gunner	WENTE ADOLPHUS
Gunner	BROCKMANN ERNEST
Gunner	REISTER JURGEN
Gunner	MUFSMANN HENRY
Gunner	GRIEFS JOHN
Gunner	WESTPHAL HENRY
Gunner	PILGER JOHN
Gunner	TROBERG CHAS.
Gunner	STREMEL CHRISTN.

Gunner	KORBOSKY ALBERT
Gunner	SIELE HENRY
Gunner	PLENTJE WM.
Gunner	PETERSEN JOHN
Gunner	MULLER FERDINAND
Gunner	HOFFMANN GEORGE
Gunner	HOIRITH PETER
Gunner	STRADTMANN FRANCIS
Gunner	HENKEL HENRY
Gunner	BERNISER JOHN
Gunner	HOSSELMANN FREDK.
Driver	BAXMANN WM.
Driver	BAXMANN WM.
Driver	DENECKE HENRY
Driver	KRAGE HENRY
Driver	HANNE WM.
Driver	RUNGE LEWIS
Driver	THIELE JAMES
Driver	HUTTMANN HENRY
Driver	BLUME JOHN
Driver	BAHLFS HENRY
Driver	GERBERDING HENRY
Driver	RICKMANN HENRY
Driver	NIENSTEDT FREDK.
Driver	PINKROFS HENRY
Driver	STRUBE HENRY Gaskell Collection 1908
Driver	MEYNE HENRY
Driver	GROTE CONRAD
Driver	HARLAND CHAS.
Driver	SCHWENKE HENRY
Driver	KUNST DIEDK.
Driver	WEHRMANN HENRY
Driver	SCHMIDT VALENTIN
Driver	BUSCH CHRISTR.
Driver	DEBUCK PETER
Driver	DANN JOHN
Driver	SCHISTEL FRANCIS
Driver	ZUBER BALTHAZER
Driver	WITCHEGODSKY PEAFSE
Driver	ADAM DEDRIC
Driver	GILBERT LEWIS
Driver	MEYER HENRY
Driver	TOLKE WM.
Driver	PFINGSTON HENRY
Driver	SANTHOFF FREDK.
Driver	BADEN CHRISTR.
Driver	DECKE HENRY
Driver	FREDERICKS JOHN
Driver	KOHLER WM.
Driver	DIERS FREDK.
Driver	SUMENING JOHN
Driver	BRASE HENRY
Driver	RUST HENRY
Driver	ROTERMMED FREDK.
Driver	GELIS FREDK.
<u>2nd Troop</u>	
Captain	KUHLMANN HENRY
2nd Captain	WIERING GEORGE
Lieutenant	SPECKMANN THEODOR
Lieutenant	MEYER GEORGE
2nd Lieutenant	WISSELL V. LEWIS
Sjt.Major	KONECKE LUDOLPHUS
Q.M.S.	WOHLER HENRY
Serjeant	LANDERS JUSTUS
Serjeant	NEINBURG FERDINAND
Corporal	REESE CHRISTN.
Corporal	MEYER FREDK.
Corporal	MULLENHOFF THEODOR
Corporal	SCHARER BENDICT.
Bomber	NOLTE CHRISTN.
Bomber	BIESTER CHRISTR.
Bomber	WINKELMANN HENRY
Bomber	MEYER JOHN
Bomber	BODE HENRY
Bomber	RAHLFS HENRY
Bomber	SCHIELE HENRY
Farrier	KNUTTEL CONRAD
Smith	DIEDRICH JOHN
Smith	BECKMANN CHRISTN.
Smith	BRANS DIEDK.
Coll.Maker	HARTMANN FREDK.
Wheeler	BALKE FREDK.
Trumpeter	SENDER HENRY
Gunner	LUHMANN HENRY
Gunner	BECKER GEORGE
Gunner	GLENE HENRY
Gunner	HARTMANN WM.
Gunner	LOHRBACH LEWIS
Gunner	CLAUSING DEIDK.
Gunner	KORFF CHRISTR.
Gunner	WAHLBAUM FREDK.
Gunner	RIECKENBERG FREDK.
Gunner	WENTE ALBERT
Gunner	ZUBERBIER FREDK.
Gunner	BERGMANN HENRY
Gunner	MEYER HENRY
Gunner	HARKE HENRY

Gunner	KRUGER FREDK.
Gunner	RESTENPART WM.
Gunner	BARTELS CONRAD
Gunner	BOHLE HENRY
Gunner	ELGES HENRY
Gunner	LAUS HENRY
Gunner	REICKENBERG HENRY
Gunner	WIEDENROTH HENRY
Gunner	ISLEMANN LEWIS
Gunner	GARTNER CONRAD
Gunner	MULLER HENRY
Gunner	VOLGER HENRY
Gunner	DUENSURG FREDK.
Gunner	GRIEME LUDOLPHUS
Gunner	HUNDERTMACH FREDK.
Gunner	HORNEMANN GEORGE
Gunner	BROCKMANN CONRAD
Gunner	BENERMANN LEWIS
Gunner	JUHNEMANN HENRY
Gunner	RITTER HENRY Whitaker Collection 1908
Gunner	FEDDERKE HENRY
Gunner	STELLMANN HENRY
Gunner	SENDER HENRY
Gunner	MAHLMANN CHRISTN.
Gunner	LINNEMANN HENRY
Gunner	HOLLE FREDK.
Gunner	SCHELE HENRY
Gunner	BLUME FREDK.
Gunner	REIGER LEWIS
Gunner	MEYER PETER
Gunner	SCHMIDT JOHN
Gunner	NIEMEYER HENRY
Gunner	RUFSE JOHN
Gunner	TRENCH JUSTUS
Gunner	SCHMIDT ESBANUS
Gunner	HOPKE HENRY
Gunner	BOLTE WM.
Gunner	ROST WM.
Gunner	BALHAUS ANDREW
Gunner	WAGNER JOHN
Gunner	TOLLER JACOB
Gunner	PUDER REINHARD
Gunner	STOOT JACOBUS Gray Coll.1908
Gunner	HARRIE ELBERT
Gunner	ANTHE PHILIP
Gunner	ANTHONITZ WM.
Gunner	SWEERINK HENRY
Gunner	ENDERLY MARTIN
Gunner	STORR JOSEPH
Gunner	STUHNDKE FREDK.
Gunner	BEISTER FREDK.
Drummer	TIMPE JURGEN
Drummer	MORTFELD CONRAD
Drummer	SCHRADER HENRY Gray Coll.1908
Drummer	KNUSH LEWIS
Drummer	BIERMANN HENRY
Drummer	DIERKS HENRY
Drummer	MINNKE HENRY
Drummer	SUSTRAT GEORGE
Drummer	HAUSE HENRY
Drummer	MOLTHAN HENRY
Drummer	HEINEMANN HENRY
Drummer	HARTMANN GODFREY
Drummer	DEMEYER CHRISTR.
Drummer	RONGE FREDK.
Drummer	ZABITZER EDWD.
Drummer	BUSKING JOHN
Drummer	MEYER JOSEPH
Drummer	JACOBI JOHN
Drummer	TAPKING FREDK.
Drummer	KUDER JOHN
Drummer	KENTZ HENRY
Drummer	JUNG HENRY
Drummer	HOOPS JOHN
Drummer	PREFSELLY JOSEPH
Drummer	STEEGE HENRY
Drummer	RIECHMANN HENRY
Drummer	GULLAS WM.
Drummer	MILLER CHAS.
Drummer	MAJER FREDK.
Drummer	RIESEBERG ANDREW
Drummer	GALTHORN CHRISTN.
Driver	ISEN CHRISTN.
Driver	PIEPHO CHRISTN.
Driver	BERGAMNN JOHN
Drummer	MATTIES CHRISTIAN
Driver	MARHENKE WM.
Driver	BRUNS JURGEN
Driver	HUGO HENRY
Driver	SCHLUTERBUSCH FREDK.
Driver	REDECKE FREDK.
Driver	BUSKING DIEDK.
Driver	MINED FREDK.
Driver	HARTMANN FREDK.
Driver	HIRCHKOFF JURGEN

1st Company

2nd Captain	ERYTHROPEL FREDK.
Corporal	LOHMANN WM.

Corporal	MARLCH HENRY
Bomber	KAHLE HENRY
Bomber	HULSEMANN WERNER
Drummer	EBENHARHT CHAS.
Gunner	BRIX JOHN
Gunner	CLEMENS WM.
Gunner	KARBER HENRY
Gunner	KIRCHOFF GOTTLIEB
Gunner	KIPP HENRY
Gunner	LUHRSEN WM.
Gunner	MERKEL JOHN
Gunner	SCHWIENING CHRISTN.
Gunner	SCHMINK JOHN
Gunner	ANGEWORTH ARNOLD
Gunner	BALORE JOHN
Gunner	CORNS PETER
Gunner	HOFFMANN GEORGE
Gunner	HAMM JOSEPH
Gunner	HEROLD HENRY
Gunner	FUNSTEIN MICHL.
Gunner	KAHLE ADOLPHUS
Gunner	MANN JOHN
Gunner	MENJES VALENTIN
Gunner	WEXEL BERND.
Gunner	FISCHER GEORGE
Gunner	SCHWERDLFEYER ERNEST
Gunner	HUCH JOHN
Gunner	KENECKE JOHN
Gunner	WESTPHAL HENRY
Gunner	ERNST HENRY
Gunner	GIESECKE HENRY
Gunner	SCHAFER CHRISTN. Gaskell Collection 1908
Gunner	RIDDER HENRY
Gunner	MEYER LEWIS
Gunner	LAAKEMANN HENRY
Gunner	ACKERMANN HENRY
Gunner	WIEZMANN HENRY
Gunner	SCHARNHORST ERNST
Gunner	LUTEFINK ANTHY.
Gunner	TRAPHAGEN CONRAD
Gunner	GREMET AUGUSTUS
Gunner	KIEN FREDK.
Gunner	ALDENHOFEN ANTHY.
Gunner	LAWRENT CHRISTN.
Gunner	FLECHSIG JOHN
Dr.Serjeant	DEICHMANN HENRY
Dr.Corporal	DUENSING JOHN Gaskell Collection 1908
Farrier	SEETIG HENRY
Smith	OHEROGGE JURGEN
Driver	AHRENS HENRY
Driver	BISCHOFF JOHN
Driver	BRENNING HENRY
Driver	BOHN WILLIAM Cheylesmore Coll.1908
Driver	BORCHERS FREDK.
Driver	EHLERS HENRY
Driver	EHLERS FREDK.
Driver	HANKE ANDREW
Driver	HAGEN JOHN
Driver	HAUSE CHRISTN.
Driver	KRENTZKAM HENRY
Driver	PAPE HENRY
Driver	BOHRIG HENRY
Driver	SAUER GEORGE
Driver	STRUBE HENRY
Driver	AHRENS LEWIS
Driver	BARTLING FREDK.
Driver	GEHRKE HENRY
Driver	LEFFHERTZ HENRY
Driver	MEYER JOHN
Driver	NEBER FREDK.
Driver	POLLMANN GEORGE
Driver	PLATTE JOHN
Driver	RIEBOCK HENRY
Driver	STUCKE HENRY
Driver	SCHMITZ WM.
Driver	SIEMER CHRISTN.
Driver	WALTER GODFREY
Driver	WIEGMANN FREDK.
Driver	WITTE HENRY
Driver	NELSON S.
Driver	BIERMANN FREDK.
Driver	MENSING HENRY
Driver	SIEVER LEOPOLD
Driver	BAUMGARTER HANS
Driver	GRAUE WM.

2nd Company

Lieutenant	HARTMANN HENRY
2nd Lieutenant	HEISE LEWIS
Corporal	BUSSMANN FREDK.
Corporal	SCHIELE FREDK.
Bomber	KRUGER HENRY
Gunner	STURMER FRANCIS
Gunner	TANKE JAMES
Gunner	SCHRADER FREDK.
Gunner	DIERKS FREDK.
Gunner	RAALEE HENRY
Gunner	DETTMER HENRY
Gunner	HOFFMANN FREDK.

Gunner	WILHELM FREDK.
Gunner	KONIG WM.
Gunner	DIEDRICH JOHN
Gunner	MATERNE CHRISTN. Payne Collection 1911
Gunner	LINNENP V.D. PETERS
Gunner	WARMS FERDINAND
Gunner	DIEPER BATIST
Gunner	DIESER CONRAD
Gunner	VAHREN CASPER
Gunner	GEHSE PHILIP
Gunner	POETSCH JAMES
Dr.Serjeant	GORLICH FREDK.
Dr.Corporal	BECKERS FREDK.
Dr.Corporal	SCHMUPHASE HENRY
Smith	WITTE HENRY
Farrier	HESPOS CONRAD
Coll.Maker	LUTYENS GEORGE
Coll.Maker	ROSE FREDK.
Driver	HEYER CHRISTN
Driver	HOLBORN HENRY
Driver	HARTMANN CHRISTR
Driver	HANNAMANN FREDK.
Driver	CRAMER HENRY
Driver	GEELE DEDRICK
Driver	HUTH ADOLPHUS
Driver	JURGENS CHRISTN.
Driver	KIRSCHNER SEBASTIAN
Driver	HANACK MICHL.
Driver	KALTWASSER ANDREW
Driver	WORMS FREDK.
Driver	HAAKE HENRY
Driver	BRETSCHNEIDER LEWIS
Driver	SPORLEDEN ERNEST
Driver	ZIMMER JOHN
Driver	WIEGAND CHRISTR.
Driver	MEINECKE CONRAD
Driver	KOCH HENRY
Driver	KORFF FREDK.
Driver	SCHULZE HENRY
Driver	STUNKEL HENRY
Driver	WILDHAGEN HENRY
Driver	KUHE FREDK.
Driver	SCHMIDT HENRY
Driver	MEYER HENRY
Driver	JACOBS WM.
Driver	SEFKE HENRY
Driver	ROSENBACH WM.
Driver	PROPSING JOSEPH
Driver	MACHEBEN HENRY
Driver	BUSKING LEWIS
Driver	WALTER FREDK.
Driver	RUTH JOHN

<u>4th Company</u>

Captain	CLEEVES ANDREW
Lieutenant	MIELMANN HENRY
2nd Lieutenant	LUDWITZ HERMANN
Serjeant	DUENKING HENRY
Serjeant	BRACKE FREDK.
Corporal	ALFKEN DEDRIC.
Corporal	KONECKE HENRY
Corporal	SCHLUTER HENRY
Bomber	BOSENBERG HENRY
Bomber	STAHL FREDK.
Bomber	HUNTE JOHN
Bomber	HAMELBURG HENRY
Bomber	LIND PETER
Drummer	JECK JACOB
Gunner	BOHLE HENRY
Gunner	BOHNE PETER
Gunner	BRUNOTTE HENRY
Gunner	BOCK CHRISTN
Gunner	BODE HENRY
Gunner	BREMER WM.
Gunner	CORDES FREDK.
Gunner	DREYER FREDK.
Gunner	DENECKE CHRISTOPH
Gunner	DETTMER LEWIS
Gunner	DELIAN ALBERT
Gunner	EHLERS JOHN
Gunner	FEHRMANN JOACHIM
Gunner	FELLERMANN HENRY
Gunner	GARTNER HENRY
Gunner	GODECKE CHRISTN.
Gunner	HEINE JOHN
Gunner	HARKE HENRY
Gunner	HUPE HENRY
Gunner	HAAKE AUGUSTUS
Gunner	HEMME GEORGE
Gunner	HAVERBECK HENRY
Gunner	KOHLER HENRY
Gunner	KRONE GEORGE
Gunner	LANDWEHR WM.
Gunner	LUTZIE ANDREW
Gunner	LEONHARDT CHRISTN.
Gunner	LESEBERG HENRY
Gunner	MEYERFELD CONRAD
Gunner	MEYER WM.

Gunner	MULLER CHRISTN
Gunner	MOHRHOFF HENRY
Gunner	MULLER DIEDRK.
Gunner	MENSEMANN HENRY
Gunner	PFINGSTEN CONRAD
Gunner	PETERS HENRY
Gunner	RIECKENBERG CHRISTN.
Gunner	SCHULZE CHAS.
Gunner	SCHUFSLER CHRISTN.
Gunner	STEINLADE HENRY
Gunner	SCHNEIDER FREDK.
Gunner	WOLTMANN JOHN
Gunner	WILDTHAGEN CHRISTN. Glendining's sale Jan 1910
Gunner	WEDEMEYER FREDK.
Gunner	BENSCH JOSEPH
Gunner	BAUMANN JOHN
Gunner	DIEBOLT ALBERT
Gunner	EICHHORN PETER
Gunner	FINGER JOHN
Gunner	JAHNS FREDK.
Gunner	KAYSER JOHN
Gunner	MEISTERLING GODFREY Watters sale June 1913
Gunner	SATE CONRAD
Gunner	SEMMEL FRANCIS
Gunner	SCHEERE GEORGE
Gunner	TIPPELSMANN HENRY
Gunner	WEGMANN ROMBERT
Gunner	ZIMMER JOHN
Dr.Serjeant	GOING FREDK.
Dr.Corporal	TINKE HENRY
Dr.Corporal	DRANGMEISTER CHRISTN.
Smith	MEYER RUDOLPHUS
Smith	SWERTEZKY ANTHY.
Coll.Maker	KREICH GEORGE
Coll.Maker	FUNK HENRY
Wheeler	DUSCHE THIELO
Wheeler	GURSKY JOHN
Driver	ASCHE JOHN
Driver	ANTHOFF JOSEPH
Driver	BATTERMANN HENRY
Driver	BEHRENS HENRY
Driver	BRUNS JOHN
Driver	BALTE FREDK.
Driver	BORGES HENRY
Driver	BOHLMEYER AUGUSTUS
Driver	COORS CHRISTR.
Driver	DEHN JOHN
Driver	ELSE JOHN
Driver	EICKMANN LUDOLPHUS
Driver	ESSER JOSEPH
Driver	ENGELMANN HENRY
Driver	FREISE WM.
Driver	FATEMANN CHRISTR.
Driver	GASTMANN HENRY
Driver	HAFSELMANN MARTIN
Driver	HAUSS MARTIN
Driver	HELLMER LEWIS
Driver	HINSBERG MATHEW
Driver	LANGWERTZ FREDK
Driver	LINNEMANN FREDK.
Driver	LANGLOTZ DANIEL
Driver	MEYER FREDK.
Driver	OHLHERST HENRY
Driver	PAYMANN HENRY
Driver	PLATE ERNEST
Driver	POHLE CONRAD
Driver	ROCKAR WM.
Driver	REINECKE FREDK.
Driver	RUPETZKY JOACHIM
Driver	SCHACHT JOHN
Driver	SCHAFER FREDK.
Driver	STAPES CONRAD
Driver	SPANGENBERG FREDK.
Driver	SCHMIDT WM.
Driver	SCHMIDT CHRISTN Col.Gaskell's Sale 1911
Driver	STEINMETZ HENRY
Driver	SCHRODER DIEDRICK
Driver	THIELKE ADAM
Driver	WEDEMEYER CHRISTN
Driver	WIELAND CHRISTN.

5th Company

2nd Lieutenant	HAARDT LEWIS
Serjeant	SCHNEIDER HENRY
Corporal	KASTNING ERNEST
Bomber	STUNKEL HENRY
Bomber	ENGELKE CHAS.
Bomber	KNIPSCHER HENRY
Gunner	BLICK JOSEPH
Gunner	LORJE JACOB

6th Company

Captain	RETTBERG V. CHARLES
Lieutenant	HUGO ANTHONY
Bomber	LOHMANN FREDK.
Bomber	PRANGE HENRY
Gunner	SCHULENBERG LEWIS
Gunner	KUNTZE HENRY
2nd Lieutenant	HEISE HENRY Record Office

ROYAL HORSE & FOOT ARTILLERY

Lieutenant EVANS MATTHEW Gaskell Collec.

Lieutenant MANNERS R."K" Whitaker Collection. Killed at Quatre Bras

Ass.Com. BANT RICHARD Cheylesmore Coll.

P.Ord.P. BURCHER J. Gaskell Collection

Gunner MANNING NATHAM Glendining's sale June 1908

Lieutenant BLOOMFIELD JOHN Daltons List

2nd Captain CAIRNS ROBERT M. "K" Dalton's List

Lieutenant ORD ROBERT H. Dalton's List

Captain BEANE GEORGE "K" Dalton's List

Lieutenant CROMIE M.T. "K" Dalton's List

Captain BOLTON SAMUEL "K" Dalton's List

2nd.Lieutenant CAPPAGE BUR. Dalton's List

Captain LLOYD WM. "K" Dalton's List

2nd Lieutenant BURNABY R.B. Dalton's List

Lieutenant LEMINE WM. Dalton's List

Lieutenant TREVOR ED. Dalton's List

2nd.Lieutenant HENNIS W.H. Dalton's List

Lieutenant JORDAN MOORE ADJ. Dalton's List

Major RAMSEY NORMAN "K" Dalton's List

Lieutenant ROBE W.L. "K" Dalton's List

* * *

7th HUSSARS

JOHN HICKS Glendining's sale 21 July 1909

* * *

11th HUSSARS

Lieutenant STEWART W.H. Dalton's List "W" in Army List

* * *

12th HUSSARS

Lieutenant LINDSEY JAMES BERTIE Killed

Cornet LOCKHART JOHN ELLIOT Killed

* * *

13th HUSSARS

Captain GUBBINS JAMES "K" Dalton's List

Lieutenant GEALE JOHN "K" Dalton's List

Lieutenant PYM GEORGE "K" Dalton's List

* * *

18th HUSSARS

Lieutenant FRENCH MARTIN Dalton's List Sick at Brussels

Lieutenant GORLON JOHN ROLFE Dalton's List.

Lieutenant MONENS WM. Dalton's List Sick at Brussels

MEDICAL OFFICERS

D.I.G. BURMEISTER M.A. "W" in Army List

D.I.G. DENECKE G. "W" in Army List

Surgeon MILLIGAN J.G. "W" in Army List

Surgeon TWINING W. "W" in Army List

Surgeon WINTER J. "W" in Army List

I.G. GRANT J.R. "W" in Army List

I.G. HUNE J.R. "W" in Army List

Surgeon LYONS W. "W" in Army List

D.I.G. TAYLOR WM. Dalton's List

D.I.G. GUNNING JOHN Dalton's List

D.I.G. WOOLRICHE STEPHEN Dalton's List

Surgeon BROWNRIGG DAVID Dalton's List

Surgeon EMERY H.G. Dalton's List

Surgeon DRAPER THOS. Dalton's List

Surgeon MALING JOHN Dalton's List "W" in Army List

Surgeon HALLIDAY ANDREW Dalton's List

Surgeon SIMPSON E. O.M.D. Dalton's List

Surgeon MORGAN J. O.M.D. Dalton's List

Surgeon CHISHOLM S. O.M.D. Dalton's List

2nd HUSSARS K.G.L.

LUTTERMAN ERNEST Gray Coll.1908

2nd LINE BN. K.G.L.

Private PLAINICKE J. Day Sale 1910

* * *

1st & 2nd BATTALION GRENADIER GUARDS

Captain DISBROWE G. Gaskell Coll.1908 A.D.C. to Maj.Gen.Cooke

Lt.Colonel HARDINGS Sir HENRY Staff att.to Prussian Army. 1st Bn."W"

Captain BURY AUG.VIS. "W" Dalton's List A.D.C. to Prince of Orange

Ensign CHAMBERS COURTNEY "W" Dalton's List. 1st Bn.

Ensign SWANN F.D. "W" Dalton's List 3rd Bn.

Private CRIBB JAMS. Day sale 1910

* * *

3rd BATTALION GRENADIER GUARDS

Surgeon CURTIS WM. Dalton's List "W" Inspector Hosp.Flanders

* * *

COLDSTREAM GUARDS

Captain SUMNER EDWD. 2nd Bn. Dalton's List Died of Wounds 26 June

Captain BLACKMAN J.L. 2nd Bn. Dalton's List Killed

Ensign BUCKLEY G.R. 2nd Bn. Dalton's List Died in Paris 1815

SCOTS GUARDS

Captain	FORBES HON.HASTINGS "K" Dalton's List
Captain	CRAWFORD THOS. "K" Dalton's List
Captain	ASHTON JOHN "K" Dalton's List
Ensign	STOPFORD HON.ED. Dalton's List Acted A.D.C. Maj.Gen. Sir John Byng
Ensign	SIMPSON C. "K" Dalton's List
Ass.Surgeon	WARDE J.R. Dalton's List

* * *

3rd BATTALION 1st FOOT

Captain	BUCKLEY WM. "K" Dalton's List
Lieutenant	ARMSTRONG JOHN "K" Dalton's List
Lieutenant	O'NEIL JOHN G. "K" Dalton's List
Lieutenant	YOUNG WM. "K" Dalton's List
Ensign	ROBERTSON ALEX. "K" Dalton's List
Ensign	ANDERSON WM. "K" Dalton's List
Ensign	GLEN ALEX. "K" Dalton's List

4th Foot

Captain	SHAW H. Dr.Payne Coll.1908
Ass.Surgeon	FRENCH JAMES Daltons List

14th Foot

Ensign	ADAMSON AUG.F.F. Daltons List

23rd Foot

Ass.Surgeon	WILLIAMS JOHN Dalton's List

27th Foot

Captain	HOLMES GEO. Daltons List "K"
Lieutenant	TALBOT WM. Daltons List
Lieutenant	GARDNER ANDREW Daltons List
Ensign	IRELAND SAML. Daltons List

30th Foot

Surgeon	PEARCE ROBERT Daltons List

32nd Foot

Captain	BOYSE JAQUES Daltons List "K"
Captain	CASSAN THOS. Daltons List "K"
Captain	WHITTY ED. Daltons List "K"
Lieutenant	BARR GEO. Daltons List
Lieutenant	BOASE JOHN Daltons List
Lieutenant	McCULLOCH J.S. Daltons List
Ensign	McCONCHY JAMES Daltons List

33rd Foot

Surgeon	BLACKALL GERALD Daltons List
Pay.	STODDART ED Daltons List

35th Foot

Lieutenant	STENTON FRANCIS Daltons List

40th Foot

Major	HEYLAND A.R. Daltons List "K"
Lieutenant	FOULKES JOHN Daltons List "W" in Army List
Pay.	DURAND F.H. Daltons List

42nd Foot

Corporal	FINN WM. Gray Coll.1908 Had also Reg.Medal
Captain	MENZIES ARCHIBALD Dalton's List "W"
Major	DAVIDSON GEORGE Dalton's List "W"
Lieutenant	GORDON ROBT. Dalton's List "K"
Ensign	ĢERARD GEORGE Dalton's List "K"

44th Foot

Ensign	WILSON ALEX. Dalton's List "W" in Army List
Ensign	SINCLAIR T.A. Dalton's List
Major	JESSOP JOHN Dalton's List "W" in Army List

51st Foot

Master of B.	THOMPSON H. Gaskell Collection

52nd Foot

Ensign	NETTLES WM. Dalton's List "K"
Corporal	MOLNEUX JOHN Glendining's Sale April 1909

54th Foot

Colonel	CAMPBELL Sir NEIL DALTON's List "W" in Army List
Ensign	DOWDALL J.(Adjt) Dalton's LIst "W" in Army List

2nd Bn. 59th Foot

Ass.Surgeon	LAMBE PETER K. Dalton's List

2nd Bn. 69th Foot

Lt.Colonel	MORICE CHAS. Dalton's List "K"
Captain	CURZON Hon.W. Dalton's List "K"
Captain	HOBHOUSE BEN Dalton's Lit "K"
Captain	BLACKWOOL ROBERT Dalton's List "K"
Lieutenant	WIGHTWICH EDWD Dalton's List "K"
Lieutenant	DEIGHTON JOSEPH Dalton's List
Ensign	AINSLIE G.S.H. Dalton's List "W" in Army List
Volunteer	CLARKE CHRISTR. Dalton's List Wounded
Pay.	VIVIAN PHILIP Dalton's List

1st Bn. 71st Foot

Ensign	TODD JOHN Dalton's List "K"

2nd Bn. 73rd Foot

Major	MACLAINE ARCH.J. Daltons List Wounded
Captain	ROBERTSON ALEX. Daltons List "K"
Lieutenant	STRACHAN J.W.H. Dalton's List "K"
Lieutenant	ACRES JOHN Dalton's List "K"

Lieutenant	HOLLIS MATTW. Dalton's List "K"
Lieutenant	BROWNE DONALD Dalton's List Wounded
Lieutenant	STEWART ROBT. Dalton's List "W" in Army List
Ensign	LOWE WM. LAWSON Dalton's List "K"
Ensign	PAGE CHAS. Dalton's List "K"

1st. Bn. 79th Foot

Captain	CAMPBELL NEIL Dalton's List "W"
Captain	SINCLAIR JOHN Dalton's List "W"
Captain	CAMERON JOHN Dalton's List "W"
Lieutenant	CAMERON DONALD Dalton's List "K"
Lieutenant	McPHERSON DUNCAN Dalton's List "K"
Lieutenant	KYNOCH JOHN Dalton's List "K"
Lieutenant	POWLING JOHN Dalton's List "W"
Lieutenant	CAMERON JAMES Dalton's List
Lieutenant	KENNEDY EWEN Dalton's List "K"
Ensign	CAMPBELL JAMES Dalton's List
Volunteer	CAMERON ALEX. Dalton's List "W" in Army List

92nd Foot

Ensign	BEECHER ABEL Whitaker Coll. 1908 Killed in Action
Colonel	CAMERON JOHN Dalton's List "K"
Captain	GRANT WM CHAS. Dalton's List "K"
Captain	LITTLE WM. Dalton's List "K"
Lieutenant	CHISHOLM J.J. Dalton's List "K"
Lieutenant	GORDON ALEX. Dalton's List
Ensign	McPHERSON J.M.R. Dalton's List "K"

95th Foot

Private	STEPHENS JAMES Glendining's sale June 1908

3rd Bn. 95th Foot

Private	HACKETT J. Cheylesmore Collection 1908

Casuals

Serjeant	CAMPBELL ALEX. 77th E.J. Needes Collection 1909 Gen.Pictons orderly
Lieutenant	CAMPBELL R.P. 7th Gaskell Coll. 1908 A.D.C. to Maj.Gen.F.Adam
Captain	LANGTON 61st & 8th Record Office Super. List Pg.72
Major	GROVE J.C. Record Office
Captain	McPHERSON J. 21st Record Office

1st Light Dragoons

Private	ACKER JOHANNES Glendining's Sale January 1910

1st Hussars K.G.L.

Private	DENFER JACOB Whitaker Collection 1908
Private	FAIRLSCH JOSEPH Gray Collection 1908
Private	HALTER MATTW. Gaskell Collection 1908
Private	RAMBENTHAL HENRY Day Sale 1910

* * *

Lightning Source UK Ltd.
Milton Keynes UK
UKOW010811050213

205843UK00006B/72/A